RED SEA CARAVAN

THE STORY OF ADEN AIRWAYS

DACRE WATSON

AN AIR-BRITAIN PUBLICATION

Copyright ©2008 by Dacre Watson

Published in the United Kingdom by
Air-Britain (Historians) Ltd

Registered Office: Victoria House,
Stanbridge Park, Staplefield Lane,
Staplefield, West Sussex RH17 6AS
www.air-britain.co.uk

Sales Department: 41 Penshurst Road, Leigh,
Tonbridge, Kent TN11 8HL
sales@air-britain.co.uk

Correspondence regarding this publication to:
D.Watson, St.Johns House,
Lechlade, Gloucestershire GL7 3AS
dacrewatson@btinternet.com

All rights reserved. No part of this publication may be reproduced, stored in a retrieval system or transmitted, in any form or by any means, electronic, mechanical, photocopying, recording or otherwise, without the prior written permission of Air-Britain (Historians) Ltd.

ISBN 978-0-851-30409-0

Printed and bound in Poland
www.polskabook.pl

Origination: David Partington
Cover design: Steve Partington

Front cover:
BOAC / Aden Airways publicity photograph, 1952.
Captain John Pascoe is at the controls.
(British Airways Archives)

Back cover:
DC-3 of Aden Airways en route from Mukeiras to Aden.
Original painting by Les Vowles

RED SEA CARAVAN

THE STORY OF ADEN AIRWAYS

"CARAVAN ....A company of merchants, pilgrims, etc travelling together for safety especially through desert". (Oxford English Dictionary) Appropriate BOAC publicity photograph of Aden Airways Captain Harry Mills with traditional camel driver. 1951. (Harry Mills)

CONTENTS

Foreword 5

Preface 6

Introduction 8

Acknowledgements 10

Chapter 1   Before Aden Airways; Early aviation in Aden; The birth of BOAC;
            The early years 11
Chapter 2   1946: A false start 17
Chapter 3   1947: Laying down the guidelines 19
Chapter 4   1948: BOAC in the Red Sea; Clairways of Kenya 23
Chapter 5   1949: The start of Aden Airways; January to March 1950 ...31
Chapter 6   1950-1951: 39
Chapter 7   1951-1952: 45
Chapter 8   Air Djibouti 51
Chapter 9   1952-1953: The Hermes operation 1952; Use of JATO by Ethiopian Airlines;
            The Haj and the Pilgrimage of 1952; The venture into Ethiopia 1952-1953;
            Proposed merger with Cyprus Airways 55
Chapter10   1953-1954: Aircraft Chartering 1953-1954; Pilot's operating rosters and
            Air Hostesses' operating rosters 4th October 1953 69
Chapter 11 Arab Airways (Jerusalem) Ltd 1953-1956 81
Chapter 12 1954-1955: 89
Chapter 13 1955-1956: 101
Chapter 14 1956-1957: 109
Chapter 15 1957-1958: 115
Chapter 16 1958-1959: 123
Chapter 17 1959-1960: 129
Chapter 18 1960-1961: Argonauts 133
Chapter 19 1961-1962: 139
Chapter 20 1962-1963: 145
Chapter 21 1963-1964: Viscounts 151
Chapter 22 1964-1965: 159
Chapter 23 1965-1966: 165
Chapter 24 1966-1967: 171
Chapter 25 1967: The last three months 177

Aircraft Histories and Accidents 181

Bibliography 192

Appendices 193

Index 211

Colour sections will be found following pages 64, 112 and 160

FOREWORD

In this materialistic century, the term Labour of Love is almost a meaningless cliché; but this effort by Dacre Watson challenges such cynicism as—to quote another well-worn phrase—his book is an exception to the rule. With full knowledge that his subject would be familiar only to a restricted audience, he has compiled the history of a relatively small airline that ceased operations several decades ago. Furthermore, even among knowledgeable aviation historians, Aden Airways is little known today, and its story could only have been written by someone who was deeply fascinated by the subject, and recognised its importance. Dacre must have realised that this long-forgotten airline—whose home base city is no longer named on 21st century maps—should be added to the wealth of literature devoted to chronicling the complete history of commercial air transport.

As an airline historian myself, I plead guilty to have been one of those who had not given Aden Airways the attention it deserved. In my 1964 book *A History of the World's Airlines*, I devoted a mere half-paragraph to it. My only excuse is that, more than 40 years ago, airline records, especially to those in the then more remote corners of the world, were not easily accessible. In the case of Aden Airways, its parent corporation B.O.A.C. did not promote its associated companies with enthusiasm.

Dacre Watson has, in full measure, filled a valuable gap in the historical archives of airline history. A port at the southern tip of the Arabian peninsula, and at the southern end of the Red Sea, Aden was a vital staging point and coaling station on the British Empire's shipping route to India and the Far East. Geographically, it was situated between the two main trunk air routes to Asia and to India, and was the key to direct transport communication between the two continents. When aeroplanes complemented and succeeded ships, Aden Airways, like East African Airways, and Central African Airways, was an important link in the chain of British airlines that served the Empire upon which the sun never set.

But its existence covered the years of a setting sun, and it was in an area where British rule and influence was diminishing within a hostile environment. Much has been written about the role of the Chinese Airline, C.N.A.C., surviving valiantly during the Second World War; and the Australian QANTAS was described, in its wartime role in the south-western Pacific, as "front-line airline." The same was true of Aden Airways. For in maintaining an air route structure that linked southern Arabia with the countries of the Persian Gulf with Egypt, the eastern Mediterranean, and Kenya, it was, towards the close of its life, in the front line, and, to extend the metaphor, too often embroiled in trench warfare.

The author has told this story of an airline, first at peace, and later having to endure wartime conditions in a hostile environment. He drew the facts from official records, B.O.A.C.'s reports and correspondence, and from the log-books, diaries and reports of Aden's pilots, especially those of Captain Vic Spencer, some of whose entries could have been written by the local military police. Flying into isolated desert communities in what is now Yemen's Hadramaut coast and hinterland, the crews had to be armed for self-defence as the guerrilla fighters of the Front for the Liberation of South Yemen (FLOSY) were never far away. Additionally, among the civilian population in the city of Aden itself, even airline employees, it was sometimes difficult to identify friend from foe.

Yet with a fleet of aircraft which most airlines would have retired as time-expired, and low on the list of B.O.A.C.'s cast-offs, this beleaguered airline managed to sustain airline services throughout the region. It was closed down only before, not to exaggerate unduly, it would have been shot down.

To write this book was indeed a labour of love. A pilot of much experience—he retired as a Boeing 747 captain after 26,000 flying hours and 39 years with B.E.A., B.A. and Singapore Airlines – Dacre Watson has told a tale that contains as much adventure as it does a narrative of cold facts and figures. A pilot's mind is evident throughout, including the justified view that those in the flight deck had to keep the faith with the travelling public, even if the management often seemed to be at odds with common sense, and a handicap to their devotion to the cause. As I read Dacre's disciplined narrative, I often felt that I was there myself, on a veteran DC-3 coming in to land on a strip more suited for a jeep than an aeroplane, or catching a few hours sleep at the airline's fortress headquarters with a .45 revolver close at hand.

I heartily recommend this book to airline aficionados and to all those readers who enjoy a good yarn as well as a good history.

R.E.G.Davies,
Curator of Air Transport, Smithsonian Institute, Washington, DC.
July 2008.

PREFACE

Aden Airways : An appreciation

Anyone who lived upcountry in the Western Aden Protectorate, as we did-mostly-from 1962 until 1967 had good cause to be deeply grateful for the service provided by Aden Airways. All my stations, as a Political Officer, had an airstrip with the exception of Abyan where the beach was the only link to Aden some 45 miles away. I had two postings to Dhala, three to Habilayn (Radfan), one to Loder and one to Beihan. Being Political Officer Loder involved frequent visits to Mukeiras with its terrifying airstrip very near the plateau top of the 7,000ft Audhali Kor. I was somewhat comforted by the Mukeiras version of the law of aerodynamics: any plane, however overloaded, flying towards the cliff and seemingly well below the top, would, at the last moment, be carried on a thermal up and over the top. Or so the pilots used to say. I used to worry about a last moment possible suspension of the law but it always seemed to work. Almost as worrying was the return trip when the DC-3 seemed to drop a thousand feet or so once clear of the cliff top.

Dhala was a particularly remote post from the point of view of road communications. Only a little more than 120 miles from Aden, the road was poor and from 1965 onwards subject to ambush and mining by the 'dissidents'- rebel tribesmen supporting the anti-governmental 'revolutionaries'. We would fly to Aden as often as we could and were dependent on Aden Airways for a regular supply of groceries and above all for the mail, personal and official. During my year's engagement to my wife throughout 1964 when I was in Dhala, in Radfan and in Beihan we wrote to each other every day and on one memorable afternoon in mid-November my diary records that 11 letters from my fiancée arrived on one Aden Airways flight to Beihan.

The weekly flight (perhaps it was twice a week) to Dhala was quite an event. Many people went out to meet the plane. The airstrip was a target for the insurgents and the Amir of Dhala had employed (at the Political Officer's expense) a team of Special Guards - local tribesmen who would patrol the airfield and protect it from potential mine layers. That was the theory but we were never too sure on whose side these 'loyal' mercenaries really were. Mines were occasionally 'found' buried in the runway just in the nick of time although I had my suspicions as to who the layers were. A double game was quite a profitable business as the official reward for finding and handing in an anti-tank Mark II (British manufactured) mine was 15 rifles and 15,000 rounds of ammunition (weapons being a sort of alternative currency in a region where everyone was armed as part of their national dress and tribal lifestyle) worth about £1,000 in local purchasing power, 1965 prices, to the lucky claimant. And you could not be sure that a special guard had not received even more, or had been intimidated into **not** finding a well-concealed mine which would certainly have destroyed the undercarriage of any aircraft unlucky enough to hit it. And at high speed that would have been a major disaster.

As it happened Aden Airways escaped fairly lightly during the years of insurgency. Only one plane was destroyed by an airborne time-bomb leading to the death of a senior state servant from the Wahidi Sultanate and, amongst many others, Tim Goschen, one of my colleagues in the political service. But it was a constant threat of terrorist action which must have been a major pre-occupation of Aden Airways and a source of worry for their pilots. Nevertheless the service was regular and usually punctual. I can think of very few occasions when we were let down by the non-arrival of a scheduled flight and you could organise itineraries for VIP visitors on the fair assumption that timings would be adhered to and you would not be stuck with difficult guests and not enough food to feed them.

One memory. Waiting on board for a plane to take off from Dhala. The starter motor whining away but to no effect. Suddenly the pilot came out of the cockpit, exited by the rear door, climbed up onto the wing and hand-cranked the port engine until it fired. The starboard one started in sympathy and away we went.

My wife has another. Staring out of the window at the wing rivets, high above the Radfan mountains, and watching the rivets vibrating, apparently steadily unscrewing themselves.

But they never did.

Peter Hinchcliffe. CMG CVO
Former Political Officer at Dhala, later HM Ambassador to Jordan and Kuwait.

INTRODUCTION

Probably the most frequent question asked of me has been: "Why Aden Airways?" Well, there were two reasons; the first was reading Neville Shute's book "*Round the Bend*" which served to fire my imagination of the period in the Middle East. Yes, the setting in the book was Bahrain, but it could just as well have been in Aden.

The second reason was that in late 1964, as a newly-qualified pilot, I was offered a job by Aden Airways, and I was captivated by what I (wrongly) imagined to be the romance of flying in that part of Arabia. Fortunately, common-sense prevailed, and when I was invited to join BEA I did so. Nevertheless, the question of "What if….?" remained with me throughout my career as a pilot, and this book is really a natural progression from the step I might have taken almost 45 years ago.

Though BOAC had maintained a considerable presence in the Middle East throughout the war and, amongst other routes, had a regular service to Karachi via Aden, it was perceived in 1945 by the Colonial Office and the Ministry of Civil Aviation that something more permanent than a "presence" in the Red Sea was required, and with BOAC being an instrument of Government policy, the result was a decision to set up a subsidiary airline to be based in Aden.

Aden Airways was registered as a wholly owned company in Aden on 7th March 1949. It had six DC-3s which had been "sold" by BOAC and which remained on the British register until 30th March, 1950 when both registrations and flight numbers were transferred to Aden.

The first Managing Director of Aden Airways was Richard de Graaff Hunter, a charismatic if somewhat mercurial man; highly educated and of great foresight and originality of thought, he was thus well equipped to stand up to BOAC when he thought the situation merited it, as it often did.

During the early years of its existence, there was little to distinguish the airline from any other small operator, but as the surrounding countries developed their own often more modern airlines, Aden Airways with their DC-3s began to lose market share on the prestigious routes up through the Red Sea and other markets had to be developed. Firstly, three DC-3s were converted to 40 seaters and placed on the local routes where traffic warranted it. An additional refinement was that any number, or all, of the seats could be quickly removed to provide space for freight depending on the load. This concept was particularly useful as the routes were developed within the Protectorates, both for the isolated villages and, from the 1950s, the oil exploration work for the various petroleum companies.

It can be difficult to think of a British airline involved in the drug running business, but the airline approached this nettle with a vigour only a good profit can induce. Qat, a soporific drug cultivated in both Yemen and Ethiopia was much in demand by the population in Aden Colony and Aden Airways ran daily services from Dire Dawa to Aden specifically to cater for this demand. In a fit of political correctness, the Government disallowed the use of the drug but the effect was so great on the economy of the Colony that it was reinstated a few months later.

Development within the Protectorates went on as well during the late 1950s; hitherto trade was by time-honoured camel train crossing different tribal boundaries and arid deserts. Flying from barely prepared strips on the desert or wadi floor, the DC-3s suddenly brought Aden within two hours flying time and while the movement of people and goods was the primary aim, it also meant prompt medical attention could be available if required and this did much to win hearts and minds. The oil exploration companies drilling deep in the interior of the Eastern Protectorate and Dhofar, in Oman, provided good revenue for the company which used the DC-3s virtually as aerial trucks to transport all the machinery, fuel, prefabricated buildings, food and personnel from Sallalah to whichever site needed replenishing. Ten round trips in a day were common. In order to provide fresh meat, the animals, usually goats and sheep, were flown in live and kept until needed.

But as the years marched on, it became clear that Aden Airways was steadily losing competitiveness with its DC-3s. At last, in 1960, BOAC sold three surplus Canadair Argonauts to the airline, though as will be seen, these were a mixed blessing and were withdrawn after three years due to corrosion. Fortunately, in 1963 two Viscount 700s became available and at long last the airline was flying modern equipment and the scheduled loads began to pick up again.

Sadly, Arab nationalism had been sweeping the region, aided and abetted by Egypt; the National Liberation Front and Front for the Liberation of South Yemen, as Aden was looked upon, were extremely successful in their activities of fomenting strikes, violence and assassinations of both Europeans and Adenis, including employees of Aden Airways. When a DC-3 en-route from Maifah to Aden was blown up in November 1966 sabotage was suspected and though the cause was rather more prosaic (the local Sheikh was on board and it is believed that his son wished to hasten the succession) there was a total loss of confidence from the travelling public and load factors fell dramatically.

During the same year the Labour Government under Harold Wilson had agreed to grant independence to Aden, but this only served to heighten the violence rather than calm it as the two Fronts fought each other for political dominance.

BOAC, meanwhile, had seen the writing on the wall and faced with mounting and unending losses decided to close the airline down on 30th June 1967. As if to hurry the end along, on the last day of operations a Viscount was blown up by sabotage as it sat in the quarantined pan after engineering work had been completed.

Thus ended the life of an airline the activities of which encompassed every aspect of civil aviation. It operated in one of the harshest environments in the world and was rightly awarded the Cumberbatch Trophy by the Guild of Air Pilots and Air Navigators in 1961. Probably its greatest contribution was to open the Protectorates to the advantages of aviation, to the benefit of the people living there whose lives were changed by it.

I hope that readers will not be disappointed by the fact that I have not given a deep analysis of the political events which took place in Aden from the early 1960s onwards. Not only would this have lengthened the book considerably, but the subject has been very well covered in other books by those with a far deeper knowledge than mine. I am deeply indebted to the British Airways Archives whose director, Paul Jarvis, gave me unfettered access to the information held there and who had the confidence in me to know that that it would be used with discretion.

I make no apology for the frequent references to the diaries of Vic Spencer. He was an inveterate recorder of events which occurred in the airline and day-to-day flying. His slides are unique and my great regret is that he has not lived to see the book which at every stage he encouraged me to write. I am indebted to his family for allowing me to use both the diaries and photographs.

This book is also a tribute to those thousands of people who lived and worked in Aden. Many served in the armed forces, equal numbers worked to maintain the infrastructure of the Colony and, of course, many worked for Aden Airways. The airline was an integral part of everyone's lives, whether they were starting their leave in Europe or Africa, or whether they needed to visit one or other of the Protectorates. From 1961 to the end in 1967, the security situation became progressively more difficult, and it would be fair to say that during the last few months, a siege atmosphere existed with many British people being murdered, both civilian and military, and I pay tribute to their bravery as they went about their normal lives.

Finally, the title of the book, "*Red Sea Caravan*". From ancient times, a branch of the Silk Route came down from Samarkand, passing through what is today Oman and the Hadramaut on its way to the old city of Medina. While Aden Airways never replaced the camel trains entirely, it did succeed for a time in easing the transport of goods within the Aden Protectorates. For some years the services operated by the airline within the Protectorates were referred to as the "Caravan Routes", and I commemorate these flights in the title.

As in any book of this nature, mistakes will be noted, even though it has been proofed by a number of experts in their respective fields. Please, by all means feel free to advise me of any which are found. Place names, too, have changed over the years; for instance, Ataq has also been named as Attak and Bahrain was also once spelled as Bahrein. I have used the spelling in use at the time so that atlases of the period may be referred to easily. However, a good number of maps have also been reproduced for easy reference.

Writing this book has been a pleasure and, for me, the end of a journey which began all those years ago.

Dacre Watson. July 2008

ACKNOWLEDGEMENTS

To:

My wife, Ann, and daughters Alexandra and Abigail.

Captain Vic Spencer, MBE
Pilot with Aden Airways from 1953 to 1967, and Chief Pilot from 1963 to the last day of operations. Without his logbooks, diaries and photographs, this book would have been much less interesting.

Harry Pusey.
Former Commercial Officer and Assistant General Manager with Aden Airways, later Resident Adviser in Jordan and first Chief Executive Officer of Kuwait Airways. His knowledge of the people involved and recall of events made it possible to explore the dynamics of civil aviation in the region in the detail it would not otherwise have been possible.

My thanks, too, for all the help received from the following people:

Former employees of Aden Airways:
Captain Peter Austin (1959-1964); Captain Tom Beale (1947-1952); Captain Alan Elgee and Mrs Elgee; Captain John Lightfoot (1953-1957); F/O Tony May (1965-1967); Captain Harry Mills (1947-1958) and Mrs Joan Mills; Captain John Pascoe (1950-1958); Captain Ian Stewart (1957-1960); Captain Ian Walbran (1948-1952); Captain Robert Wigley (1948-1965); Captain David Willmott (1963).

Stewardesses: Ann Atkinson (Berryman) 1954-1955; Jennifer Drummond Harris (Venning) 1964-1965; Wendy Hayden Sadler (Locke) 1963-1965; Christine MacIntyre (Dent) 1960-1964; Sheila Pratt (Munro) 1963-1967.

Ground staff: Trevor Austin (1963-1967) Admin Manager; Basil Bradley; John Burley (Operations Manager); Sue Douet (Russell) (1963-1964); Michael Gardner (1959-1963) Engineer; Pat Kennedy (1957-1958) Traffic Officer; Bill McGarry (1963-1967) Security Officer; Carlo Moretti (1954-1967) Traffic Officer; Mr Payne (1954-1955) Trainee Engineer, Aden.

Peter Arnold; Rachel Bannister (typing); Antonin Besse; Alan Bushell (photo printer); Vic Camden; Roger Carvell (maps); Harold Clark (RAF); Paul Colvin; Bob Cook (CAA Library); John Cork (RAF); Elizabeth Cox; John Cox; Ron Davies (Curator of Air Transport, Smithsonian Institute); Jim Davies, John Davis; Ray Deacon (RAF); Tony Doyle; Malcolm Fillmore; Roger Gilbert; Dr Roger Green; Guild of Air Pilots and Air Navigators; William Harrison (RAF); Angela Harvey (proof reading); John Havers (technical proofing); Keith Hayward, Ray Hayward; Michael Hedges (RAF); Peter Hinchcliffe CMG CVO; Sarah de Graaff Hunter; Graham Jackson (RAF); Paul Jarvis, Robert Kirby; Guy Kremmer; Malcolm Lacey; Bernard Lewis, Inmaculada Munoz, M Olden; Ian O'Neill; Captain Richard Pascoe; Peter Pickering (Aden Society, Australia); Graham Pybus; Gill Richardson; Douglas Rough; Jack Sayer (RAF); Don Schofield (proof reading); Brian Sears; Peter Skinner (Croydon Airport Society); Colin Smith; Alan Thatcher (indexing), Hendrik Van der Veen; Klaus Vomhof; Les Vowles (cover painting); David Watson; Peter Webber; John Wegg; Maurice Wickstead; Luc Wittemans.

Photographs, timetables and other memorabilia which are not otherwise credited are from the Author's collection.

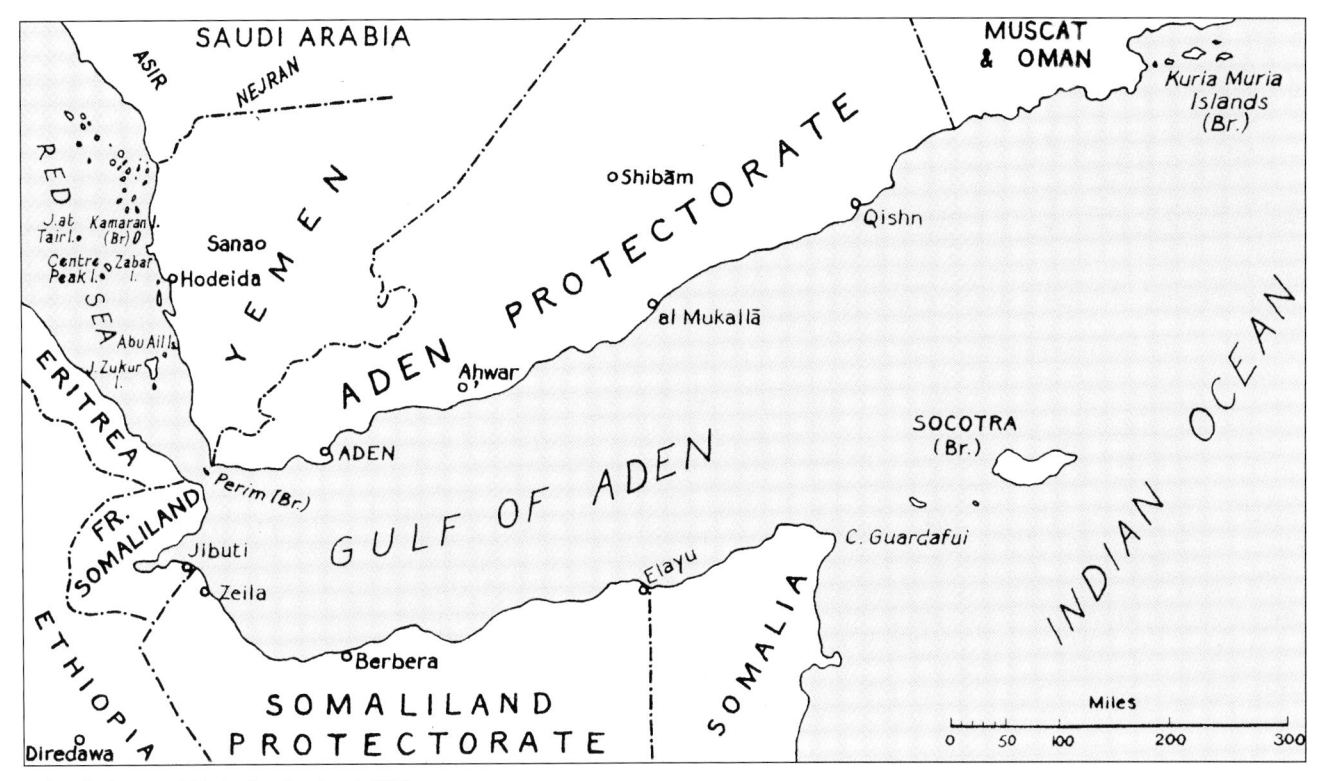

Aden Colony and Protectorate about 1950.

Chapter 1:
BEFORE ADEN AIRWAYS

Better known as a seaport, Aden was never likely to be in the forefront of commercial aviation development. Yet for some 20 years after the Second World War, it flourished in the form of an airline named Aden Airways, before independence in the region brought about its demise as the British withdrew from Southern Arabia.

An ancient land
Situated along the north coast of the Gulf of Aden, the port itself is first mentioned in the First Testament (Ezekiel) as one of the two principal termini of the Spice Road from western Arabia, and in use as such until the third century A.D. During the following centuries, Aden remained an important trading centre under the influence of the Yemenis, Arabs, Ethiopians, Turks and, eventually, the British.

In the late nineteenth century, France and Britain competed for empires, and only after Napoleon had conquered Egypt in 1798 did the British take the threat to their lines of communication with India seriously, and did so to the extent that a garrison was set up in Aden in 1802. Once the Suez Canal was opened in 1869, the port of Aden developed as a coal bunkering station and its future, for the time being, was assured. At one stage it was the fourth busiest port in the World.

In the meantime, the British Colonial Office had, between 1868 and 1888, consolidated its hold on the region by the purchase of a number of adjacent mainland areas, and in 1937 declared Aden and its territories to be a British Crown Colony.

Early aviation
Aden was too far south for it to be included in the expansion of the various European airlines before the Second World War. Air France, Imperial Airways and KLM all served territories in the Far East and preferred to route their flights through Cairo, Bahrain and Basra on their way through India to the Far East. Similarly, there was little incentive for Aden to be included on the southern routes to Africa, being so far to the east of the Cape to Cairo route via Nile. The only pre-war airline which operated regular services to Europe was the Italian airline, ALA Littoria, which flew a twice-weekly service to Rome from Asmara, the capital of what was then Italian Eritrea.

Once Aden had become a Crown Colony in 1937 however, an attempt was made to start a local scheduled airline service. The first civil aircraft to be kept in Aden had arrived in 1936, purchased by Antonin Besse, a well-known and influential businessman who had established A Besse & Co (Aden) some forty years earlier. He had purchased a General Aircraft Monospar ST-25, G-AEJB, which he was able to keep at Khormaksar (courtesy of the RAF) and which was used by him to communicate with his interests within the Aden Protectorate.

In June 1937 a local airline was proposed to be formed to fly from Aden to Khartoum to connect with the Imperial Airways flights

Steamer Point, Aden, 1954. (Ann Atkinson)

Arabian Airways General Aircraft Monospar ST-25 G-AEJB, initially purchased by Antonin Besse, which ended its days in Ethiopia.
(via John Havers)

Short Scion G-AEOY was acquired by the newly-formed Arabian Airways in 1937 but unfortunately had a very short career with them.
(via John Havers)

which passed through that city from Africa to Europe. On 30th September 1937 experimental flights began to the Eastern Protectorate and Djibouti, using the existing Monospar and a newly-arrived Short Scion, G-AEOY.

These experiments were successful enough for a company to be formally registered in London on 27th October 1937 [1] under the name of Arabian Airways Ltd with Antonin Besse as Chairman, who had done so much to promote civil aviation within the Colony of Aden and the Protectorate. He still owned his own aircraft there after the War and was on the Aden Airways Board from its inception. Sadly, he died in July 1951.

Regular weekly services started to Mukalla and Seiyun in the interior of the Hadramaut, departing from Aden on a Thursday and returning the next day. Unfortunately, the Scion was not to last long in service as it crashed on takeoff at Terim on 17th December. A replacement Scion, G-AEIL, arrived in Aden in mid-March 1938 together with two new pilots, and services were resumed, though initially with mail only.

There were continuing difficulties in establishing any permanence with the route to Djibouti, because the French wished to have reciprocal rights to Palestine. Eventually, on 21st June 1938, formal approval was given, but by this time the company was short of aircrew. The situation was further undermined as the RAF had agreed to carry the mail to Mukalla whenever it operated there. The war looming in Europe made further aircrew recruitment difficult and, with losses rising and no subsidy from the UK government forthcoming, all services were abandoned for the time being.

Another Scion, G-AEIL replaced Arabian Airways' G-AEOY.
(via John Havers)

Early days of BOAC

BOAC was formed as Britain's state-owned "chosen instrument" on 1st April 1940; its antecedents are well documented elsewhere, and the fledgling airline was unfortunate to be plunged into wartime operations at its birth. But it had a well-established route structure within Africa, through one of its predecessors, Imperial Airways, and this network was to continue throughout the war with its headquarters in Durban, South Africa.

For its military operations, Britain had a large base in Cairo which was well serviced through France and North Africa until June 1940, when France was overrun by Germany. A further setback was the entry of Italy into the war, also in June, with the result that the Mediterranean ceased to be a line of communication to Africa. Nothing daunted, BOAC was still able to fly from its southern headquarters in Durban to Cairo and then eastwards to Australia in what was to become the famous Horseshoe Route.

BOAC Lodestar G-AGCM over Cairo about 1947. *(British Airways Archives)*

Over the next two years, the western desert of North Africa was the scene of Allied advances and retreats, but early in 1941 the situation was sufficiently safe to transfer the BOAC headquarters from Durban to Cairo, where there was a pressing requirement for a communications base to serve the Middle East. However, this move was rescinded as the Axis armies moved eastwards towards Cairo, even though it remained an important, if temporary, base run by Robert Maxwell of BOAC. Of interest for the future of the region, though Cairo was the centre of operations, the military situation prevailing at the time was volatile, and it was therefore decided (by Air Marshal Tedder) to set up an engineering base in Asmara, in Eritrea, recently liberated from the Italians.

Gradually, more civil aircraft became available from various sources, and the demand for capacity was mounting rapidly. Accordingly, Tedder proposed that a joint BOAC/RAF transport organisation should be set up in Cairo under Maxwell, and for this service he was presented in June with nine Lockheed Lodestars, a number which had risen to 21 by December 1941. Asmara assumed a greater importance within the scheme in that, by October, it had become the main overhaul base for BOAC landplanes in Africa (2). Not only that, and as a result of Axis successes in the desert to the west of Cairo, the Tedder plan now established Asmara as the centre of communication flights, operated by Lodestars.

Though BOAC was very much under RAF control, as far as possible it operated as an airline with regular routes from Cairo to:

Wadi Halfa-Port Sudan-Asmara (starting 12th September)
Baghdad-Tehran (starting 3rd September)
Lydda-Adana (3rd September)
Asmara-Khartoum.

In early 1941, the revolt in Iraq had caused some concern when the landing field at Habbanniya was lost to the insurgents, with a consequent threat to the Horseshoe Route from Cairo to India via the Persian Gulf. The only alternative routeing was along southern Saudi Arabia, the Hadramaut coast, across the Persian Gulf south of Muscat to Jiwani and on to Karachi. This route was explored at the time, and it would come to influence much of the thinking over the next 25 years. It was first flown on the 29th/30th May 1941, from Karachi to Aden by Captain L A Egglesfield, flying a Douglas DC-2, in order to survey the route via the Hadramaut coast with landings at Jiwani, Sallalah and Riyan (3).

At one stage, flying boats were thought to be the best option, but the final decision was taken to set up the ground organisation for a landplane route from Aden to Riyan, Sallalah, Masirah Island, Ras el Hadd and Jiwani, and finally to Karachi.

The route was ready by May 1942, and the first flight was made from Cairo on 11th May by Lockheed Lodestar G-AGBX; further flights followed at monthly intervals. Though in theory all flights were to start in Cairo, Asmara remained the official departure point and a variety of aircraft ranging from Lockheed 14s to Armstrong-Whitworth Ensigns flew the route, depending on what was available and the load required.

In May 1943, Viscount Knollys was appointed as Chairman of BOAC. He had been Governor of Bermuda until shortly before and his assistant there was a certain Richard de Graaff Hunter whom he brought with him to BOAC and who would become the first Managing Director of Aden Airways, though this was not yet part of the planning.

Miles	Airports of	Service ...	9R		Airports of	Service ...	10R	
0	CAIRO	...dep	5 30	Alternate Fri. B	KARACHI	...dep	8 0	Alternate Tues. C
316	LUXOR	...arr	7 25	,,	JIWANI	...arr	10 5	,,
	,,	...dep	8 0	,,	,,	...dep	10 45	,,
830	PORT SUDAN	...arr	10 50	,,	MASIRA	...arr	11 20	,,
	,,	...dep	11 30	,,	,,	...dep	12 0	,,
1144	ASMARA 🛏	...arr	14 25	,,	SALALAH 🛏	...arr	14 25	,,
	ASMARA	...dep	8 0	Alternate Sat.	SALALAH	...dep	8 0	Alternate Wed.
1590	ADEN	...arr	10 35	,,	RIYAN	...arr	9 5	,,
	,,	...dep	11 15	,,	,,	...dep	9 45	,,
1909	RIYAN	...arr	13 15	,,	ADEN	...arr	11 35	,,
	,,	...dep	13 45	,,	,,	...dep	12 15	,,
2269	SALALAH 🛏	...arr	17 0	,,	ASMARA 🛏	...arr	14 55	,,
	SALALAH	...dep	8 0	Alternate Sun.	ASMARA	...dep	8 0	Alternate Thur.
2672	MASIRA	...arr	10 30	,,	PORT SUDAN	...arr	8 55	,,
	,,	...dep	11 15	,,	,,	...dep	9 30	,,
3029	JIWANI	...arr	...	,,	LUXOR	...arr	12 25	,,
	,,	...dep		,,	,,	...dep	13 0	,,
3351	KARACHI	...arr	16A15	,,	CAIRO	...arr	14 55	,,

A 70 minutes later if call made at Jiwani.   **B** From 16th August.   **C** From 20th August.
Free baggage allowance 30 kgs.   🛏 Overnight stop.

BOAC Cairo to Karachi services 9R and 10R, August 1946. (Source: Bradshaw)

With the defeat and expulsion of the Axis forces from North Africa, Cairo once again became the centre of air communications for Africa as a whole. As a result, all operational staff were moved from Asmara, and the engineering base there was transferred to Almaza, outside Cairo, where it was to remain for a number of years. However, the Lodestar flights to India via the Hadramaut coast continued, the only difference being that they now started from Cairo, flying via Port Sudan, Asmara and Aden and then following the previous route to Karachi.

Cairo increased in importance in 1944 while the Red Sea routes continued largely unchanged; early in the year, No 5 Line came into existence and would only cease in November 1947, when the DC-3s from No 1 Line replaced them. On 31st October, Kamaran Island became a port of call after Asmara and before continuing on to Addis Ababa. There were two purposes for this call, the first being the potential for increased contact with the Yemen, and the second, the increasing desire for luxury goods (in this case natural pearls) as the end of the war came in sight.

The war in Europe came to an end in May 1945 and, for the Red Sea area, there was little change from previous years, but in London thoughts were now turning to the future development of air transport in the region.

The early years
By early 1945 European minds were turning once again to the re-establishment of air routes to former colonies and overseas territories; they also sought to establish and, if possible, expand areas of influence. It was for this reason the governments were the instigators through their colonial offices rather than the airlines themselves, though this was a moot point because airlines in Europe, in general contrast to the USA, were instruments of government policy anyway, and had always been so.

In October 1945 the secretary of BOAC received a letter from the Ministry of Civil Aviation (4):

"I am directed to inform you that this Ministry has been considering, in conjunction with the Colonial Office, the future requirements for British air transport in the Red Sea area.....

The Civil Air Attaché in the Middle East has now been instructed in conjunction with the local representatives of the Corporation and the local Colonial authorities to investigate the traffic possibilities of local services based at Aden as well as a link with Jeddah and Palestine......

As you will be aware, the American company, Transcontinental and Western Air, (TWA) is actively pushing its own interests in the whole of the Middle East area and it is, accordingly, Lord Winster's wish that the investigation referred to above should be completed as rapidly as possible."

This last paragraph was significant; the expansion of American commercial interests which had hitherto been primarily confined to

BOAC Lodestar G-AGIL at Addis Ababa, Ethiopia, about 1947. (British Airways Archives)

that continent, South America and latterly the Pacific. For the next 30 years or so they would dominate the airline world, while during that same period most European airlines were subject to the political wills of their various governments.

BOAC kept flying throughout the war, though its network waxed and waned depending on the Allies' fortunes. But once hostilities were over, the company was quick to re-establish old routes, and while in some ways it was "business as usual" in relation to the pre-war years there had also been profound changes technically, politically and socially, all of which were to guide post-war development during the rest of the century.

The catalyst for airline development during the Twenties and Thirties was communication with far-flung colonies. KLM, Air France and Imperial Airways all had interests in the Far East with well-established schedules on these routes. Pan American was essentially a Latin American enterprise, and only started to expand across the Atlantic in 1939. In addition, both the UK and France had extensive interests in Africa and airlines to service them.

In the case of the UK, much of the pre-war Empire still existed, but clearly the former colonies would not allow themselves to remain so for much longer. Airlines were still instruments of government policy, of which BOAC was a particularly fine example. A different approach had to be initiated and the result was the setting up of companies associated with BOAC, effectively as subsidiaries (BOAC Associated Companies did not come into existence until 1957). The aim was to set up airlines in various colonies which were about to become independent, or self-governing. There was, naturally, an advantage to BOAC in this apparently altruistic approach, and this fact is acknowledged in the annual report for 1949-50 (5):

"An important aspect of the policy of the Corporation is to take a prominent part in the development and integration of air communications throughout the British Commonwealth of Nations and the Empire. To this end, the operational and commercial experience of the Corporation is made available to foster the development of services connecting with the Corporation's trunk routes……."

The war had brought about technological and national development to such an extent that traditional routeings, traffic rights and national loyalties were all thrown into a melting pot. It became a question of holding on to what one already had and grasping whatever other opportunities seemed to present themselves. If this meant an involvement in the aviation aspirations of a newly-emerging state, then perhaps that would be of mutual interest as one might be able to control the direction of their competitive instincts, not only to protect one's traffic but also to achieve some materialistic return for co-operation in their development. A somewhat cynical view perhaps, but current at the time.

BOAC was not the only company which was to become involved in the Middle East and North Africa. Over the following two decades Skyways would become active in both Libya and Africa generally, taking over the Kuwait Oil Contract in 1948 from Airwork, which itself had become active in Egypt and Sudan as well as Southern Arabia. However, in late 1951 Skyways passed the Kuwait Oil Contract on to British International Airlines which was 100% owned by BOAC. Other airlines active in the area were Silver City with a large fleet in Libya, Air France in Lebanon and Syria, Pan American with a temporary involvement in Middle East Airlines, Transocean in Djibouti, and later in Jordan, and, of course, TWA as technical adviser to Ethiopian Airlines and Saudia.

There was the considerable danger of duplication as well as conflicts of interest between the various airlines, so an organisation named Associated British Airlines (Middle East) Ltd was set up in co-operation between BOAC, BEA, Hunting Clan and Skyways, the purpose of which was to co-ordinate the activities of the airlines involved. Though initially successful, it flew in the face of emerging national identity and the desire for independent development in Middle East countries, with the result that there was considerable resentment, particularly as the British government was seen to have some control over the companies involved. It died a quiet death in March 1959.

BOAC had always perceived the area as one under British influence describing it as "The Southern Red Sea Group". True, there were French Somaliland and Ethiopia, but the former was run casually from Paris, while the latter had only just emerged from occupation by the Italians. Eritrea and its important capital, Asmara, were under British supervision. Aden, therefore, with its port and military presence, was seen as the natural centre for the region; it had the further advantage in that it was the natural outlet for the Yemen, at the time ruled by a reclusive and inward-looking Imam.

Early studies brought mixed conclusions (6):

1)   Air communications within the Aden Protectorate were essential, with the RAF no longer willing to provide internal aerial transport. A weekly service from Aden to Dhala, Mukalla and Riyan was thought to be the minimum.
2)   The surrounding countries of Eritrea, Ethiopia, French and British Somaliland and the Yemen were seen as barren areas for air travel with the result that considerable long-term investment would be needed.
3)   There was a high demand for travel from both service and colonial personnel as they moved about the region, or returned to and from the UK. Similarly, with a large Indian trading influence in Aden, a route to India could be viable, particularly if it was extended to Lagos in West Africa. In fact, a Lockheed Lodestar operation from Cairo to Karachi had already been in place for some time, taking three days each way and, rather grandly, named the "The Hadramaut Route".
4)   It was suggested that, should the route from India be extended across Africa, it would head westwards from Asmara to Khartoum, where it would join up with the flight by West African Airways Corporation, (WAAC) to El Fasher and Lagos. In fact, this route never did get off the ground, though Aden Airways did operate a number of special Haj flights during the 50s.

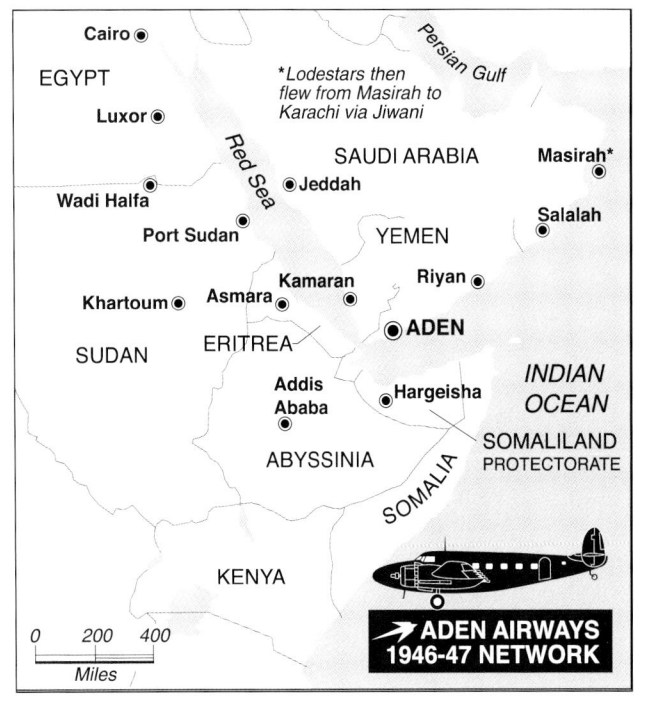

1946 BOAC network, No.5 Line　　　　　　　*(Roger Carvell)*

Miles	Airports of	Service	1R				Airports of	Service	2R		
			B	E					K	L	T
0	CAIRO ... dep		5 0	7 0	,,	...	ADEN ... dep		12 0	...	...
316	LUXOR ... arr		...	...	...	...	KAMARAN ... arr		13 50	...	...
	... dep		...	...	...	...	,, ... dep		14 30	...	...
821	JEDDAH ... arr		9A 40	...	...	...	ASMARA ⌂ ... arr		16 5	...	...
	... dep		10A 30	...	...	...					
1006	PORT SUDAN ... arr		11A 15	11x30	...	...	ASMARA ... dep		...	7 45	7 45
	... dep		11A 45	12x15	...	...	PORT SUDAN ... arr		...	8 40	8 40
1320	ASMARA ⌂ ... arr		14A 40	15x10	...	...	,, ... dep		...	9 15	9 15
					K		JEDDAH ... arr		...	11 0	...
	ASMARA ... dep		...	...	6 45	...	,, ... dep		...	11 30	...
1566	KAMARAN ... arr		...	...	8 20	...	LUXOR ... arr		12 10	13 55	...
	,, ... dep		...	...	9 0	...	,, ... dep		13 0	14 30	...
1870	ADEN ... arr		...	...	10 55	...	CAIRO ... arr		14 55	16 25	...

A 70 minutes later if call made at Luxor. **B** Mon. **E** Sun. **K** Mon., Tue. **L** Wed. **T** Tue.
x 50 minutes later if call made at Luxor. Free baggage allowance 30 kgs. ⌂ Overnight stop.

BOAC Cairo - Aden services 1R and 2R, August 1946. (Source: Bradshaw)

5) Granville estimated that the two main passenger flows would be from Asmara to Europe (Rome) and from India and the Middle East to West Africa. He suggested a route from Karachi to Khartoum via Riyan, Aden and Asmara, and at Khartoum passengers would have a choice of either Europe, South Africa or West Africa. This made sense at the time (1945) as Khartoum was at the centre of airline traffic to all points in Africa and was relatively well developed.

6) In conclusion, Aden local services were planned to be (7):

6.1 Aden-Kamaran-Asmara-Khartoum twice weekly.
6.2 Aden-Hargeisa-Addis Ababa-Asmara-Khartoum twice weekly.
6.3 Aden-Riyan-Aden-Kamaran-Jeddah once weekly.

A fairly modest beginning.

Footnotes, Chapter 1:
(1) Aeroplane, 3rd December 1937, p549
(2) History of BOAC, Bray, p26
(3) John Stroud, Annals of British and Commonwealth Air Transport, p182
(4) Letter from MCA (Dunnett) to BOAC Ref R913/2, 31st October 1945
(5) Annual Report 1949-50, p16
(6) Memo by Keith Granville, Manager Middle East, later Chairman of BOAC, 19th December 1945
(7) CMF.8.445, 17th January 1945

Miles	Airports of	Service	5R		Airports of	Service	6R	
0	CAIRO ... dep		6 30 Tue.	5 0 Fri.	ADDIS ABABA ... dep		7 15 Thur.	7 15 Sun.
316	LUXOR ... arr		... ,,	...	HARGEISA ... arr		9 25 ,,	9 25 ,,
	... dep		... ,,	...	... dep		10 15 ,,	10 15 ,,
591	WADI HALFA ... arr		...	8 15 ,,	ADEN ... arr		11 50 ,,	11 50 ,,
	... dep		...	8 45 ,,	... dep		12 45 ,,	12 45 ,,
1007	PORT SUDAN ... arr		11A 0 ,,	...	ASMARA ⌂ ... arr		15 25 ,,	15 25 ,,
	... dep		11A 45 ,,	...				
1420	KHARTOUM ... arr		...	11 20 ,,	ASMARA ... dep		7 0 Fri.	7 45 Mon.
	... dep		...	12 15 ,,	KHARTOUM ... arr		8 30 ,,	...
1846	ASMARA ⌂ ... arr		14A 40 ,,	15 45 ,,	... dep		9 30 ,,	...
					PORT SUDAN ... arr		...	8 40 ,,
	ASMARA ... dep		7 0 Wed.	7 0 Sat.	... dep		...	9 15 ,,
2292	ADEN ... arr		9 35 ,,	9 35 ,,	WADI HALFA ... arr		12 5 ,,	...
	... dep		10 15 ,,	10 15 ,,	... dep		12 45 ,,	...
2529	HARGEISA ... arr		11 45 ,,	11 45 ,,	LUXOR ... arr		12 10 ,,	12 10 ,,
	... dep		12 15 ,,	12 15 ,,	... dep		15 0 ,,	12 45 ,,
2897	ADDIS ABABA ... arr		14 20 ,,	14 20 ,,	CAIRO ... arr		16 55 ,,	14 40 ,,

A 50 minutes later if call made at Luxor. Free baggage allowance 30 kgs. ⌂ Overnight stop.

BOAC Cairo - Addis Ababa services 5R and 6R, August 1946. (Source: Bradshaw)

This later view of Aden from the south with the port area and part of the town in the Crater district in the foreground and the former RAF Khormaksar close by, lying across the mainland end of the peninsular at the top of the picture.
(Roger Gilbert)

Chapter 2 :
1946: A FALSE START

In June 1946 the Ministry of Civil Aviation (MCA) issued a request that a survey of the Red Sea routes be made by BOAC with the remit:

"..........*advising on the commercial possibilities of establishing an airline based in Aden to operate local services between there and neighbouring countries, particularly Addis Ababa.*" (8)

The subsequent report by R M Hilary was based on a survey done by him of the area and conducted from Cairo during September and October 1946 on which he was accompanied by Captain H Lazelle, the pilot of the Lodestar in which the group travelled, and Mr R Griffiths from the operations staff in Cairo.

The report was comprehensive and had both as its strength and its weakness the fundamental thinking of the day: the preservation of the dominance of Empire, and by implication, its instrument in the form of BOAC. While on the one hand there was an understanding of the changes wrought in people's minds as a result of the war, with the consequent sensitivity needed towards countries which only recently were part of the Empire, there was also a somewhat naïve assumption that any developments would be subservient to the needs of BOAC. Intermingled with this was an awareness of the strategic needs for the future as a result of the emerging tensions between East and West, though the official "cold war" was some way off.

The particular problem of a local airline based in Aden was part of an altogether wider subject: the entire network of British associated air services within a general area encompassing Cairo, Nairobi and Aden, and this network would have to have a twofold objective:

1)   It would have to provide feeder services to the main trunk routes and to other parts of the World.
2)   It would have to serve the local administrative and commercial needs of the area itself.

To add to the difficulties, the "local area" in regard to Aden consisted of Eritrea, British Somaliland, Ethiopia and, to a lesser extent, Kamaran Island. The military held sway in this part of the world and all travel during the immediate post-war era was based on a priority basis with all military and colonial service personnel having the highest priority. In fairness the RAF did not see its function as providing a transport service to these two arms of government and had already expressed a desire to terminate its weekly service between Aden and Nairobi. This would create a void which, incidentally, Clairways of Kenya was keen to fill.

Further to this, the BOAC base in Cairo, operating Lockheed Lodestars, was military in origin and political pressures were developing within Egypt for this to cease. A possible solution was to set up an airline in Cairo to be named Egyptian Airways which would fly the Red Sea routes as far as Aden, up the Nile to Nairobi and to Eritrea and Ethiopia. However, this plan never really materialised because of political events in Egypt, and fortunately it did not do so as would be borne out by the events of 1952.

Originally, the recommended network of British routes in Northern Africa as suggested by Hilary was for all air services to be under the umbrella of BOAC, and would employ Egyptian Airways, Sudan Airways, West African Airways and Aden Airways. East African Airways had not yet matured sufficiently to be considered a player in this field. An unusual departure for BOAC was the inclusion of Haj flights which were to become such a central part of operational life in Aden Airways in later years; for instance, in October, 1946 three Lodestars were employed to bring pilgrims to Jeddah from Baghdad with their return some weeks later.

Aden's main problems at this time were twofold; first, there was little accommodation for company employees and, second, the airport at Khormaksar was owned and operated by the RAF which was reluctant to share either the facilities or the available accommodation.

The report envisaged the use of two Bristol 170 Wayfarers for Aden Airways. This was an aircraft which had first flown during December 1945 and was being actively developed for precisely such an area of operations. The Wayfarer never did come to Aden since there was some doubt as to its single-engine performance from the hot and high airfields which Aden Airways would be flying into. Further, it was a little slower in comparison to the DC-3s already flown by the local opposition, Ethiopian Airlines.

A further suggestion was that, in the event of a failure in the formation of Egyptian Airways, three Lodestars would be sent to Aden Airways for services from there. In the event, the company in Egypt failed to materialise and the Lodestars were not needed as No 5 Line converted to the DC-3 in November 1947.

Two further points had to be considered if Aden were to be the base for operations. The first referred to which routes would be flown along the Hadramaut coast, and on which Hilary was unable to see any commercial reason for doing so; the RAF already operated a regular communications flight to Riyan and Mukeiras from which it had already expressed a desire to withdraw.

The second consideration was whether a route from Aden to Bombay should be established. It was accepted that at this stage (1946) there were no aircraft adequate for the route but, once they were to become available, then the much-vaunted "Ivory route" from West Africa to India could be re-launched. This route was to remain a long term wish for the airline, but it never did come to fruition, even after the arrival of the Argonauts in 1960.

And there the matter rested. The RAF proved to be unwilling, or unable, to share the facilities at Khormaksar, nor could it see its way to allowing any of its buildings to be used by Aden Airways employees. Quite simply, there were no base facilities for an airline to become established.

Footnote, Chapter 2:
(8) Report by R M Hilary, October 1946

Lodestar of BOAC's No.5 Line over Cairo, 1947, with the Ibn Tulun mosque dominant below. (British Airways Archives)

CHAPTER 3: 1947: LAYING DOWN THE GUIDELINES

The DC-3 operations of Ethiopian Airlines were already causing concern within BOAC in 1947, a significant factor in the setting up of Aden Airways to compete in the region. ET-ABI is seen here in 1960s colours at Addis Ababa. *(via O G Nordbø)*

Chapter 3 :
1947: LAYING DOWN THE GUIDELINES

Not until August 1947 did things get under way again and, in a letter from the MCA to Whitney Straight, it was revealed that negotiations with the RAF regarding the civil use of Khormaksar were now complete, "*....I am happy to say that these difficulties are now being overcome, and the way is now clear for us to proceed with the project for a local company.*"(9) Some urgency was required since the Middle East Air Transport Board (MEATB), which was controlled by the military authorities, was soon to be discontinued and a new company was needed if there was to be a seamless changeover.

Another reason for urgency was that Ethiopian Airlines, under the management of TWA, had developed rapidly and aggressively throughout the region and even up to Riyan in the Aden Protectorate; "*.....If Aden Airways does not get started fairly quickly, Ethiopian Airways (sic) may have established an unassailable position.*"(10) This may have been gentle arm-twisting as the MCA went on to suggest that, if BOAC did not have the resources to provide the start-up costs for a new airline in Aden, then the project could perhaps be offered to Airwork. "*Naturally, I would prefer to avoid this alternative, but……….*"(11)

In his next report of 15th September 1947, Hilary again affirms the need for a British presence in the Red Sea area, acknowledging the failure to create Egyptian Airways which would have taken over the No 5 Line routes out of Cairo. While this was not a disaster to the ambitions of BOAC, he now believed that "*an Aden unit cannot now be planned in isolation; it must be considered in relation to other existing, or planned, British airline enterprises in the Middle East.*"(12) He was very aware of the dominance established on international routes by Ethiopian Airlines which now had a good reputation throughout East Africa and the Red Sea. It was somewhat galling for Hilary to see this airline flying a successful service within the Aden Protectorate between Addis Ababa, Aden and Riyan. Even though in 1946 and 1947 Ethiopian Airlines had

to use the airport at Sheikh Othman, rather than Khormaksar, while BOAC were able to make use of the latter with all its advantages.

There was still some discussion on exactly which routes BOAC would continue to fly and which would be operated by the new airline. To compete effectively with Ethiopian Airlines, a fast service from Cairo to Addis Ababa and Aden, both via Asmara, would have to be set up. Clearly the Bristol 170 Wayfarer, with its 140 knots cruising speed could not provide this level of service, so it was thought that these two routes would be flown by BOAC as extensions of its London-Cairo flights, while Aden Airways would fly the much slower way, calling in at Kamaran, Asmara, Port Sudan and Jeddah, where there was plenty of intermediate freight and passenger traffic. (In fact the B170 did make a tour of the Red Sea including Jeddah, Asmara and Aden during January 1949 which appears not to have been successful).

BOAC soon realised that a complete re-think was needed as to what the future plans would be and the result could best be summarised in a memorandum from Whitney Straight dated 25th September 1947: (13)

"*1) The need to counteract the ever expanding activities of the TWA-sponsored Ethiopian Airlines.*
2) The increased strategic importance of East Africa, Aden and the Horn of Africa which seems likely in the future.
3) The value of air transport as a means of modernising and improving the usefulness of the port of Aden."

Further, it was at last decided that the Bristol Wayfarer, which was still under development, was too uneconomic for the planned route structure and, as a new aircraft, would be an expensive investment, quite apart from its unproven technical reliability in terms of single-engine performance. As a result, it was decided that the DC-3 would be used, a sensible decision bearing in mind that they

BOAC No.5 Line services between Cairo and Aden, January 1947, including onward flights to Karachi and Addis Ababa, operated with Lodestars. (Source: Bradshaw)

would come from the parent company as they became surplus to requirements.

At first the aircraft would be operated by BOAC, flying out to Cairo on a normal service, where they would be integrated into the Red Sea network until the hours flown would require a major check, whereupon they would return to the UK again on a normal Cairo-London service.

There were to be three primary routes:

1)   Cairo-Asmara-Addis Ababa-Nairobi.

2)   Cairo-Asmara-Aden.

3)   Cairo-Jeddah-Port Sudan-Asmara-Kamaran-Aden.

All routes would be flown weekly and, in the first instance, would be seen as an extension of the London-Cairo service, until a headquarters could be set up in Aden itself. Other routes under consideration for future development would be to Hargeisa, Riyan, Berbera and Mogadishu.

At this stage the choice was made for the appointment of the first General Manager for the new airline. This was to be Richard de Graaff Hunter who had been assistant to Lord Knollys when the latter was Governor of Bermuda and, later, Chairman of BOAC.

Overall, the plan had become more ambitious. Comparing the anticipated revenue and expenditure based, in the first instance, on the two Wayfarers and later on the four DC-3s:

	1946 Plans	1947 Plans
Total hours flown	2,500	6,410
Total mileage flown	113,400	864,921
Revenue	£100,000	£305,000
Expenditure	£120,000	£340,000
Deficit	£20,000	£35,000

Neither calculation took into account any revenue to be earned from carrying mail, freight and pilgrim charters.

In conclusion, the memorandum recommended that:

1)   A further survey should be carried out by R M Hilary to gauge the facilities available for these more ambitious plans, and that it should be concluded by the end of November 1947.
2)   The target date for the start of these services should be 1st January 1948.

Plans were now moving on apace. Richard de Graaff Hunter, the new General Manager of the proposed Aden Airways, moved out to Cairo on 5th November 1947 where he assumed the day-to-day planning for the coming year.

The Lodestars would not remain in service beyond the end of the year; they had been flying the Middle Eastern routes continuously since 1944 and, apart from being uncompetitive, were becoming expensive to maintain. Accordingly, the decision was made that the No 5 Line aircraft would be replaced by the DC-3s of No 1 Line, and that the changeover would take place on 15th December 1947.

On 17th October BOAC held a meeting which was attended by officials from the Colonial Office, the Air Ministry and the Ministry of Civil Aviation. That these last three organisations were present at all must come as something of a surprise to today's reader, but in those days immediately after the war the colonies were an important part of the economy and civil aviation was very much an instrument of government. At this meeting the Hilary proposals were agreed, though modified where necessary by his forthcoming report in November.

The survey trip lasted from 9th November until 1st December 1947 utilising one of the Lodestars from No 5 Line under the command of Captain C N Pelly who, apart from the flying, would report on the technical aspects of the installations en route as well as the airfields to be visited. Included in the party was de Graaff Hunter who was along in order to familiarise himself with the area.

It might have been assumed that not much had changed within the region since the previous year, but, apart from the progress made by Ethiopian Airlines, Clairways of Kenya had established a firm foothold in Somalia (14) transporting colonial and service personnel within the territory, as well as operating weekly services from Nairobi to Aden and Mogadishu. There was no doubt that Hilary viewed this latter development in particular as a serious hindrance to the successful establishment of an airline operating out of Aden and he saw the relatively lucrative and regular traffic between that port and Nairobi as an important lynchpin in the future success of Aden Airways.

"The most important point which arose from our visit to Nairobi was the future of the route between Nairobi and Aden via Mogadishu and Hargeisa. The East African Authorities were disappointed not to have received a clear-cut injunction from the Colonial Office and MCA about the licence which Clairways were seeking over this route. This development constituted such an obvious threat to both EAAC and BOAC (for the Aden Airways project) that we sought immediate permission from London to introduce a weekly BOAC Dakota service from the Aden end."

Chapter 3: 1947: Laying Down The Guidelines

In Somalia: *"We took the Chief Administrator into our confidence over our attempt to oust Clairways from the route through his territory. He said that the Clairways Anson services were popular, their main advantage being that they operated with good regularity compared with the extreme unreliability of the RAF Dakota service. Nevertheless, he would welcome the greater experience and resources which he expected that a chosen instrument would provide."*(15)

In French Somaliland, Djibouti was also seen as a good source for potential revenue, not only for freight between there and Addis Ababa but for passenger traffic as well. Air France was about to withdraw its Lodestars which operated a spur out of Khartoum to Addis Ababa via Asmara and Djibouti, while the two Ju-52s flown by the French Air Force only operated to Aden occasionally and then only for mail and official passengers. Ethiopian Airlines had been given a licence by the Aden Government to fly between Djibouti and Aden in August 1947 and this was seen as a good lever to secure traffic rights for Aden Airways between Djibouti and Addis Ababa.

Khormaksar, in Aden, continued to present something of a problem. True, the RAF had now agreed to share facilities and, indeed, was willing to provide a certain amount of accommodation as well as a Bellman hangar and stores building which could also be used as a workshop. But, beyond that, additional buildings and services would have to be found or constructed, for which there was no money available from BOAC. The problem was solved with the decision to set up two bases, one at Aden and the other in Asmara.

Apart from the brief period during the late Thirties when Arabian Airways Ltd was flying out of Aden, the port had never been considered as a centre for an airline; it did not even have an Air Licensing Board, as the Governor of the region was the authority who issued licences to operators. Other than BOAC, only two airlines had been given licences:

1) Ethiopian Airlines, which had three permits between Aden, Addis Ababa, Riyan and Djibouti.

2) Clairways which had a licence to fly a weekly service between Nairobi and Aden via Mogadishu, which had been granted on 27 May 1947 for a period of one year; this was not renewed in 1948 after pressure had been applied by BOAC.

Interestingly, another airline, Mistri Airlines of India, had applied to fly from Bombay to Aden via Karachi, but this application had been passed on to diplomatic channels and had been lost somewhere within the bureaucracy there. This airline had started operations in October 1946 flying from Bombay to Calcutta via Nagpur, but in 1947 the name was changed to Indian Overseas Airlines, taking on the night mail services, before ceasing operations in 1950.

Asmara airfield presented itself as the obvious choice for an alternative base to Aden. Situated at 7,000 feet, it had an ideal climate, had been the capital of the Italian colony of Eritrea before the war and, with its good supply of skilled Italian labour, could provide the airline with all the technicians it might need. As Eritrea was now under British administration no diplomatic negotiations would be necessary to set up a base or living quarters.

The airfield itself had become the prime BOAC base after 1941 when Cairo had become threatened by the Italian and German forces under Rommel as they advanced eastwards across North Africa. Even when BOAC had moved back to Cairo after 1943, the airfield had remained under the management of International Aeradio and the MCA and was in excellent condition in 1947. Hilary suggested that BOAC should continue to run the airfield under licence from the MCA as well as operate it as a base for the new airline.

There were other good reasons why these arrangements should continue. There was already a sizeable traffic load between Asmara and Rome to which the newly created Italian airline, Alitalia (in which BOAC had an investment), wished to have access. Hilary saw considerable benefit in this, because a reciprocal agreement could then be negotiated to allow the Red Sea services to link with the BOAC flights out of Cairo, which would then transit Rome en route to London.

Originally, the new Red Sea services should have started on 1st January 1948. However, Hilary thought that this would be premature and suggested 21st January might be more appropriate. In the meantime, No 1 Line DC-3s would continue the interim programme, adding both Jeddah and Addis Ababa to the route structure.

Ethiopian Airlines services to Aden and Mukalla by DC-3 in September 1947. (Source: Official Airline Guide)

As a result of the survey, and the market research which was undertaken, the following route recommendations were made:(16)
Furnished Dakotas:
1) Cairo-Asmara-Addis Ababa   Once weekly
   Extended to Nairobi   Once fortnightly
2) Cairo-Asmara-Aden-Nairobi   Once weekly

Unfurnished Dakotas:
1) Cairo-Jeddah-Port Sudan-Asmara-Kamaran-Aden
                                      Once weekly
2) Aden-Riyan   Once fortnightly
3) Aden-Addis Ababa   Once weekly
4) Aden-Djibouti-Addis Ababa   Once weekly
5) Aden-Hargeisa-Addis Ababa   Once weekly

The changeover in Cairo from the No 5 Line Lodestars to No 1 Line DC-3s went smoothly. Training, where necessary, was completed at Almaza airfield and the final flights of the Lodestars were planned as follows (17):

Flight No:	1R	ex Cairo	11.12.47
	2R	ex Aden	12.12.47
	5R	ex Cairo	12.12.47
	6R	ex Hargeisa	13.12.47

New flight numbers were introduced and these were to be Cairo-Aden 15/16R, Cairo-Nairobi to be 17/18R and Cairo-Aden to be 19/20R. Due to the politics of the Clairways licence, however, the 17/18R would only operate as far as Hargeisa until political clearance could be obtained to fly through to Nairobi.

The introduction of the DC-3s was to be as follows (18):
Flight No 17/18R Cairo-Hargeisa ex Cairo Monday   15.12.47.
           15/16R Cairo-Aden   ex Cairo Wednesday 17.12.47.
           19/20R Cairo-Aden   ex Cairo Saturday   20.12.47.

Note on 17/18R: The route to Nairobi had not yet been approved.

The Timetables were to be as follows (19): (All times in GMT)

Flight No 17/18R.
Monday	0530 dep	Cairo	arr 1345
	arr	Luxor	dep 1130
	dep	Luxor	arr 1055
	0910 arr	Wadi Halfa	dep 0955
	0945 dep	Wadi Halfa	arr 0825
	1235 arr	Khartoum	arr 0530 Saturday
			(Nightstop)
Tuesday	0600 dep	Khartoum	arr 1055
	0840 arr	Asmara	dep 0800
	0930 dep	Asmara	arr 0710
	1205 arr	Aden	dep 0400 Friday
Wednesday	0145 dep	Aden	arr 1425
	0330 arr	Hargeisa	dep 1245
	0415 dep	Hargeisa	arr 1215
	0730 arr	Mogadishu	dep 0845
	0815 dep	Mogadishu	arr 0800
	1210 arr	Nairobi	dep 0330 Thursday

Flight No 15/16R.
Wednesday	0400 dep	Cairo	arr 1330
	0605 arr	Luxor	dep 1115
	0645 dep	Luxor	arr 1045
	0955 arr	Port Sudan	dep 0715
	1030 dep	Port Sudan	arr 0640
	1235 arr	Asmara	dep 0430 Friday
Thursday	0330 dep	Asmara	arr 1405
	0510 arr	Kamaran	dep 1215
	0545 dep	Kamaran	arr 1140
	0745 arr	Aden	dep 0930 Thursday

At some stage, Jeddah would come on line, and the schedule would change to:

Wednesday	0300 dep	Cairo	arr 1540
	0505 arr	Luxor	dep 1325
	0545 dep	Luxor	arr 1245
	0845 arr	Jeddah	dep 0915
	0930 dep	Jeddah	arr 0830
	1055 arr	Port Sudan	dep 0715
	1130 dep	Port Sudan	arr 0640
	1335 arr	Asmara	dep 0430 Friday

Asmara/Kamaran/Aden would remain unchanged as above.

Flight No 19/20R.
Saturday	0330 dep	Cairo	arr 1600
		Luxor	dep 1345
		Luxor	arr 1310
	0710 arr	Wadi Halfa	dep 1115
	0745 dep	Wadi Halfa	arr 1040
	1035 arr	Khartoum	dep 0745
	1115 dep	Khartoum	arr 0655
	1355 arr	Asmara	dep 0400 Monday
Sunday	0330 dep	Asmara	arr 1405
	0510 arr	Kamaran	dep 1215
	0545 dep	Kamaran	arr 1140
	0745 arr	Aden	dep 0930 Sunday

Other routes which had still to be finalised were as follows, though these were radiating out of Aden where accommodation remained uncertain (20).

Route 4: (in abeyance)
0630	Aden	1445
0835	Mukalla	1100

Route 5:
0345	Aden	1445
0500	Djibouti	1330
0545	Djibouti	1245
0830	Addis Ababa	1000

Route 6:
0500	Aden	1355
0840	Addis Ababa	1015

Route 7: (in abeyance)
0345	Aden	1500
0530	Hargeisa	1320
0615	Hargeisa	1235
0840	Addis Ababa	1015

It has to be said that none of these routes or schedules were cast in stone, though many were actually flown in early 1948.

Footnotes, Chapter 3:
(9) R.20608/46 Ministry of Civil Aviation to Whitney Straigh, 25th August 1947.
(10) Ditto
(11) Ditto
(12) R M Hilary: Confidential Report to the BOAC Board, September 1947.
(13) Outline proposals for the operation of BOAC services in the Red Sea area, September 1947.
(14) See chapter on Clairways, p27.
(15) Report on Nile Valley and Red Sea Tour. R M Hilary, November 1947.
(16) Appendix C Planning Misc. (47) 25.
(17) AMEE.CS.4.511 S W Hemmings, Schedules Officer, 12th December 1947.
(18) Ditto.
(19) AMED.CS.4.539. S W Hemmings 23rd December 1947
(20) Source: BOAC Planning Office 29th December 1947

BOAC DC-3 of No.1 Line refuelling at Entebbe in late 1948. (Harry Mills)

Chapter 4 :
1948: BOAC IN THE RED SEA

The introduction of the DC-3 on the Red Sea routes was a success, though there were some cancellations and withdrawals. On 10th February, BOAC withdrew one service from Cairo to Hargeisa (21), a decision based partly on the increased frequency from Aden, and partly on the higher capacity of the DC-3 over the previously-flown Lodestars.

On 16th February, flight 21R, later to become flight BO 453, was introduced. This was to fly a weekly service from Cairo to Nairobi (22) via Wadi Halfa, Port Sudan, Asmara and Aden where the aircraft would night-stop before proceeding the next morning to Nairobi via Hargeisa and Mogadishu. The return flight would follow the same routeing in reverse, except that Wadi Halfa was to be omitted in favour of Luxor, where there was a compulsory quarantine check as a result of the frequent outbreaks of cholera in Ethiopia and Somalia. However, as stated before, there was a conflict with Clairways which already had the licence, and therefore the service terminated in Hargeisa for the time being.

On 21st February flight 23R, later to become flight BO 451, which had been suspended during November the previous year, started to operate from Cairo to Addis Ababa via Wadi Halfa, Khartoum and Asmara where a night-stop was made before proceeding at 0600 the next morning to its destination. The flight returned to Asmara on the same day as 24R for another night-stop before proceeding up through the Red Sea to Luxor for more quarantine checks prior to arrival in Cairo, where passengers could connect with flights to Europe.

Also on 21st February, a weekly flight from Aden to Addis Ababa via Djibouti was brought in as flight 27R, later flight BO 459, though this service was withdrawn in January 1949 and not reopened until December of the same year.

Within the Protectorate, a service to Riyan for Mukalla was started on 15th March as the BO 460/461, though this service was also suspended on 15th November for economic reasons and not restarted until June 1949.

Meanwhile, the discussions on setting up Aden Airways progressed. With the appointment of de Graaff Hunter as future General Manager of Aden Airways, a subtle conflict between BOAC and its creation would emerge. BOAC assumed that any subsidiary was there for the benefit of the parent company, subservient to that company's needs and wishes. de Graaff Hunter, however, was his own man and the tensions which would first

BO457 to Addis Ababa		DAKOTA SPEEDBIRD		BO456 to Aden	
G.M.T.	L.T. Thu.			L.T.	G.M.T.
03.45	06.45	dep. ADEN	arr.	15.15	12.15
07.00	10.00	arr. ADDIS ABABA	dep.	12.00 Thu.	09.00

BO459 to Addis Ababa		DAKOTA SPEEDBIRD		BO458 to Aden	
G.M.T.	L.T. Sun.			L.T.	G.M.T.
04.15	07.15	dep. ADEN	arr.	17.40	14.40
05.25	08.25	arr. JIBUTI	dep.	16.30	13.30
06.15	09.15	dep. JIBUTI	arr.	15.45	12.45
08.40	11.40	arr. ADDIS ABABA	dep.	13.30 Sun.	10.30

BOAC : Local Aden services, January 1948, flown by No.1 Line.

MIDDLE EAST LOCAL SERVICES

BO463 to Addis Ababa		DAKOTA SPEEDBIRD		BO462 to Cairo	
G.M.T.	L.T.			L.T.	G.M.T.
	Tue.				
05.00	07.00	dep. CAIRO	arr.	15.45	13.45
—	—	arr. LUXOR	dep.	13.30	11.30
—	—	dep. LUXOR	arr.	12.50	10.50
10.10	12.10	arr. PORT SUDAN	dep.	09.20	07.20
10.50	12.50	dep. PORT SUDAN	arr.	08.40	06.40
12.55	15.55	arr. ASMARA	dep.	07.30	04.30
	Wed.			Mon.	
05.00	08.00	dep. ASMARA	arr.	16.55	13.55
08.25	11.25	arr. ADDIS ABABA	dep.	13.30	10.30
				Sun.	

BO465 to Aden		DAKOTA SPEEDBIRD		BO464 to Cairo	
G.M.T.	L.T.			L.T.	G.M.T.
	Thu.				
05.00	07.00	dep. CAIRO	arr.	15.40	13.40
—	—	arr. LUXOR	dep.	13.25	11.25
—	—	dep. LUXOR	arr.	12.25	10.25
08.30	10.30	arr. WADI HALFA	dep.	10.20	08.20
09.10	11.10	dep. WADI HALFA	arr.	09.45	07.45
11.55	13.55	arr. KHARTOUM	dep.	06.45	04.45
	Fri.			Wed.	
05.00	07.00	dep. KHARTOUM	arr.	14.30	12.30
07.55	10.55	arr. ASMARA	dep.	12.50	09.50
08.35	11.35	dep. ASMARA	arr.	12.10	09.10
10.15	13.15	arr. KAMARAN	dep.	10.30	07.30
10.55	13.55	dep. KAMARAN	arr.	09.55	06.55
12.50	15.50	arr. ADEN	dep.	08.00	05.00
				Tue.	

BO467/469 to Nairobi		DAKOTA SPEEDBIRD		BO466/468 to Cairo	
G.M.T.	L.T.			L.T.	G.M.T.
	Sun.				
04.30	06.30	dep. CAIRO	arr.	16.15	14.15
—	—	arr. LUXOR	dep.	14.00	12.00
—	—	dep. LUXOR	arr.	13.00	11.00
09.15	11.45	arr. JEDDAH	dep.	10.05	07.35
10.00	12.30	dep. JEDDAH	arr.	09.25	06.55
11.20	13.20	arr. PORT SUDAN	dep.	07.30	05.30
				Sat.	
12.00	14.00	dep. PORT SUDAN	arr.	14.25	12.25
14.05	17.05	arr. ASMARA	dep.	13.15	10.15
	Mon.				
05.00	08.00	dep. ASMARA	arr.	12.15	09.15
07.25	10.25	arr. JIBUTI	dep.	09.50	06.50
08.05	11.05	dep. JIBUTI	arr.	09.10	06.10
09.15	12.15	arr. ADEN	dep.	08.00	05.00
	Tue.			Fri.	
02.30	05.30	dep. ADEN	arr.	17.20	14.20
04.10	07.10	arr. HARGEISA	dep.	15.40	12.40
04.50	07.50	dep. HARGEISA	arr.	15.00	12.00
08.20	11.20	arr. MOGADISHU	dep.	11.40	08.40
09.00	12.00	dep. MOGADISHU	arr.	11.00	08.00
13.05	16.05	arr. NAIROBI	dep.	07.00	04.00
				Thu.	

Continued on next page

BOAC Red Sea services, January 1948.   (BOAC timetable)

Richard de Graaff Hunter boarding the Alitalia Lancastrian service at Asmara for Mogadishu.   (Sarah de Graaff Hunter)

become evident in 1948 would be indicative of how role perceptions between the two companies were to differ.

By August, the requirements for the new airline were becoming more clearly defined. At a meeting in London on 17th August 1948 between BOAC and de Graaff Hunter, a plan was arrived at whereby six DC-3s would be transferred to the company, with a seventh if needed. With up to 1,200 hours of annual utilisation planned, a minimum of eight full crews (Captain, Co-pilot and Radio Officer) would be needed, with ten being preferable to give sufficient slack for charters and leave etc.

Cairo was to become the main engineering base, while Aden and Asmara would share the day-to-day engineering functions. An Operations Officer, Traffic Officer and an Accountant would all be required, seconded from BOAC, initially for two years, though this was to be flexible, as was the question of outside recruitment, should enough volunteers not be forthcoming.

Setting up the Red Sea services as a separate unit was now urgent because BOAC wished to replace the DC-3 on the London-Cairo sectors with Avro Yorks. The problem was that, until then, a DC-3 would initially operate from London to Cairo where it would be integrated into the Red Sea network, within which it would fly until approaching a major check. It would then leave the network at Cairo and fly the scheduled service back to London where it would undergo major maintenance. In a letter during September, the Technical Manager, Eastern Division, urged a resolution to the continuing delay: (23)

1) "………it is essential, operationally, that aircrew should be in a position at Asmara to start flying on the routes from about 1st November
2) Any delay may result in us being forced to maintain additional Dakota services UK/Cairo instead of allowing Yorks to take over these Dakota services completely.
3) Similarly, it is essential that Cairo be in a position to fully maintain the Dakotas remaining on the Red Sea services as from about the same date."

There was considerable discussion as to, firstly, just how many DC-3s would be needed; secondly, what equipment would be needed from the standard BOAC DC-3; and, thirdly, how many crews would be required in order to fulfil the obligations of the operation.

In the end, it was decided to have seven aircraft serviced by 10 crews, plus a Chief Pilot who was to be Captain J. L. C. Banks from BOAC. The DC-3s were to be purchased from BOAC but would require considerable modification for their new role in an essentially high humidity environment, even though much of the flying would be conducted over desert-like terrain. For instance, oxygen provision was to be removed, as were the de-icing kits. Toilets were to be modified to reflect the more spartan operation and the furnishings were to be partly stripped in order to achieve a greater flexibility in the passenger/freight ratio.(24)

Compared with BOAC's cabin standards, Aden's were austere.

In October, final plans were made to hand over the schedules though the flights would be given BOAC flight numbers (BO) which they would retain until the route licences were handed over and Aden Airways flight numbers (AD) allocated. (25) The last flights under the BOAC numbers were to be flown during the first two weeks of November and the first Aden flight numbers during the second and third week of that month.

The plan was that the changeover would commence on 14th November and the last flights under the numbered line services would be as follows:

BO 455/020	ex Cairo	11th November
BO 454/029	ex Aden	14th November
BO 453/028	ex Cairo	8th November
BO 452/028	ex Nairobi	11th November

CHAPTER 4: 1948: BOAC IN THE RED SEA

Aden DC-3 interior, 1948. The ceiling and walls were powder blue and the seats dark blue. (British Airways Archives)

Aden DC-3 aft end with the galley on the right and baggage stowage on the left, 1948. The entrance door is behind the galley. (British Airways Archives)

BO 451/028	ex Cairo	6th November
BO 450/028	ex Addis Ababa	7th November
BO 457/456/028	ex Aden	6th November
BO 459/458/028	ex Aden	9th November
BO 460/461/014*	ex Aden	8th November

*Note that this flight was to be discontinued after 8th November. Numbers after flight prefixes are sequential flights.

The first Aden Airways flights would operate as follows:

Main Line Service No 3, Southbound ex Cairo, 14th November
Main Line Service No 4, Southbound ex Aden, 16th November
Main Line Service No 4, Northbound ex Nairobi, 18th November
Main Line Service No 3, Northbound ex Aden, 19th November
Main Line Service No 1, Southbound ex Cairo, 16th November
Main Line Service No 1, Southbound ex Mogadishu, 21st November
Main Line Service No 2, Southbound ex Cairo, 18th November
Main Line Service No 2, Northbound ex Aden, 23rd November

Local services out of Aden would commence:

Aden - Addis Ababa - Djibouti - Aden would commence on 14th November, weekly.
Aden - Addis Ababa - Aden would commence on 17th November, weekly.
Aden - Mukalla - Aden would commence, if flown, on 15th November, fortnightly.

The final piece of the jigsaw was to get pilots to "volunteer" to fly for the new airline:

"Out of the blue in November 1948, I and several crews were told we were being posted to Asmara to be seconded to Aden Airways. We were only given two or three weeks to make arrangements for transfer; my wife, Joan, and I were accommodated in Asmara in a block of flats by the name of Palazzo Falletta, an old Italian building where hot water was only available at 6 o'clock each evening. Aden Airways had about 20 families based in Asmara. At the beginning they were all seconded from BOAC to Aden Airways, supposedly for two years. Some preferred to stay on and others came home, gradually numbers of BOAC personnel were replaced by direct contract staff with Aden Airways who had no connection with BOAC (Elgees, O'Neills, and Groves). The reason for being based in Asmara and not Aden was that BOAC had property available there but not in Aden."[26]

As in the best laid plans, BOAC had not taken into account the dynamism and energy of its new appointee in Aden. Though BOAC's motives in setting up a new airline had been driven by good intentions, one also has to remember that these motives were not altogether altruistic. The new airline (or division as it still was) had amongst its primary objectives the feeding of traffic and revenue into the mainline operation. And yet, it had also been the intention that Aden Airways would be autonomous once it was up and running and would be entirely responsible for its profits and losses. Indeed, once the licences had been transferred to the new

Crew photograph at Asmara, probably late 1948. Capt. Harry Mills, second from the right, was one of the first pilots seconded to Asmara and Aden Airways. He stayed for rather longer than most and did not return to BOAC until 1958. His last two years were spent as Chief Pilot of the airline. (Harry Mills)

Aden Airways office, Asmara, 1953. (Vic Spencer)

company, it would also be responsible for its own negotiations, though whether through the Aden Government or as a separate entity was not made clear. de Graaff Hunter had been over enthusiastic, or perhaps the limits of his responsibility had not been sufficiently defined, but during October and November he had undertaken negotiations in both Jeddah and Addis Ababa to discuss licences. He had also proposed to the Civil Air Attaché in Cairo that a subsidiary company could be set up in Mogadishu which would then circumvent the complications of negotiating traffic rights in Addis Ababa.

To give some idea of the reactions to these initiatives, all three embassies in these countries contacted the Foreign Office in London wanting to know what was going on. Probably unknown to de Graaff Hunter, there was some very delicate negotiating going on at the same time in terms of the Anglo-Egyptian bilateral agreements, conducted by the Ministry of Civil Aviation; the Egyptian negotiator had, understandably, been somewhat put out by what had occurred.(27)

Once again, to be fair to de Graaff Hunter, he had been led to believe on a number of occasions that Aden Airways would come into being on 1st November 1948. Firstly, on 20th August when he was advised by Captain W Armstrong, Deputy General Manager Eastern Division, that:

"The date on which Aden Airways might be prepared to take over full responsibilities for these new services appears not to have been considered. It is therefore suggested that as the Cairo Base is intended to be ready from the 1st November, that this date be accepted as that on which Aden Airways should be prepared to take over the full responsibility for Aden Airways operations." (28)

And secondly, in a letter from Captain Armstrong during September, it was confirmed that the start date would be 1st November: (29)

"Target date (will be) the 1st November when Aden Airways should take over full responsibility. We are therefore planning to move crews and aircraft to arrive in Cairo to take up the services from No 1 line by this date."

Even as late as the third week in October, it was stated at a meeting that: (30)

"It was agreed that the date of takeover of responsibility of Aden Airways from the Corporation would be the date of the registration of the company. The company's registration was expected within the next two weeks"

In the event, on 11th November, a further letter from Captain Armstrong acknowledged that the planned starting date could not be achieved and that the Red Sea services would continue as a BOAC unit with de Graaff Hunter as Manager. (31) It was further agreed at this meeting that the proposed winter timetables, using BO flight prefixes, due to start on 1st November, would be accepted at least until the airline was operational and in a position to define its own needs.

Eyebrows were raised at BOAC headquarters when de Graaff Hunter sent in a bill during late November when, at the request of BOAC, "Aden Airways" had supplied a DC-3 to operate a special flight (1XP.202 by G-AGMZ) carrying a set of Constellation passenger steps to Basra on 1st November, and a replacement Hercules engine from Luxor to Port Bell on 23rd November. (32)

Chapter 4: 1948: BOAC In The Red Sea

On 3rd November, de Graaff Hunter announced that the airline (or division as it really was) would no longer fly to Mukalla. At this time the only real interest in this destination was from the Aden Government and the RAF, and the latter had already given notice that it would no longer be able to supply fuel at Riyan, the airfield for Mukalla. The real reason for the cancellation was that the fares which had been charged hitherto were more a reflection of international rates and which were more than the route could bear, and: *"unless our fares can be made competitive with those charged by the local dhow services, we stand little chance of any improvement before the beginning of the next Monsoon period"*. (33) The route was re-opened on 5th June 1949 with a more realistic fare structure, but the timetable in October had been:

BO 460 dep 0700 Aden   arr 1225
BO 461 arr 0915 Mukalla dep 1015

On 25th November, the Cairo-Aden-Nairobi service was suspended in accordance with the Anglo-Egyptian bilateral agreement but a route from Aden to Nairobi was instituted in its place. The first service operated 30th November Aden-Nairobi via Mogadishu and Hargeisa, but then carried on to Cairo under a different flight number the following day (BO 468/466).

And so 1948 came to a close. Despite the many trials and confusions, BOAC had achieved a great deal in not only retiring the Lodestars and their replacement with the DC-3s, but also in placing Richard de Graaff Hunter in charge in Aden to take the new company on. He was the right man for the occasion.

Aden Airways Initial operating plan for November, 1948
All times are in GMT.

Service No: Main Line No 1.   Frequency: Once weekly.
Tuesday   0500 dep Cairo   arr 1345
                arr Luxor   dep 1130
                dep Luxor   arr 1050
           1010 arr Port Sudan   dep 0720
           1050 dep Port Sudan   arr 0640
           1255 arr Asmara   dep 0430 Monday
Wednesday 0315 dep Asmara   arr 1410
           0640 arr Addis Ababa dep 1045
           0730 dep Addis Ababa arr 0955
           0955 arr Hargeisa   dep 0730
           1035 dep Hargeisa   arr 0650
           1405 arr Mogadishu   dep 0330 Sunday

Earliest Sunset is 1443   Latest sunrise is 0313.

If permission to operate to Mogadishu has not been received by the effective datefor the introduction of this service, it will terminate at Addis Ababa on Wednesday, standing by in Addis Thursday, Friday and Saturday for local flights before resuming the schedule as above on Sunday. It is intended later to extend this service to Nairobi.

Service No: Main Line No 2.   Frequency: Once weekly.
Thursday   0500 dep Cairo   arr 1340
                arr Luxor   dep 1125
                dep Luxor   arr 1025
           0830 arr Wadi Halfa   dep 0820
           0910 dep Wadi Halfa   arr 0740
           1155 arr Khartoum   dep 0500 Wednesday
Friday   0500 dep Khartoum   arr 1210
           0755 arr Asmara   dep 0950
           0835 dep Asmara   arr 0910
           1015 arr Kamaran   dep 0730
           1055 dep Kamaran   arr 0655
           1250 arr Aden   dep 0500 Tuesday

Service No: Main Line Nos 3 and 4.   Frequency: Once weekly.
No 3
Sunday   0430 dep Cairo   arr 1415
                arr Luxor   dep 1200
                dep Luxor   arr 1100
           0915 arr Jeddah   dep 0735
           1000 dep Jeddah   arr 0655
           1120 arr Port Sudan   dep 0530 Saturday
           1200 dep Port Sudan   arr 1240
           1405 arr Asmara   dep 1030
Monday   0500 dep Asmara   arr 0930
           0740 arr Djibouti   dep 0650
           0820 dep Djibouti   arr 0610
           0930 arr Aden   dep 0500 Friday

No 4
Tuesday   0230 dep Aden   arr 1420
           0410 arr Hargeisa   dep 1240
           0450 dep Hargeisa   arr 1200
           0820 arr Mogadishu   dep 0840
           0900 dep Mogadishu   arr 0800
           1305 arr Nairobi   dep 0400 Thursday

Local Services.
Aden - Mukalla - Aden.   Frequency: Once fortnightly.

Monday   0400 dep Aden   arr 0925
           0615 arr Mukalla   dep 0715

Aden - Addis Ababa - Aden.   Frequency: Once weekly.

Wednesday 0345 dep Aden   arr 1215
           0700 arr Addis Ababa dep 0900

Aden - Djibouti - Addis Ababa - Aden.   Once weekly.

Sunday   0415 dep Aden   arr 1430
           0525 arr Djibouti   dep 1330
           0615 dep Djibouti   arr 1245
           0840 arr Addis Ababa dep 1030

(Source: BOAC Archives)

Clairways of Kenya, 1946-1948

In planning the formation of Aden Airways, it was always BOAC's intention to fly a route from Aden to Nairobi as an extension of its service from Cairo. The flight would be via Mogadishu and Hargeisa to take advantage of the considerable military and civil service traffic between these points.

Unfortunately, there appears to have been considerable confusion within East Africa as to which company had licences, granted by whom and applicable to whom. For a start, the RAF had been active on this route for a number of years, transporting personnel and freight between Aden, Mogadishu, Hargeisa and Nairobi on a weekly schedule. On occasions the flights would also take in Addis Ababa, depending on demand. While these services could be described as scheduled, they had originally been intended to fill a vacuum during the War when normal airline services had largely ceased. However, flights were still operated on a wartime basis whereby military and government passengers had priority over civilians, and it was not entirely suitable for the needs of businessmen. Late in 1947 the RAF announced its intention to reduce the service to once a fortnight, thus leaving the area without adequate air services.(34)

With BOAC unable to provide a service between Aden and Nairobi, the best placed company to fill this void was Clairways of

NAIROBI — MOGADISHU — ADEN CLAIRWAYS			347					
		②	⑤				⑦	③
— NAIROBI .... dep		09 00	09 00	ADEN .... dep			09 00	......
— KISMAYU	arr	12 00	12 00	BERBERA	arr		🌙	......
	dep	13 00	13 00		dep		🌙	......
— MOGADISHU ...🚌	arr	15 00	15 00	HARGEISA	arr		11 00	......
	dep	......	08*00		dep		12 00	......
— HARGEISA	arr	......	12*15	MOGADISHU ...🚌	arr		16 15	......
	dep	......	13*15		dep		08*00	08 00
— BERBERA	arr	......	🌙*	KISMAYU	arr		🌙10*00	10 30
	dep	......	🌙*		dep		🌙11*00	11 30
— ADEN .... arr		......	15*15	NAIROBI .... arr			14*15	14 30

TARIFF (🧳 and F are per lb.) 📦 44 lbs.

Nairobi:—	→ E.A. Sh.	↔ E.A. Sh.	🧳 E.A. Sh.	F E.A. Sh.	Nairobi:—	→ E.A. Sh.	↔ E.A. Sh.	🧳 E.A. Sh.	F E.A. Sh.
Kismayu	14/-	25/20	1/30	1/30	Berbera	—	—	—	—
Mogadishu ...	22/-	39/60	2/-	2/-	Aden	47/-	84/60	4/-	4/-
Hargeisa	40/-	72/-	3/50	3/50					

🚌 details on application

Clairways flights between Nairobi and Aden, February 1948. (Source: Official Airline Guide)

Nairobi. Clairways traced its origins to C. L. Air Surveys Ltd, a company which had been formed in the UK on 28th June 1939 by Colonel Charles Lloyd as part of No 9 Reserve Flying School headquartered at the airport in Doncaster. He had acquired four war-surplus Ansons which he used for survey work and charters within East African territories but had moved into scheduled flying when the opportunity presented itself. By October 1st 1947 the company had a route structure of 1,430 miles and was flying a weekly schedule of some 4,200 miles.(35) (C. L. Air Surveys went into receivership on 17th December, 1947).

Early in 1947 Clairways, as it had become, negotiated a contract with the Chief Administrator, British Military Administration (BMA), Somaliland, to fly once a week on the route Nairobi-Kismayu-Mogadishu, on which the anticipated traffic would be six passengers consisting of military and civilian officials, plus one ton of freight. Further to this, the BMA in Somaliland had allocated £5,000 per annum to pay for further charters within the territory, transporting Civil Administration Officers.(36) The first flight to Hargeisa took place on 19 September, 1947, and operated weekly with a night-stop at Mogadishu in both directions.

Apart from this, a further weekly service was also operated between Nairobi and Aden, calling at Mogadishu and Hargeisa, on a contract to the postal service for East Africa, connecting with the BOAC flights to and from Aden. Commercial passengers were also carried and, up to November, 1947 loads had averaged 50%. Revenue for the year for all these services had been £84,000, resulting in a profit of £24,000.

Notwithstanding his initiative, it would appear that Col. Lloyd had been somewhat imaginative in his dealings with various officials. At a meeting with Mr R D Stewart on 12th November 1947 he claimed that Clairways had been granted a full licence by the east African authorities, in this case the Director of Civil Aviation (DCA), to operate the schedules described above and which were valid until October 31st 1948. In fact, there was some confusion in Kenya as to whether this was truly the case, and it would appear that he had been given a temporary licence instead.(37)

He further stated that Skyways, a British charter company, had offered to purchase Clairways by which means it would also acquire that company's licences. Whether this statement was true or not is open to conjecture since, at the same time, he suggested that there would be benefits if Clairways and BOAC were to operate in pool. He may well have been trying to unsettle the latter, as there is also evidence which suggests that, despite his success so far, Clairways was seriously undercapitalised.(38)

Captain Malin Sorsbie (39) warns Granville (40) that, should Skyways be successful in investing in Clairways, DC-3s would certainly be employed on the route to Aden. Perhaps he made this statement to galvanise BOAC into bringing forward the start of operations on this route, as East African Airways (EAAC) saw here an opportunity to operate in pool with BOAC with the three Lodestars which were to arrive soon.

There were, however, further complications which favoured Clairways. Not only had it established contracts with the military in British Somaliland and the East African Postal services, but Col. Lloyd had also successfully approached the Office of Civil Affairs in Nairobi which, in the absence of a BOAC and EAAC presence on the route, stated that it would accept the company as their preferred carrier, though it would appear that Clairways had rather

NAIROBI — MOGADISHU — ADEN CLAIRWAYS — ✈ H, NA—Avro Anson				347					
	📦 44 lbs. 🚌 provided free		①	③ Alt. ③—A			②	⑥ Alt. ④—B	
mls.			✈ H	NA			✈ H	NA	
0	NAIROBI .... dep		07 00	07 00	ADEN .... dep		......	12 45	
390	KISMAYU ...... { arr dep		↓	↓	BERBERA .... { arr dep		....	14 15 14 45	
630	MOGADISHU ... { arr dep		12 00 13 00	12 00 13 00	HARGEISA ...... { arr dep		...... 07 00	15🌙30 07*00	
1161	HARGEISA ...... { arr dep		17 00	17🌙00 09*00	MOGADISHU .... { arr dep		11 00 12 00	11*00 12*00	
1251	BERBERA .... { arr dep		....	09*45 10*15	KISMAYU ...... { arr dep		↓	↓	
1411	ADEN .... arr		......	11*45	NAIROBI .... arr		17 00	17*00	

A—Dep Nairobi Oct. 26th, Nov. 9th, 23rd, etc. B—Dep Aden Oct. 27th, Nov. 10th, 24th, etc.

Clairways planned services between Nairobi and Aden, October 1948. (Source: Official Airline Guide)

Chapter 4: 1948: BOAC In The Red Sea

bullied these authorities into acceptance.(41) That said, it would also appear that Sorsbie, at a meeting with the East African Director of Civil Aviation, stated that he would not oppose an application by Clairways as the company did not yet have the spare capacity to fly Nairobi to Aden.

Prompt action was required by BOAC and on 10th December 1947, Hilary held a meeting in Fayid with the directors of both Military and Civil Affairs during which it was agreed that, while BOAC and EAAC would be welcomed on the route, there would be some embarrassment as a result of the agreements already put in place at the earlier meeting on 29th October, particularly since that meeting had been chaired by the DCA in Nairobi. The RAF openly stated that it "*would reduce their flights still further in favour of BOAC, whom they would prefer to see on the route rather than any charter operator like Clairways.*"(42)

Events moved quickly after this. On 23rd December 1947 Sorsbie had a meeting with the DCA in Nairobi during which it was agreed that a licence would be issued to BOAC at a public hearing in January 1948. The DCA went on to express the view that a good deal of embarrassment could be avoided, were BOAC to enter into a working agreement with Col. Lloyd, bearing in mind that the latter already held the licence in question until October 31st 1948, but it was quite clear that there was no intention to do so by either Sorsbie or Hilary.(43)

A few days later, the UK MCA, in a letter (44) to R D Stewart, stated that it, too, would support the application. At the public hearing in January, BOAC was granted a licence to operate a scheduled

Clairways services in October 1949 only extended from Nairobi as far as Hargeisa. (Source: Official Airline Guide)

service between Nairobi and Aden, the first flight taking place on 22nd January 1948 operating in competition with Clairways which also had a departure on the same day. (45)

Clairways, with its Ansons, could not compete effectively with the DC-3s brought in by BOAC and withdrew its service to Aden shortly afterwards, though it did continue to fly to Mogadishu in support of their original contract. Clairways would probably not have been successful in the long run. Possibly, if Skyways had bought the company it might have worked, but BOAC and EAAC would have ensured that this would not happen. The company limped on for a time but there was not sufficient traffic to warrant two airlines, particularly bearing in mind the discrepancy in equipment. By 1950 the company had disappeared.

Footnotes, Chapter 4:
(21) John Stroud, Annals of British and Commonwealth Air Transport, p 234.
(22) Ditto, p 332.
(23) ED.T.4.36. 17th September, 1948. Technical Manager, ED, Brentford
(24) TD.2.1470 Capt. Armstrong to Manager Aden Airways 28th September 1948.
(25) Aden Airways: Initial operational plan, H F G Hooke, 4th November 1948.
(26) Captain Harry Mills.
(27) MDEA.2.3095. R Maxwell to R M Hilary, 18th November 1948.
(28) ED.DM.24 Capt. W Armstrong to Manager Aden Airways, 20th August 1948.
(29) TD.2.1470 Capt. W Armstrong to Manager Aden Airways, 28th September 1948.
(30) Item 1 of Minutes of meeting held to consider transfer to Aden AW, 21st October 1948.
(31) ED.W.1.2754, Capt. W Armstrong to Manager No 1 line, 11th November 1948.
(32) MA.1138, RGH to Manager, Middle East, 24th November 1948.
(33) RGH to Manager Middle East Division, 3rd November 1948.
(34) MME.1421 23rd November 1947. RM Hilary.
(35) World Aviation Annual, 1948.
(36) Report by Col. C Lloyd, 12th November 1947.
(37) MDEA.2.1812 Letter to MCA, London 18th November 1947.
(38) GMEA.1443 Sorsbie to Granville 22nd November 1947.
(39) Captain Malin Sorsbie, General Manager of East African Airways Corporation (EAAC)
(40) Keith Granville, Manager Cairo and Red Sea Services.
(41) No.N/2360/73/CA 3rd December 1947.
(42) RM Hilary: notes on meeting at Fayid, 10th December 1947.
(43) GMEA.1628 Sorsbie, 23rd December 1947.
(44) R.7788/45/BOA1 MCA 24th December 1947.
(45) CO937/601 National Archives.

BOAC DC-3 on turnaround during Red Sea service. This must be G-AGNB, later Aden Airways VR-AAF, but see opposite. (Harry Mills)

Early colour scheme of Aden Airways DC-3 with two back-to-back 'Speedbirds' and blue cheatline in 1950. (Harry Mills)

Pilgrims departing for Jeddah, probably from Khartoum and believed to be in 1949. The fin markings declare BOAC ownership but G-AGNB is clearly chartered to Sudan Airways from Aden Airways for the Haj. (Sarah de Graaff Hunter)

Chapter 5 :
1949: THE START OF ADEN AIRWAYS

If 1948 had come to an end with a sense of irritation on the part of BOAC towards its offspring, the new year did not bring a great deal of relief either. In December 1948 the Commercial Manager of BOAC had written to de Graaff Hunter seeking confirmation of the final route structure for Aden Airways on behalf of the MCA. Clearly, and notwithstanding the language of the day, there was some frustration: *"I cannot trace having seen any reply to General Manager's E.D.M. 1769 of 11th October on the subject of projected routes………"*(46)

In his reply to the above letter (and incidentally two others in the same vein) de Graaff Hunter produced a robust defence of his approach and how he intended to run his new company. (47) As the man on the spot and he had cultivated relationships in a number of countries and with those who mattered to the interests of Aden Airways. He could react far more spontaneously to events than anyone else in London possibly could.

(1)   *"All Aden Airways services must commence in Aden, therefore route No 1 is not feasible".* (Route No 1 (see 1948) operated between Cairo and Mogadishu, with a night-stop in Asmara and not even passing through Aden. This assertion seems a little strange bearing in mind that Asmara at the time was the main base for the airline, and was, indeed, where de Graaff Hunter himself lived for most of the year.)

(2)   *"Aden-Mukalla is not a route which affects anybody but the Aden Government. It is intended to be included as one of the intermediate points to Karachi and Bombay".* (De Graaff Hunter always dreamed of establishing this route; he never did so, but it was to come up time and again over the years.)

(3)   *"Dire Dawa was of great interest to us before the slump descended upon Ethiopia, but today we can attach little importance to it".* (In fact, this destination was later to be one of the more lucrative ones for Aden Airways as it was the main point for the onloading of Qat, the soporific drug so loved in that part of the world.)

(4)   *"Unless we are looking ahead a couple of years or further, any rights in the Yemen would be pointless to seek now. We can do better business through Mukeiras and Kamaran with the Yemen than by any other means open to us at the present time, and no rights have to be given away for these destinations".*

He goes on to discuss future plans for the airline, in particular regarding the route to India: *"You specifically ask for intermediate points on the Hadramaut route to India, but you go on to say that, in your opinion, this route should not be operated until we have 4 engine aircraft. Aden Airways are unlikely to have 4 engine aircraft for at least five years, and the Hadramaut is clearly an Aden Airways prerogative. Indian Overseas Airlines have been operating Dakotas for the past 18 months between Bombay and Nairobi on a regular 10 day schedule and Ethiopian Airlines are commencing a fortnightly service this week, also with Dakotas. Air India talk of using Constellations from Bombay to Nairobi while I remember being told by their own representative that Nairobi is unsuitable at the moment for this type of aircraft. Therefore, they may operate Dakotas too. I do not know what further convincing the Ministry are going to require with this evidence before them. I can only say that Aden Airways would not be satisfied to sit by and watch other operators, employing 2 engine aircraft, on a route we claim for ourselves. Have the Ministry forgotten that Lodestars operated the Ivory Route with considerable success during and after the end of the War?"*

(5)   *"Aden Airways have a special working agreement with Alitalia whereby the latter are foregoing their rights to fly South of*

Asmara, leaving this to us on the understanding that the Rome traffic from Mogadishu, Addis Ababa and Aden will be fed into their Lancastrian direct service from Asmara. So far, the arrangement has worked rather clumsily because of failure on our part to obtain the necessary permissions to fly Addis Ababa-Hargeisa-Mogadishu on the present Cairo-Addis Ababa service upon which our Alitalia agreement was based. Our proposals go deeper than would appear (to you) on the surface.

I should like to impress on you the need for preserving flexibility in the way our proposals are presented to the Ministry. The running of local services in this area is subject to the local vagaries of the local trade conditions as well as to the violence of some of the seasons. A service which is routed one way to give the best commercial results at one time of the year may well have to be routed another during the rest of the year if the traffic is to be properly served and the best commercial gain had out of it. I realise that this is not how trunk route operations are planned or run, but when you say that you wish to avoid proposals now, which we may later wish to amend, I am afraid that I cannot give you such assurances as you require.

Therefore, we wish to retain the right to switch intermediate destinations from one route to another in order to provide the public with the best combination of services as well as ourselves with the best commercial prospects.

I have already discussed the probable future requirements of Aden Airways with the Director of Civil Aviation, Government of Aden, at his request and he, in turn, will have notified the Colonial Office as is his prerogative. Will we not be crossing wires if applications are made from several directions, especially if they are not up to date?"

This was strong stuff, bearing in mind the attitudes of the day. The wording may not have endeared him to the management of the parent company, but his thoughts would not have been out of place today. The tone of this letter must have come as a considerable surprise to the board of BOAC. It could have been seen as a declaration of independence by an airline not yet officially in existence and which was to be subservient to the needs of the parent company.

But de Graaff Hunter was right to be assertive. Aden was a great distance from the bureaucratic monolith in London and he had just the right swashbuckling instincts necessary at that time and in that environment. As will be seen later, these qualities did not serve him well after the airline had become established, but in these early days, his quick brain, willingness to challenge the established procedures and to take risks were exactly the attributes required of a manager in such an embryo enterprise.

Nevertheless, he did appear to have an obsession with the Aden-Bombay route. That other airlines, such as Indian Overseas Airlines (formerly Mistri) and Ethiopian Airlines, flew DC-3s on this route must have been particularly galling to him, while the proposed Air India Constellation service was something he could only dream of competing with. However, the figures simply did not add up and he was fortunate that the BOAC Commercial Planning department provided him with the comparative figures for DC-3s and Lancastrians flying the route.(48)

Briefly, the problem for the DC-3 was that, flying between Masirah Island and Bombay, only 850kg, or about 8 passengers, could be carried, on average. Were the flight to be operated via Karachi, 14 passengers could be carried, but this ignored the political considerations raised by the recent partition of India.

On the other hand, were a Lancastrian to be bought or hired from BOAC the costs appeared to be better, though whether it made economic sense to especially invest in one or two such aircraft for a specific route was open to question, particularly bearing in mind the technical unreliability of those days. In any case none were

Mr & Mrs de Graaff Hunter at Asmara in 1949.
(Sarah de Graaff Hunter)

available. The new Convair 240, as flown by Ethiopian Airlines, might have been a viable proposition, but the foreign exchange was simply not available in the UK at that time.

The comparative figures (per round trip) were: (49)

	Revenue	Costs
DC-3: Excluding Karachi	£ 45,760	£ 72,000
Via Karachi	£ 80,080	£ 83,500
Lancastrian to Karachi:	£ 2,016	£ 2,000

As important to de Graaff Hunter was the route to Nairobi. In March, he wrote to the General Manager (R M Hilary) suggesting a second route to Kenya *"as soon as possible"* (50). With the withdrawal of Clairways from the route north of Mogadishu, the way was now clear for Aden Airways to expand southwards, but, instead of the second service to Nairobi, his proposal was that the route would be flown from Aden to Mombasa via Hargeisa, Mogadishu and Kismayu, (flagstop). East African Airways would co-operate with a shuttle between Nairobi and Mogadishu with Lodestars, which would connect with the flights to and from Aden.

There is no record of the decisions reached by BOAC on that route. But it did not appear in the timetables for 1949, though it did appear on the route map for the same period.

The beginning of Aden Airways

March 7th 1949 was a momentous day for de Graaff Hunter. On this day Aden Airways Ltd was registered as a wholly-owned company, though still a subsidiary of BOAC, with a working capital of £225,000. For historical reasons, the company was incorporated in Aden under the Indian Companies' Act of 1913, an anachronism left over from that period when Aden's commercial administration came under the jurisdiction of India.

Chapter 5: 1949: The Start Of Aden Airways

The first meeting of the Board of Directors of Aden Airways Ltd was held in Aden on 10th March and present were Richard de Graaff Hunter and V K Joshi. The purpose of the meeting was to set up procedures, banking arrangements, allocation of shares and the appointment of officers, namely Mr P B Putt as Company Secretary and Miss E M Hornsby as his Assistant.

Of more interest to the historian, perhaps, was the selection of the company seal which was to be a diagrammatic "Aden dhow" supporting the company initials in the form of its sails. Similarly, the company trademark was also approved, the basic motive of the design provided by two elongated Speedbirds joined at the longest measurement and superimposed on a circle of smaller measurement. (51) The correct address was to be "Aden Airways Ltd, Aden, Arabia", while the telegraphic address was to be "Adenair".

The second Board Meeting took place on 30th July, in Asmara. Once again, only de Graaff Hunter and V K Joshi present as Board Members. The only significant decision was the acceptance of Al Chark to be the advertising agents on a yearly contract from 1st May 1949, with a spending limit of £15,000 per year, to include all administration fees and expenses. A photograph of a suggested colour scheme for the airline was also produced by this company, but not accepted.

On 1st October, Aden Airways began operations (52) with British-registered DC-3s acquired from BOAC. There could be some understandable confusion here as to the exact date that the company came into being as, in a letter to H O Houchen in November, de Graaff Hunter accepts that 1st January 1950 would be the date of transfer of both aircraft and licences to Aden Airways. (53) He further acknowledges that 30th November would be the date when the existing Cairo-Addis Ababa service should be terminated as a result of the proposed Anglo-Egyptian Bilateral agreement which was under discussion at the time. In fact, the last service, the BO 463, left Cairo on 25th November to be replaced on 6th December by the new "Express" Cairo-Aden flight with a connection to Addis Ababa. This second route proved to be more successful than the original.

The new company was responsible for its own finances from 1st October, and the first quarter figures were reassuring, to say the least, and were to continue into the new year up to 31st March 1950. Revenue was £216,409 against an expenditure of £213,145, giving an overall profit of £3,264. Much of this success was as a

Left: The Certificate of Incorporation of Aden Airways Ltd, dated 7th March 1949.

Below: Aden Airways timetable, June 1949, with services still flown under BOAC codes. (BOAC timetable)

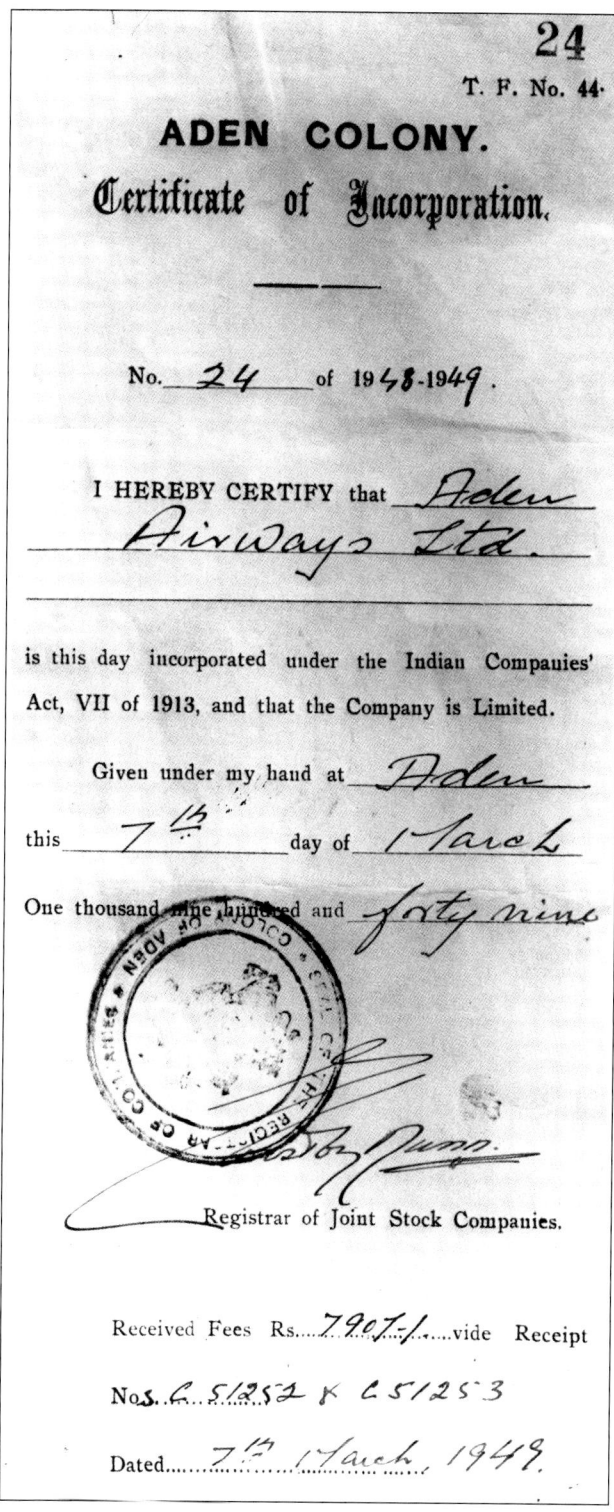

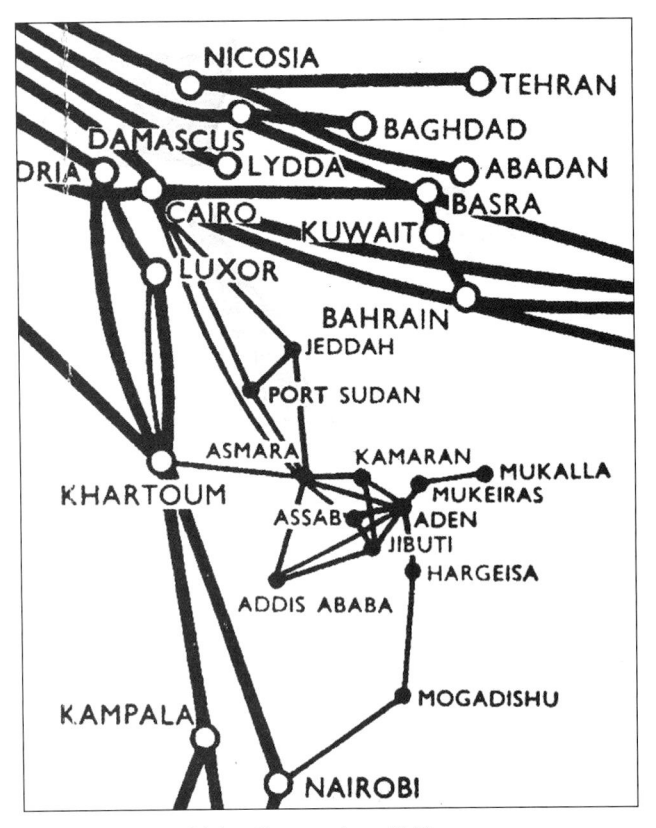

Route structure of Aden Airways, June 1949.

Looking up into the newly-refurbished cabin of an Aden Airways DC-3 while an employee tends to a floral decoration.
(Sarah de Graaff Hunter)

result of the pilgrim flights which took up some 700 flying hours and, while it stretched the integrity of the network, the additional revenue played an important part in the financial results, as it would over the coming years. The following flights are on record as having been Haj flights: (54)

27 flights from Damascus to Jeddah carrying 850 passengers;
3 flights from Baghdad to Jeddah carrying 75 passengers;
2 flights from Tehran via Beirut to Jeddah carrying 50 passengers;
There were no flights from Egypt because of the quarantine in that country.

1st January, 1950 to 31st March, 1950
After having been given operating autonomy the previous October, the crucial issue was now the transfer of the route licences to Aden Airways. January 1st 1950 had been the original promise, but negotiations with the various governments around the Red Sea had not proceeded smoothly, and the Anglo-Egyptian Bilateral negotiations were still dragging on, to the extent that Aden Airways had to clear every flight into and out of Cairo through the British Embassy there, describing each flight as a charter rather than a scheduled service. In both Saudi Arabia and Sudan de Graaff Hunter's personal intervention had smoothed the way sufficiently for an easy transition. In the end, 1st February 1950 was to be the date when the aircraft would be transferred to the Aden register, all flights would then operate under the AD callsign and route licences would be in the company's name.

However, Egypt was now also establishing a presence in the countries surrounding the Red Sea, and in particular up the Nile to Khartoum. As it claimed cabotage rights on this route it was irritated by the presence of Aden Airways. The retaliation was to place obstacles in the way of Aden Airways whose AD 472 had to pass through Luxor on its way to Cairo, such as by delaying flights for clearances onwards or lengthy health checks. Ever resourceful, de Graaff Hunter could now capitalise on his previous negotiations with the Sudanese and thereby fulfil his commitment to West African Airways Corporation (WAAC). He was able to provide a trans-Africa link between Accra, Lagos, Kano, Khartoum and Damascus via AD 478. It was a very lengthy journey, as can be seen from the relevant timetables, but it did provide the essential connection between West Africa and the Levant. The connection to Aden was also the fortnightly service which flew from Aden to Assab, Asmara and Khartoum where it made the above connection. It would seem, though, that the ulterior motive behind this was de Graaff Hunter's ambitions to make a further connection from Khartoum to India via Aden, but, once again, he was to be frustrated.

One innovation was the inauguration, on 1st January, of a local freighter service, the BO 476/477, connecting the smaller stations

West African Airways Corporation (WAAC) Accra to Khartoum service connecting with Aden Airways flight to Damascus, December 1950.

CHAPTER 5: 1949: THE START OF ADEN AIRWAYS

TABLE No. 16

	BO 471		BO 475		BO 473		BO 467				BO 466		BO 472		BO 474		BO 470	
Days	L.T.	Days	L.T.	Days	L.T.	Days	L.T.			L.T.	Days	L.T.	Days	L.T.	Days	L.T.	Days
②	00.30	Alt.⑥	23.30	⑦	02.00	④	02.00	dep. CAIRO arr.		19.00 ▲		19.30 ▲		20.00 ▲		22.00 ▲	
	—		—		—		—	arr. LUXOR dep.		—		—		17.45		—	
	—		—		—		—	dep. LUXOR arr.		—		—		17.10		—	
	—		—		07.15		07.15	arr. JEDDAH dep.		14.45		15.15		—		—	
	—		—		08.15		08.15	dep. JEDDAH arr.		13.45		14.15		—		—	
	—		—		09.05		—	arr. PORT SUDAN dep.		11.50		12.20		—		16.50	
	—		—		09.50		—	dep. PORT SUDAN arr.		11.05		11.35		—		16.05	
	—	Alt.⑦	03.00		—		—	arr. WADI HALFA dep.		—		—		—		—	
	—		03.30		—		—	dep. WADI HALFA arr.		—		—		—		—	
	—		06.15		—		—	arr. KHARTOUM dep.		—		—		12.40		—	
	—		07.45		—		—	dep. KHARTOUM arr.		—		—		11.40		—	
	08.10		11.40		11.40		12.55	arr. ASMARA dep.		09.55		10.25		10.00		14.55	
	09.10		12.45		12.45		13.55	dep. ASMARA arr.		08.55		09.05		09.05		13.55	
	—		14.25		14.25		—	arr. KAMARAN dep.		—		—		—		—	
	—		15.20		15.20		—	dep. KAMARAN arr.		—		07.00		07.00		—	
	—		—		—		—	arr. ASSAB dep.		—		06.40		06.40		—	
	▼12.00		▼17.00		▼17.00		▼16.45	arr. ADEN dep.		06.00 ①		05.30 ⑤		05.30 Alt.⑥		11.00 ③	

TABLE No. 17

	BO 457		BO 459		BO 476		BO 469				BO 468		BO 477		BO 458		BO 456	
Days	L.T.	Days	L.T.	Days	L.T.	Days	L.T.			L.T.	Days	L.T.	Days	L.T.	Days	L.T.	Days
②	13.00	④	07.45	②	08.00	⑤	06.00	dep. ADEN arr.		17.50 ▲		11.25 ▲		18.05 ▲		10.00 ▲	
	—		08.55		09.10		—	arr. JIBUTI dep.		—		10.15		16.55		—	
	—		09.35		09.50		—	dep. JIBUTI arr.		—		09.35		16.15		—	
	▼16.30		▼12.00		—		—	arr. ADDIS ABABA dep.		—		08.50		14.00	④	06.30	③
					—		—	arr. ASSAB dep.		—		08.20		—			
					11.40		—	dep. ASSAB arr.		—		—		—			
					12.20		—	arr. KAMARAN dep.		—		—		—			
					▼14.00		—	dep. KAMARAN arr.		—		—		—			
							—	arr. ASMARA dep.		—		—		06.15	③		
							07.40	arr. HARGEISA dep.		16.10							
							08.20	dep. HARGEISA arr.		15.30							
							11.50	arr. MOGADISHU dep.		12.10							
							12.30	dep. MOGADISHU arr.		11.30							
							▼16.30	arr. NAIROBI (Eastleigh) dep.		07.30 ⑦							

Aden Airways international services, January 1950, still under BOAC codes.

of the Red Sea between Aden and Asmara. This was in fact a mixed passenger/freight service carrying up to 10 passengers amid the freight. Later, this service was continued up to Cairo.

Operations to Mukeiras and Mukalla still gave some cause for concern for a number of reasons. In the case of Mukalla, there was simply not enough traffic willing to pay the relatively expensive fares when there were much cheaper dhows which plied between there and Aden.

On the other hand, Mukeiras was an important border point into the Yemen, and though there was sufficient traffic for this route, the landing strip there was dangerous and difficult to approach. After representations to the Aden Government by de Graaff Hunter, improvements had been made and services resumed in November 1949. There was also the intention to combine these two services in order to try to make them profitable, but a report to the Board by Captain Colvin, who had become Chief Pilot, expressing his concern on the safety of flights into Mukeiras resulted in a decision to discontinue flights to this destination on 27th March 1950. (55)

Another innovation was the introduction of stewardesses who had been recruited in Asmara, which at this time was the main base for the airline. They were well received on the routes, notwithstanding the high percentage of Muslim passengers carried, particularly within the Protectorate. The vast majority of the girls were of Italian origin as a result of the immigrant population in this former Italian colony, though there was a sprinkling of other nationalities. Later, once the airline had moved its main base of operations to Aden, most of the stewardesses came from British backgrounds and were from families working there.

At this stage the pilots were all seconded from BOAC, and while there had been an element of coercion in their involvement in Aden Airways, all seem to have enjoyed the experience:

"Generally, the flying was routine, operating the Aden Airways route structure. In those days there were few charters other than Haj flights to Jeddah. There was, however, one special flight which I was called out to do, and that was a trip up to Dolal, in North Eastern Ethiopia, in order to pick up the Italian Manager of a

The introduction of stewardesses on Aden Airways routes was well received. Here one poses beneath the company insignia displayed by DC-3 VR-AAF at Riyan in 1951. (British Airways Archives)

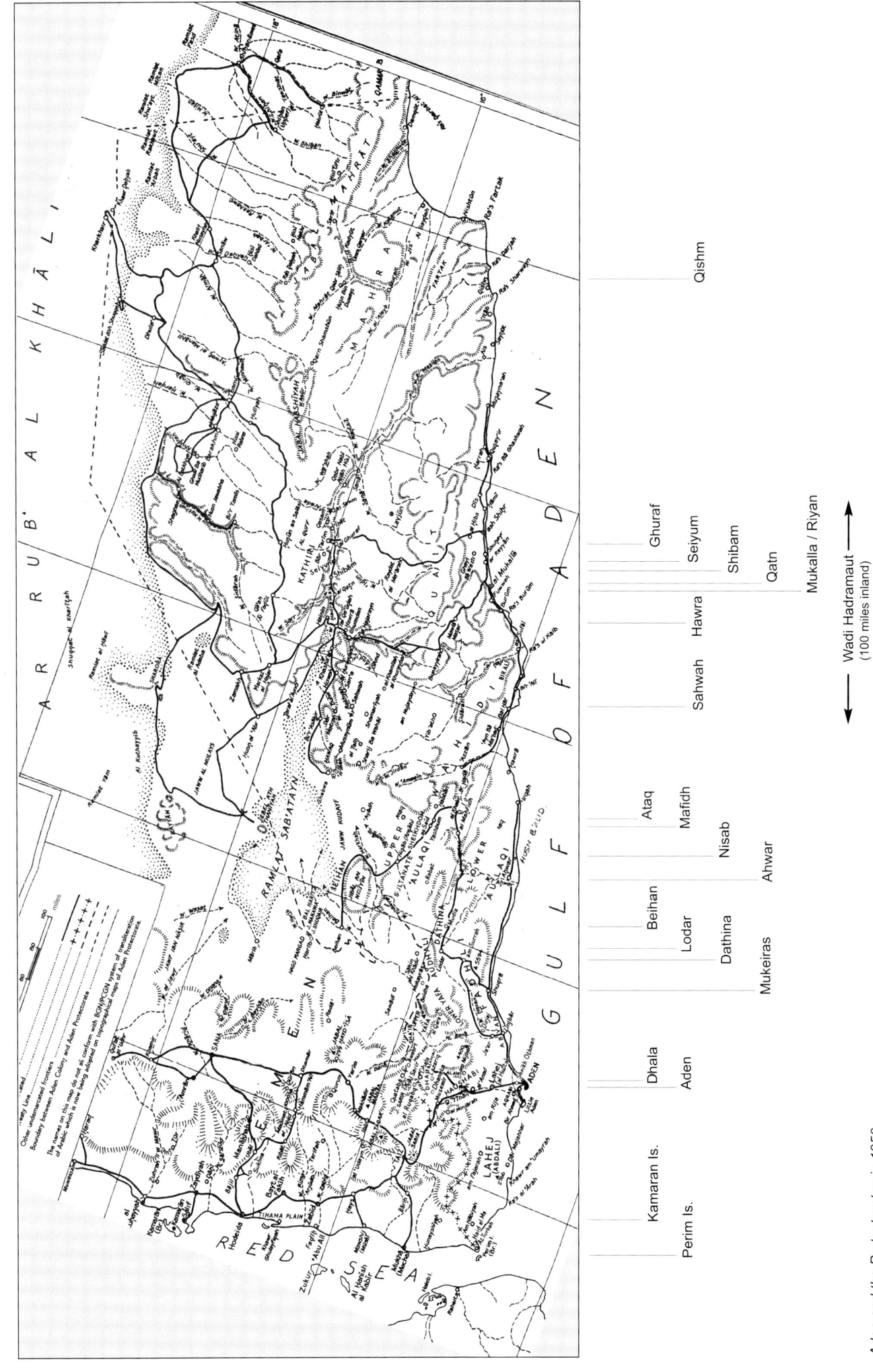

Aden and the Protectorates in 1950

CHAPTER 5: 1949: THE START OF ADEN AIRWAYS

Asmara Civil Airport about 1950. Capt Harry Mills is on the right, his wife Joan beside him. (Harry Mills)

Miss Jones, at Asmara in 1949, was one of the first stewardesses to be employed by the airline. (Sarah de Graaff Hunter)

sulphur mine who was seriously ill. The landing and takeoff were completed on a dried-up salt lake which was solid enough to carry the weight of a DC-3. When we departed for Asmara, the temperature outside was well over 100°F, and on takeoff we didn't even look at the engine gauges since they were all exceeding their limits anyway. The flying was certainly very different." (56)

Charters were also successfully sought, one of the first being with ARAMCO, an American oil exploration company which needed personnel carried between Jeddah, Asmara and Aden.

Once again, though, the Aden to India route was never far from de Graaff Hunter's mind:

"Likewise, our interest for some time had been directed upon the India/East Africa traffic, and numerous attempts have been made by this company to open up this service, which on all occasions have been turned down by the Corporation on the grounds of the unsuitability of Dakotas for the Hadramaut portion of the route.
Recently, Air India International have inaugurated a fortnightly service, which together with that of Ethiopian Airlines, adequately covers the traffic at present offering. In order not to be left out altogether, however, we have concluded a General Agency agreement with Air India International, and they have placed their representative in our office to our mutual benefit. Our desire to run the route jointly with them, employing their aircraft on a cost plus basis, was rejected by the British Government on the grounds that, if agreed in this case, Air India International may press for the formula to be applied also in other theatres where it may not be so much to the advantage of British interests. We regard this as unfortunate: the question is not yet settled and it may be possible to revive the issue by a suitable interpolation in the agreement."(57)

These problems were to beset Aden Airways throughout its early existence through the conflicting perceptions of why the airline was established, firstly by the British Government which merely saw it as an extension of foreign policy and influence, and secondly, the remit given to de Graaff Hunter whereby he was to establish an airline which was expected to stand on its own two feet. That he was clearly deeply frustrated by the constant constraints imposed by his masters in London is evident, and this continued between the two parties as time progressed.

In Khartoum, agreement had been reached with the Sudanese Government granting terminating rights at that station (to connect with the West African Airways flights from Kano and Lagos) and equal traffic rights between Asmara and Khartoum which then allowed the company to carry passengers on up to Damascus, thus creating a direct service, albeit with a change of aircraft, from West Africa to the Levant. It gave de Graaff Hunter some considerable satisfaction that the Egyptian airline, Misrair, had been totally excluded from these agreements. Revenge was to come later in the form of equally total exclusion of Aden Airways from the Nile route between Khartoum and Cairo as a result of the signing of the Anglo-Egyptian bilateral agreement some time later.

Engineering, too, was threatening to become a major cost problem in the sense that BOAC had contracted to carry out all major work for the airline in Egypt. However, on 1st November 1949 the company had ceased to maintain the workshops at Almaza, just outside Cairo and, on behalf of Aden Airways, had contracted the work to be done with a new company, Egyptian Aircraft Engineering Company (EAEC). While the engines would continue to be overhauled at Treforest, in Wales, Aden Airways was now contracted to have all their major checks completed by the new company in Almaza.

"In order to give E.A.E.C. the best opportunity of establishing itself, the terms agreed between BOAC and them on our behalf have not been as favourable financially as we would wish. It is estimated that the cost to the company of this arrangement will be in the neighbourhood of £10,000 in excess of the best terms which might have been procured had we been free to call for competitive tenders in the open market." (58)

Bearing in mind that Asmara was once the main engineering base for the Middle East during the war years, it might well have been of greater benefit to Aden Airways had an engineering unit been established there where it could also have gained revenue by contracting out services to other carriers in the area.

By now the airline had established employment bases in a number of cities: Aden, Asmara, Cairo and Addis Ababa, and the total numbers of employees were: Aden 81, Asmara 71, Cairo 14 and Addis Ababa 6, giving a total of 172. Flying crew, both pilots and radio officers were, of course, seconded at this stage from BOAC, though this was to change later. Property was being purchased in Aden for restoration as offices, namely the ex post office at Khormaksar and the Exchange Bank of India in Crater. Residential property, known as Handa's House, had also been acquired in Crater and was suitable for three families, though it would be some considerable time before Asmara lost its position as a main base, well after the federation between Ethiopia and Eritrea, in September, 1952.

So, by the end of the first six months of existence, Aden Airways had established itself well, mostly through the dynamism of its

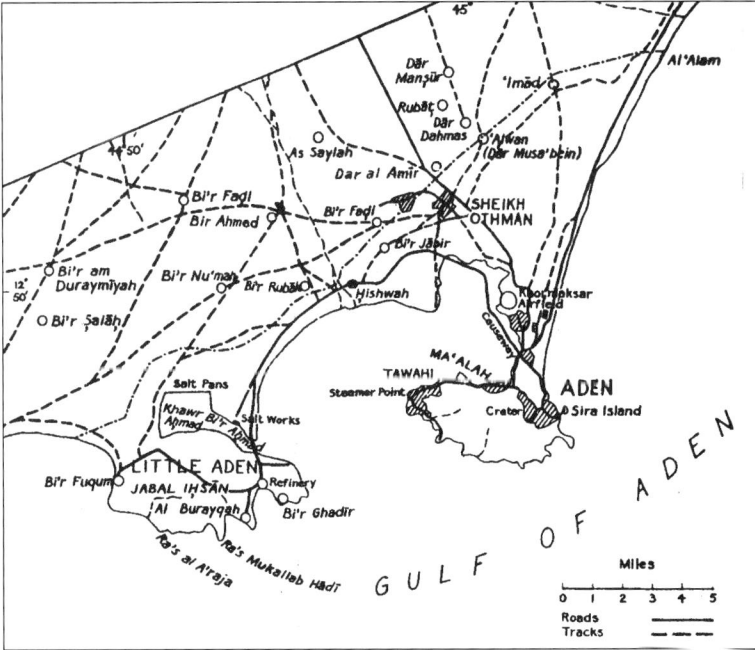

Crater, Aden, in 1951. Property was difficult to find here with crew and passenger accommodation particularly lacking.   (British Airways Archives)

The port of Aden and environs. Khormaksar Airfield can be seen on the peninsular connecting Crater with the mainland.

General Manager, de Graaff Hunter. On a total revenue of £216,409, a profit of £3,264 had been made. Six DC-3s were now on the Aden register, three of which were 21-seat full-service passenger aircraft while the other four were equipped with a flexible seating plan of 10 to 33 passengers, depending on the freight requirement at the time.

Footnotes, Chapter 5:
(46) ED.CP.439 Commercial Manager to RGH, 14th December 1948.
(47) MA.136 RGH to Commercial Manager BOAC, 7th January 1949.
(48) E.FE.80 Project No 35; Aden - Bombay, 2nd February 1949.
(49) Ditto
(50) MA.1382 de Graaff Hunter to Hilary, 4th March 1949.
(51) Article 12, First Board Meeting, 10th March 1949.
(52) Stroud, Annals of British and Commonwealth Air Transport p332.
(53) GM.ASM.304 RGH to Deputy Manager Middle East, 7th November 1949.
(54) "Flight" magazine 17th November 1949.
(55) 7th Board Meeting, item 7/92, 23rd March 1950.
(56) Captain Tom Beale was seconded from BOAC in 1948, returning there in 1952. He had come from No 5 Line in Cairo, flying Lodestars, before converting to the DC-3 of No 1 Line. During 1947, he had also been seconded for a few months to Orient Airways in Pakistan.
(57) General Manager's Report for 1st October 1949, to 15th March 1950.
(58) Ditto.

Aden Airways DC-3 taxying out at Asmara in 1951. (British Airways Archives)

Chapter 6 :
ADEN AIRWAYS 1950 - 1951

At the start of the new financial year, Aden Airways could reflect well on its achievement so far, particularly the first six months of operation. The company had six DC-3s, all fully paid for and debt was negligible, a full complement of crews on secondment from BOAC and there was a sound management structure which used local people (Antonin Besse as chairman and V K Joshi as Legal Adviser). It had a reasonable, if expensive, engineering facility in Egypt and though Aden lacked the accommodation to house all the staff, Asmara was an ideal second base from which to concentrate flights. The profit from the first six months of £3,264, though modest, boded well for the future.

Above all, the company had a dynamic and innovative Managing Director in de Graaff Hunter who, as a result of his background, upbringing and previous experience in BOAC, was quite prepared to exercise his full authority in negotiating within the region for what he believed was in the interests of Aden Airways.

He would not endear himself, however, to the BOAC parent corporation which was accustomed to a greater degree of subservience from its subsidiary companies. Thus, while de Graaff Hunter was to have a profound and positive effect locally, he may well have been sowing the seeds for his own dismissal some four years hence. Nor were all of his ideas successful. However, at this initial stage of Aden Airways' development, this was his airline, and he was very much in charge.

While the general route structure had already been well defined by previous operations with BOAC, de Graaff Hunter quickly realised that a combination of freight and passengers could successfully serve many of the smaller airfields, particularly in British and French Somaliland where the internal infrastructure was poor and subject to weather closures. For instance, a fortnightly freighter flight from Aden to Berbera was started on 26th April 1950, using a DC-3 with 14 seats. This allowed space for sufficient freight to be flown to make the flight worthwhile. Even though no fuel was available in Berbera, there was still sufficient capacity to carry 2,449 kg out of Aden and 2,731 kg out of Berbera.(59)

As mentioned previously, Mukeiras, near the border with Yemen, was a semi-official source of communication with that country, and was considered essential for trading. Yet, as reported by Captain Colvin, it was unfit for flight operations. As a result, the authorities were advised that flights there would cease from 1st April and not be resumed until such time as the airfield was considered safe. In fact, flights to Mukeiras had been linked with those to Mukalla but, from this date on, the AD 460/461 only operated to the latter destination. This action seems to have galvanised the Aden Government into resolving the issue and it immediately put arrangements in hand to remedy the situation; by June, the airfield was made serviceable and the service reinstated as the AD 462/463 and as a destination in its own right.

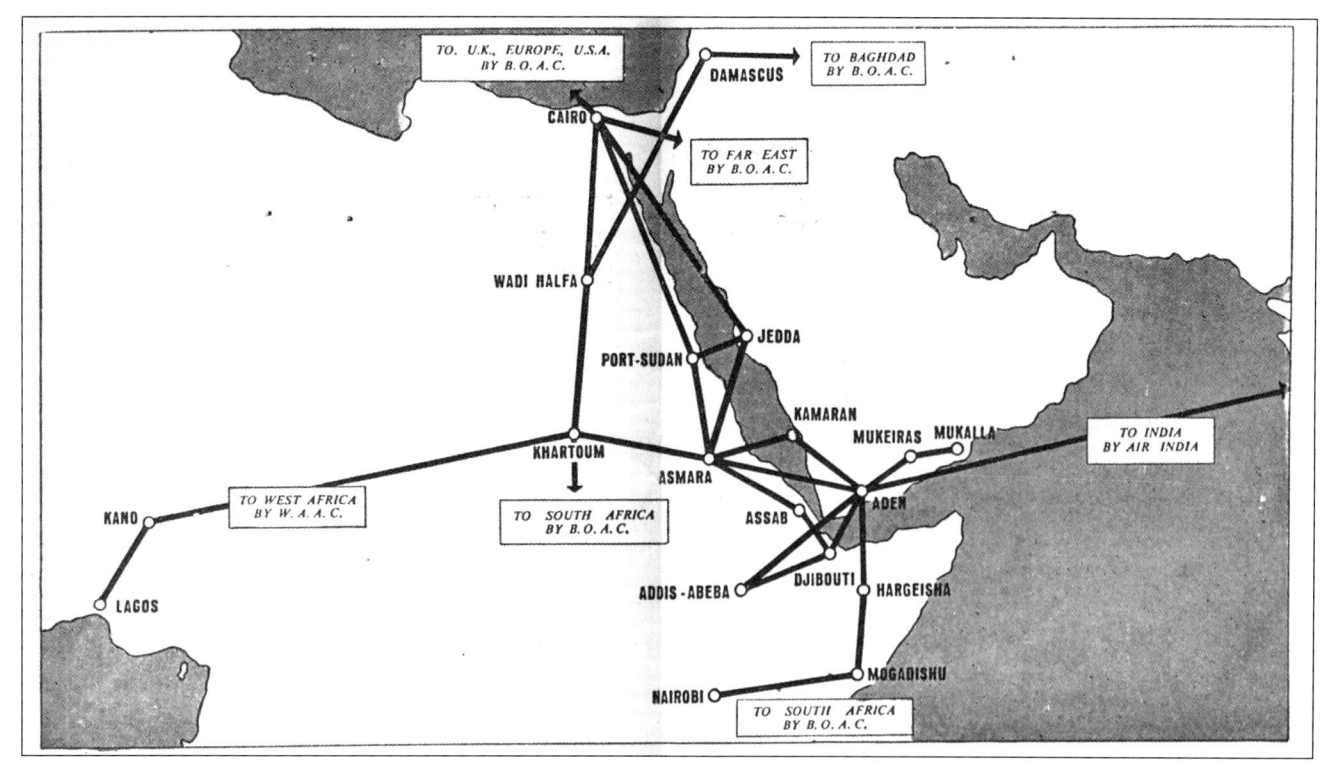

Map from Aden Airways Timetable of International Routes in June 1950.

Before the transfer of operations from BOAC, de Graaff Hunter had noted that within the Protectorate the fares were unrealistically high, reflecting more international standards, with the result that the local population were unable to afford to travel by air. Indeed, on 3rd November 1948 he had suspended the Mukeiras service for this reason, much to the chagrin of the local government. The only solution was to lower the fares to: *"levels comparable to those of surface transport, (dhow and/or camel), and from which we have found a new market from which a growing revenue is resulting"* (60). Load factors to both Mukeiras and Mukalla rose to an average of 90%, resulting in these two routes successfully sustaining dedicated services to each.

Many years later this innovative train of thought was to be the basis for the low-cost carriers we have today.

With this success behind them, the aforementioned route to Berbera was given the same treatment and with similar results, so much so that the route was extended to Hargeisa during June 1950 where it continued to be a success notwithstanding that Somaliland had come under Italian administration after the departure of the British military authorities.

The year continued to be successful. Once again, a difference in approach by de Graaff Hunter compared to BOAC was to drive costs lower and improve efficiency (this was simply not possible in the UK in the prevailing political climate) and this was measured in a number of ways. The most telling was the revenue rate per hour; for instance, the budgeted figure was £51.8 per hour, while the actual came to £59.53 per hour, an improvement of almost £8 for every flying hour completed. Similarly, expenditure for the first six months of the year was £54.62 per hour compared to the previous six months when the expenses were £60.02 per hour. This close attention to costs and revenue resulted in a consistent profit during the first half of the year to 31st September, except for July when a small loss was incurred.

	Profit	Loss
April	£2,006	
May	£2,145	
June	£2,578	
July		£775
August	£4,549	
September	£8,668	
	£19,946	£775

Richard de Graaff Hunter, centre, with his wife and baby daughter Sarah, Asmara 1951.
(Antonin Besse)

Chapter 6: Aden Airways 1950 - 1951

ADEN to/from EAST AFRICA, EGYPT, ERITREA, ETHIOPIA, SAUDI ARABIA, SOMALILAND, SUDAN, SYRIA & WEST AFRICA

*AD. 479	AD. 475	AD. 477	AD. 473	AD. 471	AD. 467	DAKOTAS		AD. 466	AD. 470	AD. 472	AD. 476	AD. 474	AD. 478*
Fortnightly services													Fortnightly services
(6) 13.00			(7) 01.00	(2) 00.01	(4) 01.00	Dep. CAIRO	Arr.	19.00	21.30	22.00			
N/S 18.25						Dep. DAMASCUS	Arr.	^	^	^			11.30
(7) 04.00					v	Arr. WADI-HALFA	Dep.						(6) 06.15
						Dep. WADI-HALFA	Arr.						N S 20.00
v					06.45	Arr. JEDDAH	Dep.	15.00		18.00			^
06.45					07.45	Dep. JEDDAH	Arr.	14.00		17.00			
0.745	(7) 07.45					Arr. KHARTOUM	Dep.	^		^			17.20
			v			Dep. KHARTOUM	Arr.					15.40	15.40
v	v		08.05			Arr. PORT SUDAN	Dep.	11.45	16.20	14.45		^	^
			08.50	v		Dep. PORT SUDAN	Arr.	11.00	15.40	14.00			
11.40	11.40		11.55	07.30	10.30	Arr. ASMARA	Dep.	10.00	14.40	13.00		14.00	14.00
13.00	13.00	(2) 13.00	13.00	08.30	11.30	Dep. ASMARA	Arr.	08.55	13.40	12.00	11.30	12.00	12.00
					13.05	Arr. KAMARAN	Dep.	^	^	^	09.55	^	^
		v			13.55	Dep. KAMARAN	Arr.				09.05		
		15.00				Arr. ASSAB	Dep.			09.55	^	09.55	09.55
		15.30				Dep. ASSAB	Arr.			09.30		09.30	09.30
		16.25				Arr. DJIBOUTI	Dep.			08.45		08.45	08.45
v	v	17.05	v	v		Dep. DJIBOUTI	Arr.			08.05		08.05	08.05
15.50	15.50	18.15	15.50	11.20	15.30	Arr. ADEN	Dep.	(1) 06.00	(3) 10.45	(5) 07.00	(2) 07.30	(5) 07.00	(5) 07.00

AD. 465	AD. 462	AD. 460	AD. 459	AD. 457	AD. 469	DAKOTAS		AD. 468	AD. 456	AD. 458	AD. 461	AD. 463	AD. 464
(3) 14.30	(1) 05.30	(1) 09.00	(4) 08.00	(2) 12.30	(5) 06.00	Dep. ADEN	Arr.	18.30	09 45	18.15	13.55	07.40	17.40
v	06.15					Arr. MUKEIRAS	Dep.	^	^	^	^	(1) 07.00	^
15.40		v				Arr. BERBERA	Dep.						(3) 16.30
		11.05				Arr. MUKALLA	Dep.				(1) 12.00		
			v			Arr. DJIBOUTI	Dep.			17.05			
			09.05			Dep. DJIBOUTI	Arr.			16.20			
			09.45	v		Arr. ADDIS ABABA	Dep.		(3) 06.30	(4) 14.00			
			12.00	15.30	v	Arr. HARGEISA	Dep.	16.50					
					07.40	Dep. HARGEISA	Arr.	16.05					
					08.30	Arr. MOGADISHU	Dep.	12.45					
					11.40	Dep. MOGADISHU	Arr.	11.30					
					13.00	Arr. NAIROBI	Dep.	(7) 07.30					
					16.45								

*THE FORTNIGHTLY SERVICES TO AND FROM DAMASCUS OFFER A THROUGH CONNECTION AT KHARTOUM BETWEEN THE LEVANT AND WEST AFRICA, OPERATED IN CONJUNCTION WITH W.A.A.C., KHARTOUM/DAMASCUS 12th. 26th MAY, 9th, 23rd JUNE. DAMASCUS/KHARTOUM 13th, 27th MAY, 10th, 24th JUNE.

Aden Airways International Services, June 1950.

Bearing in mind that a loss of £12,834 had been budgeted for these six months, this was a creditable result.

During July, return fares between Djibouti and Asmara were further reduced from £28 to £20, and a similar reduction was made in the return fare between Nairobi and Mogadishu from £34 to £25 (61). This was to compete with the fares charged by Clairways which was still flying Ansons up to Mogadishu, having been forced off the Aden sector some time before.

In promoting a new airline, de Graaff Hunter wished to attach a clear non-BOAC identity to the many schedules now flown by Aden Airways. Accordingly, he ordered that from October of that year, the various flights were to be given the following names:

Service	Name
AD 456/470	"Cairo Express"
AD 471/457	"Addis Express"
AD 458/459	"Addis Freighter"
AD 460/461	"Mukalla Air Coach"
AD 462/463	"Mukeiras Air Coach"
AD 464/465	"Hargeisa Air Coach"
AD 466/467 & 468/469	"Nairobi Special"
AD 472/473	"Cairo Freighter"
AD 474/475	"Sudan Special"
AD 478/479	"Levant Special"

It gave a cachet to travel plans: "Yes, I'm catching the Cairo Express tomorrow". But a more serious reason was that the only aircraft on offer were DC-3s, and quite old second-hand ones at that. The whole idea was to create an impression that these were the fastest flights available to a particular destination and thus a little glamorous. Aden Airways flew these aircraft hard on all the schedules such as the AD 470 from Aden to Cairo with only two stops, at Asmara and Port Sudan.

"The operational method employed for our Express services is one which would normally not be attempted by operators employing Dakotas in these parts on account of the economic characteristics of this type of aircraft. We fly extremely long sectors and operate equally by night and by day. For we have been obliged to face facts as we find them and to be ready to compete with superior aeroplanes having higher speeds and greater range. We are, in fact, stretching the performance of our fleet as well as the endurance of our aircrew to their safe commercial limits." (62)

The terminal at Ghuraf in 1951. Richard de Graaff Hunter is on the right of centre and Captain Steve Colvin, Chief Pilot, is on the left. In the background is DC-3 VR-AAC. *(British Airways Archives)*

De Graaff Hunter had to cope with other problems, mainly political. For instance, after the Arab/Israeli war of 1948, there remained a deep and fanatical resentment, particularly in Saudi Arabia and Egypt, of all things Israeli and towards those perceived to have sympathies in that direction. Aden Airways had applied to fly to Israel, and had already lodged an application to do so through the MCA in London. However, the route along the Red Sea would have involved both landing in, and over-flying, Arab countries hostile to the idea of such a connection and which would not have permitted such flights to do so.

Similarly, the route from Aden to Damascus via Khartoum, AD 478, was prevented by the Egyptian Authorities from making a technical refuelling stop in Cairo, with a result that a stop had to be made in Sudan, at Wadi Halfa, with a consequent loss in payload because of the longer sector to Damascus.

Another example was an application to fly from Nairobi to Cairo via Addis Ababa, a route much coveted by BOAC which, if it was allowed to fly the route, would then have to grant reciprocal traffic rights into London to Ethiopian Airlines. In theory, this route was a "British" one and the idea was that the MCA in London, through BOAC, would make the application but not designate the airline and, if successful, Aden Airways would be the designated carrier. Understandably, neither the Ethiopians nor the Egyptians were particularly pleased at the prospect of this subterfuge, and fought hard, and successfully, against it when the application was received in Nairobi and Cairo.

There had been problems in a number of other areas as well. The airline derived considerable revenue from the Haj pilgrimage flights in August and September. Notwithstanding the arrangements which the airline had previously made with the Saudi Arabian authorities, and the promises made by them, the Saudi Government refused at the last moment to allow pilgrim charters to be flown to Jeddah from Arab countries unless the flights were made in Arab-registered aircraft. (This sort of late change in arrangements was to plague Haj flights for years to come). Though there was some compensation from the fact that a number of flights were flown by Aden Airways aircraft from West Africa, Turkey, Pakistan, India and the Persian Gulf, a profit of only £8,668 was made when, overall, the financial return should have been considerably greater. Not only was the airline denied the ability to fly pilgrims from Arab countries with whom it had already made a contract, the airline had to find substitute aircraft by charter in order to honour its obligations to these pilgrims.

For the BOAC seconded crews, the pilgrim flights were a huge change from the rather more luxurious flying they had been used to in earlier years, and Harry Mills describes such a season:

"The pilgrim pickup points were quite varied such as Damascus, Cairo and Kano and the crews could be based at these destinations

Captain Harry Mills in the cabin of an Aden Airways DC-3 in 1950. *(Harry Mills)*

CHAPTER 6: ADEN AIRWAYS 1950 - 1951

ADEN to/from EAST AFRICA, EGYPT, ERITREA, ETHIOPIA, SAUDI ARABIA, SOMALILAND, SUDAN, SYRIA & WEST AFRICA
ALL SERVICES ARE WEEKLY UNLESS OTHERWISE SHOWN

ASSAB AIR COACH AD 455	(F) LEVANT SPECIAL AD 479 (A)	(F) LEVANT SPECIAL AD 473 (A)	(F) SUDAN SPECIAL AD 475 (B)	CAIRO FREIGHTER AD 473	ADDIS EXPRESS AD 471	NAIROBI SPECIAL AD 467			NAIROBI SPECIAL AD 466	CAIRO EXPRESS AD 470	CAIRO FREIGHTER AD 472	(F) SUDAN SPECIAL AD 474 (C)	(F) LEVANT SPECIAL AD 478 (D)	(F) LEVANT SPECIAL AD 478 (D)	ASSAB AIR COACH AD 454
				(7) 0145	(7) 01.00	(2) 00.01	(4) 01.00	Dep. CAIRO Arr.	21.30	21.15	21.30	22.00			
	(6) 13.00	(6) 13.00						Dep. DAMASCUS Arr.	∧	∧	∧	∧	11.30	11.30	
	18.15	18.15						Arr. WADI HALFA Dep.					(6) 06.30	(6) 06.30	
	(7) 04.00	(7) 04.00						Dep. WADI HALFA Arr.					20.00	20.00	
	06.45	06.45	07.30					Arr. KHARTOUM Dep.				15.55	17.20	(5) 17.20	
	Change to W.A.A.C													Change to Aden Airways	
	(7) 08.00	0830	08.30					Dep. KHARTOUM Arr.				15.00	15.00	16.15	
	11.05							Arr. EL FASHER Dep.				∧	∧	13.00	
	11.45							Dep. EL FASHER Arr.						12.05	
	16.00							Arr. MAIDUGURI Dep.						(5) 05.30	
	16.45							Dep. MAIDUGURI Arr.						17.25	
	18.50							Arr. KANO Dep.						15.15	
	(1) 09.00							Dep. KANO Arr.						13.45	
	12.20							Arr. LAGOS Dep.						10.15	
	13.00							Dep. LAGOS Arr.						09.15	
	13.40							Arr. ACCRA Dep.						(4) 06.30	
				06.45		06.45		Arr. JEDDAH Dep.	17.45		17.45				
				07.45		07.45		Dep. JEDDAH Arr.	16.45		16.45				
				08.05				Arr. PORT SUDAN Dep.	14.30	16.15	14.30				
				08.50				Dep. PORT SUDAN Arr.	13.45	15.30	13.45				
				11.55	07.30	10.30		Arr. ASMARA Dep.	12.45	14.30	12.45	13.20	13.20		
(3) 08.00	12.15	12.15	13.30		08.30	11.30		Dep. ASMARA Arr.	11.20	13.30	11.30	11.30	11.30		12.45
∨	13.30	13.30				13.05		Arr. KAMARAN Dep.	09.45			∧	∧	∧	∧
09.55						13.55		Dep. KAMARAN Arr.	09.05						(3) 10.50
	15.25	15.25	15.25					Arr. ASSAB Dep.							
	15.55	15.55	15.55					Dep. ASSAB Arr.				09.00	09.00	09.00	
	∨	∨	∨					Arr. DJIBOUTI Dep.				08.05	08.05	08.05	
	17.00	17.00	17.00		11.15	15.30		Dep. DJIBOUTI Arr.	(7) 07.30	(3) 10.45	(5) 07.00	(5) 07.00	(5) 07.00		
								ADEN { Arr. Dep.							

Hargeisa Air Coach AD 465	Mukeiras Air Coach AD 462	Mukalla Air Coach AD 460	Addis Freighter AD 459	Addis Express AD 457	Nairobi Special AD 469			Nairobi Special AD 468	Cairo Express AD 456	Addis Freighter AD 458	Mukalla Air Coach AD 461	Mukeiras Air Coach AD 463	Hargeisa Air Coach AD 464
(2) 06.30	(1) 05.45	(1) 12.30	(4) 08.30	(2) 12.30	(5) 06.00	Dep. Arr.		17.30	09.45	17.30	17.30	08.10	12.20
			09.35			Arr. DJIBOUTI Dep.		∧	∧	16.25	∧	∧	∧
			10.15	∨		Dep. DJIBOUTI Arr.				15.50			
		06.30	12.30	15.30		Arr. ADDIS ABABA Dep.			(3) 06.30	(4) 13.30			
			14.35			Arr. MUKEIRAS Dep.						(1) 07.30	
						Arr. RIYAN Dep.					(1) 15.35		11.10
07.40						Arr. BERBERA Dep.							10.25
08.15					∨	Dep. BERBERA Arr.							(2) 09.45
09.00					07.40	Arr. HARGEISA Dep.		15.55					
					08.30	Dep. HARGEISA Arr.		15.15					
					11.40	Arr. MOGADISHU Dep.		12.00					
					12.30	Dep. MOGADISHU Arr.		11.20					
					16.15	Arr. NAIROBI Dep.		(6) 07.30					

NOTES : (F)   FORTNIGHTLY
         (A)   DAYS OF OPERATION : JANUARY 6th, 20th — FEBRUARY 3rd, 17th — MARCH 3rd, 17th, 31st
         (B)   DAYS OF OPERATION : JANUARY 14th, 28th — FEBRUARY 11th, 25th — MARCH 11th, 25th
         (C)   DAYS OF OPERATION : JANUARY 12th, 26th — FEBRUARY 9th, 23rd — MARCH 9th, 23rd
         (D)   DAYS OF OPERATION : JANUARY 5th, 19th — FEBRUARY 2nd, 16th — MARCH 2nd, 16th, 30th.

CONNECTIONS AT CAIRO, KHARTOUM AND NAIROBI
TO ALL PARTS OF THE WORLD
BY
B. O. A. C.

Aden services in February 1951, showing their new, named, identities.

for up to a month at a time. The pilgrims, it has to be remembered, were relatively primitive people who had saved all their money to make this journey of a lifetime and for whom the geography of such a trip was difficult to comprehend. On one occasion the aircraft had to stop in Luxor on its way to Jeddah in order to refuel; the pilgrims, thinking they had arrived at their destination, began en masse to remove their clothes in order to don their white pilgrim robes, and it took a great deal of persuasion to convince them that they still had some way to go.
On another flight, the aircraft appeared to be flying very tail-heavy, and when the radio officer went back to investigate, he found that a number of pilgrims had set up a primus stove on the floor at the back and were making themselves some tea."

Nor were the Egyptians about to become more accommodating, insisting on what they perceived to be their rights. For instance, Aden Airways had entered into a charter arrangement with Arab Airways Association in Jerusalem, whereby an Aden-registered aircraft was to operate the bulk of that company's scheduled services on an hourly charge. After the first flight from Jerusalem, the Egyptian authorities forbade any Jordanian traffic to land in Cairo if it had an Aden registration, even though Arab Airways Association already had permission to do so.

In another case, Aden Airways had a contract to transport passengers from a cruise ship company in which the passengers were to be flown from Luxor to Cairo; the Egyptian authorities insisted that Misr should carry them between these two points.(63)

Whether or not these episodes were a result of the confusion of the times, or were entered into with exaggerated optimism, is a moot point, but it does reinforce the isolation in which Aden and its airline found itself once the umbilical cord to BOAC had been cut. But within the region Eritrea and British Somaliland were governed under British mandate, as was Aden, so there was considerable official leave traffic to be carried between their

Aden Airways crew and VR-AAE at Kamaran Island in 1951. *(British Airways Archives)*

respective territories and the UK hitherto either by charter flights or by ship. By offering a scheme whereby Aden Airways would offer fares to London considerably below those charged previously, the three Governments would take it upon themselves to co-ordinate traffic up to Cairo by Aden Airways and onward by BOAC, with some considerable sums being allocated to the local airline.

Perhaps one of the most far-reaching changes made by de Graaff Hunter was the division of the network into areas of responsibility. Previously, the airline had employed agents who were based in the more important cities to which the airline flew. They worked on commission and clearly their loyalties could be dependent on the amount of commission an airline was prepared to pay. (In fact, things have not changed that much in the last 50 years). From now on, each area was to have a Superintendent who was employed by the company and who would promote the business within his area, with due consideration for the company as a whole, taking into account the other areas. This experiment had already been tried in both Addis Ababa and Port Sudan with excellent results and was now extended throughout the network.

Thus, the areas were divided in the following manner: (64)
Cairo: To cover all operations in Egypt.
Asmara: To cover Eritrea, the Sudan, Jeddah & Damascus.
Aden: To cover the full Protectorate of Aden, Kamaran Island, British Somaliland, the Hadramaut coast, Persian Gulf and India.
Addis Ababa: Ethiopia and French Somaliland.
Nairobi: The whole of East Africa south of Parallel 4°N.

Another source of increasing costs was in the secondment of staff from BOAC. All pilots, technical and senior management were employed in this way with consequent high expatriate allowances and other benefits which were more appropriate to a larger airline than Aden Airways. De Graaff Hunter had sought permission from BOAC to employ such staff under local contracts as periods of secondment came to a close. Considerable benefits could be gained in this plan, not only for the company, but also for the locally employed staff as pension and medical schemes would have to be set up for them as well as for any new arrivals. Aden Airways was probably one of the first companies to set up a scheme whereby its staff would benefit from a bonus based on company performance. Sadly, this last initiative was to be short-lived because the parent company did not approve of such advanced thinking, probably for fear of the idea filtering back to London.

No year would be complete without a mention of the route from East Africa to India via Aden. It must appear to us, today, that this route had taken the form of a "Holy Grail", but de Graaff Hunter was correct to emphasise this potentially lucrative source of traffic. No four-engine equipment was likely to come his way, so his solution was to suggest a third-class service in order to compensate passengers for travelling on a DC-3 as opposed to an Air India Constellation. In offering such a service, Aden Airways sought a fare differential of 25%, but unfortunately the Indian authorities would only agree to one of 15%. Impasse. Once again, the ever-resourceful de Graaff Hunter then sought to operate to Riyan, Bahrain, Sharjah and from there to Karachi and Bombay. In anticipation of this plan, a service opened on this route as far as Bahrain on 25th April 1951 but there were to be more obstacles in the way.

Footnotes, Chapter 6:
(59) Notification No 29, 18th April 1950.
(60) General Manager's Report, para 21, 31st October 1950.
(61) AD/COML/FR/4/50. Fares and rates Notice, 3rd July 1950.
(62) General Manager's Report, para 25, 31st October 1950.
(63) General Manager's Report, para 11a, 31st October 1950
(64) General Notice No 14, 21st November 1950.

CHAPTER 7: ADEN AIRWAYS 1951 - 1952   45

Aden Airways ground staff at Khormaksar in 1951.   *(British Airways Archives)*

Chapter 7 :
ADEN AIRWAYS 1951 - 1952

During the early part of the financial year, Egypt continued to refuse traffic rights through Cairo to Damascus on the AD 478 northbound from Khartoum; this was not surprising bearing in mind the ambitions they held for their own airline, Misr (later named Misrair), over a route it considered to be its own. Accordingly, Cairo was omitted and a nightstop at Wadi Halfa introduced, though this did curtail the available load somewhat.

Elsewhere, though, loads were improving, such as between Djibouti and Hargeisa, with the result that the AD 455/454 from Asmara to Assab and Djibouti was extended in June to Hargeisa in order to offer extra capacity over the 14-seat freighter used hitherto.

The service to Bahrain and which had been intended to carry on to India started in April. It quickly ran into objections from the Saudis. By June 1951 Aden Airways had still not received traffic rights from either India or Pakistan for the airline to fly there via the Persian Gulf, with the result that the airline had to terminate the flights at Bahrain, with the occasional extension to Sharjah when the traffic warranted. However, during June, the airline was advised through diplomatic channels that the Saudi Arabian government objected to their country being overflown on the sector between Riyan and Bahrain. Initially, these objections were ignored but after further diplomatic pressure, BOAC instructed the company to withdraw the service, which it duly did on 2nd July. A further potential complication was that BOAC already had an interest in Gulf Aviation (later the airline Gulf Air) based in Bahrain which flew Ansons from there to Sharjah.

The airline continued to conduct a safe operation throughout what was considered to be a hostile environment. Occasional damage could often occur as a result of poor runway conditions but, apart from the odd burst tyre, the airline flew quite smoothly. However, on 22nd June, the northbound AD 478 (VR-AAC), from Aden to Damascus suffered an engine failure shortly after take-off from Asmara and had to return there for an emergency landing - not an easy feat considering the 7,000 foot elevation there. No spare aircraft were available and this, perhaps, highlights the problems

BOAC publicity shot of Captain Harry Mills and ground crew at Aden in 1951.   *(Harry Mills)*

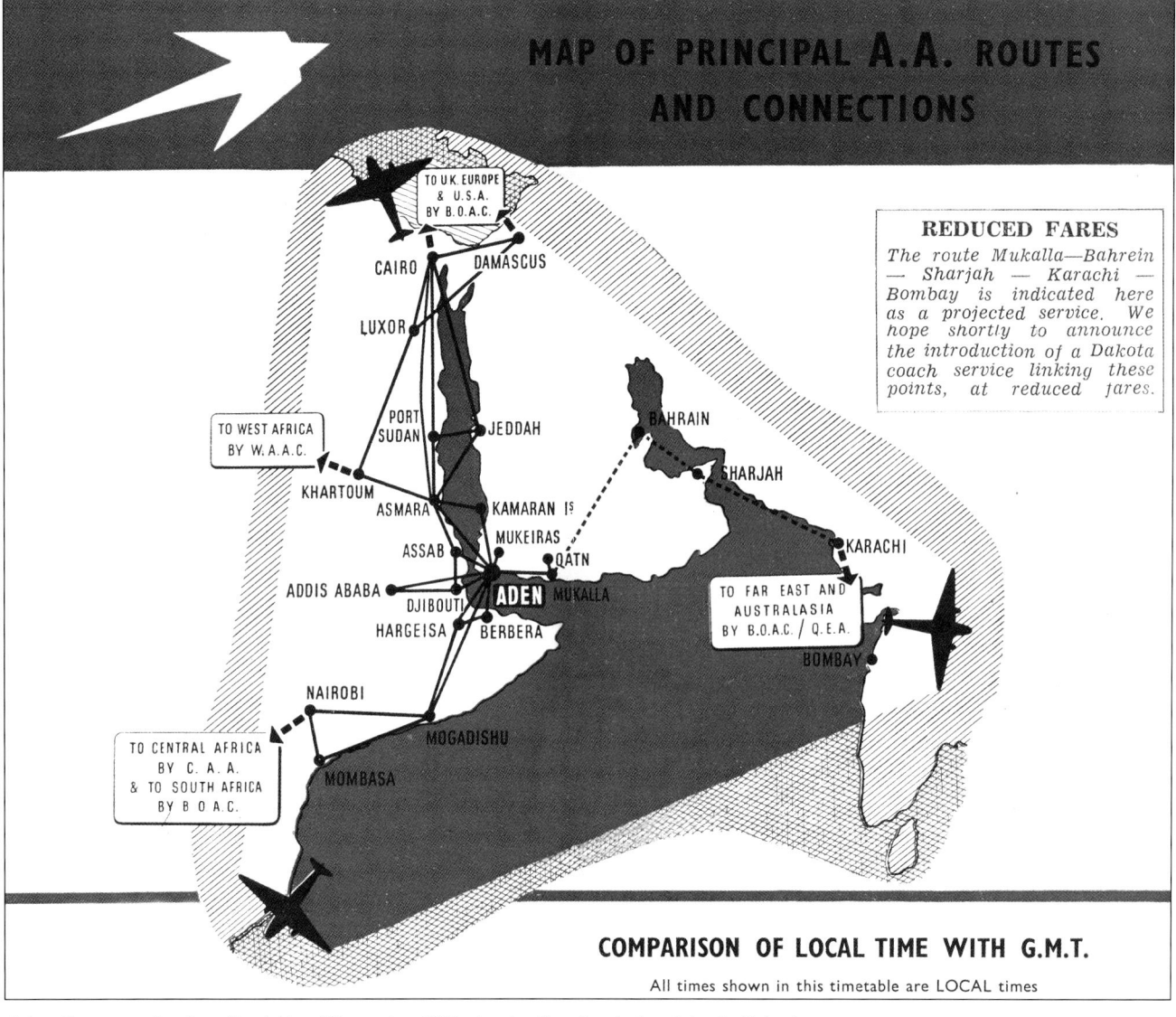

Aden Airways routes from timetable of November 1951 showing the disputed routeing to Bahrain.

experienced by the airline in running such a tight schedule. The only way to solve the problem was to charter a C-46 from Air Djibouti, a rather galling solution for de Graaff Hunter considering his antipathy towards this airline.

More seriously, on 2nd July 1951 VR-AAD, flying the AD 466 from Aden to Cairo, suffered damage to the undercarriage on take-off from Kamaran Island, similar to the incident experienced in Nairobi the previous February. The aircraft, flown by Captain Ian Walbran and First Officer Lovell, continued on to Asmara where there were good engineering facilities and where a successful emergency landing was carried out, even though the undercarriage collapsed at the end of the landing roll. Temporary repairs were made before the aircraft was ferried to Cairo for a new wing. (See page 188).

Nevertheless, the aircraft was out of service for eight days which meant that a lucrative and long-term charter for an oil company to Basra had to be cancelled with a serious loss of revenue.

Misr Viking SU-AGO photographed at Beirut, August 1952.

Competition was now increasing from Ethiopian Airlines and Misr. The former had previously operated onward to Riyan from Aden and, as well as being aggressive in their sales tactics, it was also flying recently purchased Convair 240s on the route. Nevertheless, in a protective move, the Department of Civil Aviation in Aden restricted the flights into and through Aden to six per week in an attempt to level the playing field.

Misr was now flying Vickers Vikings from Cairo to Aden via Jeddah, and was advertising itself as "The Moslem Airline" to echo the antipathy towards those whose sympathies lay with Israel. This was a powerful advertising message and the services did well at the expense of Aden Airways. Despite this, the company held their own with an average of 12 passengers and 1,070 kgs of freight and baggage on each service.

Weather was also a serious factor in Aden operations. The popular concept of the Red Sea is one of unrelenting sunshine but, at certain times of the year, the Saudi winter for instance, heavy thunderstorms can affect navigation aids and landing conditions. At times, airfields such as Dire Dawa were rendered unusable for weeks at a time. Similarly, routes were made seasonal, a good example being Addis Ababa which was affected by the monsoon as it moved north for the northern summer. Nairobi and Mogadishu were equally affected. During these times, services were curtailed as passengers chose to travel less, because of the unreliability of flights. This then allowed the crews and aircraft to be used on charters into the Protectorates as well as pilgrimage work.

CHAPTER 7: ADEN AIRWAYS 1951 - 1952

Cholera was part of life within the region and Luxor was a compulsory calling point on the way to Cairo so that the Egyptian authorities could perform quarantine checks on passengers. An outbreak of bubonic plague in eastern Saudi Arabia during July demanded further checks to be carried out in Jeddah.

With the advent of the Haj pilgrimage in August 1951 the plague had particular consequences for Aden Airways. The company had already contracted to carry 2,200 pilgrims between Bahrain and Jeddah, in addition to those from West Africa, Sudan and the Aden Protectorate itself. Unfortunately, the York which had been promised from BOAC did not materialise and so, once again, Air Djibouti was called on to assist in flying pilgrims between Bahrain and Jeddah, a route it was familiar with because of its cargo operations between these two points. A further complication was the Pakistani insistence on severe quarantine requirements, producing delays which affected the productivity of the whole operation.

Despite all these problems, the pilgrimage operations went well and the numbers were greater than in any year hitherto. Fortunately, none of the difficulties experienced with the Saudis in previous years had arisen, and a total of 2,626 pilgrims were flown in on 73 separate flights. The outward flights from Jeddah were completed by 25th October, 1951 in which 74 flights returned 2,454 pilgrims to their countries of origin. Sadly, many of the pilgrims were elderly and some simply died from the strain of travel as well as succumbing to disease. Such a high mortality rate was not uncommon.

All flights to Jeddah from: Bahrain   27   (11 by Air Djibouti)
                             Aden   15
                             Kano   6
                             Mukalla   8
                             Khartoum   7
                             Asmara   3
                             Others   7

Five complete crews had been based in Jeddah for the duration of the Haj and the whole fleet involved had averaged 20 hours flying per day, a figure rather better than most airlines achieve today. Clearly, there were crew limits as to the number of hours they could fly in a month, but this minor problem was surmounted by a visit to the doctor as the monthly limit was reached and *"after a quick medical, flying was resumed."* (65)

For the company, the gross revenue exceeded £120,000, from which a profit of approximately £55,000 was derived.

Despite this success, clouds were looming on the horizon. The airline simply did not possess competitive equipment. Not only that, of the six DC-3s, only two were laid out in "proper" passenger configuration, while the rest were mixed passenger and freight services which did not really compare well with contemporary standards, especially as the competition was becoming better organised. Ethiopian Airlines had, as already mentioned, bought two CV-240s from the USA which were relatively fast twin-engine aircraft (240 mph v 160 mph) and, being pressurised, made the journey from Asmara to Cairo both quicker and more comfortable. Misr on its Viking service to Aden via Jeddah was not only offering a superior service but, by emphasising Moslem origins, had much more appeal to the local populations. In October 1951, Saudi Arabia had also filed for traffic rights between Jeddah and Aden and planned to use the DC-4 on this service, an aircraft which, though it was not pressurised, was faster than the DC-3 and had the added cachet of being 4 engined. These traffic rights were granted.

On the much sought-after route to Karachi and Bombay, Air India, with its Constellations, had established total dominance and was solidly booked for months at a time. Ethiopian Airlines was also

Stewardess service in 1951, Hargeisa.   (British Airways Archives)

Ethiopian Airlines DC-3 ET-ABX at Addis Ababa, taken some years later.

now seeking to upgrade its equipment on this route from the DC-3 to the CV-240 and planned to fly from Addis Ababa to Aden, Riyan and Karachi, a plan in which it was successful from early 1952. Further north, Gulf Aviation had also been successful in blocking Aden Airways from flying between the Persian Gulf and India, not unreasonably as both companies were subsidiaries of BOAC. Further pressure was to come from another BOAC Associated Company, Cyprus Airways, based in Nicosia, which objected to Aden Airways competing on the Khartoum-Damascus route, resulting in the forced withdrawal from this lucrative route in January 1952. This deprived the company of some £24,000 in annual revenue, as well as cutting a vital link which it had forged with West African Airways the previous year.

World events had also conspired against the company. Fuel prices had risen on three separate occasions so operating costs had risen from £9.90 per flying hour during 1950/1951 to £12.39 during the current year, a factor which further increased annual cost by £ 22,000. (66)

Within the Red Sea area, during the summer months of 1951 increasing unrest in Egypt had escalated into full-scale and violent rioting in January and February 1952. The AD 472, 474 and 466 to Cairo had been one of the most lucrative routes, not only as a result of the normal commercial traffic but also for the military and civil service personnel from the surrounding states, such as Eritrea and British Somalia. As a result of the riots there were no Aden Airways services to or from Cairo for a period of six weeks, and even after resumption, services were sporadic. The losses in revenue stemming from these events were estimated to be more than £ 11,000. (67)

Yearly profits came from revenues from charters and pilgrimage flights. In the financial year 1950/1951 operating revenue on scheduled services resulted in a loss of £34,663, a sum which reverted to a profit when the surplus of £55,877 from the pilgrim and charter flights was added. By October, 1951, but for the revenue from these flights, the losses would be unacceptable; at year's end, a loss of £112,319 on scheduled services was offset by a sum of £123,879 earned on pilgrims and charters, for an overall profit of £11,470.

To be fair to the Aden Airways Board, it had been aware of the impending financial problems for some time and, to keep a closer track of income and expenditure, a new accounting system had been introduced in July in Aden and during August at other main stations.

The Board was also increasingly aware of the uncompetitive position into which the airline was being forced because of the lack of good four-engined aircraft. Indeed, at the 12th Board meeting held in Aden on 30th April 1951, the Board requested that the Managing Director, de Graaff Hunter: *"...bring to the notice of BOAC the need for replacing our fleet by suitable aircraft in view of the growing competition. The Board considered that any delay in this process may eventually lead to more and more losses every year and to loss of traffic which may not be retrieved as other airlines would by then be fully established on our network."* (68)

A further complication during the year had been the failure of the General Post Office (GPO) in the UK to forward the full payments for mail carried during the previous financial year. The onus was on BOAC to pay this money to Aden Airways, but only £10,000 of £40,547 had been paid by 30th April. Also, during October 1950, BOAC had advised the company that it wished to have its outstanding loan of £90,000 repaid by 30th September 1951, (69) an almost impossible task for the airline to honour.

By early October 1951, the results were announced to the Aden Board at the 14th Meeting of the Board of Directors, held in London on 7th November. The Chairman of the Meeting was Sir Miles Thomas DFC, and his message was one of drastic cuts: (70)

"The Chairman outlined the future policy for Aden Airways as follows:
1) BOAC would take over the route Nairobi-Aden-Cairo for operation by Hermes aircraft on a once-weekly frequency. Aden Airways to waive handling fees and commission in Aden in respect of Hermes service and its traffic.
2) Revenue earned on the sectors Nairobi-Aden-Cairo to be trisected, one part being payable to Aden Airways and two parts to BOAC.
3) Aden Airways to discontinue the Nairobi-Aden 468/469 and the Aden-Asmara-Cairo 470/471 routes as from the start of the Hermes operations planned for the 1st April, 1952, or earlier if possible.
4) Aden Airways would not operate a Dakota service beyond the Persian Gulf to Karachi and Bombay, but the British rights on this route should be maintained in any future review of the Anglo-Indian Bilateral Agreement so that 4-engined high density aircraft of BOAC can be put on it whenever a suitable opportunity occurs.
5) Aden Airways may be called upon to provide an aircraft and crew for service in the Gulf under charter to the Gulf Aviation Company, in which case a service between Aden and Bahrain would be operated as a means of positioning for these operations
6) The establishment of the company must be immediately reviewed with special attention to retrenchment. As many aircrew as possible should be returned to the Corporation forthwith, two pilots of which being earmarked for the Gulf Aviation Company.
7) The managing director of the company was instructed to negotiate with the Gulf Aviation Company in respect of the purchase of Anson aircraft for taxi and general communications work in Aden Airways.
8) An immediate reduction in the Aden Airways fleet must be made. One Dakota must be dispensed with forthwith, either by charter to Gulf Aviation Company, or by sale on the open market and a further aircraft to be disposed of as appropriate when the company becomes wholly centralised in Aden.
9) In view of this drastic curtailment of equipment and manpower, Aden Airways would not be able to engage in future Pilgrimage operations with the remaining aircraft and crews. Sir Miles Thomas promised Aden Airways, in compensation, the use of York aircraft and crews for pilgrimage work next year (1952) and in succeeding years at a basic charter rate from which BOAC would not expect to derive any profit or contribution towards standing charges."

Transfer of headquarters.

That BOAC had been considering this course of action for some time is obvious; what is less evident is that the Board of Aden Airways had no idea of what was about to happen until the meeting itself and it must have come as a considerable shock to most of them, though it would appear that de Graaff Hunter must have had some inkling of what was in store. BOAC may have been fair to its subsidiary but it might have been a way of cutting de Graaff Hunter down to size. He had pursued his own desires for the company, and had not been afraid to make decisions without reference to the parent company in London, for example in varying the services from passenger to part freight/passenger to full freight and, indeed, cancelling services when they proved to be uneconomic.

On the other hand, there might have been a desire to help the smaller (and more pliable?) company in Bahrain, while de Graaff Hunter may also have made himself unpopular with his preoccupation for better equipment and the route to India. True, there was now to be four-engine equipment on the most lucrative sectors between Nairobi, Aden and Cairo, but only 33% of the revenue would come to Aden Airways and no income from interline traffic as there was before, when traffic transfer to BOAC took place at Cairo. Also, the Hermes flights would only be once weekly and, while this aircraft would fly this prestigious direct flight, Aden Airways would still be obliged to continue with the frequent stoppers as before (AD472/474 and AD 466). Gulf Aviation would benefit to a considerable degree in that it would be "provided" with a DC-3 and crew, and the question of who would pay for this was never made clear. Gulf Aviation would, but there was some doubt whether they could afford the annual fees of £20-40,000, depending on utilisation, which would have been payable to Aden Airways.

Also, as described in paragraph "7)" of Miles Thomas' instructions above, Aden Airways was required to purchase two Ansons from Gulf Aviation, aircraft which were totally unsuitable for the route structure within the Aden Protectorate or indeed on any other routes. The purchase of these two aircraft might have offset to some extent the cost of hiring the DC-3, but there was no evidence of a firm agreement on this question. The Ansons did arrive in Aden, but were never used because of their unsuitability.

The airline was to be left with only four DC-3s and, while this number was enough to operate within the much reduced network, no resources would be left to fly either charters or the pilgrim flights for 1952. Nor was there any slack built in for technical failures. The promise of a York from BOAC would prove to be a

CHAPTER 7: ADEN AIRWAYS 1951 - 1952

Unloading at Ghuraf, April 1952. VR-AAC has no airline titles on the roof. (British Airways Archives)

mixed blessing, as indeed would the arrival of the Hermes, as we shall see later.

As in any dark cloud, there were some glimmers of a silver lining in the form of benefits to be derived from this drastic cutback, the main one being the relocation of all staff to Aden where the shortage of accommodation would no longer be so severe, because of fewer staff. This move would have had to come anyway, as Eritrea was due to federate with Ethiopia in September of the following year.

If the sole purpose of this plan was to ensure the continuing positive income flow from Aden Airways, then there was some cause for optimism, at least in the short term, when the finances resulting from the cutback had been analysed.

Assuming:
Revenue from Hermes to be £23,000 and
Revenue from Pilgrim flights, in 1952 using the York, to be £35,000.
There were three options:

	No of aircraft	No of crews	Hours flown	Profit/ (Loss)
(1)	6	11	7,540	(£24,000)
(2	5	6	5,735	(£36,000)
(3)	5 (with GA charter)	6	6,000	(£7,000)

Weighing the load in the Hadramaut, a matter of considerable interest to all present. (British Airways Archives)

Richard de Graaff Hunter in the Hadramaut amid a group of local tribesmen, April 1952.
(British Airways Archives)

Revenue from Hermes operation and York charter was forecast to be £58,000, resulting in a profit of £51,000 for the year. (71)

Two other more important changes before the year's end were a contribution to profitability. The first was to convert the remaining DC-3s into 40-seaters, to carry more people at lower fares, needed for the services within the Aden Protectorate and the closer destinations in Africa such as Berbera, Djibouti, Hargeisa and Dire Dawa.

These modifications consisted of a rearrangement of the radios so that the radio officers could be dispensed with which, in turn, enabled the forward bulkhead to be moved forward, thus providing space for an extra row of seats. The toilet was also moved to allow a further row of seats to be installed while at the same time all unnecessary weight was to be removed to allow a greater payload to be carried. The work was to be done by Scottish Aviation at Prestwick, Scotland, and would cost, in all, some £40,000 paid for by BOAC. (72)

Closer to home, in December, 1951 Aden Airways got together with Ethiopian Airlines in an attempt to bring some order to the frequently difficult issue of rights between the two countries as well as those connecting routes within the surrounding territories. After much discussion, an agreement emerged in which Ethiopian was to be given full Fifth Freedom rights through Aden to Dhahran and Karachi. In return, and in anticipation of the federation of Eritrea and Ethiopia due the following year, Aden was to be given the same rights through Asmara. (73)

A further meeting the following January confirmed that Aden Airways would be given the rights to operate three flights per week between Aden, Djibouti and Dire Dawa with full traffic rights, particularly important bearing in mind the very lucrative Qat cargo traffic from the last location. In addition, the local routes between Aden and Addis Ababa, as well as to other points such as Massawa, Asmara, Assab and Djibouti, were to be liberalised between the two airlines to the extent that each was free to operate daily services, on demand, for both passengers and cargo. (74)

By the end of the financial year, Aden Airways was in as good a position as it could expect to be, considering the body blow it had received from its parent company. But without the ability to compete with the equipment flown by its rivals, Ethiopian Airlines, Misrair and Air France, it was a sensible rationalisation.

Footnotes, Chapter 7:
(65) Captain Vic Spencer, former Chief Pilot.
(66) Director's Report to Shareholders, 31st March 1952.
(67) Ditto.
(68) 12th Board Meeting held in Aden, 30th April 1951.
(69) Ditto. Ref 12/173
(70) 14th Board Meeting, London, 7th November 1951, 14/211
(71) Statement of proposals and analysis with Hermes weekly flight, October 1951.
(72) 15th Board Meeting, AOB, November 1951
(73) Meeting held at Asmara between Aden Airways and Ethiopian Airlines, 22nd December 1951.
(74) Meeting held at Addis Ababa between Aden Airways and Ethiopian Airlines, 18th January 1952.

Air Djibouti was a division of Transocean Air Lines Inc of Oakland, California, operating Curtiss C-46s such as N68964 seen here.
(Peter R Arnold)

Chapter 8 :
AIR DJIBOUTI

It would have been naïve of Richard de Graaff Hunter to assume that he (and BOAC) were the only ones to have identified a niche for an airline based in the Gulf of Aden, bordering both the Horn of Africa and the Arabian peninsula. Indeed, it would be fair to say that it was surprising that there were no others apart from local national airlines such as Ethiopian Airlines, Misr of Egypt and Saudi Arabian Airlines. That said, though, the Gulf of Aden was considered a British sphere of influence and the arrival of competitors was viewed with some alarm by de Graaff Hunter; in a telegram to Richard Hilary dated November 4th 1950 he speaks of his *"apprehensions regarding Air Djibouti's proposal"* (75) to set up services in the area, albeit at the time based in Djibouti and not Asmara, where Aden Airways was, at the time, headquartered.

After the war, a large number of transport aircraft had become available, together with an equally large surplus of demobilised pilots to fly them, particularly in the United States. The US Government made special arrangements whereby ex-US Army personnel could buy war-surplus equipment at specially discounted rates. As a result, a whole host of small airlines emerged, usually flying cargo and run on a shoestring. Few survived for very long, but some did prosper and became large airlines which, through mergers, still exist today.

A good example was Flying Tigers, which was eventually absorbed into FedEx. The founder of Flying Tigers was Major General Chennault, who had commanded the US Army unit of that name, which operated both fighters and transport aircraft over the "Hump" from eastern India to Kunming in southern China, where Chiang Kai-hek was leading the Nationalist forces against the Japanese. Most of the early post-war work was ad hoc freighting across the Pacific and Atlantic Oceans where sea rates were abnormally high.

Another company was Indamer in India, of which more later, set up by two gentlemen by the names of Baldwin and Koszarek, who were later involved in setting up another airline in Afghanistan. Indamer was able to acquire 13 DC-3s from various sources and was successful in gaining an Indian Army contract supplying troops in Assam by parachute drop. Later, it was instrumental in saving the 1952 Haj for Aden Airways when the York provided by BOAC was inadvertently released back to London too soon.

Under these circumstances Transocean Air Lines was started by Orvis Nelson, a former US Army pilot and pre-war mail pilot. At that time, he flew anything and anywhere, so long as it was profitable; with the rise in the search for oil in the Arabian peninsula, he identified a need for the supply of fresh produce from Eritrea to the oil companies based in Saudi Arabia and the Gulf states, as well as those US forces already stationed in the area. To quote Nelson: *"We set up the Air Djibouti division of Transocean in the late summer of 1949 to engage in operations in the Middle East, with particular emphasis on East Africa and the Arab countries".*(76)

Djibouti was under the jurisdiction of France as French Somaliland and was thus the easiest state under which to register and base an operation. The French Bureau de Securite would appear to have been under the impression that the American CAB was monitoring this new airline and, conversely, the Americans believed that the French had everything under control. The result was that this swashbuckling airline was able to do as it liked.

The aircraft in use were Curtiss C-46s, rather more powerful, and carrying twice the load of the DC-3s operated by Aden Airways. However, because of to the climate and lack of general maintenance facilities in Djibouti, the airline soon decamped to

Asmara, Eritrea, where more support was available and, more importantly, most of the cargo originated. Fresh fruit, vegetables and meat were the normal cargoes which were then flown on to Jeddah and Bahrain.

By moving to Asmara, conflict between the two airlines became inevitable; because of the dispute with Clairways in Kenya, Aden Airways had not yet had time to set up a proper East African network which would also connect onwards from Asmara into the Red Sea route structure which it jealously guarded as its sphere of influence.

On November 9th 1950 a memorandum, from the Station Manager in Bahrain to Maxwell, BOAC General Manager, Middle East, announced that Air Djibouti had *"applied to the Resident for full rights Nairobi-Mogadishu-Asmara-Dhahran-Bahrain once weekly"*. It also went on to say that Morton, the Resident, was recommending *"permission (for the) carriage (of) fruit, vegetables, meat, poultry and other produce, but refused permission (for) carriage of passengers or other types of cargo"*. (77) Flights to Bahrain by Air Djibouti began on November 10th 1950, and continued on a weekly, if at times sporadic, basis. The British were put in a difficult position by this turn of events as they did not yet have either the capacity or the route structure to justifiably demand a denial of the Air Djibouti licensing request. The dilemma is best illustrated in a letter from R M Hillary to de Graaff Hunter in November 1950: *"The need for fresh foodstuffs in the Persian Gulf is, of course, a real one, and we know that it is difficult to oppose projects designed to meet this need. Nevertheless, this particular operation of Air Djibouti's does seem to have come about in a rather haphazard way, and we would be interested to know what means you can suggest for controlling it, quite apart from controlling the other ambitions of this rather peculiar company"*. (78)

Later, during February 1951, J W S Brancker, in writing to the Ministry of Civil Aviation in London, states that, as Aden Airways would be operating from Aden to Bahrain in the near future, Air Djibouti should be restricted to charter flights only, and not to a regular schedule as was proving to be the case. *"Their existing flights should also be regarded with considerable suspicion and should be restricted by the authorities in Nairobi and elsewhere to strictly charter operations........We should regard Air Djibouti as a complete parasite which merely takes traffic which would have otherwise travelled by Aden Airways"*. (79)

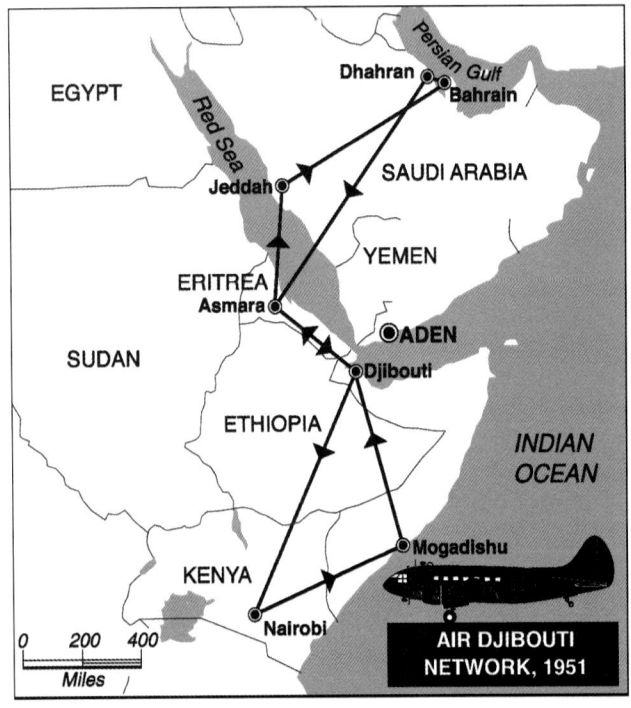

Air Djibouti route map, Nairobi to Bahrain, 1951. (Roger Carvell)

This was harsh criticism, smacking of petulance, as Air Djibouti was only filling a gap in the market and, indeed, would have been considered normal today. Air Djibouti's timetable, as shown below, and fare structure were both efficient and substantially below the fares charged by Aden Airways.

Bahrain	Depart	Tuesday	1630
Dhahran	Arrive		1700
	Depart	Wednesday	0730
Asmara	Arrive		1230
	Depart	Saturday	0630
Djibouti	Arrive		0830
	Depart		0930
Nairobi	Arrive		1500
	Depart	Monday	0630
Mogadishu	Arrive		1015
	Depart		1100
Djibouti	Arrive		1445
	Depart		1530
Asmara	Arrive		1730
	Depart	Tuesday	0630
Jeddah	Arrive		0900
	Depart		1000
Bahrain	Arrive		1530

The real threat was the route between Asmara and Nairobi on which Aden Airways was planning to fly in the near future; Air Djibouti's fares were substantially lower and also allowed passengers to carry up to 66 lb of baggage. Cargo fares, too, were more competitive.(80) Furthermore, the Kenyan Civil Aviation authorities were sympathetic to the service as, indeed, were the Aden government representatives, though this might have had more to do with the poor relationship between de Graaff Hunter and the Governor of the Protectorate. Once again, the Licensing Authorities were not even-handed, as Aden Airways had been refused these very same charter licences a few months previously.

Meanwhile, political events in the region, and in Eritrea in particular, were changing rapidly. After the war, Eritrea was administered by the British, under a United Nations mandate, hence the ease with which Aden Airways was able to set up their headquarters in Asmara, and the indignation felt when Air Djibouti also moved in. In September 1952, Eritrea and Ethiopia were federated and Ethiopian Airlines (EAL), now under the active management of Trans World Airlines (TWA), wished all foreign airlines to quit Asmara. It was made very clear to Aden Airways that it would have to move its base of operations to Aden, which it started to do shortly after, though not until 1956 was the airline entirely based there. Air Djibouti was doubly unfortunate; not only was TWA involved in the management of EAL but it was involved with Saudi Arabian Airlines as well. No time was lost in advising Transocean that, not only must it return its base of operations to Djibouti, but its cargo traffic rights between Asmara and Jeddah were cancelled, as EAL would now provide the service.

At Transocean, Orvis Nelson was nothing if not resourceful and during the latter half of 1951, perhaps perceiving the forthcoming chain of events, Air Djibouti had approached the Afghan government in Kabul seeking sponsorship for a weekly service Kabul-Kandahar-Zahedan-Bahrain using the soon-to-be-redundant C-46s. The proposed schedule was not ambitious, as can be seen from the timetable below, but the idea was greeted with enthusiasm by BOAC as this would connect with the BA 775 to Europe, as it was assumed most passengers would fly on from Bahrain to the financial gain of the company. This change would not wholly answer the question for Aden Airways, because a utilisation of only two days per week was hardly sensible for Air Djibouti and until its ejection from Asmara, it continued to pose a threat. Even then, de Graaff Hunter displays a certain pragmatism and, in a letter to Whitney Straight (81) of BOAC, he describes the situation:

CHAPTER 8: AIR DJIBOUTI

"You will have heard of Air Djibouti, a charter company employing C-46s and backed by Transocean, which in fact has its home in America and not Djibouti, as the name might suggest. Air Djibouti has, during the past two years, built up a special line of business which, principally, consists of flying vegetables grown in Eritrea to destinations in the Red Sea and the Persian Gulf, where they command high prices. On return flights, and at various other times in the past too, they have much annoyed us by carrying coolie traffic to and from the Persian Gulf, mostly emanating from the Aden Protectorate, and in doing so, cut into our Aden/Bahrain service which, as you know, we are no longer operating.

By constant vigilance, we kept this buccaneer American company out of Aden to a large extent and only permitted them to do business there when the traffic was controlled by us. In this way latterly, we were able to employ their highly economical aircraft and operating methods to our advantage without incurring, of course, any of the risks. In fact, during the last Pilgrimage, when Yorks from BOAC failed to turn up as promised, we being already committed by contract, we harnessed Air Djibouti at the eleventh hour and made some £ 15,000 clear profit out of them. EAL, however, did not employ the same tactics as us, and their relationship with Air Djibouti gradually worsened to a point where they are forbidden to enter Ethiopian territory. Bearing this in mind, and in view of the imminence of the federation of Eritrea and Ethiopia, Air Djibouti have been driven to seek new fields and have already started to withdraw from this end of the Red Sea. It appears that they intend to centre themselves somewhere in the Middle East and will seek to continue in the vegetable trade by supplying Gulf stations from Damascus." (82)

Air Djibouti did, indeed, go to the Middle East but while the company headquartered itself in Beirut, their real intention was to establish a base in Jordan, which it promptly did by entering into a partnership with a local businessman, Ismail Bilbeisi, to form an airline to be named Air Jordan. This arrangement ignored the fact that already another airline was present in Jordan, named Arab Airways Association, in which there were British interests.

A tacit agreement between the Americans and the British agreed that neither country would attempt to intervene in a country, or area, where the other already had an interest. In this case, the Americans used the disingenuous argument that as Arab Airways was clearly about to fail, the agreement was invalid. Arab Airways was in a precarious financial state, but the threat from Transocean was considered so great that the British Civil Air Attaché for the Middle East requested that de Graaff Hunter examine the case for Aden Airways supporting Arab Airways; this, notwithstanding the fact that BOAC had only recently decided not to do so. After a visit to Amman by de Graaff Hunter and Middleton (83), it was decided that Aden Airways would invest in the company and change the name to Arab Airways (Jerusalem) Ltd.

De Graaff Hunter sent his planning manager, Harry Pusey, to finalise the deal, which he did, but in an unorthodox way:

"I was sent to Jordan to finalise the deal and arrived simultaneously with Orvis Nelson. We both stayed in the Amman Club Hotel in Salt Road, and we breakfasted together and talked about all subjects under the sun except why we were there. We agreed that we would each meet with the directors of Arab Airways that day and we would make it clear to them that this was a make or break day, and whoever lost the deal would quickly go away and cease making overtures to Arab Airway., Orvis told me that, as a Quaker, I could accept his word that he would abide by that understanding.

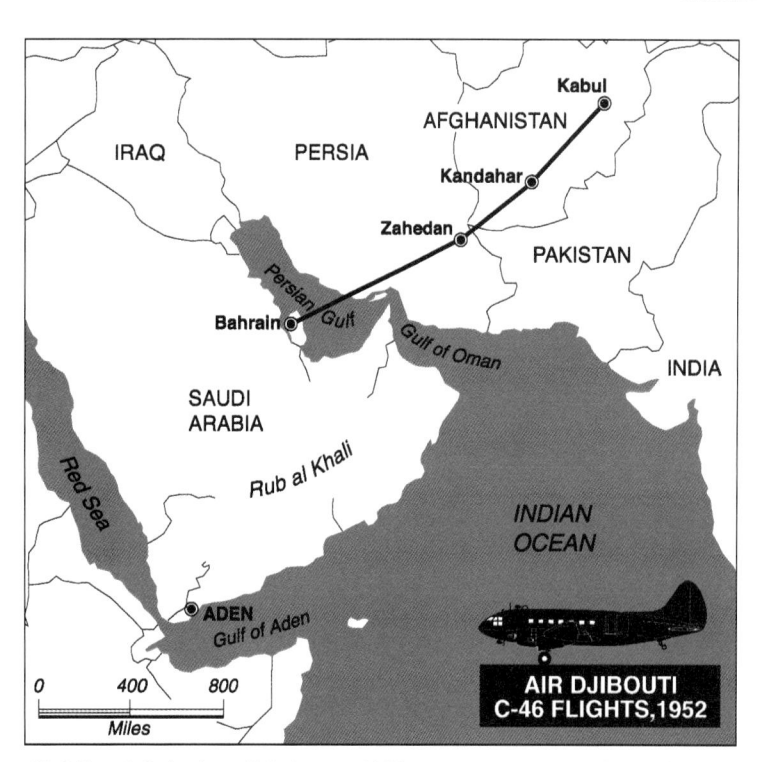

Air Djibouti, Bahrain to Kabul route, 1952. (Roger Carvell)

In the event, I won that discussion and Arab Airways (Jerusalem) Ltd was born. Orvis kept to his word and retreated, but not entirely since he kept alive his company, Air Jordan which, years later, became part of the national airline of Jordan".

Air Djibouti timetable from Bahrain to Kabul.

Tuesday			Wednesday		
Bahrain	Departure	0730	Kabul	Departure	1100
Zahedan	Arrival	1100	Kandahar	Arrival	1230
Zahedan	Departure	1200	Kandahar	Departure	1330
Kandahar	Arrival	1415	Zahedan	Arrival	1410
Kandahar	Departure	1515	Zahedan	Departure	1510
Kabul	Arrival	1645	Bahrain	Arrival	1830

Footnotes, Chapter 8:
(75) Telegram to Hilary from RGH, 4 November, 1950.
(76) Transocean: The story of an unusual airline; p 165.
(77) Signal No BH/M/2798/3898, 9 November, 1950.
(78) CSC.880 RMH to RGH, 15 November, 1950.
(79) C.949 J W S Brancker to Miss S Brown, MCA, 7 February, 1951.
(80) Air Djibouti Timetable and fares 28 November, 1950.
(81) Deputy Chairman of BOAC.
(82) MD 1691 de Graaf Hunter to Whitney Straight, 28 December, 1951.
(83) Secretary and Chief Accountant of Aden Airways.

BOAC / Aden Airways publicity photograph, 1952. Captain John Pascoe is at the controls. (British Airways Archives)

Aden Airways offices in Aden, 1952. (Michael Hedges)

Chapter 9 :
ADEN AIRWAYS 1952 - 1953

After the Board meeting of November 1951, the new financial year was bound to be difficult; consolidation and a certain amount of reflection were to be required for the enterprise to go forward. Two events were significant: the 1952 Haj and the Hermes operation described on page 57. There were also significant changes within the region, of which the most important was the federation of Eritrea and Ethiopia.

Before the war, Italy had colonised Eritrea as part of its grandiose plans for an African empire, taking over the country by expropriating land for the Italian immigrants who were sent out there, many of whom elected to remain there after the eviction of Italy by British forces in 1941. Asmara, the capital, had flourished under Italian influence and a well-educated urban middle class had grown with it, together with a well-established airfield which had been set up by the Italians and which was used by BOAC as its main engineering base while Cairo was threatened by German forces in North Africa. Sound engineering expertise was thus available for Aden Airways when the company came into being in 1949.

During the decade following the end of the war, Eritrea remained under British administration, much to the advantage of Aden Airways in terms of a centre of operations and traffic rights for both freight and passengers. Ethiopia, however, with no access to the sea, had campaigned vigorously for approval to annex the former Italian colony, claiming sovereignty on the basis that in ancient times the two countries had been one. In retrospect, this would have been difficult to justify as Eritrea was essentially a Muslim country with a poor record of tolerance towards other religions, while Ethiopia was Christian

Nevertheless, in 1950, the United Nations resolved that the two countries should be joined in a Federation which would provide Eritrea with autonomy under its own constitution and elected government. A new Eritrean assembly was elected in 1952 and the new constitution was adopted in July of that year. The Act of Federation was ratified in September and the British authorities officially relinquished control on 15th September 1952.

The effects on Aden Airways were immediate, quite simply because its main base, Asmara, was now in a foreign country. Also, the traffic generated by the former British Administration was lost after 15th September, resulting in an annual loss of some £18,000 in revenue.(84)

All traffic rights which had hitherto been enjoyed by the company within and from Eritrea were now ceded to Ethiopian Airlines, including the lucrative route between Asmara and Assab, which represented a further annual loss of an estimated £10,000. Clearly, the company had to rethink its future and it turned now to the development of its routes within the Aden Protectorate, based on Aden, where profits could be found if the price was right and the service offered was suitable. The first step was to convert the DC-3s to 40 seats, a configuration which could be altered at short notice depending on the amount of freight and passenger mix which was to be carried on a particular day or route.

"The 40-seat configuration was normally used when operating schedules outside the Protectorate. Of course, we also had the daily flight (by two aircraft) as freighters only, at first to Djibouti, but later on direct to Diredawa to pick up Qat. Otherwise the mixed freighters usually had seats along the left hand side and the freight was carried in large plastic bins along the other."(85)

On 19th October 1952 VR-AAE force-landed near Assouan while on a delivery flight from Prestwick after a C of A renewal, and was declared a total write-off, though it was in fact repaired and flew for a number of years after this mishap. There is an amusing side to this story in that a short time before this accident, the insurance value

VR-AAE lying in what appears to be a burial area after its forced-landing near Assouan on 19th October 1952. All airline markings had been quickly painted out.
(British Airways Archives)

of 'AAE had been increased from £10,000 to £30,000.(86) However, the assessor, after his initial appraisal, which was accepted by Aden Airways, decided that the aircraft was repairable after all, and offered to do the work for the company. But de Graaff Hunter insisted on the money instead making a profit of £20,000 in the process. (See pages 88, 89 for the full report)

On the scheduled routes passengers carried (87) declined by 15%, mostly because of a reduction in the schedule between Aden and Cairo from three to two per week, as well as the replacement by the Hermes between Aden and Nairobi on its weekly London- Cairo- Aden-Nairobi flight. As agreed by BOAC, between 1st May 1952 and 31st January 1953, the company was compensated for this change to the extent of £21,641, while a further £10,189 was paid over for February and March 1953 when the Hermes terminated at Aden.

While on the surface this might appear to have been a godsend to Aden Airways, it was something of a mixed blessing. Although there was a substantial increase in revenue, the airline suffered from the repercussions in passenger perceptions that Aden Airways had become very much a "local" carrier and therefore made their travel arrangements to take advantage of the superior BOAC service offered. Aden Airways still flew between Aden and Cairo, with a number of stops en route, but these tended to generate intersector travel rather than the more lucrative Aden to Cairo passenger through flights.

Some relief came in the decision by the Anglo-Iranian Oil Company to build a refinery at Little Aden; initially, much of the traffic generated by this enterprise was satisfied by the Hermes operation but, once the actual construction got under way, there was a considerable requirement to import labour from the Levant to the benefit of both Aden Airways and, later, Arab Airways (Jerusalem) Ltd.

As mentioned earlier, with some surplus capacity, the opportunity was presented to further develop services into the Hadramaut. For instance, between Aden and Mukeiras on the Yemen border,

passenger numbers increased by 48% to 47,775 over the previous year, and on the AD 452 and AD 462 from Aden to Riyan, Qatn and Ghuraf there was an increase of 7% to 127,757. (88) In addition to this effort, there were charters to oil companies into the deep interior, as well as other points within the Protectorate when opportunities presented themselves and a sufficient load could be found though these flights could be very different:

"Some of the routes were the same, like Nairobi and Khartoum, but at other times we flew into the Protectorate; early on destinations within the Protectorates were relatively few, such as Ghuraf, Qatn, Riyan and Mukeiras, but as the airline became more accepted as a form of transport other smaller and more remote strips were developed. Once again the unusual could occur such as when the aircraft was on a turnaround at a strip, there was a bearded gentleman sitting under the wing of my Dakota who nonchalantly took a shot at something with his rifle. I went up to him to remonstrate only to find that he was the local sheikh for the area and who was not about to be told what he could do in his own territory!

On another trip from Addis Ababa to Aden I had a passenger, a lion cub accompanied by a keeper, with the keeper sitting on one seat and the cub in a cage beside him. I went back and the keeper asked if he could let the lion out of its cage as it was perfectly tame, and he would have it on a lead. It was a present from the Emperor Haile Selassie to the King of Saudi Arabia. I checked with the other passengers who had no objection and so gave him permission. Later I went back again and there was the young lion sitting next to his keeper, erect and dignified whereupon I gently stroked him and he licked my hand." (89)

On the local routes from Aden to the Horn of Africa, services to Berbera and Hargeisa were increased, while Dire Dawa in Ethiopia came on line for the lucrative Qat traffic, as well as general freight/passenger flights. Other flights to Dire Dawa returned to Aden via Djibouti. Though Nairobi had been discontinued in favour of the Hermes, a weekly service continued to Mombasa via Hargeisa and Mogadishu which was popular with both military and civilian personnel taking a break from the oppressive climate of

CHAPTER 9: ADEN AIRWAYS 1952 - 1953

Captain Ken Bulmer and his wife Elsa arriving at Asmara, 1952,
(Paul Colvin)

Aden. Damascus was taken off-line because of poor loads and the intransigence of the Egyptian authorities who refused landing rights for Aden aircraft stopping for fuel enroute from Khartoum.

1952/53 had thus proved very much to be a year of transition and consolidation. The events in Eritrea forced the company to rethink its policies in that, for instance, all engineering up to Check 4 could now be done "in house", thanks to the improved facilities both in Asmara and Aden, as well as the skills of those Italian engineers who were happy to relocate. Perhaps one of the most important decisions to be made was the move from Asmara to Aden where, notwithstanding the climate, the costs were lower and from where a greater sense of identity could be derived.

Hermes Operation, April-December 1952

The repercussions from the 14th meeting in November 1951 continued to be felt into the following year. During the months before the meeting, the Aden Airways Board had repeatedly advised BOAC of its increasingly uncompetitive position as a result of operating inferior equipment compared to those of their competitors on the prime routes from Aden to Cairo and, southwards, to Nairobi. The consequences of the enforced cutbacks from six DC-3s to four merely served to exacerbate their worsening position.

During the northern summer of 1951, BOAC had experienced a surge of traffic to East Africa where it already operated seven flights per week to Nairobi via Khartoum and Entebbe. For 1952/53 nine services per week were proposed, one of which would operate through Aden. Initially, this was perceived to be something of a mixed blessing by Aden Airways; on the one hand, it would give the passengers out of Aden to Nairobi and Cairo a much better ride in the pressurised Hermes but, on the other hand, it would take traffic away from the company where the DC-3 still

Carlo Moretti, Traffic Officer at Asmara in 1952.   (Carlo Moretti)

flew three services a week to Cairo and one to Nairobi, albeit via a number of intermediate points.

It was a complex issue. With the forthcoming federation between Eritrea and Ethiopia, Aden Airways would be obliged to move from its former base in Asmara to the rather less congenial surroundings of Aden where personal accommodation was inadequate, the airport facilities were rudimentary and hotel space was scarce.

There does seem to have been a general lack of awareness within BOAC as to exactly what they were taking on in routing through Aden. It would appear that no-one had thought of hotel accommodation in the event of aircraft unserviceability (not uncommon in those days) and, in a rather exasperated letter, H M Harman, BOAC reservations superintendent, complains:

"*I assume Aden Airways mean that they are unable to provide hotel accommodation on Sundays. This is rather a peculiar*

A BOAC Hermes, G-ALDW, at London Airport in August 1953

The terrace at the Aden Airways mess at Khormaksar, February 1956. Earlier, in 1953, BOAC passengers had been obliged to sleep on this terrace when the Hermes they were travelling on became unserviceable. *(Vic Spencer)*

Passengers disembarking from a BOAC Hermes at Khormaksar, 1953. *(Michael Hedges)*

attitude, because if it is an unscheduled nightstop, they would surely have to do something about it and I think we should be unhappy to leave it like this"(90) . This was less than two weeks before the planned starting date of the service, which in fact would be delayed until well into May for aircraft technical reasons.

Similarly, in a letter to BOAC, de Graaff Hunter explains the situation thus:

"Regarding passenger accommodation, I must ask you to forbid your Hermes from breaking down in Aden because it would not be possible to accommodate more than a handful of passengers here, even with prior warning. In extreme emergency, passengers could, of course be accommodated in dormitory fashion on the verandahs of our crew mess, but I fear that the consequences of such an arrangement would be severe criticism against both our airlines." (91)

The comments on this attempt at humour were not long in coming; R M Hilary, who had, after all been in at the early planning of the airline, replied:

"I hope no one imagines that we are routing one of the East African Hermes services through Aden just for the fun of it, or because we think that it is a brilliant idea. You may know how it all arose: Aden Airways' fear that their Dakotas were becoming uncompetitive, and their request for four-engine aircraft, the desire to cut Aden Airways down from the point of view of crew requirements, and the difficulty of providing accommodation for a concentrated unit at Aden itself. If the experiment proves unsatisfactory, we shall have to scrap it and think again." (92)

Aden Airways was being severely tested by the competition on both the routes from Aden to Nairobi and up through the Red Sea to Cairo. On the former, Air India had place its newly-acquired Constellations which flew from Bombay direct to Aden and then non-stop to Nairobi; these aircraft were also faster and were pressurised and, with the strong Indian community in Aden and Kenya, there was a ready source of passengers who wished to fly on this superior service, compared to that of Aden Airways which flew there via Hargeisa and Mogadishu. Similarly, Ethiopian Airlines with the Convair CV-240 on its routes out of Asmara to Cairo, and though there was a weight penalty for the flight at Asmara because of the altitude, there were many who preferred the option of a direct flight to Cairo, or a quick refuelling stop in Port Sudan, to the rather longer and sedentary progress of the DC-3s. The result of this was that while Aden Airways was able to pick up point-to-point intermediate traffic, the lucrative long-distance passengers were choosing to fly with the opposition.

Once again, it was left to Aden Airways to make the compromises, which it did to its advantage. First, a fare differential of 15% was

Ethiopian Airlines Convair 240 ET-T-20 at Nairobi in 1953. The type offered pressurised, faster competition for Aden's DC-3s.

Chapter 9: Aden Airways 1952 - 1953

Four Engined Pressurised Hermes operated jointly by BOAC and Aden Airways Between London and Aden, Calling at Rome and Cairo.

ALL TIMES ARE LOCAL TIMES

BA 324/AD 471				BA325/AD 470	
Day LT.				LT. Day	
Wed.					
1200	dep.	LONDON	arr.	0625	
1735	arr.	ROME	dep.	0215	
1835	dep.	ROME	arr.	0115	
Thur.					Sat.
0125	arr.	CAIRO	dep.	1925	
0225	dep.	CAIRO	arr.	1825	
1020	arr.	ADEN	dep.	1220	
					Fri.

Aden Airways provides direct connections with this service in Aden.

Details of connections with B.O.A.C. routes to Europe, U.S.A., East and South Africa and W.A.A.C. routes to West Africa can be obtained from any Aden Airways or B.O.A.C. Booking Offices.

FOUR ENGINED PRESSURISED ARGONAUT OPERATED JOINTLY BY BOAC AND ADEN AIRWAYS BETWEEN LONDON AND ADEN, CALLING AT ROME AND CAIRO.

ALL TIMES ARE LOCAL TIMES

BA 324/AD471				BA325/AD 470
Wed.				
1845	dep.	LONDON	arr.	0640
2305	arr.	ROME	dep.	0210
0005	dep.	ROME	arr.	0110
Thurs.				Sat.
0645	arr.	CAIRO	dep.	1945
0745	dep.	CAIRO	arr.	1845
1535	arr.	ADEN	dep.	1300
				Fri.

Note: The above local times are effective 1st May 1953.

ADEN AIRWAYS PROVIDES DIRECT CONNECTIONS WITH THIS SERVICE IN ADEN.

BOAC / Aden Airways timetables for London to Aden joint service, showing (above) the Hermes service as operated in February and March 1953, and (right) the Argonaut service which replaced it in April as seen in the May 1st issue. Direct comparison of timings requires application of time zones and of BST.

placed on the Hermes flights which did deter some passengers, though not many. Second, there would be all the handling charges of aircraft turnarounds in Aden, providing engineering cover there, fuel and the commission on ticket sales. An added incentive was that BOAC agreed to hand over 33% of all revenue generated by the Hermes in compensation for the loss of traffic; this alone produced revenue of £31,830 for the airline.

With the benefit of hindsight, the Hermes was probably not the best aircraft to have on these routes. It was new in design and was the first pressurised passenger aircraft to be produced by Handley Page. The onboard systems were driven by microswitches which did not fare well in the hot and humid environment which was experienced in Cairo, Aden and Khartoum, while additional problems were to be found at hot and high airfields such as Nairobi. The Argonaut, a proven, if noisy, design would have been better suited.

The service had been due to start on 1st April 1952 but was postponed until 1st May as a result of a number of problems involving availability of fuel, diplomatic clearances, and crew slips in Cairo, because, in the last case, of continuing unrest in Egypt. After 8th August, the flight operated through Khartoum for crew slips en-route to Aden, though on the winter schedules the flight reverted back to Cairo again.

There were a number of problems with the service, culminating in an embarrassing experience in September when a Hermes broke down in Aden on its way to Nairobi; de Graaff Hunter's predictions came true and there was a considerable delay in getting the passengers on to their destination, though this was not entirely the fault of either BOAC or Aden Airways as EAAC could not transfer another aircraft.

By the end of 1952, it was decided that the BA 163 would no longer operate onwards from Aden to Nairobi. Loads had been insufficient between these two points for some time and the service was proving to be uneconomical. Accordingly, the last flight to leave London as the BA 163 departed Heathrow on 31st January 1953, and the last one from Nairobi was the BA 164 on 30th January. As from February, a new service number was given to this flight which became the BA 324/325, and flew under this prefix to Cairo where it would then adopt the Aden Airways callsign as the AD 471, before proceeding to Aden. The return flight would be the AD 470 to Cairo and the BA 325 onwards to London.(93)

A further change was made on 1st April 1953, when the Argonaut took over the Red Sea route.

It had been a bold experiment on the part of BOAC to try to compensate Aden Airways for the rather savage cutbacks imposed in November 1951. There were undoubted benefits to passengers, at least on the Red Sea routes, but Aden-Nairobi alone was never likely to generate the loads required to keep an aircraft such as the Hermes profitable. Air India was able to benefit because of the ethnic connections and loyalties in all three countries, while BOAC was really dependent on passengers who preferred to travel on the more direct Nile route to London, instead of the dog-leg via Aden. It was questionable as well whether Aden Airways benefited in any real way from having what was effectively another company flying on its routes; when passengers travelled on the BA 164 to Cairo, they were choosing to travel on BOAC and not an Aden Airways flight as such. A third of the revenues was cold comfort when it was still perceived by the travelling public to be a small and very local airline. Having the main base at Asmara did not help either as that is where Ethiopian Airlines competed most effectively.

Once again, and through no fault of their own, Aden Airways was required to pick up the pieces on the Nairobi route, with a much depleted fleet.

It is an interesting aside that during February 1952, after much pleading from de Graaff Hunter, BOAC made a feasibility study (94) of placing either the Hermes or the Argonaut on the route from Nairobi to Bombay. The flights would go via Bahrain to Karachi and Bombay, thus honouring the original route which had been much sought after two years previously and denied. In the end, the route was considered to be unproductive because of the difficulty

Yemeni DC-3 YE-AAC at Aden 1955 with a BOAC Hermes in the background. *(Ann Atkinson)*

The timing of the planned winter schedules differed slightly from the original times because of the changes in the wind components from summer to winter. Effectively, the flight departed on 1 November at 1145 and, flying via Rome, Cairo and Aden, arrived in Nairobi at 1600. The return flight to London departed on 31 October at 1030 and, following the same route, was scheduled to arrive in London at 1040.

When the decision was made to terminate the Hermes service in Aden, the operation from the first week in February 1953 was as shown on the previous page. When the Hermes was replaced by the Argonaut, at the beginning of April 1953, the times changed again as shown in the second table.

of integrating either the Hermes or the Argonaut into the BOAC route structure both in the Middle East and in East Africa, partly because of the impending arrival of the Comet 1 and partly because of switching the Hermes to Middle East routes. The proposed timetable is shown below.

The first services from London were on 2nd May 1952, and the return from Nairobi on 4th May. All times are local.

	BA 163				BA 164	
Saturday	1145	dep	London	arr	1130	
	1605	arr	Rome	dep	0625	
	1705	dep	Rome	arr	0525	Saturday
	2359	arr	Cairo	dep	2340	
Sunday	0115	dep	Cairo	arr	2225	
	0845	arr	Aden	dep	1635	
	0945	dep	Aden	arr	1535	
	1435	arr	Nairobi	dep	1030	Friday

On 29th July 1952, slip crews were transferred to Khartoum due to unrest in Cairo. (95)

Saturday	0945	dep	London	arr	1315	
	1405	arr	Rome	dep	0825	
	1505	dep	Rome	arr	0725	
	2100	arr	Cairo	dep	0040	Saturday
	2215	dep	Cairo	arr	2325	
Sunday	0300	arr	Khartoum	dep	1830	
	0415	dep	Khartoum	arr	1730	
	0755	arr	Aden	dep	1335	
	0855	dep	Aden	arr	1235	
	1340	arr	Nairobi	dep	0730	Friday

Ethiopian Airlines use of JATO 1952

Ethiopian Airlines had ordered the Convair 240 from the USA, placing two of them into service in December, 1950. Pressurised and fast, the aircraft had by 1952 gained some considerable commercial advantages over Aden Airways and its DC-3s, particularly on their prime route from Asmara to Cairo which it could fly non-stop, though, because of the high elevation of Asmara, not always with a full load which seemed to negate the aircraft's inherent advantage.

The answer was to use Jet-Assisted-Take-off (JATO) and this system was installed on ET-T-21 (later ET-AAW) where it proved to be an immediate and great success. However, on 29th June 1952 this aircraft suffered considerable damage when one of the JATO bottles happened to be misaligned on takeoff and blew a large hole in the fuselage. A new mid-section was obtained from Convair and following the rebuild ET-T-21 returned to service, without JATO, in February 1953.

Until then Aden Airways was considering its use, but gave up the idea after this particular incident. The company did, however, consider using the French Turboméca Palas jet unit which had been successfully pioneered in France by the Air France Night Mail DC-3s. Unfortunately, being fitted underneath the centre section, and extending downwards some way, it was considered too dangerous in the event of a wheels up landing. The ARB resident in Cyprus was also less than enthusiastic about it and after the Ethiopian incident the idea was quietly shelved.

Ethiopian Convair 240 ET-T-21 demonstrating the use of Jet Assisted Take-Off (JATO) in 1952. *(via O G Nordbø)*

Chapter 9: Aden Airways 1952 - 1953

The Haj and the pilgrimage of 1952

As became evident during the year 1950/1951, the major share of the profits was derived from the Haj pilgrim flights; but for this revenue, the airline would have run at a substantial loss. Before the official start of Aden Airways, in October 1949, this segment of the market had been largely ignored by BOAC, but thanks to the lateral thinking on the part of de Graaff Hunter the airline undertook these flights and was able to profit from them to the extent it did.

The concept of the Haj itself is an interesting phenomenon, as Harry Pusey writes:

"The Haj traffic was something special, as were the Hajis themselves. In the early years, before air travel was accepted as commonplace, the Haj traffic was limited and there was little problem with the Saudis as their airline was basically a special service for the Great King, as Abdul Aziz Ibn Saud was fondly known. The airline was under the command of General Ibrahim Tassan who was one of Ibn Saud's comrades when they took over Saudi Arabia during the 1920s and banished the Hashemites, (Abdullah and Feisal who had held the holy places in the Hejaz since records began), to Jordan and Iraq respectively.

In 1950, Jeddah was the port of entry and at that time had a population of some 50,000, though this number was never discussed since it could lend doubt to the Great King's statement that he could and would provide an army of some two million soldiers to fight a Jihad for control of the Holy Lands.

As such, there were few restrictions, if any, on what an airline could carry, the only real stipulation being that the Pilgrims had to have valid passports, a Pilgrimage Certificate endorsed by a Saudi consular official, to have paid to that official the visa fee and the mitawif fee, to be vaccinated against smallpox and cholera and to have a valid return ticket. In addition, the airline had to agree that it would take out of Saudi Arabia all the people it had brought in, and at the end of the Haj, not weeks or months later.

The Saudi Government was, therefore, reasonably content; it had its visa fees, the Haji guide—the mutawif, had his fee, there was a reasonable protection against health risks and the far more serious risk of illegal immigration was also dealt with. This last was simply because Saudi Arabia was seen by other Moslems as being immensely wealthy when compared with conditions within the Hadramaut and elsewhere.

Initially, Aden Airways took Pilgrims from Aden and the Hadramaut, though some came across the border from Yemen. This initial success led the airline to expand the operation to other Moslem areas such as East Africa, mainly Mombasa and Dar-es-Salaam, and the Somalilands. Further expansion was made into Nigeria, with an occasional foray into the Middle East and Afghanistan.

The Saudis began to wake up, particularly so in the case of Kamal Sindi, clerk and translator to General Tassan, and a man who was eventually to become the head of Saudi Arabian Airlines. New rules were introduced whereby Saudi Arabian Airlines became entitled to carry 50% of the pilgrims from each country. Pilgrims could be flown into Saudi Arabia by either Saudi Arabian Airlines or by an aircraft of national registration of the country from which the pilgrims began their flights. These rules were introduced after the main operations of the 1952 Haj had begun, and which ensured that several fraught meetings took place during which a deal was hammered out whereby Aden Airways would fly all the pilgrims in as arranged, and Saudi Arabian Airlines would fly them out. But when the Saudis reneged on the deal, 13 DC-3s had to be hired from Indamer of India to carry all the pilgrims back to their country of origin.

After this fiasco, and in order to safeguard future Haj operations, Aden Airways made a further deal with the Saudis whereby Aden Airways would pay them £1 for each pilgrim flown in and another £1 for each one flown out. This was an unofficial arrangement and was thus a cash transaction carried out by suitable agents with nothing appearing on paper.

There were other subterfuges which ensured that things went smoothly. For instance, the Hadramaut had always given problems, and on each return Haj flight we had young men in proper Saudi dress, a typical Saudi beard as well as other Saudi mannerisms who represented themselves as the pilgrims we had taken in that year. In fact these were people who had gone in two or three years previously, had made their money, and in order to simplify problems had bought the return half of the ticket from a fellow tribesman who had gone in that year. In fact, the Hadramis found it difficult to raise a return fare in any case. So, using our agent in Ghuraf, a man named Al Khaff, we met with the village headmen and agreed to issue return tickets for a single fare provided the headman agreed to pay the return fare if the pilgrim was apprehended by the Saudi authorities and sent back or, indeed, when that pilgrim returned. This system worked well; the pilgrims made their Haj, some stayed on to work while others returned and Aden Airways made a profit. Sadly, a later company manager thought this too underhand and the direct Hadramaut pilgrimage ceased.

In Jordan we had an easier problem. In Aden I had met a gentleman by the name of Abdul Manaf Mohager, and whose family had connections going back to Mohammed in Jeddah and Medinah, and as a result was a man of some influence. His main interests were in Northern Persia and there are various Holy places between there and Mecca. So, together, we organised bus and truck travel from Northern Persia to Isfahan, from there to Kerbala and Nejjaf in Southern Iraq, from there to the Khadaman Mosque in Baghdad and then on to the Omayyad Mosque in Damascus; from there they travelled on to the Dome of the Rock in Jerusalem and the Tomb of Abraham in Hebron from where they were transported to Amman Airport. They then became airborne pilgrims and we flew them to Jeddah for a return fare of £48, of which Abdul Manaf received £3.

As part of our customer relations, each pilgrim received a certificate with his photograph on it and signed by the aircraft Captain with a quotation from the Holy Koran:

"Blessed is he who in a single night flew from the most Holy and most inviolate sanctuary to the distant most Holy and inviolable sanctuary. Blessed also shall be.................. who has flown between.............. and.............. on this day by Arab Airways (Jerusalem) Ltd"

These arrangements were made entirely by word of mouth and on personal honour, and Mohager always paid; a little late at times, but it always arrived."

The 14th Board Meeting on 7th November 1951 was a watershed for Aden Airways and a stunning reminder of just how precarious an existence they had under a mercurial owner such as BOAC.

The proposed cutback to 4 DC-3s meant that there was insufficient capacity to carry out the pilgrim flights for 1952, and under these circumstances BOAC promised: *"York aircraft and crews for pilgrimage work next year (1952) and in succeeding years, at a basic charter rate from which BOAC would not expect to derive any profit or contribution towards standing charges."*(97) From this wording, de Graaff Hunter seems to have inferred that several, or certainly more than two, Yorks would be available, but in the end it only two appeared.

The planning for this operation started in January 1952. The two Yorks would be used on the pilgrimage from West Africa, through Khartoum to Jeddah. The dates for the 1952 Haj were to be 1st to 27th August for the inward (to Jeddah) flights and 3rd to 30th September for the outward flights.

The potential for misunderstandings between the two companies was considerable, and, in particular, the offer from BOAC for Yorks, or similar aircraft, to be available in subsequent years. In fact, the Yorks would not be available after 1952 because of their impending retirement, nor would there be any other suitable aircraft as a result of the shortage created by their very retirement. (98) This situation could not have been foreseen in November 1951 and obviously was not deliberate, but it did highlight the precarious consequences of the decisions from the 14th Board Meeting.

Nor did de Graaff Hunter make it easy for the BOAC Board. Perhaps to take advantage of their apparent magnanimity, he requested a further two Yorks with the intention of using them as freighters out of Asmara under the auspices of a separate Eritrean company controlled by Aden Airways. Whether BOAC would ever have approved of one of their subsidiaries controlling another subsidiary is open to question and was potentially fraught with difficulties. But de Graaff Hunter, with his entrepreneurial spirit, would certainly not have seen it this way. He had overlooked the fact that, at over 7,000 feet, Asmara was unsuitable for such an operation with Yorks, particularly in the case of engine failure on take-off. BOAC, under a Captain Houston, carried out a technical survey of the operating parameters for the York out of Asmara and other hot and high airfields and concluded that, while flights could be made safely, loads would be so restricted as to render the services uneconomical. Nevertheless, de Graaff Hunter persisted, suggesting through Captain Colvin (Aden Airways' Chief Pilot) that Gura could be used instead as it had an elevation of only 6,300 feet and a longer runway. Clearly, there was some exasperation settling in at BOAC headquarters with the bombardment of ideas by de Graaff Hunter, and in a letter from Whitney Straight, the parent company did not mince their words:

"*Thank you for your letters of the 12th and 15 January. We now understand your requirements.*

The York investigation done by Captain Houston so far has shown a pretty unsatisfactory state of affairs at Asmara. Captain Houston is sending you a memorandum on this and until you have had a chance of considering it I do not think you should enter into any commitments, least of all with Count Davicos. (A wealthy local merchant of Italian descent)

The Chairman did promise you two Yorks for the pilgrimage season, and here again I think you should be careful what payload you offer pending Captain Houston's memorandum.

You talk as though the Eritrean company was in fact a going concern. There have been so many propositions of this sort in various parts of the World in the past that, quite frankly, I am a little cynical and would like to see something really firm before the Corporation undertakes any commitment. It would be interesting to have the views of your local diplomatic representative on this." (99)

Considerable planning for the Haj flights from Nigeria was involved. The two Yorks were to be provided with 46 seats, together with five crews, three ground engineers and a suitable amount of spare parts, these last two to be based in Khartoum. The routeing was to be as follows:

	Capacity to Jeddah (kgs)	Flight time hr.min	Capacity from Jeddah (kgs)	Flight time hr.min
Kano-Maiduguri	6050	1.30	6070	1.30
Maiduguri-El Fasher	4420	4.05	4000	4.05
El Fasher-Khartoum	4790	2.20	5290	2.20
Khartoum-Jeddah	5400	3.05	5440	2.55
Khartoum-Kano		7.30		7.30

(100)

Three crews were to be based at Kano to fly to Khartoum and back, while the other two crews would fly the Khartoum-Jeddah-Khartoum sectors. The ground engineers and spares would, as mentioned, be based in Khartoum, but available for anywhere along the route should anything untoward occur. The total number of round trips would work out at 40 and would cost £69,500 in all at £1,060 per round trip plus other costs. Each round trip would take approximately 21 flying hours.

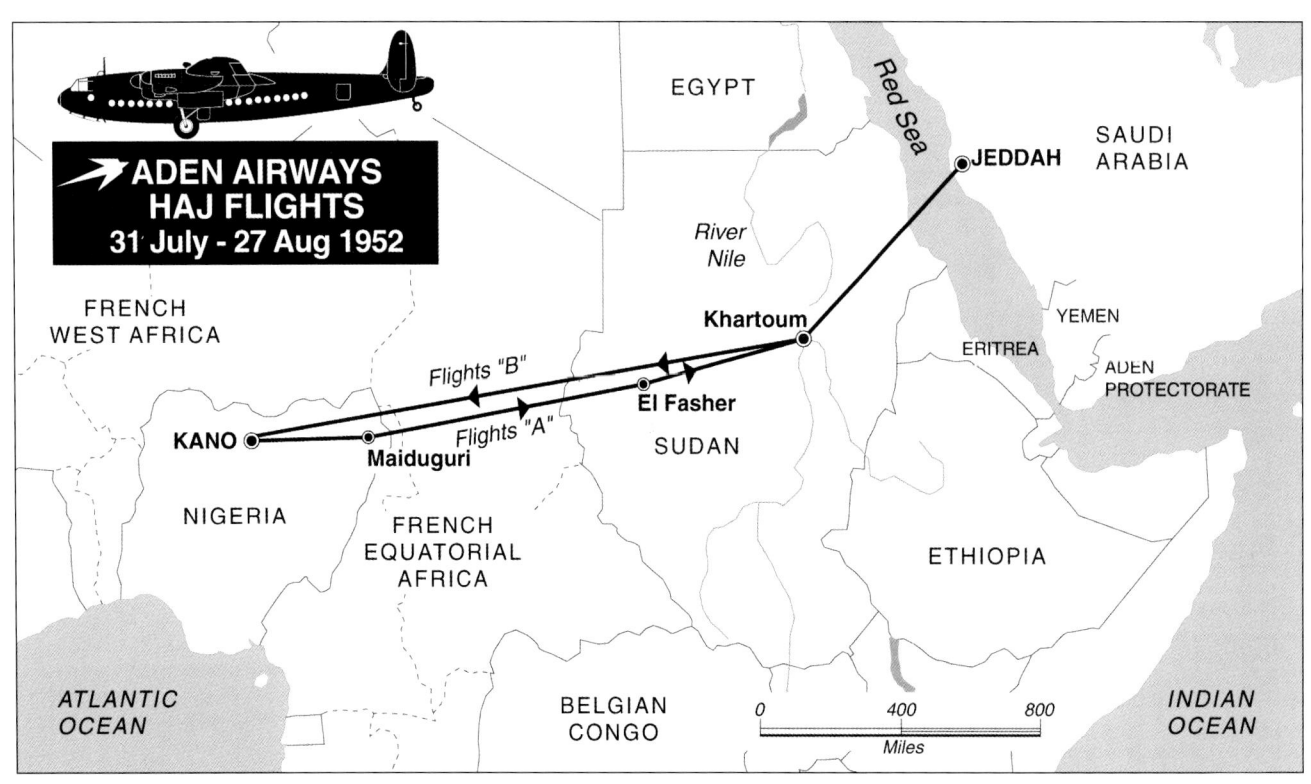

The 1952 trans-Africa Haj routes flown with Yorks. (Roger Carvell)

Chapter 9: Aden Airways 1952 - 1953

Avro York G-AGSO was one of the two used for the 1952 Haj.

The timetable reflected the fact that the Haj would have two distinct phases. From 31 July to 27 August, the pilgrims would travel to Jeddah, after which the main celebrations would be held followed by the return exodus to Nigeria. Thus, the flights from Kano to Jeddah had to stop and refuel frequently, but on the return to Kano the York was able to fly direct from Khartoum to Kano: (101)

B	A				A	B
2200	2015	dep	Kano	arr	1055	1125
	2155	arr	Maiduguri	dep		1000
	2355	dep	Maiduguri	arr		0800
	0410	arr	El Fasher	dep		0410
	0510	dep	El Fasher	arr		0310
0610	0745	arr	Khartoum	dep	0330	0050
1600	0845	dep	Khartoum	arr	1535	2350
1900	1145	arr	Jeddah	dep	1245	2100

Flights "A" were the inbound to Jeddah at the start of the Haj, while flights "B" were the outbound ones at the end. The Flight numbers were rather more complicated, being odd numbers eastbound and even numbers westbound, so that on the initial flow to Jeddah, the numbers were to be YCS 195/1 eastbound for the first flight and YCS 195/2 for the westbound flight to collect more pilgrims for the YCS 195/3, and so on. For the homeward flights at the end of the Haj, the flights were numbered YCS 196/2 westbound, and YCS 196/1 eastbound. Some form of record had to be kept, and this was the best way. (102)

In June, BOAC had advised Aden Airways that 48 flights could now be accomplished, instead of the original 40, resulting in 984 hours of flying, of which 856 would be revenue-producing, while 128 were for positioning the aircraft. The total cost was to be £78,000. All seemed to be set.

The first inkling that the best laid plans might not go so well arrived in an innocuous letter from the MCA in London during July, only a few days before the Haj flights were due to start.

"The Saudi regulations require that application for permission for such flights should be made by your agents in Jeddah direct to the local authorities. For traffic rights at Kano, you should obtain permission from the West African Air Transport Authority, c/o Department of Civil Aviation, Lagos, Nigeria. Finally, you are advised to obtain permission for the flights through the Sudan either from the Sudan Agency in London, or from the Civil Secretary, Sudan Government, Khartoum." (103)

The local authorities in Jeddah were represented by none other than General Ibrahim Tassan, referred to previously by Harry Pusey and, as he has already pointed out, the Saudis were already waking up to the fact that they were not only seriously losing out to other airlines in terms of revenue, but were also seen to be losing face within the larger Arab community. Thus when Aden Airways sought a meeting with General Tassan on 27th July to confirm permission for the whole Haj operation, he was ready with demands of his own. After considerable negotiation, an agreement was hammered out whereby: (104)

1) Aden Airways was to bring pilgrims in from Aden, Mukalla, Kano and Khartoum, plus from any other points, provided permission was granted by the Saudi Authorities, in other words General Tassan.

2) No other British-registered airline was permitted unless operating on behalf of Aden Airways.

3) The return fares payable to Aden Airways were:
Khartoum £ 30   Aden   £ 44
Mukalla   £ 53   Kano   £105

Half of these receipts would be paid to Saudi Arabian Airlines which would now return the pilgrims to their points of origin; in other words, Aden Airways would lose all their returning flights **and** the revenue.

This was a severe blow to the airline, but there was more to come. The second half of the BOAC York charter was cancelled and, after completing the Kano to Jeddah phase of the charter, both aircraft returned to London.

Unfortunately, shortly after General Tassan had made his ruling, it became obvious that the fledgling Saudi airline simply did not have the capacity to repatriate all the pilgrims who had been brought in, and the Saudi Government was faced with the slightly ridiculous situation of thousands of pilgrims, having completed their pilgrimage, having no means of leaving. So the Saudis did the next best thing; they reneged on the deal and advised Aden Airways that they were responsible, after all, for the return flights and that if they did not undertake this task they would lose all traffic rights in the future. (105) De Graaff Hunter made frantic efforts on 19th August for the return of the Yorks but they had by now flown back to the UK and their crews dispersed back to the fleets from whence they had come.

Fortunately, the American/Indian charter company, Indamer, based in Bombay, was able to supply a number of DC-3s to help out; in fact, because of the Saudi rules previously described, no less than 13 Indamer aircraft were leased and placed on a temporary Aden register in order to comply. So Aden Airways was able, by the skin of its teeth and a great deal of luck, to save the day. All the pilgrims were eventually returned to their points of origin, particularly to Nigeria.

There were, however, some repercussions. All the Nigerian pilgrims had been ticketed by WAAC (West African Airways Corporation) and these pilgrims had not been impressed by the means and uncertainty of their return from Jeddah. WAAC were not impressed either, as evidenced by a letter from its General Manager to the BOAC Sales Director when discussing the plans for the following year:

"I am anxious that there shall be no third party, as was the case this year when Aden Airways sub contracted to BOAC and Indamer. If BOAC can undertake the work, I want to negotiate direct with them and cut out Aden Airways. I shall ask Brown to go to Jeddah and try and tie up once and for all whether Saudi Arabian Airlines will insist on carrying half the pilgrim traffic themselves without making the same kind of haphazard and arbitrary arrangements which they instituted this year, and which the Saudis cannot honour when it comes to the point." (106)

While this exemplified the sense of frustration felt by all concerned, it was also unfair criticism of Aden Airways and its Managing Director, de Graaff Hunter, who had rescued the situation from potential disaster. So ended what was, probably, the most fraught pilgrimage so far. Future pilgrimages were to prove easier to handle.

A venture into Ethiopia, 1952-1953
This was one of the more curious episodes during the early years of Aden Airways. Right from the beginning, Ethiopian Airlines had been the arch rival within the region and its management under TWA had pursued an aggressive policy of competition on every front, particularly after September, 1952 when Eritrea, and therefore Aden Airway's base in Asmara, ceased to be under British jurisdiction.

In December 1952 news came to de Graaff Hunter that Ethiopian Airlines was sustaining heavy losses which were blamed on the fact that the TWA management fees were too expensive as were the high salaries enjoyed by the Captains seconded from the parent company. De Graaff Hunter wrote to the Chairman of BOAC (107) informing him of the situation, advising that Aden Airways, if asked, could, and should, fill the vacuum were TWA to depart.

Early in January of the following year, de Graaff Hunter was approached by *"two different responsible quarters in the Ethiopian Government"* (108) that separately made specific enquiries as to the ability of the Aden Airways Management to replace TWA if it was asked to do so.

On the 8th February de Graaff Hunter had visited Addis Ababa where, with the active participation of the British Ambassador, meetings were quietly held with the latter's American counterparts during which it was agreed that should TWA be denied a new contract, then Aden Airways would step in.

"After discussions with the Ambassador we decided upon the policy to let our purpose be known quite widely; but that it was not our intention to be used as a bargaining counter by the Ethiopians against the American interests. Neither would we secretly bid against them to seek to capture the agency. In the event of negotiations between the Americans and the Ethiopians breaking

The Ethiopian Emperor, Haile Selassie, touring the Aden Airways facilities in January 1953. Richard de Graaff Hunter is on the right and Chief Pilot Captain Steve Colvin in the centre.
(British Airways Archives)

down, however, we were willing and ready to consider drawing up specific proposals for official study. Meanwhile we would do nothing in the matter.
Our Ambassador emphasised this to the American Ambassador and I, in turn, to the General Manager of Ethiopian Airlines. The understanding we reached with them was that we would be informed immediately by them if it looked likely that they would not be able to secure the renewal of their contract, in fact before the Ethiopians themselves knew." (109)

During this visit to Addis Ababa de Graaff Hunter also met Count Von Rosen, the Swedish Director General of the Ethiopian Air Force, who was also interested in bidding for the management of Ethiopian Airlines. The plan hatched between these two unlikely allies was that whichever one of them won the contract, Aden Airways would take over all external routes while the domestic routes would be operated by Count Von Rosen with the help of Air Force personnel; in effect by the Air Force. This collaboration was considered essential bearing in mind that other airlines such as KLM, Pan American and Scandinavian Airlines were also interested in bidding at the time.

At the same time, A C Middleton, Accountant and Company secretary to Aden Airways, was invited to meet the Ethiopian Director-General of Civil Aviation who *"left no doubt whatsoever about his Government's dissatisfaction with the TWA past agreement and, indeed, their latest proposals. He hoped that Aden Airways would now come forward with a plan and he felt confident that were we to do so it would be very favourably considered".* (110)

No plans of such magnitude could be decided upon until the Emperor, Haile Selassie, had himself seen and approved of them or not. It was he who made the final decision and to whom de Graaff Hunter sent the submission: (111)

1) Aden Airways would assume full commercial, operational and financial responsibility for the international routes, leaving to a re-constituted Ethiopian Airlines the responsibility for the operation and development of services internally within Ethiopia.
2) Ethiopian Airlines would dispose of its two CV-240s and would standardise on the DC-3 for both international and domestic routes.
3) Although Ethiopian Airlines would be relieved of financial responsibilities for international routes, it would be politically desirable that these routes be operated under the Ethiopian flag thus assuring political continuity and an uninterrupted link with Ethiopia in the eyes of the foreign countries served.

COLOUR SECTION 1

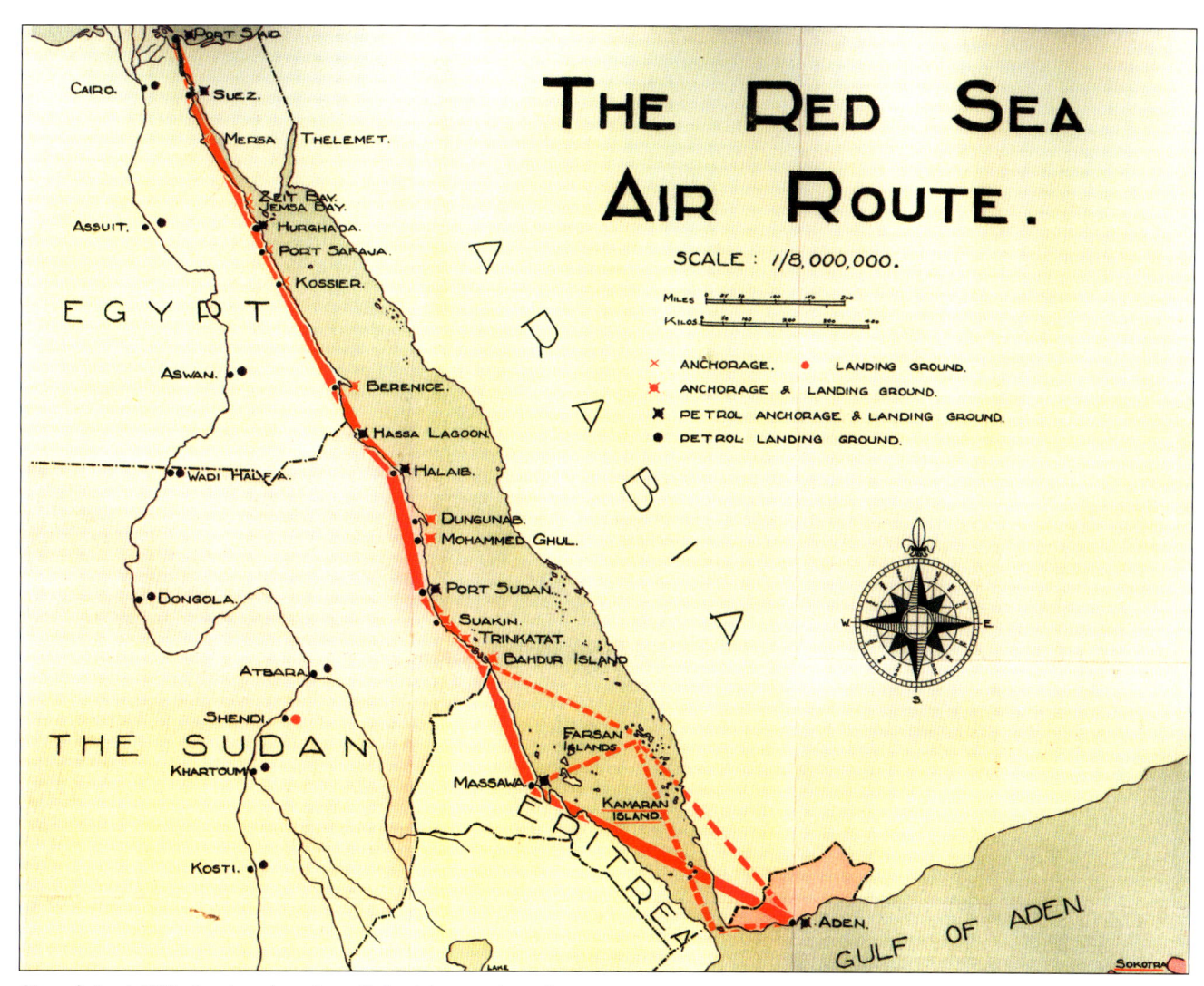

C1

Map of about 1935 showing air routes with landplane and seaplane destinations along the Red Sea.

Alitalia schedule in 1949 for Rome – Cairo – Asmara operated by Avro Lancastrian aircraft.

Map from Ala Littoria timetable of October 1937. Most of the African routes were flown with Fokker F.VII trimotors, with Cant Z 506 trimotors to Bengasi and Savoia Marchetti S73 trimotors to Addis Ababa.

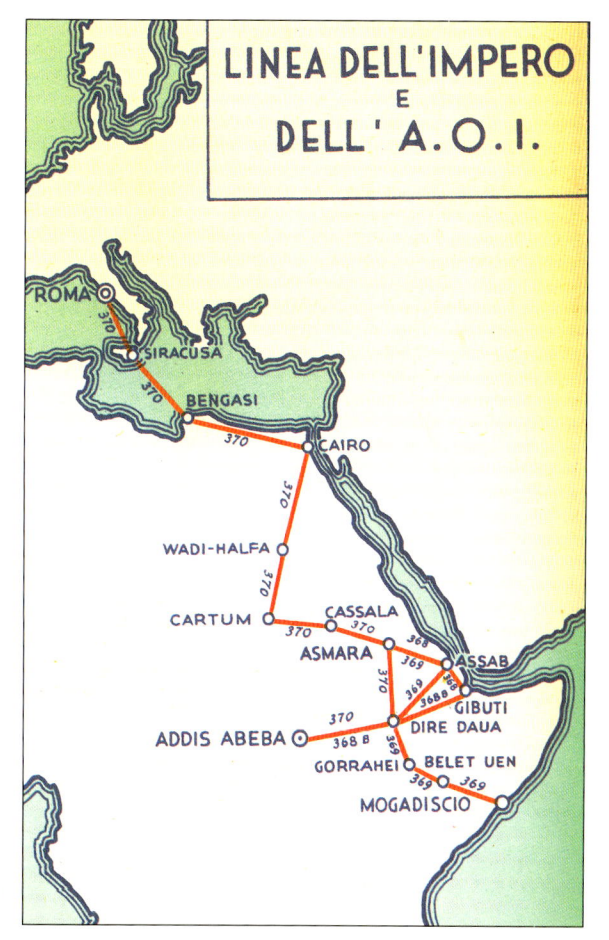

Timetable from 1st June 1950.

The first baggage label from the early fifties. (Dacre Watson)

A Maria Theresa Thaler, the accepted currency amongst the tribes of the Hadramaut. (Wendy Hayden Sadler)

A baggage label from the fifties. (Dacre Watson)

A ticket from 1950 for a journey from Aden to Damascus and return. The flight number is for the AD 478. (Dacre Watson)

Colour Section 1

Aden Airways experimental colour scheme 1950, on hand-painted print of VR-AAC. (British Airways Archives)

Timetable for 1st November 1951

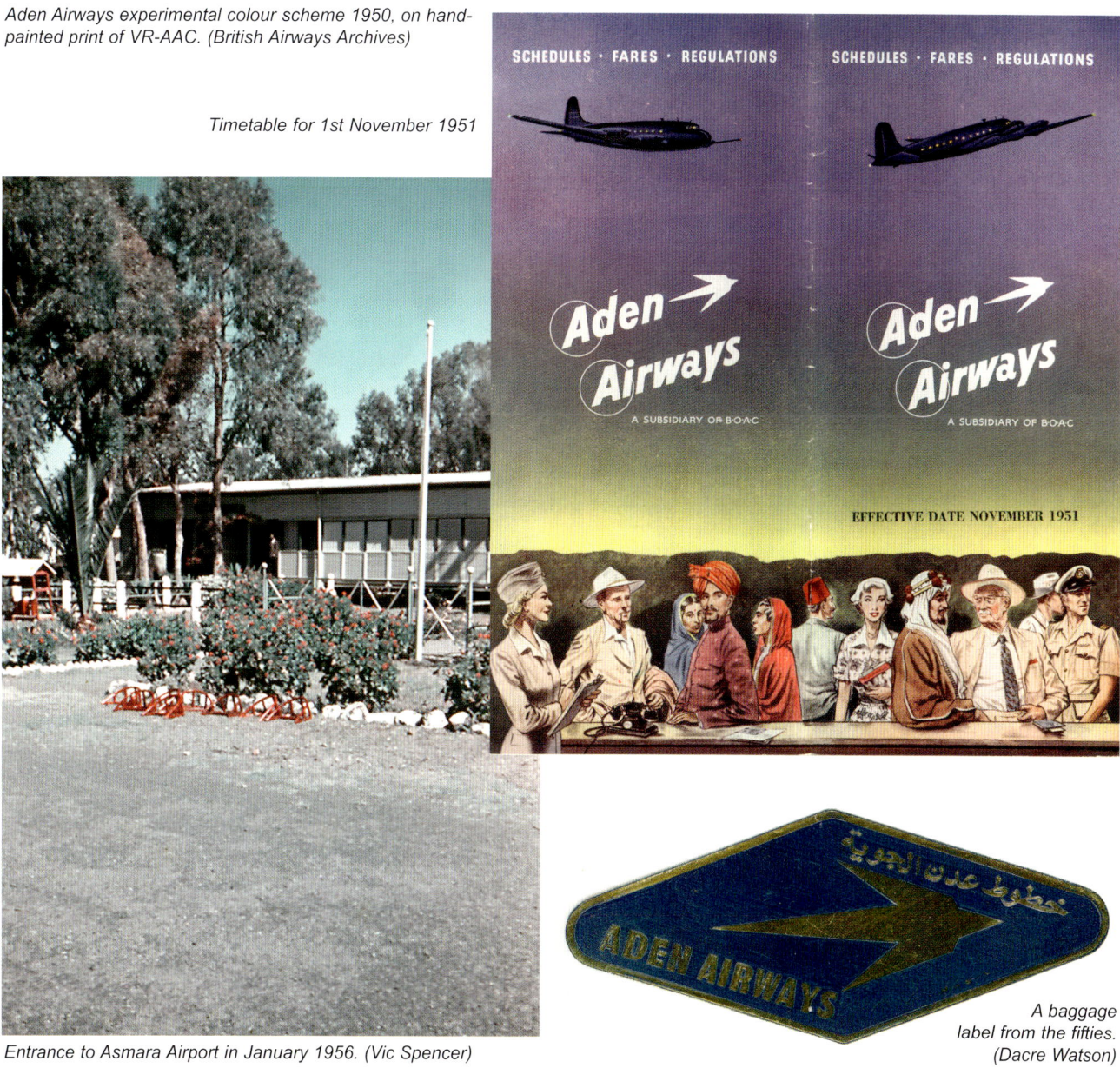

Entrance to Asmara Airport in January 1956. (Vic Spencer)

A baggage label from the fifties. (Dacre Watson)

Aden Airways offices in Asmara, April 1956 (Vic Spencer)

Vic Spencer in the uniform worn when operating scheduled routes out of Asmara, January 1956. When flying from Aden into the Protectorates the uniform was shorts and shirt. (Vic Spencer)

An evocative view of a DC-3 taxying out at Asmara, April 1956. (Vic Spencer)

Qat, a mainstay of Aden Airways' economy.

Asmara control tower, April 1956. (Vic Spencer)

Crew transport to the airport, July 1956, Alan Jennings about to board. (Vic Spencer)

Carlo Moretti (Traffic Officer) and Alan Elgee (F/O) at Asmara Airport, April 1956. (Vic Spencer)

THE QAT TRADE:
Upper: Loading Qat at Dire Dawa in April 1956. Alan Jennings is standing in the aircraft doorway.
Lower: Sacks of Qat waiting to be loaded at Dire Dawa. Ideally the Qat was picked when the morning dew was still on it; the flights from Aden landed just after dawn and were off back to Aden within 20 minutes. (Vic Spencer)

VR-AAA has just been flown into Mukeiras by Vic Spencer. The usual crowd has gathered around to observe. (Vic Spencer)

Ethiopian Airlines CV-240 ET-T-21 on turnaround at Asmara, April 1956. (Vic Spencer)

DC-3 at Ataq airport June 1956 with the fort in the background. (Vic Spencer)

Above: The fort at Ataq, June 1956.
Below: VR-AAM being unloaded at Ataq, the view is from the fort. (Vic Spencer)

COLOUR SECTION 1

C7

A camel train sets off after unloading at Beihan, July 1956. An RAF Valetta stands in the background. (Vic Spencer)

Alan Elgee and Capt Ken Balsden at Beihan, both in standard uniform for the Protectorates. (Vic Spencer)

VR-AAF being unloaded at Beihan, July 1956. Vic Spencer is admiring the donkey. (Vic Spencer)

The arrival of an Aden DC-3 always generated a small crowd. (Vic Spencer)

Unloading was a very manual process in the Protectorates, Beihan 1956. (Vic Spencer)

VR-AAF refuelling at Asmara, July 1956. (Vic Spencer)

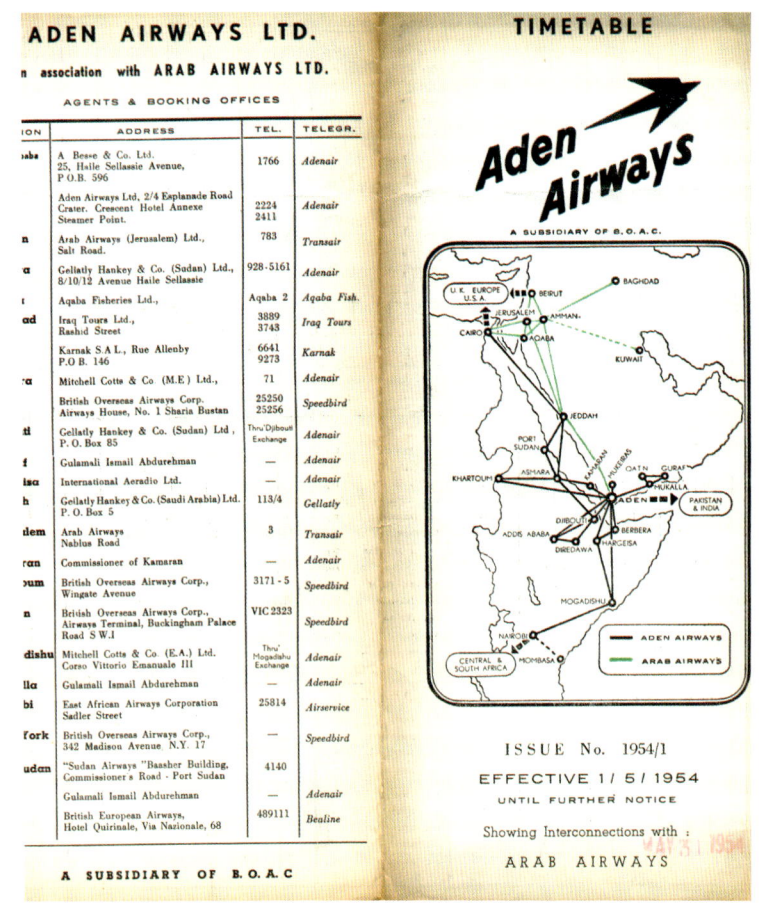

Above: Aden Airways and Arab Airways timetable, May 1954.

Below: Aden Airways timetable for period commencing May 1st 1955.

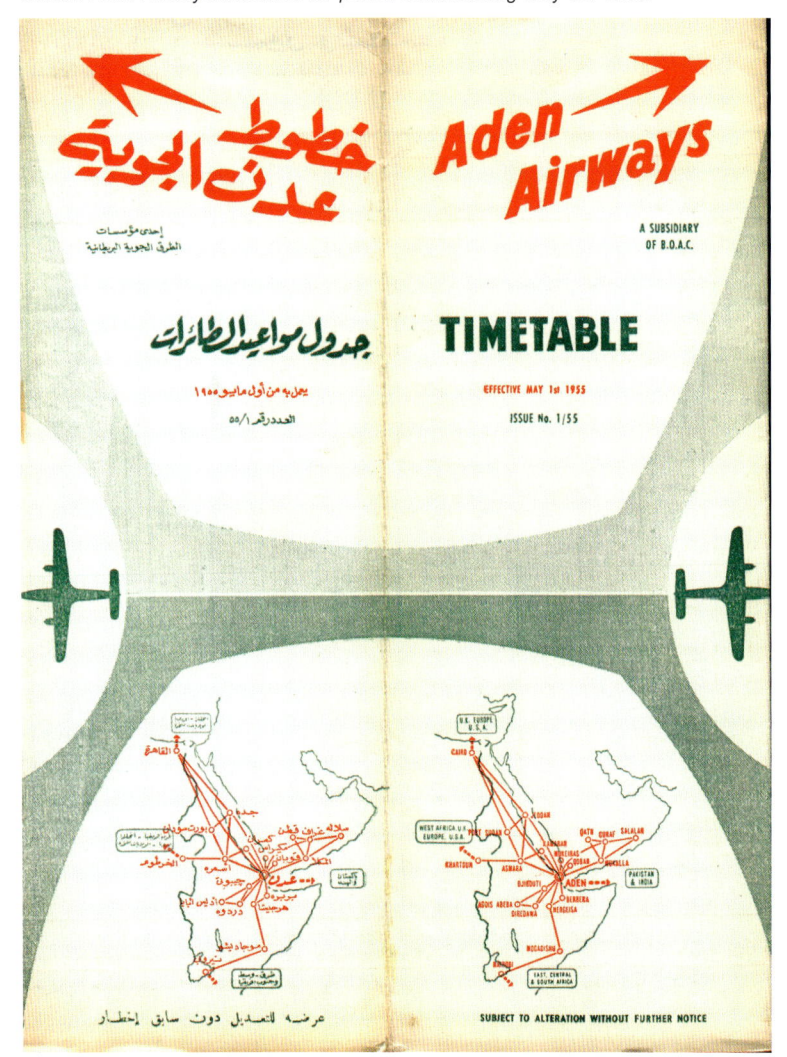

Ticket for Aden-Khartoum-London, flight number BA 321, in 1957. English version above with Arabic version on reverse side shown below. (Brian Walker).

COLOUR SECTION 1																																																																																																																																																																																																					C9

Ras Boradli - the General Manager's house refurbished at very great cost by Richard de Graaff Hunter. It remained the home of all future General Managers. (Vic Spencer)

Aden Airways Headquarters in April 1956. (Vic Spencer)

Mary Spencer, Di Dowle and Captain Harry Mills at Goldmohur Beach, July 1956. (Vic Spencer)

View of the dhow building yards from Crater Pass, Aden, January 1956. (Vic Spencer)

Looking back at Crater Pass from the dhow building yards. (Vic Spencer)

Unloading the aircraft at Ghuraf while the passengers sit under the wing in the shade as they wait to board, May 1956. (Vic Spencer)

VR-AAI being unloaded at Ghuraf, May 1956. This would have been a mixed passenger/freight flight, hence the steps. (Vic Spencer)

Duqa Askari tribesmen deep in the Eastern Protectorate. Note the very different style of dress from area to area. (Vic Spencer)

Above left: Ghuraf was the only destination within the Protectorates which had a formal building as an airport terminal. It stands here in solitary splendour, May 1956. (Vic Spencer)

Above right: F/O Frank Gouws in the right-hand seat of the DC-3. (Vic Spencer)

VR-AAI at Hargeisa, British Somaliland, with the company emblem atop the flagpole, June 1956. (Vic Spencer)

COLOUR SECTION 1

C11

The Dragon Rapide VR-AAL on turnaround at Qatn in April 1956. (Vic Spencer)

The British Political Officer checking his Hadramaut Bedouin Levies in April 1956. (Vic Spencer)

Houses at Qatn, April 1956. (Vic Spencer)

Haura, the Arab District Commissioner's house there, April 1956. (Vic Spencer)

Qatn, tombs just outside the city. (Vic Spencer)

Vic Spencer with VR-AAL at Hargeisa in March 1956. Clearly visible beneath the tailplane is the "BOAC Subsidiary" emblem. (Vic Spencer)

Refuelling at Riyan. (Vic Spencer)

Left: VR-AAM supplying the oil exploration rigs at Marmul, Dhofar, in May 1956. (Vic Spencer)

F/O John Kay flying a DC-3. (Vic Spencer)

Jack Stovall, rig boss at Marmul. (Vic Spencer)

Vic Spencer in a DC-3, March 1956. Note the Very Pistol behind his head. (Vic Spencer)

Dragon Rapide VR-AAL by the flagpole at Hargeisa, British Somaliland. (Vic Spencer)

COLOUR SECTION 1

C13

An atmospheric view of the Dragon Rapide VR-AAL at Raudah, July 1956. (Vic Spencer)

The terrain between Raudha and Aden did not make for a comforting thought in the event of a forced landing, particularly in the Rapide. (Vic Spencer)

Alan Elgee on the DC-3, July 1956. (Vic Spencer)

Alan Jennings in May 1956. (Vic Spencer)

Riyan, and the Rapide receiving maintenance on its hydraulics by engineer Pete Smale, April 1956, (Vic Spencer)

The harbour at Mukalla. The port was the main commercial centre on the eastern coast after Aden and was served by the airport at Riyan inland. (Vic Spencer)

Above: A camel train entering the main gate at Mukalla.
Left: The harbour at Mukalla with steep mountains behind. (both, Vic Spencer)

Flying over the Farsan Islands en route from Jeddah to Aden by DC-3, July 1956. (Vic Spencer)

Mukalla, the British Residency in April 1956. (Vic Spencer)

COLOUR SECTION 1   C15

*On the ground at Mukeiras and flying the flag. Alan Elgee takes advantage of the shade.
(Vic Spencer)*

*Mukeiras, January 1956, and VR-AAA is met by the usual large group of curious tribesmen.
(Vic Spencer)*

VR-AAM unloading at Mukeiras with Levies in attendance. (Vic Spencer)

Mukeiras tribesmen, June 1956. (Vic Spencer)

F/O Bob Wigley in the DC-3. (Vic Spencer)

Notwithstanding the peaceful scenes, Mukeiras was not far from the border with Yemen, incursions were frequent and a British army presence was essential. July 1956. (Vic Spencer)

The stewardess, Mary Spencer, attending to the pilots' needs in flight. (Vic Spencer)

CHAPTER 9: ADEN AIRWAYS 1952 - 1953

Asmara Airport scene, 1953. *(Vic Spencer)*

4) Twelve crews would be supplied by Aden Airways for international routes and would be paid the same salaries as those from that company, presenting a considerable saving on the costs of American pilots. For domestic services, Aden Airways would supply eight Captains who would also be responsible for bringing on an equivalent number of Ethiopian co-pilots for eventual command.
5) Ground staffing levels would be completely reorganised with agents being used at all domestic airports, rather than airline staff, who would be paid by the amount of traffic generated. The headquarters would be established in Addis Ababa and would be the only location where airline staff would be employed.
6) A proposal for a joint engineering operation would be studied with a view to serving both airlines.
7) Policy would be laid down by the Ethiopian Government which would also be responsible for all costs incurred. However, no fees would be payable to Aden Airways unless a profit was made, in which case all profits would be shared equally and which would constitute the fees payable.

Overall, it was a good plan, and de Graaff Hunter could see that by controlling Ethiopian Airlines he could eliminate the only real competition in the Horn of Africa, apart from Air Djibouti, at that time. The sale of the two CV-240s would have eliminated the technical advantage held by Ethiopian Airlines, though Aden Airways might not have taken them on as part of its own fleet instead. Overlapping routes would have been re-organised to the benefit of Aden Airways, and indirectly Ethiopian Airlines, to the advantage of both parties.

Whether the Ethiopian Government would have been prepared to countenance the dismissal of as many staff as de Graaff Hunter had in mind is questionable, if only for social reasons, and it is hard to believe that the Government would not have seen the advantages to Aden Airways whatever benefit they received.

Sadly, all this did not happen as not long afterwards TWA were offered another contract.

Would de Graaff Hunter's plan have worked? This is hard to say bearing in mind his handling of the investment later in the year in Arab Airways (Jerusalem) Ltd. On the other hand, the latter investment might then never have taken place with the result that the drain on Aden Airways' finances during the coming years would have been avoided, while the local competition would have been eliminated. That said, though, de Graaff Hunter was not known for his willingness to grasp the detailed minutiae of daily operations and his grand scheme may well have become mired within the complexities of the Ethiopian bureaucracy.

Proposed merger between Aden Airways and Cyprus Airways 1952-1953

By the middle of 1952 BOAC controlled four companies in the Middle East: Aden Airways (100%), Gulf Air (51%), Kuwait Unit under the auspices of British International Airlines, (BIAL) (100%) and Cyprus Airways (23%). By and large these companies operated successfully, but there would inevitably be some conflict on the routes such as that flown by Aden Airways between Khartoum and Damascus (as an onward flight from West Africa) which was also flown by Cyprus Airways, connecting Khartoum with Nicosia. The latter objected to the invasion of what it perceived to be its territory and, on the instructions of BOAC, Aden Airways was obliged to withdraw. Similarly, when Aden Airways wished to fly from Bahrain to Sharjah and Karachi, Gulf Aviation also objected successfully.

On the political front, Asmara, where Aden Airways was based, was about to become Ethiopian territory as a result of the federation between that country and Eritrea in September, 1952. Had Eritrea remained under British administration, a merger could have taken place between Aden Airways and East African Airways (EAAC) as both airlines were African-based and there was considerable scope for synergy with common route structures and interests. However, this merger did not take place and although the Ethiopian Government was accommodating towards the airline after federation took place, the change in currency resulted in inflation and increasing costs. Also, though Ethiopian Airlines was a government-owned enterprise, it was managed by TWA which quite rightly regarded Aden Airways as a serious competitor and behaved accordingly.

The proposed move to Aden was also proving problematical because of the lack of suitable available accommodation. The land on which to build had to be purchased and this, together with the building costs involved, threatened to be a serious capital cost to BOAC and in which neither the Aden Government nor the Colonial Office in London wished to participate.

The setting-up of the engineering base in Asmara, though sound in principle, would still prove to be a costly exercise in terms of attracting the right personnel and importing the necessary equipment.

Finally, in moving the relatively short distance to Aden, the airline's geographical base would change substantially from an "African" airline to a Red Sea one with all the implications this meant for operating in a primarily Arab environment.

Having established these subsidiaries, BOAC had come to realize that some consolidation would be desirable, partly to cut costs and partly, one is led to suspect, to exert a greater control by the parent company:

> *"There appears to be too great a fragmentation of BOAC subsidiary interests, and upon a general examination of the subject, there seems to exist a strong case to rationalize the operations of Cyprus Airways and Aden Airways, if this can be brought about.*
>
> *The advantages would be that two small British airlines in the Middle East, each with a good reputation built up over the past few years, but each too small to remain economic over the foreseeable future, could be joined into one reasonably-sized unit, based in Cyprus, operating a network of routes which, when joined together, would provide scope for development under a British aegis for years to come."* (112)

There were many advantages to consolidation in Cyprus, the climate and accommodation being just two of them. Both airlines flew the same equipment to the same standards set by the MCA and good maintenance facilities were already in place which would cost relatively little to upgrade. Both airlines were making profits from gross revenues of £400,000 for Cyprus Airways and £600,000 in the case of Aden Airways.

The plan would be that aircraft would shuttle to Aden to operate local services there and return to Nicosia whenever a major check was due. A similar arrangement could be devised for BIAL in Kuwait which was contracted to the Kuwait Oil Company.

However, some serious difficulties would have to be overcome before all these plans could be put into place. BOAC did not have traffic rights at Nicosia and only had a minority share of 23% in Cyprus Airways. BEA, the Cyprus Government and private shareholders held the rest and it was believed that BEA would be unwilling to dilute its influence without some compensating accommodation by BOAC.

At the Airline Chairman's Committee meeting in August 1952 BEA, while accepting in principle that BOAC could have additional points of call within Europe, was adamant that any agreement would be conditional on BOAC withdrawing its claim for traffic rights in Nicosia.(113) Understandably, there was some political manoeuvring here by BEA as it was known that it wished to extend its route structure into the Persian Gulf region, either in its own name or through Cyprus Airways; clearly, this would be unacceptable to BOAC as the situation stood at the time. There were to be significant consequences from this impasse. BOAC delayed the expenditure necessary on the proposed engineering base in Asmara and temporarily shelved the plans to purchase both land and buildings in Aden with the result that it left the management of Aden Airways in a difficult position when it came to financial planning for the following year.

In November 1952, the London Manager Subsidiaries, Captain V Wolfson, reported back to the Board with his proposals for a merged unit which included not only Cyprus Airways and Aden Airways but also BIAL in Kuwait as well. (114)

Wolfson proposed that, in addition to the existing route structure flown by Cyprus Airways, it would also adopt the external routes flown by Aden Airways, but starting from Nicosia where they could be integrated into the BOAC system. The Aden regional routes within the Protectorate (Mukeiras, Ghuraf, Riyan and Qatn) and the immediate African hinterland (Berbera, Hargeisa, Dire Dawa and Djibouti) would be flown from Aden. BIAL would fly between Kuwait, Beirut and Baghdad.

At the time, Cyprus Airways operated six DC-3s, Aden Airways a further six and BIAL had two. The plan was that these would be allocated as follows: seven to Cyprus Airways operating out of Nicosia, one in Aden and two in Kuwait. The four surplus aircraft would be sold, while a total of 17 Captains, 14 First Officers and 12 Cabin Crew would be required. It was quite extraordinary from this perspective that BOAC really envisaged that the Aden hub could be flown with one DC-3 with no allowance for breakdowns or ad hoc charters within the region, let alone the Haj pilgrimage flights which brought in such significant amounts of revenue. Captain Wolfson suggested that the two Ansons which Aden Airways had been obliged to accept as part of the November 1951 rationalization could be used in this role, but he also seems to have been unaware that these aircraft were completely unsuitable for the hot-and-high environment to be found within the Protectorate. In fact they were never used by the airline.

It was further estimated that an expenditure of £100,000 would be required in order to upgrade the engineering facilities in Nicosia to the standard required for heavy maintenance, as well as new buildings and workshops - about one third of the investments originally proposed in Asmara and Aden. A calculation of revenue versus expenditure predicted a profit of some £70,000 per annum

Cyprus Airways operated six DC-3s in British marks during the fifties. G-AKGX "Curium" shown at Beirut 21.11.55.

for the new company which would be named British Levant Airways. That the figures produced were deeply flawed does not appear to have deterred either Captain Wolfson or anyone else on the Board at the time. In a similar vein, the existing shareholders were expected to exchange their shares for 5.5% preference shares, though it was hoped that the Cyprus Government would retain their share, *"...it would be desirable for them to do so from a point of view of support for the new company."* (115)

The original stumbling block, the denial of traffic rights to BOAC in Nicosia, had been resolved, in principle, by the agreement with BEA that the three existing companies would pool the revenue created, though no mention is made of what would happen in the event of losses. It was also agreed that the two Corporations would have equal shareholdings in the new company though, once again, no mention is made of what the Cyprus Government might think of this arrangement.

Like so many undertakings by BOAC, many assumptions were made and it never seemed to occur to them that their plans might not be so palatable to others. For instance, BEA seems to have been a reluctant recruit to the concept of the amalgamation; after all, it was already a large shareholder in a profitable airline and exercised considerable influence within the region as a result, while BOAC could be seen as muscling in for its own benefit, which of course it was. On 30th September 1952 Sir Miles Thomas had informed the Governor of Aden of the plan to merge the two companies. The Governor was not enthralled by the idea, and replied that he *"....strongly objected to the merger on the grounds that (he) would not favour the prospect of local air services affecting his territory being controlled from Cyprus"*.(116) In fairness, though, BOAC was facing an expenditure of £300,000 to move the operating base of Aden Airways from Asmara to Aden, and to which the Aden Government had declined to make a contribution. (This was in contrast to the situation in the more affluent, oil-rich Bahrain where the Government there provided all the staff accommodation for Gulf Aviation. (117))

Together with the Cyprus Government, BEA had proposals of their own which, among others, proposed a Board of 12 Directors of which only three would be from BOAC. This was an impossible proposal for BOAC which had presumed to dominate the new airline.

Red Sea politics also played a significant part. Aden Airways, notwithstanding problems in Egypt, had always operated comfortably within the Arab world and was accepted by all the countries bordering that sea. Cyprus Airways, however, had strong ties with Israel, and bearing in mind the strong anti-western rhetoric emerging from Egypt under Nasser, Cyprus Airways could not have undertaken the same operation. In a letter to the BOAC Board, de Graaff Hunter wrote: *"The Saudi Arabians would not favour allowing an airline, based in Cyprus, taking part in the annual pilgrimage traffic to Mecca due to the boycott which (has) recently developed against the island of Cyprus in retaliation for this Colony's trading with Israel."* (118)

Finally, BEA, which had been asked to concede traffic rights in Nicosia, had stated their intention to charter Viscounts to Cyprus Airways which would fly into the Middle East, thus penetrating an area BOAC considered as its own. To them it was inconceivable that a subsidiary should be seen to operate more modern equipment than the parent company.

By this time, enthusiasm had waned in the face of insurmountable obstacles, at least to BOAC, the primary one being that it would not have absolute control of the new company. Though there were proposals made of pooling crews, maintenance and aircraft, these came to naught simply because of the logistics and political considerations involved.

BOAC quietly shelved the Cyprus-Aden merger idea when a new plan emerged in the form of an investment in Jordan through Aden Airways to form Arab Airways (Jerusalem) Ltd.

A further view of the apron at Asmara in 1953, two DC-3s awaiting passengers. *(Vic Spencer)*

Footnotes, Chapter 9:
(84) Director's Report to Shareholders 31st March 1953.
(85) Captain Peter Austin.
(86) Director's Report to Shareholders, page 2, 31st March 1953.
(87) Ditto, page 3.
(88) Ditto.
(89) Captain Harry Mills reminiscences.
(90) SSR.2.1034 H M Harman to Sales Director (Planning). 17th March 1952.
(91) ASA.348 de Graff Hunter to Sales Director (Planning) 4th April 1952.
(92) SP.184 R M Hilary to Administration Manager. 8th April 1952.
(93) SPE. 1787 From Sales Director (Planning) 19th January 1952.
(94) L.1..PL.2429. Operations Planning 28th April 1952.
(95) OPL.5439, H Ball Wilson for Operations Planning Manager, 29th July 1952.
(96) 'Bringing Africa together'. Ethiopian Airlines booklet, 1988.
(97) 14th Board Meeting, Para 14/211 (g). 7th November 1951.
(98) SPE.991 A Wheeler (Assistant Sales Director to General Sales Manager), 26th August 1952.
(99) Letter from Whitney Straight to R de Graaff Hunter, 21st January 1952.
(100) L.2.0.6.111 (JS) Fleet Manager Hermes and Yorks to Operations Planning Manager 5th February 1952.
(101) L.I.PL.2373, E T House to F S Osborne, Operations Planning Officer, BOAC. 12th March 1952.
(102) OPL. 5395, H Ball Wilson, Operations Planning, to Operations Accountant. 16th July 1952.
(103) AS/54/150/01/ASC1, the MCA to The Secretary, BOAC, 2nd July 1952.
(104) Agreement signed on 4th August 1952 between General Ibrahim Bey Tassan and Richard de Graaff Hunter.
(105) Source: Harry Pusey.
(106) GM.3447 General Manager of WAAC Keith Granville of BOAC, 29th September 1952.
(107) MD.2211, R de Graaff Hunter to Whitney Straight, 22nd December 1952.
(108) MD.2445, R de Graaff Hunter to Captain V Wolfson, London Manager Subsidiaries, 19th February 1953.
(109) Ditto.
(110) MD.2445, de Graaff Hunter to Captain V Wolfson, 19th March 1953.
(111) Submission made by de Graaff Hunter to the British Ambassador to Ethiopia, March 1953.
(112) Minutes of BOAC Board Meeting 10th July 1952.
(113) Minutes of BOAC Board Meeting 11th September 1952. (3231)
(114) Minutes of BOAC Board Meeting 13th November 1952. B4 (11/52)
(115) Ditto
(116) Minutes of BOAC Board Meeting, 9th April 1953. B7 (4/53)
(117) Minutes of BOAC Board Meeting 13th November, 1952. 3250
(118) Minutes of BOAC Board Meeting 9th April 1953. B7 (4/53/10)

Aden Airways DC-3 VR-AAE between flights, Asmara 1952. *(British Airways Archives)*

VR-AAC being loaded with freight and mail while passengers and onlookers remain in the shade, Aden 1953.   (British Airways Archives)

Chapter 10 :
ADEN AIRWAYS 1953 - 1954

The year began well enough. The company was by now well established within the region, and notwithstanding the lack of competitive equipment available to it, it was holding its own by a careful combination of mixed passenger and freight services which it was able to vary according to the route, the season and the day-to-day demand.

The loss of VR-AAE during October 1952, reducing the fleet to five aircraft, did result in some loss of flexibility for ad hoc flights and charters, but the financial compensation from the insurance write-off went some considerable way to mitigating any losses incurred in this way. Even then, when an aircraft became unserviceable the airline found that it did have to charter replacements to fulfil its obligations, a problem which was to become increasingly significant as the year progressed.

While not spectacular, the profit of £9,475 (119) for the first four months of the year (April to July inclusive) was considered to be good, and this sentiment was fortified by a further profit of £9,127 in August. With the *"second half of the pilgrimage to come, our position this year is most encouraging"* wrote the secretary and accountant, A C Middleton, when making his monthly report to London. (120)

The first signs of concern came in the report for September. Notwithstanding a further profit of £11,059 for the month, most of which came from the recently concluded Haj flights, *"disconcerting features of the September accounts are the failure to contribute to overheads on the Aden-Khartoum and Aden-Addis Ababa services which showed load factors of 35.3% and 48% respectively"*.(121)   Middleton goes on to give as reasons for this situation the continued disadvantage to Aden Airways presented by the operation in direct competition by the Ethiopian Airlines CV-240 together with the latter's refusal to consistently apply the fare differential which had been agreed upon the previous year. Aden Airways had responded with some success by increasing the freight capacities on these routes, but the continuing perception by the travelling public was still to view the company as a secondary carrier.

The situation was not improved with the October results (122). Not only was there a deficit of £454 reported, not unusual for the time of year, but this had occurred despite a credit of £12,000 commission from Indamer Company Ltd. (This had been earned as a result of Aden Airways having agreed to place the Indamer Independent Afghanistan Pilgrimage uplift under the Aden Airways umbrella politically, thus enabling Indamer to obtain rights at Jeddah which they would not otherwise have secured). But for this commission losses for the month would have been substantial, and while other factors were involved, mismanagement throughout the previous year would appear to be the prime cause.

A strategy for dealing with events was not evident. For instance, when VR-AAE was lost the previous year, de Graaff Hunter accepted the insurance money rather than having the aircraft repaired and, while the repairs would have taken some time to be completed, the result would effectively have been a new aircraft. Secondly, when de Graaff Hunter was negotiating the contract to

Air Traffic Control Centre, Aden 1953. (Michael Hedges) *Frank Marlow, Aden Airways radio operator, 1953.* (Michael Hedges)

ADEN AIRWAYS LTD.

TEMPORARY SCHEDULES EFFECTIVE 2nd FEB. 1953 UNTIL FURTHER NOTICE

to and from Aden, East Africa, Egypt, Eritrea, Ethiopia, Saudi Arabia, the Somaliland- Protectorate, French Somaliland, Somalia and the Sudan.

NOTES

(A) Service AD452/453 terminates at Qatn and Ghuraf alternately; calling Qatn 14/2, Ghuraf 7/2.

(B) Same day connections to Addis Ababa, with the BOAC Hermes Service from London, Rome, and Cairo.

(C) Same day connection (Friday) from Addis Ababa, Diredawa and Djibouti with the BOAC Hermes service Cairo, Rome & London.

(D) Immediate connection with E.A.A.C. service to Nairobi, (as shown) and Tanga and Dar-es-Salaam.

(E) Overnight connection with E. A. A. C. service from Nairobi (as shown).

SYMBOLS

(1) = Monday.
(2) = Tuesday.
(3) = Wednesday.
(4) = Thursday.
(5) = Friday.
(6) = Saturday.
(7) = Sunday.

	AD 475	AD 473	AD 467			AD 466	AD 472	AD 474
		(4)	(2)	Dep. CAIRO Arr.		2000	1745	
		0100	0100	Arr. JEDDAH Dep.		1615	↑	
		0645	0645	Dep. JEDDAH Arr.		1530		
		0730	0730	Arr. PORT SUDAN Dep.		1315	1245	
		0745	0745	Dep. PORT SUDAN Arr		1245	1215	
	(7)	0815	0815	Dep. KHARTOUM Arr.		↑	↑	1400
	0815	↓	↓	Arr. ASMARA Dep.		1145	1115	1215
	1200	1115	1115	Dep. ASMARA Arr.		1050	1015	1120
	1300	1215	1215	Arr. KAMARAN Dep.		↑		
		1350		Dep. KAMARAN Arr.				
		1430		Arr. DJIBOUTI Dep.				0905
	1515			Dep. DJIBOUTI Arr.		↓		0835
	1545	↓	↓	Arr. ADEN Dep		0700	0730	0730
	1650	1605	1500			(7)	(2)	(5)

LOCAL SERVICES BASED ON ADEN

AD 452	AD 462	AD 465	AD 459	AD 479	AD 459	AD 469	ALL TIMES ARE LOCAL TIMES	AD 468	AD 458	AD 478	AD 464	AD 463	AD 453
(6)(A)	(1)(6)	(1)	(7)(B)	(2)	(4)	(3)	Dep. ADEN Arr.	1710	1115	1115	1520	0810	1645
0945	0600	0945	1100	0600	1100	0600	Arr. DJIBOUTI Dep.	↑	1010	1010	↑	↑	↑
			1205		1205		Dep. DJIBOUTI Arr		0940	0940			
			1235		1235		Arr DIRE DAWA Dep.		0840	0840			
			↓	0800	↓		Dep. DIRE DAWA Arr		0800	(2)			
			1450		1450		Arr. ADDIS ABABA Dep.		0630				
	0645						Arr. MUKEIRAS Dep.		(1)(5)(C)	↑		0730	
↓							Arr MUKALLA/RIYAN Dep.					(1)(6)	1445
1145							Dep. MUKALLA/RIYAN Arr.						1415
1215							Arr. QATN GHURAF Dep.				↑		1330
1300							Arr BERBERA Dep.				1410		(6)(A)
		1055					Dep BERBERA Arr.				1340		
		1125					Arr. HARGEISA Dep.	1530			1200		
		1205				0735	Dep. HARGEISA Arr.	1500			(1)		
						0805	Arr. MOGADISHU Dep.	1150					
						1115	Dep. MOGADISHU Arr.	1110					
						1200	Arr MOMBASA Dep.	0730					
						1540		(4)(E)					
						(D)	Dep. MOMBASA Arr.	1515					
						1630	Arr. NAIROBI Dep.	1330					
						1805		(3)					

LOCAL SERVICES BASED ON ADEN

H.H.P. 12/1/53.

Aden Airways temporary timetable commencing 2nd February 1953 to cover aircraft shortage.

Chapter 10: Aden Airways 1953 - 1954

set up Arab Airways (Jerusalem) Ltd in Amman, he agreed that two DC-3s would be transferred from Aden Airways to the new airline. The effect of these two events was to reduce its fleet to three aircraft which was inadequate to fly the scheduled routes, let alone any charters, and made no allowances for either scheduled servicing or aircraft unserviceability. The result was that, not only did aircraft have to be hired from Indamer to cover the Haj, but a further two DC-3s had to be chartered at expensive rates, one from British West Indian Airways (BWIA) and another from Eagle Aviation Ltd, solely to fly the normal scheduled services.(123) During the seven months to 31 October, £18,626 were spent on these charters, excluding those from Indamer, while the revenue from the hire purchase of the two DC-3s to Arab Airways (Jerusalem) Ltd merely generated an income of £3,800. (124)

Aden's income was also falling, not only because of the competition from Ethiopian Airlines, but also because of increasing nationalism within the countries bordering the Red Sea led by the anti-western rhetoric emanating from Egypt under Colonel Nasser, with the result that agents within those countries were reluctant to book passengers on the more lucrative Aden Airways flights from Cairo, Jeddah and Port Sudan.

Costs were increasing dramatically too. Development of the new engineering base at Asmara had stalled as a result of BOAC not fulfilling its promise to fund the project, though the staff had been hired and equipment ordered. The intention had been for Aden Airways aircraft to be serviced there, but work for third parties would also be offered; instead, the company had to resort to sending its own aircraft to either Cairo (politically difficult) or Prestwick which virtually doubled the servicing costs.

Seconding crews from BOAC was costly. Many of these pilots were relatively senior within the parent Corporation and their salaries were higher than those which would normally be paid to a locally-engaged pilot in a small company such as Aden Airways. In addition, they received personal allowances under their BOAC contract and all these costs were borne by Aden Airways thus placing it in an increasingly difficult position as these pilots also received their annual increments.

Early in 1953 de Graaff Hunter had secured an agreement from BOAC for Aden Airways to employ pilots from other sources. One of the first pilots to join under these circumstances was Vic Spencer who joined in December 1953. He had previously flown in the Navy, developed air services in the Falklands and had latterly flown as a co-pilot in BEA. He was to remain with Aden Airways until the airline was closed down in June 1967, becoming Chief Pilot in 1964, and holding various posts in flight training before that. Throughout his time he kept a diary and from this source, together with his logbooks, much of the operational information for this account of the company has been obtained.

As a result of his previous experience in BEA, his training was rather brief and almost haphazard; a supernumerary ride from Aden to Asmara with Captain John Pascoe who had recently been appointed Chief Pilot, followed by further training under Captain Les Ward which involved flying both Aden routes and those of Arab Airways (Jerusalem) Ltd. Later there was route familiarisation around all the scheduled routes flown by the airline after which he was released to the line as a co-pilot.

A lucky break came his way when, on a night-stop in Cairo, he met Captain Alan Bodger who had flown previously with Aden Airways but had recently been appointed Chief Pilot of Arab Airways (Jerusalem) Ltd. He offered Vic an immediate Command if he would agree to be based in Amman, though still technically employed by Aden Airways, for a certain period of time. This was too good an opportunity to miss and Vic started his Command training under Captain Harry Mills which consisted of 19 sectors

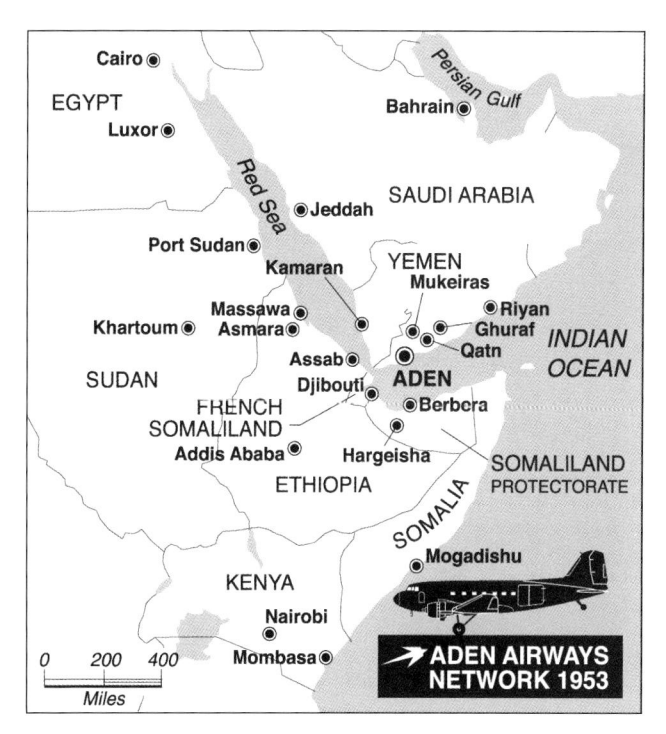

Aden Airways network of scheduled destinations, 1953.
(Roger Carvell)

visiting every airfield on the network, including Mukeiras, Qatn, Riyan and Ghuraf which were the only regular destinations within the Protectorate at that time. The final check was unusual in that it consisted of a delivery flight for G-ANAE from Asmara to Blackpool in the UK where the aircraft was to be returned to its owners, Lancashire Aircraft Corporation, after being chartered to Aden Airways.

This flight left Asmara on 18 April 1954 at 0915 (Z), 1215 local time, routeing to Port Sudan and Cairo where it arrived at 1710 (Z), a flight of 7.20 hours during which Vic completed a radio telephony check as well as an instrument rating as P1, Captain.

Departure from Cairo on the 19th was at 0435 (Z), arriving at Benina for refuelling at 0935 (Z) before departing for Rome 50 minutes later, landing there after a flight of 5.15 hours, most of it being accomplished without the benefit of radio communications as a result of failure of the onboard radios. The final day started at 0700 (Z) when the aircraft took off for Nice and Southampton before flying on to Blackpool where it arrived at 1705 (Z).

Vic passed his Command Check and Captain Pascoe promoted him on the spot so that when he arrived back in Cairo he operated his first flight in command in VR-AAI to Jeddah, Port Sudan and Asmara with First Officer Castle as co-pilot and Air Hostess Attie looking after the passengers. Radio Officer McGarry handled the radios.

In Aden, the November figures were even more disappointing. The loss for the month was £12,107, of which almost £5,000 were

DC-3 G-ANAE was returned to Lancashire Aircraft Corporation from Aden charter by Vic Spencer in April 1954 and is shown operating a Blackpool - IoM service at Ronaldsway 22.7.55.   (Dave Partington)

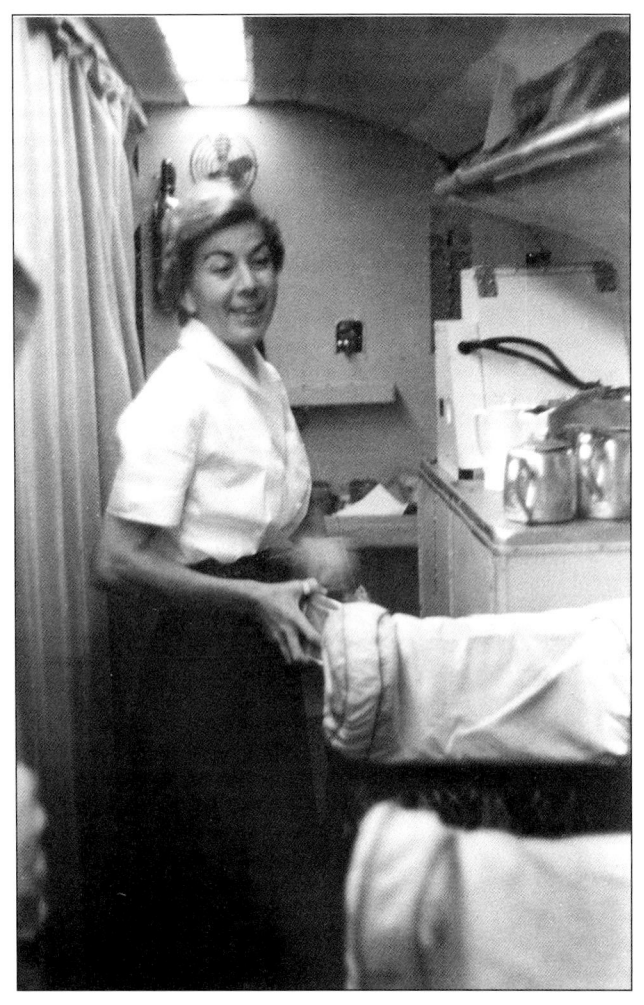

Jean Attie at work on board a DC-3, 1953.   (Vic Spencer)

IAL International Aeradio Ltd wireless operators, 1953.
(Michael Hedges)

Unloading scene at Mukeiras, September 1954.   (Vic Spencer)

losses incurred by Arab Airways (Jerusalem) Ltd from its inception in August until the end of November. (125) By now, only the two Aden-Cairo stopping services and the Aden-Mukeiras services were covering overheads (though not making a real profit); all other services were operating at a loss.

Thus what at first promised to be a profitable year was rapidly sinking into serious deficit. The overall surplus for the first eight months of the year had been only £7,864, with no improvement forecast for the remaining four months. By January, 1954 the situation was dire and de Graaff Hunter was concerned enough to write to Whitney Straight to warn him that Aden Airways was unlikely to make a profit for 1953-1954. He sought to excuse the situation by pointing out that, while BOAC was pursuing other projects, Aden Airways had been left in an uncertain position as to their status and future. (126)

"(I wish to bring to your attention) the seriousness of our present financial position. This has been largely caused through the policy occasioned by our earlier plans for a merger with Cyprus Airways. These plans deterred us from purchasing an aircraft to replace our Dakota VR-AAE which crashed towards the end of 1952 and caused us to depend on chartered aircraft to fulfil our basic commitments. Furthermore the establishment, in all but its final features, of our C of A base in Asmara, which in fact has not yet come into operation, because of similar considerations, has cost us £10,000 per annum whilst our Cs of A continue to be undertaken in the United Kingdom.

The capitalisation of Arab Airways out of Aden Airways revenue through the sale to them of two of our fleet and the need which this has created latterly for the chartering of further aircraft to take their place on our routes, although realising a considerable profit on realisation which will be reflected in our capital account, nevertheless is found as an adverse feature in our Profit and Loss Account, adding an additional expense upon our current trading figures.

These handicaps have made themselves felt to the extent of reducing us to a position today where I doubt we can show any surplus in our accounts at the time of writing."

This was the beginning of an increasingly acrimonious squabble between the two men and one which would contribute to a large extent towards the forced resignation of de Graaff Hunter in May, 1954. Among many inaccuracies in his letter he cites the departure of the two DC-3s to Amman as one of the reasons for Aden's predicament. Yet he himself had gone to Amman to supervise the investment in Arab Airways (Jerusalem) Ltd. He must have foreseen the effect of reducing the Aden Airways fleet to three aircraft. Similarly, it was he who negotiated the leasing arrangements of the two aircraft to Arab Airways, and to state that it was a sale was quite simply untrue.

He may have expected the proposed merger with Cyprus Airways in which case he would not have had a need for more than three aircraft based in Aden. But, as we know, BOAC prevaricated for a long time and did not proceed with the merger plans (on the advice of de Graaff Hunter, for one), but there is no evidence that he was actually thinking this way. The fact was that de Graaff Hunter had spent far too much time in Amman during the second half of 1953, leaving the day-to-day running of the airline to his accountant and company secretary, A C Middleton, who was good at his job but who was also overwhelmed by the sheer volume of work which presented itself during the Managing Director's long absences in Amman. He could not cope with it, particularly after he began to

Chapter 10: Aden Airways 1953 - 1954

Aden Airways Chief Pilot, Captain Steve Colvin, far right, at a formal dinner in Asmara, 1952. (Paul Colvin)

Armed tribesman at Nisab, September 1954. (Vic Spencer)

realise that the company was slipping into serious deficit. He returned to England in early January, 1954 for health reasons.

The other senior manager in Aden was the Chief Pilot, Captain Steve Colvin. There were deep personal tensions with de Graaff Hunter, a situation which was only worsened as time went by and he, too, returned to England in 1953. Upon their separate returns to BOAC, both men wrote damning reports on both the administration of Aden Airways and of a more personal nature about de Graaff Hunter himself.

Looking back, communications between BOAC and Aden Airways were already beginning to break down during the early part of the financial year, as much because of the former's preoccupation with other matters such as the proposed merger with Cyprus Airways, as de Graaff Hunter's tendency to take matters into his own hands without consulting London. With the Aden headquarters left largely unattended and rudderless, the losses of the second part of the year went unchecked. Reports were already being received in London which were giving rise to some unease at BOAC, and in January 1954 it was decided that de Graaff Hunter should be replaced in Aden. (127) At this stage the intention was to bring him back to Head Office, though whether he was aware of these plans is difficult to say. Certainly, he became more combative in his correspondence with London.

In his explanations for these losses (128) de Graaff Hunter cites the increased living costs in Aden as a result of the arrival of the Anglo Iranian Oil Co. which was about to build a refinery at Little Aden. Secondly, he castigates BOAC for encouraging the creation of the engineering base at Asmara and then failing to provide the capital to complete it. Yet the missing capital was only £3,000 which could easily have been provided by Aden Airways itself. A further bone of contention was the operation of the Hermes flight between Cairo and Aden. The revenue distribution of this service had been agreed at the November 1951 Head Office meeting, but once it was realised that Aden Airways was making good profits, BOAC unilaterally reduced the amount it was willing to make to the company and while this did not greatly affect the company that year (1952-1953), it made a considerable difference when losses were being experienced.

In his reply, (129) Smallpiece was uncharacteristically forthright in questioning de Graaff Hunter's business acumen in agreeing to a contract with Arab Airways (Jerusalem) Ltd in which two DC-3s were made available at such easy terms, to the financial detriment of Aden Airways. He was dismissive of the suggestion that Aden Airways should be further compensated for the Hermes operation and its effect on Aden Airways' traffic. *"As you know, the task of local management is to see that the company pays its way. I am sure that staff morale will respond to the fact of that achievement much better than to any artificial manipulation of accounts".*

In his reply, de Graaff Hunter, perhaps suspecting that a decision on his future had already been made, was equally forthright: (130)

"Your letter of 29th January was frankly a disappointment. I must have failed to make myself clear.

If we were to go back to the intention behind the formation of Aden Airways, it would be found that this was to muster traffic in our area and to feed it into the Corporation's trunk routes operating at the perimeter of the area at points such as Cairo, Khartoum and Nairobi. It was never the thought at that time that the Corporation would in fact wish to operate a trunk service right into the heart of the area itself. Clearly the doing of this is in the public's interest as well as that of the Corporation, but inevitably it is against the interests of Aden Airways whose obsolescent Dakotas could never compete with the Corporation's Argonauts. What in fact is now taking place is that the Corporation is removing the very traffic upon which the airline was built and upon which it must depend, and in return is only paying us at a rate equivalent to our gain from this one route alone judged at a time when the traffic had only just begun to develop. The fact is that our costs everywhere have continued to mount and so would our mainline revenue had it not been for the introduction of your service. Now as your revenue increases, ours must diminish as our traffic is progressively drained away by you from our two main routes.

Since what we are discussing is Corporation money, it might be said that it makes little difference as to its distribution, but if our revenue cannot be matched to our costs because a part of it is no longer under our control, whilst our costs mount with a trend of the times, it is obvious that neither the staff of the Company nor the Corporation itself will be pleased with the results. In short, Aden Airways is left with a receding scale of 1950 revenue to meet 1954 costs."

This letter would seem to be a very good summary of the raison d'etre of Aden Airways and the effect of the introduction of mainline services into the area. BOAC had behaved badly in this case, indeed one could say that this situation had its origins in the fateful meeting during November 1951 when Aden Airways were given instructions to run the company in a manner they would not have chosen, and in which no choice was given. Equally, BOAC

Freight at Nisab in the Protectorate, September 1954. Rex Barnes is on the right. (Vic Spencer)

would not have seen this behaviour in any way as arrogant, and to admit any fault would not have occurred to them, even in the way the basis of remuneration to Aden Airways for the operation of the Hermes was changed.

It would also be true to say that de Graaff Hunter had sowed the seeds for his own downfall. His ostentatious lifestyle, his inability to work easily with those in Government in Aden, a tendency to make decisions without reference to London and his long absences from Aden itself during 1953 did not endear him to those around him, while his obvious intelligence was frequently intimidating to those who might have wished to guide him.

On 10th January, 1954 Comet 1, G-ALYP, came down just off the coast of Elba, Italy. All on board were killed, including the London Manager Subsidiaries, Captain V Wolfson. His replacement in this position was Gilbert Lee who, until 1952, had been General Manager of West African Airways Corporation and who was experienced in the problems of running local airlines.

By this time, mid-February, Middleton had written his 20-page report which was highly critical of the administration of Aden Airways and personally of de Graaff Hunter. Alarm bells were ringing in London with regard to the true state of the accounts and Smallpiece suggested to Lambert (131) that he should write to both C Vincent (132) and de Graaff Hunter *"as it seems that the accounts to 31st December of Aden Airways and Arab Airways (Jerusalem) Ltd do not reflect the situation you outline"*. (133)

On 24th February, Smallpiece wrote to E D Hone (134) in the Government Offices in Aden advising him of the new appointment and that a complete reappraisal of Aden Airways was about to take place: (135)

"We have now taken the first step and appointed someone to take over Captain Wolfson's job. He is Mr Gilbert Lee who was, until 1952, General Manager of WAAC. I am sure you will like him and find him anxious to assist you and the Government of Aden in dealing with aviation problems. As I have said before, we regard it as our business, whether as BOAC or through our subsidiary Aden Airways Ltd, to provide the Colony and Protectorate of Aden with the service it requires, subject to reasonable economic considerations, and you will find that Mr Lee is fully imbued with this idea."

Mindful of the fact that de Graaff Hunter and the Government of Aden had rarely got on well, either on a personal or a business basis, Smallpiece went on to say:

Chapter 10: Aden Airways 1953 - 1954

"You can rest assured that we are bearing in mind the necessity for finding someone whom we believe would be capable of working with you and other officers of the Aden Government, and of establishing the Company on the basis you and we would like.

I hope that it will be possible to implement fairly soon the suggestion that a Government nominee should take his (de Graaff Hunter's) place on the Board of Aden Airways, and if it were possible it would be nice to get your nominee (and I hope you will put Dutton forward) appointed to the Board Meeting which Gilbert Lee will be attending when he is out in Aden next week.

I fear the affairs of the Company are in a most unsatisfactory state, and the sooner we can get a new General Manager appointed and everything straightened up, the better it will be all round."

None of the contents had been intimated to de Graaff Hunter and he must have been deeply wounded at the treatment being meted out to him: (136)

"............In Lee's last signal he mentioned something about the appointment of a Government nominee upon our Board which again came as somewhat of a surprise. The last communication on this subject from London was from Mostert when he asked me to clear the matter in principle with our local directors, and then to consider the question of amending our Articles of Association.

I think it is a great pity that our first meeting at which the Government Director will be present, we will have had so little time for preparation. I hope he will get no impression that the Company always operates in this rush and unpreparedness. Presumably he is Dutton, in which case he will certainly be critical."

Of course it was Dutton who was appointed, a particularly galling experience for de Graaff Hunter since the two men had never got on well. (137)

There was more to come. When the accounts for January and February arrived in London discrepancies were found to the extent that up to December 1953 the losses had been understated by some £50,000 (138). Further investigation of the accounts indicated that the real cause was not so much a decline in revenue, but runaway expenditure which had been incurred by the need for continuous chartering of several aircraft (not just two as had been intimated earlier) at any one time to fly the schedules. In fact the costs for hiring aircraft, excluding pilgrimage charters, had exceeded the budgeted figure by over £100,000. As Lambert dryly observes: *"It is interesting to compare the amount received from AAJ (for the charter of two DC-3s), £3,800, with these larger charter costs."* (139)

There was little more to say except: *"I have Mr Lambert's memorandum to you, dated 7th April. I am horrified, as you must be, at the disastrous results suddenly revealed from Aden. It is obvious that the management of the Company has been incredibly lax."* (140)

De Graaff Hunter left the employ of BOAC the following month.

The Annual Accounts for that year laconically stated: *"A loss of £140,595 was incurred during the year against a profit of £22,817 for the previous year. Steps have been taken to re-organise and rehabilitate the Company."* (141)

Aden Airways Timetables September 1953.   International services.

AD458 5	AD475 4	AD473 4	AD467 1		<Days of operation>		AD466 7	AD472 2	AD474 4	AD459 3
		0100	0100	dep	Cairo	arr	2000	1930		
		0345	0345	arr	Jeddah	dep	1315	1245		
		0430	0430	dep	Jeddah	arr	1230	1200		
		0745	0745	arr	Port Sudan	dep	1315	1245		
		0815	0815	dep	Port Sudan	arr	1215	1215		
				arr	Khartoum	dep				
1100	0800			dep	Khartoum	arr			1645	1430
1600				arr	Addis Ababa	dep				1130
0800*				dep	Addis Ababa	arr				1040
	1145	1115	1115	arr	Asmara	dep	1145	1115	1500	
	1245	1215	1215	dep	Asmara	arr	1050	1015	1400	
	1515			arr	Djibouti	dep			1130	
	1545			dep	Djibouti	arr			1105	
		1350		arr	Kamaran Island	dep	0915			
		1430		dep	Kamaran Island	arr	0835			
1110	1650	1605	1500	arr	Aden	dep	0700	0730	1000	0730

*next day

Aden Airways Timetable September 1953. **Local and African Services**

| AD462 | AD452 | AD452 | AD465 | AD469 | | | | AD468 | AD464 | AD453 | AD453 | AD463 |
1,3,6	6	2	6	4		<Days of operation>		5	6	2	6	1,3,6
1300	1100	0700	0700	0600	dep	Aden	arr	1705	1215	1510	1630	1510
1345					arr	Mukeiras	dep					1430
	1305	0905			arr	Riyan	dep			1315	1335	
		0935			dep	Riyan	arr			1245		
						Qatn	dep			1200		
						Qatn	arr			1130		
		1020			arr	Ghuraf	dep			1050		
			0810		arr	Berbera	dep		1115			
			0830		dep	Berbera	arr		1045			
			0915	0735	arr	Hargeisa	dep	1525	1000			
				0800	dep	Hargeisa	arr	1455				
				1110	arr	Mogadishou	dep	1145				
				1140	dep	Mogadishou	arr	1115				
				1525	arr	Nairobi	dep	0730				

Aden Airways Timetable October 1953. **International Services**

| AD458 | AD475 | AD473 | AD467 | | | | AD466 | AD472 | AD474 | AD474 | AD459 |
5	4	3	1		<Days of operation>		7	2	2	4	3
		0100	0100	dep	Cairo	arr	2010	2000			
		0345	0345	arr	Jeddah	dep	1325	1315			
		0430	0430	dep	Jeddah	arr	1240	1230			
		0745	0745	arr	Port Sudan	dep	1325	1315			
		0815	0815	dep	Port Sudan	arr	1255	1245			
				arr	Khartoum	dep					
1100	0800			dep	Khartoum	arr				1645	1450
1600				arr	Addis Ababa	dep					1150
0800*				dep	Addis Ababa	arr					1050
	1145	1115	1115	arr	Asmara	dep	1155	1145		1500	
	1245	1245	1215	dep	Asmara	arr	1100	1050	1050		
1015	1530	1530		arr	Djibouti	dep		0820	0820		0835
1045	1600	1600		dep	Djibouti	arr		0750	0750		0805
			1350	arr	Kamaran Island	dep	0925				
			1430	dep	Kamaran Island	arr	0845				
1150	1705	1705	1630	arr	Aden	dep	0645	0645	0645		0700

*next day

Aden Airways Timetable October 1953. **Local and African Services**

| AD462 | AD452 | AD452 | AD465 | AD469 | | | | AD468 | AD464 | AD453 | AD453 | AD463 |
1, 6	6	2	5	2		<Days of operation>		3	6	2	6	1, 6
1300	0930	0930	1600	0600	dep	Aden	arr	1705	0815	1400	1740	1510
1345					arr	Mukeiras	dep					1430
	1135	1135			arr	Riyan	dep			1205	1545	
		1205			dep	Riyan	arr				1515	
						Qatn	dep				1430	
						Qatn	arr				1400	
		1250			arr	Ghuraf	dep				1320	
			1710		arr	Berbera	dep		0705			
			1730		dep	Berbera	arr		0645			
			1815	0735	arr	Hargeisa	dep	1525	0600			
				0800	dep	Hargeisa	arr	1455				
				1110	arr	Mogadishou	dep	1145				
				1140	dep	Mogadishou	arr	1115				
				1525	arr	Nairobi	dep	0730				

Chapter 10: Aden Airways 1953 - 1954

Aircraft Chartering for 1953-1954

When VR-AAE was lost near Assouan in October 1952 Aden Airways requested that a replacement should be sent out from London as soon as possible. This was a fairly canny move by de Graaff Hunter because the insurance money for the lost aircraft had come to Aden Airways and not to London. At the time, DC-3s were at a premium and good examples were hard to find. Not only that, but a new aircraft would have to be set up for operations in the much harder environment in which Aden Airways flew, rather than the European theatre where one was likely to be found.

In May 1953 BOAC leased G-AMYJ (C/n 32716) from Transair and sent it out to Aden as the replacement for 'AAE. However, this aircraft turned out to be totally unsuitable and had to be sent back to the UK. Perhaps BOAC did not understand that Aden Airways required an exact replacement for 'AAE. In a letter to J Lobley of BOAC, Capt J G Pascoe (who had replaced Captain S Colvin as Chief Pilot) wrote: (142)

"I have been requested by Managing Director to inform you that Aden Airways insist on an exact replacement for VR-AAE and after the inspection I carried out at Aden it is regretted that this will not meet our requirements for several reasons.

Firstly, the conversion is quite different from our own fleet and will complicate our operations. The conversion is unsuitable for the rough conditions under which we operate. It will be quite impossible to stow enough baggage in the three small holes* on this aircraft to carry its full complement of 32 passengers. Secondly, the seats are different from ours. Thirdly, the radio is unsuitable for two-crew operation. Fourthly, this is a very heavy conversion. Fifthly, this is a restricted aircraft.

As stated in previous correspondence, Aden Airways require an exact replacement for VR-AAE."

*   He probably meant holds.

With that, the aircraft was returned to London.

Earlier in the year, BOAC had taken back a DC-3 (VP-TBJ) from BWIA (143), and it was decided that this aircraft would be handed over to Aden Airways after suitable refurbishment had been completed by Scottish Aviation at Prestwick which would also complete a C of A at the same time. The aircraft was transferred to Aden Airways on 1st May, but the work which had to be carried out took much longer than anticipated and not until the end of July was it ready for positioning to Aden where, in the meantime, other aircraft had to be chartered from Indamer. (144)

Aircraft deliveries were different in those days. The policy was, if at all possible, to achieve some revenue from the flight to defray costs as much as possible. In this case a charter was obtained from George Wimpey, the construction firm, which wished to send a team to Aden where they would be involved in the building of the new refinery at Little Aden. The charter contract was CH-OC-21 and was scheduled to depart from London Heathrow on 27th July bound for Aden via Rome, Nicosia, Cairo and Port Sudan. On arrival the aircraft would be re-registered as VR-ABJ.

The fee to Wimpey was to be £1,300, though all passenger, crew and nightstop expenses would be taken out of this sum. Interestingly, the catering load out of London was to be 12 dozen bottles of beer, six each of gin and whisky, 2,000 cigarettes and 23 lunchboxes. Supplies were to be replenished en route. (145)

The flight finally left London at 0900 on 1st August, routeing to Rome via Nice for a night stop, from whence it flew to Cairo via Benina for another nightstop before proceeding via Port Sudan to Aden where it landed at 1700 local time. Accompanying Captain Purvis was F/O John Lightfoot who had literally just joined the Company and for whom this was to be Line Training. (146)

After receiving the rather abrupt letter from Captain Pascoe, BOAC then approached Eagle Aviation Ltd for a DC-3 and was successful in finding G-AMYB (C/n 33346) which was then on hire to Iraqi Airways and based in Baghdad. Not only did it fulfil Aden Airways' requirements, but it was also cheaper and easier to position to Asmara for the start of its period of hire which was to start on 15th July and would last until 30th September (147). It was a dry lease, i.e., no crews were supplied and the hourly charge was to be £20-9-0 (£20.45 in decimal currency).

In fact, de Graaff Hunter had hoped to buy the aircraft from Eagle Aviation and made an offer of £14,000 which was refused (148). He than raised the offer to £15,000, but this, too, was refused. This was just half the sum Aden Airways received for the crashed 'AAE.

However, even with the arrival of this aircraft, de Graaff Hunter realised that it was imperative to acquire more equipment, but this could only be done through Captain Wolfson, London Manager Subsidiaries.

"……..we have no whole-time spare aircraft in our fleet, which is an essential, not only owing to the possibility of breakdowns, but because of the constant absence on maintenance of at least one of the five for which the commitment is unavoidable." (149)

But de Graaff Hunter had already committed two of the Aden Airways fleet to Arab Airways (Jerusalem) Ltd.

Cyprus Airways was unable to help either as it, too, was fully committed to its scheduled summer programme, and though it was able to offer an aircraft after November, this would be too late for the Aden Airways Haj flights which were imminent. So de Graaff Hunter did the next best thing; he reneged on the Eagle Aviation contract and simply did not return their aircraft on the appointed date of 30th September.

Harold Bamberg was not amused by this and made his feelings known in no uncertain manner: (150)

"I would like to place on record our complete astonishment that this aircraft was not returned to Base on the 30th September and that on the 1st October we were formally advised that you required to keep it for a further period of six weeks."

The aircraft was eventually returned to the UK in November, leaving Asmara on the 12th and routeing via Wadi Halfa and Benina where it stopped for the night before proceeding the next day to Malta and Nice for a further night. It arrived at Blackbushe at 1400 on 14th November. The aircraft was flown by Captain M Lipkin and F/O Everest.

Indamer Charters 1953

Once the Haj pilgrimages were over and the Indamer aircraft had been returned to Bombay, Aden Airways was still faced with the problem of fulfilling its normal scheduled requirements, and with only three very tired aircraft now available, and Eagle Aviation not inclined to put its trust in the company any longer, it had to return to Indamer for more chartering. However, while the company had on previous occasions chartered for the Haj, it had not done so for normal operations. A ticklish problem was in which country the aircraft should be registered because bilateral agreements generally insisted that aircraft flew schedules for a particular route with an aircraft registered in the country of that particular airline's origin. Nor could Aden Airways purchase these aircraft, temporarily or otherwise, from Indamer; had they been able to do so they would have been registered in Aden.

Indamer DC-3 VT-DGP photographed at Beirut 20th November 1953.

In October, de Graaff Hunter advised Lobley (151) in London that he intended to enter into negotiations with Indamer to charter three DC-3s. The terms on offer were particularly favourable at £6-10-00 (£6.50 in decimal currency) per flying hour, as opposed to over £20 per hour for G-AMYB (which had been leased from Eagle Aviation). While two of the aircraft would be used on the company routes, the third one would be sub-chartered to the United Nations in Kashmir, for which BOAC had successfully tendered earlier in the year. This DC-3 would become UN-650 for the duration of this particular charter.

The Indian Government was, however, reluctant to allow the two other aircraft to be re-registered in Aden. The Indian Minister for Communications, Mr J Ram, had ruled that de-registration from India, however short-lived, would be considered to be an export, and because of the recent nationalisation of the many Indian airlines and the resulting compensation that would have to be paid to those companies which had forfeited their aircraft, all aircraft exports were banned. The compensation which the Indian Government intended to pay to these airlines for the loss of their aircraft was well below the true value that could be obtained on the world market, so by not allowing the aircraft to be sold abroad the airlines could not claim a higher value. (152)

So the two DC-3s came to Aden wearing Indian registrations. The Ethiopian authorities made their feelings known through the British Ambassador in Addis Ababa, and he in turn passed on these concerns to the MCA in London (re-designated MTCA in October 1953) which passed them on to BOAC. (153)

"As you know, Indamer is an American Company operating in India and the Ethiopians were, we understand, reluctant at first to allow Aden Airways to use the chartered aircraft. Although they eventually agreed, the matter does not seem to have been closed. There must, we assume, have been good reasons for these arrangements, but we are told that the Ethiopians, who are guided by appearance rather than reality, look upon the whole issue as rather questionable and they are inclined to think that Aden Airways are "operating on a shoe string", although we know, of course that the facts belie this."

It is hard to discern whether this was gentle sarcasm or not, but this did seem to galvanise BOAC into putting an effort into the purchase of DC-3s to make good the loss of 'AAE and the hire purchase of the two aircraft to Arab Airways (Jerusalem)Ltd.

"We have endeavoured to avoid purchasing (an aircraft) in the hope that aircraft will become redundant in Cyprus and also waiting for the market to fall. The time has now come to replace the crashed Dakota and the purchase of one aircraft is being arranged through Supplies Department, BOAC." (154)

The two Indamer aircraft were returned to Bombay in March of the following year, but Aden Airways continued to make regular use of their aircraft over the coming years.

Aden Airways:
Pilots' operating schedule 4th October 1953

Trip	Local time Pick up/ETD	Day	Route	Service No
A	1115/1215	Mon	Asm/Aden	AD 467
		Tues	Aden/Riy/Ghu/Qatn/Riy/Aden	AD 452/453
		Weds	Ad Hoc (Diredawa)	
			Aden/Muks/Aden	AD 462/463
		Thurs	Aden/Dji/Asm	AD 474
B	1015/1115	Tues	Aden/Pzu/Jda/Cai	AD 472
		Weds	Cai/Jer/Bei/Jer	JE 014/006/005
		Thurs	Jer/Jda/Aden	JE 007
		Fri		
		Sat	Aden/Brx/Hgs/Brx/Aden	AD 465/464
		Sun	Standby	
		Mon	Ad Hoc (Diredawa)	
			Aden/Muks/Aden	AD 462/463
		Tues	Aden/Asm	AD 472
C	1115/1215	Weds	Asm/Kam/Aden	AD 473
		Thurs	Aden/Hgs/Mog/Nai	AD 469
		Fri	Nai/Mog/Hgs/Aden	AD 468
		Sat	Ad Hoc (Diredawa)	
			Aden/Riy/Ghu/Qatn/Riy/Aden	AD 452/453
		Sun	Aden/Kam/Asm	AD 466
D	1145/1245	Thurs	Asm/Dji/Aden	AD 475
		Fri	Ad Hoc (Diredawa)	
		Sat	Aden/ Jda/ Jer	JE 008

CHAPTER 10: ADEN AIRWAYS 1953 - 1954

			Sun	Standby	
			Mon	Standby	
			Tues	Jer/Cai	JE013
			Weds	Cai/Jda/Pzu/Asm	AD473
E		1130/1230	Thurs	Asm/Ktm	AD 478
			Fri	Ktm/Ads	AD 458
			Sat	Ads/Aden	AD 458
				Aden/Muks/Aden	AD 462/463
			Sun	Ad Hoc (Diredawa)	
			Mon	Standby	
			Tues	Ad Hoc (Diredawa)	
			Weds	Aden/Ads/Ktm	AD 459
			Thurs	Ktm/Asm	AD475
F		1045/1145	Sun	Asm/Pzu/Jda/Cai	AD 466
			Mon	Cai/Jer/Bag	JE 014/012
			Tues	Bag/Jer	JE 011
			Weds	Standby	
			Thurs	Standby	
			Fri	Standby	
			Sat	Jer/Bei	JE 006
			Sun	Bei/Jer/Cai	JE 005/013
			Mon	Cai/Jda/Pzu/Asm	AD 467

Key:
Ads	Addis Ababa	Jda	Jeddah
Asm	Asmara	Jer	Jerusalem
Bag	Baghdad	Kam	Kamaran Is
Bei	Beirut	Ktm	Khartoum
Brx	Berbera	Mog	Mogadishou
Cai	Cairo	Muks	Mukeiras
Dji	Djibouti	Nai	Nairobi
Ghu	Ghuraf	Pzu	Port Sudan
Hgs	Hargeisa	Riy	Riyan

Air Hostess operating schedule 4 October, 1953

Trip	Local time Pickup/ETD	Day	Route	Service No
A	1100/1215	Mon Tues	Asm/Kam/Aden	AD 467

		Weds	Aden/Asm/Ktm	AD 459
		Thurs	Ktm/Asm	AD 475
B	1000/1115	Tues	Asm/Pzu/Jda/Cai	AD 472
		Weds	Cai/Jer/Bei/Jer	JE 014/006/005
		Thurs	Jer/Jda/Aden	JE 007
		Fri		
		Sat		
		Sun	Aden/Kam/Asm	AD 466
C	1100/1215	Wed	Asm/Kam/Aden	AD 473
		Thurs	Aden/Hgs/Mog/Nai	AD 469
		Fri	Nai/Mog/Hgs/Aden	AD 468
		Sat		
		Sun		
		Mon		
		Tues		
		Weds		
		Thurs	Aden/Dji/Asm	AD 474
D	1130/1245	Thurs	Asm/Dji/Aden	AD 475
		Fri		
		Sat	Aden/Jda/Jer	JE 008
		Sun	Standby	
		Mon	Standby	
		Tues	Jer/Cai	JE 013
		Weds	Cai/Jda/Pzu/Asm	AD 473
E	1115/1230	Thurs	Asm/Ktm	AD 474
		Fri	Ktm/Ads	AD 458
		Sat	Ads/Aden	AD 458
		Sun		
		Mon		
		Tues	Aden/Asm	AD 467
F	1030/1145	Sun	Asm/Pzu/Jda/Cai	AD 466
		Mon	Cai/Jer/Bag	JE 014/012
		Tues	Bag/Jer	JE 011
		Weds	Standby	
		Thurs	Standby	
		Fri	Standby	
		Sat	Jer/Bei	JE 006
		Sun	Bei/Jer/Cai	JE 005/013
		Mon	Cai/Jda/Pzu/Asm	AD 467

(Source: British Airways Archives)

Footnotes, Chapter 10:
(119) F.23.0507 A C Middleton to Basil Smallpiece, 7th September 1953.
(120) F.23.0609 A C Middleton to Basil Smallpiece, 7th October 1953.
(121) F.23.0863 A C Middleton to Basil Smallpiece, 30th October 1953.
(122) F.23.1090 A C Middleton to Sir Miles Thomas, 25th November 1953.
(123) VP-TBJ from BWIA, registered as VR-ABJ, and G-AMYB from Eagle Aviation Ltd.
(124) LMS.1.382 to London Manager Subsidiaries, 7th April 1954.
(125) F.23.1261. A C Middleton to Sir Miles Thomas, 29th December 1953.
(126) MD.2976 de Graaff Hunter to Whitney Straight, 6th January 1954.
(127) Confidential Letter from Whitney Straight to Basil Smallpiece, 9th January, 1954.
(128) MD.3047, de Graaff Hunter to Basil Smallpiece, 17th January 1954.
(129) F.1478. Basil Smallpiece to de Graaff Hunter 29th January 1954.
(130) MD.3070. de Graaff Hunter to Basil Smallpiece, 4th February 1954.
(131) A J Lambert, Accountant to London Manager Subsidiaries, Captain V Wolfson.
(132) The Accountant who had been sent out to Aden in order to replace A C Middleton.
(133) F.1524. Basil Smallpiece to de Graaff Hunter and C Vincent, 12th February 1954.
(134) E D Hone CMG, OBE. Aden Government Secretariat.
(135) Private letter from Basil Smallpiece to E D Hone, 24th February 1954.
(136) MD.3125. de Graaff Hunter to Basil Smallpiece, 27th February 1954.
(137) Source: H Pusey.
(138) LMS.1.382. A J Lambert to Gilbert Lee, 7th April 1954.
(139) Ditto.
(140) F.1646. Basil Smallpiece to Gilbert Lee, 13th April 1954.
(141) BOAC Annual Report and Accounts: 1953-1954, p 27.
(142) CP.91 J G Pascoe to J Lobley of BOAC, 5th June 1953.
(143) British West Indian Airways, a wholly-owned subsidiary of BOAC based in Trinidad.
(144) F.26.0361. A C Middleton to J Lobley, 8th July 1953.
(145) GMS.2.935. J Lobley to Captain Purvis, Captain of the flight, 27th July 1953.
(146) GMS.2.943. J Lobley to de Graaff Hunter, 31st July 1953.
(147) Personal letter from Eagle Aviation to J Lobley, 22nd June 1953.
(148) MD. 2659 de Graaff Hunter to J Lobley, 28th July 1953.
(149) MD.mo de Graaff Hunter to Captain V Wolfson, 7th August 1953.
(150) HB/LAS Harold Bamberg to P T Griffiths of BOAC, 2nd October 1953.
(151) Cable HERCC de Graaff Hunter to J Lobley 25th October 1953.
(152) DEL/M.18/794 B W Galpin (BOAC Manager, India) to de Graaff Hunter 28th November 1953.
(153) S 3081 L T Scott (MTCA) to J Lobley (BOAC) 23rd December 1953.
(154) Gms.397 J Lobley to Basil Smallpiece, 30th December 1953.

The Queen and The Duke of Edinburgh departing Aden on a BOAC Argonaut, April 1954. (Michael Hedges)

Passengers disembarking from Arab Airways DC-3 TJ-ABN at Amman in 1954. (Harry Pusey)

Chapter 11 :
ARAB AIRWAYS (JERUSALEM) LTD, 1953 - 1958

What initially strikes one as strange is that a wholly-owned subsidiary of BOAC should get involved in the setting up and running of another subsidiary, but there were compelling reasons to do so, not least the "request" by BOAC, the parent company, that Aden Airways should at least make a feasibility study of the proposal.

In 1952, BOAC had been invited by the Foreign Office to examine the possibility of providing support for Arab Airways Association, an airline in Jordan which was under severe threat from another Jordanian company, Air Jordan, itself supported by none other than Transocean Airlines under Orvis Nelson. (See Chapter 8, Air Djibouti). The survey team sent out from London by BOAC were not impressed by what they found and recommended to its Board that it should not become involved. However, the Foreign Office, with the active encouragement of the British Embassy in Amman, pleaded with the company to reconsider its decision, citing the very real threat of loss of British influence within the region. The company did reconsider, but in doing so suggested to Richard de Graaff Hunter, managing director of Aden Airways, that it would be good for that company, as well as the region, if it would support the setting up of an airline in Jordan.

Firstly, though, a brief history of the development of civil aviation in post-war Jordan would be useful in understanding the situation pertaining at the time of Aden Airways' involvement in there.

The first development in civil aviation in what was then the Emirate of Trans Jordan was the formation on 21 December 1946 of a small company, Arab Airways, which operated from Amman to neighbouring Arab capitals with leased aircraft. Most of the capital was publicly subscribed, but the Jordan government was also involved. The Technical manager was an Englishman who had no commercial experience, a deficiency compounded by a management which equally had no experience in aviation matters. At the time, no facilities for civil aviation existed in Jordan and the company undertook what would normally be the responsibility of the state in providing the first airstrip in Amman, together with hard standing, hangarage, a terminal building and all the office requirements of an airline; the estimated cost to this start-up airline was £24,000, no small sum at the time. Unfortunately, the airline did not acquire safeguards against these facilities being used later, without any fees, by other companies, including competitors, or against appropriation by either the Government or military authorities. Not only this, the terms of hire of its aircraft were very hard on the Arab company and by 1947 it was almost bankrupt.

In the meantime, a group of Arab businessmen in Palestine had established an Arab secular airline, Eastern Airways, which was to compete with the Jewish internal airline, Arkia. Eastern Airways did not operate, mainly because the Government of Palestine, under a League of Nations Mandate to Great Britain, did not wish rival Arab and Jewish airlines to develop and compete with each other. But, with the worsening political position within Palestine, the directors of Eastern Airways agreed a merger with Arab Airways in Jordan, with the new company to be named Arab Airways Association.

The result of this merger was to bring considerable financial resources to the company from Eastern Airways in return for one-third representation on the Board of Directors of the new company, which now for the first time had Palestinian as well as Jordanian membership.

Amman Airport in 1955. (John Lightfoot)

Arab Airways Association Dragon Rapide TJ-AAE "Moab". The registration prefix TJ- was for Trans Jordan and was changed to JY- in 1954.
(via John Havers)

During its first year of operation (1948) Arab Airways Association suffered a deficit of just over £8,300; not in itself a bad performance, but the management problems within the old Jordanian company still existed. These were aggravated by the political uncertainties of the area as a result of the British withdrawal from Palestine, the Arab-Jewish conflict which led to the setting up of the state of Israel and the eventual armistice which was not recognised by the Arab states. Instead, Israel was referred to at that time as Jewish Occupied Palestine.

Several international airlines were asked for financial and technical assistance, but the Jordan government was cautious after the recent war and refused to admit outside capital, stating that it intended, instead, to form a state airline which would merge with the Arab Legion Air Force. With this in mind, the latter had acquired transport aircraft which were maintained on the civil register, surveyed by the British Air Registration Board and operated on civil as well as military services. It also competed with Arab Airways Association. What advice was asked for by the government, and given, went unheeded, nor did the plans for a new national airline come to fruition.

The Airport Commandant at Amman, 1955. *(John Lightfoot)*

As a result of the Arab–Jewish conflict, a new airfield was needed to serve Jerusalem and other parts of Palestine which now formed part of Jordan. Kalundia, an airfield built during the War, and roughly midway between Jerusalem and Ramallah, was found to be suitable for development, and, once again, Arab Airways Association helped to finance the provision of facilities. Yet again, national pride took the place of common sense and national interest, and this airport, which should have been designated as an internal airport, was nominated as an international one. The drawback to this strategy was that with all the religious and tourist sites being in the vicinity of the West Bank of Jordan and Jerusalem, and the area being rather more prosperous than Amman itself, foreign airlines with more modern equipment started to use Jerusalem as a gateway to Jordan rather than Amman.

The strains began to show and in 1950 a rift developed between the management of the company and the Arab directors and, taking advantage of a longstanding feud between prominent local businessmen, a new company, Air Jordan, was formed. This company also operated a mix of Consul and Rapide aircraft, but fell into financial difficulties rather more rapidly, and would probably have collapsed in 1952 had it not received outside financial assistance which, by then, the Jordan government was prepared to allow. This outside assistance was from Transocean which had come up from Djibouti.

Transocean background

As a result of the Second World War, Eritrea had been transferred from Italy and placed under United Nations trusteeship and British administration. The more important regional airlines serving the area were Ethiopian Airlines, a state organisation managed by Trans World Airlines, and Aden Airways, a wholly-owned subsidiary of BOAC. The former was based in Addis Ababa and the latter in Asmara where the facilities and climate were infinitely better than in Aden itself. In 1950, a new company was formed and registered in Djibouti, French Somaliland, under the name of Air Djibouti and under the auspices of Transocean Airlines led by the redoubtable Orvis Nelson. Despite its name, this company was also based in Asmara and employed some of the senior staff of both Ethiopian Airlines and Aden Airways as management. Its interests were wide but generally centred on the local vegetable produce traffic, the Aden entrepot and developing oil traffic, as well as the increasing Muslim pilgrimage traffic between British East Africa, the Somalilands, Aden, the Hadramaut and the Hejaz.

Chapter 11: Arab Airways (Jerusalem) Ltd, 1953 - 1958

Airspeed Consul TJ-AAY, one of several operated by Air Jordan in the early 1950s. *(via John Havers)*

Aden Airways and Ethiopian Airlines contrived to put all possible obstacles in the way of this company, but it was not until the federation of Eritrea and Ethiopia in September, 1952, that Air Djibouti's operations could be curtailed by executive action from the Ethiopian Government. In its search for a new base in the Middle East, Transocean came into contact with Air Jordan, and by the end of 1952 had formed a new company, the Air Jordan Company, introducing DC-3 and C-46 equipment.

By early 1953 the revitalised Air Jordan was well established and Arab Airways Association now not only had foreign competition using superior equipment, but also the Arab Legion Air Force operating in a civil guise. By March its liabilities exceeded its assets by some £25,000 and it appealed for outside assistance from British sources.

Politically, there was much to justify this assistance being given. At this time Jordan was still in the British sphere of influence and the British maintained units of their own Army and Air Force in Jordan, as well as paying for the Arab Legion. They also contributed grants in the form of aid and loans for economic development, and any budgetary losses were covered by annual subventions. Official payments to Jordan were £13,000,000 per annum while personal investment by the expatriate community would have amounted to a further £7,000,000. (155)

Commercially, there were other reasons for the British to give assistance. With the type of equipment then in common use in the Middle East, Jordan was conveniently situated at the crossroads between Lebanon and Syria to the North, Aden to the South, Egypt to the West and Iraq, Kuwait and the Persian Gulf to the East. It had the major religious shrines of Islam and Christianity and was on the major pilgrimage routes to Saudi Arabia. Following the Egyptian revolution in 1952, many of the international trunk route services transiting the Middle East had been rerouted via Beirut which was conveniently close. The existence of this considerable traffic was evidenced by the very high load factors of the twenty 28-seat DC-3/Viking services per week between Jerusalem and Beirut, and the twelve 28-seat DC-3/Viking services between Jerusalem and Cairo at the beginning of 1953, together with other busy, though less frequent, services to Damascus, Jeddah and Baghdad. The only note of caution, which would have repercussions in the future, was that only some 20% of passengers were full-fare-paying load.

Apart from the general commercial aspect, Aden Airways had further interests to safeguard. With the impending development of the refinery at Little Aden, with its requirement for a large Levantine labour force, as well as large British communities in Cyprus, Jordan, Aden and East Africa, it would not be able to resist indefinitely the applications by Air Jordan for traffic rights to Aden. In addition, there were indications that Hunting Clan were becoming interested in Jordan and, were this company to be successful in achieving its aims, it could be damaging to Aden Airways as well as to the wider interests of BOAC.

There was, then, a degree of political pressure, but there was also a commercial opportunity to be taken advantage of and, with the assurances that the Jordan Government wished to see a monopoly airline under British influence thrive within the region, Aden Airways entered into an agreement with Arab Airways Association.

A further condition within the original draft agreement was that the BOAC General Sales and Traffic Handling Agencies in Jordan would be given to the new company. In the event this was not done, nor did the Jordan Government take the action promised to establish Arab Airways (Jerusalem) Ltd as the monopoly national airline. The new airline was thus unable to establish the vital foothold in its early days. The major reason for Aden Airways'

Harry Pusey meeting an arriving flight at Amman, 1954. With him is the Airport Commandant. *(Harry Pusey)*

Harry Pusey's car was transported from Aden to Amman by DC-3; here the car is tied down towards the front of the cabin.
(Harry Pusey)

decision to establish a joint venture with Arab Airways Association was commercial but the political aspects could not be overlooked and would assume a greater importance later.

A "gentleman's agreement" had reputedly been reached earlier between the British and American governments to the effect that neither would encourage interference in any Arab state in direct competition with the established interests of the other. Whether it was the Transocean agreement with Air Jordan which constituted the first breach of this agreement, or whether it was the Aden Airways agreement with Arab Airways Association, will remain in dispute. It was, however, sufficiently disputed that the Arab partners of both companies, and, indeed, the Jordan Government, were able to use the "difference" between the Americans and the British to serve their own purposes and avoid taking any positive decisive action in favour of one side or the other.

From left to right, Harry Pusey, Richard de Graaff Hunter and the airline Manager in Jordan, 1954. *(Harry Pusey)*

Structure of Arab Airways (Jerusalem) Ltd

The terms of the Jordan agreement in the arrangement were that Aden Airways would "sell one DC-3 on hire-purchase terms extended over a period of five years;" this aircraft was to be fully furnished and equipped with 36/40 seats and Aden Airways would be fully responsible for its operations and engineering requirements, which would be charged to Arab Airways (Jerusalem) Ltd. (156)

An amendment to the original contract offered a second DC-3 under similar circumstances, except that Aden Airways also reserved the right to take back the aircraft should Arab Airways (Jerusalem) default on the hire purchase at any time; also, a clause was inserted which allowed Aden Airways to make use of this aircraft at any time that it was not being employed by the Jordanian company. (157) A third aircraft was hired by the airline from Indamer in India.

Of the nominal capital of £100, 51% was held by the Jordanian interests and 49% by Aden Airways which had complete financial and management responsibility for the new company and whose shares were later transferred to Associated British Airlines (Middle East) Ltd, an association of BOAC, Skyways and the Hunting Group. Eventually, these shares were transferred to BOAC Associated Companies Ltd. In the event of an operating loss, which turned out to be the normal case, Aden Airways and BOAC would meet it, while profits, if any, were to be shared equally between the three companies.

The Board of Directors consisted of four members nominated by Arab Airways Association and two nominated by Aden Airways. The Jordanian complement was to include two members from Eastern Airways, the original Palestinian company, and also Jordan's Director of Civil Aviation. Very quickly, a law was passed in Jordan whereby the General Manager of this new company was required to be a Jordanian and, for this reason, the Secretary, W Salameh, was appointed to this role, the terms of reference being that he would *"act only on the advice of the resident adviser and follow that advice in all respects"*. (158)

The quorum for a Board meeting was two Arab Directors and one British one. The political uncertainties at the time meant that, for a brief period, the Resident Adviser was an alternate Director, but this was cancelled in April, 1954. This was a wise move as it meant that it was then possible to avoid Board meetings being called at short notice by the Arab Directors during politically embarrassing times. An example was when, at the time of the Suez crisis, in November, 1956, the Chairman and other Arab Directors decided that all British personnel were to be dismissed and repatriated. A further precaution was that the basic agreement had contained safeguards against differences in commercial policy, in that Aden Airways and BOAC were protected against financial results arising from actions or decisions against their advice, either at Board or local management level, but political disturbances had not been foreseen on such a scale.

In practice two Board meetings a year were held, one to approve the budget for the following year and the second to approve the accounts for the previous year. Generally speaking, control was exercised by the Resident Adviser with reference to London when necessary. (159)

Organisation of Arab Airways (Jerusalem) Ltd

For organisational purposes, the company was divided into four sections:

1) Administration and Commercial: At headquarters level, this unit was very small, consisting of the Resident Adviser and Manager, two secretaries and a clerk. No specialist sales staff were

Chapter 11: Arab Airways (Jerusalem) Ltd, 1953 - 1958

employed, though in Amman and Jerusalem the company maintained its own booking and aircraft handling units. At all other stations, local sales agents and handling agents were used, while in Beirut and Cairo, the two main traffic generating points, representatives were employed to deal with both interline traffic and local bookings.

2) Accounting: The company was completely self-accounting and based upon the system which had been instituted within Aden Airways some time before, whereby actual revenue figures per month were compared to the standard costs for the same month together with the variances available within the standard month. This meant that decisions could be made quickly if costs were exceeding revenue by too much, which they nearly always did.

3) Engineering: The engineering section was fairly small, consisting of a seconded BOAC engineer assisted by two locally-engaged expatriate engineers. Although on the Jordanian register, the aircraft were under the supervision of the British Air Registration Board. Inevitably, this meant that the company endured higher maintenance costs compared to their rivals who did not follow the same practice. All attempts to persuade the Jordanian authorities to change this state of affairs proved unsuccessful. The plus side was that the company aircraft proved to be more reliable in operation than those of its competitors, but the costs were high, nevertheless.

4) Operations: Originally, the operational plans for the company had been that the aircraft would be based in Aden and crewed from there. This soon proved to be costly and impractical and a separate unit was established in Amman. All aircraft were fitted with duplicated Collins R/T equipment so that only two-man crews were required and the radio officer dispensed with. A single Jordanian stewardess flew on each flight.

Seven crews in all were employed and, though at first they were seconded from Aden Airways, it was later necessary to employ them from other sources. Pilot utilisation was some 850 hours per year, a high figure bearing in mind that little flying was done at night and each pilot was given eight weeks leave per year. Later, political developments such as during the aftermath of the Suez Crisis in 1956, made it necessary to employ what were euphemistically referred to as "neutral" crews, in other words, non-British, French or Australians. Fortunately, the company had one Irish Captain at the time, and he, together with his Lebanese co-pilot, who was himself on loan from Middle East Airlines, kept the daily Jerusalem-Amman-Beirut service going, together with the four weekly flights from Jerusalem and Cairo. Later, a Dutch and two Swiss pilots were taken on and this relieved the load somewhat.

Operational Patterns

The first flight of Arab Airways (Jerusalem) Ltd took place on 23 August, 1953 and was operated by DC-3 TJ-ABN from Amman to Jerusalem and Beirut. In addition to the DC-3, the initial fleet consisted of the two Rapides which had come from Arab Airways Association, but these two were sold in 1954 with the arrival of two further DC-3s.

Other services were flown to Aden via Jeddah, through which the airline had full fifth freedom rights, three services per week between Jerusalem and Beirut, and two per week to Cairo, all of which were flown with one DC-3 with a second in reserve. However, it was clearly not competitive at this stage with the daily flights mounted by the competition in the form of Air Jordan, Air Liban and Middle East Airlines between Jerusalem and Beirut, nor the frequent services of Air Jordan and Misrair to Cairo. Furthermore, under pressure from the Jordan Government, and always with the implied (but never fulfilled) promise that, once the

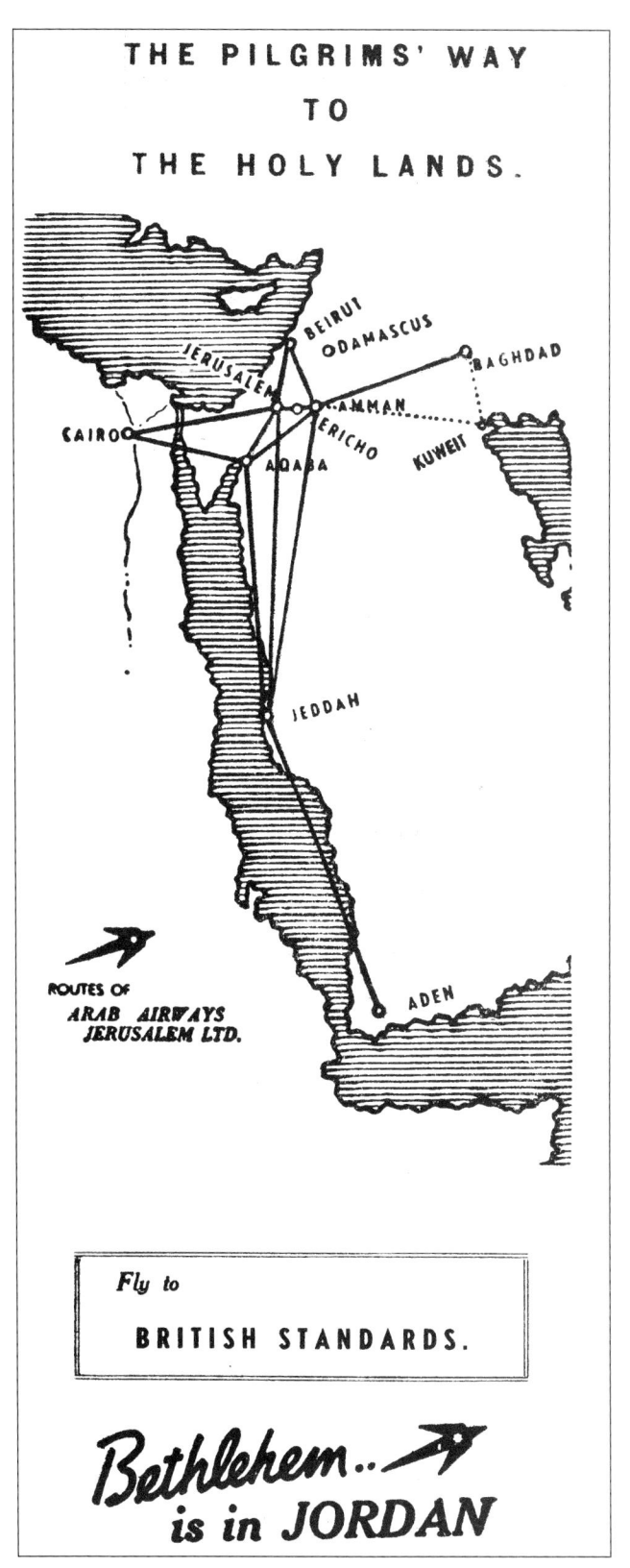

Arab Airways (Jerusalem) Ltd route map, April 1956.

airline had proved itself, Air Jordan would be forced to cease operations, Arab Airways felt obliged to expand further. With the arrival of the third DC-3, this expansion took place to include the following:

Jordan-Beirut	7 weekly
Jordan- Jeddah-Aden	1 weekly
Jordan- Cairo	4 weekly
Jordan-Kuwait direct	1 weekly
Jordan- Jeddah	1 weekly
Jordan- Baghdad- Kuwait	1 weekly
Jordan internal services	2 weekly

ADEN AIRWAYS MAIN LINE SERVICES

JE.008/6	AD. 470	AD. 474	AD. 472	AD. 466	DAKOTAS		AD. 467	AD. 473	AD. 475	AD. 471	JE.005/7
4	5	3	2	7							
0600	1400	0830	0800	0645	Dep. ADEN	Arr.	1745	1755	1700	1150	1720
↓	↓	↓	↓	↓	Arr. DJIBOUTI	Dep.	↑	↑	1555	↑	↑
					Dep. DJIBOUTI	Arr.			1520		
		1030			Arr. KAMARAN	Dep.			1340		
	ARGONAUT	1100			Dep. KAMARAN	Arr.			1310	ARGONAUT	
		1235		0930	Arr. ASMARA	Dep.	1500	1510	1135		
		1325	↓	1020	Dep. ASMARA	Arr.	1410	1420	1045		
			1125	1120	Arr. PORT SUDAN	Dep.	↑	1120	↑		
			1155	1150	Dep. PORT SUDAN	Arr.		1050			
		1510	↓	↓	Arr. KHARTOUM	Dep.		↑	0700		
1030			1410	1405	Arr. JEDDAH	Dep.	1135	1035	▲		1230
1115			1500	1455	Dep. JEDDAH	Arr.	1045	0945			1145
	1945		1845	1840	Arr. CAIRO	Dep.	0500	0400	0400		
							1	3		5	

ARAB AIRWAYS CONNECTING SERVICES

		JE. 014/006	JE. 014/012	DAKOTAS		JE. 013	JE. 011/013		JE. 011	
		3	1							
		0745	0745	Dep. CAIRO	Arr.	1540	1715			
1500		↓	1015	Arr. JERUSALEM	Dep.	1310	1445			
1540		↓	1100	Dep. JERUSALEM	Arr.	1240	1415			
		1015	1125	Arr. AMMAN	Dep.	1215	1350			0600
										3
		1100	1200	Dep. AMMAN	Arr.	↑	1315		1315	1615
		1125		Arr. JERUSALEM	Dep.		↑			1550
		1200		Dep. JERUSALEM	Arr.					1515
1755		1415	↓	Arr. BEIRUT	Dep.					1500
			1615	Arr. BAGHDAD	Dep.		1100		1100	
						7	2		2	2

Aden Airways main line routes with Arab Airways connecting services in May 1954.

The arrival of the first service to Beirut. Harry Pusey is second from the left, Captain Harry Mills in the centre. The aircraft is TJ-ABN.
(Harry Pusey)

Operational record

1953-1954: As in any airline, the start-up costs were high mainly because, initially, the crews were based in Aden; also, the previous airline, Arab Airways Association, bore little goodwill or expertise to the operation with the result that a loss of £27,000 was made in the first year. The government was ambivalent on its stated intention of giving the airline a clear path as the national carrier. On the other hand, the construction of the oil refinery in Little Aden required a steady flow of labour from the Middle East and that route at least was profitable.

Politically, there had been some turmoil, such as the Kibya village massacre followed by Jordanian retaliation, which would have a negative effect in the coming year.

1954-1955: That said, the early part of the financial year was successful as a result of a rapprochement between the Arab world and the West. Not for long, though. Severe rioting broke out in Amman during the general election there in October; a curfew was imposed and flight operations were suspended by the government, which in turn had a depressing effect on business and on the Christmas and Easter Christian pilgrimage traffic. Even then, only a small loss of £7,000 occurred for this year.

1955-1956: Tensions within the Middle East were growing as Egypt, under Nasser, sought to become the leader in the region. The Baghdad Pact, negotiated between the UK and Iraq (which was still a monarchy) was seen as a deliberate attempt to undermine Nasser, as well as protecting its oil interests there. Egyptian retaliation in the form of anti-Iraq and anti-UK propaganda unsettled the region and matters were only made worse when Jordan also joined the Pact. The Palestinian refugees were encouraged by Egypt to believe that the British were responsible for their predicament, with the result that rioting, even more severe than the previous year, broke out again in Jordan. Once again, a curfew was imposed, relations with Egypt were broken off and air services cancelled. The situation was considered so unstable that

Chapter 11: Arab Airways (Jerusalem) Ltd, 1953 - 1958

The composer/songwriter Cole Porter (with a cane) and his group travelled from Jerusalem to Petra on 16th April 1955. DC-3 "Bethlehem" was JY-ABS. Note the Aden Airways insignia on the nose with the inscription 'AAJ' for Arab Airways Jerusalem below. *(John Lightfoot)*

the American Government even advised a travel ban on the region for its citizens, which was not lifted until January 1957. Even the special relationship which existed between the UK and Jordan was not immune and when General Glubb Pasha was dismissed from his position as head of the Arab Legion in March 1956, the British withdrew their liaison officers and personnel. Once again, a loss was recorded for the year, this time for £46,350.

1956-1957: There had already been a loss of confidence in the Middle East. What really affected air services, though, was that the main users were the foreign nationals, whether for business or tourism, while the loss of local traffic was as bad, as this was the sector of society which was the most air-minded. Even then, and despite a relatively poor pilgrim season to Jeddah, the company made a profit of some £2,000 during the first six months of the year.

However, July saw the start of the Suez Crisis which culminated in the invasion of Sinai on 30th October, Anglo-French air operations against Egypt on the 31st, followed by the invasion on 5th November. Jordan was seen as a British sympathiser and the Egyptian rhetoric intensified. A curfew was imposed throughout Jordan, and the aircraft of Arab Airways (Jerusalem) Ltd were impounded lest they be taken from the territory to be used by British pilots in support of British forces. Syria, Egypt and Saudi Arabia closed their borders and airspace to British aircraft and crews. With the open condemnation of Anglo-French actions by the American Secretary of State, John Foster Dulles, Air Jordan, with its American crews, was in a better position to meet the limited demands for air travel which still existed. Even so, Arab Airways (Jerusalem) Ltd had regular services up and running first with internal flights on 20th November; to Baghdad and Kuwait on 21st November; through Jeddah to Aden on 26th November and to Beirut and Cairo on 10th December.

At the end of the year the losses amounted to £ 47,000.

1957-1958: This financial year was to be no different to the last. In April 1957, an attempt to overthrow King Hussein by a Col. Ali Abu Nawar, even though it failed, once again perpetuated the sense of uncertainty within the kingdom. Learning from the past, perhaps, the company had budgeted for a loss of £9,550 for this financial year but, with the philosophic optimism which seems to have been a feature of this part of the world, confidence was slowly returning to the Jordanian economy. A study was carried out into the feasibility of buying out Air Jordan which had also suffered the tribulations of the last months and years. The study was encouraging and revealed that, as a result of rationalising frequencies and days of operation, and by greater utilisation of aircraft and staff, a profit could be made of up to £34,000. Nothing came of these negotiations which may have been influenced by BOAC's increasing interest in Middle East Airlines in Beirut, an altogether more progressive and profitable airline flying from what was then a rather more stable country. Rumours had also been circulating which indicated that King Hussein was about to nationalise the two airlines anyway.

More was to come. Early in 1958, the United Arab Republic was formed between Egypt and Syria, and increased propaganda from Egypt called for revolution within Jordan to overthrow the King and for that country to become a part of the United Arab Republic. Egyptian and Syrian airspace was again closed to Jordanian civil traffic and there were demonstrations and civil unrest within the country. Perhaps as a precaution, Jordan entered into a federation with Iraq, but this was short-lived as a result of the Iraqi revolution in mid-July, when the monarchy was deposed by General Kassem. This isolated Jordan from her neighbours even further, and further restrictions were imposed by Saudi Arabia which, it would appear, did not wish to offend the Egyptians. As if this was not enough,

Arab Airways (Jerusalem) Avro York JY-AAC on lease from Skyways for the Haj in 1957.   (via John Havers)

Below: Amman, 1955. Left to right: Emile Farqe, Theresa Saad and Captain Jimmy Gross.
(John Lightfoot)

Air-to-air view of Arab Airways Association Dragon Rapide TJ-AAE in flight.   (via John Havers)

civil war broke out in the Lebanon, further restricting flights in that direction, and thus, without the remotest possibility of a viable and profitable operation being possible within the foreseeable future, BOAC did not renew the contract at the end of the five-year period.

Arab Airways (Jerusalem) Ltd ceased operations on 31st October 1958, and the company was wound up on 31st July 1960.

Conclusions and aftermath

With the benefit of hindsight it would be difficult to imagine that this venture would ever have been successful, bearing in mind the economic and social upheavals which were bound to take place within the region. BOAC had already declined to take an interest in Arab Airways Association as far back as 1952, and only under pressure from the Foreign Office did BOAC suggest to de Graaff Hunter that Aden Airways might benefit from such a venture. The politics of both the region and the Jordanian Government would militate against it from the start. The BOAC General Sales and Traffic Handling agencies in Jordan were not awarded to the Arab Airways (Jerusalem) Ltd; after all, the airline was a subsidiary, albeit indirectly.

The original mandate given to Aden Airways by BOAC was that its experiment in Arab Airways was not to continue beyond a loss of £10,000. Although the company lost some £27,000 during its formative seven months, the option to cease operations was not exercised. Politically, such action would have been undesirable because the implied agreement to transfer all agencies in Jordan to Arab Airways would have given considerable economic power to BOAC.

BOAC was also somewhat ambivalent in its support of the airline; had their General Sales and Traffic Handling Agencies been given to Arab Airways from the start of the operation, there would have been considerable revenue from interline sales as well as through traffic. Furthermore, there was a distinct lack of commercial support from the parent company towards Arab Airways. For instance, there were many cases when BOAC traffic was booked for onward travel from, say, Beirut or Cairo on Air Jordan, when flights were available on Arab Airways at equally convenient times. (160)

Perhaps the agreement should have been called off at the time of the Suez Crisis, in November 1956 and, while this would have been justified on commercial grounds, political pressure was applied on the company to remain, as it represented the last vestiges of British activity in the region. BOAC was still a state corporation and thus representative of the British government. Despite promises from the King, Arab Airways never had the monopoly which might have made it a viable proposition.

Ironically, Arab Airways Association, as the company had reverted to in name, and Air Jordan did amalgamate after all. Under the management of Transocean, the new company became Air Jordan of the Holy Land. It was given the monopoly so sought after by Arab Airways (Jerusalem) Ltd, and was profitable from the start. Sadly, though, with no internal competitive standard to be matched, operational regularity and maintenance standards declined after a time. Nevertheless, the company continued in operation until 30th August 1961, when the Jordan Government cancelled its licence before licensing its own company, Jordan Airways, to start operations on 29th September 1961. In 1963, after another reorganisation, this became Royal Jordanian Airways and, later, Royal Jordanian Airlines.

Footnotes, Chapter 11:
(155) Civil Aviation in Jordan. H Pusey, 1963.
(156) Terms of agreement between Aden AW and AA(J) Ltd 30th July 1953.
(157) ZMD.AMM 0501. Letter from de Graaff Hunter to AA(J) 15th August 1953.
(158) Harry Pusey records.
(159) Civil Aviation in Jordan, H Pusey, 1963.
(160) AA(J) Ltd: An appreciation by de Graaff Hunter to the Aden Board. Secret. January 1954.

An interestingl sight at Ghuraf in August 1954; an Indamer DC-3 VT-DGP (apparently with Aden Airways titles for the Haj) along with Aden Airways VR-AAA whose passengers are taking advantage of the only available shade! (John Rush)

Chapter 12 :
ADEN AIRWAYS 1954 - 1955

The BOAC Board then had to set about rectifying a situation for which they, as much as anyone in Aden Airways, were responsible. de Graaff Hunter had been given too much authority and a long leash which suited his style perfectly, but which had, for reasons already described, led to the virtual collapse of the airline.

The post of Managing Director was abolished with the result that the new manager would be appointed as General Manager instead and would not even have a seat on the Aden Airways Board. He would be answerable to the London Manager Subsidiaries (L.M.S.) and work through the Board in Aden on which the L.M.S would sit as Chairman. (161)

Gilbert Lee, the new L.M.S., was invested with the task of creating a new policy (162) for the airline in accordance with the views and desires of the office of the Governor of Aden and the new General Manager of the airline, Stephen Broad. Barney Dutton would remain on the Board as the Aden Government representative.

The Aden Government had definite policies in mind concerning civil aviation in Aden and in particular Aden Airways. They had long disagreed with de Graaff Hunter's desire for Aden Airways to be seen as a major player within the orbit of Red Sea and East Africa. Instead they preferred the concept that BOAC would have full responsibility for operating the route between London and Aden via Cairo which of course they had been doing for some time with the Hermes and Argonaut. While the longer Aden Airways routes to Cairo, Khartoum and Nairobi were considered desirable, they were not seen as vital to the Colony's aviation future; indeed the DC-3s had for some time been uncompetitive with other airlines within the region, and these once-profitable routes were now losing both money and reliability. Once again, it was suggested that BOAC would do well to include these three destinations as part of the network of routes through Aden. In fact, BOAC did fly from London to Aden via Khartoum later on in 1957.

In contrast, the Aden Government was very supportive of the success Aden Airways had experienced in developing the local routes within the Colony and Protectorate as well as neighbouring countries such as Somalia and Ethiopia. The view was that this should be the prime function of the airline and thus be an extension of the Government's communication and administrative functions, as well as providing an easy way to maintain internal security with the new airfields that the company was laying down. The term "airfield" was something of a euphemism since many were mere strips in the desert which had been cleared of stones.

There were two further areas where it was perceived Aden Airways would do business profitably. The first was in charters to the oil exploration companies and the second the Haj Pilgrimage.

With oil and gas believed to be available in large quantities within the Protectorate (and later in Oman), oil exploration companies were keen to make exploratory bore holes deep in the interior which would, in turn, need regular supplies of men, machinery, fuel and food. Obviously there were no roads and it was therefore much easier to lay out a strip on the desert floor and have everything flown in by DC-3. One such place, for instance, was Midway (so named because it lay midway between Aden and Masirah Island) which lay some 20 minutes flying time from Salalah, but up to three days by truck. As will be seen later, it became a vital part of Aden Airway's source of revenue.

Less certain for the future was the annual Haj. Certainly in earlier years the revenue derived from this source kept the company in profit, the scheduled routes only just breaking even. But other countries bordering the Red Sea had also realised that there were profits to be made and were now beginning to introduce protective measures which would favour their own airlines (Egypt and Sudan) or would ensure that airlines over-flying their countries on the Pilgrimage would share the profit in the form of overflight charges. It was foreseen that at some stage in the not too distant future Aden Airways would only be allowed to carry pilgrims from the Colony, Protectorate and any remaining British territory as well as from outer fringes where other companies would not be particularly interested. And, of course, the Saudis did tend to make up the rules as they went along as was seen in 1952 and 1953.

In fact, de Graaff Hunter had already secured the West African pilgrim traffic from Nigeria for 1954 using Yorks chartered from Skyways, and a profit was envisaged for the year.

A further policy decision under Gilbert Lee was to concentrate all resources in Aden instead of splitting them between the Colony and Asmara, with the result that land was acquired and permission to build staff housing was to be sought. Accounting was to be

Far Left: *John Rush in Asmara when he was flying as an Aden Airways copilot, 1954.* Left: *Mrs John Rush, Asmara 1954.* Above: *Bahobescia Apartments, Asmara 1954, where the Rushes rented accommodation.* (all: John Rush)

transferred as soon as possible, while engineering functions such as daily maintenance would be carried out at Khormaksar with major engineering to follow as soon as suitable hangars and stores became available. By and large, most of this was achieved by 1956.

This also involved a greater presence by the airline in Aden itself for ticket selling and marketing, initially with an office at Steamer Point and later in Crater. Ann Berryman was recruited to work there and she gives some idea of what it was like to live there:

"When I was 17 in 1954 I was back in Aden for what was to have been a last holiday before University, but which turned out to be an interlude before marriage. If a girl had to spend her teens anywhere then there can be no better place than Aden. All men and no girls to put it bluntly. Life was one long party whether Sunday morning breakfast picnics at Goldmohur, or the Thursday evening dance nights on the roof of the Crescent Hotel in Steamer Point. Land Rover days out to Lahej or just travelling into the desert. My photo albums are full of snaps of parties, same people, different venues. My father insisted that I get a job to fund my decadent lifestyle so I started working for Aden Airways and have been in the travel industry ever since and am still at it after 50 years. My Aden Airways office was in the Crescent Hotel, managed by the Volpe family of Italian descent, and I spent a happy 18 months there – when they were short of stewardesses I dashed out to the airport and went to Assab and Asmara, Addis Ababa, Khartoum and Cairo, even to Jeddah and Kamaran Island.

In early 1954 I started as a reservations clerk at the office in the annexe to the Crescent Hotel in Steamer Point working for a short time with Betty Hudson and then for an elegant and delightful lady called Joan Goldsmith. She was originally from South Africa. I started at the bottom doing filing by the hour and gradually learning how to compute fares by mileages, eventually how to issue tickets, answer the telephone and how to deal with the public who were mostly business men and Government officials passing through who needed changes to their tickets. I earned what was to me a large salary of £17 per month to start with. I seem to remember that after a year it was raised to £21 per month. My uniform was a white linen skirt, white shirt, black epaulette with a stripe and a revolting black forage cap.

Joan was due to leave Aden due to ill health towards the end of 1954 and return to South Africa, so Jack Chambers decided that I should take over the running of the Crescent Hotel office and to this end I was sent away for further training. At 17 off I went to Khartoum for a week in the BOAC office, followed by another week in the BOAC Cairo office, and then for two weeks at BOAC in London where my time was spent between the office in Regent Street and the main flight allocation office for the whole world which was near Heathrow. Now in the computer age it is hard to see how the "Sell and Record" booking system managed to work, but it did and I was never aware of an overbooking problem or undersold flights.

Back to Aden where I continued in the Crescent Hotel office, but was very occasionally asked to fill in as a stewardess when there was a problem. I say very occasionally as I did not acquit myself well on my first flight. By now, 1955, the flight stewardesses and admin people were Italians – very suave and elegant in their khaki green uniforms. I was phoned at the office one morning and told to close up and get to Khormaksar right away, collecting a passport en route and to go as the only stewardess on the morning flight to Assab and Addis Ababa, overnighting there and returning the next day via Asmara. So off I dashed in my white uniform, grabbed my passport and toilet bag and probably a clean pair of

Khartoum Airport. An Avro York on charter from Skyways to Aden Airways during the Haj in October 1954. (John Rush)

Chapter 12: Aden Airways 1954 - 1955

Ann Berryman wearing her uniform as a Ground Stewardess, 1955.
(Ann Atkinson)

knickers, and was almost pushed into the Dakota without a word of explanation of which was what other than "Here are the Ship's Papers." I hadn't a clue what they were!

The plane was full, would there have been about 20 passengers? What was I supposed to do with/for them? There were sandwiches and biscuits in a cupboard in the galley and great urns of what was cold water. I had to go to ask the Captain what I was supposed to do and how to make the water hot.

On arrival in Assab I was asked for the ship's papers. Ah yes, I knew where they were so I handed them out of the aircraft. After unloading cargo we departed and then eventually landed in Addis where again I was asked for the ship's papers. Oh dear, I had left them in Assab!!! The rest of that flight seemed a nightmare to me and the final straw was on returning to Khormaksar and opening the door of the aircraft. The soignée lady Italian supervisor took one look at me and said my white uniform was filthy, why wasn't I wearing proper khaki flight uniform? Ah well, we live and learn and after 50 years of travel industry travelling I always take a spare outfit with me wherever I go. I never did get a khaki uniform.

On other occasions flights took me to Mogadishu, Jeddah, Kamaran Island, Cairo and Khartoum.

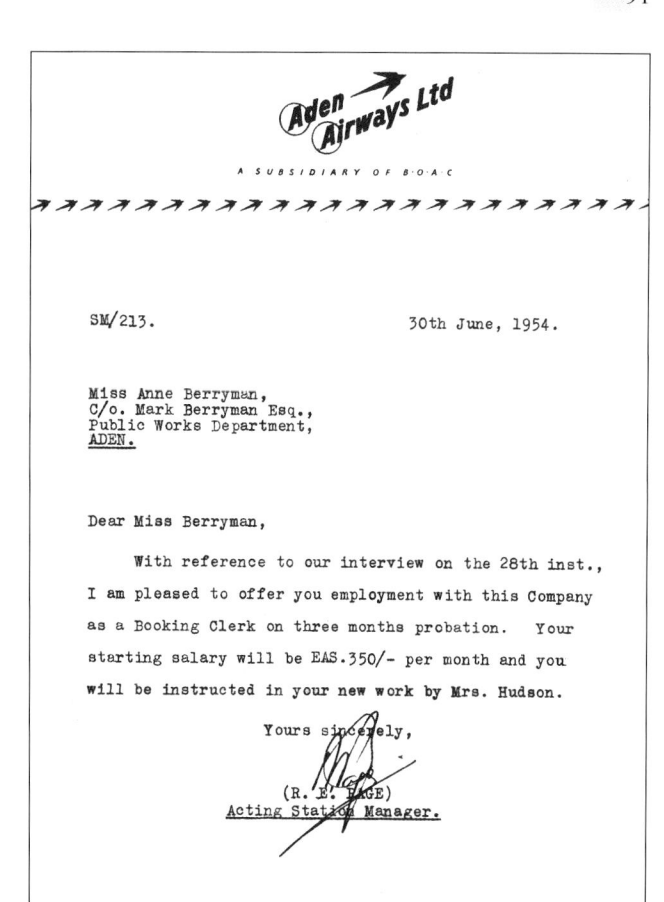

Anne (sic) Berryman's formal offer of employment as a Booking Clerk, June 1954. She was also required to fly as a Stewardess when the occasion demanded. *(Ann Atkinson)*

At sometime during this period 1955/56 the office in the Crescent Hotel annexe was closed and I moved into the main hotel where we had an office behind a counter in the reception area of the hotel and I was joined by a young man called Andy Anderson who worked for Besse. I think he must have had something to do with freight which is why he was in the Aden Airways office. He had a motor scooter, one of the first in Aden - my parents were horrified when he gave me a lift on it." (163)

One of the weakest areas of the company during previous years was the poor quality of administration. This was not necessarily the fault of the individuals concerned, but more because they had ill-defined duties and responsibilities, with de Graaff Hunter both a strong and somewhat mercurial manager. BOAC, too, had to take some of the blame.

Aden ground staff meeting a Hermes from London. Ann Berryman is on the left of the pair, Joan Goldsmith on the right.
(Ann Atkinson)

TIMETABLE

Aden Airways

A SUBSIDIARY OF B.O.A.C.

ISSUE No. 1954/1

EFFECTIVE 1/ 5/ 1954

UNTIL FURTHER NOTICE

Showing Interconnections with :

ARAB AIRWAYS

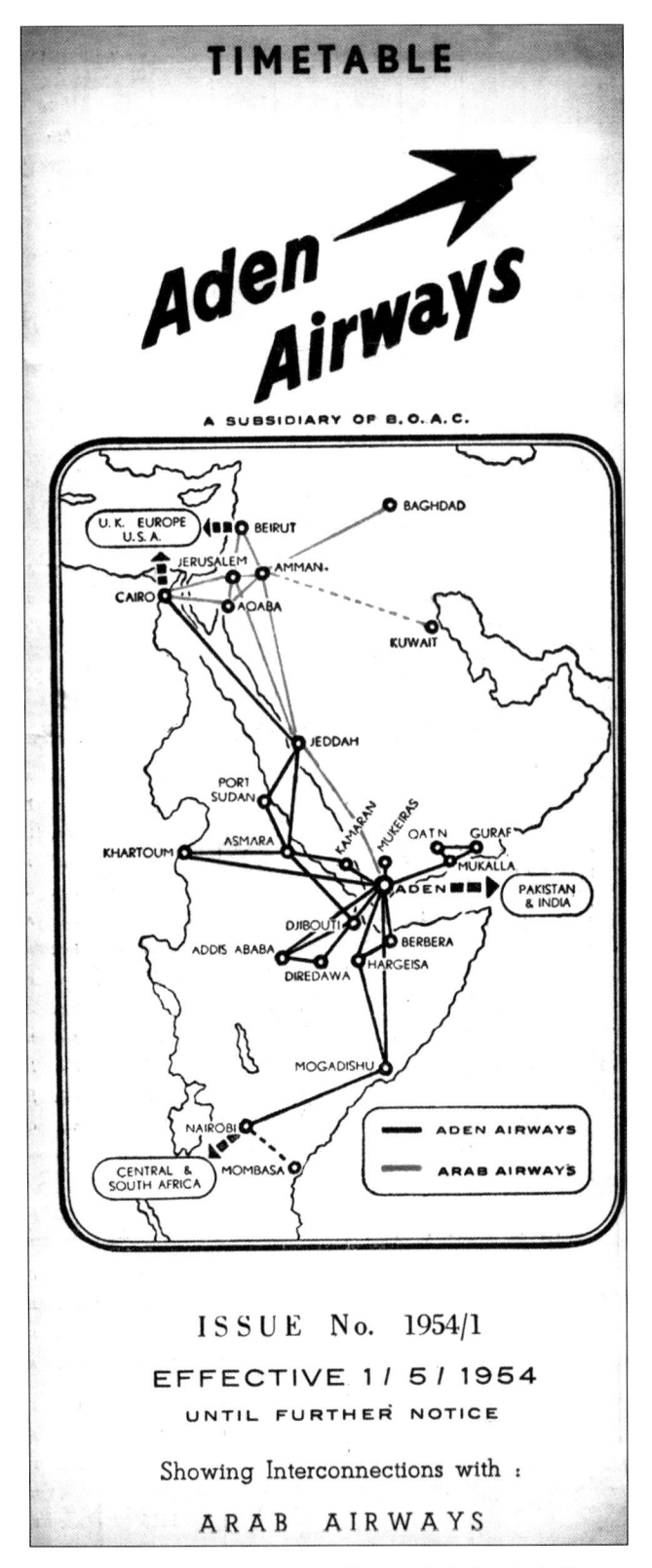

May 1954 route structure of Aden Airways, including Arab Airways (Jerusalem) Ltd routes, as shown on timetable cover.

Now, with de Graaff Hunter gone, Wolfson dead, Colvin no longer Chief Pilot and Middleton back in London, Lee could start afresh. The new structure at managerial level ensured that Stephen Broad would stay focused in a way de Graaff Hunter had not, while the accounting section was to be tidied up under the temporary Chartered Accountant, Mr Vincent. Engineering would continue under the competent Mr Martin while Mr Page would oversee the implementation of the move from Asmara, in terms of housing, furniture and office supplies. Lee was less sanguine about his Chief Pilot, John Pascoe, who had been appointed after the departure of Captain Steve Colvin the previous year.

A further concept, new at the time, was to be a possible share participation in the company by commercial interests within the Colony, though this was not acted upon for fear it might impair the commercial judgement of the Board.

Finally, the relationship with Arab Airways (Jerusalem) Ltd was to be put on a sounder footing; it should be more of a separate entity not managed from Aden except in terms of broad policy. BOAC was concerned that, with the rise of nationalism within the Arab world, Jordan remained the only country within the region that was well-disposed towards Britain, and British influence there was to be maintained almost at all costs. (165)

There still remained, of course, the question of the Indamer debt, some £50,000, which was owed to Aden Airways as a result of the 1953 Haj charters. There was no suggestion that Indamer had in any way been devious in their dealings with Aden Airways, it simply reflected the financial chaos which had developed the previous year in the absence of de Graaff Hunter and the overwhelming work, previously discussed, in the financial department in Aden.

In fact, de Graaff Hunter had somewhat belatedly dealt with this problem. In negotiations with Indamer it was agreed that six DC-3s would be chartered for the Haj, together with their crews (which was known as a "wet lease"), and this would provide some 760 hours of flying for the 1954 Haj. In addition, Indamer would continue to provide two DC-3s for the UNO charter, awarded to BOAC but handed on to Aden Airways, of which one aircraft (UN 640) was based in Beirut and the other (UN 351) in Kashmir. (165) Finally, £20,000 was to be repaid in cash by Indamer in two stages, April and May 1954.(166) It is interesting to note that the UNO charters, while not particularly lucrative, did provide a net income of £1,000 per month to Aden Airways.

In all this upheaval, it was clear that both the results for 1953/54 and the budget for 1954/55 would take some time to be resolved and it was not until June 1954 that the company would start to look forward again. The previous year's results were worse than had been feared. Originally the loss was estimated to be £105,986 (167) but turned out to be £140,595 of which £25,562 was attributable to the losses at Arab Airways (Jerusalem) Ltd.

The budgeted loss for 1954/55 was now expected to be £25,804 made up as follows. (168)

The scheduled routes would lose £61,336 which would be offset by a profit of £35,532 for the pilgrimage operations. This elicited a comment from Gilbert Lee (169):
"It is true to say that this follows the pattern of previous years, but it is a somewhat disturbing state of affairs in as much as we now know that the Pilgrimage business is becoming more and more difficult, and that greater financial risks are consequently involved in dealing with the business."

In fact, it was anticipated that the Pilgrimage traffic would bring in revenue of some £378,000 against expenditure of £342,000 for a profit of £36,000. However, the bulk of this operation would originate from West Africa where the company had obtained (through de Graaff Hunter) a monopoly of the traffic by negotiation with the local authorities. Once again, Lee raised doubts as to the sense of relying on such a wayward source of income, prophetically as it turned out.

In respect of Arab Airways (Jerusalem) Ltd, this company was no longer to be a liability on Aden Airways in terms of losses, and although Aden Airways would continue to hold 49% of the shares, any losses would be borne by BOAC. Further, a new manager, Mr John Linstead, was to be installed in Amman, initially for six months.

Chapter 12: Aden Airways 1954 - 1955

Mukeiras: Mrs Chloe Bishop, Mr Henderson (Political Officer) and Captain Vic Spencer, September 1954. (John Rush)

The finances of the company were not the only problem; staff moral had fallen, particularly amongst the pilots. In keeping with the reduction in numbers of pilots seconded from BOAC, replacements had been taken on as direct entry from other airlines and countries with none of the loyalty and "respect" for the motives of BOAC in its ambitions in setting up associated companies such as Aden Airways. They were assertive in their views as to how things should be done, particularly in the area of flight operations.

John Pascoe, on the other hand, was a BOAC seconded pilot imbued with that company's ethos and it must have come as some surprise to him to find many pilots were less than happy at his way of doing things. Into this area walked the new General Manager, Stephen Broad, who for all his experience in airline matters had little experience in dealing with industrial relations. BALPA by now had a presence in Aden Airways and while this fact should not have been a cause for disharmony, it did provide a conduit for them to voice their frustrations. It was at such a meeting in Aden during early July that Stephen Broad was present while his Chief Pilot had remained in Asmara.

There were a number of bones of contention, but the main one was the increased take-off weights out of Mukeiras. Until recently, the company had simply used Official Regulated Take-Off Weights (RTOW) which were used on a seasonal basis taking into account, among other things, temperature and elevation and which, in simple terms, allowed the aircraft to climb away safely after an engine failure immediately after take-off. Mukeiras is at a high elevation (7,000 ft) and already this made the take-off fraught in the event of engine failure, though there was an "escape route" down a valley (see colour photo page C41).

Added to this, the engines on the DC-3 were well past their prime and would not necessarily work at their theoretical best. To therefore increase the maximum take-off weight was, in the opinion of the pilots, foolhardy.

There was, though, a reason for the increased weight. (170) One of the Aden Airways Board members, Mr A S Hasanali, had a farm near Mukeiras producing vegetables; the company had agreed to guarantee him 500 kg of freight space on a weekly basis for the transport of his produce to Aden and this was in addition, of course, to the normal commercial loads. While there was no impropriety suggested, and the transport would have been paid for, there would appear to have been a lack of understanding of the implications of over-loading an aircraft, particularly flying out of Mukeiras.

Who made the agreement is not known, but until the take-off weights went back to their original figures considerable difficulties

Mukeiras: passengers ready for boarding, 1954. The Flight Clerk was responsible for ensuring the there were no bullets in the breech of any rifles. (John Rush)

had been created when Captains off-loaded commercial traffic in order to keep the weights within limits.

Other points voiced by the pilots were two-crew operations (i.e. with no radio operator) and the lack of suitable radio equipment when flying to Nairobi and Cairo. In turn, the pilots felt that in operating flights without a radio officer they should receive some financial compensation for the saving involved. Another issue was with the unrealistic schedules whereby if the crews were to complete the flights on time they would have to fly at higher power settings. This in turn meant higher fuel consumption and lower engine life, yet they were constantly being exhorted to save on both.

There were other issues of lesser importance and on which Stephen Broad wrote in strong terms to his Chief Pilot. He also made the mistake of circulating the letter to a number of those present at the meeting, thus undermining the position of this individual and eventually his own.

By this time the company had started to settle into its new direction and status as envisaged at the beginning of the financial year. As was always the case, in addition to the Indamer aircraft, all Aden Airways crews and aircraft, when not flying the scheduled routes, were involved in the Haj operation. This year the inbound flights to Jeddah were from 5th – 26th July. In addition to the six Indamer aircraft mentioned earlier, two Yorks were chartered from Skyways for the West African uplift.

As always during the Pilgrimage, the flying days were long and hard and the crews quickly exceeded their monthly flying limits of 100 hours. The solution to this minor inconvenience was to give them a medical, find them fit and on they flew. 120 hours in a month was certainly not unusual, and 130 hours were achieved on occasion.

Interestingly, though the charters were done on a "wet" basis, where the chartered aircraft came supplied with their own crews,

Flying over harsh terrain; a mountain village NE of Aden, 1954.
(John Rush)

Mukeiras: initially sheep were wrapped in sacks ready for air transport. *(John Rush)*

some of the Aden crews also flew the chartered aircraft. For instance, on 12th July Captain John Pascoe flew an empty York (G-AHFF) from Jeddah to Kano via Port Sudan, returning there on 15th July with a full load of pilgrims in York G-ANGL via El Fasher and Khartoum. Again on 25th July, he flew VT-DGP (Indamer) from Aden to Jeddah carrying a group of Adeni pilgrims, and again on 31st July he flew VT-DGT to Jeddah, this time from Asmara.

The "outbound" return flights of the pilgrims took place from 9th – 31st August and once again Captain Pascoe flew VT-DGQ from Jeddah to Asmara. Naturally, he and other Aden Airways pilots flew Aden-registered aircraft as well, but it was unusual to fly the chartered ones.

By 30th August, the chartered aircraft were being returned to their owners, all except for VT-DGT which was flown from Asmara to Aden on 17th September where it was given an air test after engineering work on 26th November and sent to Kashmir for the ongoing UN charter there as UN 601.

Gilbert Lee's forebodings on the results of the Pilgrimage revenue were well-founded however, when, later in the year, the results showed that the earlier revenue forecasts had been wildly optimistic, particularly in relation to the West African operation organised by de Graaff Hunter before his departure from the company. The forecast profit had been £17,370 (171) but in fact turned out to be a mere £933. The pilgrims simply weren't there or had made other arrangements and, of course, this resulted in lower flying hours, which meant that penalties had to be paid to Skyways since the minimum guarantee of 1100 hours had not been reached. In fact, on a budgeted profit of £35,532 on the pilgrim charters, a profit of only £4,791 was made, a huge disappointment and calling into question the future of pilgrim charters from anywhere other than the Colony and Protectorate.

However, there was a gleam of light emerging from these disappointing results and that was an unexpected profit of £13,000 from charter work during the months of June and July. (172) This reflected the new direction the company wished to go as it partially withdrew from its loss-making scheduled services and concentrated its resources closer to its base of Aden. Cairo, Nairobi and Khartoum services did continue, but at a lower frequency and with a greater concentration on a mix of freight and passengers.

At a meeting of the Board in Aden on 28th October (173) Stephen Broad outlined his views on how he wished to proceed: an increase in charter work particularly to the oil exploration companies. For this he would need a fifth DC-3 as well as a smaller aircraft such as the Rapide. Whether he took advice on the purchase of a Rapide is not known, but as will be seen later it was not to prove a success. However, on the advice of the Aden Board, the BOAC Board agreed in November to the purchase of a Rapide Mark IV with spares for a sum of £5,500. (174)

During the year Mukeiras, entry point to the Yemen, Riyan (for Mukalla) and Qatn had become regular destinations within the Protectorate. Ghuraf, Ataq, Nissab and Beihan were visited on an irregular basis, though they too would receive regular schedules in the near future.

The weather at African destinations was much affected by the seasonal movement of the monsoon in a similar pattern to that which affects India. Thus the Somali and Ethiopian destinations

Mukeiras: all freight had to be laboriously weighed before loading; even so turnarounds were short. VR-AAA, July 1954. *(John Rush)*

Mukeiras resident, 1954. *(John Rush)*

CHAPTER 12: ADEN AIRWAYS 1954 - 1955

Loading freight at Beihan, October 1954. (John Rush)

Mukeiras: though much of the freight would be brought by truck, donkeys were also important and here they wait for their loads. September 1954. (John Rush)

are subject to heavy rain and thunderstorms in July and August. While Aden itself suffered under very high temperatures and humidity at this time, flying conditions were generally much better while, within the Protectorate, the arid landscape was hardly conducive to monsoon conditions. However, turbulence due to thermal activity could be a factor and did on a number of occasions cause landings to be aborted.

That said, it did rain at times within the hinterland, the results of which could be devastating for the populations involved and disruptive to air transport. During the week ending 14th August the heavy rains at Mukeiras waterlogged the runway there and no services could be flown in for 10 days.

In October, much of the flying in the Horn of Africa was disrupted by weather with the result that Djibouti, Berbera and Hargeisa were frequently unusable. One has to remember, too, that radio navigation aids were rudimentary with, at best, only an NDB available with its correspondingly high limits.

However, progress was being made and the Aden Government was true to its word in aiding the company to promote travel between the Colony and the Protectorate. While word travelled slowly from tribe to tribe, it did travel, and it did not take long for the tribal leaders to realise that there could be distinct advantages in moving goods by air rather than a long and uncertain journey by caravan.

The way it worked was that a tribal leader would contact the Local Government Officer, often far away, and advise him that there were goods to be flown to Aden, or, indeed, goods were required from there. A cost would be arrived at for which the leader was responsible and, if a landing strip could be cleared of stones and rubble, a very basic survey would be made and a flight sent up. Often the strip was sprayed with used vehicle oil, since not only did this make it more visible, but it also kept the dust down. There were no radio aids and all flying was visual which meant that familiarity was the key.

When Vic Spencer operated the first flight to Beihan on 26th September in VR-AAF, the strip proved to be somewhat difficult and short; *"a little bit exciting"* was the record in his diary. Another such flight was to Qaban on 3rd October, but the strip could not be found and the aircraft returned to Aden.

Trevor Adams on the flight deck of a DC-3, July 1954. (John Rush)

Aden Airways Planning Office at Khormaksar, March 1955. (Vic Spencer)

Above: *F/O Alan Jennings in the cockpit of a DC-3, September 1955.* *(Vic Spencer)*
Above, right: *Engineer Lombardini, a Mr Farrell and Stewardess Vera Merlo during an oil company charter to Kuwait, October 1954.*
Right: *Captain Vic Spencer and Engineer Lombardini in Baghdad during an oil company charter, October 1954.* *(Both: John Rush)*

A further idea of the problems involved in finding these strips can be gained by an entry in John Pascoe's logbook for 19th January 1955 when he flew to Lamsoon in VR-AAA for the first time. All he had to go on were the coordinates and the magnetic direction of the strip, in this case N 14° 14´ E 47° 37´ 1,200ft long RW 36/18 (north/south).

The setting up of strips for the exploration companies was altogether more difficult. Where an exploratory well site was to be established it was usually in an utterly desolate area and literally every item had to be flown in. There was no local tribal labour with a vested interest in the future, and suitable landing sites had to be reasonably close to the oil rig. This involved many hours of flying over the Wadi Hadramaut trying to find landing grounds. These charters could also be open-ended with the exploration company deciding what would be done on the next day and where the flights would, within reason, go to.

One of the first areas covered was on 16th October when Vic Spencer flew VR-AAA from Aden to Salalah with a party of geologists and engineers employed by the Kuwait Oil Co. Normally the direct flight took 4.30 hours but on this occasion the party asked to see as much of the Wadi Hadramaut as possible from the air with the result the flight was 6.35 hours long.

This was always going to be a long charter because the oil company had to react to the need for discussions with engineers and local authorities. Under the circumstances Vic remained in Salalah together with the aircraft and his crew (F/O Rush, Air Hostess Merlo and Engineer Peter Lombardini) receiving signals from Aden as to what the next days would involve. Eventually, on 22nd October the aircraft flew from Salalah to Kuwait (5.20 hours) where they dropped off the first party, and remained for four days waiting for a second charter party.

Unlike today, the two pilots were expected to look after the aircraft and help the engineer do running repairs (spark plugs needed changing, as did several cockpit instruments which had become unserviceable). The Captain was also expected to liaise with the charter group as to times of departure and even where they could or could not go. For instance, the second charter party wished to fly to Dhahran in Saudi Arabia, but the closest the flight was allowed to get to that destination was Bahrain whence the party would fly on by ARAMCO DC-3.

On the 27th the new party flew to Baghdad for more talks followed by a flight to Beirut on the 28th where, on arrival, the crew were each given a "tip" of $500 by the charterer. The rest of the charter was completed on 30th October when the party flew to Cairo and the crew returned the aircraft to Asmara on 1st November in a direct flight of 6.40 hours after two weeks away.

This success with charters was not confined to supplying capacity to the oil companies. For some time the RAF had been reducing their passenger transport capabilities within the region with the result that when the army wished to move troops it was more convenient (and cheaper) to charter a DC-3 from Aden Airways for this purpose. One such flight was made on 11th December when VR-AAA with Vic Spencer flew non-stop from Aden to Sharjah to pick up 28 soldiers bound for the garrison in Aden. It was a long day for the crew which, with a refuelling stop at Salalah on the return flight, meant over 10 hours flying that day. Most charter days were similar in length and, as during the pilgrimage flights, the crews quickly ran out of hours creating more problems for the company as pilots decided to leave or requested higher salaries in compensation.

The job of supervising the construction of the landing sites within the Protectorate fell to the Chief Pilot, John Pascoe. As the company AOC holder he had to approve the technical aids (though there were precious few of those) as well as ensuring that refuelling facilities and fire extinguishers were adequate for the job in hand.

On 9th February 1955 he took VR-AAI to Riyan and Salalah and then on to the Wadi Hadramaut and the Dhofar region to survey the three new, and as yet unnamed, strips in that region for Dhofar Air Services. (175)

Again, on 23rd February, he flew in VR-AAI once more to Riyan and Salalah to negotiate with the RAF authorities there for

Chapter 12: Aden Airways 1954 - 1955

Mr Albert Young, Aden Airways Agency Manager in Addis Ababa, was responsible for the export to Chicago of this Abyssinian cat which started its journey with Aden Airways in October 1954.
(British Airways Archives)

Aden Airways timetables for 15th November 1954. On the right are the International Schedules and below are the "Caravan" routes within the Protectorates.

ADEN AIRWAYS MAIN LINE SERVICES & CONNECTIONS

AD. 475	AD. 473	AD. 467	B.A. 324 / AD. 471	DAKOTAS			AD. 470 / BA. 325	AD. 466	AD. 472	AD. 474
Sun.	Thur.	Tue.	Thur.							
			1400	Dep.	LONDON	Arr.	0655			
			2020 Fri.	Dep.	ROME	Arr.	0205 Sat.			
	0530	0630	0400	Dep.	CAIRO	Arr.	1915	2020	1940	
	1130	1230	↓	Arr.	JEDDAH	Dep.	↑	1620	↑	
	1220	1320	ARGONAUT	Dep.	JEDDAH	Arr.	ARGONAUT	1530		
0600	↓	↓		Dep.	KHARTOUM	Arr.		↑	↑	1840
↓	1235	↓		Arr.	PORT SUDAN	Dep.		1425	↑	↑
↓	1305	↓		Dep.	PORT SUDAN	Arr.		1355		
0945	1610	1600		Arr.	ASMARA	Dep.		1250	1250	1700
1025	1700	1650		Dep.	ASMARA	Arr.		1200	1200	1605
↓	↓	↓		Arr.	KAMARAN	Dep.		↑	↑	1430
↓	↓	↓		Dep.	KAMARAN	Arr.		↑	↑	1400
1325	2000	1950	1145	Arr.	ADEN	Dep.	1315 Fri.	0900 Mon.	0900 Wed.	1200 Sat.

AD. 459	AD. 469	AD. 459	AD. 459				AD. 458	AD. 468	AD. 458	AD. 458
Sun.	Sat.	Thur.	Fri.							
1400	0700	1310	1310	Dep.	ADEN	Arr.	1130	1735	1110	1110
1505	↓	1415	1415	Arr.	DJIBOUTI	Dep.	↑	↑	1005	1005
1525	↓	1445	1445	Dep.	DJIBOUTI	Arr.	↑	↑	0945	0945
↓	0840	↓	↓	Arr.	HARGEISA	Dep.	↑	1555	↑	↑
↓	0910	↓	↓	Dep.	HARGEISA	Arr.	↑	1525	↑	↑
↓	↓	↓	↓	Arr.	DIREDAWA	Dep.	0930	↑	0845	0845
↓	↓	↓	↓	Dep.	DIREDAWA	Arr.	0900	↑	0815	0815
↓	1220	↓	↓	Arr.	MOGADISHU	Dep.	↑	1215	↑	↑
↓	1250	↓	↓	Dep.	MOGADISHU	Arr.	↑	1145	↑	↑
1740	↓	1700	1700	Arr.	ADDIS ABABA	Dep.	0730	↑	0645	0645
	1635			Arr.	NAIROBI	Dep.		0800 Fri. Sun.	Mon.	Sat.

ADEN AIRWAYS "CARAVAN CLASS" SERVICES

AD. 462	AD. 462	AD. 450	AD. 465	AD. 456	AD. 452	AD. 454	DAKOTAS			AD. 455	AD. 453	AD. 457	AD. 464	AD. 451	AD. 463	AD. 463
Fri.	Mon.	Mon.	Thur.	Alt. Wed.	Fri.	Alt. Wed.										
0630	1200	1450	0630	0630	0945	0630	Dep.	ADEN	Arr.	1710	1725	1130	1200	1750	1405	0840
0715	1245	↓	↓				Arr.	MUKEIRAS	Dep.	↑	↑	↑	↑	↑	1325	0800
		1605	↓				Arr.	QOBAN	Dep.					1635	Mon.	Fri.
			0740				Arr.	BERBERA	Dep.				1050	Mon.		
			0800				Dep.	BERBERA	Arr.				1025			
			0845				Arr.	HARGEISA	Dep.				0940			
				0835	1150	0835	Arr.	RIYAN (MUKALLA)	Dep.	1515	1530	0935	Thur.			
					1220	0905	Dep.	RIYAN (MUKALLA)	Arr.	1445	1500	Alt. Wed.				
					↓		Arr.	QATN	Dep.	↑	1415					
					↓		Dep.	QATN	Arr.	↑	1355					
					1305		Arr.	GHURAF	Dep.	↑	1335					
						1125	Arr.	SALALAH	Dep.	1225 Alt. Wed.	Fri.					

AD. 454 / AD. 455 - Alternate Wednesdays - Commencing 17th November 1954
AD. 456 / AD. 457 - Alternate Wednesdays - Commencing 24th November 1954

servicing and refuelling facilities, particularly at Salalah which, for a number of years, would be the centre from which oil exploration servicing flights would be made.

He also took the time to survey the new strip at El Gheida on 16 March in VR-AAF but not all went to plan in that a tyre burst on landing at Salalah, and it was not until 18th March that a replacement could be brought up. From then on, all such oil charters carried the required spares and engineer.

From 28th February to 2nd March, Captain Pascoe chartered an aircraft, a Beech Bonanza, N3608B, to fly from Aden to Salalah from where, during the next few days, he inspected the strips at the new Duqa and Midway rigs as well as landing at and marking out a number of additional strips in the Dhofar area for possible future use.

The effect on the company's finances was instant. A profit of £7,183 in October (budgeted loss of £3,786) mostly thanks to the charters followed by a further profit of £6,612 in November. The future was starting to look better and at the January BOAC Board meeting it elicited the comment:

"There is every indication that the oil prospecting that is going on in the Hadramaut may be greatly increased, resulting in additional long-term business for the company."

Further monthly profits were posted and the company now found itself in the rather surprising position of quite possibly making a

Away from Aden itself, fuel supplies were scarce and the refuelling process could be rudimentary. The refuellers shown here are at Salalah in March 1955. *(Vic Spencer)*

profit for the year instead of losing £25,000 as budgeted. There were however, some clouds on the horizon and, in a letter to Gilbert Lee, Broad expressed his unhappiness on a number of points: (176)

1)   More aircraft were needed because of the shortage of DC-3 aircraft and the costs of chartering aircraft from Indamer were becoming high.
2)   The Captains were leaving because of the high work load as much as the low salaries.

The best way to keep meat fresh at Midway was to keep the animals alive until they were needed. Here some goats are being transported from Salalah. The animals travelled at the back of the aircraft and any passengers were in front. *(Vic Spencer)*

3)   A lack of clear policy as to Aden Airways responsibility for Arab Airways (Jerusalem) Ltd and potential losses there (£6,980 for 54/55).
4)   His ongoing problems with his Chief Pilot.

On this last point, John Pascoe was about to leave the company at the end of his secondment from BOAC. He had joined Aden Airways in April 1950 and had been there throughout a difficult latter period, contributing a great deal to the company. His last flight with Aden Airways was on 30th March 1955 when, after a test flight on JY-ABN at Asmara, he flew VR-AAC from there back to Aden.

The plans for the entry into service of the Rapide did not receive a full welcome from those who would be closely involved with it - the pilots and engineers. It also meant that a complete inventory of spares would have to be acquired, training for engineers provided and it was dubious whether it was suitable for operations into the Protectorate.

While two aircraft were bought, VR-AAL and VR-AAP, only the former entered service. The mark IV Rapide was different from its stable-mates in that it had Proctor engines (210 hp Gipsy Queen 2) with variable-pitch propellers. Take-off weight was 2,727kg, maximum speed 156 mph and range only 573 miles (177). Another fuel tank had to be installed in the cabin just behind the cockpit, further lowering the useful load which could be carried from the hot and high airfields to be found in Somalia and the Protectorate.

Some pilots were asked if they would be prepared to fly both the DC-3 and the Rapide, but few volunteered. One of those asked to fly it was Captain Spencer - *"I didn't really want to fly it; I was*

CHAPTER 12: ADEN AIRWAYS 1954 - 1955

Eric Borsberry at Thamud when he was a copilot in March 1955.
(Vic Spencer)

pushed." (178) Nevertheless, he and the two others took the ARB exams in Asmara on 8th February and then qualified on the aircraft itself at Khormaksar because Asmara was too high.

During March 1955 the charters continued to increase and the Aden Government, in the absence of available RAF equipment, was using Aden Airways more frequently. On 2nd March VR-AAI flew to Riyan and Thamud with a party of Government officials and local freight. This was a new destination and the Government was keen to see at first hand how well the new policy of opening up the Protectorates to air travel was working.

The main thrust at this time, though, was in keeping the oil exploration companies well supplied from Salalah. An example of one such trip was the departure on 30th March of VR-AAF from Aden just before first light (03.30Z) en route to Ghuraf where it would drop off goods ordered from Aden and then, after 15 minutes on the ground, carry on to Riyan and Salalah. Once there, freight consisting of fuel supplies, vegetables, meat, machinery, oil and personnel would be loaded on for the 25-minute flight to the main rig at Midway. On this particular day, Captain Spencer made two

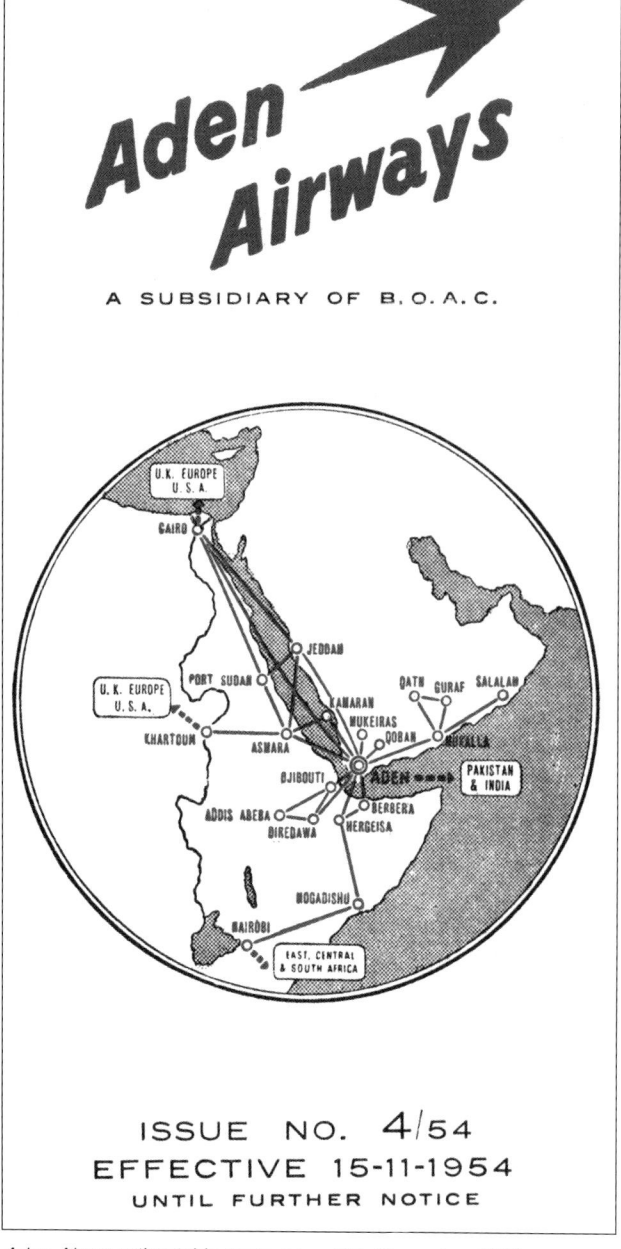

Aden Airways timetable route map, 15th November 1954.

DH Rapide VR-AAL in the hangar at Khormaksar, September 1955. Mary Spencer is standing in front of the aircraft. *(Vic Spencer)*

Mukeiras: unloading freight, July 1954. (John Rush)

Transporting a Pratt & Whitney engine on a DC-3, June 1955. Note additional seats in front of the engine. (Vic Spencer)

Aden Protectorate Levies (enlisted men) at Ghuraf, August 1954. (John Rush)

DC-3 interior during flight, November 1955. (Vic Spencer)

return flights to Midway with similar loads before ending the day at 1410Z.

The next day, 31st March, he flew seven return flights between Salalah and Midway and a further four on 1 April before returning to Aden via Riyan that evening, transporting personnel on leave and one oil rig worker who had been injured at Midway. The crew had flown a total of 32 take-offs and landings in three days. *"Good fun at first, but very tired in the evening."* (179)

As the year drew to a close, Stephen Broad had every reason to be pleased with what had been achieved. Notwithstanding the losses experienced on the scheduled services and the disastrous pilgrimage season, the company had made a profit of £599 instead of a forecast loss of some £25,000, mostly as a result of the new charter work which was proving to be a godsend. BOAC, too, was keeping its side of the bargain in that the finance had been made available for the purchase of land, the building of some 54 apartments of various sizes and the purchase of six vehicles in the form of two Harrington crew buses, three Bedford vehicles and one Bedford three-ton truck. On the administrative side, the engineering function was about to move to Aden and the finance section had already moved.

Footnotes, Chapter 12:
(161) Minutes of meeting held in London on future of Aden Airways, 25th February 1954.
(162) Report on Aden Airways policy for the future G Lee (L.M.S.), 9th April 1954.
(163) Ann Berryman went to Aden in 1947 at the age of 10 with her parents; her Father, a civil engineer with the Colonial Office, was involved in extending the water wells in the gardens at Sheikh Othman. The family lived in Crater next door to the Sultan's palace, and she went to school at the Franciscan Convent in Steamer Point and afterwards in the UK.
(164) Meeting at Stratton House 9th March 1954.
(165) These charters had been in a place for a year and the aircraft were flown by Aden Airways or Arab Airways (Jerusalem) Ltd crews on secondment either to Kashmir or Amman.
(166) MD.3184 de Graaff Hunter to Gilbert Lee 28th March 1954.
(167) Profit and Loss statement March 1954.
(168) Report to the Board Commercial and Economics Committee, 10th June 1954.
(169) Ditto.
(170) GM. 270 Stephen Broad to Captain John Pascoe (Chief Pilot), 12th July 1954.
(171) Board Commercial and Economics Committee 11th November 1954.
(172) Board Commercial and Economics Committee 9th September 1954.
(173) Aden Board Minutes 28th October 1954.
(174) Board Commercial and Economics Committee 11th November 1954.
(175) This information is taken from Captain Pascoe's logbook, and he may have meant Dhofar City Services.
(176) GM. 998 Stephen Broad to Gilbert Lee 19th February 1955.
(177) Ref "The DH Dragon Rapide family" by J F Hamlin, Air-Britain page 50.
(178) Conversations with Captain Spencer June 2005.
(179) Captain Spencer diaries 31st March 1955.

An unusual event, with an RAF Valetta parked at Ataq together with an Aden DC-3 during October 1955. (Vic Spencer)

Chapter 13 :
ADEN AIRWAYS 1955 - 1956

The results of the previous year did more than uplift the morale of the Aden Airways Board. The success made others wonder why more could not be done in other areas, while there were also covetous eyes from other quarters. For instance, for some time Aden Airways had enjoyed a lucrative vegetable charter from Asmara and Massawa to Aden. Previously while the Governor had been able to "run" Aden colony in his own way, the Legislative Council in Aden had increasingly become more assertive in questioning how agreements were made, and in the case of Aden Airways why there should not be more competition, rather than the monopoly enjoyed hitherto. There were fears that Besse & Co might well wish to start competing services, particularly in the carriage of freight and vegetables and at lower cost than Aden Airways.

A second local irritant was the fact that Air India was not permitted to pick up passengers in Aden for Nairobi on their Constellation service from Bombay. Instead passengers from Aden were obliged to travel on an Aden Airways DC-3 via Hargeisa and Mogadishu at a higher fare than they would with Air India. Barney Dutton left Aden in early April carrying a letter [180] from Stephen Broad in which he pleaded for more modern aircraft to be made available for the trunk routes from Cairo to Aden, and in particular onwards to Nairobi, since he did not think he could resist the pressure from the council for the lifting of the cabotage enjoyed by Aden Airways.

He was not alone in voicing these concerns. V K Joshi, one of the original Aden Airways Board members, cited the meeting of the Legislative Council on 28th March [181] during which a number of members questioned the right of the Government to continue in preventing Air India boarding passengers between Aden and Nairobi. He wrote: [182]

"Though the Government has stalled the questions for the time being I am afraid they may not be able to do that for very long. If we are unable to provide an equivalent service to Air India's Constellation service, I am afraid that these questions may be persisted on and enough pressure may be brought on the Government to modify our cabotage rights. I therefore suggest that we bring the matter up before the next Board Meeting.

In this respect I would again refer to the question of introducing a service between Nairobi/Aden/Bombay and vice versa. I know that this question was discussed by you with Mr Lee some time ago and the result was in the negative. I however think that it may be useful to discuss this also at our next Board Meeting. I still believe that the Nairobi/Bombay route is a gold mine which we have failed to exploit."

In his reply Stephen Broad quoted the BOAC reasoning: [183]

"East African Airways have for some time been thinking about providing a service parallel with the Air India Constellation one between Bombay/Karachi/Nairobi. They have not been able to do anything yet about it as they have no suitable aircraft, but when BOAC have Argonauts to spare East African Airways are likely I believe to obtain two or three of these aircraft for use by themselves. It would certainly be nice to see Aden Airways on the route instead, but we should have to have a very careful commercial assessment prepared before BOAC would I think be willing to agree, and at the present fare rate in force with Air India, the proposition I believe is not exactly an attractive one."

At the Board Meeting held in Aden on 28th May, Barney Dutton expounded the views held by the Government stressing that Aden Airways must now build on its success of the previous year and produce greater reliability and efficiency. Further, he fully endorsed the proposal that two more DC-3s should be acquired for the fleet so that less ad hoc chartering would have to take place; *"most important, we should not have foreign (e.g. Indamer) aircraft and crews flying under Adenair's flag in the area."* [184]

Air India L749 Constellation VT-DEO refuelling at Khormaksar, 1955. (Ann Atkinson)

Nor did he hold back in his criticism of BOAC on the India/Aden/Kenyan service:

"I do not consider that this is a route which Adenair should contemplate operating. Where I agree with Mr Joshi is that I think it is high time that Adenair's Dakota service to Nairobi is replaced by a BOAC service using the faster and more modern aircraft. You will note that Government has stated that "BOAC have recently sought and have been granted permission to operate a direct and fast service over the route between Aden and Nairobi." If BOAC do not now intend to go ahead with the service for which they sought and obtained a licence, someone ought honestly to say so quickly or there is going to be more mud-slinging from which Adenair will suffer more than BOAC. As you know I do not believe that Adenair's interests will best be served by continuing to shelter behind the cabotage rule which prevents Air India from having rights. I incline to the view that we should take the initiative in saying that we would not be opposed in the circumstances to Air India being given temporary rights pending the introduction by the national airline of a more satisfactory service."

During these discussions, the airline continued to fly its schedules as well as an increasing number of charters and not only for the petroleum companies but also for the Haj which started in April 1955. That month, a profit of £2,000 was made from charters, while £3,000 was contributed by early pilgrims to Jeddah.

While the normal schedules through the Red Sea and the Horn of Africa were maintained, more flights were taking place within the Protectorate. These could involve very long days such as on 13th April when Vic Spencer flew to Riyan in VR-AAA, starting at 0300 Z (0600 local) and then on a charter to Jeddah which took 4.40 hours before returning to Aden the same day at 1515 Z; 11.15 hours flying. Nor was it easy since the flights flew direct to Jeddah over a particularly hostile part of Arabia where, as a result of the high mountainous terrain, an engine failure could create real difficulties. Not only that, over-flying Yemen without permission was fraught in itself, not that that country could do much about it at the time.

F/O Robby Robinson at the controls of a DC-3 in June 1955. (Vic Spencer)

The Aden Protectorate Levies fort and camp at Ataq. (Vic Spencer)

Once again, Salalah and Midway featured prominently in most pilots' rosters at one time or another. However, it was rarely routine and when an oil company geologist from Midway became lost, Captain Spencer in VR-AAF spent the whole day searching for him while flying between Duqa, Midway and Salalah on normal charter work; as a result the normal 25 minutes between Midway and Salalah became 1.30 hours. Eventually the geologist was found after Captain Spencer and his co-pilot David O'Neil had completed 10 sectors and over 11 hours of flying that day.

A new aircraft, G-AIWC, was leased from British International Airlines (BIAL) Ltd on 13th May. This aircraft had just finished a lease to KNA (Kuwait National Airways) and was to be leased to Aden Airways until April 1958. It was collected from Kuwait on 12th May by Captain Spencer who then flew it to Cairo in 6.45 hours and onwards the following morning in a non-stop flight to Asmara in 6.45 hours. F/O Robinson was co-pilot and R/O McGarry the Radio Officer.

Later in the month, on 18th May, Captain Spencer flew VR-AAF from Aden to Salalah via Ghuraf where 18 live goats and other fresh produce were loaded for transport to the oil drilling rig at Midway. Of course, loads did not simply consist of freight but passengers who were generally the workers on the oil rigs throughout the area. One of the problems which emerged later as a result of carrying both livestock and construction materials was that, inevitably, some of the bags of cement would tear and cement dust would collect on and below the floor of the aircraft. Naturally the goats urinated during the flight and this would mix with the accumulated cement dust and set into a hard surface. Although this didn't matter too much on the floor of the cabin, it played havoc with the control lines located below the floor and it was only discovered after there had been numerous Technical Log reports by the pilots of "heavy controls experienced" that the cause dawned on the engineering branch. From then on, the goats were transported in large trays.

On 19th May, a charter was flown from Salalah to Bombay via Masirah Island. Once again, Captain Spencer was flying VR-AAF, which had had its seats replaced after the freighter service the day before, with a flying time to Masirah of 2.40 hrs and a further 5.40 hrs to Bombay. A replacement load of Indian oil rig workers was taken back to Salalah the next day. That was a relatively pleasant part of the charter, since on 21st May, six round trips were flown between Salalah and Midway in temperatures of over 45°C.

By this time Ataq was a scheduled destination on a once-weekly basis, though if the agent there could find a reasonable load, an extra charter was flown on demand.

During late May, the Company's Rapide, VR-AAL, was delivered, though it would be some time before it was fully in use because the engineers needed time to acquaint themselves with the airframe and engines, the traffic staff had to work out load sheets and, not least, the pilots had to learn to fly it.

Chapter 13: Aden Airways 1955 - 1956

Not only were refuelling methods primitive away from Aden, but so was routine maintenance. Here the tail-wheel of a DC-3 is being changed at Salalah in May 1955. *(Vic Spencer)*

Later, on 22nd June, a second DC-3, G-AMVK, was transferred from BIAL which was to become VR-AAM. Not only was this last aircraft a 32-seater, which meant that it would have to be modified for Aden Airways operations, but both recently-acquired aircraft had previously been flown with a Radio Officer. Modifications had to be made to the radio systems in order to bring them into line with the two-crew system already in place and this was to cost £7,400, though the withdrawal of radio officers would save the Company £5,500 pa.

During the first three months of the financial year (April, May and June) Aden Airways made good profits of £13,630 (185) though it has to be remembered that the major part of the Haj pilgrimage had taken place during those months.

As the monsoon moved north, the flights into the Protectorate were affected by the seasonal change:
1st July: *"Very rough run around the Hadramaut. Unable to land at Ghuraf due to turbulence."*(186) Simply a reflection on the trials

It was unusual for a European stewardess to fly as cabin crew on a service into the Protectorates. Here Mary Spencer, surrounded by children, heads off to the fort at Ataq in March 1955. *(Vic Spencer)*

The Wali of Salalah arriving at Duqa on one of his tours of inspection in 1955. (Vic Spencer)

and tribulations effected by the monsoon weather which brought low cloud and drizzle at places such as Salalah, but high temperatures, wind and turbulence inland.

In all of this, neither the oil drilling companies nor the airline had forgotten that they were dependant on the goodwill of the local tribal leaders, both for permission to explore for oil and also to fly the services between drilling camps and Salalah. On 14th July, in the middle of a week-long charter between Salalah and Midway, Captain Spencer was asked to take the Wali of Salalah and the resident government representative on an inspection trip to Midway and then on to Duqa where a new oil exploration site was being set up.

July and August were hard-working months for pilots. Not only were the normal schedules flown but the charters, already mentioned, took up many flying hours. Even though aircraft were chartered from Indamer on a wet lease, Aden crews were at times called upon to fly these Indian-registered aircraft, even though this was not strictly legal, with the result that the monthly flying-hour limits (100 hours) were often exceeded. This could play havoc with the schedules as in the case of F/O Wood who was due to operate from Aden to Asmara and on to Cairo via Jeddah and who had to delay the flight by 45 minutes so that he could have a medical to clear him to fly that day. (187) However, with a flying time of 9.45 hours planned for the return to Asmara via Jeddah next day, the flight had to be delayed for one hour because of crew fatigue. An example of just how tight the rostering was. In fact, during July, Captain Spencer's total was 133.40 hours.

Other than the Qat from Dire Dawa, other freight flights were for fresh vegetables which were all imported to Aden. The main source of these were from Massawa on the Eritrean coast, a mere 25 minutes flying time from Asmara but another climate away bearing in mind Asmara's elevation of over 7,000 feet. Generally the flights left Asmara at 0930 Z and Massawa at 1020 Z for the vegetables to be on sale in Aden either that evening or next day.

Captains Harry Mills, Frank Gauws and Jack Lawson relaxing at the Aden Mess between flights in November 1955. (Vic Spencer)

Nor were the night-stop hotels of a standard flying crews expect today. While Cairo and Nairobi had adequate accommodation,

CHAPTER 13: ADEN AIRWAYS 1955 - 1956

Loading VR-AAF at Ghuraf in May 1955. Weather conditions could make this and similar sites inaccessible by air. (Vic Spencer)

crews based in Jeddah during the Haj were lucky to get hotels with air-conditioning. At other times in Addis Ababa the crews were often expected to search for and find a hotel when the regular one was over-booked. On 14th August, Captain Spencer and his crew consisting of F/O Borsberry and F/O Elgee flew to Dire Dawa for an early departure back to Aden laden with Qat and had to share a room between them, though no mention is made of the number of beds.

The charters were not the only flights with interesting incidents. On 19th September, Captain Spencer was due to go to Cairo from Asmara via Jeddah on VR-AAC, but was delayed for an hour waiting for the Emperor's (Haile Selassie) lions to be brought to the aircraft. They were intended as a gift for the King of Saudi Arabia and, apparently, such gifts were not uncommon.

On 27th December 1955, Captain Spencer converted to the Rapide VR-AAL under the supervision of Captain Ted Parker. After a supernumerary trip to Dhala in the morning, he completed eight landings at Aden that afternoon (one of them single-engine) followed by five landings at night of which one was on a single engine. His conversion consisted of 1.30 hours of which 35 minutes were at night.

On 2nd January 1956, Captain Spencer again flew the Rapide to Dhala, 50 minutes from Aden which he described as *"quite an experience."* A small band of pilots flew both the DC-3 and the Rapide and alternated between the two fairly often in order to stay current on both types, particularly bearing in mind the difficulties operating within the Protectorate.

Loading Qat at Dire Dawa for delivery to Aden, November 1955. (Vic Spencer)

Ethiopian DC-3 ET-T-3 parked beside an Aden aircraft at Dire Dawa in September 1955. (Vic Spencer)

That month Captain Spencer flew to Dhala on a number of occasions, but he also operated to Djibouti and Berbera. On one trip to Djibouti, on 16th January, he records the *"port engine giving trouble on the return sector and very worried all the way back"* as well he might have been flying over the Gulf of Aden. On another occasion, 18th January 1956 he flew up to Dhala and *"waited there for two hours but no pax turned up and felt quite foolish on my own."*

However, the charters to the oil companies were always part of the operation and hard work too; over the four days from 31st January to 3rd February, Captain Spencer flew 23 sectors out of Salalah to Midway, Duqa and (a new location) Shaum transporting personnel, food and machinery for the drilling teams. This continued to be lucrative work for Aden Airways but was also hard on both aircrew and aircraft.

The Rapide VR-AAL at Dhala in January 1956. (Vic Spencer)

Chapter 13: Aden Airways 1955 - 1956

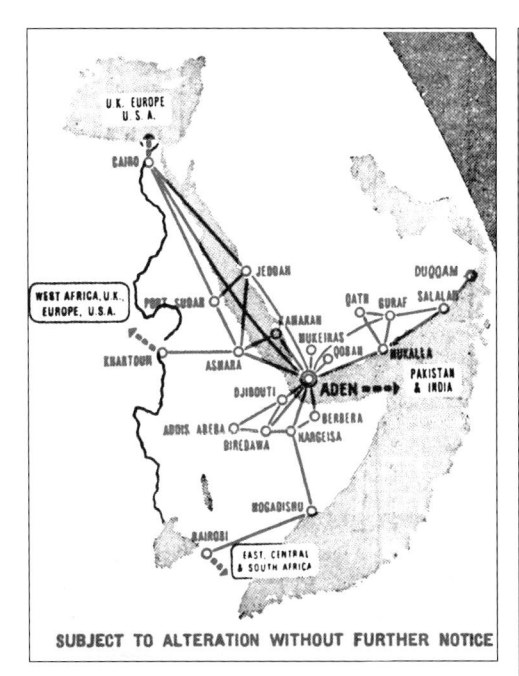

Above: *Aden Airways route structure as shown in their timetable of 1st October 1955.*

Right: *Timetables for 1st October 1955 with International services above and "Caravan Class" services in the Protectorate and Somaliland below.*

Below: *Flying over Steamer Point, Aden, in November 1955.* (Vic Spencer)

ADEN AIRWAYS - MAIN LINE SERVICES & CONNECTIONS

	AD.471	AD.475*	AD.473*	AD.467*	BA.324*	DAKOTAS		BA.325*	AD.466*	AD.472*	AD.474*	AD.470
	Mon.Fr.	Sun.	Thur.	Tues.	Thurs.							
					11.45	Dep. LONDON	Arr.	08.05				
					15.55	Dep. FRANKFURT	Arr.	05.50				
	(see Note)				19.45	Dep. ROME	Arr.	01.25				
	(3)				Fri.			Sat.				
			05.30	06.30	03.25	Dep. CAIRO	Arr.	18.50	18.30	18.30		
			11.30	12.30		Arr. JEDDAH	Dep.	↑	14.30	14.30		
			12.10	13.20		Dep. JEDDAH			13.40	13.50		
		06.00				Dep. KHARTOUM	Arr.				18.15	
			12.25			Arr. PORT SUDAN	Dep.		11.35		↑	
			12.55			Dep. PORT SUDAN			11.05			
		09.45	16.00	16.00		Arr. ASMARA	Dep.		11.00	10.00	16.35	
	14.00	10.15	16.30	16.30		Dep. ASMARA	Arr.		10.30	09.30	16.05	13.30
	14.20					Arr. MASSAWA	Dep.	ARGONAUT				
	14.50					Dep. MASSAWA						
						Arr. KAMARAN	Dep.				14.30	
						Dep. KAMARAN					14.00	
	17.40	13.15	19.30	19.30	11.10	Arr. ADEN	Dep.	12.40	07.30	06.30	12.00	10.30
								Fri.	Mon.	Wed.	Sat.	Mon.Fr.

	AD.459*	AD.469*	AD.459*	AD.459*	DAKOTAS		AD.458*	AD.468*	AD.458*	AD.458*
	Sun	Sat.	Thur.	Fr.						
	13.50	07.00	12.50	12.50	Dep. ADEN	Arr.	11.30	17.20	11.10	11.10
	14.55	13.55	13.55	Arr. DJIBOUTI	Dep.	↑	10.05	10.05		
	15.15		14.15	14.15	Dep. DJIBOUTI			09.45	09.45	
		08.40			Arr. HARGEISA	Dep.		15.40		
		09.10			Dep. HARGEISA	Arr.		15.10		
					Arr. DIRE DAWA	Dep.	09.30		08.45	08.45
					Dep. DIRE DAWA		09.00		08.15	08.15
		12.20			Arr. MOGADISHU	Dep.		12.00		
		12.50			Dep. MOGADISHU			11.30		
	17.30		16.30	16.30	Arr. ADDIS ABABA	Dep.	07.30		06.45	06.45
		16.35			Arr. NAIROBI		07.30			
							Fri.	Sun.	Mon.	Sat.

NOTES: 1. — Hostess service and bar facilities are provided on services marked*
2. — Free Baggage allowance on all Main Line services is 30 kilos.
3. — Service AD. 471 is a Contract Cargo flight. No passengers may be accepted.
4. — All times are Local Times except Jeddah which is shown as for Aden (i.e. G.M.T. plus 3 hours).
5. — Timings shown for Argonaut service BA.324/325 become effective on 3rd November 1955.

ADEN AIRWAYS "CARAVAN CLASS" SERVICES

AD.462	AD.462	AD.450	AD.465	AD.461	AD.456	AD.452	AD.454	AD.448	DAKOTAS		AD.449	AD.455	AD.453	AD.457	AD.460	AD.464	AD.451	AD.463	AD.463
Fri.	Mon.	Mon.	Thur.	Sun.	Tue.	Fri.	Tue.	Sat.											
06.30	12.00	14.30	06.30	13.30	06.30	09.45	06.30	07.00	Dep. ADEN	Arr.	12.50	09.30	17.25	13.30	09.40	12.00	17.50	14.05	08.40
07.15	12.45	↓	↓	↓	↓	↓	↓		Arr. MUKEIRAS	Dep.							16.35	13.25	08.00
		16.05							Arr. ATTAK (Qoban)	Dep.									
			07.40						Arr. BERBERA	Dep.	↑				10.50				
			08.00						Dep. BERBERA	Arr.					10.30				
			08.45	15.10				See	Dep. HARGEISA	Arr.	See				08.00				
				15.40				Note	Arr. HARGEISA	Dep.	Note				09.45				
				16.40				7	Arr. DIRE DAWA	Dep.	7	15.30	11.35		06.30				
					08.35	11.50			Arr. RIYAN (Mukalla)	Dep.		15.00	11.05						
					09.05	12.20			Dep. RIYAN (Mukalla)	Arr.		14.15							
									Dep. Q A T N	Arr.	↑	13.55							
					09.50	13.05			Arr. Q A T N	Dep.		13.35	10.20						
								10.00	Arr. GHURAF	Dep.									
							12.00	10.30	Dep. THAMUD	Arr.	09.50	↓							
								13.20	Dep. THAMUD	Arr.	09.30	06.00				See			
								13.50	Dep. SALALAH	Arr.	08.30					Note			
								15.50	Arr. DUQQAM	Dep.	08.00					6			
											06.00								
											Sun.	Fri.	Fri.	Tue.	Mon.	Thur.	Mon.	Mon.	Fri.

ALL TIMES SHOWN ARE LOCAL TIMES

NOTES: 6. — Free Baggage allowance on Caravan Class services is 15 kilos.
7. — AD. 448/449 operates Aden/Duqqam as a Contract Service. Commercial Traffic must not be accepted unless prior approval is obtained from Aden Airways Head Office.

F/O Roger Grove in August 1955. (Vic Spencer)

The company was now experiencing some success on their scheduled routes and on 15th February, a new midweek (AD 476) service commenced between Aden and Nairobi via Hargeisa and Mogadishu (188). This inaugural flight was flown by Captain Spencer in VR-AAF, though the return flight (AD 482) over-flew Mogadishu (no passengers) and landed in Hargeisa after a flying time of 5.30 hours. Whether this was a good idea was questionable since not only was there no suitable weather alternate in case the aircraft was forced to divert, but the radios at Hargeisa were unserviceable that day and the aircraft landed there with no air traffic control facilities.

A further new service was to Nisab, up in the Protectorate, started on 19th February and flown once again by Captain Spencer in VR-AAK, a flight of an hour each way, though he did record having some trouble finding his destination. Beihan was next to get a regular service, instead of charters, on 21st February.

The Rapide was taken up to Asmara on 21st February with Captain Spencer in command. During the flight of 3.30 hours the aircraft continued to give problems when the fuel from the long-range tank failed to feed, a serious prospect bearing in mind the high terrain at Asmara. Later, Captain Spencer took the Rapide to Kamaran Island and back on 4th March, its first visit there.

Despite the fact that the DC-3s were worked hard, the overall standard of engineering in both Asmara and Aden was good. There were minor problems but engine failures were relatively uncommon. However, on 18th March VR-AAF had to return to Nairobi while operating the AD 468 to Aden via Mogadishu and Hargeisa. On 20th March, a substitute aircraft VR-AAI was flown by Captain Spencer from Asmara to Nairobi, picking up the delayed passengers in Mogadishu en route. The next day after an air test, VR-AAF was returned to Aden in a non-stop flight of 6.50 hours.

As the year came to an end, the oil charter out of Salalah continued. On 24th March, two new exploration sites were visited by Captain Spencer in VR-AAM, these being Camp 2 and Ras Duqam.

During the northern summer months Aden Airways went from strength to strength, partly as a result of having a fleet of DC-3s large enough to fly the schedules without bringing in additional capacity from Indamer.

In July, the profit was £37,075 (£21,000 better than budget), £14,348 in August and £10,338 in September. October and November were traditionally quiet months, yet produced profits of £730 and £1,261 respectively. (189)

Above: *Gilbert Lee who became London Subsidiaries Manager after the sacking of Richard de Graaff Hunter.* (Sarah de Graaff Hunter)
Left: *V K Joshi, one of the first and most influential members of the Aden Board.* (Sarah de Graaff Hunter)

Footnotes, Chapter 13:
(180) GM.1070. (confidential) Stephen Broad to Gilbert Lee, 1st April 1955.
(181) Legislative Council Meeting 28th March, 1955 Questions 32 & 33 by J R Kynaston.
(182) AA/16/195/55 VK Joshi to Stephen Broad, 13th April 1955.
(183) GM. 1127/SE 16 Stephen Broad to VK Joshi, 25th April 1955.
(184) Minutes of Aden Airways Board Meeting, 28th May 1955.
(185) Minutes of BOAC Board Meeting, 31st August 1955.
(186) Captain Spencer diaries.
(187) Ditto.
(188) Source Captain Spencer diaries
(189) Sources: BOAC Board Meetings 138, 139, 140 and 141.

Captain Jack Lawson handing over ship's papers to Abdul Rahim at Aden in February 1956. Engineer Volpe is on the right. (Vic Spencer)

Chapter 14 :
ADEN AIRWAYS 1956 - 1957

With the expansion of the oil exploration charters, an increasing amount of work was being flown out of Salalah. Marmul and Ghudu were two new sites visited for the first time on 3rd April in VR-AAM. The operation was basic and repetitive which had its advantages as exemplified on 4th April when F/O Lorrimer had to go off sick in Salalah and Vic Spencer took both the CO of RAF Salalah and the Aden ground engineer with him for 11 sectors around Midway and Duqam as his co-pilots. *"A good day, though very tired."* (190)

The Rapide now tended to be used only in an exploratory role. When a new landing strip was notified as being ready for use Vic Spencer would be sent into the Protectorate to check its suitability. On 14th April he flew the aircraft to Riyan and the next day he set out for Khareba from which he had to return as an inspection pass showed that the strip was still not ready for use. Later in the morning, an attempt to land at Shir had the same result.

On 16th April, instead of flying to Aiwa, he took a Land Rover in order to inspect it, though the drive there was so rough that it only reinforced the enormous difference air travel would make to these communities. Later that day on his return to Aden he flew into Qatn and on to Lamsoon in order to give the latter an inspection and approval for use by the DC-3.
"These days were different from the normal scheduled flights we did out of Aden; one became aware of the enormous benefit that we as an airline, and as individuals, could bring to these isolated communities in the Protectorates." (191)

The scheduled flights continued up the Red Sea to Jeddah and Cairo, but by now the General Manager of Aden Airways, Stephen Broad, was aware of the diminishing appeal of the DC-3, when compared to the Viscounts and CV240s of the opposition. He had been given a quotation from MEA for the hire of a Viscount which he proposed to use between Aden and Cairo, but BOAC put a stop to this for fear it would compete with their own Argonaut service. (192)

So the DC-3s soldiered on and during the Haj in June, after their trips around the Protectorates and elsewhere, the aircraft were used at night to fly between Aden and Jeddah. On normal flights up to Cairo the service was conducted in daylight with the advantage that coastline could be easily seen on one side or the other. At night, though, it was a different matter and the navigation was somewhat more challenging due to the few aids available:

8 July *"Back to Aden from Jeddah, good run but no fix all the way."*
9 July *"Flew up to Jeddah at night. Good trip but completely lost for most of the way."*
10 July *"Back from Jeddah, good run but again no fix all the way."*
(193)

A good moon and the absence of cloud made an enormous difference.

But the success of the Haj depended on the availability of the Indamer aircraft and the charter costs were particularly high during

Engineers working on a Pratt & Whitney engine at Khormaksar, March 1956. (Vic Spencer)

Right: Fernanda Rizzi and Alan Jennings at Asmara Airport, March 1956. (VS)

Alan Jennings and the doctor's wife at Beihan, September 1955. (Vic Spencer)

this season. Stephen Broad's attempts to modernise his fleet came to naught.

At this time, there were eight DC-3s in the Aden fleet and though the average utilization was only some four hours per day, BOAC seemed unable to appreciate the conditions under which the airline was obliged to operate, i.e. basic airfields, few landing aids, little infrastructure at many of the destinations and, in the case of the Protectorates, purely visual flying. The oil charter supply flights had no facilities whatsoever for night flying.

"Although limitation of flying to daylight and other reasons is a handicap, your daily utilisation of a little over four hours is less than one would hope for." (194)

Nevertheless, approval was given for the purchase of a ninth DC-3 and though Broad wished to purchase the aircraft which was on charter from Indamer for the UN subcharter in Kashmir, this was denied by head office. (Just as well since BOAC lost the contract in 1957).

During August, Duncan Cumming visited Aden and quite clearly there was a "meaningful" discussion between him and Stephen Broad on the role Aden Airways would play not only within the region but also in relation to the other companies in which BOAC had an interest, such as those in Bahrain, Kuwait and Beirut.

*"BOAC require the General Manager to make a financial success of the company within the limits of the present pattern of its services and with the fleet of eight Dakotas and two Rapides.
It is not intended that Aden Airways should be given four-engined equipment in the immediate future, but you will be considering the pros and cons of a partnership with EAAC to which Aden Airways would contribute if they had four-engined equipment to put in any pool based on EAAC."* (195)

The letter goes further to discuss Aden Airways' attempt to gain the contract supplying IPC (International Petroleum Company) from Azaiba (Muscat) into the interior of Oman.

"The development of aviation in Muscat depends on the result of oil exploration now in progress. If this is successful it is probable that the Ruler of Muscat will be asked to take an interest in Gulf Aviation and that Gulf Aviation will establish scheduled services from Bahrain to the new airport at Azaiba near Muscat."

In other words, Aden Airways was not to encroach in Gulf Aviation's territory if that would be contrary to the interests of that airline. In fact, Aden Airways did receive the contract and operated successfully out of Azaiba in much the same way as it did out of Salalah.

Finally, in terms of contradictory instructions, the following paragraph must have made Stephen Broad realise what De Graaff Hunter was up against in the early years of the company; Broad, however did not have the strength of character to resist.

"It is not intended that you should continue scheduled services which become uneconomic due to changed circumstances and competition from other airlines which have more advantageous operational patterns and more advanced equipment. At the same time Aden Airways' responsibilities as a common carrier under the

CHAPTER 14: ADEN AIRWAYS 1956 - 1957

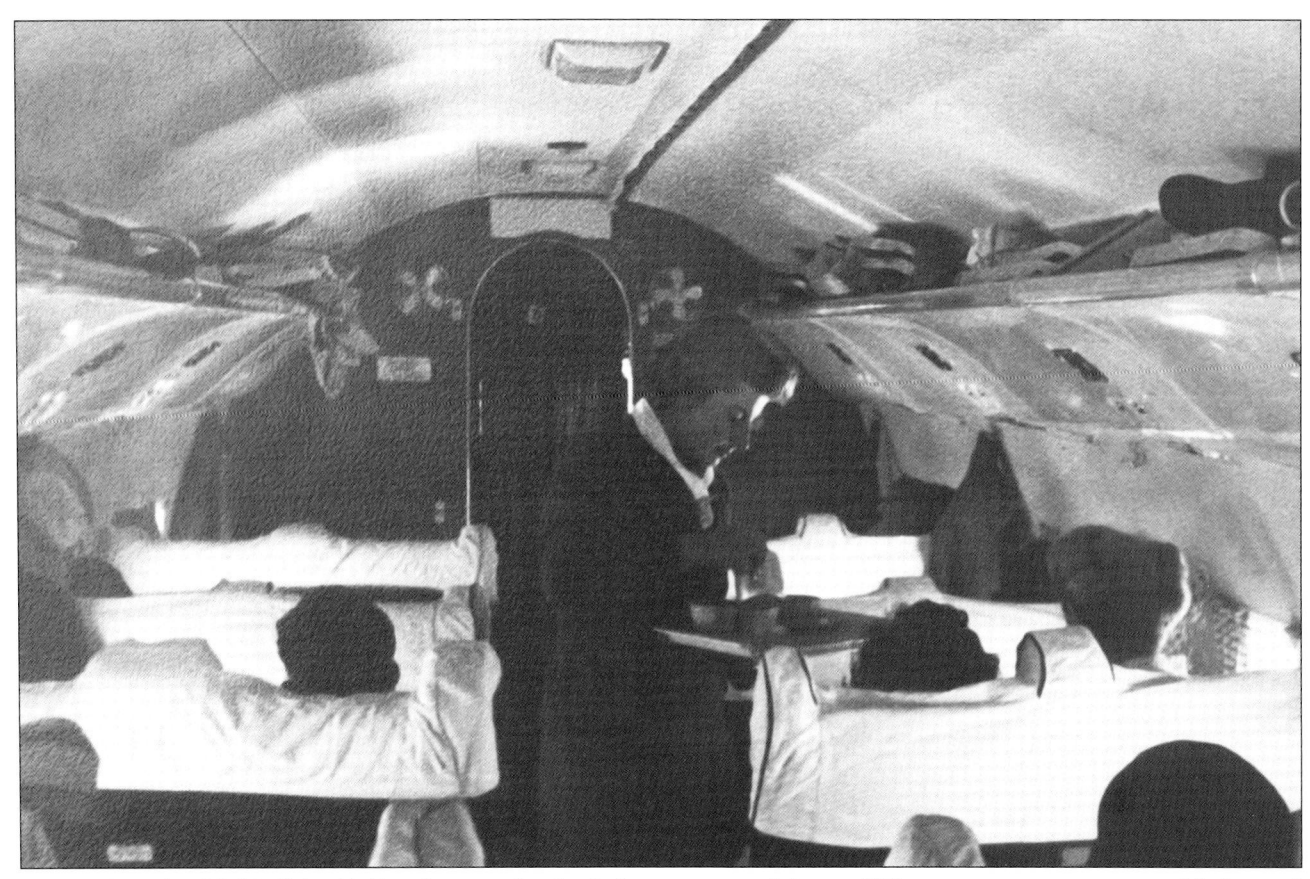

Interior of an Aden DC-3 in flight with Mary Spencer attending to the passengers, February 1956. (Vic Spencer)

monopoly granted to them by the Aden Government must be taken into consideration." (196)

This last statement completely ignored the fact that Aden Airways' profits were largely due to Haj charters, the carriage of Qat and the oil charters.

Further south there was oil exploration in Somaliland and Aden Airways had the contract to supply transport for the Amerada Petroleum Corporation. Because surface transport conditions were far better here than in the Protectorates, the Rapide was used a great deal more as its role was limited to casualty evacuation and the movement between sites of small numbers of personnel.

In Aden, casualty evacuation of injured troops from Dhala was a regular occurrence for which the Rapide was ideal. On 27th November Shell chartered the aircraft for a flight to Berbera and Hargeisa in order that executives could negotiate exploration rights. On 15th December the Amir of Dhala travelled from Aden to visit his territories i the Rapide, flown as always by Vic Spencer who received a large pot of honey as thanks.

Above, Western Protectorate services and below, Hadramaut and Somali services, May 1956. (Source: Official Airline Guide)

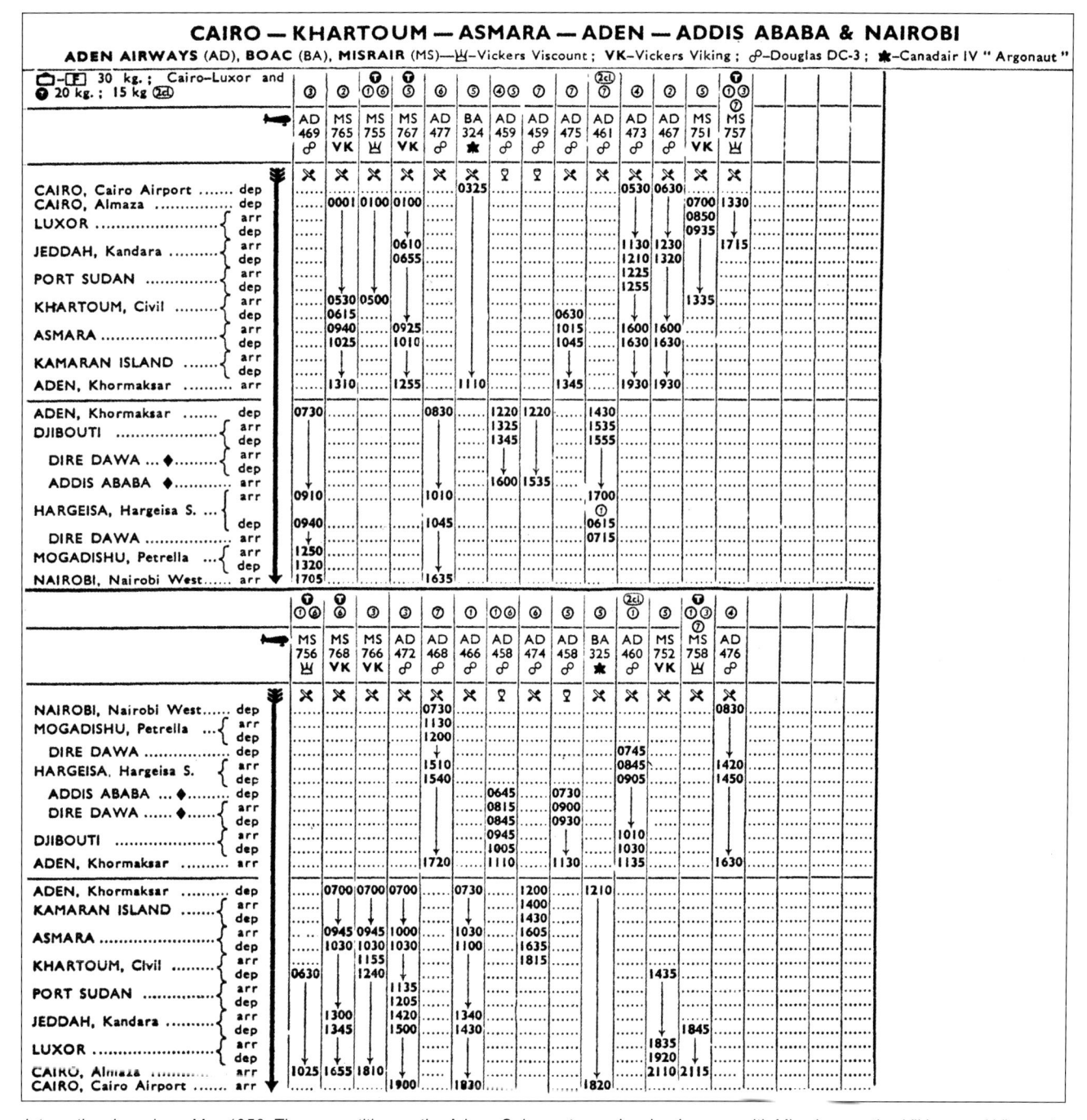

International services, May 1956. The competition on the Aden - Cairo route can be clearly seen, with Misrair operating Vikings and Viscounts and BOAC employing their Argonauts while Aden Airways were restricted to DC-3s. (Source: Official Airline Guide)

On 3rd December Shell chartered the aircraft to fly executives from Aden to Perim Island and on to Assab and Asmara. While it was employed flying this type of charter, there were none of the problems with performance which would come the following year, and the aircraft earned its keep.

On 26th July 1956, Colonel Nasser of Egypt had announced the intention that Egypt was to take over the Suez Canal and nationalise it. Britain and France were outraged, and colluded with Israel to wrest back possession of the canal. The Israelis invaded on 29th October followed by Britain and France on 31st October. It was an uneven contest and the fighting was over by 8th November.

For Aden Airways the repercussions were considerable. Though Cairo airport was closed by the fighting, it reopened fairly quickly to civilian traffic. However, all French and British airlines were banned from Egyptian airspace and this included Aden Airways (though not Arab Airways (Jerusalem) Ltd). They were now deprived of their most prestigious (and lucrative) route because Saudi Arabia had also closed its airspace to British interests and, while the company was able to increase its frequency to Khartoum (for onward flight to Europe), this did not compensate for the loss of the Red Sea routes.

While this setback had given the company more opportunity to continue developing flights into the Protectorates, the lack of delivery of two DC-3s ordered earlier in the year had meant that more charters had to be made from other airlines which was an expensive option for the airline.

Nevertheless, on 23rd January 1957, Hamq was flown into for the first time by Vic Spencer in VR-AAK. At other destinations nearer to the border with Yemen, the loads were more frequently gasoline and ammunition, a reflection of the tensions created within the region by the events the previous year:

"Did Beihan with ammo and petrol. Asmara (flight) cancelled. Future for Adenair (sic) looks very bleak and no prospect of new aircraft or routes." (197)

COLOUR SECTION 2 C17

VR-AAA at Ghuraf, about to embark the local tribal leader, March 1957. (Vic Spencer)

Checking the magnetos. Performing a ground run at Djibouti after maintenance, March 1957. (Vic Spencer)

Las Anod, Somalia, exploratory drilling ground, May 1957. (Vic Spencer)

The drilling rig at Las Anod, March 1957. The Rapide came here frequently, usually for casualty evacuation. (Vic Spencer)

Mukeiras tribesmen watching the turnaround, August 1957. (Vic Spencer)

Nisab. A Bedouin waiting to load his camel. November 1957. (Vic Spencer)

Ataq. Two local boys come to see the fun, May 1957. (Vic Spencer)

French Air Force AAC 1 (Junkers Ju 52) visiting Asmara in January 1957. (Vic Spencer)

Vic Spencer on turnaround at Ataq, May 1957. (Vic Spencer)

F/O David O'Neill in the DC-3, March 1957. (Vic Spencer)

F/O Trevor Hamblin, March 1957. (Vic Spencer)

Captains Howard Benton and Dick Larcombe at Asmara in winter uniform, January 1957. Asmara, at 7,000 ft, was cold in winter. (Vic Spencer)

VR-AAI parked and unloading at Ataq, March 1957. (Vic Spencer)

COLOUR SECTION 2

An unusual sight, VR-AAM photographed from VR-AAO when flying from Salalah to Midway, May 1957. (Vic Spencer)

VR-AAO loading diesel fuel for transport up to Midway in the Hadramaut. (Vic Spencer)

Problems at Salalah with a flat tyre, May 1957. (Vic Spencer)

VR-AAM unloading at Party 2, having flown up from Salalah, May 1957. (Vic Spencer)

Over-flying an unidentified village near to Raudha in November 1957. (Vic Spencer)

Above: Aden Airways Air Mail label. (David Watson)
Below: Sheet of Air Mail labels. (Dacre Watson)

Timetable cover for 1st January 1961.

Above and below: Timetable cover and route map, 21st September 1957.

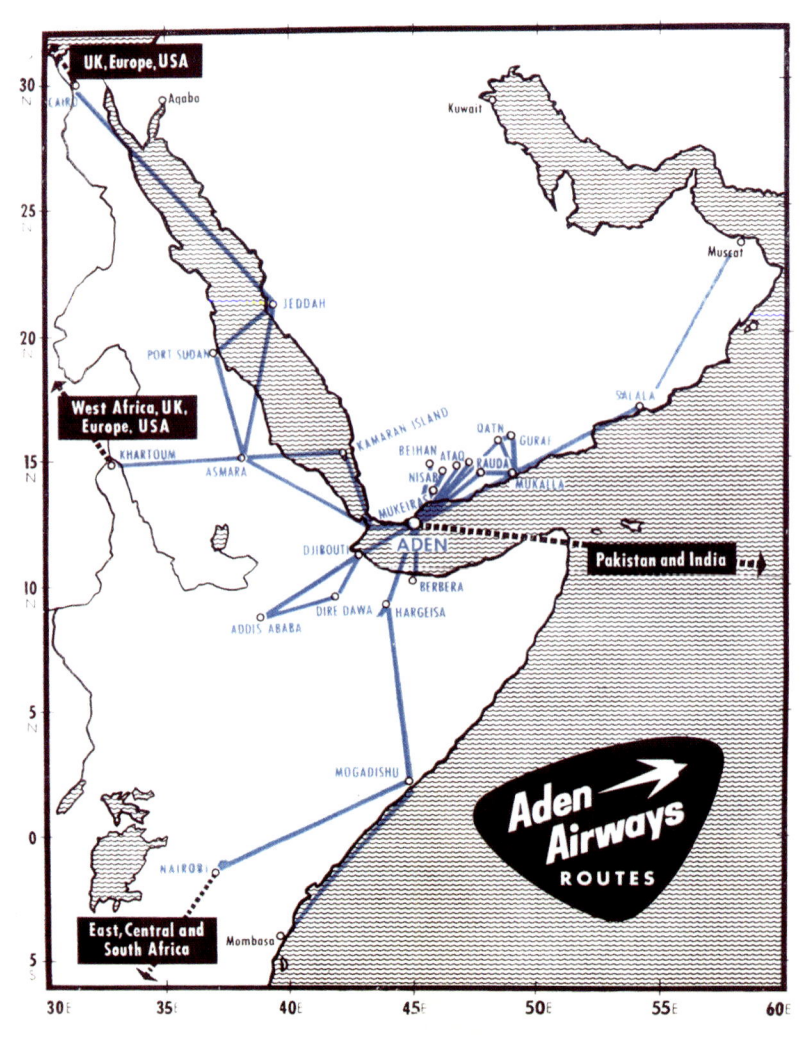

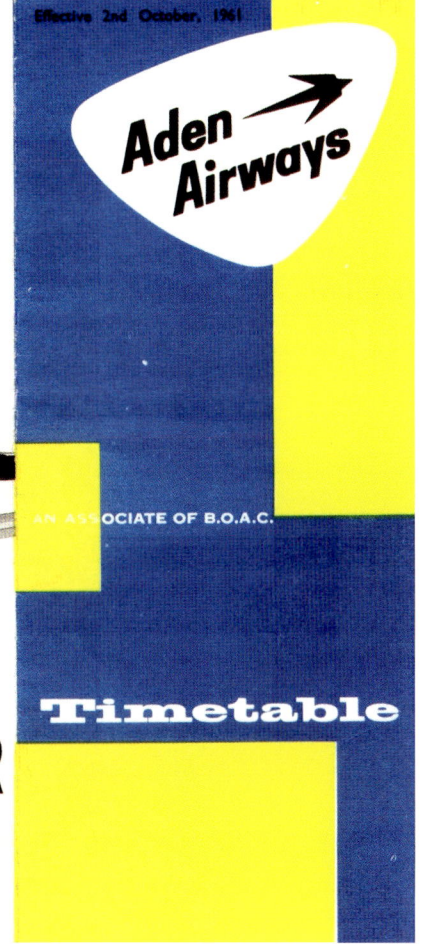

Colour Section 2 C21

Timetable cover, 2nd October 1961

Timetable cover, September 1963

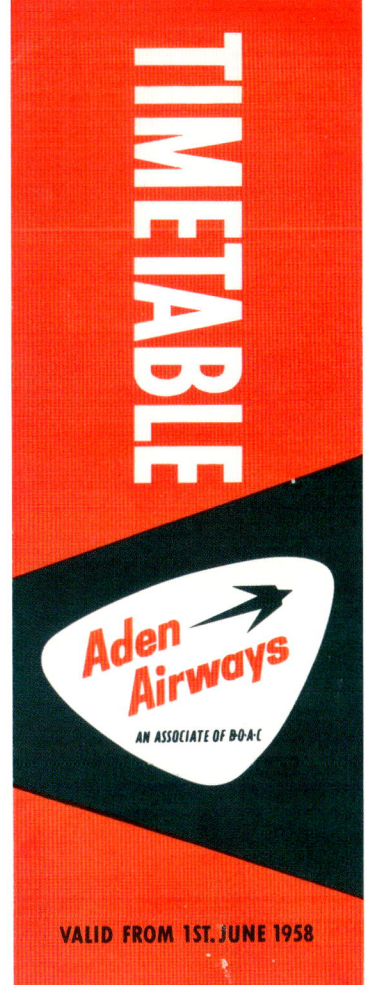

Timetable cover and route map, 1st June 1958.

Khormaksar terminal building from the apron, May 1957. (Vic Spencer)

Aden Airways staff apartments built in 1956. Cathay House, photographed in March 1957. (Vic Spencer)

Cathay House interior, March 1957. (Vic Spencer)

The terrace of Cathay House. Left to right: Syd Martin, Mary Spencer, Rise Martin and unknown. (Vic Spencer)

Vic Spencer at home with his Pi dog, Brandy, April 1959. He is wearing the uniform used when flying the scheduled routes out of Aden. (Vic Spencer)

Eric and Betty Borsberry at Goldmohur Beach. February 1958. (Vic Spencer)

Frank and Doreen Gouws at Goldmohur Beach, with Mary Spencer on the right, March 1959. (Vic Spencer)

COLOUR SECTION 2   C23

Unloading a jeep the hard way at Mukeiras in August 1958. The 'driver' appears to be about to reverse - but what happens next? (Vic Spencer)

DC-3 parked at Mafidh, April 1959. (Vic Spencer)

DC-3 by the walls of Mafidh fort. (Vic Spencer)

Mafidh town well, April 1959. (Vic Spencer)

The town of Mafidh in April 1959. (Vic Spencer)

Aden fishermen setting out, January 1959. (Vic Spencer)

Boy with fishing boat on Perim Island, January 1957. Located at the entrance to the Red Sea, Perim was an essential navigation fix before setting course up to Jeddah. (Vic Spencer)

Argonaut G-ALHR at London prior to delivery to Aden to become VR-AAR. (William Harrison)

G-ALHR newly-arrived on the Khormaksar tarmac in March 1960. (Vic Spencer)

Another view of G-ALHR after arrival in Aden. (Vic Spencer)

A fine shot of the Argonaut, its Merlin engines and the BOAC name "Antiope" still carried on the nose when it arrived. (Vic Spencer)

VR-AAI at Masirah, 1960. Note the RAF Beverley behind. (John Cork)

VR-AAM at Salalah in 1960. Capt Parker is on the left and the CO Salalah is on the right. (John Cork)

COLOUR SECTION 2

VR-AAT parked on the Khormaksar stand in October 1961. (Vic Spencer)

VR-AAF being refuelled at Khormaksar, December 1961. (Vic Spencer)

The RAF station at Masirah, 1960. (John Cork)

VR-AAA painted with "Father Xmas Special" titles for a special flight operated by Aden Airways in December 1960. (Vic Spencer)

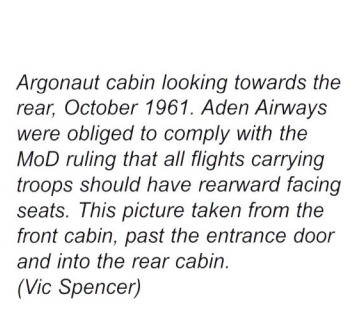

Argonaut cabin looking towards the rear, October 1961. Aden Airways were obliged to comply with the MoD ruling that all flights carrying troops should have rearward facing seats. This picture taken from the front cabin, past the entrance door and into the rear cabin.
(Vic Spencer)

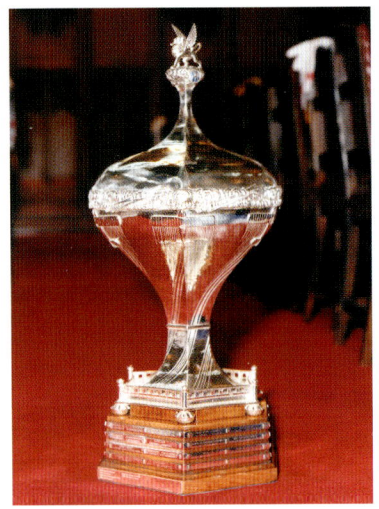

VR-AAN at Riyan with Vic Spencer wearing Protectorate flying uniform. (Vic Spencer)

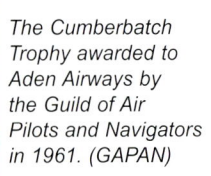

The Cumberbatch Trophy awarded to Aden Airways by the Guild of Air Pilots and Navigators in 1961. (GAPAN)

The Aden Yacht Club. March 1962. (Vic Spencer)

Argonaut G-ALHS flying south over the Alps at the start of its charter to Aden Airways in March 1962. (Vic Spencer)

Colour Section 2

AD-2, probably from early 1960s.
(Dacre Watson)

AD-5, early 1960s.
(Dacre Watson)

Arab Airways JO-2 of 1954.
(Dacre Watson)

Aden Airways, unclassified. (David Watson)

Air Jordan JO-10, about 1953. (Dacre Watson)

Aden - Khartoum flight AD474 baggage label about 1955. (Dacre Watson)

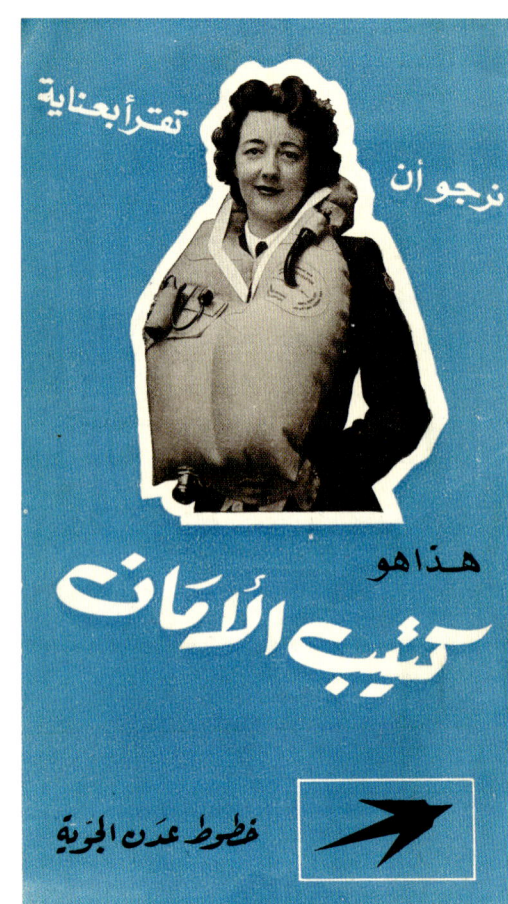

Above left: Aden Airways route map cover of 1960. (Dacre Watson)
Above right: Safety Card of 1958. (Dacre Watson)

Passenger ticket for an Aden - Mombasa forces leave charter, flight nos AD489/AD490. (Dacre Watson)

Aden Airways - the link between two continents. Practical route map in the form of a fan.

COLOUR SECTION 2

C29

Aircraft arrival at Ataq, followed by identification and sorting of baggage. July 1962.
(Dr Roger Green)

The Officers' Mess at Dhala village, 1962.
(Dr Roger Green)

The "Contractor's House", Ataq, 1962. (Dr Roger Green)

The fort at Ataq. (Dr Roger Green)

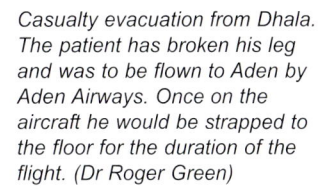

Casualty evacuation from Dhala. The patient has broken his leg and was to be flown to Aden by Aden Airways. Once on the aircraft he would be strapped to the floor for the duration of the flight. (Dr Roger Green)

A Beverley of No.48 Squadron, RAF, at Beihan in January 1963. (Dr Roger Green)

Argonaut VR-AAT on arrival at Nairobi in February 1963. (Dr Roger Green)

Below, left: Argonaut cabin looking rearwards in August 1963. The partition between the cabins has been removed. (Vic Spencer)
Below, right: F/O Robby Robinson on the Argonaut flight deck, August 1963. (Vic Spencer)

Above, left: F/O David O'Neill and un-named stewardess on the Argonaurt, September 1963. (Bob Wigley)
Above, right: Trevor Hamblin on the Argonaut, October 1963. (Bob Wigley)

A fine view of Aden as the Argonaut makes an approach to Runway 09. (Wendy Haden Sadler)

COLOUR SECTION 2
C31

Sue Russell escorting passengers across the tarmac at Khormaksar, 1963. (Sue Douet)

Below, left: Khormaksar Airport in 1963. (Wendy Hayden Sadler)
Below, right: Mogadishu Airport terminal building from the apron. (Wendy Hayden Sadler)

Aden Airways Argonaut VR-AAT on turn-around at Mogadishu Airport., 1963. (Wendy Hayden Sadler)

Below, left: Sue Russell who was a ground hostess from 1963 to 1965. (Sue Douet)
Below, right: Khormaksar Airport civil side in 1963. (Peter Pickering)

Loading awkward freight at Salalah c.1960. (Alan Elgee)

Refuelling at Salalah was an entirely manual task. (Alan Elgee)

Passengers from a British Eagle Britannia, probably a trooping flight, arriving at Khormaksar. (Christine McIntyre)

The British Eagle crew passing VR-AAS on the apron at Khormaksar, 1962. (Christine McIntyre)

Hand-operated fuel pump at Salalah. (Alan Elgee)

The famous sign on Kamaran Island erected by the Governor, Major Thomson, 1962. (Christine McIntyre)

BOAC Comet 4 G-APDN on the apron at Khormaksar in 1963. (Alan Elgee)

CHAPTER 14: ADEN AIRWAYS 1956 - 1957

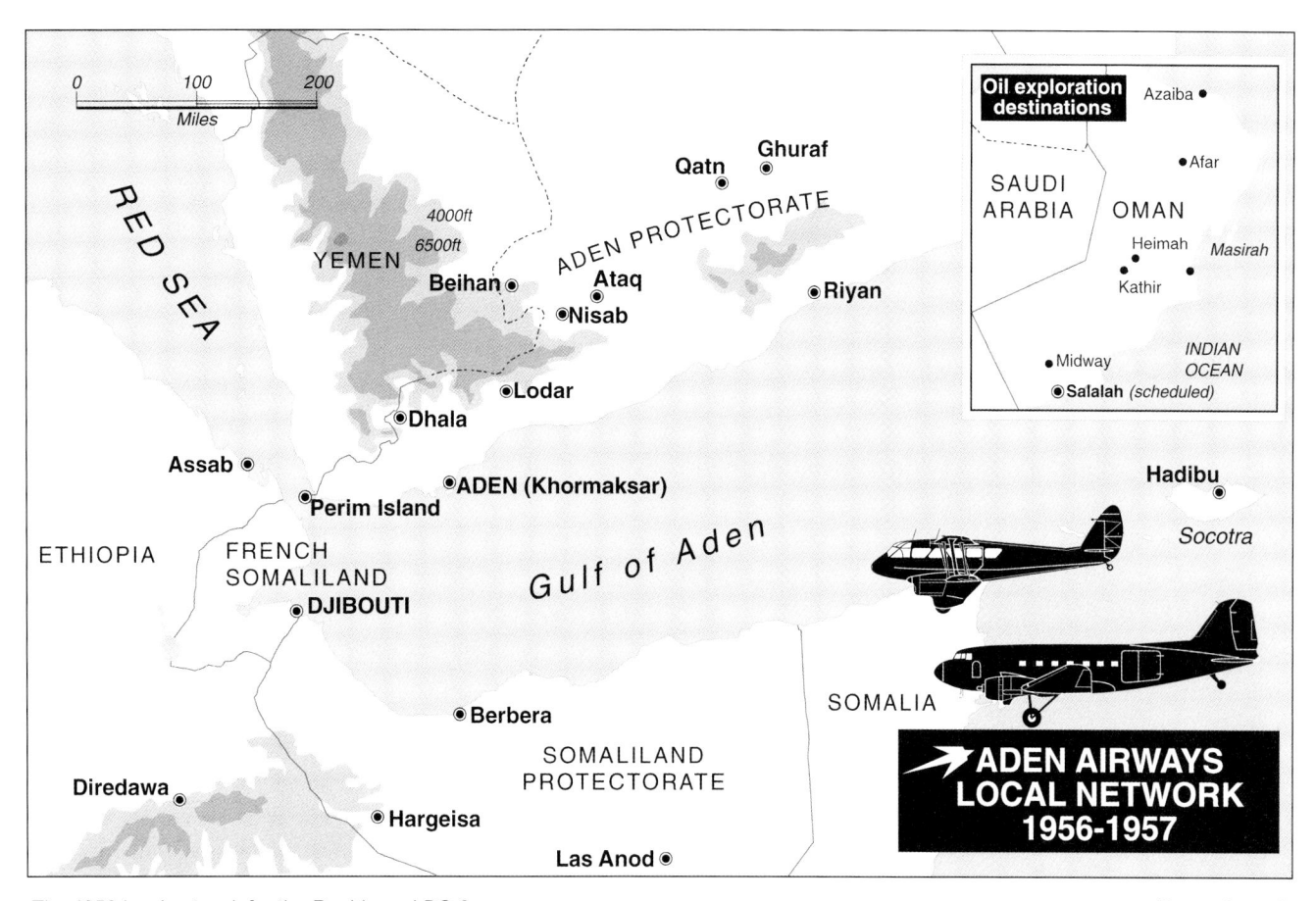

The 1956 local network for the Rapide and DC-3. (Roger Carvell)

This bleakness was shared by others of the expatriate employees. Not only could they not fly through much of the Red Sea, Misrair, EAL and EAAC were not only able to do so, but were operating much better equipment.

Profits had fallen dramatically and for the last four months of the financial year, serious losses were incurred. Much of the increased expenditure was as a result of moving base from Asmara to Aden, in particular the entire engineering function. The expatriate personnel moved into newly-built apartments along the coast southwest from Khormaksar airfield which were a pleasant surprise to most.

"Specially-built blocks of flats were built in Aden in 1956 on the East coast for the airline staff. The accommodation consisted of six blocks of two-storey apartments right on the beach from where advantage could be taken of the prevailing wind in order to alleviate the heat. Most people found them to be pleasant to live in." (198)

The new Aden staff apartments being built in November 1955. (Vic Spencer)

Footnotes, Chapter 14:
(190) Vic Spencer diaries.
(191) Conversations with Vic Spencer 2005.
(192) TA/113 letter from HWC Alger to Stephen Broad, 5th April 1956.
(193) Vic Spencer diaries.
(194) M.1963 Duncan Cumming to Stephen Broad, 22nd June 1956.
(195) Aden Airways Policy. Duncan Cumming to Stephen Broad, 10th August 1956.
(196) Aden Airways Policy, 10th August 1956.
(197) Vic Spencer diaries, 1st March 1957.
(198) Captain Harry Mills, reminiscences.

Rapide VR-AAL being refuelled at Kamaran, February 1956. (Vic Spencer)

Frank Gauws in the co-pilot's seat, March 1956.
(Vic Spencer)

Post-1955 advertisement for Aden Airways internal services.

ADENAIR – an important part of Aden's future

Aden Airways' internal services are an important feature of the Company's operations. They have played their part in the development of Aden's expanding economy by opening up large areas of the Protectorate to fast, modern transport, and providing the freight and passenger service essential to present-day commercial needs.

Aden Airways are proud to have played their part in the story of Aden's progress, and hope to play an increasingly useful part in the future.

ADEN AIRWAYS LIMITED

سافر
Aden Airways
AN ASSOCIATE OF B·O·A·C
خطوط عدن الجوية

Due to the lack of hangar space at Khormaksar, much of the lighter work took place outside early in the morning. (Brian Sears)

Chapter 15 :
ADEN AIRWAYS 1957 - 1958

During the last days of March, DC-3 G-AOJI was delivered from the UK to Aden to become VR-AAO. The F/O on that flight was Ian Stewart and his account of the delivery and indeed his recruitment to the company makes for interesting reading, giving an indication of the relaxed nature of Aden Airways:

"During January 1957, and being at that time employed by Air Charter (Freddie Laker) on MoD trooping contracts to the Middle and Far East operating Avro Yorks and DC4s, I was approached by Howard Benton, an earlier acquaintance from Hamble (AST) days. He proposed that I replace him as F/O on an Aden Airways DC-3 then sub-chartered to the UN in Kashmir. He had apparently been told that he could only leave the Kashmir job if he could find a replacement! After not too much thought (I was then regularly away from home more than three weeks every month) I agreed, was interviewed and accepted by BOAC Associate Companies and told to report to Blackbushe March 14th to meet Capt Harry Mills, then Chief Pilot, who would be ferrying an Aden Airways DC-3 back to Aden after major overhaul. We duly departed for Nice and a night stop and then continued by stages to Malta, Benina, El Adem, Wadi Halfa and eventually Aden.

After leaving El Adem, with Harry flying that leg, he asked me to go back into the cabin seated in which there were three or four other pilots returning from leave, and bring the navbag back up to the flight deck. Quite unable to find it, I was told by Harry to take control while he looked for it. "I'll find it. I brought it on board". Some time later he returned to the flight deck. No navbag to be found! "Can't understand it, I put it there myself". Situation a little fraught as no navbag and therefore no charts! Conference of all on board and the decision was made to continue on present south-easterly heading. As someone pointed out "if we keep going on this heading we're bound to reach the Nile – after all it's 4,000 miles long, we can hardly miss it!" Good thinking! We continued thus for several hours and eventually the river came in sight. Great relief all round until the question arose, "well, which way do we turn, north or south?" Good question, particularly as the fuel situation would shortly become critical and so far as we knew there were no other fields within range. No VHF contact at this stage and no beacon. We knew that the prevailing wind would have probably taken us north of track, so South it was and within ten minutes the lights of Wadi came in sight, it being pretty well dark by this time. During the landing run one of our tyres burst thus bringing to an end an interesting day which might possibly have ended very differently. Wadi Halfa incidentally is now under 20 or 30ft of water at the bottom of Lake Nasser. Contents of the hotel bar suffered a glancing blow that evening. We continued to Aden the following morning without further ado.

I spent the next ten days being indoctrinated into Aden Airways procedures and then went as pax to Karachi and on to Rawalpindi where the UN flight (UN351) was then based, accommodated in Flashman's Hotel (a name of some repute)." (199)

BOAC had for some time successfully bid for UN charters, though there was no obvious reason why they should have done so except

The UN mission at Srinagar was operated by Aden Airways on a subcontract from BOAC. The three crew members, from left to right Captain Frank Whittaker, F/O Ian Stewart and R/O McGarry, are seen here with the aircraft in the background. (Ian Stewart)

UN 351 is seen here at Srinagar. The aircraft was actually leased by Aden Airways from Indamer of Bombay. (Ian Stewart)

possibly to give work to subsidiaries. The first charter was based in Beirut where the work was subcontracted to Arab Airways (Jerusalem) Ltd and another in Kashmir where the flying was subcontracted to Aden Airways. Having no aircraft to spare, Aden Airways hired a DC-3 from Indamer (believed to be VT-DGT) which they based in Rawalpindi together with a crew:

"The aircraft was at that time captained by Frank Whittaker with the support of a Radio Officer and a Ground Engineer. I joined them as the First Officer. We were based in Rawalpindi during the winter and in Srinagar in the summer months – it was under deep snow most of the winter. This arrangement was intended to keep everyone happy as Pindi was in Pakistan and Srinagar on the Indian side of the cease-fire line. This line had been established shortly after the British departure in 1947 when there had been controversy over which country Kashmir should join. The Maharajah had opted for India, he being a Hindu, the majority of people wished to be part of Pakistan as they were mainly of the Muslim faith. After one or two minor skirmishes between the two armies the UN was persuaded to establish a cease-fire line to be policed by military officers from various countries - Canada, Poland, Brazil, Indonesia amongst many others. One of the services carried out by UN 351 was to ferry departing and arriving officers to and from Delhi and Karachi. The flying was hardly demanding as, apart from these ferry flights, our other job was to fly every Tuesday morning between the two bases acting as a communications flight when weather permitted. The scenery, particularly when flying eastwards towards Srinagar, was quite stunning with an inspiringly wonderful view of the Western Himalaya with the great single peak of Nanga Parbat at nearly 26,000 ft standing out in prominent isolation.

Whilst in Srinagar in the summer of 1957 we lived on a houseboat originally on the River Jhelum, a tributary of the Indus, and later our boat was towed out to a mooring on Neguin Bagh (Lake). We were fortunate enough for a few months to live an idyllic life of fishing (trout in the streams), golf and mountain walking. Shikara wallahs (selling from small boats) brought us an endless succession of fruit, flowers, wood and ivory carvings, carpets and general groceries and virtually anything else that might take one's fancy. Sometime during midsummer the aircraft had to be flown to Bangalore for a major check taking three weeks. We were told to amuse ourselves as best we could until UN351 was ready for service so I decided to take off to Chittagong and stay with friends working with Burmah Oil. I managed to hitch-hike most of the way on various DC-3s of which, in those days, there were many, mainly on charter work, plying Indian skies.

Sadly for us, BOAC lost the UN contract when it came up for renewal at the end of the year – undercut by a bid from the Italian Air Force! We were told by Aden Airways to return the aircraft to Indamer, the original owners, from whom it had been chartered for the period of the contract. We flew it to Bombay and regretfully returned ourselves to Aden. Quite a shock to be pitched into the desert after the surroundings to which we had become used. Fortunately it was winter so Aden was not at its hottest and most uncomfortable. It could reach 45°C in midsummer. Very little air-conditioning in those days, generally just the main bedroom, otherwise fans and sea breezes were all our comfort. At that time all crew, in fact nearly all staff, were housed in comfortable flats near the airport and named after it as Khormaksar flats." (200)

There were two major events in the previous year (1956–57) which were to affect Aden Airways. The first one was the invasion of the Suez Canal area in November 1956 which served to unite the Arab nations bordering the Red Sea into banning all flights by UK-registered aircraft into those countries or indeed over-flying them, though Aden Airways was allowed to re-start flights to Jeddah in May 1957. The second issue was the breakdown of the bilateral agreement between Ethiopia and the Aden Government which resulted in the suspension of air services between Aden and Addis Ababa in June.

That said, the lack of suitable equipment for the longer routes such as these was always a handicap against the company, bearing in mind the Viscounts which Misr were now operating in the region.

Financially, the year was going badly for the company and in a letter to the MTCA, Duncan Cumming was forced to admit that:

"The losses sustained by the company from April to December of the current financial year amount to £56,698 and there is every reason to believe that the final figure will be substantially greater than this." (201)

Pilots' children, early residents at the purpose-built Khormaksar apartments. (John Lightfoot)

Chapter 15: Aden Airways 1957 - 1958

*F/O David O'Neill at Salalah.
(John Lightfoot)*

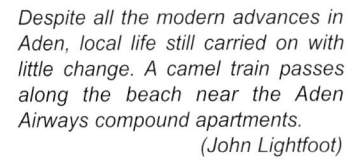

*Despite all the modern advances in Aden, local life still carried on with little change. A camel train passes along the beach near the Aden Airways compound apartments.
(John Lightfoot)*

However, there were glimmers of light and, while he suggested that profits would continue to be made on schedules and charters within the Protectorate and Somaliland, he was also concerned that, should Aden Airways cease to fly international routes, they might well lose the operating rights for the future. In fact, the MTCA were sympathetic to the situation (probably aware that no other British airline was likely to want these routes anyway) and Aden Airways was allowed to retain them.

To put the foregoing into perspective, most of the scheduled flying was now within the Protectorate and to the Horn of Africa. The oil exploration charters based on Salalah continued to expand, particularly to places such as Midway where up to seven return flights were made very day, taking up rig supplies, food and personnel. Masraq was a frequent destination for the same purpose while on 20th April 1957 Duqam, Alam and Azaiba (Muscat) were visited by Vic Spencer in VR-AAM before returning to Aden the next day via Duqam and Salalah. Other flights were via Riyan to Museifa, as Camp 2 was now called.

Not all the oil charters were into the Protectorate though; the Rapide was frequently flown into Somaliland via Hargeisa, a flight for which it was most unsuited because the high elevations at both Hargeisa and Las Anod where the exploration rigs were then placed. On 4th May the Rapide was damaged in a landing incident at Las Anod when it scraped a wing-tip in windy conditions.

On the other hand the Rapide based in Hargeisa had its uses in that it could be used as a cheap communications vehicle. For instance, on 15th May VR-AAI went unserviceable at Hargeisa on the run to Nairobi and the Rapide was used to fly back to Aden to fetch an engineer for the repair. Similarly, on 17th May, it was used to fly to Las Anod to pick up an injured oil worker and bring him to Hargeisa for onward transportation to hospital in Aden.

May is a bad time in Somaliland for weather; there are frequent thunderstorms with torrential rain which quickly renders dirt strips unusable, or at best treacherous. Obbia was an oil exploration site up on the Somali plateau at over 5,000 ft and subject to the weather conditions described. On 18th May Vic Spencer refused to fly there from Hargeisa citing the en-route weather and landing conditions at destination, and again on the 19th he refused to go in heavy rain.

Two days later, on a trip to Las Anod, *"I had a big run-in with Weathersby of Armadea over flight to Obbia."* (202) The next day he returned to Aden where he *"Saw Harry* (Mills, Chief Pilot) *re cable from oil company. I stated to him that we were unable to continue Rapide flying in Somaliland."* (203) The dispute rumbled on and BALPA became involved as time went on through May into June. *"Convinced now over Rapide operation and gave Alan Castle a note to BALPA if I am rostered out in the Rapide."* (204) In the end, the Rapide was withdrawn from use in July, though it remained on the register until September 1958.

There were, however, other hazards when flying within the region: *"An occasional stop en route to Nairobi was made at Hargeisa, the then capital of British Somaliland – now Somalia. A particular hazard here was created by the local tortoises which often took it into their heads to amble across the runway. As their shells were pretty well indestructible, striking one during take-off or landing caused the aircraft to make a most disconcerting leap into the air, becoming either prematurely airborne or experiencing a heavy bounce landing plus possible damage to the undercarriage. A lookout was normally posted to warn of this problem. This area also suffered from swarms of locusts at certain times of the year. To meet one of these whilst airborne could be a little disconcerting as the noise of the bodies hammering on the windscreens was deafening, but greater risk was of the blockage of the oil coolers under the engines and subsequent overheating calling for rapid descent and landing, sometimes on one engine."* (205)

While this dispute continued, the DC-3 operations to the Protectorate and Oman survived. Riyan and Salalah with their relatively good facilities remained the centres of operations for flights to Sahna, Azaiba, Marmul and Masraq in support of the oil exploration companies, but even then flights to the outlying strips could be fraught. Sahna was described as having a strip which was *"dangerously soft."* (206) Unlike today, Captains often had to make decisions based on their judgement and experience. Rules could be bent if the alternative would cost the company extra money in sending another flight to a particular destination. It was under these circumstances that Vic Spencer states in his diary for 14th June that at Beihan he *"uplifted an overload of 400kg"* in VR-AAA and in so doing he was aware of the potential consequences of an engine failure on take off.

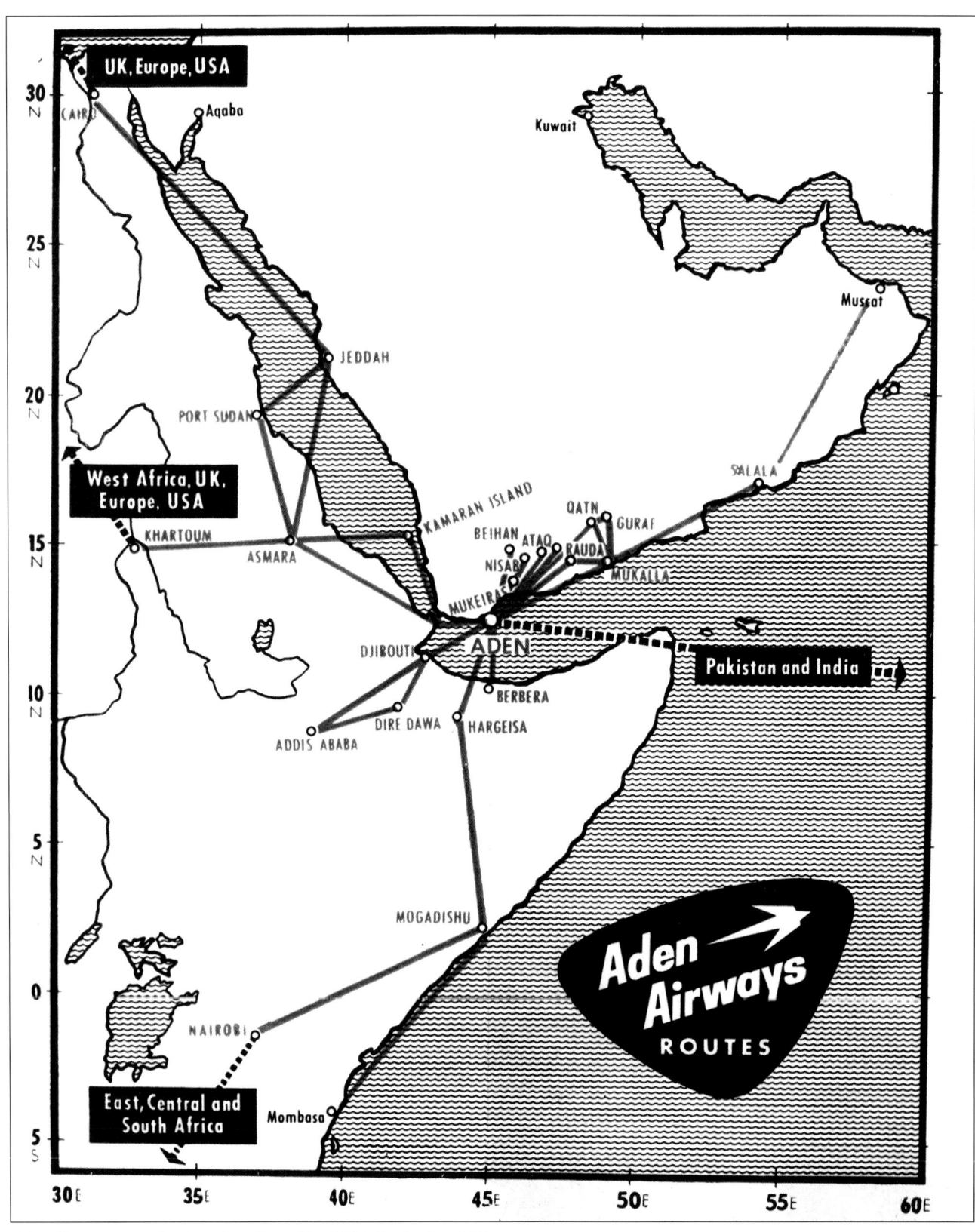

Aden Airways route structure, from timetable of 21st September 1957.

By 15th June the 1957 Haj had swung into its stride and any spare aircraft were fully employed in flights between Aden, Riyan, Asmara and Jeddah. The flights between Riyan and Jeddah were an example of a "needs must" approach. Legally, the flights should have proceeded down the Western Protectorate coast and past Aden to Perim Island before turning up the Red Sea to Jeddah. Instead the operation could be far more profitable if they were flown, illegally, direct from Riyan to Jeddah since *"this usually involved a night flight across the corner of Southern Arabia, crossing the Yemen mountains and by modern standards was a bit dodgy as the chances of getting over the hills in a loaded Dak in the event of an engine failure would not have been good."* (207)

As in previous years, the flying hours were high and for June Vic Spencer flew over 116 hours. *"Out to Jeddah and back via Asmara, 10.20 hrs. Now left with 8.45 hrs until 4th July, so no Jeddah tomorrow"* (208), stated with obvious relief.

The Haj was always different and *"produced good revenue for the company every year involving the carriage of pilgrims to Mecca – we actually carried them to Jeddah and brought them home again ten days later. This was known as the Haj and used most of the available aircraft over a period of perhaps two weeks each way. On these trips the passengers were always keen to know when we were within half an hour of landing as it was necessary for them to*

Chapter 15: Aden Airways 1957 - 1958

MAIN LINE SERVICES

AD.475x	AD.475	AD.475	AD.473	BA.230		DAKOTAS		BA.231	AD.472	AD.474	AD.474	AD.474x
Mon.	Sat.	Thurs.	Tue.	Thurs.								
				1700	Dep.	LONDON	Arr.	2050				
				2020	Dep.	ROME	Arr.	1625				
			0600	Fri.	Dep.	JEDDAH	Arr.	↑	1700			
			↓	0510	Arr.	KHARTOUM	Dep.	0950	↑			
0800	0800	0800		0555	Dep.	KHARTOUM	Arr.	0905		1750	1815	1745
1145	1145	1145	0940		Arr.	ASMARA	Dep.			1605	1630	1600
1245	1245	1245	1045	BRITANIA	Dep.	ASMARA	Arr.	BRITANIA		1505	1545	1500
↓	1420	↓	↓		Arr.	KAMARAN	Dep.			1330	↑	↑
	1450				Dep.	KAMARAN	Arr.			1300		
1545	1650	1545	1345	1000	Arr.	ADEN	Dep.	0700	1300	1100	1245	1200
								Sat.	Mon.	Wed.	Fri.	Sun.

A.D.481	AD.481	AD.469	AD.477		DAKOTAS		AD.468	AD.476	AD.480	A.D.480
Sun.	Tues.	Wed.	Sun.							
1730	1500	0700	0700	Dep.	ADEN	Arr.	1720	1705	2020	1750
1835	1605	↓	↓	Arr.	DJIBOUTI	Dep.	↑	↑	1915	1645
		0840	0840	Arr.	HARGEISA	Dep.	1540	1525		
		0910	0910	Dep.	HARGEISA	Arr.	1510	1455		
		1220	1220	Arr.	MOGADISHU	Dep.	1200	1145		
		1250	1250	Dep.	MOGADISHU	Arr.	1130	1115		
		1635	↓	Arr.	NAIROBI	Dep.	0730	↓		
			1635	Arr.	MOMBASA	Dep.		0730		
							Thurs.	Mon.	Sun.	Tues.

Mainline services, 21st September 1957. All times are local. Note that the BOAC London - Rome - Khartoum - Aden BA230/231 service is shown as operated by Britanias (sic).

change into clean white clothing before arrival, providing the stewardesses with some interesting scenes in the cabin." (209)

Once the Haj was over at the end of July, the company could concentrate again on operating to new destinations within both the Protectorate and Oman for the petroleum companies and for those communities that requested a service. Tufluk (alias Party II), an exploration site, was an extension from Riyan and first flown to on 18th September. Djibouti, Asmara and Massawa were sources of vegetable charters as was Assab.

On 22nd September a new service (AD 477/476) was started to Mombasa which for a while replaced the Nairobi service. The purpose of this destination was to cater for the increasing numbers of oil company employees who wished to have a holiday away from the heat of the desert or humidity of Aden. The route was via Hargeisa and Mogadishu, took some eight hours of flying time by DC-3 and while popular through lack of an alternative, was not a comfortable one.

In Oman, Ghubara and Heima were visited for the first time on 2nd November en route to Azaiba. From Salalah, Khasfa came on line on 11th January 1958, Salasil on 21st January and Ramlat Rkhot from Riyan on 29th January.

In Somaliland there was increasing activity out of Hargeisa in support of the oil exploration with visits to Buran (*"...found with some difficulty"* (210)) and Erigavo which became a regular destination as a source of labour for Aden.

Khartoum airport was undergoing repairs at this time, so it was temporarily closed to air traffic with the result that schedules were now flown to Wadi Seidna where the facilities were minimal.

However, back in London there were changes afoot which would bring the Company under increasing scrutiny and pressure in the forthcoming years.

CARAVAN CLASS SERVICES

ALL TIMES ARE LOCAL STANDARD TIMES.

WESTERN ADEN PROTECTORATE

AD.440	AD.462	AD.444	AD.470	AD.450	DAKOTAS			AD.451	AD.471	AD.444	AD.462	AD.440
Mon.	Tue. Thur. Fri. Sun.	Fri.	Mon. Sat.	Mon. Sat.				Mon. Sat.	Mon. Sat.	Fri.	Tue. Thur. Fri. Sun.	Mon.
0630	0630	0700	0600	1015	Dep.	ADEN	Arr.	1330	0915	0950	0840	1030
0710					Arr.	LODAR	Dep.	↑	↑	↑	↑	0955
0755	↓	↓			Dep.	LODAR	Arr.					0910
0810	0715				Arr.	MUKEIRAS	Dep.				0800	0855
		0805	↓		Arr.	NISAB	Dep.			0845		
			0715		Arr.	BEIHAN	Dep.		0800			
				1130	Arr.	ATAQ	Dep.	1215				

EASTERN ADEN PROTECTORATE, MUSCAT & OMAN-PERSIAN GULF

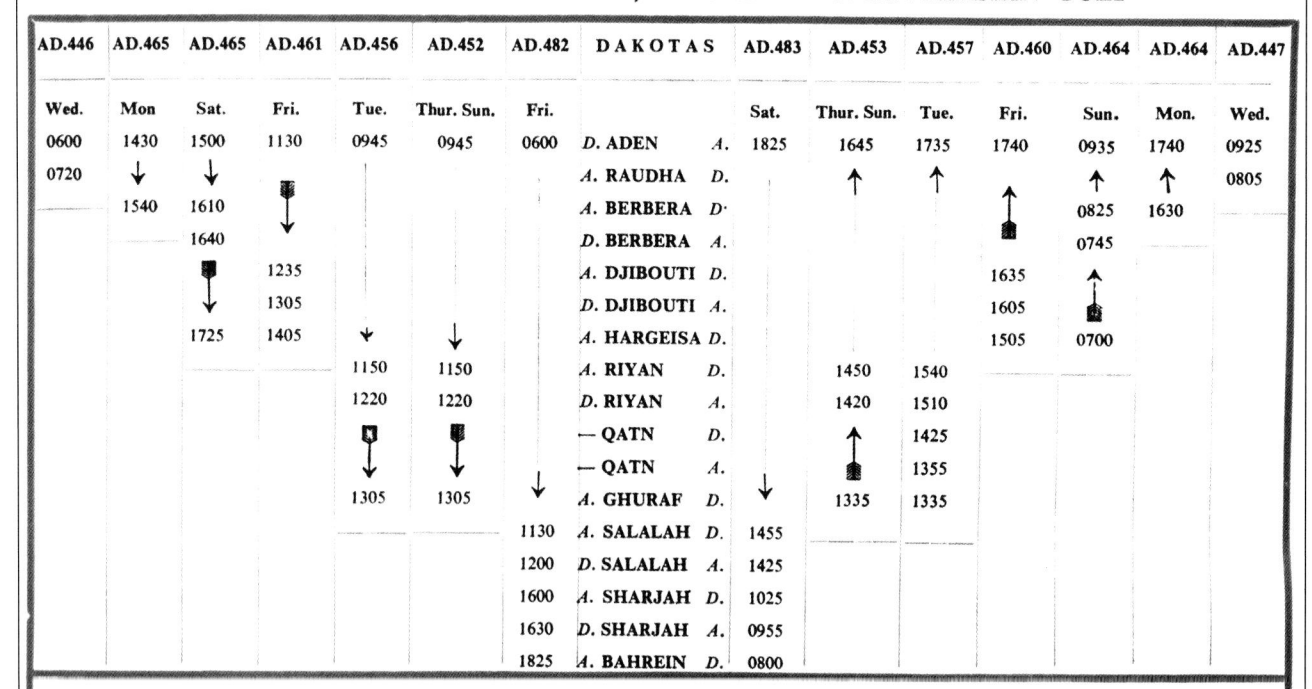

AD.446	AD.465	AD.465	AD.461	AD.456	AD.452	AD.482	DAKOTAS			AD.483	AD.453	AD.457	AD.460	AD.464	AD.464	AD.447
Wed.	Mon	Sat.	Fri.	Tue.	Thur. Sun.	Fri.				Sat.	Thur. Sun.	Tue.	Fri.	Sun.	Mon.	Wed.
0600	1430	1500	1130	0945	0945	0600	D.	ADEN	A.	1825	1645	1735	1740	0935	1740	0925
0720	↓	↓					A.	RAUDHA	D.		↑	↑		↑	↑	0805
		1540	1610				A.	BERBERA	D.					0825	1630	
			1640				D.	BERBERA	A.					0745		
							A.	DJIBOUTI	D.				1635			
			1235				D.	DJIBOUTI	A.				1605			
			1305				A.	HARGEISA	D.				1505	0700		
			1725	1405												
				1150	1150		A.	RIYAN	D.		1450	1540				
				1220	1220		D.	RIYAN	A.		1420	1510				
							—	QATN	D.		↑	1425				
				↓	↓		—	QATN	A.			1355				
				1305	1305		A.	GHURAF	D.		1335	1335				
						1130	A.	SALALAH	D.	1455						
						1200	D.	SALALAH	A.	1425						
						1600	A.	SHARJAH	D.	1025						
						1630	D.	SHARJAH	A.	0955						
						1825	A.	BAHREIN	D.	0800						

Notes:
(1) Free Baggage Allowance on Caravan Class services, with the exception of our AD. 482 - 483 Aden-Bahrein services, is 15 kilos - 33 lbs. (On Aden-Djibouti sector only Baggage Allowance is 30 kilos-66 lbs.)
(2) Passengers transferring from Caravan Class to Main Line Services and v. v. are not entitled to free hotel accommodation unless they are travelling on through published fares e.g. (Hargeisa/Aden/London & V. V.)
(3) Our AD 482-483 Bahrein services, are "B" class. Hostess-Steward and Bar facilities are available. Baggage Allowance is 30 Kilos.

Caravan Class services, timetable of 21st September 1957.

Creation of BOAC. Associated Companies (BOAC.AC)

In October Aden Airways, together with all the other subsidiary companies, came under "new management" so to speak.

During 1951 the BOAC Board had become increasingly concerned at the amount of time it had to spend on subsidiary companies' affairs, often to the detriment of running BOAC itself. A report was commissioned which recommended that one full-time executive would be responsible for the subsidiary companies and he would report to the BOAC Board. In February 1952, Captain V Wolfson was appointed General Manager: Subsidiaries (GMS) and he continued in this position until his death in a Comet crash in February 1954. The vacancy created by his death was not filled, but instead Gilbert Lee was appointed to the new position of London Manager Subsidiaries (LMS).

Even then the many companies proved to be unwieldy and a decision was made that those subsidiary companies located in the Middle East – Aden Airways, Arab Airways, British International Airlines, Gulf Aviation and Middle East Airlines would all come under one umbrella named Associated British Airlines (Middle East) Ltd (ABAMEL). Also included was a maintenance company, Mideast Aircraft Service Company (MASCO) which was intended both to service the aircraft of these companies and to buy aircraft for leasing.

Chapter 15: Aden Airways 1957 - 1958

Mr Harvey, BOAC Station Engineer at Khormaksar, descends from Argonaut G-ALHS, 1957. (Brian Sears)

ABAMEL came into being in September 1955 under the chairmanship of Sir Duncan Cumming, and the transfer of shares from the companies mentioned took place in November.

As in any reorganisation, there were some advantages to be gained and in the case of Aden Airways it meant that the losses being sustained by Arab Airways (Jerusalem) Ltd (in which Aden Airways had held a 49% stake) became the liability of the new company. Less successful was MASCO which never fully realised the purpose of its creation. There is no record of discussion of the investment in the engineering base of Asmara.

However, the original reasons for putting in place a separate profit centre, as outlined above, remained relevant in 1957 as senior BOAC executives were still finding themselves preoccupied by the minutiae of such a widely-scattered and diverse collection of companies.

In June 1957 Sir George Cribbett made a proposal to the BOAC Board suggesting that a separate company be set up, with a separate Board under the name of BOAC Associated Companies that would be responsible to the BOAC Board. The proposal was accepted and the new company was incorporated on 6th September 1957 and held its first meeting on 14th October of that year with Sir George as Chairman and Sir Duncan Cumming as Managing Director. This new Board then took over the day-to-day running of all the associated companies of which ABAMEL was one; however there was little need now for the latter company and it quietly ceased to exist in March 1959.

Major aircraft checks were now carried out by MASCO in Beirut and the first Aden Airways aircraft to be serviced in this way was VR-AAF which arrived there in late September. On 28th October Vic Spencer flew VR-AAA to Beirut, via Jeddah, in 9.15 hrs for a major check and to collect VR-AAF for the return flight to Aden.

The first meeting of the BOAC.AC Board took place on 14th October 1957 and one of the main points on the agenda was a discussion of a suitable replacement for the Aden Airways DC-3s. At the time the two aircraft under consideration were the Fokker Friendship with Rolls-Royce Dart engines and the Handley Page Herald with either two Dart engines or 4 Alvis Leonides piston engines.

"... none of these aircraft was sufficiently suited to Aden Airways' requirements to justify its replacement of the DC-3 at present operated. Meanwhile, however, the Chairman would endeavour to ascertain what, if any, operating limitations were likely to be placed on the DC-3 by the Ministry of Transport and Civil Aviation in the near future." (211)

These limitations on the DC-3 were due to be implemented by 1st January 1959 and would affect Aden Airways in particular, since it operated almost wholly from hot and/or high airfields.

Over the next series of Board meetings, the question of re-equipment frequently arose. The Aviation Traders Accountant was considered and discussed, as was the Leonides-powered Herald; the Airspeed Ambassador was also rejected on the grounds that it was too large and expensive to purchase at £150,000 per unit. (212) Once again, it appeared cheaper to modify the existing DC-3s to more powerful engines at £44,600 for each aircraft. In fact, at this stage it was calculated that purchasing four Heralds to replace six DC-3s would cost an additional £87,000 p.a. plus an introductory

Pilots at Salalah, 1957. *(John Lightfoot)*

DC-3 VR-AAO between tasks, 1957. *(John Lightfoot)*

cost of £100,000 in the first year alone. (213) Costs which such a small airline could ill afford.

These possible costs had become particularly relevant of late. Associated Companies had undertaken a financial review of all the subsidiary companies and while not alone, Aden Airways had suffered badly. In a letter to the MTCA, Sir Duncan Cumming commented: (214)

"The losses sustained by the company from April to December of the current financial year amount to £56,698 and there is every reason to believe that the final figure for the year will be substantially greater than this."

The letter acknowledges the loss of the routes to Cairo and Addis Ababa, but also points out that these two routes had already operated at a loss and, should resumption occur, it would only lead to a greater deficit.

A similar letter was also sent to Barney Dutton, the Aden Government representative on the Aden Airways Board, informing him that the only way the Company could stop the losses would be to *"reduce the scale of the company's operations in such a way that Aden Airways would become a local operator within the Aden Protectorate and Somaliland"* (215) which would mean a reduction in the fleet from six to four DC-3s.

There were good reasons for the losses. In addition to the loss of Cairo and Addis Ababa, in a dispute with Ethiopian Airlines the company had been prevented from flying to Asmara while the lucrative Qat traffic from Ethiopia to Aden had also been stopped by the Aden Government which did not wish to be seen aiding and abetting the trafficking of a drug. The loss of an oil exploration contract, Dhofar City Services, together with a reduction in pilgrim traffic had also contributed to a serious shortfall in revenue.

Some thought was given at the Board meeting of 11th March 1958 to replacing the General Manager of Aden Airways (Capt Alger) but this decision was deferred. Nevertheless, in contrast with a budgeted loss of £25,000, the final figures for 1957-58 were a loss of £124,709.

Footnotes, Chapter 15:
(199) Captain Ian Stewart, 1957-1960.
(200) Captain Ian Stewart.
(201) X.1641 letter to M Custanco (MTCA) from D Cumming, 5th February 1958.
(202) Vic Spencer diary, 21st May 1957.
(203) Vic Spencer diary, 22nd May 1957.
(204) Vic Spencer diary, 1st June 1957. This was in case he crashed and was killed.
(205) Captain Ian Stewart.
(206) Vic Spencer diary, 8th June 1957.
(207) Letter from Vic Spencer, 4th April 2004.
(208) Vic Spencer diary, 30th June 1957.
(209) Captain Ian Stewart.
(210) Vic Spencer diary, 11th February 1958.
(211) First BOAC.AC Board meeting, 14th October 1957 (1/14).
(212) Third BOAC.AC Board meeting, 10th December 1957 (3/2).
(213) Fourth BOAC.AC Board meeting, 7th January 1958 (4/2).
(214) X.1641 letter to M Custanco (MTCA) from Sir Duncan Cumming, 8th February 1958.
(215) Copy of letter to B Dutton from Sir Duncan Cumming, 5th February 1958, presented to BOAC.AC Board 11th February 1958 (5/8).

VR-AAN in the new BOAC.AC colour scheme at Nisab, 1958. (Bill Harrison)

Chapter 16 :
ADEN AIRWAYS 1958 - 1959

After the high losses experienced by Aden Airways the previous year, the BOAC.AC Board decided that two of the eight DC-3s had to be sold. During April, VR-AAK was sold to British Aviation Services (Engineering) Ltd for £33,500 while Skyways Ltd had expressed an interest in the second one though, in fact, this DC-3 was retained by the company.

One of the main causes for the losses the previous year had been the poor utilisation of the existing fleet of eight DC-3s. While the Board had planned a reduction to four aircraft flying 2,000 hours p.a. each, it took no account of unserviceability or maintenance requirements, so it was decided that a reduction to six aircraft, also averaging 2,000 hours p.a. each would produce a more effective revenue rate if the extra work could be found.

The Aden Board had also proposed a budget loss for the coming year of £83,000 and they were promptly advised that this would not be acceptable. Shortly afterwards a new projected loss of £53,000 had been suggested which was accepted in London.

There were good signs of economic upturn as well, though not from a source one normally expects from an established airline. The previous year, the general consensus between the Aden Government, Aden Board and the BOAC Board was that Aden Airways should not be seen to be supplying a soporific drug to the population of Aden. Qat was officially banned in Aden, though obviously it did still arrive clandestinely, and the effect in loss of revenue to the Aden exchequer was so great that a tax of 6d per gallon (or about 5 pence today) had to be placed on gasoline.

Fortunately, the Government saw some sense and from 1st July 1958 allowed this drug to be flown in but only by Ethiopian Airlines, as it would not be seemly for the local airline to be involved. Fortunately, Aden Airways was later allowed to resume the services to Dire Dawa with a consequent large increase in freight revenues.

The scheduled routes were picking up as well, particularly the one to Bahrain. This service had been started on 27th September 1957 and was in response to the increasing numbers in the oil business who wished to travel between the two centres. It was a long flight and involved flying from Aden to Riyan (though it sometimes called at Salalah instead) to Sharjah (to avoid Saudi airspace) and Bahrain, a flying time of some 10 hours each way.

Generally speaking, Aden Airways flights flew without serious mishap despite the relatively primitive airports and facilities available, as well as the less than hospitable terrain overflown. However, an incident occurred on 13th April during flight AD 474 between Aden and Khartoum, via Asmara. About an hour after take-off from Asmara, Vic Spencer with F/O Bob Wigley in VR-AAN collided with a large bird which caused considerable damage to the nose radome and the aircraft had to make an emergency landing at Kassala, just inside the Sudan border. Fortunately once on the ground he was able to contact Aden on the aircraft HF radio, but the passengers and crew were obliged to spend an uncomfortable night as best they could since there were no facilities whatsoever.

Early the next morning, a relief plane flew in from Aden bringing a new radome and an engineer to fix it. The passengers transferred to the serviceable aircraft and carried on to Khartoum while the engineers repaired 'AAN which then took the remaining freight on to the original destination before flying back to Aden the same day.

By now, Vic had become one of the more experienced captains with the airline and it frequently fell to him to operate into and assess new destinations, particularly if they were for the oil companies, though the social intention of making the Protectorate villages more accessible had not been forgotten. On 17th April, two new destinations came up in the Eastern Protectorate, Mahfid and Ahwar, both of which came onto the schedules the following year.

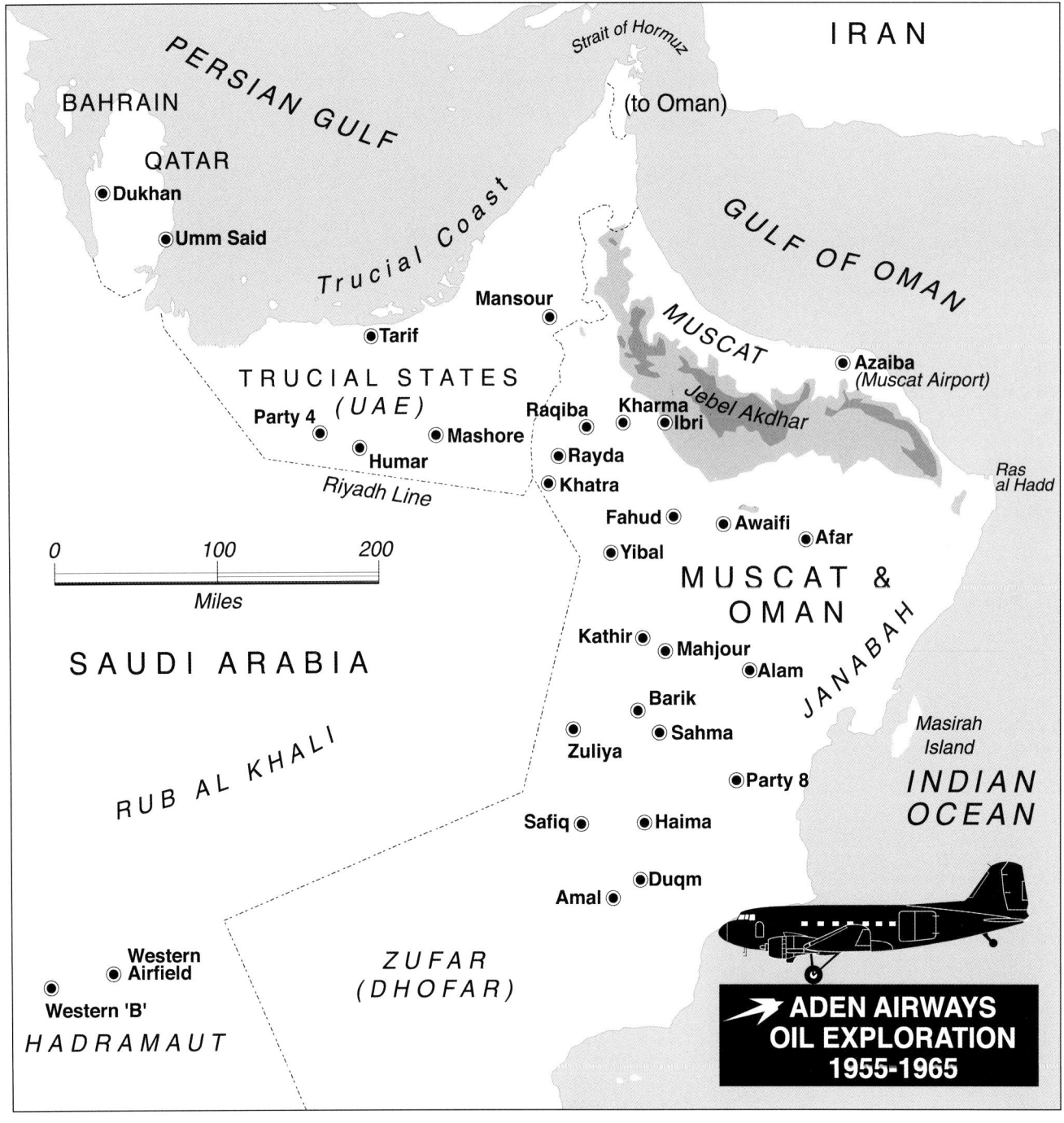

Map of oil exploration sites, 1955-1965. (Roger Carvell)

There was also a greater concentration in oil exploration in the state of Oman where operations were based in Azaiba, where Muscat is today. From late April Sauqira and Heima were opened to air supply, followed shortly by Gharb, Afar, Ibri and Dhahir.

"One trip enjoyed by most was the week spent in Azaiba just outside Muscat (now the site of the main airport). Each week an aircraft was despatched from Aden to be used in supplying the desert camps at which exploration, mainly for oil, was taking place. Apart from charts, which were not a lot of use flying over the desert, the only way to locate a camp was either by sighting a burning oil drum or hoping to be close enough for low-power NDB reception. There were occasions when both failed and we gave it a miss and pressed on to the next camp. Landings were made on the desert, nearly always flat and hard, wind direction given by oil smoke. Our arrivals with loads of laundry, mail, beer and newcomers always welcome, particularly to those being flown out. Load and trim sheets were somewhat cursory for these trips." (216)

Even here it is quite remarkable that there were so few mishaps. On 27th April, while landing at Ibri, the first stop of the day, the left wheel oleo lost all pressure and went flat. It would have been bad enough on a modern metalled runway, but in this case the operation was from rough desert floor from which only the larger stones had been removed, and on this particular day the aircraft had to continue to five more oil rig sites before it returned to Azaiba where it was repaired next day.

Somaliland was also opening up when a charter to Burhisso was made from Hargeisa on 29th May in VR-AAA, while a further charter was flown to Yagouri on 31st July in VR-AAN. Both charters were flown on behalf of Amerada, the oil and gas exploration group.

In August Captain Harry Mills, the Chief Pilot of Aden Airways, returned to BOAC on the termination of his secondment which had been unusually long. Captain George Dyer was selected to replace him, an unusual appointment as he had been one of the first recruits

Chapter 16: Aden Airways 1958 - 1959

after the decision by the company to seek pilots from sources other than BOAC. At the same time, it was recognised that with the large increase of charter work the job had become too much for one man, and Captain Vic Spencer was promoted to be his deputy.

The finances of the company, the source of much disquiet the previous year, had by now improved considerably. While it had been suggested that the General Manager, Captain W Alger, might be replaced, this proposal had been discarded and, instead, a new Chief Engineer had been brought in who had successfully brought the spiralling costs under control in that department. *"Engineering costs were being considerably reduced and the company hoped to carry out its own check IVs by October 1958."* (217)

Better news was on the way though. As mentioned earlier, Ethiopian Airlines had been given permission by the Aden Government to fly in Qat from Dire Dawa, though it still preferred at the time not to allow Aden Airways to be associated with this trade. However, once it was realised just how much profit was available from this market, and bearing in mind the parlous state of Aden Airways' finances, the Government relented. However, the Ethiopian Government was no longer prepared to allow Aden Airways to simply fly into Dire Dawa to pick up the Qat there and an impasse quickly developed whereby neither Government would allow the other's airline to transport the drug. Fortunately, a compromise was reached whereby EAL would fly the Qat load from Dire Dawa to Djibouti in a CV-240 where to be met by an Aden Airways DC-3 for onward transportation to Aden.

The first Qat flight under the new arrangements was flown on 18th August by Vic Spencer in VR-AAN: *"To Ataq with Bob (Wigley) and then to Djibouti for first load of Qat. Got 2,250 kg and expect 6,000 kg tomorrow."* (218)

There were problems in this arrangement; the EAL CV-240 would carry a greater load of Qat than the DC-3 so at times it would arrive in Djibouti presenting the Aden crew with a problem; either overload the DC-3 or leave some of the Qat behind where it would become useless if there was not a second flight from Aden soon after the first one. Often the EAL flights would be delayed or even not turn up at all. *"Up at 4.45 but again no flying. Later to Djibouti and waited 2.20 hours on the ground for EAL."* (219) Next day: *"to Djibouti with Bob (Wigley). Usual delay for EAL."* Later still, *"VR-AAM in (to Nissab) from Aden with new engine (for VR-AAO). Left them to it and took Mike (Scott) direct Nissab-Djibouti. Some trouble re Qat. Rather worried about overload. In Aden, tail-wheel broke and fell off."* (220) In the September accounts revenue was £15,215 above budget which was attributed to the carriage of Qat after the lifting of the ban.

Fuel drums at Salalah ready for transport to Midway.
(John Lightfoot)

Notwithstanding the improvement in the finances generated by the cost-cutting in the engineering section, together with the additional revenue from the Qat traffic (some £30,000 p.a.) the company finances were still in a fragile state. In a paper presented to the BOAC Board in September, Sir Duncan Cumming, General Manager of BOAC.AC makes the following observations:

"Examination has shown that economics of the order contemplated by the management will not be achieved and new Anglo/Ethiopian Bilateral limits the prospects of restoring revenue. The Company is therefore unlikely to become self-supporting because:- (221)

i) *its revenue is decreasing through restriction of routes*
ii) *its overheads were established at too high a level in the early years of its operations when it had access to revenue of which it has been deprived*
iii) *the transfer of its engineering base from Asmara to Aden has led to a substantial increase in maintenance and engineering costs. Experience indicates that Aden is an unsuitable place for maintaining aircraft*
iv) *its Dakotas are no longer competitive on external routes although they are the most suitable aircraft for the internal routes."*

EAAC had expressed an interest in adding the Aden Airways services to their own in return for a share in the Company. While on the surface this would appear to be an eminently sensible solution, there were other considerations to be borne in mind:

1. BOAC still wished to retain the traffic between London and Aden. Were EAAC to own 90% of Aden Airways then it, too, could expand onto the route and compete against BOAC.

The new Air Stewardess uniform, June 1958. *(British Airways Archives)*

A view of the Khormaksar parking area containing VR-AAF and VR-AAN, August 1958.
(Bill Harrison)

2. A vital consideration for BOAC was that if the Middle East and Eastern Mediterranean were to become closed to BOAC (as it had after Suez) then Aden would become a focal point in its new routings to the Far East and a new company under foreign ownership could block this.

3. While BOAC did not at the time envisage a route London-Aden-Bombay or Ceylon (Sri Lanka), it also did not want the new owner of Aden Airways to develop such a route.

As had always been the case, BOAC appeared unable to decide exactly what it wanted :

"By far the best arrangement would be if EAAC can take over the full control of Aden Airways leaving us with, say, 10% or 15% and agree, without compensation, not to open up a service either in competition or in partnership with us between Aden and London." (222)

Certainly, Aden Airways had an unwieldy cost versus revenue structure and one could arguably refer back to the days when de Graaff Hunter successfully reduced fares in order to stimulate traffic. But that was some six years earlier and the traffic and competition had matured in the meantime.

At that time, fares were calculated on a mileage basis and set by The International Air Transport Association (IATA). Aden Airways did not belong to this organisation with the result that it could charge whatever fare it wished. Bearing in mind the age of the fleet of DC-3s this made sense particularly within the Protectorate. However, the company also extended this policy to its international routes with the result that revenue was lower than it need have been. For instance, Aden to Hargeisa, a distance of 239 miles, was charged at £8 – 10s, 19% below the IATA fare and onward to Nairobi was £19-15s, 17% below the IATA fare. (223)

The consequences were that Aden Airways continued to be considered a second-rate operator picking up fares discarded by the other companies, an image which had persisted for some time. Still, the company successfully continued doing what it was best at: servicing the small settlements within the Protectorate.

By November, the talks between BOAC.AC and EAAC had broken down when the latter refused the conditions under which it would be obliged to operate. Also, MASCO, the engineering company based in Beirut and which was contracted to carry out major checks for Aden Airways, had not been successful either financially or technically.

At the same time, September 1958, the company in Aden advised BOAC.AC that the state of the Aden Airways hangar was causing serious concern and that it had become necessary, as a matter or some urgency, to carry out repairs and improvements. Indeed the ARB representative who had responsibility for East Africa, of which Aden was considered to be part, had intimated that maintenance approval might have to be withdrawn from Aden Airways if no improvements were made.

The result of all these circumstances was that Aden Airways and EAAC would explore the possibilities of establishing a centralised maintenance unit based in Nairobi. In fact this did occur insofar that EAAC became responsible for the major checks at Aden Airways and while the airline were short of an aircraft, EAAC would charter a DC-3 to them. In November VP-KLA arrived in Aden for a duration of six weeks.

By this time, there was room for optimism within the airline - Qat was producing excellent revenue while the charters were increasing in number and frequency. A third boost came when the airline was awarded a contract in October to carry RAF personnel to Mombasa on leave, a contract which would provide a regular monthly income.

The Mombasa flights were flown via Hargeisa and were generally about 7.30 hrs southbound and 8.30 back. Nevertheless, they were

Engine out: maintenance work taking place in the Aden Airways hangar at Khormaksar. (Brian Sears)

Chapter 16: Aden Airways 1958 - 1959

The condition of the Aden Airways maintenance hangar was criticised in 1958, Here, the DC-3 being serviced appears to have recently had the company name applied in Arabic above the English version. (Brian Sears)

enjoyed by the crews who, in addition to a night stop in pleasant surroundings, were able to bring back to Aden suitable quantities of meat, oysters and lobsters.

It is interesting to note that for the month of October the Qat traffic produced revenue of £14,828 for 130 hours flying and the Mombasa charter made revenue of £8,550 for 138 hours flying.

As so often seems to have happened to Aden Airways, just when things were starting to go well again, yet another problem raised its head.

When the airline was started in 1949 the flying manuals and procedures were taken directly from BOAC. Little change had occurred in the Flight Operations department during its first 10 years as the airline became more involved with flights into the Protectorate. Standard Operating Procedures are a relatively new concept in airline flying and they certainly weren't part of Aden Airways' operation during the 50s. *"We just flew as we knew how; we were doing 1,000 hours a year on short sectors and into airports and strips with which we were familiar. Co-pilots learned on the job and if we had an engine failure, we simply feathered the engine. Experience and airmanship were the common denominator and as far as I remember, we had no formal checklists."* (224)

However, once Aden Airways had been given the contract to carry RAF personnel on leave, the Ministry of Transport and Civil Aviation (MTCA) became interested in the operational aspects of the airline. Although the head office was in London, the MTCA also had a representative in Nairobi.

On 9th December, Captain R L C Branson, a Flight Operations Inspector from the Ministry of Transport and Civil Aviation arrived in Aden in order to carry out an audit on the company's operations. Vic Spencer records his visit (though he still used the term 'MCA'):

9th December: *"To office and hangar in morning and again at night over MCA Inspector scare. Worked till 10pm; hope for best tomorrow."*

10th December: *"To office with George (Dyer) and saw Branson of MCA. Complete Ops Manual to be re-written and spent most of the day in the office."*

11th December: *"Up early and to the office with George and Branson. Still going through the mill. Then to Khartoum in the evening. A relief."*

While the responsibility rested on the shoulders of Captain Dyer since he was, after all, the AOC holder, he was not best equipped to deal with the detail required by the MTCA; nor was he a mild-mannered man, so the vast amount of work fell upon the shoulders of his deputy, Vic Spencer, who over the next two months, spent his time in the office re-drafting the Emergency notes and

Captain George Dyer flying as a passenger during May 1955. In 1958 he became Chief Pilot of Aden Airways. (Vic Spencer)

Khormaksar: passengers walking out to board an Air India Super Constellation flight, 1959. (Colin Smith)

checklists as well as the Operations Manual and with only the occasional day flying.

By some coincidence, on 18th December he flew to Nisab where he had the opportunity to use his new Emergency Checklist when he had an engine failure on take-off but returned safely to Nisab on one engine and spent the night with his crew in the Government Guards Fort there. *"A hard bed and very basic"*, he records.

By the end of December, Captain Dyer had had enough and asked Vic to take over his job of Chief Pilot. It wasn't really within the gift of Captain Dyer to do this, but his recommendation would carry weight. In the end, Vic agreed that he would remain as Assistant Chief Pilot and oversee the introduction of all the new paperwork required by the MTCA, which now included the construction of Weight and Temperature (WAT) graphs for take-off weights at hot and high airfields as well as load sheets, not something the company had concerned itself with too much in the past. The manuals were eventually finished the following March.

Notwithstanding the jolt provided by the inspection of the operating standards by the MTCA, the company ended the year on a high note. Charters to Oman in particular were increasing with Ghaba, Rayda, Khama and Kathir becoming destinations out of Azaiba, Rujeima and Anaqein out of Salalah.

Financially and thanks to the Qat and military traffic, the company made a profit of £29,751 (after a loss of £103,000 the year before), but it did highlight the vulnerable conditions under which the airline operated.

Aden Airways advert for 'leave' services to East Africa.
(via Peter Pickering)

Fly with ADENAIR for your leave in East Africa!

A chance to spend a holiday in the world's safari centre is one which might never come your way again! From famous snow-capped Kilimanjaro to the warm tropical coast, East Africa is rapidly becoming one of the world's foremost tourist attractions, where a camera is all you need to capture the unique flavour of an entirely *different* leave!

Exciting East Africa is only a few hours away by Aden Airway's fast leave charter flights or regular scheduled services.

ADEN AIRWAYS LTD.
KHORMAKSAR
ADEN

FLY Aden Airways
AN ASSOCIATE OF BOAC

Footnotes, Chapter 16:
(216) Captain Ian Stewart.
(217) BOAC.AC minutes 10th Board Meeting, 8th July 1958 (10/12).
(218) Vic Spencer diary 18th August 1958.
(219) Vic Spencer diary 26th August 1958.
(220) Vic Spencer diary 18th December 1958.
(221) Paper presented to BOAC Board by Duncan Cumming, 11th September 1958.
(222) Report by Keith Granville to BOAC Board, 28th August 1958.
(223) Source: Comparison of International Fares (AC.11/10).
(224) Conversations with Captain Vic Spencer 2004.

Khormaksar Airport scene in 1959 with a DC-3 undergoing routine maintenance on the apron. (William Harrison)

Chapter 17 :
ADEN AIRWAYS 1959 - 1960

By April the frenzied activity in the office had abated. The manuals had been written to the satisfaction of the ARB and a new set of procedures set in place in which all pilots would have to undergo a route check on the aircraft once a year to any destination on the network. In addition to this, a six-monthly check would also be carried out on the aircraft at Khormaksar during which engine failures on take-off together with single-engine approaches and landings would have to be flown. Though these checks would not be carried out on passenger flights, they could be done on freighters and thus Vic Spencer found himself flying from Aden to Djibouti with the Chief Pilot, George Dyer, and experiencing a failed engine on take-off out of Aden, restarting the engine in flight to Djibouti and stopping it again for the approach and landing. On the return Vic checked Captain Dyer in the same way. (225)

A whole new department had to be created in order to carry out the checks regularly and it fell to Vic Spencer, as Assistant Chief Pilot, to organise and carry out the majority of these checks.

There was more to come. Normally the company's operating licence issued by the Aden Government would be for five years but on this occasion when the renewal was granted in June, it was only for a period of one year. *"The Aden Government had indicated that this limited renewal was associated with the absence of plans made by Aden Airways for introducing new equipment"*. (226)

This thinly-disguised ultimatum had a galvanising effect on the Associated Companies Board. At the meeting on 7th July, Mr J W Booth (227) was asked to expedite Aden Airways' recommendations as to the suitability of the Avro 748, of which they would require three. The other two aircraft which would be examined as well would be the Handley Page Dart Herald and the de Havilland DH. 123 with twin Gnome engines.

While this debate continued, the Haj season was about to start. By now most of the other airlines bordering the Red Sea had their own programmes for flying the pilgrims to Jeddah and Aden Airways was largely confined to picking up loads from the Protectorate and Somaliland. Aden was the hub to which pilgrims would be brought and from there the flights would usually depart during the late afternoon for the four-hour flight to Jeddah and return to Aden for early morning. There were two good reasons for this pattern, the first being that all the DC-3s were being heavily utilised on normal operations during the day and, secondly, the NDB at Kamaran Island was unserviceable at the time. This meant that flights to Jeddah had to leave Aden at such a time that daylight would still be available at the turning point at Perim Island which was located at the entrance of the Red Sea; an accurate fix was essential so that the aircraft could avoid straying into Yemen airspace with all the diplomatic consequences that would result.

Routes into the Protectorates also continued to be developed, though this type of flying was obviously more demanding than the normal schedules flown to Nairobi and Cairo. The only aeroplane capable of this type of operation was, and would remain, the DC-3.

"The flying was interesting and varied not to say challenging at times in that we were frequently taking off from and landing into short desert strips which took some finding with no nav aids other than a chart. Arrival was greeted as often as not by a fusillade of rifle shots from excitable tribesmen (generally not aimed at the aircraft). Passengers would at times bring aboard chickens, and goats were by no means rare. These latter caused our engineering department considerable problems as their urine would drain through the floor and cause corrosion in the control runs beneath the floor giving rise on occasion to unexpectedly heavy elevator and rudder controls. Loaded rifles were another hazard, no tribesman being willing to be parted from his gun on boarding. It was also not unknown for paraffin stoves to be lit in flight when the owner felt in need of a brew-up. We always carried an Arab steward on these particular flights, he usually being the only one of us who could communicate with the passengers and attempt to instil a little order and discipline.

One particular trip involved flying about 100 miles inland from the coast and landing on the pancake-flat floor of the Wadi Hadramaut. This wadi was some 250 miles long, ran parallel to

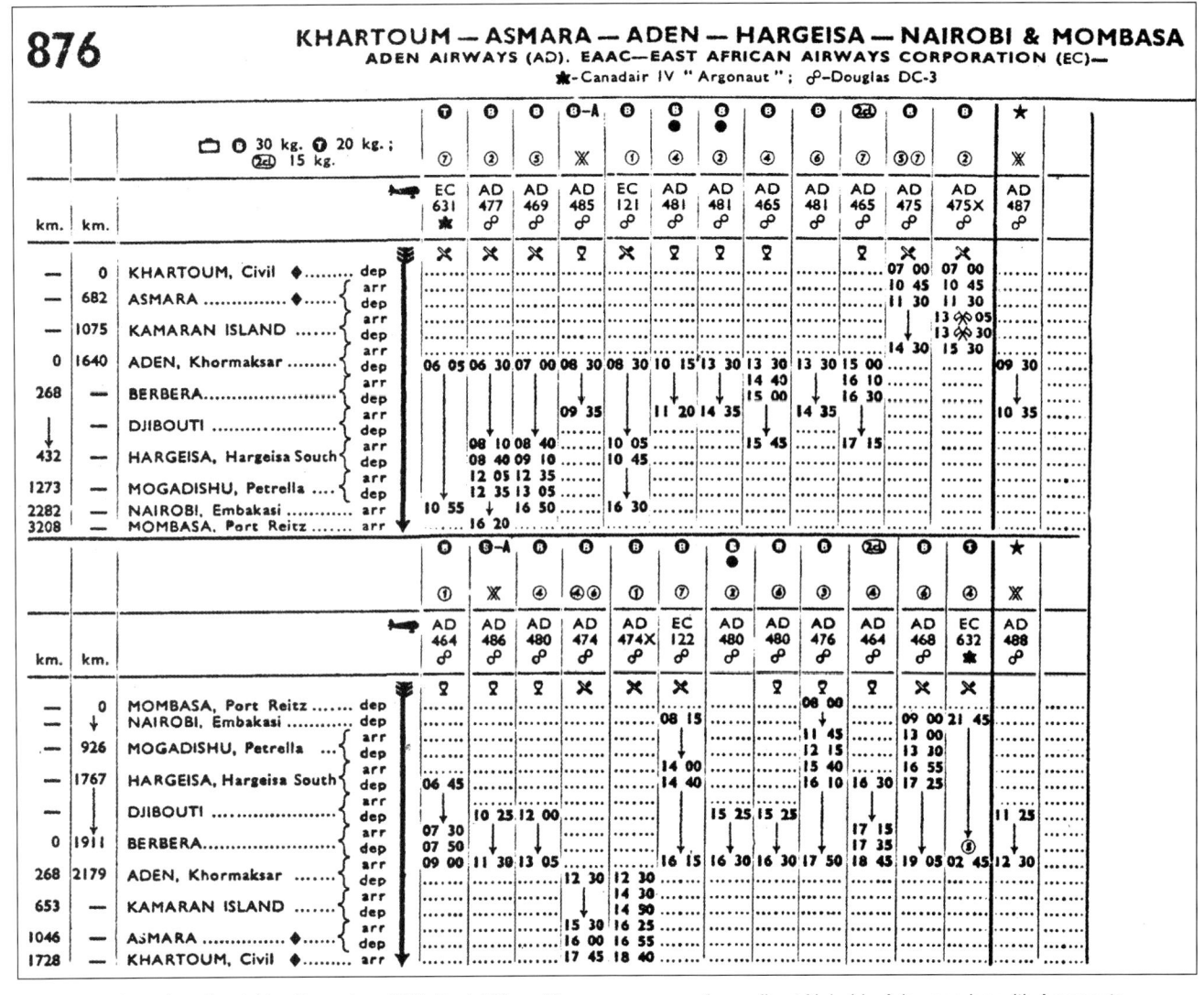

876 KHARTOUM — ASMARA — ADEN — HARGEISA — NAIROBI & MOMBASA
ADEN AIRWAYS (AD). EAAC—EAST AFRICAN AIRWAYS CORPORATION (EC)—
★ –Canadair IV "Argonaut"; ♂ –Douglas DC-3

km.	km.			EC 631 ★	AD 477 ♂	AD 469 ♂	AD 485 ♂	EC 121 ♂	AD 481 ♂	AD 481 ♂	AD 465 ♂	AD 481 ♂	AD 465 ♂	AD 475 ♂	AD 475X ♂	AD 487 ♂
—	0	KHARTOUM, Civil ♦	dep											07 00	07 00	
—	682	ASMARA ♦	arr / dep											10 45 / 11 30	10 45 / 11 30	
—	1075	KAMARAN ISLAND	arr / dep											13 05 / 13 30		
0	1640	ADEN, Khormaksar	arr / dep		06 05	06 30	07 00	08 30	08 30	10 15 / 13 30	13 30	13 30	15 00	14 30	15 30	09 30
268	—	BERBERA	arr / dep							14 40 / 15 00		16 10 / 16 30				
↓	—	DJIBOUTI	arr / dep				09 35		11 20 / 14 35		14 35					10 35
432	—	HARGEISA, Hargeisa South	arr / dep		08 10 / 08 40	08 40 / 09 10		10 05 / 10 45			15 45		17 15			
1273	—	MOGADISHU, Petrella	arr / dep		12 05 / 12 35	12 35 / 13 05										
2282	—	NAIROBI, Embakasi	arr		10 55		16 50	16 30								
3208	—	MOMBASA, Port Reitz	arr		16 20											

km.	km.			AD 464 ♂	AD 486 ♂	AD 480 ♂	AD 474 ♂	AD 474X ♂	EC 122 ★	AD 480 ♂	AD 480 ♂	AD 476 ♂	AD 464 ♂	AD 468 ♂	EC 632 ★	AD 488 ♂
—	0	MOMBASA, Port Reitz	dep									08 00				
—	↓	NAIROBI, Embakasi	dep					08 15				↓		09 00	21 45	
—	926	MOGADISHU, Petrella	arr / dep							11 45 / 12 15		13 00 / 13 30				
—	1767	HARGEISA, Hargeisa South	arr / dep	06 45			14 00 / 14 40			15 40 / 16 10	16 30	16 55 / 17 25				
—	—	DJIBOUTI	arr / dep		10 25	12 00				15 25 / 15 25					11 25	
0	1911	BERBERA	arr / dep	07 30 / 07 50							17 15 / 17 35					
268	2179	ADEN, Khormaksar	arr / dep	09 00	11 30 / 13 05	12 30	12 30 / 14 30		16 15	16 30	16 30	17 50	18 45	19 05	02 45	12 30
653	—	KAMARAN ISLAND	arr / dep				14 90									
1046	—	ASMARA ♦	arr / dep				15 30 / 16 00	16 25 / 16 55								
1728	—	KHARTOUM, Civil ♦	arr				17 45	18 40								

International services timetable, November 1959. East African Airways was operating a direct Nairobi - Aden service with Argonauts.
(Source: Official Airline Guide)

the coast and contained several villages with multi-storey mud skyscrapers. The cliffs on either side of the wadi were at least 1,000 ft high. Not too difficult to find but a bit unnerving in the event of a sandstorm blowing up.

Mukeiras was one of the closest destinations to Aden being less than half an hour's flying away but it was also 7,000 ft above sea level (amsl) and close to the Yemen border where there lurked some fairly unfriendly customers. It was by no means unknown to find bullet holes in the wings and elsewhere on return. I believe one captain discovered after landing that a bullet had passed through the fuselage immediately behind his seat." (228)

The Associated Companies Board continued to give consideration to the DC-3 replacement for some time and by the time it was ready to make a decision both the Dart Herald and the DH.123 has been cast aside in favour of the Avro 748 equipped with Mark 7 Dart engines.

The DH.123 simply did not put forward the necessary improvements over the DC-3 to justify the cost; it was only 10kts faster and would offer only a marginal increase in payload, particularly from the hot and high airfields from which it would be required to operate. It was also limited in range so that payload would suffer on the longer sectors to Jeddah and Cairo.

Though the purchase price of the Herald was some £17,000 less than the Avro 748, its slower speed would result in higher flying costs in fuel and crews. Secondly, its payload, though at sea level marginally higher than the 748, would be reduced to well below the payload capacity of the other aircraft when operating from the important high-altitude airports of Asmara, Nairobi, Mukeiras and Hargeisa.

By September, the Board had come to some sort of conclusion as to what the equipment plans would be for the coming decade. The intention would be to buy three Avro 748s with Dart 7 engines which would operate beside a reduced fleet of three DC-3s.

The company could offer delivery of the Dart 6 powered aircraft in mid-1961 and the Dart 7 version during early 1962. There was a clear advantage in the latter aircraft in that it offered higher block speeds (190kts v 160kts) and greater payloads from the high altitude airfields which would adequately compensate for the higher costs involved. Also, as time went on and daily utilisation increased from five hours per day to just under seven, revenue rate was forecast to increase by some 30% in the third year. (229) On this basis it was decided to seek approval from the BOAC Board for funds to purchase the aircraft. The Herald was rejected simply on the grounds of operating costs which were calculated to be 5.5% higher than the Avro 748.

The problem, though, was that while the Herald could be delivered the following year, 1960, the 748 would not be available until 1961 at the earliest, and Aden Airways was coming under pressure once more to upgrade their equipment in the short term if they were not

Eastern Protectorate and Bahrain services, November 1959.
(Source: Official Airline Guide)

to lose the Service Leave charters to Central African Airways which had made a very competitive bid for them. It just so happened that BOAC had started to retire the Argonaut fleet and this was seen as the ideal short-term solution to the company's problems.

As if on cue, there was a further problem with the ARB surveyor from Nairobi. On 10th October, VR-AAF landed back at Aden with a load of Qat from Djibouti when a routine inspection was requested into all the paperwork pertaining to the flight as well as the aircraft technical state. The service was found to have been seriously overloaded on this occasion which was not reflected in the loadsheet information and the result was that the Inspector threatened to take legal action which might not only have cost the company a heavy fine, but could eventually lead to closure. As it was it could be shown that the error had arisen in Djibouti where poor weighing procedures were to blame, but the event was a salutary lesson and a reminder that the company would have to take its responsibilities more seriously if it was to operate more modern equipment in the near future. (230)

Even then the Company had a relaxed approach to training newly-arrived pilots. One such was Peter Austin, who joined as a copilot in August 1959:

"When I joined I was already rated and current on the DC-3, and last flew it with my previous employer about six weeks earlier. My training in Aden consisted of an instrument rating (duration 35 mins) and then straight out on service. When I was selected for a Command, I operated as P1 (under supervision) for the 12 sectors on May 28/29/30th 1961 prior to my promotion, followed by a base check of 35 mins on June 1st. I then operated six sectors in command on the same day." (231)

The request to the BOAC Board for capital sanction for the purchase of the three Avro 748s was made on 5th January 1960 (for delivery in July 1962) when a sum of £880,000 was requested for three aircraft at £218,400 each, three spare Dart 7 engines at £27,800 each and spares. To back up the request, figures suggested a surplus on 748 operations of £34,000 in the first year based on five hours utilisation per day, and £131,600 in the second year when utilisation would have built up to 6.7 hours per day.

During the first year the routes would be as follows:- (232)

Once a week to Khartoum and Nairobi; Bahrain; Ghuraf and Qatn.
Five times a week to Mukeiras.
Daily to Djibouti.

Together with charters these would amount to 5,488 hours per year. The 3 DC-3s would continue to fly into the Protectorate and to Djibouti for Qat.

In addition, the second year would see:-

Cairo and Ataq would be added twice a week and Hargeisa and Berbera once a week.

At the same time, two Argonauts were requested from BOAC with a third as an option. In fact, it was decided at the same meeting to order the third aircraft since few were now left; a number of UK airlines in the "independent" sector had purchased nearly all of them. The price was to be £102,000 for all three aircraft plus £50,000 for 16 spare Merlin engines which might seem a large number, but which were needed. (233)

On 31st October a party was held at the Crescent Hotel to celebrate the 10th anniversary of the founding of the company. By all accounts it was not a sparkling event and there was a great deal of uncertainty about the future. Financially, the previous few months had only been profitable as a result of the carriage of Qat and the future looked bleak – *"Not a very gay party."* (234)

When, in April 1960, it was announced that the Avro 748 had been ordered, the delivery date was too far in the future for any real excitement to be generated and many pilots feared that the

Mock-up of the Avro 748 in Aden Airways colours at the SBAC show, Farnborough, 1960.

Aden Airways first Argonaut, VR-AAR, with basic tailfin colour scheme.

company might have ceased to exist before then. Nor was the prospect of three Argonauts greeted with enthusiasm amongst the staff. Further disruption would be caused when the main runway was closed for strengthening, resurfacing and lengthening to 8,386 feet so that it could handle the heavier aircraft which were expected to pass through Aden in the future such as the Boeing 707 and DH Comet. The temporary runway of 6,000 feet would become a taxiway for the new 08/26 runway when the work was completed some nine months later.

It wasn't difficult to understand this lack of euphoria. The cheap offer from BOAC was not all it might have seemed as the Argonauts had been brought back into service as a result of the Comet 1 disasters of 1954 and were tired after being worked so hard (the last service flown by BOAC with the type was in April 1960 in G-ALHG). The airframes were of old design (from the DC-4) and the engines were Rolls-Royce Merlins which had first seen service during the war on Lancaster bombers. Nevertheless, their arrival would represent an advance of sorts in that they were pressurised and faster than the DC-3s to Nairobi, Mombasa and Bahrain. There were misgivings amongst the pilots summed up by: *"I hope for the best but fear for the worst."* (235)

Vic Spencer was asked to be Chief Pilot for the Argonaut fleet, and he would also keep his position as Deputy Chief Pilot of the company and fly the DC-3 as well. He and the other pilots who were due to convert onto the Argonaut started their course on 13th January 1960 under the care of BOAC instructors sent to Aden for that purpose. For those pilots involved, this was the first time they had been obliged to attend formal classes for an aircraft conversion and they were expected to study for eight hours a day and then again at home in the evenings, a work rate unheard of in that climate.

The first aircraft, VR-AAR, arrived in Aden on 18th February, 1960 and spent 10 days with the engineers and traffic staff to become familiar with the airframe, engines and loading techniques. After this it was available for crew training.

The Chief Pilot, George Dyer, had already been checked out by BOAC and was therefore the first to be qualified on the type, not only to fly it commercially, but also to help train the others, and it was he who operated the first Argonaut in Aden Airways livery when he flew from Aden to Bahrain via Riyan and Sharjah (AD482/483) on 28th February 1960.

On 1st March, Vic Spencer describes his first flight as *"a bit of a handful, but OK"*, though on 3rd March he wrote *"Ground school in the morning and the Argonaut again. Not doing so well. Did baulked take-off, 3-engine overshoots etc. Read notes in the evening"*.

On 4th March *"Beginning to feel very tired of Argonaut course. School in morning, flying at night. Not too well on 3-engine landing."*

However, the final technical exam was on 18th March and all but one passed that side of the course. After this, Vic resumed flying the DC-3 while some of the others undertook line operations on the aircraft itself when it had supplanted the DC-3 on the route to Cairo. Vic Spencer himself travelled to Cairo on the first passenger flight there in order to pick up a DC-3 from MASCO in Beirut (VR-AAB) after a C of A check. His departure from Beirut had to be delayed 24 hours by weather and when he did leave the next day, he had to return because of heavy icing while en route to Damascus. The contrast with the Argonaut was clear.

Khormaksar terminal building in 1959. (Colin Smith)

Footnotes, Chapter 17:
(225) Vic Spencer diaries, 31st March 1959.
(226) Report by J W Booth at 21st Board Meeting of BOAC.AC, 7th July 1959 (21/10).
(227) Associated Companies Board Member responsible for Aden Airways.
(228) Captain Ian Stewart.
(229) BOAC.AC analysis, 9th September 1959 (AC/22.4).
(230) Vic Spencer diaries 10-15th October 1959 and conversations 2004.
(231) Peter Austin joined Aden Airways in August 1959 and left to join Air Kruise in January 1964.
(232) BOAC.AC Board Meeting, 15th March 1960.
(233) BOAC.AC Board Meeting 15th March 1960 (AC.28/4).
(234) Vic Spencer diaries, 31st October 1959.
(235) Vic Spencer diaries, 30th December 1959.

Passenger unloading at Beihan, April 1960. *(British Airways Archives)*

Chapter 18 :
ADEN AIRWAYS 1960 - 1961 : ARGONAUTS

The arrival of the Argonaut in early 1960 gave great cause for optimism to the management of Aden Airways, but the realities were substantially different and the aircraft was to prove a constant drain on the company's finances.

It had been hoped that all three aircraft would be available for the start of the summer programme commencing on 1st April 1960. However, only VR-AAR was airworthy with the other two being obliged to have Check IVs completed before they could be delivered to Aden and, though the Aden to Bahrain (AD482) service was inaugurated on 28th February, most of the flying was being done locally to Djibouti and return in order to complete the training sectors as quickly as possible. Another reason for selecting Djibouti as a training destination was that the aircraft could be loaded up with Qat for the markets in Aden, thus saving several flights by DC-3.

Training was initially conducted by Training Captains on a temporary secondment from BOAC who also had the additional task of training and checking Aden pilots for that role. Captain George Dyer had completed his course in London, but by May 1960 Captains Jack Lawson, Pete Williamson and Vic Spencer had been trained and took over the responsibility. However, because the flight from Aden to Bahrain was direct, there was for some time a requirement for navigators, also on loan from BOAC.

The second Argonaut, VR-AAS, became available in Aden on 2nd May after its Check IV and flew its first service that day from Aden to Cairo via Jeddah (AD479) under the command of Captain George Dyer. Two days later VR-AAR flew the first Argonaut service to Nairobi (AD478) via Hargeisa and Mogadishu with Captain Mike Murray in charge.

While the arrival of the second aircraft gave some flexibility, it was 21st July before the third aircraft, VR-AAT, was ready for service and this delay had already created some dismay within the travelling public. The reinstatement of the service to Cairo on 2nd May was intended to herald a new period of better travel, but this had already been achieved by both United Arab Airlines with their Viscounts while Middle East Airlines were operating both chartered Britannias and Viscounts.

Later in the year, there were two flights per week to Cairo, one via Jeddah (AD472/473) and the other, a direct flight (AD466/467) departing Aden at 1630 and arriving in Cairo at 2245 in order to connect easily with the passing flights to Europe. The return flight departed Cairo at 2300 arriving in Aden at 0715 the next morning.

Similarly, Nairobi was to receive two Aden flights per week (there were an additional two flights by East African) with stops at Hargeisa and Mogadishu on the AD468/469 and only calling at Mogadishu for the AD480/481.

Service Leave charters would not be given to Aden Airways unless four- engined and pressurised equipment was available. With the Argonaut now in service this condition could be fulfilled and the first such charter departed to Mombasa on 4th July in VR-AAR under Captain Dick Larcombe. Flying time was five and half hours each way with the flight departing Aden at 0700 and returning at 1830. This was a particularly lucrative charter, providing some £200,000 revenue per year.

For the first few months of the financial year the company made good profits. The DC-3s in particular were kept busy on more local services across the Gulf of Aden to Djibouti, Berbera and Hargeisa as well as up into the Protectorates where regular schedules were flown to a number of settlements which, together with the RAF, had come to depend on the air services provided to Riyan, Salalah and Masirah Island.

"I made my first encounter with Aden Airways Ltd during my National Service in the Royal Air Force from 1959 – 1961. In particular, I remember flying from Aden's Khormaksar Airport during August 1960, to a small remote island called Masirah off the

Argonaut cockpit details, as exemplified on G-ALHX later VR-AAS:

Top left: *Captain's instrument panel, containing basic flight instruments such as ASI, altimeter, rate of climb, ILS, turn and bank, pitch and trim and directional gyro. The rudder pedals are hinged to provide hydraulic braking.*

Top right: *Co-pilot's instrument panel contains the same basic instrumentation as the Captain's with the addition of the fuel gauges on the right.*

Left: *Cockpit rool panel. Immediately above the windscreen in the centre are the four sets of engine monitoring instruments, with cabin heat controls to the left and cabin pressure gauges to the right. The main roof panel includes the internal and external lighting controls and the engine radiator switches.*

Bottom left: *Cockpit pedestal, on top of which are the duplicated throttle levers with elevator trim wheels either side and propeller controls between them. Radio controls are found in the centre and at the bottom is the autopilot controller. The lever to the left of this is for the landing gear and to the right is the flap selector.*

Bottom right: *Centre panel contains mostly rpm, fuel and oil pressure gauges, with the throttles and propeller controls visible below.*

(Vic Spencer)

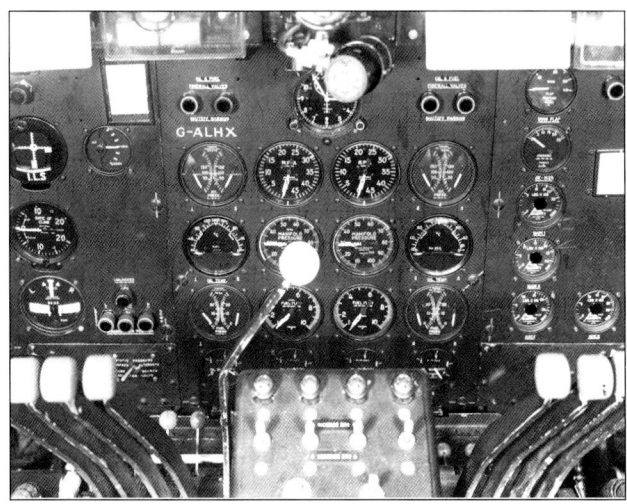

Chapter 18: Aden Airways 1960 - 1961 : Argonauts

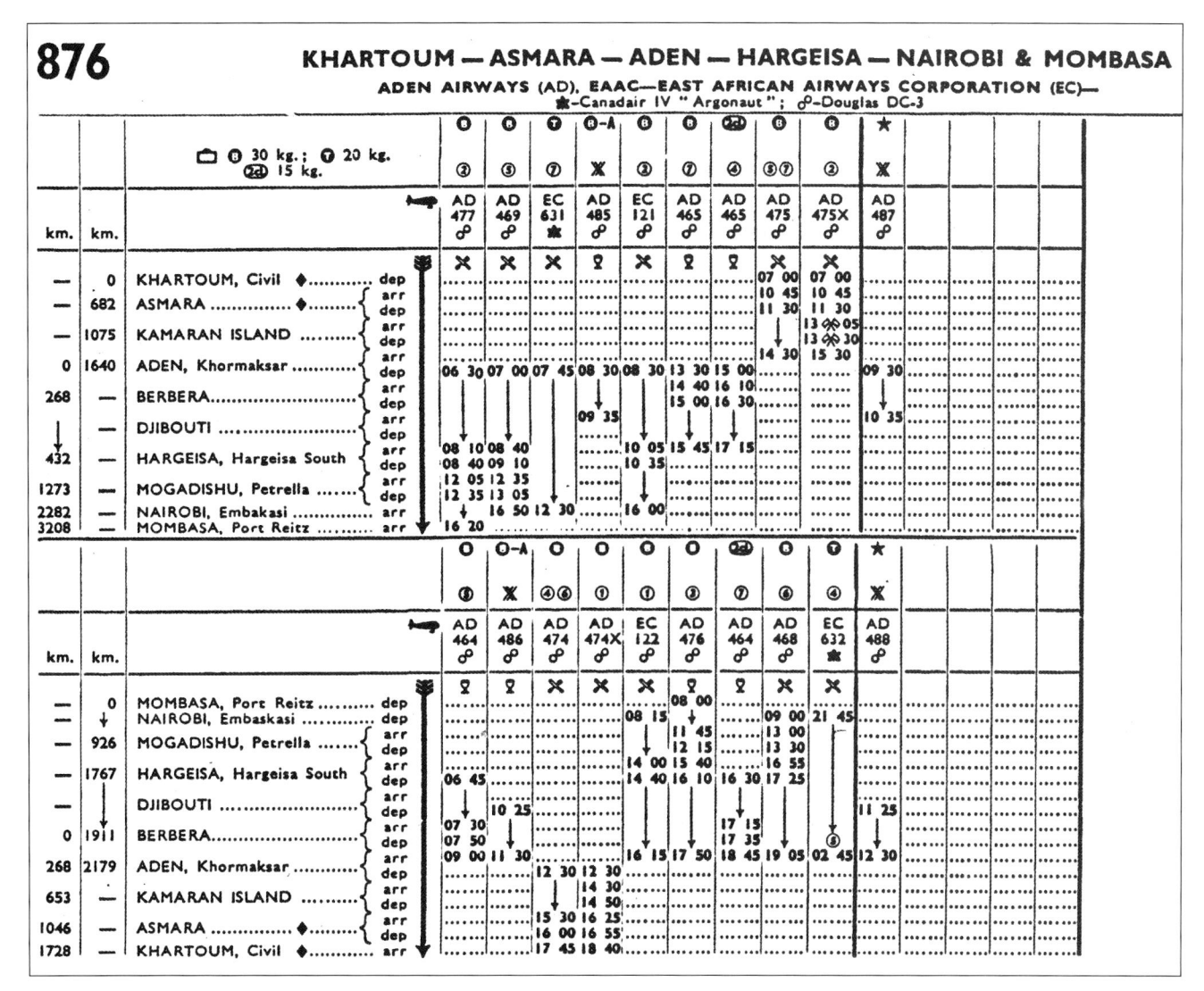

876   **KHARTOUM — ASMARA — ADEN — HARGEISA — NAIROBI & MOMBASA**
ADEN AIRWAYS (AD), EAAC—EAST AFRICAN AIRWAYS CORPORATION (EC)—
★-Canadair IV "Argonaut"; ⚙-Douglas DC-3

km.	km.			AD 477	AD 469	EC 631 ★	AD 485	EC 121	AD 465	AD 465	AD 475	AD 475X	AD 487				
—	0	KHARTOUM, Civil ♦	dep								07 00	07 00					
—	682	ASMARA ♦	arr / dep								10 45 / 11 30	10 45 / 11 30					
—	1075	KAMARAN ISLAND	arr / dep								13※05 / 13※30 ↓						
0	1640	ADEN, Khormaksar	arr / dep	06 30	07 00	07 45	08 30	08 30	13 30	15 00	14 30	15 30	09 30				
268	—	BERBERA	arr / dep						14 40 / 15 00	16 10 / 16 30			↓				
—	—	DJIBOUTI	arr / dep				09 35						10 35				
432	—	HARGEISA, Hargeisa South	arr / dep	08 10 / 08 40	08 40 / 09 10			10 05 / 10 35	15 45	17 15							
1273	—	MOGADISHU, Petrella	arr / dep	12 05 / 12 35	12 35 / 13 05												
2282	—	NAIROBI, Embakasi	arr	↓	16 50	12 30		16 00									
3208	—	MOMBASA, Port Reitz	arr	16 20													

km.	km.			AD 464	AD 486	AD 474	AD 474X	EC 122	AD 476	AD 464	AD 468	EC 632 ★	AD 488				
—	0	MOMBASA, Port Reitz	dep					08 00									
—	↓	NAIROBI, Embakasi	dep				08 15	↓			09 00	21 45					
—	926	MOGADISHU, Petrella	arr / dep				11 45 / 12 15			13 00 / 13 30							
—	1767	HARGEISA, Hargeisa South	arr / dep	06 45			14 00 / 14 40	15 40 / 16 10		16 55 / 16 30	17 25						
—	↓	DJIBOUTI	arr / dep		10 25						17 15		11 25				
0	1911	BERBERA	arr / dep	07 30 / 07 50							17 35						
268	2179	ADEN, Khormaksar	arr / dep	09 00	11 30		16 15	17 50	18 45	19 05	02 45	12 30					
653	—	KAMARAN ISLAND	arr / dep			12 30	14 30 / 14 50										
1046	—	ASMARA ♦	arr / dep			15 30 / 16 00	16 25 / 16 55										
1728	—	KHARTOUM, Civil ♦	arr			17 45	18 40										

Aden Airways international services timetable, May 1960. The Argonaut is not yet scheduled but does operate EAAC's Nairobi service.

Protectorate services in May 1960 showed that the Mahfid (AD454/5) links had been deleted. On the other hand the services from Aden to Riyan, Ghuraf, Sharjah and Bahrain remained exactly as shown on Table 1052, page 131.
(Official Airline Guide)

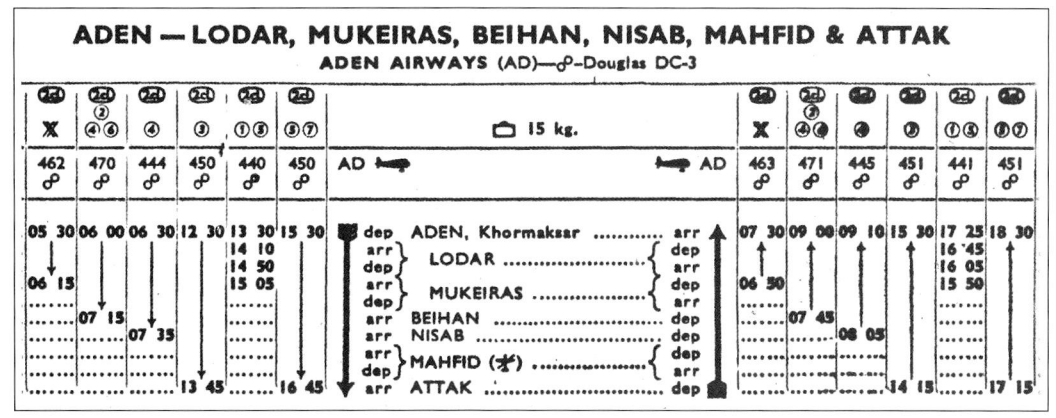

ADEN — LODAR, MUKEIRAS, BEIHAN, NISAB, MAHFID & ATTAK
ADEN AIRWAYS (AD)—⚙-Douglas DC-3

	462	470	444	450	440	450	AD			AD	463	471	445	451	441	451
dep ADEN, Khormaksar arr	05 30	06 00	06 30	12 30	13 30	15 30					07 30	09 00	09 30	10 30	17 25	18 30
arr/dep LODAR dep/arr				14 10 / 14 50											16 45 / 16 05	
arr/dep MUKEIRAS dep/arr	06 15			15 05							06 50				15 50	
arr BEIHAN dep		07 15										07 45				
arr NISAB dep			07 35										08 05			
arr/dep MAHFID (★) dep/arr																
arr ATTAK dep				13 45		16 45								14 15		17 15

coast of Oman, some thousand miles from Aden. The aircraft was a DC-3 Dakota of Aden Airways on charter to the Royal Air Force. While entering the aircraft at Aden I noticed a row of seats on the port side and a row of dustbins (attached) on the starboard side. These bins, I was told, contained fresh food and vegetables for the RAF stations on route, namely Riyan, Salalah and Masirah. Goods, mail and personnel were carried at least twice a week by these workhorses, commonly known as the RSM. For passengers on my flight there was myself and a replacement Commanding Officer for Riyan.

On one occasion on Masirah, an Aden Airways pilot (Mike Warrington) did a wonderful "beat up" of the Masirah control tower, much to the delight of those watching. The previous night in the Officers Mess he had been drinking a fair amount of alcohol which was not unusual in that part of the world. He was otherwise a very likeable character sporting a full black beard, as far as I can remember. However, the Squadron Leader CO at the time did not appreciate this and quite rightly sent a stiff note to Aden Airways Ltd reprimanding this pilot. It so happens that some time later this same CO finished his tour and was taken back to Aden by the same pilot. It was no surprise that it turned out to be quite a bumpy ride, more than the usual amount of turbulence." (236)

The oil exploration charters appeared to be doing well and the Qat traffic provided the second largest source of income after the service leave charters. Even the Haj was proving to be profitable with the Argonauts available from time to time.

Other interests were coming to the fore. On 1st July 1960, the independence of British and Italian Somaliland came into effect. Naturally the routes within Somalia, as it was to become, were

VR-AAS with the company logo on the fin and the Associated Companies badge below the registration.

cabotage which not only affected the route between Hargeisa and Mogadishu, but also those routes to Berbera, Burao and Erigavo. The drawback for the new Somali Government was that navigation aids and airports were rudimentary (though Aden Airways had been content to use whatever was available for a good number of years), nor was money available for new aircraft or the training of personnel.

A plan was proposed by the Aden Airways Board that, with the arrival of the Argonauts, there would be spare capacity in the DC-3 fleet and this could be utilised by chartering aircraft, crews and ground staff to a new airline to be named Air Somali.

There was an element of urgency and common sense in this proposal. Politics and nationalism were increasingly coming into play within the Red Sea region, mostly led by Egypt under Colonel Nasser but with the active support of Russia. Already the Somali Government had made approaches to TWA who managed EAL, East African Airways had expressed an interest and United Arab Airlines was actively lobbying the Government there. (UAA flew a regular service to Mogadishu via Aden from both Damascus and Cairo).

The BOAC.AC Board were apprehensive at this plan, as was the BOAC Board. Having burned their fingers with Arab Airways (Jerusalem) Ltd in Jordan, no-one wished to become embroiled in a similar situation. For some time the Somali Government had not allowed funds from ticket sales which were due to Aden Airways, to be transferred out of the country to Aden. Even though the new Somali Government promised that this practice would cease, there was no guarantee it would happen (in fact, it continued for some years).

However, there were clouds on the horizon. As one would expect, after their pre-delivery Check IVs by BOAC in London, the Argonauts performed well for a time. Engine failures were common while the pressurisation and hydraulic systems were tired. In his diaries, Vic Spencer reports for 10th August: *"Started for Nairobi. After Hargeisa had coolant loss warning on no 4 and returned to Aden on three engines. Overshot first approach, OK on second".*

This was not an isolated event and it did not take long for word to get around that the Argonauts were unreliable, with the result that loads began to fall. On the Cairo route passenger numbers were more often than not in single figures, Bahrain was no better though Nairobi held up reasonably well since it was seen as a holiday destination.

As a result of the Argonaut technical problems, engineering costs were rising rapidly. Not only that, a DC-3 which had been given a Check IV by MASCO in Beirut was about to incur a charge of £15,000 which was only a little less than the book-value of the aeroplane.

In order to maintain services on the Argonaut routes, aircraft had to be chartered from Ethiopian Airlines. These were more modern Douglas DC-6Bs which only served to highlight the inadequacies of the company's new fleet.

Politics were also due to play a greater part in the life of Aden Crown Colony in the coming years. On 15th August, a general strike was declared in Aden and observed by all Adeni staff who worked for the airline. Even with all the European staff helping to

VR-AAT finally entered service in July 1960. It is seen here with a rather small Aden Aiways logo on the rudder.

CHAPTER 18: ADEN AIRWAYS 1960 - 1961 : ARGONAUTS

Ethiopian Airlines leased Douglas DC-6Bs to Aden to enable services to be maintained. ET-T-26 later became ET-AAY.

Left: Captain Dick Larcombe who flew the first Argonaut Service charter on July 4th 1960. Right: Captain George Dyer who resigned as Chief Pilot in July 1960 but remained as Argonaut Training Captain.   (Vic Spencer)

*Passengers waiting to board at Beihan, April 1960.
                                                           (British Airways Archives)*

load and unload aircraft, conducting transit checks and refuelling, only a couple of services were flown each day. When the strike was over on 18th August, services resumed but the damage public confidence was done.

Problems were also beginning to emerge within the Company management. The Chief Pilot, Captain George Dyer, had been given a huge workload not only in introducing the Argonaut into operations, but it was also on his watch that the MTCA had required all the operation manuals to be re-written and, though it was not directly his fault, he had borne the brunt of the criticism. He had always been known as a man with a short fuse who did not suffer fools gladly, and when his relationship with the General Manager, Captain Jimmy Alger, had deteriorated to such an extent, it became clear that the situation could not go on. In early June matters came to a head between the two men and George Dyer was obliged to resign as Chief Pilot later that month, though he did stay on as a Training Captain on the Argonaut.

In the meantime, the General Manager had been trying to persuade Captain Spencer to take over as Chief Pilot, a request which put him in a difficult position since he believed that such as appointment would only create divisions within the pilot community. Instead, he suggested that for the time being a new Chief Pilot should be appointed from BOAC to whom he would remain as Deputy and in charge of the DC-3. This recommendation was accepted and Captain Bill Burman arrived in September in take over.

By the end of September, the BOAC.AC Board was expressing considerable concern with the financial deterioration in Aden Airways' affairs. Hitherto, the seven DC-3s had earned a steady, if unspectacular, income from flights into the Protectorates and the Horn of Africa; charters had been consistent and freight, particularly of Qat, had produced good revenue.

In November the charter to the International Petroleum Company was not renewed and this created a serious shortfall in the forecast revenue for these activities. To this disappointment had to be added the rapidly increasing costs of the Argonaut operation and suddenly the company was facing an unacceptable shortfall and an explanation was called for by the Board.

The causes for the losses on the Argonaut operations were:-

1)   The estimates for April to September were too optimistic. Revenue was expected to be £394,000 compared to actual results of £316,000.

2)   The technical problems with the aircraft meant they did not fly 440 hours of the planned 2,060 hours with a consequent loss of revenue.

3)   It had been planned that the Argonaut would fly 156 trips to Djibouti on the lucrative Qat freighters. Iin fact it only flew 17 trips since it was quickly found that the DC-3 could do multiple trips (frequency was more desirable than quantity) at a far lower cost than the Argonaut which needed a longer turnaround and more intense engineering cover.

4)   Costs which had been estimated at £150 per hour were in practice £170 per hour while revenue averaged £160 per hour. (237)

The airline pressed on;even though losses were mounting and the playing field was not always level. Middle East Airlines, a member of the BOAC.AC group, was accused of carrying passengers from

The 1961 international schedules showed the Argonauts operating on the Aden to Nairobi, Cairo and Bahrain routes. The DC-3s were then reduced to the Khartoum, Mogadishu and Djibouti sectors but still operated the Caravan class routes in the Protectorate.

TABLE No. 1a

ADEN AIRWAYS LIMITED (effective from 1st January 1961)
MAIN LINE SERVICES — WINTER SCHEDULES (NORTHBOUND)

Time deviation from G.M.T.	DAY FLIGHT NO. AIRCRAFT SERVICE		Thur AD468 Arg T	Thur AD466 Arg T	Sun AD480 Arg T	Sun AD472 Arg T	Tue AD482 Arg T	Tue AD458 DC-3 T	Tue AD474 DC-3 T	Daily AD486 DC-3 T	Sat AD474 DC-3 T
+3	NAIROBI	dep	0700		0600						
+3	MOGADISHU	arr dep	1005 1050		0905 0950						
+3	HARGEISA	arr dep						0730 1055 1125			
+3	DJIBOUTI	arr dep								1055 1200	
+3	ADEN	arr dep	1420	1630	1320	1430	0600	1305	1230		1130
+3	KAMARAN	arr dep									1330 1355
+3	ASMARA	arr dep							1530 1600		1530 1600
+3	JEDDAH	arr dep		2015 2115		1815 1915					
+2	KHARTOUM	arr dep							1745		1745
+4	BAHREIN	arr dep					1300				
+2	CAIRO	arr		2359		2200					

NOTES: (1) No traffic may be accepted between Asmara/Khartoum and Kamaran/Asmara on AD474/475 Services.
(2) Call at Kamaran on AD475 Sundays is optional.
(3) No traffic may be carried Jeddah/Cairo on AD466 service on Thursdays.

TABLE No. 1b

ADEN AIRWAYS LIMITED (effective from 1st January 1961)
MAIN LINE SERVICES — WINTER SCHEDULES (SOUTHBOUND)

DAY FLIGHT NO. AIRCRAFT SERVICE		Fri AD467 Arg T	Sat AD481 Arg T	Mon AD473 Arg T	Wed AD469 Arg T	Tue AD483 Arg T	Sun AD475 DC-3 T	Mon AD459 DC-3 T	Wed AD475 DC-3 T	Daily AD485 DC-3 T
CAIRO	dep	2300			1115					
BAHREIN	arr dep					1400				
KHARTOUM	arr dep						0700		0700	
JEDDAH	arr dep			1600 1700						
ASMARA	arr dep						1045 1130		1045 1130	
KAMARAN	arr dep						1305 1330			
ADEN	arr dep	Sat 0715	0930	2045	1000	1900	1530	1030	1430	0900 1005
DJIBOUTI	arr dep									
HARGEISA	arr dep							1210 1240		
MOGADISHU	arr dep		1300 1345		1330 1415			1605		
NAIROBI	arr		1645		1715					

NOTES: Service AD467 will call at JEDDAH during June/July 1961 to Cater for return Pilgrim traffic. Timings will be Friday Cairo dep. 2300 Saturday Jeddah arr. 0345 dep. 0445. Aden arr. 0830 then connect with AD481. Advance bookings can be accepted on AD467 ex Jeddah on Saturday 3rd, 10th, 17th, 24th June and 1st, 8th, 15th, 22nd, 29th July, 1961.

Aden to London through Beirut, as if they had Fifth Freedom rights, and this was done with the tacit acknowledgement of the BOAC Board. (238) Whether this was true or not is open to question but it would be hard to prove one way or the other.

A further cause for concern was the granting by the UK Government of Fifth Freedom rights for United Arab Airlines to pick up passengers in Aden for Mogadishu and return, a route which would normally have been Aden Airways' by right. This had occurred because BOAC wished to obtain certain rights (239) from the United Arab Republic. This would represent a loss in revenue of over £16,000 and seemed to be a most extraordinary decision to be made by the parent company.

As the year came to a close, the situation was not promising. Overall, during the last six months of the financial year, the Argonaut load factor had fallen from 44% to 37% (27% on the Cairo service). The budgeted figures for the coming year were equally gloomy with a loss of some £58,000 forecast and an overall load factor of 48% when breakeven was 49%. At the same time, it was learned that Captain Alger was to retire as General Manager in May 1961 to be replaced by Mr Donald Classey, his deputy.

Footnotes, Chapter 18:
(236) John Cork was with the RAF in Aden while doing his National Service from 1959 to 1961.
(237) AC.36/4 BOAC.AC Board Meeting, 29th November 1960.
(238) BOAC.AC minutes 39/4 para 2, 15th March 1961.
(239) BOAC.AC General Manager's report, 15th March 1961.

Jennifer Vennings, on the left, coming down the steps with Margaret Wilson, right, from an Argonaut c.1962. (Jennifer Drummond-Harris)

Chapter 19 :
ADEN AIRWAYS 1961 - 1962

The year did not start well for Aden Airways. As mentioned previously, the engineering policy was that major checks such as the Check IV would be done away from Aden because there were insufficient facilities at Khormaksar to undertake this work. For the last couple of years this work was undertaken by MASCO in Beirut and one of the DC-3s had been sent there for the Check IV work to be done in August 1960. When the aircraft was ready in March 1961 a bill was presented for £35,281; bearing in mind the sale price of a refurbished DC-3 was in the region of £17,000 the bill was considered to be ridiculous, but the company was forced to make provision for it in the accounts while it argued its case. Fortunately, VR-AAB was sold in April 1961 to Gulf Aviation for £17,500 which mitigated the situation somewhat.

Furthermore, there was increasing concern on the Associated Companies Board that the Avro 748 was not coming up to performance expectations, though the situation was expected to become clearer as the year moved on.

Additional costs also had to be met for an increase in crew salaries which was to be backdated to April 1960.

However, not all was doom and gloom in the financial arena. The Qat trade was still vibrant and while hitherto EAL had insisted that it should fly from Dire Dawa to Djibouti for onward carriage to Aden, a new agreement was put in place whereby *"both companies' aircraft will operate end to end being chartered by each other over the other's sector. It is expected that the arrangement, which had some initial opposition from our Ministry will improve Aden Airways' results by about £30,000 p.a."*. (240)

Further plans included discussions with BOAC on proposals for:
1. A pooling agreement between Aden and Cairo
2. Operation of a weekly Comet service between Cairo/ Jeddah/ Aden in Aden Airways colours
3. Operation of a weekly Comet service in Aden Airways colours between Aden and Bombay. (241)

These last two proposals would have involved a straightforward charter arrangement with BOAC and had become common practice between that company and, for instance, Air Ceylon and Malayan Airways. The added advantage was that it would go some way to dispel the image Aden Airways had acquired of being a secondary company.

Meanwhile, the Argonauts continued to give problems. On 7th May 1961 VR-AAT experienced a No.4 engine failure operating the AD 472 to Jeddah and Cairo; the crew was obliged to sleep on board the aircraft (they were not allowed to go to a hotel) before conducting a three-engine ferry back to Aden next day. On 13th May, VR-AAT had to feather No.2 engine on the AD 481 to Nairobi due to a faulty propeller governor. Despite being repaired overnight, the same fault occurred the next day on the return to Aden: *"A/C still U/S. RPM on No. 2 almost uncontrollable at times and obliged to feather it after departing Mogadishu."* (242)

Yet again, on 16th May VR-AAS suffered a complete hydraulic failure while flying to Jeddah.

Fortunately, the new Chief Pilot, Bill Burman, had taken up his position which took a great deal of the load off the shoulders of

Aden Airways Eastern Protectorate services, May 1961.

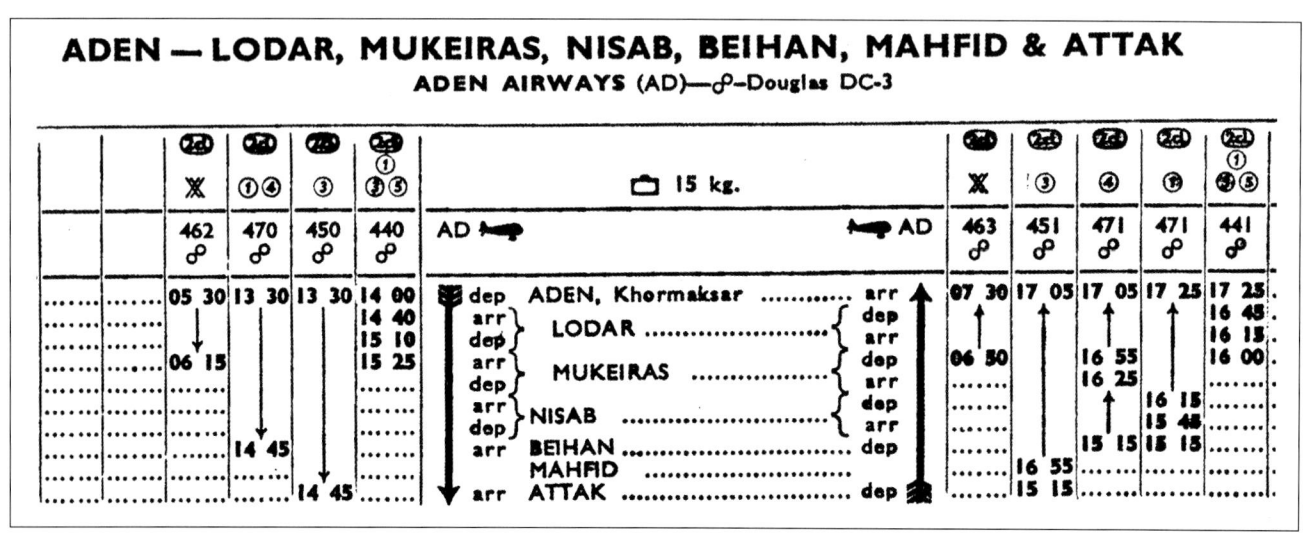

Aden Airways Western Protectorate services, May 1961. (Source: Official Airline Guide)

Captain Vic Spencer who remained as Deputy Chief Pilot overall, though in charge of both DC-3 and Argonaut fleets.

Also in May the General Manager Captain Alger retired to be replaced by Mr Donald Classey who had been his deputy for some time.

The cold war politics of the Middle East and the Red Sea area continued to move on with Egypt very much in the lead, aided and abetted by the Soviet Union as it tried to extend its influence in the region and the Western Powers, the UK in particular, sought to retain theirs. In Aden itself there was pressure within the local business community and the Legislative Council for greater participation in the affairs of Aden Airways - so far the airline had been run by BOAC through the Aden Board from the Governor's office. There was no interaction with the business and government leaders of the colony, a situation which was recognised by BOAC, and later in the year two prominent business men, Alawi Al Kaff and Antonin Besse, son of Antonin Besse who was involved with Arabian Airways in 1937, were invited on to the Aden Board.

Further north, in a foretaste of its activities some 30 years later, Iraq decided to make threatening noises towards Kuwait which it considered to be a province rather than a sovereign country. The UK had a defence treaty in place with Kuwait and as these threats from Iraq developed Aden Airways was brought into play for the movement of troops from Kenya to the Gulf. The first reinforcement flight was flown by Captain Spencer on VR-AAR when he flew to Mombasa and back on 1st July 1961 with a full load of soldiers and their equipment. The reason Mombasa was used as the Kenyan departure point was that Nairobi, where the troops were normally based, was at too high an altitude for a heavily-loaded Argonaut to take off.

More locally, an interesting development was taking place in the Yemen. During May 1961 word was received at the Ministry of Transport and Civil Aviation in London that a group of Yemeni businessmen wished to set up an independent airline in Yemen, starting with three DC-3s. The information had come from the Yemeni Director General of the Ministry of Foreign Affairs, Abu Talib, who had been instructed by the Imam himself to explore the possibilities. (243) There were some difficulties and contradictions here in that there had been tensions between the Crown Colony and Yemen. The Imam had long held claims that the Aden Protectorates were part of Yemen. Indeed, from time to time both Mukeiras and Dhala on the Protectorate/Yemen borders had come under fire from Yemen "troops" and for this reason any openly direct assistance from Aden Airways would not be acceptable. Nevertheless, the Imam had always professed a great admiration for BOAC and he also felt that relations between his country and Aden could only be improved through such collaboration.

On the other hand, there were other pressures on him. Colonel Nasser in Egypt had ambitious plans for the whole region in which he naturally would take a leading part. The Soviet Union was equally ambitious for itself and saw Nasser as an excellent medium through which to extend this influence. Accordingly the USSR had presented the Imam with three helicopters and two Ilyushin IL-14s for his airline. (244) It would not have escaped the notice of the Imam that few rulers lasted very long once the Soviets had succeeded in establishing a presence in a country and he may have been seeking to establish allies.

Nevertheless, the talks continued using a Yemeni businessman, Mr El Aghil, who had bought two of the government DC-3s and was planning to use them on the following basis: (245)

Chapter 19: Aden Airways 1961 - 1962

ADEN AIRWAYS LOCAL SERVICES — DAKOTAS

NOTE: All Times are in Local Standard Time. Jeddah Time is shown as for Aden (i.e. GMT plus 3 hrs.). Aden Airways Services are Shown in Black. Arab Airways Services are Shown in Green.

SYMBOLS:
1 - Monday
2 - Tuesday
3 - Wednesday
4 - Thursday
5 - Friday
6 - Saturday
7 - Sunday

J.E. — Arab Airways
A.D. — Aden Airways

	AD.463	AD.478	AD.464	AD.458A	AD.458	AD.453	AD.468		AD.469	AD.452	AD.459	AD.459A	AD.465	AD.479	AD.462
							3	Dep. NAIROBI Arr.	1625						
							0800	Arr. MOGADISHU Dep.	1240						
						1—5	1145	Dep. MOGADISHU Arr.	1210						
							1215	Dep. GHURAF Arr.		1235					
							1305	Arr. QATN Dep.		↑					
							1325	Dep. QATN Arr.							
							1345	Arr. MUKALLA Dep.		1150					
					5	2—6	1430	Dep. MUKALLA Arr.		1120					
					0730	0645	1500	Dep. ADDIS ABABA Arr.			1620	1700			
			7	1000			1525	Arr. HARGEISA Dep.	0900		↑	1430			
			1040	1020			1555	Dep. HARGEISA Arr.	0830			1410	0940		
			1125					Arr. BERBERA Dep.	↑			↑	0855		
			1155					Dep. BERBERA Arr.					0825		
	1					0815		Arr. DIREDAWA Dep.					↑		
	0900					0845		Dep. DIREDAWA Arr.						0800	
						0945		Arr. DJIBOUTI Dep.			1405			↑	
1—6						1015		Dep. DJIBOUTI Arr.			1335				0645
0730								Dep. MUKEIRAS Arr.			↑				0600
0810	1100	1305	1150	1120	1655	1725		Arr. ADEN Dep.	0700	0915	1230	1240	0715	0600	0600
									2	1—5	1—4	5	7	1	1—6

ADEN AIRWAYS MAIN LINE SERVICES — DAKOTAS

JE.008/6	AD.470	AD.474	AD.472	AD.466		AD.467	AD.473	AD.475	AD.471	JE.00
4	5	3	2	7						
0600	1400	0830	0800	0645	Dep. ADEN Arr.	1745	1755	1700	1150	172
					Arr. DJIBOUTI Dep.	↑	↑	1555	↑	↑
					Dep. DJIBOUTI Arr.			1520		
			1030		Arr. KAMARAN Dep.			1340		
	ARGONAUT		1100		Dep. KAMARAN Arr.			1310	ARGONAUT	
			1235	0930	Arr. ASMARA Dep.	1500	1510	1135		
			1325	1020	Dep. ASMARA Arr.	1410	1420	1045		
			1125	1120	Arr. PORT SUDAN Dep.	↑	1120	↑		
			1155	1150	Dep. PORT SUDAN Arr.		1050			
		1510			Arr. KHARTOUM Dep.		↑	0700		123
1030			1410	1405	Arr. JEDDAH Dep.	1135	1035	4		114
1115			1500	1455	Dep. JEDDAH Arr.	1045	0945		0400	↑
	1945		1845	1840	Arr. CAIRO Dep.	0500	0400		0400	
						1	3		5	

ARAB AIRWAYS CONNECTING SERVICES — DAKOTAS

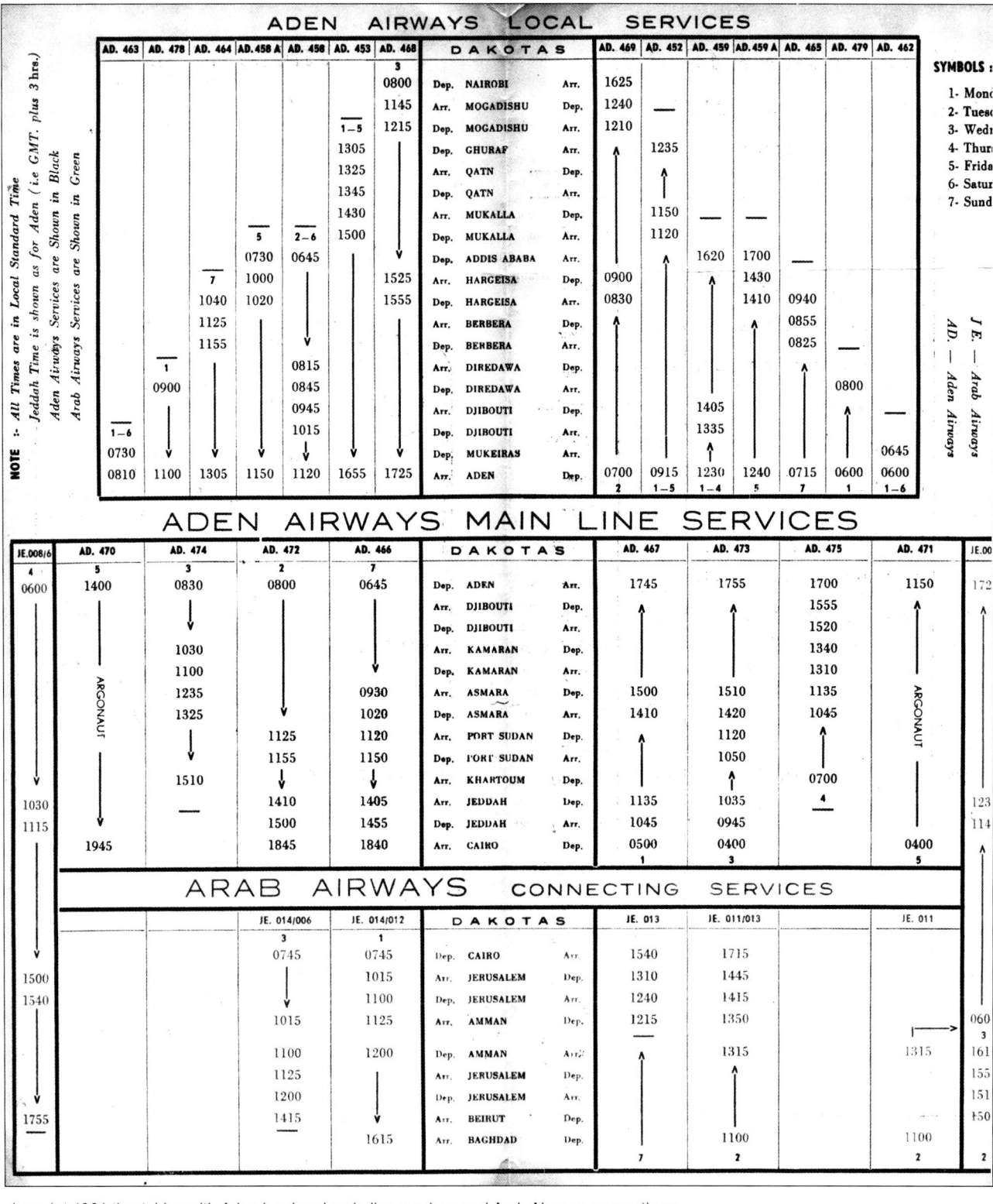

		JE.014/006	JE.014/012		JE.013	JE.011/013		JE.011	
		3	1						
		0745	0745	Dep. CAIRO Arr.	1540	1715			
1500			1015	Arr. JERUSALEM Dep.	1310	1445			
1540			1100	Dep. JERUSALEM Arr.	1240	1415			
		1015	1125	Arr. AMMAN Dep.	1215	1350			060
									3
		1100	1200	Dep. AMMAN Arr.		1315		1315	161
		1125		Arr. JERUSALEM Dep.	↑				155
		1200		Dep. JERUSALEM Arr.					151
		1415		Arr. BEIRUT Dep.					150
1755			1615	Arr. BAGHDAD Dep.		1100		1100	
					7	2		2	2

June 1st 1961 timetables with Aden local and main line services and Arab Airways connections.

1. Aden/Taiz — daily
2. Taiz/Hodeida/Sa'ana — thrice weekly
3. Taiz/Hodeida/Asmara — once or twice weekly

One of the stumbling blocks preventing any agreement was that Mr El Aghil did not seem to appreciate that Aden Airways would wish to have reciprocal rights between Aden and Taiz. In addition, the quite reasonable request that Aden aircraft should be allowed to overfly Yemen territory en route from Aden to Jeddah or Asmara, with all the time and fuel savings this involved, was flatly refused by the Imam.

Eventually, on the advice of the UK Government and BOAC, Aden Airways agreed the following: (246)

1. For six months, a daily service would be flown between Taiz and Aden using Yemeni aircraft only.

2. In the event of a Yemeni aircraft not being available, Aden Airways would supply a DC-3 on charter.

3. After Yemeni Airlines expenses of £80 per round trip, Aden Airways would receive 25% of any profit.

A separate maintenance agreement was also concluded whereby Aden Airways undertook to maintain Yemeni Airlines' DC-3s. Whether this agreement was a realistic one or not is open to question and it probably reflected an old-fashioned outlook on the part of the UK Government. The Imam died in 1961 and the country was quickly consumed in turmoil.

Although Aden Airways was a much-valued launch customer for the Avro 748 it was becoming clear in 1961 that the order for three aircraft would have to be cancelled.   (via Peter Pickering)

Meanwhile, Aden Airways had other more pressing problems. It was learned in July that delivery of the Avro 748 would almost certainly be delayed and its performance would be below estimates (247). Mr J C Dykes, an AC.Board member, had been in Aden to meet the Aden Board. His report was not encouraging when he said he *"had misgivings as to the use to which Aden Airways proposed to put the Avro 748, the manner in which the project was being handled and the adequacy of the facilities and staff available to deal with project."* (248)

This was, perhaps, an understandable view, bearing in mind the facilities with which the airline had to work at Khormaksar. In the meantime, the AC.Board found in September that: *"At the last meeting (with Avro) it was clearly established that the aircraft will not meet the performance guarantees as given in the contract."* (249) With this in mind, it was only a matter of time before the 748 order was cancelled and this was done shortly afterwards.

Aden Airways was, however, doing its best to cope with the ongoing problems. It was only a question of time before EAAC would operate the Comet between Nairobi and Aden on their way to India forcing Aden Airways to negotiate a pooling agreement as soon as possible.

Some idea of the difficulty the airline was in can be seen from the following assessment in June. (250) *"The net profit of ALL our scheduled services has been £5,700 this month. The profit from our Qat-carrying Djibouti services has been £5,850; but for the profits on this single route, our losses would have been £150."*

By August the first Argonaut, VR-AAR, was due for a Check IV. On 13th August, the aircraft flew the normal AD 472 from Aden to Cairo where it was picked up by Captains Dyer and Spencer plus R/O McGarry and flown via Malta and London Heathrow to Wymeswold, the Field Aircraft Services Ltd maintenance centre. The aircraft did not return until the 19th December leaving a severe gap in the schedule capability which meant that DC-6Bs had to be chartered from EAL.

Further bad news was to come when, in September, the company was advised by the Field Aircraft Services engineering team that extensive corrosion had been discovered in VR-AAR and not only would the work take some time to complete, but would cost a further £10,000. The other two Argonauts were also due for a Check IV during the next 12 months and it was only sensible to assume that they, too, would be affected by the Aden climate and have similar corrosion problems. Thus, while the company was making a reasonable operating profit, money had to be put aside to pay for extra engineering work.

In the meantime the DC-3s carried on doing good work in the Protectorates on both schedule routes and charters for the oil exploration companies. On 12th September the Colony's Governor and his office chartered VR-AAN for a tour of both the Eastern and Western Protectorates in order to meet the local leaders, albeit briefly. The flight took off at 0725 local time with Captains Spencer and Dinnie as pilots and Air Hostess Wilson in the cabin with Flight Clerk Fara to do the loadsheets. The flight went from Aden to Lahej and Dhala to Lodar where it remained for two hours, then on to Beihan and Ataq for lunch. The afternoon flight was on to Said, Yeshbum and Haban en route to Ahwar and then back to Aden where it landed at 1830 local time. Other flights into the Protectorates went less smoothly:

"It was interesting flying. Apart from Aden, Riyan, Salalah and Masirah all the strips were just flattened soil. There were no aids of course, and no radio. It was not unusual to have to chase off the odd camel or other wildlife before landing. Weather generally was very good, but there could be dust clouds, and locust swarms to add interest. Crosswinds on landing and take-off could be a problem, and some of the strips were a bit short. I never had to night-stop up-country fortunately, but due to aircraft unserviceability, it came close a couple of times. I remember once for example, after landing at Mahfid, I found one engine covered in oil (the scavenge pump drive had sheared). A look at the contents convinced me that I just had enough for the take-off, which I did, and feathered it immediately after becoming airborne. On another occasion, there had been very heavy rain at Mukeiras, leaving a wide-spread 'lake' on the runway. The previous Captain had asked the A.P.L. (Aden Protectorate Levies) if they could arrange to clear the water. When I arrived there, there was just one big puddle on the runway, although I didn't go through it on landing. I went to take a look at it during the turn-round and found that the obliging Levies had cleared the water by the simple expedient of digging a big hole for it to drain into. Also the hole was in the middle of the strip. On take-off I was careful to keep to one side of it. I never experienced that sort of thing at LHR, did you? The freight carried, apart from Qat, was all sorts: vegetables, live goats, gas cylinders, some other smelly nameless items, etc. I remember once an old chap had some very heavy sacks with him. When I checked, I found that they contained hundreds of Maria Theresa dollars, which were still being used in some places for currency. All dated 1814 I think!" (251)

In October, a further oil exploration charter was arranged in the Qaiti States (the area known as Qatar today) which promised some 40 additional hours per week – almost 2,000 hours per year.

By December, news was coming through from Wymeswold that all four flap jacks on VR-AAR had been cracked as a result of corrosion and while there were replacements for this aircraft, there were none easily available for any future repairs since DC-4 jacks could not be used for Canadair aircraft (The Argonaut was a Douglas DC-4 built in Canada with Rolls-Royce engines to save US dollars). There was no alternative but to pay for the work to be

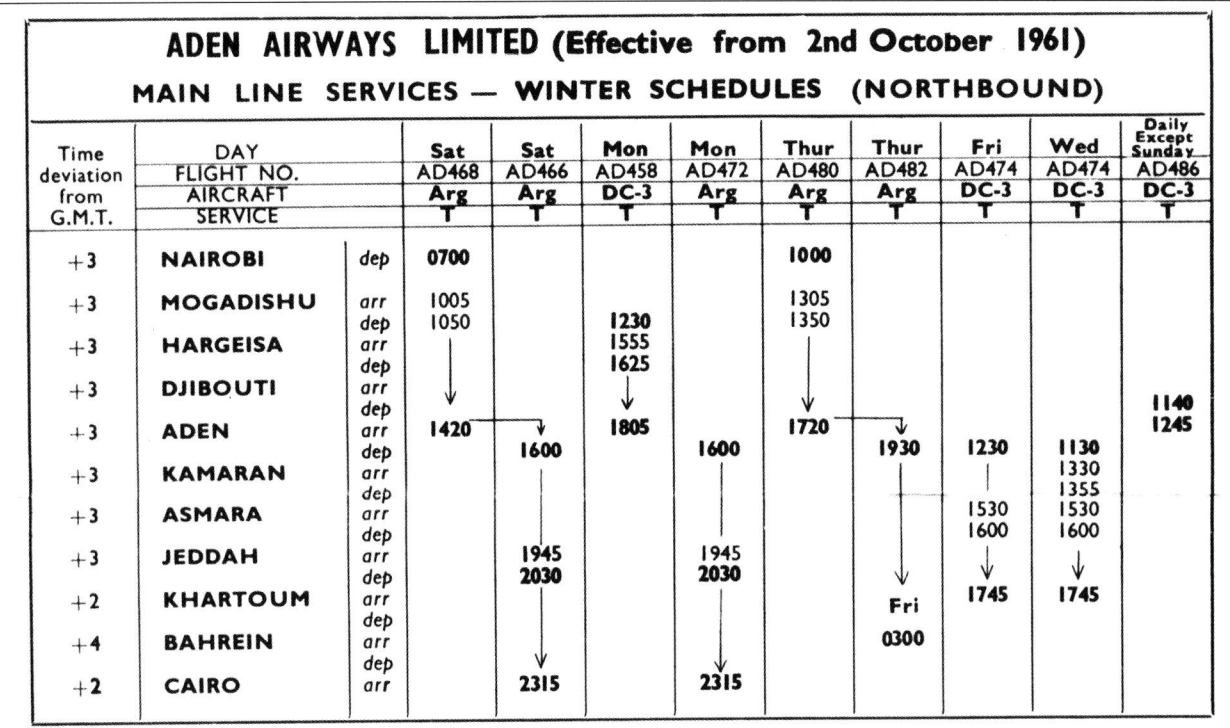

ADEN AIRWAYS LIMITED (Effective from 2nd October 1961)
MAIN LINE SERVICES — WINTER SCHEDULES (NORTHBOUND)

Time deviation from G.M.T.	DAY FLIGHT NO. AIRCRAFT SERVICE		Sat AD468 Arg T	Sat AD466 Arg T	Mon AD458 DC-3 T	Mon AD472 Arg T	Thur AD480 Arg T	Thur AD482 Arg T	Fri AD474 DC-3 T	Wed AD474 DC-3 T	Daily Except Sunday AD486 DC-3 T
+3	NAIROBI	dep	0700				1000				
+3	MOGADISHU	arr dep	1005 1050		1230		1305 1350				
+3	HARGEISA	arr dep			1555 1625						
+3	DJIBOUTI	arr dep									1140 1245
+3	ADEN	arr dep	1420	1600	1805	1600	1720	1930	1230	1130 1330	
+3	KAMARAN	arr dep								1355	
+3	ASMARA	arr dep							1530 1600	1530 1600	
+3	JEDDAH	arr dep		1945 2030		1945 2030					
+2	KHARTOUM	arr dep						Fri	1745	1745	
+4	BAHREIN	arr dep						0300			
+2	CAIRO	arr		2315		2315					

NOTES: (1) No traffic may be accepted between Asmara/Khartoum and Kamaran/Asmara on AD474/475 Services.
(2) Call at Kamaran on AD475 Thursdays is optional. When a call is made service will arrive Aden one hour later.

ADEN AIRWAYS LIMITED (Effective from 2nd October 1961)
MAIN LINE SERVICES — WINTER SCHEDULES (SOUTHBOUND)

DAY FLIGHT NO. AIRCRAFT SERVICE		Tue AD467 Arg T	Wed AD469 Arg T	Sun AD473 Arg T	Mon AD459 DC-3 T	Fri AD483 Arg T	Fri AD481 Arg T	Thur AD475 DC-3 T	Sat AD475 DC-3 T	Daily Except Sunday AD485 DC-3 T
CAIRO	dep	2300		1315						
BAHREIN	arr dep					0345				
KHARTOUM	arr dep							0600	0600	
JEDDAH	arr dep	Wed 0340 0430		1800 1845						
ASMARA	arr dep							0945 1030	0945 1030	
KAMARAN	arr dep									
ADEN	arr dep	Wed 0815	1015	2230	0600	0845	1015	1330	1330	0945 1050
DJIBOUTI	arr dep									
HARGEISA	arr dep				0740 0810					
MOGADISHU	arr dep		1345 1430		1135		1345 1430			
NAIROBI	arr		1730				1730			

Aden Airways winter international schedules, commencing 2nd October 1961

done even though it would have severe consequences on the financial results. A further cause for loss was to be the pay award to all staff backdated to 1st January 1961 and which would cost £30,000 to the bottom line.

Another blow to the company's finances was the sudden decision by the Aden Government to ban the import of Qat. As described earlier, both BOAC and the Ministry of Aviation in London had been uneasy for some time about the fact that a British airline was so deeply involved in what amounted to a drug trade, never mind that it had gone on for centuries and the only thing that had changed was the mode of transport. It will also be remembered that the revenue derived from the carriage of Qat was largely responsible for the company remaining solvent and, as before, the ban had an immediate and serious impact on the finances.

The effect in Aden was also quickly felt in that those who partook of the drug discovered the joys of beer, while the revenue, it will be remembered, which came from a tax on Qat ceased which meant that a tax had to be re-introduced on gasoline.

ADEN AIRWAYS LIMITED
WINTER SCHEDULES — CARAVAN CLASS SERVICE

Wed,Fri	Sat	Mon	Thur	Sat		DAY		Sat	Thur	Mon	Sat	Wed,Fri
AD465	AD465	AD452	AD452	AD452		FLIGHT NO.		AD453	AD453	AD453	AD464	AD464
DC-3	DC-3	DC-3	DC-3	DC-3		AIRCRAFT		DC-3	DC-3	DC-3	DC-3	DC-3
Standard	Standard	Standard	Standard	Standard		SERVICE		Standard	Standard	Standard	Standard	Standard
0530 0710	1515 1655	0700 ↓	1115 |	1115 |	dep arr dep	ADEN HARGEISA	arr dep arr	1905 ↑	1815 ↑	1400 ↑	1910 1730	0930 0750
		0905 0935	1320 1350	1320 1350	arr dep	RIYAN	dep arr	1710 1640	1620 1550	1205 1135		
		↓	↓	↓	arr dep	QATN	dep arr	!555 1525	↑	↑		
		1020	1435	1435	arr	GHURAF	dep	1505	1505	1050		

NOTES: (1) Free Baggage Allowance on Caravan Class Services is 15 Kilos (33 lb.).
(2) Passengers transferring from Caravan Class to Main Line Services and vice versa are not entitled to hotel accommodation unless travelling on through published fares.
(3) All times are Local.

Aden Airways Caravan Class services, winter timetable commencing 2nd October 1961. (Source: Official Airline Guide)

Two views of the airport terminal building at Mukeiras in April 1960. (British Airways Archives)

"One particularly profitable contract for the company involved the despatch of two aircraft to Djibouti early every morning to collect cargoes of Qat. This was mild narcotic (the shrub from which it comes being related to coffee) grown in the Ethiopian highlands and flown from Dire Dawa to Djibouti for onward delivery to the Arab customers keenly awaiting its arrival in Aden. Not a lot of work was done until the morning "fix" arrived (and not a lot after!). It arrived as small twigs and leaves bundled up in large canvas sacks; I heard later that it had been banned for some time which seemed rather foolish." (252)

Nobody was happy and by 2nd March 1962 the ban was lifted and peace of sorts was restored.

The second Argonaut, VR-AAT, went off to Wymeswold in March for a Check IV. Sure enough, severe corrosion was found in this aircraft as well and it would be some considerable time before it returned to Aden, in fact in early September. This time though, Aden Airways had anticipated the problems and an Argonaut was chartered from Derby Airways who had just received a fleet from BOAC. G-ALHS flew out from London to Cairo in 9.20 hrs on 11 March and carried straight on to Aden that evening, arriving early in the morning after a 6.45 hr flight. The aircraft remained in Derby Airways colours with Aden Airways painted on the roof and returned to the UK on 7th May when Captain Spencer flew the normal AD 472 to Cairo via Jeddah and a Derby Airways crew (Captain Van Elst) flew it home.

Thus came to an end a hard year. While there were compensations in the renewal of the service leave contract to Mombasa and a service contract to Bahrain, the loss (albeit temporary) of the Qat trade, the serious corrosion problems on the three Argonauts and the cancellation of the Avro 748 order combined to leave the company with an unpredictable future and a loss of some £50,000 for the year.

Footnotes, Chapter 19:
(240) BOAC.AC Board Meeting, 2nd May 1961 para 2c.
(241) BOAC.AC Board Meeting, 2nd May 1961 para 2d.
(242) Vic Spencer diaries.
(243) BOAC.AC Board Meeting, 6th June 1961 (42/2a).
(244) BOAC.AC Board meeting, 6th June 1961 (42/2b).
(245) BOAC.AC Board meeting, 6th September 1961 (43/3e).
(246) BT/245/830 National Archives, 29th May 1962.
(247) BOAC.AC Board Meeting, 4th July 1961.
(248) BOAC.AC Board Meeting, 4th July 1961 (42/2X).
(249) BOAC.AC Board Meeting, 6th September 1961 (42/2 IX).
(250) BOAC.AC Board Meeting, 6th June 1961 General Manager's Report.
(251) Captain Peter Austin.
(252) Captain Ian Stewart.

Argonaut VR-AAT on the tarmac at Aden with an interesting variety of other users - Curtiss C-46 Commando, Lockheed Lodestar and a Grumman Goose amphibian.
(Ray Deacon)

Chapter 20 :
ADEN AIRWAYS 1962 - 1963

The company had anticipated the reduction in the Argonaut fleet when G-ALHS was due to return to Derby Airways in May and had been negotiating for the lease of a similar aircraft from East African Airways (EAAC) in June. Sadly, on 11th April VP-KNY of EAAC crashed near Nairobi while on a training flight with the consequence that no Argonaut would be available for lease to Aden Airways.

Meanwhile the Haj started early this year, in April, and any spare capacity from either fleet was pressed into service. The inbound Haj started on 14th April when DC-3 VR-AAI flew to Jeddah from Aden with Captain Vic Spencer in command with F/O Gordon as co-pilot and Air Stewardess Seton in the cabin looking after the pilgrims. As mentioned previously, when a DC-3 was used to fly pilgrims from Riyan to Jeddah, it could be a hazardous flight if it was flown direct over Yemen because of the mountain range in between. However, in the Argonaut it was no problem and when available it was used on that route, the first time being when the Chief Pilot, Captain Bill Burman, flew VR-AAR on 29th April in 3.40 hours. Captain Vic Spencer was co-pilot and Air Stewardesses Mordini and Anastasi had the job of making sure no primus stoves were lit. There were good reasons for this vigilance since lighting up was not unknown. *"Smells of paraffin in the aircraft on this flight"* (Vic Spencer diary 18th May; Jeddah to Aden on VR-AAS).

"Trooping flights to Mombasa and Nairobi were regularly undertaken, and while these flights were invariably full, they were also very enjoyable. Less so were the Haj flights to Jeddah, usually from Aden, and where the flight was packed with extra seating; cabin service on these occasions was limited, but one had to be wary of those pilgrims who would light their paraffin stoves during the flight in order to do some cooking. Boarding the aircraft could also be eventful, and I well remember the time I was hit on the head with an umbrella during a boarding stampede." (253)

On the local scheduled routes the DC-3s remained uncompetitive compared to the equipment flown by other airlines. Ethiopian still had the use of their CV-240s on the route between Asmara and Aden and occasionally supplemented these by the DC-6B when traffic demanded. It made sense, therefore, for Aden Airways to enter into negotiation with EAL for a pooling agreement on Aden – Asmara – Khartoum. Sadly these talks were not successful and the company could only carry on with the DC-3s for the foreseeable future.

IATA, too, was putting pressure on the company to join that organisation. Fortunately the company were able to resist this pressure since joining would mean that it would have to charge the same fares on a given route as other IATA carriers, which would have placed it in a seriously uncompetitive position when one considers the rather old DC-3s in comparison with the Viscounts and CV-240s. Aden Airways' strength was that it could charge significantly lower fares for a given route, and though it would almost certainly operate at a loss unless the load factor was 90%, it made such good profits on the Qat flights, the Haj and oil exploration charters that the company's finances remained in overall surplus, though this was to be a precarious premise as time would tell.

Against the odds, the company earned its best revenue income during April, £158,918 which produced an operating profit of £20,340. But once again, engineering and leasing charges of the Derby Airways Argonaut were to reduce the figures by £4,000 and £9,000 respectively.

On 7th May G-ALHS flew the normal AD 472 service to Cairo via Jeddah with Captain Spencer in command and from there the

DC-3 landing at Ataq, September 1962. The tents are those of the Aden Levies.
(Dr Roger Green)

International services, May 1962. While Aden Airways operated Argonauts and DC-3s, EAAC had introduced Comets from Nairobi. (OAG)

aircraft was taken back to the UK by Captain Van Elste to rejoin the Derby Airways fleet. By all accounts the aircraft had performed well with relatively few failures and now Aden Airways were obliged to face the next few months with only two Argonauts. The only way to handle this shortage was to cancel services and this policy was put into force on 14th May when the Cairo flight (AD 472) was cancelled. It was more sensible to maintain the Service Leave flights to Nairobi and Mombasa which were highly profitable than to fly the scheduled flights to Jeddah and Cairo on which load factors rarely exceeded 35%. (254)

It was during May that the first good news of the year was to arrive in Aden. The company had been awarded the Cumberbatch Trophy for 1961. Awarded by the Guild of Air Pilots and Air Navigators (GAPAN), the Trophy recognised the outstanding contribution which Aden Airways had made in operating in a hostile and difficult environment such as the Arabian Peninsula without serious incident. The inscription on the Trophy reads:
"I was wrought in utmost faith and hope by command of Alice Beatrice Martha Cumberbatch in the Year of our Lord 1932 for the promotion of reliability in Civil Aviation; to the memory of those who have gone before and encouragement to those to come".

Political events were starting to make their presence felt in Aden itself even though the surrounding countries, Yemen in particular, had felt the unsubtle presence of Egypt for some time. Talks in London during June between the UK Government and the Federal Government of Aden gave rise to unrest within Aden Colony and a general strike was called for on 23rd July which grounded all flights that day with a consequent repercussion on operations for the next few days. While the DC-3 flights were flexible, most being within the Protectorate or near-African mainland, the Argonaut operation was proving to be somewhat ambitious, so when low cloud at Cairo forced the diversion of the AD 472 to Port Said on the night of 5th June, the delay meant that the Nairobi (AD 469) had to be cancelled on 6th June. Instead, it was flown on the 7th June in VR-AAS as one service, Aden – Mogadishu – Nairobi – Aden, a 15½ hour day for the crew.

VR-AAR taxying at Khormaksar in May 1962; the previous month it had made a direct Riyan - Jeddah Haj flight over Yemen. (Ray Deacon)

CHAPTER 20: ADEN AIRWAYS 1962 - 1963

ADEN — LODAR — MUKEIRAS, NISAB, MAHFID, WADI AIN, ATTAK & BEIHAN
ADEN AIRWAYS (AD)—Douglas DC-3

AD 462	AD 470	AD 450	AD 470	AD 440		AD 463	AD 471	AD 451	AD 451	AD 471	AD 441
06 30	09 30	11 30	13 45	14 00	dep ADEN, Khormaksar .... arr	08 30	13 55	15 05	15 15	17 20	17 25
				14 40	arr } LODAR .... { dep						16 45
				15 10	dep						16 15
07 15				15 25	arr } MUKEIRAS .... { dep	07 50	13 15			16 40	16 00
......				......	dep	......	12 45			16 10	......
......				......	arr } NISAB .... { dep	......		14 00			......
......				......	dep	......		13 30			......
......				......	arr } MAHFID .... { dep	......			14 15		......
......				......	dep	......			13 45		......
......				......	arr } WADI AIN .... { dep	......	12 00		↑		......
......		12 45		......	dep	......	11 30				......
......	10 45	......	15 00	......	arr ATTAK .... dep	......	↑	13 15	13 15		15 30
					arr BEIHAN .... dep		11 15				

Western Protectorate services, May 1962. One new destination listed is Wadi Ain (see map on p154). (Overseas Airline Guide)

ADEN — NISAB — RAUDHA   ADEN — RIYAN / MUKALLA — GHURAF
ADEN AIRWAYS (AD)—Douglas DC-3

AD 446	AD 452	AD 452		AD 447	AD 453	AD 453	AD 453
......	07 00	07 00	11 15	dep ADEN, Khormaksar .... arr	10 10	14 00	18 15	19 05
......	08 20			arr RAUDHA .... dep	08 50			
......	......	09 05	13 20	arr } RIYAN / MUKALLA .... { dep	......	12 05	16 20	17 10
......	......	09 35	13 50	dep	......	11 35	15 50	16 40
......	......			arr } QATN .... { dep	......			15 55
......	......			dep				15 25
......	......	10 20	14 35	arr GHURAF .... dep	......	10 50	15 05	15 05

Eastern Protectorate services, May 1962. Raudha, dropped from the winter schedule, is re-instated. (Overseas Airline Guide)

"The Argonaut was not the most reliable of aircraft by this stage of its career, and somewhat prone to engine problems. On one scheduled service to Nairobi, an engine failed about an hour into the flight, necessitating a return to Aden. Here there was an aircraft change and the flight set off again only to experience another engine failure a short time after becoming airborne. This aircraft was repaired quite quickly and on this occasion it proved third time lucky, though the service was rather late arriving at its destination." (255)

On 3rd July VR-AAT returned from its extensive Check IV in the UK. The essential repair work to the flap jacks had also been completed as had all the corrosion problems, though these last repairs would prove to be short-lived. However, a new engineering contract with EAAC meant that in future all major engineering work including Check IVs on both DC-3s and Argonauts would be done in Nairobi. In return, EAAC would lease an equivalent aircraft to Aden Airways for the duration of the work being carried out. This was a much cheaper solution than chartering an aircraft from Derby Airways who, in any case, were finding sufficient work for their own fleet. Fortunately the Board realised at this stage that a replacement would have to be found for the Argonauts. A number of types were looked at, but the problem now was not one of simple replacement in the short term, but also the very long term bearing in mind the fast moving politics of the region. Harold Macmillan's speech on "The Winds of Change" was to cause some thought-provoking discussions within Africa and which spilled over into those countries bordering the Red Sea.

As in the past, the greatest weakness of the company was its reliance on revenue from the Haj, carriage of Qat, oil exploration charters and (employing the Argonaut) the Service Leave flights to Mombasa and Nairobi. Significantly, 80% of the operational profits were made by charters using the DC-3 and the only reason

Christine Dent, above, and Fiammetta Mordini on the steps of an Argonaut, 1963. (Christine McIntyre)

DC-3 VR-AAN taxying in at Khormaksar past a pair of RAF Canberras in June 1962. (Ray Deacon)

the Argonaut made a profit on the schedule to Nairobi was that it was effectively already a charter. Otherwise all the scheduled flights generally operated at a loss or just covered their costs. Should any one of the profitable elements suffer a negative effect, then the airline made a loss, an example being when drought in Ethiopia affected Qat production, the loss was more than £13,000. Once again, the MTCA had announced the intention to limit the loads ageing aircraft such as the DC-3 could uplift by applying limits on the WAT graphs. This would have had a particularly severe limitation in Aden where many of the airfields were located over 5,000 ft above sea level as well as experiencing high temperatures. Though the MTCA intention had been shelved after some debate, it was now on the agenda again with the result that a further debate had to take place, and a decision reached as to whether the company should withdraw from the scheduled routes completely. (256)

Meanwhile the two neighbouring airlines, Yemen Airlines and Air Somali, continued to exercise the minds of Aden Airways' management. In Yemen, the three DC-3s owned by the royal flight (and which effectively operated as Yemen Airlines) had ceased flying due to poor or non-existent maintenance, with the result that Aden Airways honoured their contract and operated several flights to Sana'a on their behalf. The airline had even asked Aden Airways to recruit pilots for them. However, in July the old Imam died and was succeeded by his son; an Egyptian-backed coup followed soon afterwards and, while Yemen Airlines nominally ceased to exist, there is evidence that it continued to fly with Egyptian pilots even though there was an extreme shortage of aviation fuel in Taiz and Sana'a.

The immediate effect on Aden Airways was that the £17,000 owed to them by Yemen was lost and when a cheque for £5,000 was eventually extracted, this bounced. (257)

In the case of Air Somali, negotiations continued throughout September and October 1962 with little progress made. The proposals made by Aden Airways were that an airline could sensibly operate in Somalia on the following routes: (258)

1. Aden/Hargeisa/Mogadishu	1 per week
2. Aden/Berbera/Burao/Galkayu/Mogadishu	1 per week
3. Hargeisa/Mogadishu	1 per week
4. Mogadishu/Kisimayo	2 per week

These routes would be flown by Aden Airways crews operating two DC-3s donated by the US Government as part of an aid package on independence. However, even without the obsolescence charges on the two aircraft, the estimate was that total costs would be in the region of £140,000 p.a. against projected revenue of £130,000 p.a.

An alternative proposal was that Aden Airways would assume financial responsibility for all domestic operations in Somalia, taking a fee of 2½% of all revenue earned while any losses would be borne by the Somali Government. Not surprisingly, the Somali Government rejected both of these proposals and in February 1963 it was learned that Alitalia was about to sign an agreement to establish a national airline in which Alitalia would bear 40% of the costs and revenues as well as being responsible for all staff training.

DC-3 VR-AAF on the tarmac at Khormaksar in 1962 with Argonaut VR-AAS behind. (Ray Deacon)

Chapter 20: Aden Airways 1962 - 1963

The RAF side of Khormaksar as seen from Hunter T.7 XL613 on 14th February 1962. (Ray Deacon)

This represented the end of Aden Airways' ventures into other airlines, altogether a sensible course of action as events in Aden would require all the expertise that the management could muster.

After the general strike during July, the colony had not returned to its normal peaceful existence. The People's Socialist Party had become active and strongly opposed the inclusion of Aden in the Federation brought about by the Aden Government. Normally the airline would have remained aloof from the colony's politics, but in this case the leader of this party happened to be a Mr Al Asnag, the Senior Reservations Officer in the company's Crater office. That an employee should have a senior position within such an extreme party came as a surprise to the management and though he was arrested on 8th November on a charge of seditious publication and imprisoned for a year, it was only the start of the involvement of company employees in politics with the National Liberation Front. Subsequently, whatever industrial disputes were going on in Aden, the company would be affected some way or other.

On 13th September, Vic Spencer wrote in his diary: *"Union trouble today"*. This was followed by more unrest on 24th September when there was rioting in Aden and one person was shot. After the arrest and conviction of Mr Al Asnag in November, a strike was called in which all Adeni staff at the airport took part, with the result that no flights departed that day.

On the civil apron stewardesses Mavis Buckham and Christine Dent walk across from their aircraft in 1962. (Christine McIntyre)

ADEN — RAUDHA, BERBERA & BURAO							ADEN — RIYAN / MUKALLA — GHURAF					
		ADEN AIRWAYS (AD)—Douglas DC-3										
		② ⑦	② ①	② ⑥	② ③	② ④⑦	15 kg.	② ⑦	② ①	② ④⑦	② ③	② ⑥
		AD 452	AD 446	AD 452	AD 452	AD 445		AD 447	AD 453	AD 444	AD 453	AD 453
km.	km.											
0	0	......	06 30	09 00	11 15	12 15	13 15 dep ADEN, Khormaksar arr	12 10	14 50	18 25	19 05	19 15
304				10 20			arr RAUDHA dep	10 50		17 15		
—							14 25 arr BERBERA dep			16 45		
—							14 55 dep BERBERA arr			16 05		
—							15 35 arr BURAO dep					
—	317		08 35		13 20	14 20	arr RIYAN / MUKALLA dep		12 35		17 10	17 20
			09 05		13 50	14 50	dep arr		12 05		16 40	16 50
—							arr QATN dep				15 55	
—							dep arr				15 25	
—							arr HAURA dep		11 20			
—							dep arr		10 50			
—	412		09 50		14 35	15 35	arr GHURAF dep		10 20		15 05	16 05

Regional services, November 1962. Berbera and Burao are in Somaliland, Haura in the Wadi Hadramaut (see map p154).

(Overseas Airline Guide)

In early 1963 the decision to replace the Argonauts became more urgent when VR-AAR was found to be beyond economic repair because of extensive corrosion and the need to reseal the wing internal fuel tanks. The aircraft had been undergoing a Check IV by EAAC in Nairobi and a decision was made to scrap it immediately, thus saving some £20,000 in engineering costs.

Fortunately, EAAC was able to place a spare Argonaut (VP-KO1) as a charter to Aden Airways for a contracted 1,500 hours at £25 per hour with all checks up to Check III completed.

At the same time, the budget for 1963–64 would assume that the last Argonaut flight would take place on 30th September 1963 and the two Viscount 700s would be ordered and placed in operation on 1st October 1963.

Footnotes, Chapter 20:

(253) Christine Dent, as she then was, arrived in Aden in November 1959 when her father was posted there with the RAF. She joined Aden Airways as a stewardess shortly after the Company had taken delivery of the Argonaut, and she flew on these as well as the DC-3 to Khartoum. Training was limited and tended to be while on the job. Emergency training was rudimentary and was given by one of the First Officers. She left in 1964.
(254) BOAC.AC Board Meeting, 5th June 1962 (para 16e).
(255) Christine Dent.
(256) BOAC.AC Board Meeting, 2nd October 1962 (53/1a).
(257) BOAC.AC Board Meeting, 30th October 1962 (54/1b).
(258) BOAC.AC Board Meeting, 1st January 1963 (55/1e).

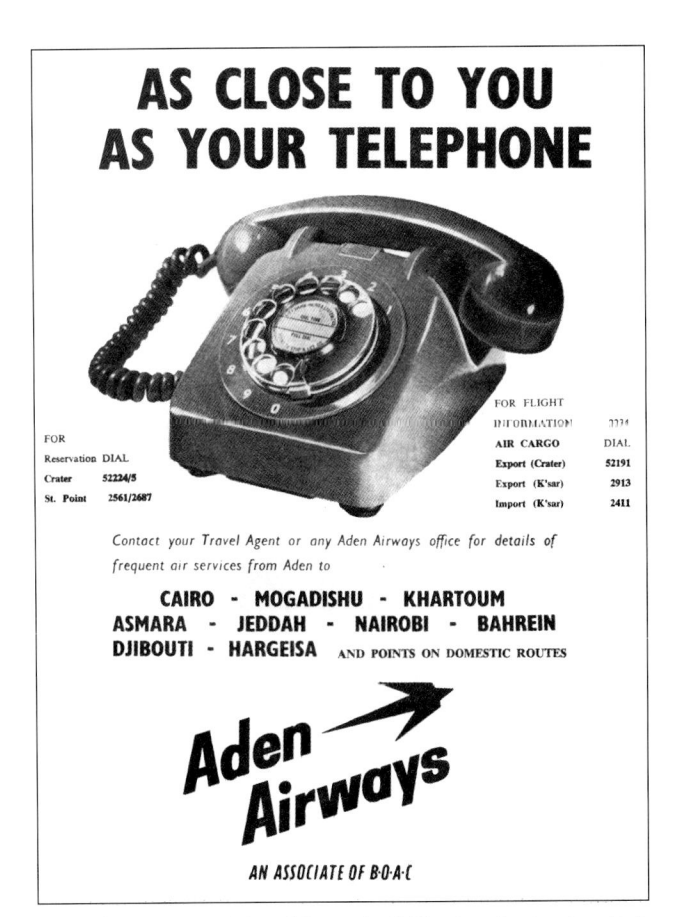

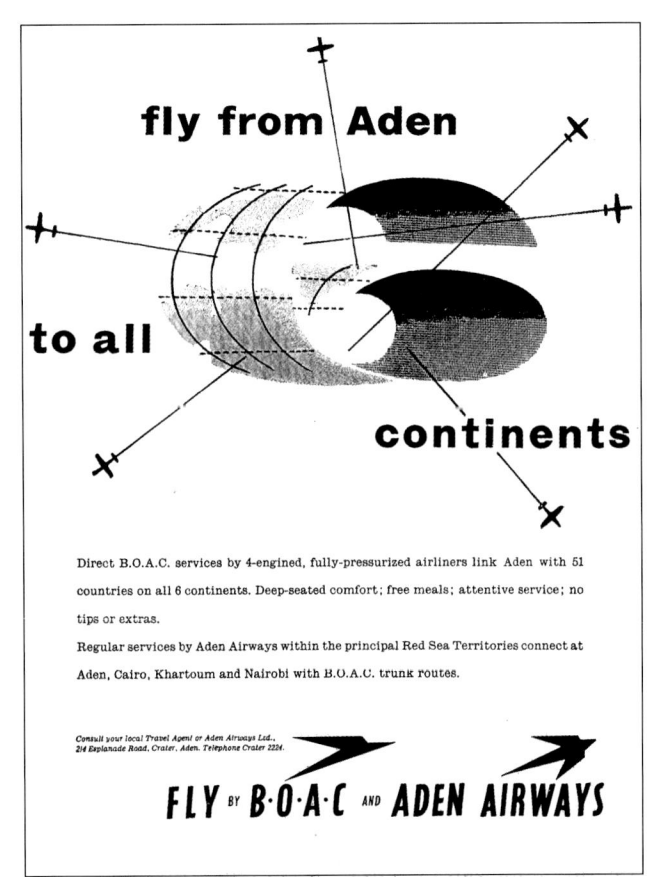

AS CLOSE TO YOU AS YOUR TELEPHONE

FOR Reservation DIAL
Crater 52224/5
St. Point 2561/2687

FOR FLIGHT INFORMATION 2224
AIR CARGO DIAL
Export (Crater) 52191
Export (K'sar) 2913
Import (K'sar) 2411

Contact your Travel Agent or any Aden Airways office for details of frequent air services from Aden to

**CAIRO - MOGADISHU - KHARTOUM
ASMARA - JEDDAH - NAIROBI - BAHREIN
DJIBOUTI - HARGEISA** AND POINTS ON DOMESTIC ROUTES

Aden Airways

AN ASSOCIATE OF B·O·A·C

fly from Aden to all continents

Direct B.O.A.C. services by 4-engined, fully-pressurized airliners link Aden with 51 countries on all 6 continents. Deep-seated comfort; free meals; attentive service; no tips or extras.

Regular services by Aden Airways within the principal Red Sea Territories connect at Aden, Cairo, Khartoum and Nairobi with B.O.A.C. trunk routes.

Consult your local Travel Agent or Aden Airways Ltd., 214 Esplanade Road, Crater, Aden. Telephone Crater 2224.

FLY BY B·O·A·C AND ADEN AIRWAYS

Aden Airways advertising of the early 1960s stressing local and international links.   *(Left, via Peter Pickering. Right, via Roger Carvell)*

CHAPTER 21: ADEN AIRWAYS 1963 - 1964 : VISCOUNTS 151

Argonaut VR-AAS, departing Bahrain for Aden, was withdrawn from use in April 1964 due to corrosion. (Ray Deacon)

Chapter 21 :
ADEN AIRWAYS 1963 - 1964 : VISCOUNTS

This year was to prove to be one of both difficulty and transition for the airline. The Argonauts had been a temporary arrangement at best, and while they had allowed the airline to progress into pressurised flight, their time in service could hardly have been counted a success. Meanwhile the Avro 748 had not come up to performance and had been cancelled. In London the MTCA had announced that from 1st January 1965 load limits were to be placed on the DC-3 which would severely limit operations within the Protectorate both in terms of passengers for the scheduled routes as well as containing vague proposals for alleviations to freight operations.

Compared to most other airlines, Aden Airways was unusual in that its operations and revenue sources were so diverse and it is worth making some comparisons and observations:

1. Revenue Source:

	Aden Airways	BOAC
Scheduled service passengers	45%	68.2%
Charters	27%	11.5%
Freight	21%	8.2%
Other (Haj etc)	7%	12.1%

2. The scheduled services comprised two categories:
a) the Protectorate routes with competition from dhows and camels and where "airfields" were only suitable for the DC-3;
b) the international routes on which, with the exception of Aden/Bahrain and the short sectors to Djibouti and Hargeisa, jet competition already existed or was imminent.

3. The airline would run at a loss overall were it not for:
a) the Qat traffic;
b) the Air Ministry leave charters which were negotiated annually and which were wholly dependent on the maintenance of British forces in Aden;
c) to a lesser extent each year, the Haj traffic.

These three sources alone maintained the profit margins and if any one were to disappear the airline could not be profitable.

A further dilemma was that there was no other aircraft available which was suitable for both the Protectorate and international routes which Aden Airways flew. Nor would the numbers of passengers on the international routes sustain the purchase of a DH Comet (whatever amount of Qat was carried), nor was there sufficient expansion of the route network possible in the foreseeable future.

Thus, with the two Viscounts due for delivery later in 1963, the airline was still in a quandary as to how to progress the future. Nevertheless, the terms of lease of the Viscounts were particularly favourable (£100,000 per aircraft, payable over three years) and with this in mind the company hoped to survive.

An alternative, was to enter pooling arrangements with competing airlines and a new agreement was concluded in April 1963 with Ethiopian Airlines over the Aden-Asmara-Khartoum route. The advantage to EAL was that the restriction which only allowed them to operate twin-engined equipment was lifted (allowing them to fly the DC-6Bs) and would benefit Aden Airways once the Viscount was on the route. Later, Sudan Airways was allowed to participate in the pool, though only on the Asmara-Khartoum sector. Overall, the benefits to Aden Airways were such that revenues on this route were to double within a year.

Aden Airways crew at Nairobi, left to right: Captain Alan Jennings, Captain Vic Spencer, Sheila Monro, Chris Chambers, Carlo Moretti (the Traffic Manager, Nairobi), and unknown. (Sheila Pratt)

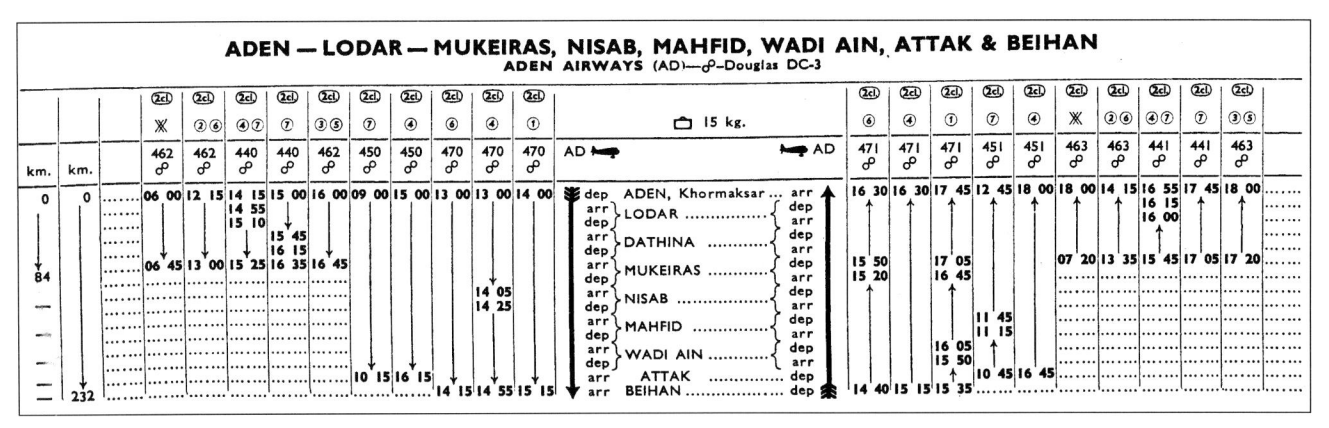

Services to the Western Protectorate, May 1963. (Overseas Airline Guide)

In the Protectorate; left: Beihan from the air and, right: the Beihan hotel. (Dr Roger Green)

This was an entirely unofficial agreement quietly made by the airlines involved. There was no bilateral agreement between the UK and Ethiopia and, in aviation terms, relations were poor between the two countries. Flights between Aden and Addis Ababa had not officially existed since early 1958 and both airlines had co-existed with connecting flights at Djibouti.

As if to add to the uncertainties, local politics began to play an increasingly important and disruptive part in Aden. Somalia had become independent the previous year and had quickly descended into political confusion. Though diplomatic relations were broken off with Britain early in 1963, Aden Airways was still able to continue flying to Hargeisa and Mogadishu, though this created uncertainty for passengers and load factors suffered.

In the Yemen, where Yemen Airlines had ceased to operate in all but name, the political rhetoric emanating from the new regime was beginning to have an influence within the Colony. The new Civil Aviation Employees Union, all of whose members worked for the airline, was becoming increasingly disruptive, complaining frequently that the company was slow to react in settling outstanding matters. For instance, in July industrial action took the form of a go-slow and an overtime ban commenced; it was led by those employees who were classed as labourers, the majority of whom were Yemenis who had no fixed abode in Aden. Accommodation would be relatively expensive for these individuals and difficult to find, so the demand was that some contribution should be forthcoming from the Company which in turn considered it to be a Government obligation. Nevertheless, the Aden Airways agreed to provide each worker with a monthly 25 shilling allowance for this purpose, though this was unsatisfactory to the Union.

Violence towards westerners had also been increasing and the Company felt that security was now becoming sufficiently important to ask for the secondment of a BOAC Security Officer to Aden Airways. This position was quickly to become a permanent one.

Meanwhile, planning for the arrival of the Viscounts continued. A training agreement for the flying crews was negotiated with Central African Airways (CAA) to coincide with the arrival of the first Viscount in September. Training would take place in Salisbury (now Harare) and would involve ground school, simulator and flying familiarisation in Rhodesia followed by line training in Aden under the supervision of Captain Heap from the CAA.

Also, further pooling arrangements with EAL to Addis Ababa were sought on the same unofficial basis as those to Asmara, though these negotiations proved to be a step too far.

The two remaining Argonauts plus VP-KOI on loan from EAAC were retained. On 17th April, 1963 VR-AAS had a Certificate of Airworthiness test lasting 1.35 hours flown by Vic Spencer who reported that the aircraft *"barely passed"* and ordered another air test which was carried out on 8th June resulting in another bare pass. The Cairo service that afternoon (AD 466) had to be postponed 24 hours so that the aircraft could be substituted by VR-AAT.

Meanwhile, flights within the Protectorates were still being developed. On 23rd April the airfield at Dhala in the Western Protectorate was opened for commercial services and the first proving flight was done by Vic Spencer in VR-AAF with Captain Elgee as co-pilot and Flight Clerk Yafai in the cabin. This was no ordinary destination since it was on the border with Yemen where there were frequent incursions of Egyptian-backed dissidents and it was to prove a contentious destination in the coming years.

The oil charters were also doing well with further exploration sites being opened up. A new one by the name of "Western" was visited on 30th April by Vic Spencer flying VR-AAI, the flight going Aden-Riyan-Thamud-Western-Aden. *"Some trouble finding Western"* was the diary entry, not surprising really bearing in mind the navigation methods in use.

Once a petroleum company had decided on a location where it wanted to explore, it set up the basic camp and levelled enough of the surrounding desert by the simple expedient of removing all the stones and rocks so that a passable runway existed which the DC-3 could use. Once this task was completed, a great deal of the equipment could be flown in, though obviously the really heavy drilling equipment could be brought in by truck if roads were available.

Finding the landing site was not always easy. In the first instance, the exact latitude and longitude co-ordinate would be worked out and passed to Aden Operations. A track and distance would then be plotted as a straight line giving a rough position on the chart. Navigation was basic in that a drift sight was used which was set up on take-off by the co-pilot and the aircraft would navigate accordingly until the pilot estimated that he was within the vicinity of the site. If things were well organised, an NDB would be in operation and its signal would guide the aircraft to the overhead position from which the pilot could then position himself for landing, always assuming he could identify the landing strip. If the NDB was unserviceable, or had not been installed, once the ground crews heard the aircraft engines spare tyres would be set on fire producing black smoke to indicate the position. This had the added advantage that it also indicated the wind direction.

"As I said, a lot of the destinations were for the oil company exploration teams. These could be anywhere in the Rub al Khalli. Their teams carried a M/F radio and they could give you weather information etc and at your request change it to a steady note so that the NDB could give you a bearing. That was all very well unless you were the first aircraft into a new position, in which case you probably had their radio on board. If it was a difficult location, they would sometimes set fire to a tyre just before your expected arrival time. You could see the plume of back smoke from many miles away on a calm day. I once landed at a new location and although I could see their caravans, I could see no sign of a marked strip. So I chose what looked like a fairly flat piece and landed there. When they met me off the aircraft, the oil chap said "I see you found the strip OK them". I replied in the negative to his surprise but then found that they had marked the sides of the strip with piles of sand. I landed around midday so the piles had no shadows so it was fortunate that I chose the right place." (259)

VR-AAA at Ataq with the "Contractor's House" in the background.
(Dr Roger Green)

Several exploration sites were named "Western" and each had a suffix code letter such as "A", "E" or "G" etc. Pilots were responsible for marking their personal charts with these positions, but it wasn't always easy. For instance, Vic Spencer marked "Western" on his chart with the frequency of the NDB 390, and the code letter (AA) and then a small note to say it was 7 nm north of Drill Co 2 (another exploration site) which could be found at Lat 17°15'N Long 51°01'E.

Deterioration of the Argonauts continued with the result that passengers' confidence in their reliability continued to fall away steadily. In July, the load factor was 47%, down from 56% the previous month, and VR-AAS which had experienced so many problems in passing its C of A had to be grounded on 26th July with severe corrosion. Fortunately, EAAC had a spare Argonaut for hire and VP-KOJ joined 'KOI in the Aden fleet. VR-AAS was sold locally for scrap, the company receiving £5,000 for the hull and spares. In the meantime, DC-6Bs were also hired regularly from Ethiopian Air Lines to fill in when the Argonauts became unserviceable.

The low level unrest continued within Aden, and in particular within the local labour force employed by the airline. In July, the UK Government, through the Foreign Office, had informed the airline that Aden Colony was henceforth to be called "Aden and the Protectorate of South Arabia" though Kamaran was to remain a separate entity for strategic reasons. For some time now, the company had also sought to bring more Adenis into responsible positions hitherto occupied by expatriate staff either seconded from BOAC or employed on a contract basis. Indeed, the Board of

VP-KOJ, an East African Airways Argonaut on lease to Aden Airways, in Aden titles, at Khormaksar in March 1964. It is accompanied by a British Eagle DC-6A and an RAF Dakota.

154

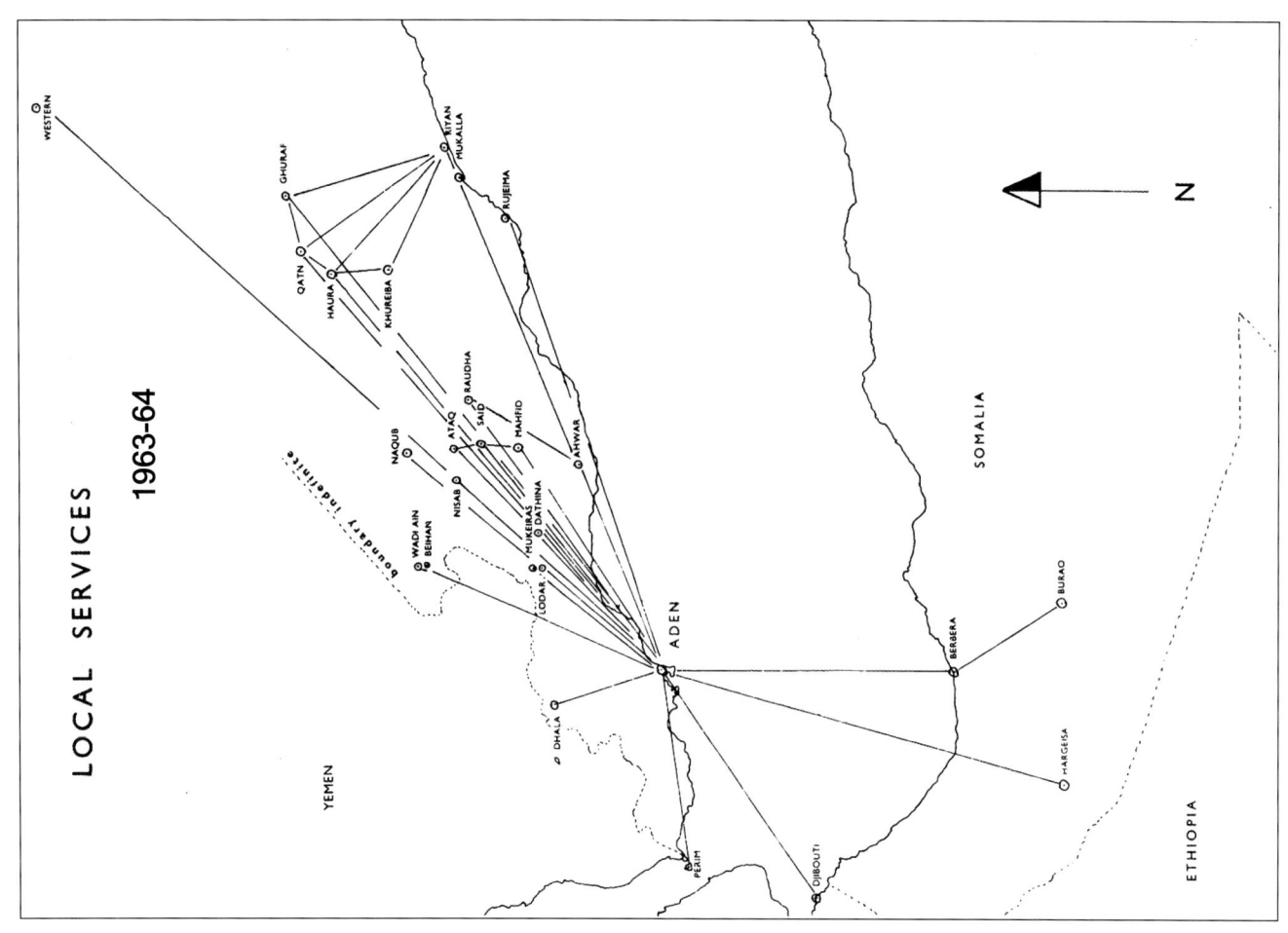

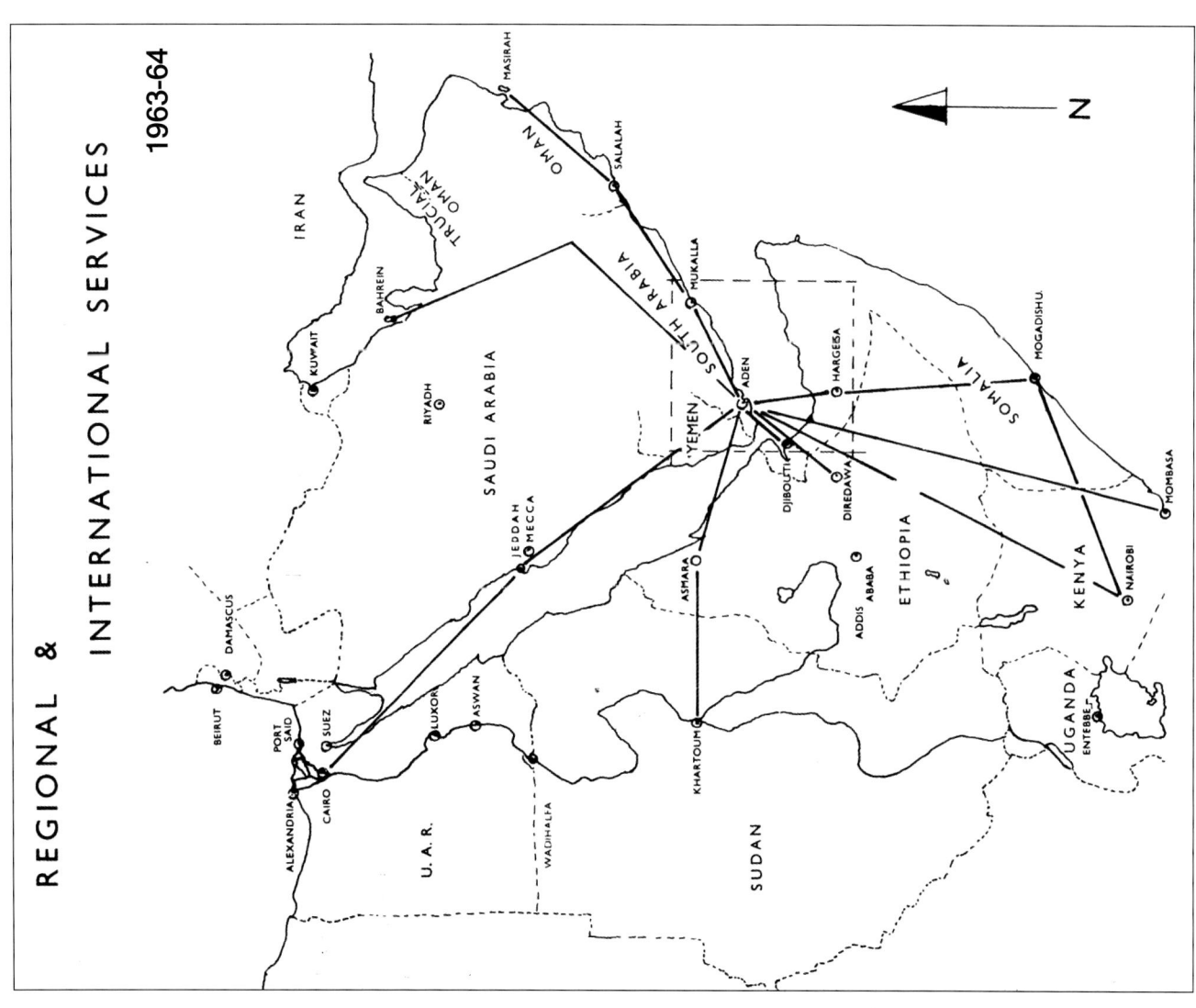

LOCAL SERVICES 1963-64

REGIONAL & INTERNATIONAL SERVICES 1963-64

Aden Airways first Viscount, VR-AAV, at Khormaksar in March 1964. (Ray Deacon)

Associated Companies had even agreed to sponsor two suitable Adeni candidates for pilot training at the College of Air Training, Hamble, which BEA and BOAC had opened in 1960. In fact, while it could not be determined how many pilots were sponsored in this way, only one Adeni Second Officer was ever employed and not until January 1967.

Nevertheless, the overall effect on the expatriate staff of these processes was to create further uncertainty in their own ranks. Added to this, there was continual pressure by the Aden Immigration Authorities for company job vacancies to be filled by Adenis and, even though this was often impossible to comply with, work permits for expatriates were becoming harder to obtain.

The result of this was a demand from the British Airline Pilots Association (BALPA) and the Expatriate Staff Association for some form of redundancy compensation scheme. In addition to this, expatriate staff had successfully argued for a large cost-of-living allowance as well as children's educational allowances, both claims adding some £19,000 to the company's annual costs.

Indeed in the monthly report to the Associated Companies Board a note of caution is made: *"net expenditure variances of the budget were £8,725 for the month of August, 5% of our budgeted costs and which introduce a disturbing note into the company's results. Flying staff pay, general administration, passenger service costs and, above all, charter of the second Argonaut from East African Airways were the main factors."* (260)

Despite these difficulties, the Viscounts were due for delivery and the first group of pilots and engineers went off to Salisbury to start their conversion courses at the CAA facility there. Vic Spencer was on the second course which started ground school on 26th August and he expressed surprise at having to attend lectures on the theory of gas turbines in general and the Rolls-Royce Dart engine in particular. Apparently there was general relief that the engine was far simpler than the Merlins of the Argonauts.

A further novelty for them was the requirement to complete the Viscount simulator course prior to doing the conversion training on the aircraft itself. These were the very early days of simulators and were archaic compared to those in use today. There was no movement, nor was there a "visual" system beyond the cockpit windows since the main purpose would have been to teach procedures such as checklists, engine starting and emergencies. This simulator phase lasted for ten days and consisted of eight details prior to completing a type rating exam for the endorsement of their licences.

This whole phase was quite a hurdle for the majority of Aden pilots as little instrument flying was required in normal operations out of Aden, and this course would have assumed a certain competency in flying procedures solely by instruments.

Also new was learning how to use Flight Planning and Performance Tables which had never really been part of the Aden Airways operation, particularly on the DC-3 where for many years a somewhat casual approach to the maximum take-off weight had prevailed.

The first Viscount 760D, VR-AAV, arrived in Aden from Singapore on 6th September, 1963. It should have gone into service on the 13th, but the aircraft had developed leaks in its fuel cells and it was not until 24th September that it was fit to fly when it operated the AD 474 from Aden to Asmara and Khartoum in place of the DC-3 service. It returned to Aden again the next day via Asmara before operating the AD 481 on 27th September to Mogadishu and Nairobi. (261)

Apart from the huge technical advance on the Argonaut, there were two very welcome additions to the aircraft equipment. The first was the installation of weather radar and the second was the use of slipper tanks, fitted to the wings, to increase the range sufficiently to reach Bahrain non-stop.

The pilots were so pleased with their new aeroplane that BALPA quickly put in a claim for a type differential for Viscount pilots of £425 p.a. for Captains and £290 p.a. for First Officers. This was over and above the £200 p.a. differential which they received for flying the Argonaut, but the pilots' argument was that they should have a share of the increase in productivity represented by the Viscount.

The second Viscount, VR-AAW, leased from BOAC.AC, arrived in Aden during the fourth week of October and was introduced into service on 13th November when it flew the AD 469 to Nairobi via Mogadishu.

The Argonauts continued in service for the Service Leave charters, though this produced fewer flying hours. During December VR-AAT was sold to Derby Airways for £5,000 and ferried back to Burnaston in the UK that month where it was scrapped and used for spares. But even these trooping charters were becoming vulnerable to industrial action. In October the Aden Airways trade union decided to support a strike by local Air Ministry employees by refusing to handle any military charters (such as leave charters) operated by the company.

The second Viscount, VR-AAW, on the tarmac at Khormaksar in April 1964. The slipper tanks, outboard of the engines, carried an extra 290 gallons of fuel resulting in a 10% increase in range. Partly visible on the right is another Viscount believed to be VP-YNA, briefly leased to Aden Airways by Central African Airways and wearing Aden stickers on the rear fuselage. (Ray Deacon)

Violence was increasing in Aden week by week. In December the High Commissioner, Kennedy Trevaskis, was leaving Aden for talks in London. As he was about to board the aeroplane, an Aden Airways employee by the name of Khalifa threw a grenade into the group and, though the High Commissioner was unhurt, one of his aides died later from his injuries. Khalifa was a senior station officer with Aden Airways, and also president of the Civil Aviation Employees Union. This was an indication not only of the strength of feeling within Aden, but also of the infiltration of dissident elements into Aden Airways which was to plague the airline in its final year.

"I was on duty when the bomb was thrown at the Governor. I was actually taking the passengers to the aircraft, and though it was still early morning, an immediate curfew was imposed. No one could get a (telephone) line in or out of the airfield and there seemed to be pandemonium. Naturally, everyone was questioned and then released, but following that incident the job became less attractive; no one seemed to trust anyone." (262)

More problems loomed for DC-3 operations within the Protectorate. The MTCA in London had finally issued its revised restrictions on DC-3 performance figures which were to be implemented by January 1965. If applied to Aden Airways routes these restrictions would invoke severe penalties on certain routes such as Mukeiras where the load could only be three or four passengers because of the airfield altitude. Other routes in the Western Protectorate would have weight penalties equivalent to 10 or more passengers.

Sensibly, the management appealed to the BOAC Board to use their influence with the MTCA not to extend these new limits to Aden Airways. It therefore came as a considerable surprise to the airline when BOAC declined to help on the premise that any advantage to Aden Airways would be reflected in a similar advantage to BOAC's competitors in the UK. How on earth the Corporation came to this conclusion must remain a mystery, but it was hardly helpful.

Nevertheless, the DC-3s continued to fly to new destinations within the Protectorates. On 24th February 1964 Vic Spencer landed VR-AAA at Said in the Eastern Protectorate: *"In the afternoon to Ataq/Mafidh and tried new field at Said. Fair with poor approaches"* (Vic Spencer diaries). Interestingly, Said was only 20

The international routes schedule for September 1963 shows how the Viscount was intended to take over services from the Argonaut.

CHAPTER 21: ADEN AIRWAYS 1963 - 1964 : VISCOUNTS

VR-AAA at Khormaksar in April 1964, still active after fourteen years of flying to Red Sea destinations. (Ray Deacon)

minutes flying time away from both Ataq and Mafidh but some days by camel. (263) On 6th February, the Chief Pilot, Bill Burman, announced his resignation from Aden Airways in order to join the UK Ministry of Aviation (as it had become) as an Inspector. BOAC also made it known that the company were reluctant to supply the chief pilots for the Associated Companies and Aden Airways was advised that, after Captain Burman's departure they would have to find their own people for this position. It came as some surprise to Vic Spencer to be offered the job of Operations Manager on 22nd February 1964 bearing in mind his refusal some time before when George Dyer was relieved. However, this time he accepted and was confirmed in that position on 1st April.

This was a time of mixed fortunes for both the Colony and the airline. The political situation had become tense within Aden and was to become more so as time went on, with inevitable consequences on labour relations in both the engineering and traffic departments. Two of the neighbouring countries, Yemen and Somalia, were increasingly turbulent. In the latter case not only had Somalia broken off diplomatic relations with Britain, but was also involved in a bitter border dispute with Ethiopia which meant that the flights from Aden to Mogadishu had to make a long detour over Somali territory to avoid flying through Ethiopian airspace.

Egypt's disruptive influence within the Red Sea countries had also resulted in Saudi Arabia breaking of diplomatic relations with that country, though this did become a benefit to Aden Airways as it meant that it became the sole airline between Jeddah and Cairo (AD 466/472) with consequent high load factors.

As a result of the increased tensions in the area, the UK Government had set up a listening post on Perim Island on the mouth of the Red Sea. In order to re-supply the outpost the Air Ministry awarded a three-year contract to the airline in March for the carriage thrice weekly of personnel and mail for the Diplomatic Wireless Service from Aden to Perim.

The downside, of course, of the unsettled atmosphere was that there would be a reduction in service leave charters to Mombasa and Nairobi as the troops were becoming increasingly busy both in Aden and the Western Protectorate where incursions from Yemen were becoming more frequent.

Notwithstanding all the difficulties that the year had witnessed, Aden Airways had done well. The profit would be almost £72,000 compared to a budgeted profit of £48,000 but the forecast for 1964/65 was not very encouraging.

Footnotes, Chapter 21:
(259) Captain Peter Austin.
(260) BOAC.AC Board Meeting, 1st October 1963.
(261) BOAC.AC Board Meeting, 1st October 1963.
(262) Mrs Sue Douet (Russell) who was a Ground Stewardess for Aden Airways at Khormaksar.
(263) Conversations with Vic Spencer, 2005.

ADEN AIRWAYS ROUTE MAP

FLIGHT INFORMATION

March 20th 1964.

FLIGHT No. AD 489   FROM Aden
                   TO Mombasa.

CAPTAIN Barnes   AIRCRAFT: Viscount VR-AAV.

ALTITUDE 16,000'   POSITION

GROUND SPEED 290 MPH. KNOTS

TIME OF ARRIVAL AT Mombasa.   11.10 G.M.T.

14.10 LOCAL TIME

REMARKS We shall be over Diredawa (in Ethiopia) at 0746 GMT (10.46 Local Time).

It gives us pleasure to welcome you on board this flight. If there is anything you require, please do not hesitate to ask the stewardess or any member of the crew whose pleasure it will be to give you assistance or advice.

In these days of moving-map computer displays it is easy to forget that in the past an in-flight log may have been passed around the passenger cabin for information. Although this example has an image of an Argonaut it clearly shows that it was issued on board Viscount VR-AAV operating the AD489 from Aden to Mombasa on 20th March 1964.   *(via Roger Carvell)*

VP-YNB, a Viscount 748D leased from Central African Airways in 1964.

Chapter 22 :
ADEN AIRWAYS 1964 - 1965

The policy initiated the year before of making strategic pooling agreements was continued. In April 1964 a Tripartite Pool was agreed between Air India, East African Airways and Aden Airways on the route Aden-Mogadishu-Nairobi. The terms were particularly favourable to Aden Airways and even though the initial agreement was for six months it would be carried on, unless one of the partners pulled out, which would be unlikely. (264)

By this time Air India were operating the Boeing 707 and EAAC the Comet, thus putting Aden Airways as a Viscount operator at a serious disadvantage. The agreement was that up to revenue of £350,000 the split would be Aden Airways 62%, EAAC 27% and Air India 11%; any revenue over £350,000 would be split 33%, 27% and 40% respectively. It might seem strange that Air India would receive such a small proportion of the Pool, but the prize for them was that they would now be able to carry originating passengers between Aden and Nairobi, an opportunity hitherto denied them. Neither Air India nor EAAC would be obliged to land at Mogadishu, which was not suitable for jets anyway.

Further cause for optimism was that the Air Ministry had renewed the service leave contracts to Mombasa and Nairobi, while the desire for Qat remained as high as ever, a desire which Aden Airways did it's very best to fulfil at a large profit.

This year the Haj started in April and made a fair contribution to the profit, though not as much as in the early days. Cairo, meanwhile, was producing good revenue even though the Egyptians and Saudis had patched up their differences and had resumed diplomatic relations and air services. Bahrain loads were poor, though, partly because the service had been increased to twice weekly and fewer people than before wished to travel between these two areas.

Labour relations with the local staff were poor, but that was more because of the political situation than anything else. More worrying was the fear of redundancy within the expatriate staff, the pilots in particular, and this would cause problems for the company as time went on, though there were still opportunities for expatriate ground-staff:

"I was interviewed by the Station Manager, a man named Khalifa. We got on well and I was offered a job as a ground hostess. Transport was provided and I worked shifts with another girl, there just being the two of us.

Most of the staff were Indian, and my duties were to check-in the passengers and get them to the aircraft so that it could leave on time. I had to learn the announcements in Arabic as our passengers were mainly Arabs; wild and woolly and always armed with daggers. The Arabic names were incredible and they took hordes of children with them, also, they could be travelling with two or three wives.

I remember we were late getting one lot of passengers on board because six hadn't turned up. I then discovered that they had six children under their clothing so as not to pay for them. There was never any feeling of urgency with them; they would just amble about and disappear into the loo when they needed to board the aeroplane." (265)

On 12th April, Captain Hamblin was operating the AD 465 from Aden to Hargeisa. The aircraft, VR-AAM, departed Aden at 1300 for the 1.40 hour flight and was due to arrive at its destination at 1440 local. Unknown to Captain Hamblin, a trench had been dug across the runway to a depth of some two feet which had not been notified to the airline. On landing the aircraft went over the trench at some speed with the left undercarriage, which promptly collapsed. Not only was the left engine damaged, but the spar was as well, with the result that the aircraft was beyond economical repair. (266) There were no injuries to the three crew and 15 passengers.

Fortunately the aircraft was insured for £21,000 and had been fully written down so there was some benefit to the company. However, the flying program planned for the year could not be flown with a fleet of only five DC-3s and two Viscounts. The Aden Board made a case for the purchase of a third Viscount, which did make sense as there had been a need to charter an Ethiopian DC-6B during the Haj season which reduced the profit from this trade.

International and regional services, May 1964. While Aden - Nairobi was operated by EAAC Comets and Aden Viscounts, the latter shared the Aden - Khartoum route with Ethiopian DC-6Bs and Sudan Airways Friendships.

(Overseas Airline Guide)

COLOUR SECTION 3

Birgit Baker on board an Argonaut. (Wendy Hayden Sadler)

Wendy Locke and Natasha Seton, 1962. (Wendy Hayden Sadler)

Aden Airways cap badge. (Wendy Hayden Sadler)

Aden Airways Stewardess badge. (Wendy Hayden Sadler)

Captain Pete Williamson and F/O Bob Wigley, 1961. (Wendy Hayden Sadler)

Wendy Locke with a passenger and an engineer. (Wendy Hayden Sadler)

VR-AAM at Hargeisa after its landing mishap on 12th April 1964. The ditch which had been dug across the runway had not been notified to the airline. (Vic Spencer)

Unfortunately the damage to VR-AAM was greater than this photo implies. (Vic Spencer)

Captain Bill Burman, Chief Pilot of Aden Airways, January 1964. (Vic Spencer)

Another view of the crippled VR-AAM at Hargeisa. (Vic Spencer)

Captain Vic Spencer in the uniform of 1964. (Vic Spencer)

Colour Section 3

Captain Dick Larcombe and VP-KOI, February 1964. (Bob Wigley)

Captain Dick Larcombe in the Argonaut. (Bob Wigley)

Argonaut VP-KOI on lease from East African Airways, 1964. Note the all-white fin and rudder. (Bob Wigley)

Stewardess Caroline Flory on the steps of a Viscount, Asmara, early 1965. (Caroline Burrows)

Sheila Munro with Captain Hewitt. 1964. (Sheila Pratt)

Top and bottom of page: Two views of DC-3 VR-AAC in the extreme conditions of the Hadramaut. (Bob Wigley)

The airport terminal at Ghuraf, the only such building in the Hadramaut. (Bob Wigley)

Unloading at Dhala. (Bob Wigley)

A discussion taking place at Beihan, 1964. (Bob Wigley)

Loading crews at Dhala. (Bob Wigley)

COLOUR SECTION 3 C37

VR-AAC taxying out at Khormaksar in 1964. (Ronald Davidson)

Captain Emmett in contemplative mood. (Bob Wigley)

Ethiopian Airlines DC-6B at Khormaksar, 1964. These were frequently chartered by Aden Airways when short of capacity. (Ronald Davidson)

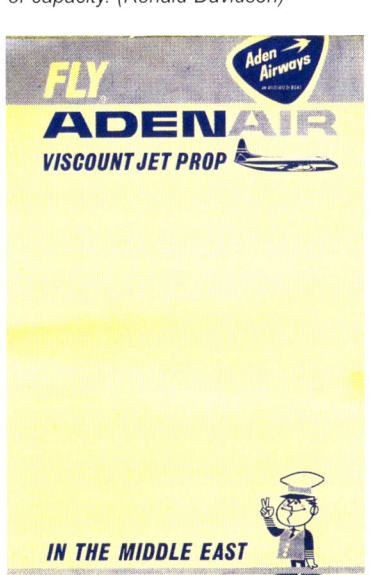

Playing cards via "Airline Playing Cards - Colour Reference Guide", Fred Chan 2007

Aden Airways notepad, 1964. (Bernard Lewis)

Book matches (Jenny Drummond Harris)

Bridge score card. (Brian Walker)

Aden Airways ashtray c.1964. (Trevor Austin)

C38

RED SEA CARAVAN

(Brian Walker)

Beer mat, 1959 (Brian Walker)

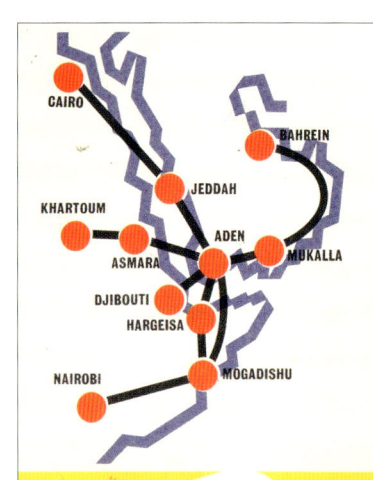

Frequent Viscount Services between Aden – Mogadishu – Nairobi – Jeddah – Cairo and Bahrein. Your Travel Agent will gladly give you details of the latest schedules and air fares.

ADENAIR

Viscount brochure c.1964

Aden Airways BRING NEW PLEASURE TO MIDDLE EAST TRAVEL

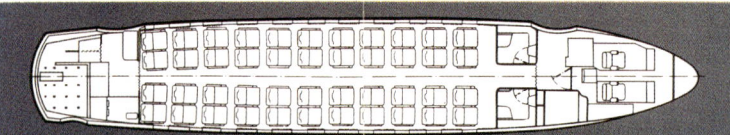

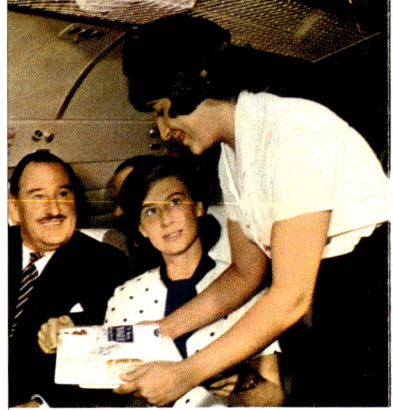

VISCOUNT JET PROP

The VISCOUNT Jet Prop is the most popular medium-range aircraft in the history of air travel —swift, silent and supremely comfortable. The Viscount is now available for your journeys by ADEN AIRWAYS, from Cairo in the north to the cool, green highlands of Kenya. **And remember,** Aden Airways crews are the most experienced in the Middle East and Adenair cabin-care is unsurpassed.

FOR SUPERB CABIN CARE - FLY **ADENAIR**

ADENAIR FLY Aden Airways VISCOUNT JET PROP

(Ray Deacon)

(Ray Deacon)

COLOUR SECTION 3   C39

Aden Airways Head Office, May 1965. (Trevor Austin)

Aden Harbour looking towards Steamer Point 1965. (Bob Wigley)

The rear of the Aden Airways compound, August 1965. (Trevor Austin)

Aden Harbour from overhead Little Aden, 1965. (Bob Wigley)

Adhal car park vendors, May 1965. (Trevor Austin)

Aden Harbour, a further view from overhead Little Aden during the approach to runway 09. (Bob Wigley)

Final approach to runway 09 at Khormaksar, 1965. (Bob Wigley)

Flying along the coastline of northern Socotra before commencing an approach to the south. (John Burley)

*The accident at Socotra, March 1965.
At the end of the landing roll, when it was feared that VR-AAA might run down an incline, the aircraft was slewed to the left and the right undercarriage collapsed under the strain. The skid marks can be clearly seen in the photograph above, as can the irreparable damage to the right wing. (John Burley)*

VR-AAA seen from the front. (Vic Spencer)

The right wheel collapsed under the fuselage. (John Burley)

VR-AAN was flown in to pick up the crew and passengers, leaving an engineering team behind who would strip VR-AAA of all useful items. (Vic Spencer)

The Sheik Othman salt mills, 1965. (Trevor Austin)

The Aden Airways accommodation blocks on Khormaksar Beach, 1965. (Bob Wigley)

COLOUR SECTION 3   C41

Berbera Airport terminal in 1965. (Bob Wigley)

Unloading army supplies at Dhala in 1965. (Bob Wigley)

Nightstop accommodation was not always up to the high standards expected today. The sleeping quarters for pilots at Thamud with Vic Spencer in the doorway, 1965. (Bob Wigley)

Airborne from Mukeiras in 1965, with a view of the valley which doubled as an 'escape route' in the event of an engine failure on take-off - see page 93. (Bob Wigley)

The "Contractor's House" next to the football field and the airstrip at Ataq, 1965. (Bob Wigley)

A terminal in the Hadramaut, location unidentified. November 1965. (Trevor Austin)

Troops transported to Perim Island, 1965. (Ingleby Jefferson)

Unloading an incoming flight, Khormaksar 1965. (Bob Wigley)

Ghuraf airport from the air in 1965. Note the oil-covered area of sand to prevent excessive dust. (Bob Wigley)

The airline offices at Hargeisa, June 1965. (Trevor Austin)

On turn-around in the Hadramaut, probably Beihan in November 1965. (Trevor Austin)

Viscount VR-AAV at Mombasa in 1965. (Vic Camden)

COLOUR SECTION 3 C43

Flying up to Mukeiras in November 1965; the difficult terrain can be seen to full effect here. (Trevor Austin)

The Crescent Hotel, May 1965. (Trevor Austin)

Steamer Point. Even in 1965 Aden was a regular port of call for passenger ships on their way to or from the far east. (Trevor Austin)

The Khormaksar Palace Hotel with an Aden Airways bus outside, May 1965. (Trevor Austin)

Goldmohur Beach Club from the sea, May 1965. (Trevor Austin)

Flying down to Africa on VR-AAV, with the aircraft fuselage reflected on the cowlings of the Rolls-Royce Darts. (Trevor Austin)

Over-flying Shebam in January 1966. (Vic Spencer)

Houses in Shebam were all built of mud. (Vic Spencer)

The Aden Airways offices in Shebam, January 1966. (Vic Spencer)

Street scene in Shebam. (Vic Spencer)

Captain Alan Jennings on the DC-3 in January 1966. (Vic Spencer)

A view of Shebam from ground level. (Vic Spencer)

Colour Section 3 C45

Street scene in Crater, Aden May 1966. (Trevor Austin)

Ready for unloading in the Hadramaut. (Trevor Austin)

S/O Tony May, June 1966. (Bob Wigley)

Stewardesses Ann Ilott and Gill Lees flying between Jeddah and Aden in March 1966. (Vic Spencer)

Airside view of Hargeisa terminal. May 1966. (Trevor Austin)

DC-3 VR-AAI during a turn-around up in the Hadramaut. 1966. (Trevor Austin)

Aden Airways head office in Khormaksar, October 1966. (Trevor Austin)

Aden Airways personnel staff in August 1966. Trevor Austin is fifth from the right. (Trevor Austin)

Captain Pete Williamson, deputy chief pilot, in February 1966. (Vic Spencer)

Don Classey, second from the left, General Manager of Aden Airways in 1966. (Vic Spencer)

Emile Tewfik at his desk in September 1966. (Vic Spencer)

Mary Warden, secretary, at Khormaksar in September 1966. (Vic Spencer)

COLOUR SECTION 3   C47

The view of Aden as a Viscount approaches for runway 09 at Khormaksar. (Trevor Austin)

VR-AAW reflected on a wet day at Khormaksar in February 1966. (Vic Spencer)

In-flight service on a Viscount, November 1966. (Trevor Austin)

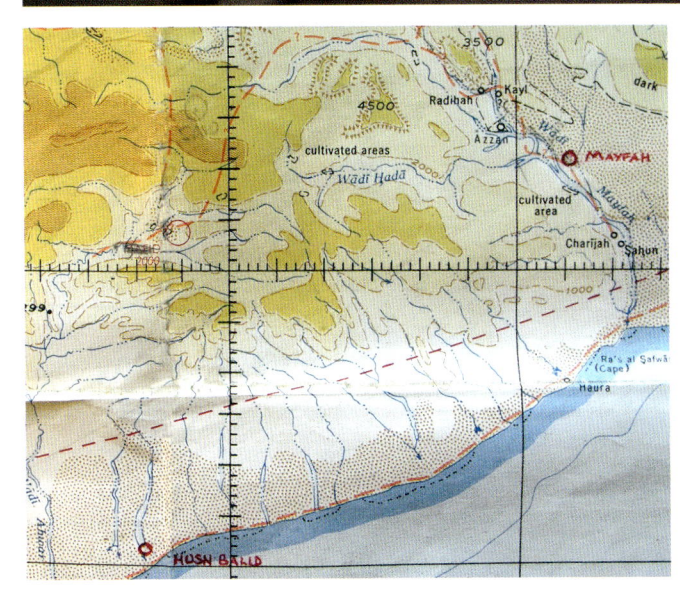

VR-AAN had taken off from Mayfah to fly back to Aden. The crash site was near Mafid, in the wadi just to the west, partly obscured by pencil on the map. (Vic Spencer)

External view of the port fuselage of VR-AAN at the approximate location where the bomb exploded. (Trevor Austin)

Trevor Austin by VR-AAC at Hargeisa, May 1967. (Trevor Austin)

Captain John Rose in a Viscount cabin, May 1967. (Vic Spencer)

Viscount VR-AAV burning fiercely a few moments after the bomb blast. (Jack Sayer)

The wreckage of VR-AAV under guard on June 30th 1967. (Vic Spencer)

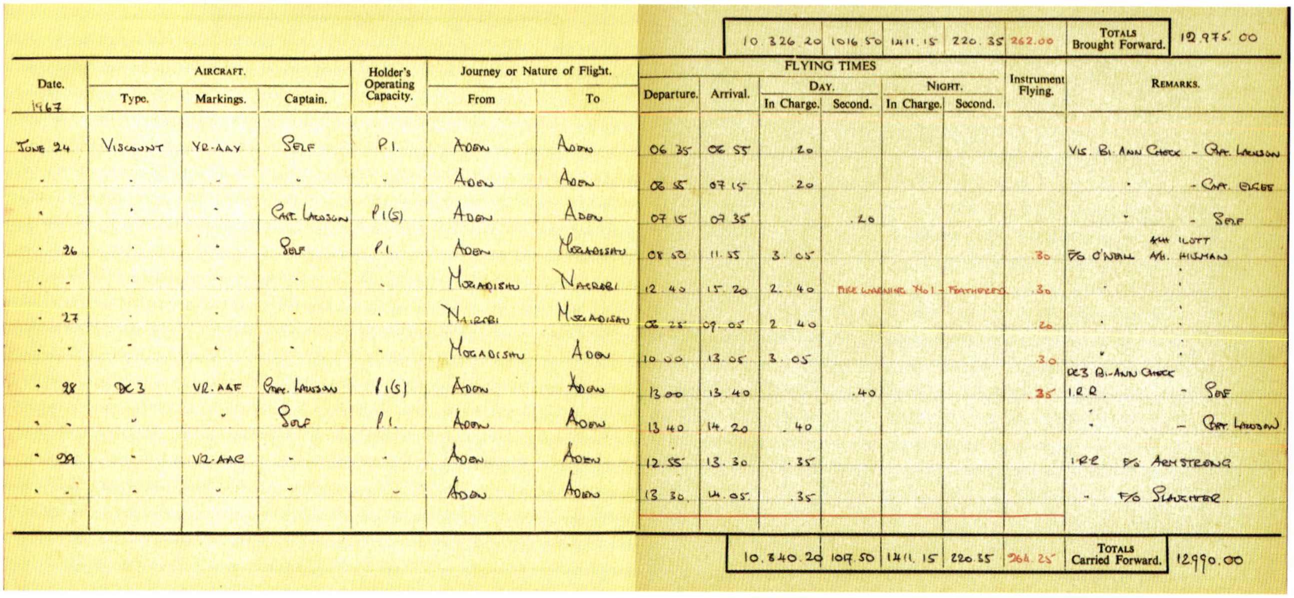

The final days of Aden Airways as recorded in Vic Spencer's log book, June 1967. (Vic Spencer)

Chapter 22: Aden Airways 1964 - 1965

On 1st April, Captain Vic Spencer was officially appointed Operations Manager for Aden Airways, although he had been doing the job since the departure of Captain Bill Burman some months before. Captain Pete Williamson was appointed as his deputy. Their first official duty was to investigate the accident at Hargeisa which was put down to lack of communication from the Hargeisa airport authorities. Occupying these positions meant that both men had to become Instrument Rating and Type Rating Examiners, meaning that they were designated to carry out the six-monthly competency checks on all the pilots in the airline. Today these checks are carried out in sophisticated simulators, but in 1964 all of these were done on the aircraft which involved considerable expense to the airline as well as time taken in the air with no revenue.

The question of a replacement for the DC-3 lost at Hargeisa had to be resolved quickly. It would take some time for a paper to be presented to the Aden Board which would then recommend it to the AC Board which, in turn, would take it to BOAC. In the meantime a Viscount, VP-YNA, was dry-leased from Central African Airways in April, followed by VP-YNC later in the year. Meanwhile, a DC-3 (OD-AAM) belonging to Middle East Airlines came up for sale - it was considered a good buy and joined the Aden fleet on 27th July as VR-AAZ. A further Central African Viscount, YP-YNB, was also leased on other occasions.

However, after the first three months of financial good fortune (ignoring the loss of the DC-3), matters started to go wrong. In fact, much of the reason for the profits then was that the Haj took place in April (with a £40,000 profit), the Qat trade was doing well and the service leave charters had been renewed on a temporary basis.

Labour problems, still a relatively new problem for the airline, began to make themselves felt. The Civil Aviation Employees Union which had already forced a 25 shilling housing allowance, was now seeking a further 80 shillings per month based on an increase in the cost of living within the Colony, and failure to pay this increase would result in a "work-to-rule" from 4th July. Eventually the Union accepted an increase of 60 shillings (£3) but even this would cost the company some £20,000 p.a.

In June, in an attempt to reduce the price of Qat imported from Ethiopia, the Qat Importing Company placed an embargo on its import from that country and turned instead to Yemen for supplies. This gave rise to some problems as officially Yemen was fomenting unrest in Aden thanks to the Egyptian influence there. Clearly Mukeiras and Dhala, both on the Yemen border, could not be the entry points because of uncertainties created by the political tensions, so Kamaran Island was chosen as the hand-over base. On the surface, this could work, but it did require some co-ordination between Aden Airways and what remained of Yemen Airlines. All too frequently the Yemen aircraft did not arrive or was hours late, which meant the Qat was hardly fresh. Often it didn't arrive at all.

The loss of revenue to Aden Airways was substantial.

Trouble with tribesmen in the Radfan in the Western Protectorate also meant that the forces could no longer release troops for leave flights to Kenya with the result that many charters were cancelled at short notice.

Suddenly the future did not look good and the company could do little about it. An interesting diversion (and one perhaps which was a foretaste of the future) came in July when the Chief Minister of Aden, Mr Baharoon, complained that the company had discriminated against a travel agency with which the Chief Minister had connections. (267) That a man in that a position should even have such connections while in office was somewhat strange.

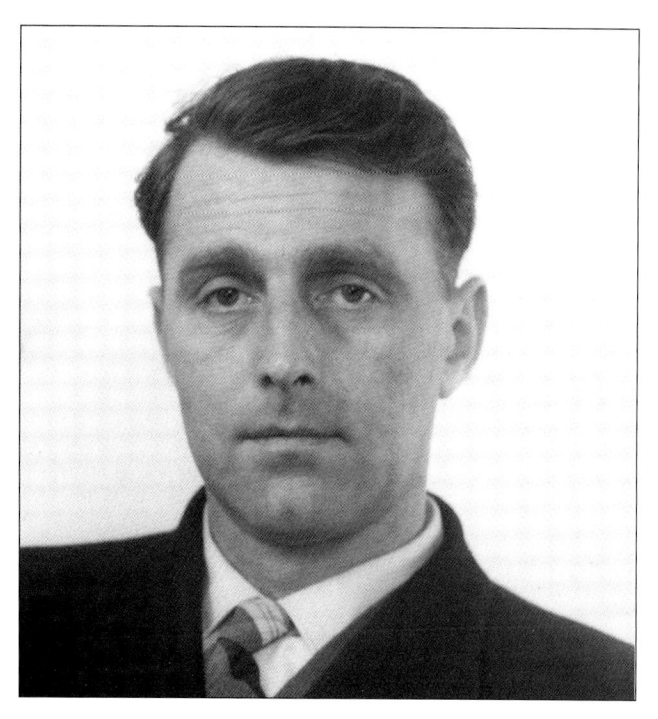

Captain Pete Williamson who became Deputy Operations Manager in April 1964.
(Vic Spencer)

The proposal to the AC Board for a third Viscount had a great deal of merit, not least because circumstances had changed considerably since the original study had been made in November 1963. The major change was the loss of the DC-3 at Hargeisa and it was perceived that a third Viscount could take over the routes from the DC-3 to Hargeisa and Djibouti. The third aircraft would give added flexibility in that it would be productive for the next Haj and there was the possible lease of some 600 hours p.a. to Air Somali on wet lease. The newly-bought DC-3 would be sold and the capital would go towards the initial cost (some £41,000 p.a.) of the Viscount which would come from Hawaiian Airlines.

Overall, it was envisaged that after all costs there would be a surplus of £8,500 p.a. instead of the loss which had been forecast the previous November. (268)

The plan was put to the AC.Board which approved it; but when it went to the BOAC Board it was turned down. This was understandable since the Aden Board had always seemed to view their plans in the best possible light. However, it would be fair to say that, even as it planned the future, the ground was being cut from under its feet. Air Somali was certainly interested in a Viscount lease, but at rates so advantageous to itself that it was hardly worth it. Secondly, the extra weekly service to Bahrein had not been a great success with average load factors falling to 34% from 42%. Thirdly, the route up to Cairo through Jeddah was already failing as a result of relations being restored between Saudi Arabia and Egypt, it being established that the inhabitants of those countries preferred to travel on their national airlines. Finally, perhaps the BOAC Board for once had a better perspective on the situation viewed as it was from London; perhaps it could see the worsening security situation and the consequent loss of both scheduled and charter revenue. There is evidence, too, that there had always been a slight distaste at the carriage of Qat and some discomfort at the dependence of the airline on this source of revenue.

Concern had already been expressed in BOAC at the direction in which the Aden Airways finances were going and the Board had become well aware, possibly through the Colonial Office, of the potential for violence in Aden and the effect it would have on Aden Airways.

Above: VR-AAI being examined after the left undercarriage collapsed on landing at Khormaksar, 2nd August 1964. (via Peter Pickering)

Right: Captain Jack Parker who was in command of VR-AAI at the time. (Vic Spencer)

A further development with the Chief Minister of Aden, Mr Baharoon, took place in discussions with the Chairman of Aden Airways and Sir Duncan Cumming in London. In his report to the BOAC Board on these discussions, Mr Cumming said of Mr Baharoon: *"As to the desirability of local (Adeni) participation in Aden Airways, it was clear that the Brothers Trading Company (of which the Minister is a large shareholder) had ambitions in the aviation world. The Minister seemed to have the erroneous impression that BOAC would not under any circumstances part with any of the shares of Aden Airways. On the assumption that he could change this outlook, he indicated that there should be no public prospectus of application for investment but that participation should be reserved for selected concerns in Aden. The first and possibly the only concern being the Trading Company.*

The Minister exaggerated Aden Airways' labour troubles and suggested these could be avoided by setting up a local handling company similar to Karnak, but of course, a subsidiary of Brothers Trading Company." (269)

After the closure of Aden Airways, Brothers Air Services took over the operations of the airline with even less success.

The whole episode left an unpleasant flavour and gave some indication of how business might be run after the British left Aden.

In another incident on 2nd August, DC-3 VR-AAI was involved in a landing accident with Captain Parker in command when the left undercarriage collapsed as the aircraft came to a halt. While there were no injuries to the crew or passengers, the left wing, undercarriage, engine and propeller were badly damaged. The aircraft was given a temporary repair at Khormaksar before being given an air test by Vic Spencer on 18th August and then flown with the undercarriage down to Addis Ababa for further repairs.

Further problems were now making themselves felt on the borders with Yemen, at Dhala in particular. This latter outpost is situated to the north of the Radfan valley (where, it will be recalled, a combined British and Federal Army Operation against rebels and insurgents had been taking place). Aden Airways had operated regular scheduled flights to this airfield since 1963, starting with one flight per week (AD 460/461) and increasing this to three per week by August 1964. While the flights carried passengers and local goods on these flights, supplies of war material were also carried for the Federal Regular Army on these and additional "freight" charter flights. On 2nd September Vic Spencer had landed there in VR-AAZ and while the aircraft was on the ground

the fire tender was mined and blew up. On the same day, an RAF Beverley also sustained a number of hits from small arms fire during take-off. (270) As Aden Airways did not have war risk insurance, operations were suspended into Dhala until cover would be arranged. Services were resumed on 14th September when Vic Spencer once again took VR-AAZ, though for understandable reasons he only spent 15 minutes there. *"To Dhala, OK but some pilots still unhappy."* On 23rd September *"To Dhala in AAF. More mining on the airfield"* (Vic Spencer diaries).

The pilots were generally very unhappy about it. BALPA had strong views, particularly as Dhala was technically a "war zone" and though the company had obtained war risk insurance, there was some doubt in the minds of the pilots that this would cover them as well as the aircraft. Several pilots refused to go and had the full backing of BALPA. However this was Aden Airways and it had a pride in flying to inhospitable places.

"In the evening saw Emsley who refused Dhala tomorrow. Will go myself." (Vic Spencer diaries 25th September). He went again on 30th September, after which he attended a meeting at Company HQ where he had arranged for a Colonel Newton to explain the safeguards put in place at Dhala for their safety. On 10th October *"Dhala flight went off OK"* (Vic Spencer diaries).

It wasn't so much any one incident which was now causing the BOAC Board to question the long term viability of Aden Airways, but it was the number of signals coming from the Federal Government, the financial results, unrest within the expatriate ranks and the ongoing industrial relations problems with local staff.

"The view of HMG as to a possible transfer of part of BOAC AC's shareholding in Aden Airways to local interests would be obtained prior to the Chairman's proposed visit to Aden in December.
A review should be made of the reasons for participation in Aden Airways and of the long-term prospects of the company. This, together with HMG's opinions, would be submitted to the BOAC Board in due course.
The Chairman of Aden Airways should be told of the Board's concern at the current results of Aden Airways and asked what proposals his Board would make to deal with the situation and what they considered the long-term prospects of the company to be. The Board did not agree that Aden Airways should acquire a third Viscount aircraft." (271)

By September the financial situation was beginning to cause concern. A loss of £6,628 was posted for the month (though a profit of £6,000 had been budgeted) because of a substantial

Chapter 22: Aden Airways 1964 - 1965

shortfall in revenue. This was from losses on the route to Cairo, fewer charters as a result of the political situation and the loss of the Qat flights to Dire Dawa on which an income of £18,800 could have been expected. Even though the drug was still available through Kamaran Island, the unreliability of the Yemen Airlines flights meant that only the costs of the flights were covered.

However, in October the airline earned its final monthly profit for the financial year (£1,498). Charter operations picked up a little though revenue from scheduled services was well down. Strangely enough, because of repairs to the runway at Mogadishu, DC-3s had to be used on the AD 469 and 481 to Nairobi on seven occasions during the month, operating at high load factors for a very good profit.

Profits or break-even continued during the next few months, but it was a constant struggle to do so in a climate of increasing violence both in Aden and along the border of the Eastern Protectorate, not only at Dhala but also in Mukeiras: *"To office and later to Mukeiras. Good run and the runway OK. Battle at Mukeiras last night"* (Vic Spencer diaries 14th October). Needless to say this caused more concern to BALPA and the pilots; meetings were frequent and most expressed a wish not to fly to Dhala where mining of the runway was almost a nightly event.

Despite these conditions, the company continued to try hard to bring local Adenis into the operation. On 26th October, seven local women presented themselves for interview as stewardesses and the next day four young men came in to try for sponsorship as pilots at the College of Air Training, Hamble. Results were mixed; it must have been difficult for these young people to try to join the "other side" and the sad fact remained that in the case of the stewardesses the experiment was not a great success. Only one pilot (S/O Wahed) succeeded in joining the airline in 1967.

Chief Pilot Vic Spencer continued to fly to many of the more unpopular destinations within the Western Protectorate, in particular Dhala, where on 10th November he took the Chairman of Associated Companies and the General Manager of Aden Airways in order to assess the situation for themselves. On 21st November, he went to Mukeiras and on to a new destination, Dathina, where he described the strip as *"not very good"*.

Ever since the RAF had reduced its transport fleet, Aden Airways had a contract to fly from Aden to Riyan, Salalah and to Masirah Island transporting men, supplies and mail on behalf of the RAF. These flights operated several times a month and were popular with both the passengers and crews. In November the company was informed that this charter would not be renewed after March 1965 (though in fact they did continue on an ad hoc basis).

During the rest of the financial year to April 1965 incidents continued Bombings in Aden, grenades thrown at expatriate groups and local industrial unrest and work-to-rule; all helped to sap the morale of the expatriate workforce. The pilots' pay claim put in during 1964 was settled at last with Captains receiving a considerable rise in salary. A new rank of Senior First Officer would allow an increase in salary as a Co-Pilot but at the expense of newly-employed First Officers who would now start their careers in the Company with the new rank of Second Officer.

From the foregoing it would be easy to assume that the Company offered a low level of service whereas in fact the leave charters had always been very popular for the service families who travelled to Mombasa or Nairobi on them.

"In February 1965 we made our way across to the civilian airport side of the Royal Air Force, Khormaksar, airfield, from where our transport to Mombasa was to be by way of an Aden Airways scheduled flight. The Vickers Viscount aeroplane that we were to

Flying in the Hadramaut - a more inhospitable landscape could hardly be imagined! (Trevor Austin)

board was standing with its dark blue and white colour scheme showing to good effect in the bright sunshine and giving a very favourable first impression.

I do recall that I was impressed by the comfort of the accommodation compared with my other experiences, either as an RAF pilot or as a passenger on BEA's DC-3s. In particular, after the heat of Aden outside, it really was wonderful to experience the air conditioning within the aircraft". (272)

Financially, the year as a whole was a disappointment. A loss during the first three months of 1965 of £15,202 brought home the sense of crisis and only the capital profits (loss of VR-AAM) permitted a profit of £5,000 to be declared for the year, though this was in contrast to a budgeted profit of some £48,000. Once again, the real weakness of the company was exposed: the loss of the Qat trade which would have brought in an estimated £172,000 in revenue. Another way of looking at it was that the profits from the drug trade subsidised the scheduled routes.

The final blow to the year came on 26th March, 1965 when DC-3 VR-AAA was damaged beyond repair while landing at Hadibo on the island of Socotra.

John Burley was on the flight:
"The flight was chartered by Pan American Hadramaut Drilling Company, which had rights in what was then the Eastern Hadramaut Province. They needed to have discussions with the Sheikh who lived on Socotra Island, just off the Horn of Africa, and the legendary site of Sinbad's shipwreck. The Sheikh was not prepared to accept the drilling company's offer to be flown to Aden itself, and so the company therefore chartered an aircraft to go up there.

The mountains in the background of the photographs are on Socotra Island, and the coastline is the North coast of Socotra.

Viscount over Kilimanjaro, August 1963. (Vic Spencer)

The accident to VR-AAA at Hadibo, Socotra 26th March 1965.

Left: The DC-3 had been landing towards the mountains in the distance. This photo taken early next morning after the occupants had slept out under the wing of the "Tilting Hilton" as they named it. (John Burley)

Below, left: Location map showing Socotra Island.

Below, right: The right undercarriage can be seen collapsed under the wing as a result of the sharp left turn on landing. (John Burley)

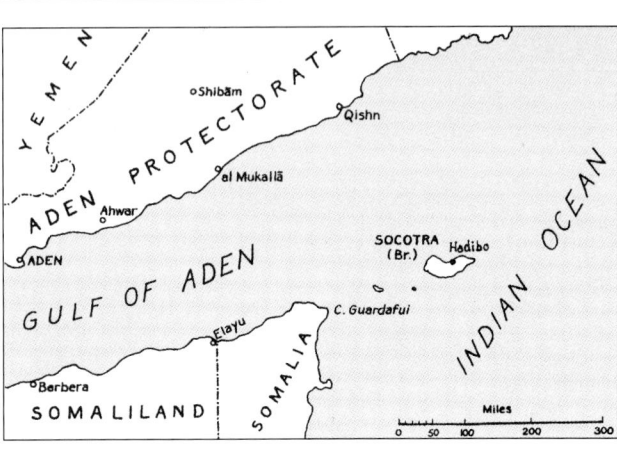

The airstrip at Hadibo was on the narrow coastal plain at the foot of the mountains, and aligned at approximately 90 degrees to the sea. There was an escarpment rising to over 1,000 feet immediately inland of the strip, making a landing towards the sea difficult as it involved a low tight turn on finals.

Normally, an arrival would have been timed to take advantage of the offshore wind in order to land into wind, and in the direction towards the escarpment, but on this occasion the diurnal change had already occurred with the result that a tailwind landing was required from the sea. The airstrip was somewhat shorter than anticipated, and with the tailwind landing being deeper than normal, together with a higher groundspeed, the result was an overrun. An additional problem was that the ground fell away steeply at the at the end of the runway, and in order to avoid this it was necessary to turn the aircraft sharply to port before sufficient speed decay had occurred. The result was that the starboard landing gear collapsed and though the aircraft was halted, it was badly damaged.

The crew was led by Captain Peter Williams, and his co-pilot was F/O Bob Wigley; the steward was a gentleman by the name of Shansan. The supernumeraries were an engineer and John Burley, the Operations Officer for Aden Airways. The passengers, about 15 in all, were shaken by the experience, but recovered sufficiently to be able to proceed as scheduled to the meeting with the Sheikh.

The airstrip was, literally, a cleared strip, with no communications and no aids, not even a windsock. There were, obviously, no accommodation facilities either. The entire complement of passengers and crew were forced to spend an uncomfortable night sleeping in the open beside the aircraft, which was christened the "Tilting Hilton" for the occasion. During the mid to late afternoon the crew were able to establish contact with an RAF plane which happened to be flying within radio VHF range and a message was relayed to Aden Airways operations in Aden.

A rescue DC-3 flown by Chief Pilot, Vic Spencer, managed to land at Socotra the next day and effect a rescue of everyone on board. As for the stricken aircraft, a skeleton team of engineers was placed on the island and they were able to strip all the recyclable equipment from it before returning to Aden. Reports received years later indicated that the aircraft was still there.

After Aden and the Aden Protectorate became independent, they united with the Yemen Arab Republic, and the country became aligned with the USSR. The island of Socotra, because of its strategic position, became a communications monitoring base for the Soviets who even established an army detachment there." [273]

Footnotes, Chapter 22:
(264) BOAC AC Board Meeting, 13th April 1964.
(265) Mrs Sue Douet (Russell), Ground Stewardess.
(266) BOAC AC Board Meeting, 28th May 1964. Also Vic Spencer diaries.
(267) BOAC.AC Board Meeting, 20th July 1964.
(268) Aden Airways proposal of a third Viscount - 20th July 1964.
(269) BOAC AC Board Meeting, 28th September 1964.
(270) BOAC AC Board Minutes, 28th September 1964.
(271) BOAC Board Meeting, 28th September 1964.
(272) Vic Campden worked for the Air Ministry Directorate in the architectural section of their offices in Aden.
(273) John Burley was Operations Officer with Aden Airways.

VR-AAF, seen here in the Associated Companies colour scheme, was used in June 1965 to investigate the possibility of upgrading the Riyan runway for Viscount use as described below.
(Author's collection)

Chapter 23 :
ADEN AIRWAYS 1965 - 1966

After the experiences of the previous year, matters could only get worse primarily because of the security situation in Aden itself and the Western Protectorate. Fortunately the Eastern Protectorate stayed relatively calm, probably because Egyptian influence there was negligible.

During the first three months of 1965, April to June, the Company lost just over £20,000, most of it in the last month. The main reason was the sudden decision by the military to cancel all service leave charters after one of the two RAF DC-3s was blown up on the civil side of the airfield at Khormaksar on 29th May. Understandably, the Forces perceived themselves to be a target and therefore any military personnel travelling on leave would be targeted too.

The loss of these charters represented a fall in revenue of £120,000 for the year and it would prove difficult to find enough employment for the two Viscounts.

One of the problems in the Protectorates was the lack of investment over the years in the transport infrastructure by both the Aden and British Governments. Perhaps they had felt that while the DC-3 had performed so well for so long there was no need to improve the runways and the flights were looked upon as a social service rather that an airline activity in the conventional sense. In contrast, the newly independent Somalia had accepted all offers of foreign aid, particularly when it came to airport improvements. Mogadishu was upgraded during the previous year and now Hargeisa could also boast a metalled runway.

The first flight to the new airfield there was made by Vic Spencer on 11th June in VR-AAI with S/O Spouce as Co-Pilot. *"To Hargeisa today to look at new runway. OK for Viscounts. Later discussed proposals to replace trooping contract, now off for good. To go to Riyan tomorrow to study possibility of using Viscount there."* He went to Riyan the next day in VR-AAF together with Captain Pete Williamson, but the runways there were unsuitable which was regrettable, as Riyan served the second most important city, Mukallah.

Understandably, public confidence continued to ebb; the three accidents the previous year had left the airline with only five DC-3s as it was decided not to replace the aircraft lost at Hadibo, but this also meant that there were not enough resources to accept the number of charters available which had always been lucrative sources of revenue.

The shortage of DC-3s also meant that if unserviceability of any kind occurred, then the rest of the flying programme was vulnerable. On 30th May, a DC-3 flown by Captain Whittaker burst a tyre on landing at Mukeiras which meant that engineering staff had to be flown up to replace the wheel. On the 1st June VR-AAZ damaged a wingtip at Nisab so Vic Spencer flew up there in VR-AAN with a replacement wingtip and brought 'AAZ back to Aden after the repair, while Captain Whittaker continued his flight in 'AAN to the original destinations.

An Aden Airways 'Best Crew' presentation; left to right: Assam (catering officer), unknown, R Wilson, Sheila Munro, Captain van der Laan, unknown.
(Sheila Pratt)

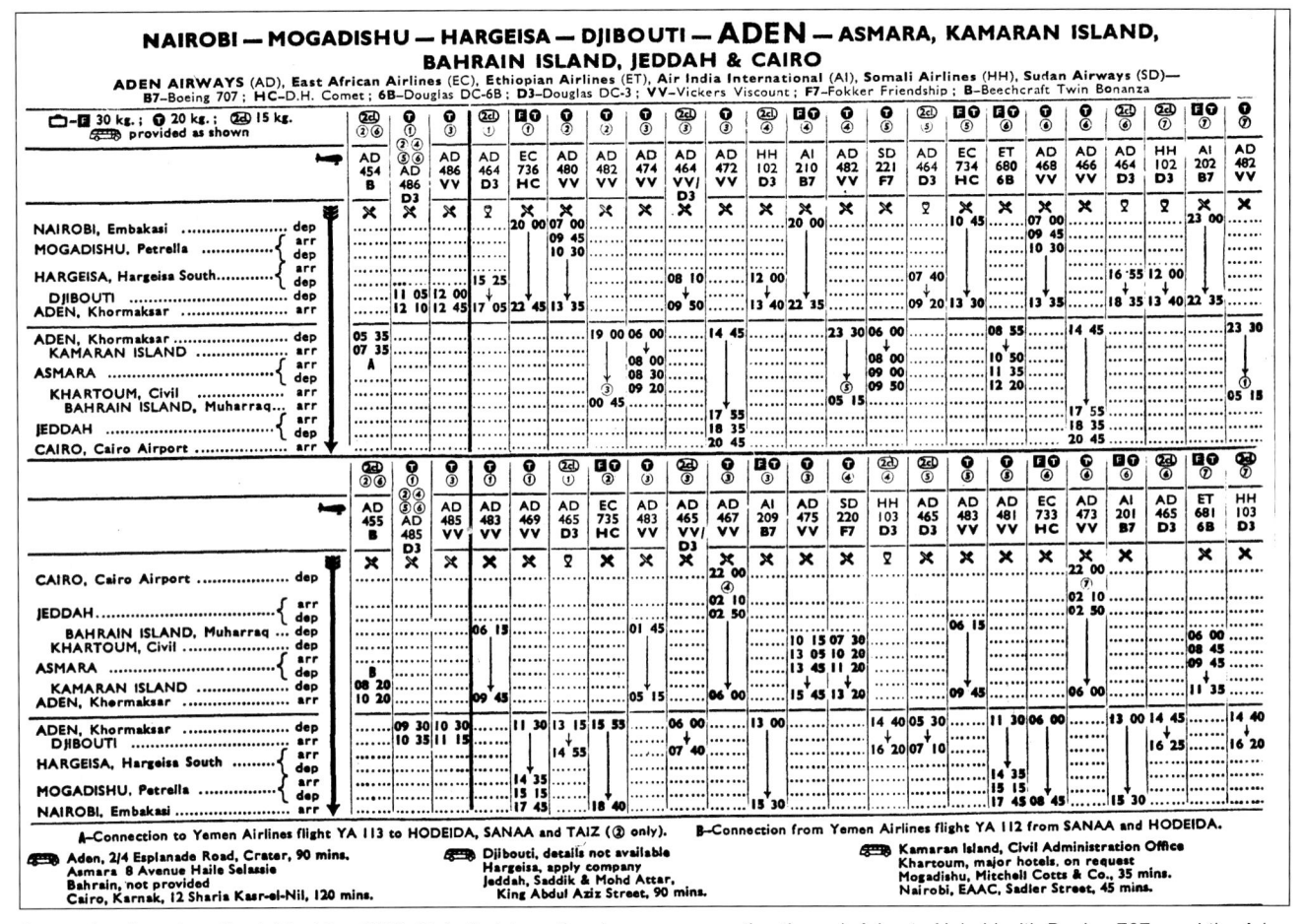

International services timetable, May 1965. Air India International are now operating through Aden to Nairobi with Boeing 707s and the Aden to Kamaran Island service, shown as being by Beech Twin Bonanza, offers Yemen Airlines onward connections. (Overseas Airline Guide)

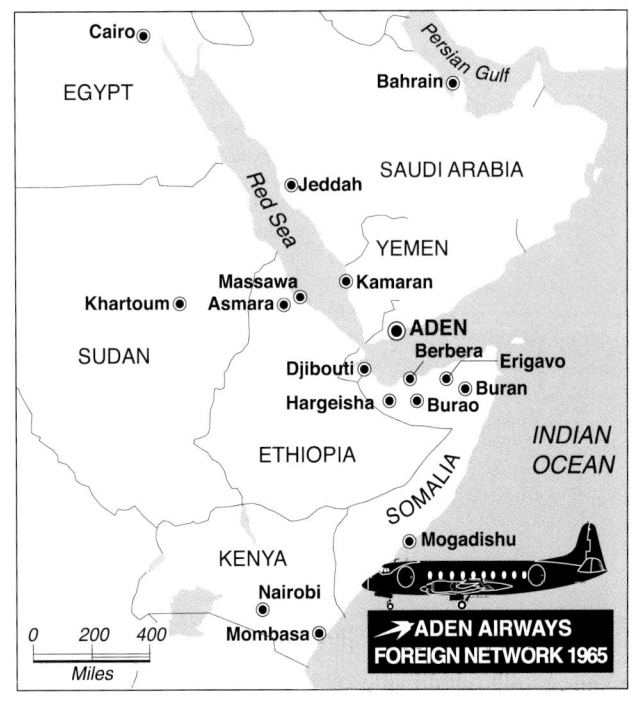

Aden Airways foreign destinations, 1965. The Somali locations appear within the regional timetable. (Roger Carvell)

The incidents of the bomb explosions and grenade throwing in Aden had increased substantially and in June, because of security risks at Khormaksar airport, all civil aircraft would henceforth be handled in the RAF terminal area. Though BOAC still continued to fly to Aden, the company decided that it was no longer safe for their crews to slip there and had them stay in Khartoum instead before flying a shuttle to Aden and back the same day. A further blow was the withdrawal (temporary at the time) of flights by East African Airlines on their route from Kenya to India. Bearing in mind the pooling agreement signed the year before and highly advantageous to Aden Airways, this was an unhappy development.

The violence was not confined to Aden itself. In a new development, a Yemeni Mig fighter carried out a brief attack on Beihan, up in the Western Protectorate. Though apparently causing little damage, it did indicate Yemeni intentions for the future.

The loss for this period was £110,782 and as always, reflected a number of factors.

On 6th July, a bomb was found on a Shell bowser at Khormaksar. This induced a walkout by all the Shell staff who had any work to do at the airport, particularly the refuelling staff. The result was that nearly all flying had to be cancelled that day and for the subsequent days until the Shell employees came back. Some flights did manage to get away:

6th July: *"Shell walkout after bomb found on bowser. Almost all services cancelled tomorrow."*

7th July: *"Operation upset badly by go-slow and Shell walkout. To meeting at Gov. House with GM this evening."*

8th July: *"Another day of go-slow and Shell strike. Managed to get Viscount away to Khartoum and a DC-3 to Riyan."*

In these circumstances, it was difficult to find replacement work for the Viscounts. The AC Board was obviously unhappy at this and in its report to the BOAC Board it voiced concern for the future:

"All avenues are being explored to find alternative work for the Viscounts in order to replace the lost military contract, but there is no doubt that this will take some time and will still further adversely affect the annual results." (274)

Chapter 23: Aden Airways 1965 - 1966

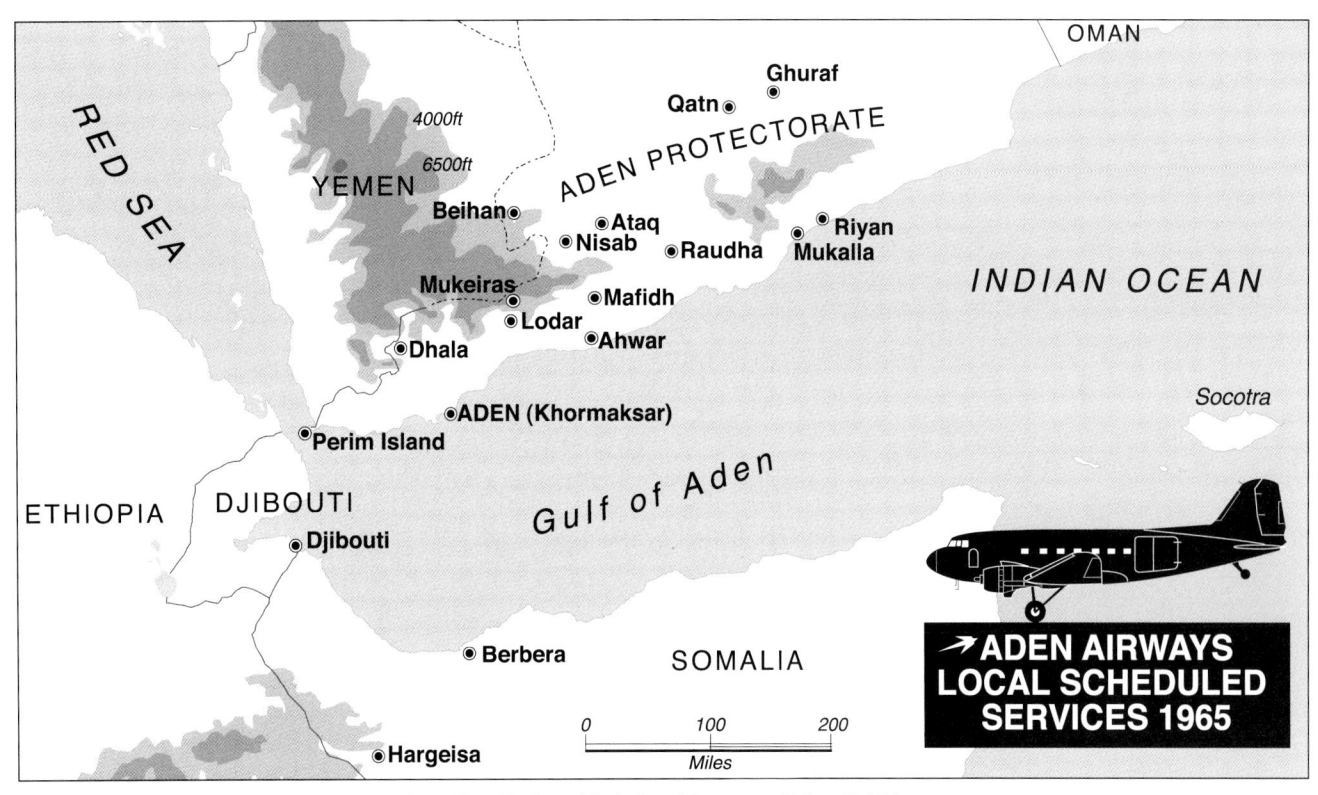

Regional destinations, May 1965 (Roger Carvell), with timetable below (Overseas Airline Guide).

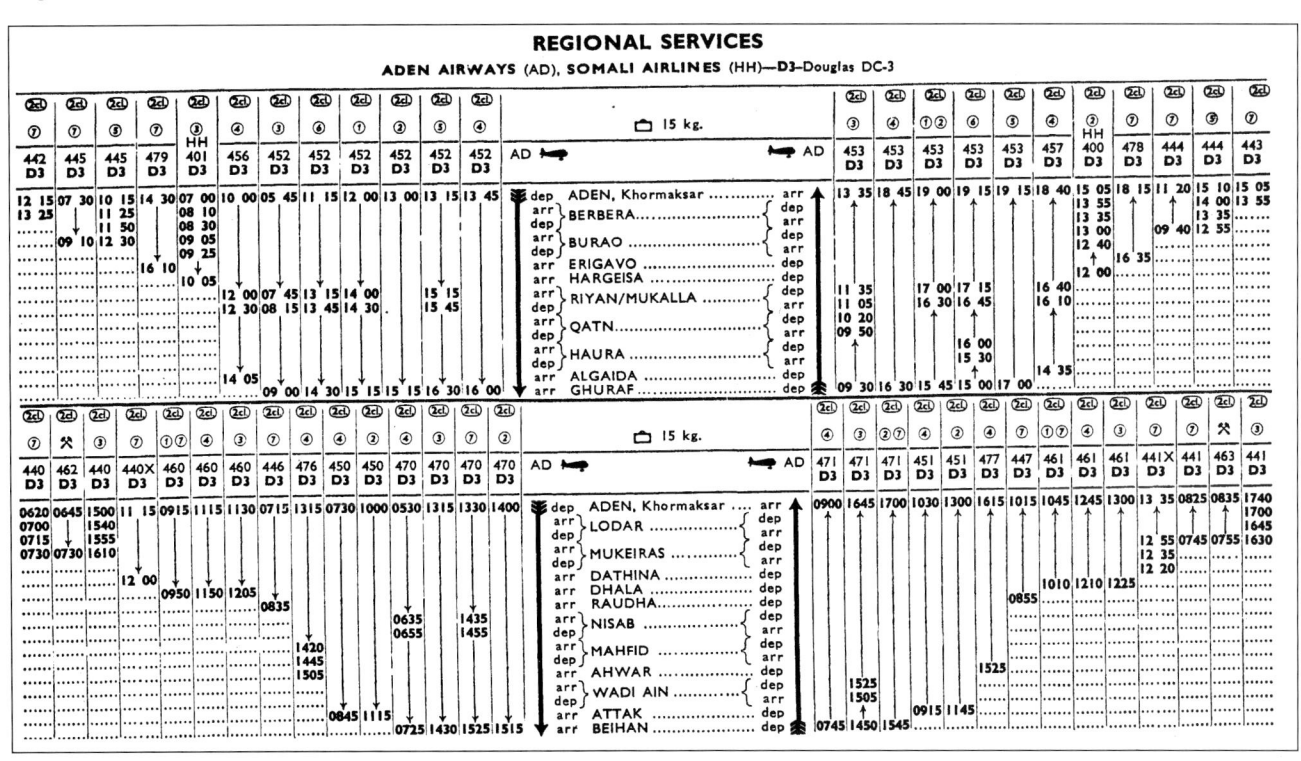

9th July: *"Still a go-slow and Shell strike. Managing a skeleton service only."*
10th July: *"Go-slow still on but Shell strike over by evening."* (275)

The go-slow activity became a feature of life at the airport. On 20th July all training flights were cancelled because of a lack of engineers. The next day *"grenade explosion while getting car out today. Troops think it was thrown from Aden Airways (housing) compound. All servants rounded up."* (276)

Other factors included the cancellation of flights to Bahrain because of a cholera outbreak there. The oil company BP cancelled a number of charters for workers, many of whom flew to and from Erigavo and Berbera and to exploration sites. The fact that other airlines were cancelling services to Aden also had an effect since Aden Airways had earned steady revenue from the handling of these flights.

By late August the company was in a difficult position and the General Manager felt that there might have to be a significant cutback in operations, possibly even a shutdown (277), but the airline managed to struggle on.

With a forecast loss for the year running to some £200,000 the question of the Government of the South Arabian Federation (as the western Protectorate had become) taking up 49% of the company's shares was now being pursued through the Government Director. Whether there was any real conviction in this line of thought is not known, bearing in mind the open suggestions by the Chief Minister the previous year.

Left: *Company crewbus in Aden, taking Sheila Munro to work.*
(Sheila Pratt)

Centre: *Captain Collin Dinnie and* Right: *Captain Alex Emmett.*
(Vic Spencer)

A second question being pursued was for some form of financial assistance to the company for services to the Protectorates, which were considered essential to the Government of the country. But the Colonial Office, which still held sway in such matters, proved to be slow to come to a decision.

Even during this time, the Aden Airways management was not receiving the full support, or understanding, of the BOAC Board. At the Board Meeting of 22nd September 1965, Mr T J Glover stated that: *"BOAC had noticed some weakness in Aden Airways management during recent weeks."* (278) This was a particularly unfair assessment of the situation. To view the situation from London in this way indicates just how divorced from the reality of Aden the BOAC Board was, and had been for some time.

In March, the Board informed the Government in Aden that *"the commercial value to BOAC of Aden Airways was such that BOAC would not be prepared to maintain its interest in the company as a wholly-owned subsidiary in the absence of Government support. The developments referred to above might make it desirable for BOAC's interest in the company to be terminated before 1968. Meantime, the authority of the Local Management would be supported and maintained."* (279)

Throughout this unhappy period, the DC-3s kept flying within the Protectorate and Somalia. Perim Island increased in importance as a listening post and Aden Airways were lucky to have the contract renewed for servicing it three times a week. As Chief Pilot, Vic Spencer went there regularly to liaise on security matters. At other times he had to fly to Dhala because of the reluctance of other pilots to fly there. On 22nd December identity cards were introduced for security reasons, but there was little evidence they were effective because they were mostly issued to the expatriate staff and they certainly did not prevent the security office at the airport from being blown up on 24th December.

On a brighter note, on 2nd January Vic Spencer operated a tourist charter flight in VR-AAN into the Eastern Protectorate. Taking off from Aden at 0615, the flight did a low pass beside the towns of Shibam and Layun before heading off to Ghuraf where the party were given an "Arab lunch". The flight departed Ghuraf at 1620 landing in Aden 2.10 hours later. Sadly, this sort of excursion was now the exception and there was little tourism in Aden.

On 5th January 1966, VR-AAW was due to return to the UK to undergo maintenance. The plan was that Vic Spencer, accompanied by Captain Pete Williamson, would fly the normal service to Cairo (AD 472) and then fly on to the UK the next day. Unfortunately, there was a strike by the Shell refuellers on that day and the aircraft was unable to uplift sufficient fuel to fly to Jeddah, the normal en-route stop. Under the circumstances, the flight had to fly first to Djibouti where it took on enough fuel for the flight to continue to Jeddah and Cairo.

VR-AAW was obliged to return to Aden almost immediately because VR-AAV had become unserviceable in Cairo and was thus unable to operate the AD 467. However, 'AAW was back in time for the flight to the UK on 7th January, taking off from Cairo at 0930 for the five hour flight to Malta where it remained for 50 minutes before departing for Castle Donington, a flight of 6.40 hours. The flight to Wymeswold continued on 9th January where it remained for three weeks, returning to Aden in early February.

As a temporary replacement for 'AAW, Aden Airways had leased a Viscount 700 from MEA (OD-ACT) which was collected from Beirut by Vic Spencer and F/O Robinson on 15th January. The previous day the two pilots had spent some hours looking around the leased aircraft and had been somewhat dismayed at what they found. Not only was it in a poor technical state, but all the systems controls were different, as were the instruments. *"Very worried about flight home. Aircraft very unfamiliar. Stewardesses able to do supernumerary flight to Jerusalem."* This last comment was because the aeroplane was scheduled to operate the AD 473 from Cairo to Aden the following night and it was essential the stewardesses were familiar with the galleys and cabin emergency procedures.

On the 15th, the intrepid crew departed Beirut at 1600 for the two-hour flight to Cairo. *"Very shaky ride in an unfamiliar aircraft. Arrived Cairo OK and departed for Aden"* (Vic Spencer diaries).

DC-3 at Qatn, Eastern Protectorate, 1960s. (Alan Elgee)

Chapter 23: Aden Airways 1965 - 1966

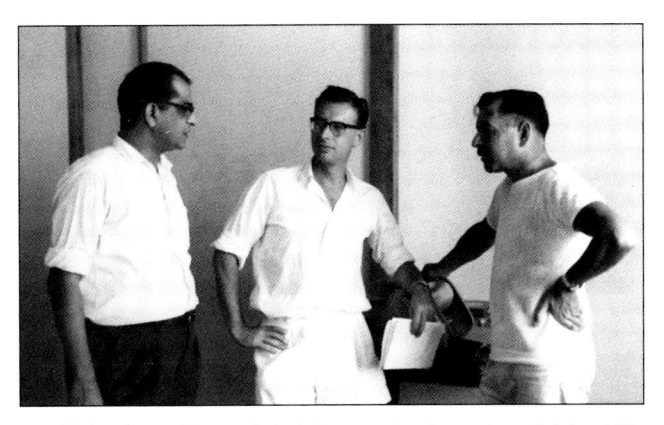

Lal Sikka, Dave Cox and Jack Lawson in discussion at Aden HQ, August 1965. *(Vic Spencer)*

The airport at Salalah in Oman. *(Alan Elgee)*

Left: *Captain Jack Lawson, and* Right: *Captain Jimmy Gross.*
(Vic Spencer)

The flight via Jeddah seems to have gone all right, but Vic reports OD-ACT as *"not so hot"*. In fact, he took it upon himself to be at the airport for every departure of this aeroplane in order to brief the crews on its characteristics.

On 28th January OD-ACT flew to Nairobi via Djibouti (Shell refuellers still on strike) and Mogadishu. Unfortunately, a brake problem developed in Nairobi and spares had to be ordered from Beirut which did not arrive for two days. This was not a happy time for the company and a further fall in confidence among employees and passengers.

On 21st February 1966 news was received in Aden that the military base there would be closed by 1968. This only confirmed what everyone had both believed and feared would happen. With the economic support military personnel gave to the airline and the Colony gone, few had any doubts as to what would happen. Only a few days later, the first pilot resignations started to come in, notwithstanding the large salary increases they had received during the previous year.

Industrially, as if to celebrate the news, a general strike was called for 26th February. One Viscount service arrived, none departed, and the same applied to the DC-3s. Such was the tension outside the airport that the cabin crew from the incoming flight had to be driven home by the managers. Early in March, more strikes were called which were totally effective.

With few services operating, there was a surplus of staff. 64 local employees were identified as no longer required, but any discussions on redundancy were thwarted by the Civil Aviation Employees Union which refused to recognise the term or negotiate.

On 19th March, Gilbert Lee arrived in Aden. As Chairman of BOAC.AC, he was determined on a confrontation if only to establish who was in charge. On 22nd March, an ultimatum was delivered to the Union which required them to call off the permanent "go-slow", not take part in strikes and return to working a normal day. 43 employees were sacked as a result and though no junior grade Adenis came to work that day, the airline managed to keep some services flying by having pilots do refuelling, taxying aircraft into position and loading them. Cabin crew organised the catering, loading of it and cleaning aircraft. On 23rd March, a further 120 local staff were dismissed as a result of the previous day's activities. In the end, a total of 255 employees were sacked over this period, some of them operations staff who were crucial to the day-to-day running of the airline.

By 26th March, most of the operations centre were out on strike, as were the HQ staff. Shell refuellers threatened to come out in sympathy and did so on 27th March.

Generally, though, the firm action applied by the company had the desired effect. Those employees who were not dismissed came back early in April. Flights returned to a semblance of normality, but resentments, understandably, remained. They would continue to do so into what was to prove to be the airline's last year.

The losses for the year were considerable, some £250,000 against which there were the capital gains from the insurance receipts for the aircraft lost at Hargeisa in March 1965 and the savings on costs associated with maintenance of that aircraft. Nevertheless, the AC.Board thought it prudent to make provision of £75,000 to cover unforeseen debts and contingencies during the coming year.

The year ended on an unhappy note. A driver was killed when a company vehicle was attacked and set on fire by a mob believed to be from the Civil Aviation Employees Union, nearly all of whom would have been employed by Aden Airways. The arrest of both the president and secretary of the Union did nothing to calm the situation.

Footnotes, Chapter 23:
(274) Associated Companies Report to BOAC Board, 20th August 1965.
(275) Vic Spencer diaries. 'Gov. House' = Government House.
(276) Vic Spencer diaries, 21st July 1965.
(277) Vic Spencer diaries, 24th August 1965.
(278) BOAC AC Board Meeting, 22nd September 1964.
(279) BOAC Board Meeting, 22nd March 1966.
(280) Vic Spencer diaries, 14th January 1966.

ADEN AIRWAYS LIMITED

From: Operations Officer.
Ref : OO/SF11/7825
Date: 25th February, 1966

To: Miss Ilott

Cabin crew roster for the period 28.2 to 6.3.1966. inclusive:-

Service		Route	STD LT.	Stewardesses	Stewards

Monday 28th February

Service		Route	STD LT.	Stewardesses	Stewards
Pan Am.CHT	(D)	Adn/	0700		Hameed
Special	(V)	Adn/Jda/Adn	0800	Anastasi/Madge	
AD485/6	(D)	Adn/Dji/Adn	0930		Abdi
AD469	(V)	Adn/Mog/Nai	1130	Seton/Wood	
AD452/3	(D)	Adn/Riy/Ghu/Riy/Adn	1200		Shamsan
AD465/4	(D)	Adn/Hgs/Adn	1315		Abdi
Standby		At Aden		Bharucha/Hillman	
Standby		At Aden Pick up	0530		Dayal

Tuesday 1st March

Service		Route	STD LT.	Stewardesses	Stewards
AD454/5	(D)	Adn/Kamaran/Adn	0545		Adan
AD485/6	(D)	Adn/Dji/Adn	0930		Hameed
AD452/3	(D)	Adn/Riy/Ghu/Riy/Adn	1200		Dayal
AD482/3	(V)	Adn/Bah/Adn	1845	Lees/Nabiha	
AD480	(V)	Nai/Mog/Adn	0700	Seton/Wood	
Standby		At Aden		Munro/Adla	
Standby		At Aden Pick up	0415		Shamsan
TRAINING AT H.Q.		"	0830	Madge	

Wednesday 2nd March

Service		Route	STD LT.	Stewardesses	Stewards
AD452/3	(D)	Adn/Riy/Ghu/Qat/Riy/Adn	0545		Adan
AD474/5	(V)	Adn/Asm/Ktm/Asm/Adn	0600	Anastasi/Hillman/Madge(Sny)	
Pan Am.CHT	(D)	Adn/	0700		Harharah
AD485/6	(D)	Adn/Dji/Adn	0930	Munro	
AD472	(V)	Adn/Jda/Cai	1745	Flory/Landez	
Special	(V)	Adn/Jda/Adn	0800	Bharucha/Adla	
Standby		At Aden		Peat/Wood	
Standby		At Aden Pick up	0415		Abdi

Thursday 3rd March

Service		Route	STD LT.	Stewardesses	Stewards
AD467	(V)	Cai/Jda/Adn	0100	Ilott/Nagat	
AD485/6	(D)	Adn/Dji/Adn	0930		Abdi
AD456/7	(D)	Adn/Riy/Algeida/Riy/Adn	1015		Shamsan
AD452/3	(D)	Adn/Ghu/Adn	1345		Harharah
AD482/3	(V)	Adn/Bah/Adn	1930	Munro/Wood	
Standby		At Aden		Seton/Hillman	
Standby		At Aden Pick up	0800		Dayal

Typewritten cabin crew roster for February/March 1966. Apart from a general reduction in scheduled services, one special flight and two oil company charters may be identified. It is clear that the stewardesses are rostered on the international Viscount (V) services while all but one of the regional flights by DC-3 (D) are operated with male stewards.

(Sheila Pratt)

VR-AAF getting airborne from Habilayne in April 1966. (Vic Spencer)

Chapter 24 :
ADEN AIRWAYS 1966 - 1967

BOAC now began to give serious thought to the future of Aden Airways and the effect of the closure of the British military base in Aden. The airline had always provided feeder traffic revenue of £50,000 p.a. to BOAC either through Cairo, Khartoum or Nairobi. In addition, BOAC had its own weekly service from London to Aden which at different times transited either Cairo or Khartoum, and which provided annual revenues of £1.4 million. A direct competitor on this route, it was estimated, could dilute this revenue by up to £400,000, thus driving BOAC into an operational loss.

"If BOAC abandoned Aden Airways it is highly probable that another company would take its place. Other existing airlines may provide the necessary regional connections now supplemented by Aden Airways but, irrespective of the presence of the British base, the political and commercial developments which have helped to build up the local services cannot be put completely into reverse. A small airline is certain to be necessary and if this were orientated towards another trunk airline, BOAC would lose revenue even without a competitor on the Aden-London route.

If the domestic routes were not sufficient attraction to a newcomer the Aden Government might offer long-distance rights as a quid pro quo for providing local services; with the imminence of independence HMG would find it difficult to refuse the reciprocal rights and the major threat to BOAC would then materialise.

The unknown factor is the extent to which air travel to and within the Aden Protectorate will be affected when the British base is closed, but until a major deterioration is seen to be inevitable Aden Airways seems to have a strong protective role for BOAC." (281)

Meanwhile, the flight operations side struggled on through general strikes, go-slows by local employees and a growing disenchantment amongst the expatriate staff.

On 8th April, the AD 450 to Ataq was forced to nightstop as a result of a taxying accident, not desperately important in itself, but indicating a worrying trend of small incidents recorded by Vic Spencer in his diary, who flew up to Ataq in VR-AAF to take a party of engineers to repair the damaged aircraft.

More problems arose both with flight crews refusing to fly and stewardesses refusing to report from standby. The sickness rate amongst the stewardesses went up to such an extent that there was trouble crewing some of the flights (282).

Within the Protectorates, all was calm in the East, but in the West both Mukeiras and Dhala came under light-arms fire on a number of occasions during April and May. On 22nd April the early morning Dhala (AD 460) was obliged to return to Aden as a result of overnight mining of the runway there.

In Aden itself, the go-slow by staff continued through April and May, while at the same time tensions in Crater and Maalla continued unabated with shootings and grenade throwing being common events. It had become the habit for many expatriate staff to carry small revolvers, both .38 and .22 calibre. Shooting practice was either at the club on the military base or on the beaches, but even in the latter areas things were not quiet. Whether these revolvers would have been of any use in an emergency could be debated, but they gave some comfort.

During the first three months of the financial year, the company lost a further £23,000. For some time BOAC.AC had been requesting financial assistance for operation within the Protectorates and the Government in Aden had made very clear that it considered the routes within the protectorates to be essential to good governance of those territories. While it had made promises to Aden Airways that the question of a subsidy would be given serious thought,

As the security situation worsened, it became common practice for the employees of Aden Airways to carry a loaded pistol wherever they went. Practice was usually carried out on the beach.
(Trevor Austin)

Left: *Captain Jimmy Wood;* Right: *Captain Rex Barnes.*
(Vic Spencer)

nothing was forthcoming by the end of June. Finally, in August, £75,000 was paid to the company towards the cost of maintaining these services with a further £75,000 to come in February 1967.

Only two payments made. By this time, though, a number of pilots had left because of the increasing dangers of living and working in Aden. It had also become difficult to attract replacement aircrew despite the high salaries on offer. The result was that flight operations were increasingly curtailed or cancelled altogether.

On 17th June Vic Spencer departed Aden on the BOAC VC-10 for London in order to go up to Wymeswold to collect VR-AAV which had been undergoing servicing since late May. A few days before, he had received a letter containing a bullet from FLOSY which had caused some consternation at home. *"This usually meant that one was being considered as a particular target; it made me feel uncomfortable, but there was little I could do except hand it in to security, make certain my own gun was always loaded and with me and be careful whenever I was driving or walking anywhere outside the living quarters."* (283)

On 23rd June VR-AAV left Wymeswold for Castle Donington whence it took off the next morning for the 5.10 hour flight to Malta and Cairo (4.15 hrs) where the crew night-stopped prior to operating the AD 473 to Aden via Jeddah.

To give some idea of the difficulty in attracting and keeping aircrew in Aden. Vic Spencer interviewed an applicant while in the UK on 18th June. He was offered a command on the DC-3 and Captain Dunsmore arrived in Aden early in July to start his line training with Vic Spencer on 15th July when they flew VR-AAC from Aden-Riyan-Ghuraf-Haura-Riyan-Aden. On the 18th July, further training consisted of Aden-Mukeiras-Aden, Aden-Djibouti-Aden and Aden-Hargeisa-Aden after which he flew as Captain. And that was his training.

By 7th September he had resigned, though the reasons for it are uncertain. Nevertheless, bringing him out to Aden, setting him up in accommodation, uniforms etc was expensive and this was beginning to happen more often.

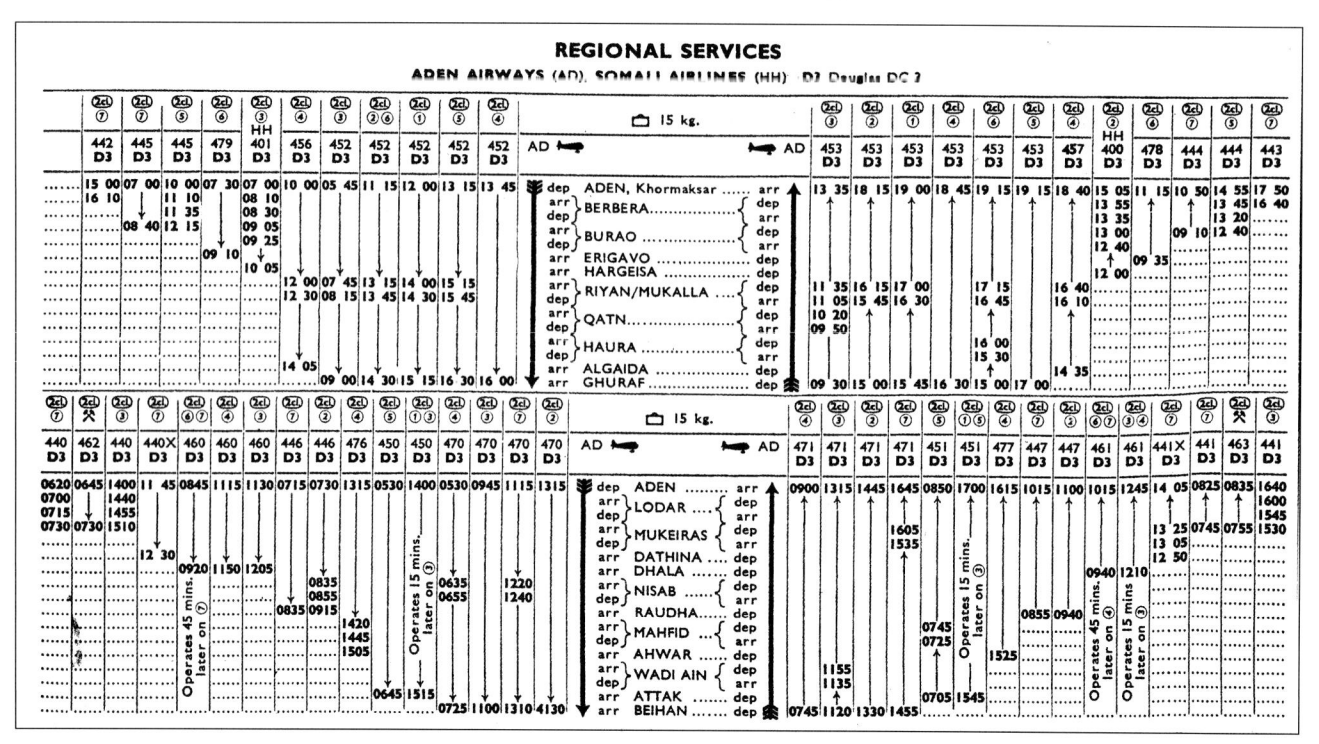

Apart from some re-timing, regional services had changed little by November 1966 for both social and political reasons.
(OAG)

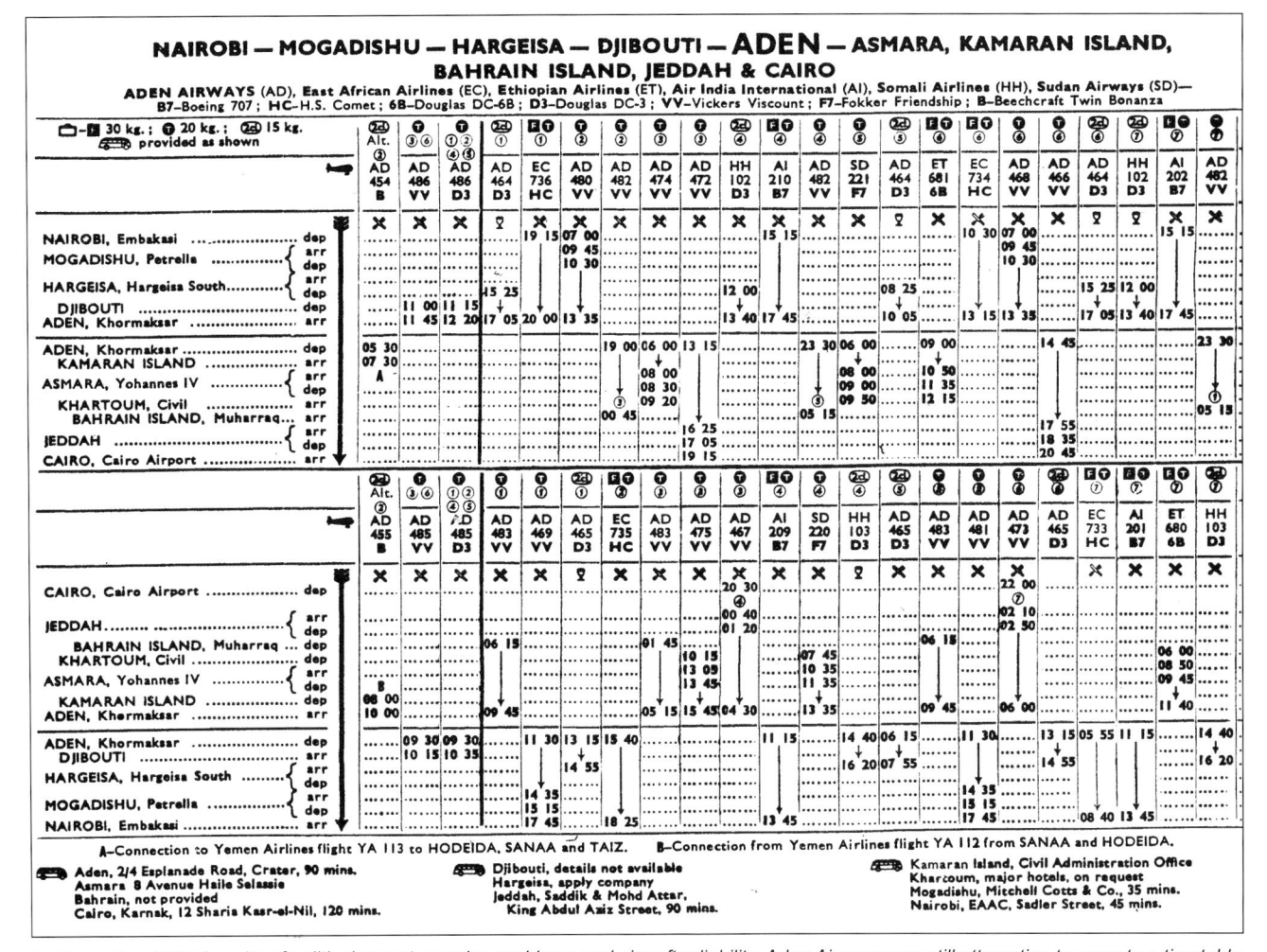

In November 1967, in spite of political unrest, crewing problems and aircraft reliability, Aden Airways was still attempting to operate a timetable similar to that of eighteen months earlier.
(Overseas Airline Guide)

Tensions were probably having an effect on the pilot group. Spencer refers to a number of incidents of drunkenness which exceeded the normal exuberant lifestyle that pilots seem to lead. Arguments and fights are often referred to and disciplinary interviews occur more frequently. Four Captains resigned in August, though not all were for disciplinary reasons.

Aircraft serviceability, too, was becoming a problem, not so much with the DC-3s, but the two Viscounts suffered mishaps. On 17th July VR-AAV burst all its tyres while landing at Aden from Cairo, the most likely reason being that the aircraft landed with its brakes applied or the brakes were applied too fiercely during the landing roll. On 23rd July, VR-AAV was delayed for 24 hours with flat batteries. On 31st July, VR-AAW was unserviceable in Jeddah for 24 hours due to a major problem on No.2 engine.

BOAC.AC had also been worried about the reliability of the Aden Airways service with the Viscounts. At one stage it had been planned that spare Trident hours from Kuwait Airways could be used for the benefit of Aden Airways, but this plan came to naught when Kuwait lost one of their Tridents in the landing accident of 9K-ACG on 30th June, 1966.

Even then, the DC-3s had their problems as well. On 30th August, VR-AAZ suffered an engine failure on take-off for Riyan (AD 452) with Vic Spencer as Captain and Captain Duirs operating as Co-pilot. The aircraft returned to Khormaksar for a single-engine landing and the service departed two and half hours later, this time in VR-AAF. Interestingly, the crew flew Aden-Riyan-Ghuraf-Qatn-Riyan-Aden, after which Captain Duirs and Vic Spencer conducted an air test on VR-AAZ which had been repaired after the engine failure earlier that morning.

The independence of South Arabia, as Aden Colony was now named, was to come in 1968 and BOAC was again becoming concerned as to what would happen to its investment in Aden Airways. Early in November the Chairman of Associated Companies, Gilbert Lee, visited Aden in order to speak with the British High Commissioner and two ministers of the South Arabian Federal Government. Mr Lee made it clear that BOAC would not be prepared to maintain Aden Airways with heavy subsidies right up to independence without some clear and agreed plan for the future. He also suggested that the Federal Government should at some time before independence acquire 51% of the company, 25% should be offered to the public leaving BOAC with 24%. Generally the idea was accepted though there was some doubt as to whether the Federal Government would be able to raise the money to buy 51%. (284)

None of these plans were to come to fruition as a result of the events of November 1966. As much in desperation as anything else, Associated Companies made efforts to interest the UK Government in buying the airline from BOAC and then making it a gift to the South Arabian Government upon independence, but for quite understandable reasons, the Government displayed little enthusiasm for this suggestion. (285)

On 22nd November came the almost inevitable disaster. At 2 o'clock in the afternoon, local time, Captain Peter Skingley lifted off the runway in VR-AAN at Khormaksar and set course to Meifah, a small settlement in the Eastern Protectorate. His co-pilot that day was Captain Warren Wilson, an experienced DC-3 pilot who had recently joined the company and who, after his line training, was being shown around the route structure within the Protectorates. In the cabin was Flight Clerk Neguib because stewardesses were not carried on internal flights of this nature.

The aircraft arrived in Meifah at 1535 hours where the entire commercial load, both passengers and freight, were taken off. For the flight back to Aden, 27 passengers boarded the aircraft which departed at 1605, half an hour after landing. At 1620 the flight called Aden by radio to give a position report and pass an estimated arrival time in Aden of 1716 local. Approximately five minutes after this call the aircraft exploded and all aboard were killed.

As Chief Pilot, Vic Spencer was called up at home to be told the flight was overdue. *"Heard of VR-AAN missing. In the evening with DCA and GM very worried. Appears probable that aircraft is lost and no survivors. Expect to go out to wreck tomorrow."* (Vic Spencer diaries 22nd November). On the 23rd: *"To Hiom B'alid by Twin Pioneer and helicopter.* (286) *Aircraft completely written off. Helped remove bodies. Looks like sabotage."*

On 24th November Vic Spencer flew up to Ahwar in VR-AAZ together with Captain Marian Kozubski, a famous wartime pilot from Poland who, after a number of adventures, had joined Aden Airways not long before. The two men then took a Land Rover to the scene of the crash where they spent the day collecting all the personal belongings of the two pilots and two European passengers for transportation back to Aden later than evening.

The repercussions of this event were, predictably, considerable. No one knew the originators of the sabotage, whether NLF or FLOSY. Despite the security precautions at Khormaksar, the explosive device might have been put on board there or at Meifah during the stop there. If the latter, then this represented a new threat as the Eastern Protectorate had been relatively unaffected by the events further west.

On 27th November Vic and Marian flew up to Meifah in VR-AAZ together where the two spent the day consulting with the local security agents and trying to ascertain whether the device had been placed on board in Meifah and by whom. Some time later it was discovered that the son of one of the passengers, a local Sheikh, had placed the device on board, his purpose being to hasten his own progression to Sheikh by killing his father .

When the assumption was made (wrongly, as it turned out) that either the NLF or FLOSY were involved, a defining moment had arrived and a line was crossed. The former Colony's airline was vulnerable to sabotage. For some days no services flown while the airline management and Government pondered the future.

On 28th November, a meeting was held at Aden HQ hosted by Vic Spencer where the options for action were laid before the pilots; tensions were high and the question was how many would leave.

Captain J Johnson, one of the directors of Associated Companies, arrived in Aden on 29th November where he immediately had meetings with both Vic Spencer and the General Manager. Included in the meetings were the heads of security, personnel and operations. The news from Captain Johnson was stark: either the airline had to start flying again or it would be shut down immediately. (287) On 30th November Vic Spencer operated the first flight since the events of the 22nd when he took VR-AAV to Nairobi (AD 481) with Captain Alan Jennings as his Co-Pilot; the cabin crew being Sheila Munro, the airline's Chief Stewardess, and Miss Chambers. Not surprisingly, the loads on both sectors were poor.

After his return from Nairobi on 1st December Vic attended a meeting for all the pilots at Ras Boradli, the General Manager's home. *"In the evening to a long meeting of pilots at Ras Boradli. Looks like the end; only 11 voted to stay and feel very depressed."*

Captain Alan Jennings who, with Chief Pilot Vic Spencer, flew the first service following the tragic loss of VR-AAN on November 22nd 1966.
(Vic Spencer)

(Vic Spencer diaries). This number would not have been sufficient to fly the four remaining DC-3s and the two Viscounts. On 3rd December two more pilots decided to stay, though even with 13 available it meant only a skeleton roster could be flown.

Eventually the first flights to the Protectorate started again when, on 7th December, VR-AAI visited Ataq (AD 450) with Vic Spencer in charge and Alan Jennings as his Co-Pilot. On this occasion no flight clerk was carried. Then, on the 8th and 9th December, two more pilots O'Neill and Lawson said they would stay. With 15 pilots in place the future began to look a little brighter.

Obviously new security measures which would inevitably impinge on the overall operation had to be put in place. It had been known for some time that the engineering department had been heavily infiltrated by the NLF. Not only had it been possible for employees there to be recruited, but it was also easy to put pressure on the less committed by threats of violence to them, their homes or their families, and if there was going to be any sabotage it was believed that this would probably be the source.

Accordingly, a system was put in place. If any engineering work had been carried out on an aircraft, it would then be moved to a secure area and quarantined for a period of 24 hours before it could operate a flight. This had a considerable effect on the flexibility of the operation, partly overcome by cutting the Cairo service and Jeddah becoming a return service. The Asmara/Khartoum service had already become a daylight return and the Bahrain was cut from two to a single weekly flight.

The first service since the accident was operated on 23rd December when VR-AAC flew up to Riyan on behalf of the RAF (though it was not extended to Salalah and Masirah).

By early January 1967 public confidence in Aden Airways had all but disappeared. Load factors hovered at about 30% on the

CHAPTER 24: ADEN AIRWAYS 1966 - 1967

The unfortunate VR-AAN, destroyed by sabotage on November 22nd 1966, seen in its mid-fifties colour scheme. (Author's collection)

international routes and, while the airline was still used for flights within the Protectorates, regular schedule-keeping was becoming increasingly difficult because of the quarantine restrictions. The occasional charters still came about to Berbera and Hargeisa to take migrant workers home and bring others to Aden. These were the exceptions, though, since it was already difficult enough to keep the DC-3 schedules going.

Over the previous year or two the company had continued its attempts to bring more Adenis into the operation of the airline. There had been problems with the engineering department and many local employees had been dismissed during 1966 during the perpetual go-slow. Though flight clerks on flights into the Protectorate had been a huge success, the recruitment of Adeni stewardesses had, for a variety of reasons, not been so. However, two young Adenis had been sent off for pilot training and on 16th January one of these, S/O Wahed, started with Aden Airways when he flew with Vic Spencer to Djibouti and Hargeisa in VR-AAI. What became of him after Aden Airways was closed down is not known.

Meanwhile, the tensions in Aden itself continued. A general strike on 19th January meant the cancellation of all flights and police throughout the Colony were out in force.

A new problem was brewing now from a more unusual quarter. Until recently there had been few female passengers on the flights within the Protectorates out of respect for Muslim sensitivities. However in January a new procedure was brought into force whereby certain flights were designated on which women could be carried at the sametime as males who, if they objected, could wait for another flight (see Appendix 3). The problem now, though, was security; while it was easy to search male passengers, women were more difficult, a problem which was never really resolved.

Viscount VR-AAV had been sent to Wymeswold for maintenance during December, 1966 and on 29th January Vic Spencer departed Aden on the MEA Comet to London via Beirut in order to fly her back to Aden. Together with Captain Dick Larcombe and R/O McGarry, the return flight departed Castle Donington at 1045 for Malta where it arrived 5.25 hours later and after a brief stop there it continued on the 4.05 hour flight to Cairo. Next day they flew on (empty of course) to Jeddah and Aden in two hops of 3.30 hours and 3.00 hours respectively.

Unrest continued in Aden with more strikes, shootings and grenade-throwing. On 9th February the flight to Dhala had to be aborted at the last moment when shooting broke out at the airfield, while the following day there were problems at Ghuraf when the airfield had been under attack the previous night, though the service did get in. (It would have been interesting for the insurgents to know that the co-pilot on that flight was an Adeni, S/O Wahed). Taxis and public transport in Aden were curfewed that night. The next day another general strike and a curfew all day which was not observed, with the result that troops opened fire on the crowds in Maalla when they became violent. All social life was cancelled and no flights took place during this period. They did not start again until 14th February.

A further general strike in Aden took place on 28th February. Vic Spencer and his crew were due to fly back to Aden from Nairobi at the time, so they decided to fly to Mogadishu and nightstop there as Aden could not accept them. It was not until 2nd March that the aircraft could be flown on from Mogadishu, the passengers arriving two days later than planned. It was experiences such as this which brought it home to some, that while the political situation continued, the days of Aden Airways were numbered. During the financial fourth quarter from January to March 1967, the airline lost £104,000 before the £45,000 subsidy from the UK Government was taken into account.

The UK Government also confirmed that it was not prepared to buy the airline and make it an independence gift to the South Arabian Government.

"The local Government have been offered the company as currently constituted and, in case finance was a major difficulty, an alternative whereby we were prepared to reduce the company to a purely domestic operation. This would have reduced the cost to the order of £200,000 and we indicated that even this figure was negotiable." (288)

"The Federal Government asked for three months until 30th June to consider this proposal. Government were told. We would wait until 30th June for their decision, if unfavourable, the airline would close on that date and that meanwhile, about the beginning of May, staff would be given notice of termination effective 30th June. This has been done and reactions have been comparatively calm. All necessary preliminaries for going into liquidation on 30th June have been provisionally completed." (289)

While these decisions were apparently made in May, the thought process within the two Boards of BOAC and Associated Companies had reached these conclusions in March. But in Aden Airways an air of detachment bordering on the plot of a Chekhov drama appears to have existed. On 24th March, the General Manager departed for London where he would officially hear the news above.

wherever your thoughts take you—

Spread your wings, fly fancy free around the world. For BOAC will fly you anywhere you want to go. Fly you in blissful comfort all the way with a cabin service—First Class or Economy—that has no equal. BOAC offer you fast, frequent services by Rolls-Royce jet 707s, Comets or jet-prop Britannias which link Aden with all six continents, all parts of the world.

YOUR GUIDE TO THE MIDDLE EAST—ADEN AIRWAYS
Throughout the Middle East and Red Sea areas, Aden Airways is your guide. In association with BOAC it offers you select services and connecting flights with the major trunk routes at Cairo, Nairobi and Khartoum.

Consult your local Travel Agent or BOAC, Barlaman Avenue (P.O. Box 250), Khartoum, Tel: 71171, 77115, 77172; Aden Airways Ltd., Air Booking Centre, Queen Arwa Road, Crater, Tel: 2224/5 and 2258.

FLY B·O·A·C WITH ADEN AIRWAYS

Aden Airways advertisements in the sixties tended to emphasise the company's BOAC association and service standards. With only one weekly BOAC flight calling at Aden the connections offered by Aden Airways to the trunk routes were vitally important.
(via Roger Carvell)

FLY BRITISH

Fly British by Aden Airways and B.O.A.C.—you'll fly swiftly, smoothly in a fine modern airliner, and enjoy attentive *personal* service throughout your journey.

Consult your local Travel Agent or B.O.A.C., 32-41 Wingate Avenue (P.O. Box 250), Khartoum, Tel: 3171 and 7172/3. Aden Airways Ltd., 2-4 Esplanade Road, Crater, Aden, Tel: 2224/5 and 2258.

FLY ➤ B·O·A·C *All over the world*
FLY ADEN ➤ AIRWAYS *To all points in the Red Sea Territories*

BRITISH OVERSEAS AIRWAYS CORPORATION IN ASSOCIATION WITH ADEN AIRWAYS

Footnotes, Chapter 24:
(281) BOAC Board Meeting, 15th June 1966 (B5-6).
(282) Vic Spencer diaries.
(283) Conversations with Vic Spencer 2005.
(284) Report by Chairman of BOAC.AC on meetings 1st – 4th November 1966 (B5-6).
(285) BOAC Board Meeting, 17th February 1967 (B5-6).
(286) The Scottish Aviation Twin Pioneer was used by the RAF for communications work in Aden and had exceptional STOL characteristics.
(287) Conversations with Vic Spencer 2005.
(288) BOAC Board Meeting, 19th May 1967 (B5-7).
(289) Ditto.

The wreckage of VR-AAV after the sabotage on 30th June 1967. (Vic Spencer)

Chapter 25 :
ADEN AIRWAYS 1967 : THE LAST THREE MONTHS

Almost appropriately, on 1st April heavy rain fell all day in Aden, to the extent that the airfield was flooded and no flights departed or arrived. The next day another general strike was due to last for an indeterminate period. Into this sad situation there came a UNO mission on 2nd April which had been appointed by the United Nations General Assembly earlier in the year.

"The final, farcical and violent end to British rule began with the visit of the United Nations Mission in April 1967, appointed by the United Nations General Assembly in February 1967 'to recommend practical steps for implementing previous United Nations resolutions on South Arabia'. The earlier resolutions had condemned the Federal government as unrepresentative. HMG accepted the mission because they hoped that it might induce the parties to negotiate more flexibly about the future. The NLF and FLOSY condemned the mission as 'UN puppets of British imperialism'; they refused to deal with them unless their claims were recognised. When the mission declined to do this, the fronts launched strikes, 'popular' riots and demonstrations. The High Commissioner had the unenviable duty of protecting the mission, which was virulently anti-British, against possible terrorist attacks at a time when most of the population was not at work. On the day the mission arrived, there were 71 security incidents in Aden. The mission told the High Commissioner that they were not prepared to have any dealings with the Federal government. When the mission visited the al Mansoura detention camp, the detainees jeered at them and refused to talk to them. When they wanted to broadcast to the nation, the Federal authorities, who controlled the broadcasting facilities, refused to let them. The frustrated UN mission then decided to leave Aden, which they did amid farcical scenes at the airport." (290)

During the following days a great deal of rioting in Crater brought in police and army detachments to try to control the unrest. No flying took place during these days and one detects an air of resignation amongst the expatriate staff: *"UN mission left in a huff today. Doesn't matter a lot."* (Vic Spencer diaries 7th April). But by 8th April the strike was almost over, and some flying took place, though the two Viscounts had been forced to stay elsewhere to wait out the strike.

Some time before, Vic Spencer had received a bullet through the post, supposedly from FLOSY. As Chief Pilot of Aden Airways he had a high profile within the company and was known to have done his utmost to keep the operation going when strikes or go-slows were on. The NLF was now influential within the airline, so it was no surprise to Vic when early in the morning of 10th April, he received a telephone call from someone in the NLF informing him that he was now a specific target for murder. Most of the expatriates had for some time now been carrying a gun for self protection; in Vic's case it was a .38 calibre pistol which he kept in a shoulder holster. *"Uncomfortable as it was, it was the first thing I put on in the morning and the last thing I took off at night. Once I had received the warning from the NLF, I also carried a .38 in my briefcase; it wouldn't have made a great deal of difference, but it made me feel better."* (291) From then on, all expatriate staff also checked under their cars for explosive devices.

By now the Viscount schedules were haphazard in spite of an attempt to maintain them. Passenger numbers on the Bahrain, Nairobi and Khartoum service were in single figures and it became more a question of keeping up everyone's spirits was difficult even though the deadline of 30th June now seemed certain to result in the closing down of the airline.

On 15th April it became known that Viscount VR-AAW would not return from its planned maintenance in the UK, leaving only VR-AAV to fly whatever schedule it could maintain. Vic flew the last service for 'AAW to Khartoum via Asmara on 19th April with Captain Alex Emmet as Co-Pilot and Air Hostesses Ilott and Adila in the cabin; the flight departed Aden at 0800, two hours late, arriving in Khartoum at 1140 local. It was back in Aden at 1800 local, 15 minutes early.

On 24th April, with Captain Gross and R/O McGarry, Vic got airborne in 'AAW at 0305 GMT bound for Jeddah, Cairo and Malta where the aircraft landed at 1615 GMT. The next morning saw it depart Malta at 0715 GMT for Nice, Castle Donington and Wymeswold, landing there at 1725 GMT and passing out of service with Aden Airways.

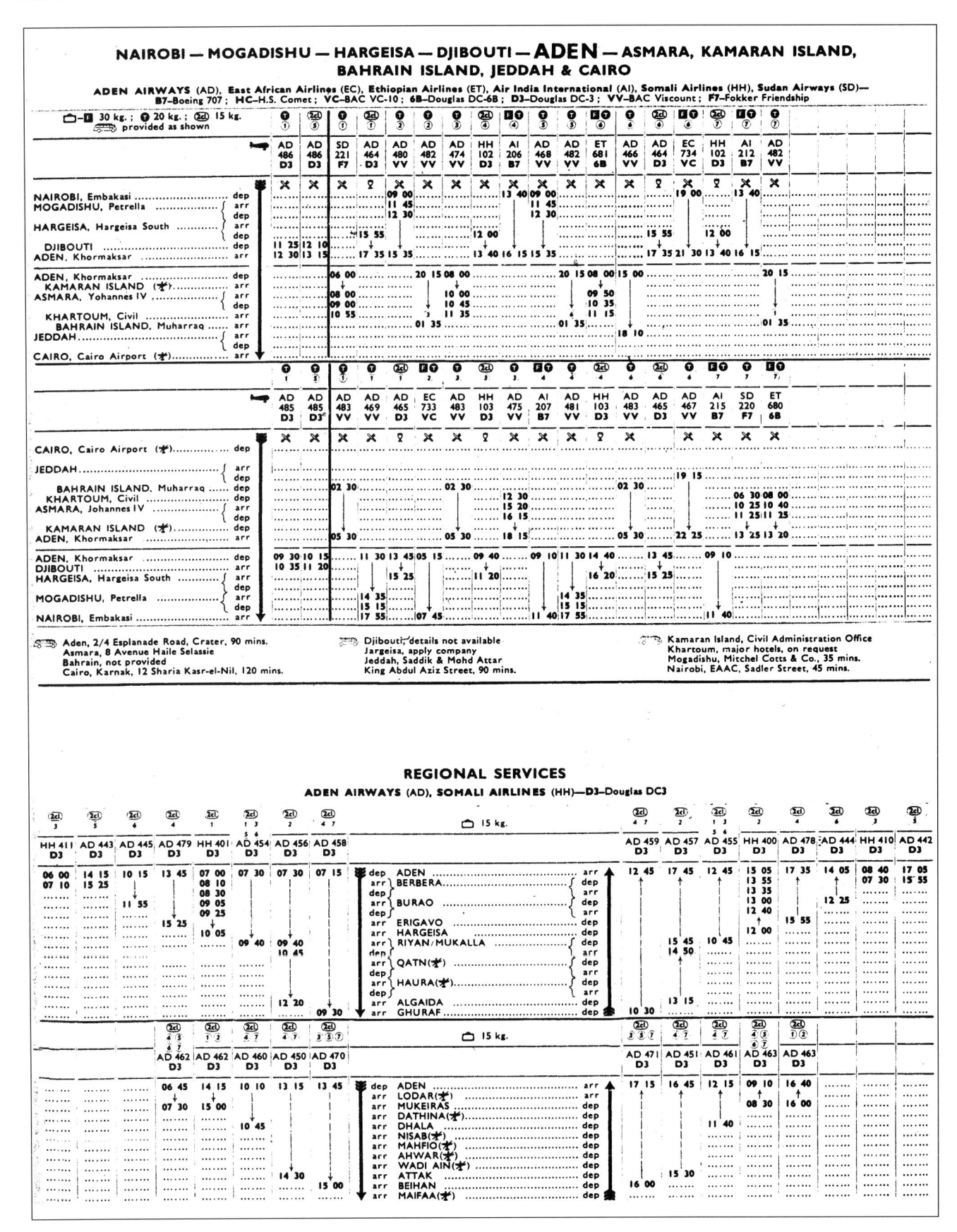

NAIROBI — MOGADISHU — HARGEISA — DJIBOUTI — ADEN — ASMARA, KAMARAN ISLAND, BAHRAIN ISLAND, JEDDAH & CAIRO

ADEN AIRWAYS (AD), East African Airlines (EC), Ethiopian Airlines (ET), Air India International (AI), Somali Airlines (HH), Sudan Airways (SD)—
B7–Boeing 707; HC–H.S. Comet; VC–BAC VC-10; 6B–Douglas DC-6B; D3–Douglas DC-3; VV–BAC Viscount; F7–Fokker Friendship

The final international and regional timetables issued in May 1967. The international section has been reduced to eleven return flights a week, none of which serve Cairo. Seven flights are operated by other airlines, amongst them EAAC who are now operating VC-10s to Nairobi. Regional services have shrunk even more noticeably and nine earlier destinations are now marked as having no service, mostly in the Western Protectorate. Four locations are jointly served with Somali Airlines.

(Overseas Airline Guide)

Chapter 25: Aden Airways 1967: The Last Three Months

Back in Aden on 28th April, the three were returned to the violent reality of life there, and on his first evening home Vic fitted new grips which he had just bought in London to his .38. On 30th April a car full of Arab children was blown up by a mine in Sheikh Ottman, killing nine of them. A general strike was called on 1st May as a result, and once again no flights operated.

The writing was on the wall now and at their Board Meeting in May, Associated Companies came to the following agreement:

"The conclusion has been reached that the Company cannot continue as a subsidiary of BOAC Associated Companies Limited if current negotiations with the South Arabian Federation Government for them to take over the Company in whole or in part do not succeed; it will be necessary for the company to be liquidated." (292)

The staff in Aden received their notices on 6th May and while there was some discussion on redundancy pay the company felt that notice had been given and that was sufficient; especially as there were extenuating circumstances. A few days later, staff in other countries were issued their notices of termination. *"To Nairobi with Kozubski, Sheila and Madge. Good run. Gave notices to Carlo (Moretti) and others. Very depressed."* (293)

Services within the Protectorate continued with the DC-3 though it was now limited by the serviceability and quarantine rules in force. There was also a sense of urgency, even when on the ground. At Dhala on 11th May the aircraft took off again only 10 minutes after it had landed. *"Too dangerous to hang around there."* (294).

Throughout May the strikes and attendant violence continued, but the airline carried on as best it could, flying the remaining Viscount when it was available and cancelling services when it was not, for example, whenever a general strike was called. But as many pilots as possible were given renewals to their instrument and type ratings in preparation for life after Aden; personal references were written and job applications were made.

On 5th June 1967 the outbreak of the Arab-Israeli six day war was a signal for further violence in Aden and, unusually, in the Eastern Protectorate, mainly in Riyan and Mukalla. The repercussions were immediate in that Saudi airspace was now closed to Aden Airways, the Jeddah services were cancelled and the Bahrain flights now had to route via Doha in order to avoid Saudi Arabian airspace. On 14th June when the AD 474 from Aden to Khartoum arrived in Asmara, the flight was not allowed to proceed and had to return to Aden.

Further violence and yet another general strike took place on 10th June when Colonel Nasser of Egypt offered to resign after his defeat by the Israelis. His 'resignation' was refused, but the action does give some idea of the support he enjoyed in other countries bordering the Red Sea. Flying into the Protectorates was no longer a pleasant experience. On 12th June Vic flew to Riyan and Mukeiras with S/O Wahed. *"Very strained atmosphere in the cockpit and Protectorates."*

Throughout the last two weeks of the airline's life, the frequency of violence, strikes and shooting gained momentum. On 22nd June Air India cancelled all its flights until further notice. On 26th June Vic Spencer operated the last flight to Nairobi and back; as if to remind him of the end, the weather was appalling in Mogadishu and a fire warning came up on No.1 engine while flying the second leg to Nairobi. David O'Neill was the Co-Pilot with Air Hostesses Ilott and Hillman looking after the few passengers on board.

Apart from the Nairobi flight, the final week was spent renewing all the pilots' ratings.

That afternoon Viscount VR-AAV was blown up as it sat in the quarantine pan at Khormaksar. The aircraft had been worked on during the previous day and earlier that morning it was towed out to the security pan for its 24 hour quarantine. About four hours later, an explosive device went off and the aircraft was destroyed.

"Intelligence had been received that, within the engineering staff, the terrorists had some influence, though whether this was because of sympathy to the cause or by coercion, no one was entirely sure. In order to safeguard the aircraft after maintenance, it was required that any aircraft which had been in the workshops should be returned to the secure aircraft movements area where they were further required to remain within a sterile area for a full 24 hours before returning to service. VR-AAV had been sterile in this way for about four hours when the bomb placed within it went off.

I was an RAF policeman on duty that day, and we were controlling a tarmac entry gate some 50 – 100 yards away from the Viscount when the bomb went off. After the explosion, there was a deathly quiet, broken within a few seconds by the sound of the Thorneycroft fire engine starting up and setting off to the scene; it arrived within three minutes of the explosion and immediately set about putting out the fire.

Understandably, the incident caused great excitement outside the secure area, and we were required to remain on duty until 2 o'clock the following morning, controlling the local crowds and preventing them from gaining entrance to the airport itself." (295)

Captain Alan Jennings flew the last scheduled flight to Mukeiras in VR-AAZ during the morning of the 30th June.

Vic Spencer's diary entry was Aden Airways' epitaph:

"Our last few days were spent in ensuring that all the pilots left with valid instrument ratings on both the Viscount and DC-3. Though many would have returned to the UK, the majority dispersed throughout the world while some left flying altogether. The last flight was to Mukeiras on 30th June and the next day the airline ceased to exist."

Footnotes, Chapter 25:
(290) *Without Glory in Arabia*. Hinchcliffe, Ducker & Holt
(291) Conversations with Vic Spencer 2005.
(292) Minutes of May Board Meeting of Associated Companies, 23rd June 1967.
(293) Vic Spencer diaries, 8th May 1967.
(294) Conversations with Vic Spencer 2005.
(295) Jack Sayer, RAF Policeman.

ADEN AIRWAYS LTD.
ADEN.

Know all men that while *Trevor James Austin* was emplaned in ADEN AIRWAYS Airliner *AD 469* on *19th June* 19*67* he/~~she~~ did join that select band of travellers who have looked at one time on both the Northern and Southern hemispheres by

➚

Crossing the Line of the Equator

at Longitude *40° 20' E*.

"Much delight attend them on their travel,
And may good fortune follow them on arrival."

In witness thereof _____
CAPTAIN

➚

Aden Airways Trans-Equatorial Service

An amazing sense of normality attended some activities. Trevor Austin left Aden on the penultimate AD 469 service to Nairobi on Monday June 19th and as a matter of course was issued with this Aden Airways "Crossing the Line" certificate.

INDIVIDUAL AIRCRAFT HISTORIES

Aden Airways

Douglas DC-3

1) VR-AAA
Constructor's No: 14141/25586

9 August 1944	Del to USAAF as C-47B-1-DK **43-48325**
11 August 1944	Del to RAF, Montreal as **KJ802** (OFZY)
21 September 1944	Del to BOAC as **G-AGKA**
22 January 1945	Registered G-AGKA to BOAC
1 February 1950	To Aden Airways as **VR-AAA**
11 September 1953	Leased to Arab Airways (Jerusalem) Ltd as **TJ-ABO**.
26 November 1953	To Aden Airways as **VR-AAA** ("Aden")
26 March 1965	Crashed at Hadibo, Socotra Island

2) VR-AAB
Constructor's No: 14361/25806.

27 August 1944	Del to USAAF as C-47B-1-DK **43-48545**
30 August 1944	To RAF, Montreal as **KJ867** (OFZU)
21 September 1944	To BOAC as **G-AGKE**
14 November 1944	Registered G-AGKE to BOAC
1 February 1950	To Aden Airways as **VR-AAB**
11 September 1953	Leased to Arab Airways (Jerusalem) Ltd as **TJ-ABN** ("Jerusalem")
April 1954	Re-registered as **JY-ABN**
14 December 1958	Returned to Aden Airways as **VR-AAB** ("Sheikh Othman")
13 April 1961	To Gulf Aviation as **G-AGKE**
9 October 1971	Cancelled as sold in Lebanon but did not leave Bahrain
	5B-CAZ applied but ntu
	N27AA World Inter Supply Services, ntu
11 July 1974	Abandoned Bahrain & sold by State
4 August 1975	Possibly registered **N94718** International Air Ltd but cancelled 10 March 76 to Malaysia
	9M-AUK allocated but ntu
October 1978	Noted derelict still at Bahrain as G-AGKE
May 1984	Taken to Kuwait and repainted as "**G-AMZZ**" in Kuwait National Airlines colours to represent their first aircraft

3) VR-AAC
Constructor's No: 14365/25810

27 August 1944	Del to USAAF as C-47B-1-DK **43-48549**
29 August 1944	Del to RAF, Montreal as **KJ871** (OFZR)
21 October 1944	Bought by BOAC as **G-AGKH**
21 February 1945	Registered G-AGKH to BOAC

24 May 1947	Leased to Iraqi Airways as **YI-GKH**
12 November 1947	Returned to BOAC as **G-AGKH**
1 February 1950	To Aden Airways as **VR-AAC** ("Mukeiras")
1953	Leased to Arab Airways (Jerusalem) Ltd as **TJ-ABQ**
By 10 December 1953	Returned to Aden Airways as **VR-AAC**
13 February 1969	Leased to Air Djibouti as **F-OCKU**
14 August 1976	Visionair International as **N9986Q**
4 November 1976	Urban L Drew, Khartoum, Sudan
December 1982	Cancelled, derelict Khartoum

4) VR-AAD
Constructor's No: 14660/26105

25 September 1944	Del to USAAF as C-47B-5-DK **43-48844**
29 September 1944	Del to RAF, Montreal as **KJ933** (OFZP)
7 November 1944	To BOAC as **G-AGKJ**
3 February 1945	Registered G-AGKJ to BOAC
1 February 1950	Registered to Aden Airways as **VR-AAD**
October 1953	To Arab Airways (Jerusalem) Ltd as **TJ-ABR** ("Amman")
April 1954	Re-registered as **JY-ABR**
1 December 1958	Registered to Air Jordan of the Holy Land
31 May 1959	Registered to Aden Airways as **VR-AAD**
	Leased as **JY-ACN**
	Returned to Aden Airways as **VR-AAD**
July 1968	To International Aviation Development Corporation as **N9895F**
1971	Diamond Leasing Corp to April 1977
	Leased to Lavco, Libya as **N488F**
23 March 1978	To ATC, Inc, Reno, NV and still on lease in Libya
July 1983	Cancelled. Taken by Libyan Army for target practice

5) VR-AAE
Constructor's No: 14978/26423

24 October 1944	Del to USAAF as C-47B-10-DK **43-49162**
26 October 1944	Del to RAF, Montreal as **KJ985** (OFZK)
29 November 1944	To BOAC as **G-AGMZ**
29 March 1945	Registered G-AGMZ to BOAC
1947	For Orient Airways as **VT-CPA** (ntu)
October 1947	Re-registered as **AP-AAA** Orient Airways Ltd
	To BOAC Associated Companies as **G-AGMZ**
1 February 1950	To Aden Airways as **VR-AAE**
19 October 1952	Ran out of fuel & f/l at Aswan, Egypt but rebuilt and became **N9935F** by March 1955
	Leased to Nadir and to Libyan American Oil Co
April 1955	Leased to Air Jordan as **JY-ABW**
25 April 1957	To Transocean Air Lines as **N9820F**
	Leased to Air Jordan as **JY-ABW**
	Oil Exploration Air Service as **N9820F**
	Sahara Petroleum Co
1965/66	International Aviation Development Co
1966/67	LAVCO (Diamond Leasing Corp, Reno)
1971	Re-registered to LAVCO as **N482F**
11 January 1977	Re-registered to ATC Inc, Valetta
	Taken by Libyan Army for target practice

6) VR-AAF
Constructor's No: 15274/26719

26 November 1944	Del to USAAF as C-47B-15-DK **43-49458**
13 December 1944	Del to RAF, UK as **KK137** (OFZH)
17 December 1944	Del to BOAC as **G-AGNB**
26 January 1945	Registered G-AGNB to BOAC
11 July 1947	Leased to Iraqi Airways as **YI-GNB** to 12 November 1947
12 November 1947	Restored as **G-AGNB**
1 February 1950	To Aden Airways as **VR-AAF**. ("Mukalla")
1953	Leased to Jordan Airways
August 1967	To Air Djibouti as **F-OCKV**, registration cancelled 24 December 1971
	French records say sold to Somali Airlines, no further information

INDIVIDUAL AIRCRAFT HISTORIES

VR-AAI   *VR-AAK*

7) VR-AAI
Constructor's No: 15770/27215

24 January 1945	Del to USAAF as C-47B-20-DK **43-49954**
30 January 1945	Del to RAF, Montreal as **KN279**, then to UK
23 June 1953	Registered to Transair Ltd as **G-ANAD**.
17 March 1954	Registered o Aden Airways as **VR-AAI**. ("Ghuraf")
27 August 1968	Registered to Air Djibouti as **F-OCKX**.
14 August 1976	To Visionair International as **N9985Q**
4 November 1976	To Urban L Drew, Khartoum
January 1979	Leased to Caprivi Airways Ltd
1981	African Air Carriers Ltd
December 1982	Cancelled, used as clubhouse, South Africa. No longer extant

8) VR-AAJ
Constructor's No: 12142

12 December 1943	Del to USAAF as C-47A-1-DK **42-92351**
8 January 1944	Del to RAF, Nassau as **FZ587**
30 January 1947	To Indian Government.
	Re-registered as **N9083C**
June 1953	To Hindustan Aircraft Ltd as **VT-DGX**
	To Indamer Co Ltd.
	Leased to Aden Airways as **VR-AAJ**
16 December 1960	To Kalinga Airways as **VT-DGX**
21 September 1962	Crashed into high ground Se La Pass, Arunachal Pradesh India-Bhutan border, 8 fatalities

9) VR-AAK
Constructor's No: 13474

31 May 1944	Del to USAAF as C-47A-25-DK **42-93550**
6 June 1944	Del to RAF, Montreal as **KG657**
2 November 1946	Bought by G. Victor
13 November 1946	Registered to Air Contractors Ltd as **G-AIWC**
6 December 1948	To Skyways Ltd ("Sky Despatch")
31 December 1951	To BOAC
3 April 1952	To British International Airlines, Kuwait
13 May 1955	Leased to Aden Airways as **VR-AAK** ("Attaq")
3 April 1958	Delivered to Silver City Airways as **G-AIWC** ("City of Lincoln")
30 October 1959	Leased to Libyan Oil Co ("City of Tripoli")
7 March 1962	Registered to SABENA as **OO-SBI**
28 March 1962	Leased to Spantax SA, del as **EC-WRZ**, registered **EC-ARZ**
1962	Leased to Air Mauretania
31 December 1964	Bought by Spantax SA
7 December 1965	Crashed nr El Ortigal, Tenerife, Canary Is.

10) VR-AAM.
Constructor's No: 15530/26975

23 December 1944	Del to USAAF as C-47B-20-DK **43-49714**
18 January 1945	Del to RAF as **KK198**
7 October 1952	Bought by Transair Ltd as **G-AMVK**
29 January 1953	Retgistered to British International Airlines, Kuwait.
16 June 1955	Registered to Aden Airways as **VR-AAM**. ("Raudha")
12 April 1964	Written off at Hargeisa, Somalia.

11) **VR-AAN**
Constructor's No: 4284:

1 April 1942	Del to US Navy as R4D-1 **4692**
September 1943	To Pan American, Alaska Div.
November 1944	Returned to US Navy
31 December 1944	SOC.
	To Pan American **NC33372**
8 August 1948	Delivered to Liberian National Airlines as **EL-AAB**
16 January 1953	Registered to Middle East Airlines as **OD-ABO**
6 April 1956	Bought by Aden Airways as **VR-AAN**. ("Nissab")
23 November 1966	Crashed Wadi Rabta due to sabotage.

12) **VR-AAO**
Constructor's No: 16411/33159

26 April 1945	Del to USAAF as C-47B-30-DK **44-76827**
4 May 1945	Del to RAF, Montreal as **KN550**
29 June 1950	SOC as spares.
	To Army Field Training School, (Mytchett, Camberley, Surrey)
10 March 1956	Rebuilt (at Ringway) with wings from G-AGIZ
4 April 1956	Registered to Eagle Aircraft Services as **G-AOJI**. (del 8 February 1957)
8 March 1957	To BOAC as G-AOJI
14 March 1957	Delivered to Aden Airways at Blackbushe
22 March 1957	Registered to Aden Airways as **VR-AAO**
17 October 1958	Registered to Salmesbury Engineering as **G-AOJI**
16 December 1958	Registered to Skyways Ltd as **VP-BAH**
31 December 1959	Registered to Bahamas Airways as **VP-BBN**
21 November 1960	Destroyed by fire on takeoff, Nassau, Bahamas

13) **VR-AAZ**
Constructor's No: 4495

6 July 1942	Del to USAAF as C-47-DL **41-18433**
11 December 1945	Foreign Liquidation Commission
24 July 1947	Registered to Air France as **F-BCYR**.
4 August 1947	Registered as **LR-AAM**. to CGT "Beyrouth"
March 1951	to Air Liban
May 1951	Re-registered as **OD-AAM**
27 July 1964	Bought by Aden Airways as **VR-AAZ**
23 July 1968	Registered to Air Djibouti as **F-OCKT**
23 July 1969	Crashed at sea 9 miles W of Djibouti 23 July 1969

Vickers Viscount

1) **VR-AAW**
V.760D   Constructor's No: 186

13 December 1956	First flown
1 January 1957	Delivered to BOAC Associated Companies as **VR-HFI**
1 January 1957	Leased to Hong Kong Airways
	To Malayan Airways as **VR-RCH** but not taken up
1 August 1959	Transferred to Malayan Airways as **9M-ALY**
	For Aden Airways lease as **VR-AAU** but not taken up
6 September 1963	Lease transferred to Aden Airways as **VR-AAW**
February 1968	Returned to BOAC Associated Companies as **G-AWCV**
7 April 1968	Leased to British Midland Airways Ltd
April 1970	Withdrawn from use at Tees-side
May 1970	Broken up

Individual Aircraft Histories

2) VR-AAV
V.760D   Constructor's No: 187

14 February 1957	First flown
28 February 1957	Delivered to BOAC Associated Companies as **VR-HFJ**
28 February 1957	Leased to Hong Kong Airways
August 1959	Bought by Malayan Airways as **VR-SEE**
September 1959	Re-registered As **9M-AMS**
September 1963	Bought by Aden Airways as **VR-AAV**
30 June 1967	Destroyed by sabotage at Aden

Avro Anson

1) VR-AAG
Constructor's No: Unknown

1944	To RAF as **NK727** (but civil registered as ex NK 787 in error)
9 September 1946	Sold (Struck off Charge)
14 November 1946	Registered as **G-AIWH** to Autowork (Winchester) Ltd "La Fort"
1 May 1947	Registered to Air Transport Association Ltd, Guernsey
20 March 1948	Registered to Morgan Aviation
15 June 1949	Registration cancelled
3 April 1951	Registration restored to Gulf Aviation Co Ltd
18 June 1952	Cancelled as sold to Aden Airways
August 1952	Delivered to Aden and registered as **VR-AAG** but not operated
1954	Cancelled & Wfu

2) VR-AAH
Constructor's No: RY/LW 2356

1942	To RAF as **DJ492**
3 September 1946	Registered as **G-AIFD** to Straight Aviation Ltd & Western Airways Ltd
2 November 1951	Registered to Gulf Aviation Co Ltd
14 July 1952	Registration cancelled as sold abroad
August 1952	Delivered to Aden and registered to Aden Airwaysas **VR-AAH** but not taken up
23 September 1953	Aden registration cancelled
2 October 1953	To Kassa Marru t/a Meat Export & Supply Co, Dire Dawa, Ethiopia as **ET-P-18**
28 November 1953	Repossessed by Aden Airways and flown Addis Ababa to Djibouti
1961	Scrapped, possibly at Bahrain 1954

3) VR-AAI
Contruction No: "7909"

1943	To RAF as **MG292**
18 August 1947	Sold (Struck off Charge)
10 March 1948	Registered as **G-AKVW** to British Air Transport Ltd, Redhill
1 August 1950	To Gulf Aviation Co Ltd.
27 January 1953	Cancelled as sold to Aden Airways to be **VR-AAI** but not taken up or delivered Broken up at Bahrain

Canadair Argonaut.

1) VR-AAR
Constructor's No: 163

23 February 1949	Registered as **G-ALHR**
14 September 1949	Del to BOAC as G-ALHR ('Antiope')
17 February 1960	Sold to Aden Airways as **VR-AAR**
18 February 1960	UK registration cancelled
21 February 1963	Withdrawn from use at Nairobi due salt corrosion

2) VR-AAS
Constructor's No: 169

23 September 1949	Registered as **G-ALHX**
27 October 1949	Del to BOAC as G-ALHX ("Astraea")
28 January 1960	Registered to BOAC Associated Companies
30 April 1960	Cancelled on sale to Aden Airways as **VR-AAS**
April 1964	Withdrawn from use due salt corrosion

3) VR-AAT
Constructor's No: 167

23 February 1949	Registered as **G-ALHV**
7 October 1949	Del to BOAC as G-ALHV ("Adonis")
15 July 1960	Sold to Aden Airways as **VR-AAT**
December 1963	Sold to Derby Airways as **G-ALHV** but not restored to UK register, intended for spares
	Transferred to British Midland Airways
	Scrapped at Burnaston

Avro 748 Srs 2

1) **VR-AAU**   Constructor's No: 1550   Ntu. To Brazilian AF as **FAB2500** November 1962

2) **VR-AAV**   Constructor's No: 1551   Ntu. To Brazilian AF as **FAB2501** February 1963

3) **VR-AAW** Constructor's No: 1552   Ntu. To Brazilian AF as **FAB2502** March 1963

de Havilland DH.89A Dragon Rapide

1) VR-AAL
Constructor's No: 6700

10 March 1944	Del to RAF as **HG715**
5 October 1953	Registered as **G-ANET** for Hants & Sussex Aviation Ltd
13 October 1953	Sold to Hants & Sussex Aviation, delivered 14 October 1953
8 March 1954	Registered to Silver City Airways Ltd
17 March 1955	Registered to BOAC
29 May 1955	Cancelled as sold to Aden Airways, modified to Mk.4, 6.55, and became **VR-AAL** ("Dhala")
	Leased to Amerada Petroleum Corpn
5 September 1958	Cancelled and registered in Ethiopia as **ET-P-22** to L Mascheroni & C Tonna, Asmara
	Reported crashed at Gondra but likely CofA lapsed 26 June 1960 at Addis Ababa
	after death of owner, C Tonna, in a motoring accident
	Scrapped

2) VR-AAP
Constructor's No: 6803

4 November 1944	Del to RAF as **NR715**
9 January 1945	Registered as **G-AGNH** to BOAC, Nairobi
11 May 1945	Allocated serial **VG764** for ferry flight Witney – Hurn – Nairobi commencing 17.5.45
	but reverted to **G-AGNH** on arrival (this registration cancelled 2.8.46)
9 August 1945	Registered **VP-KCT** to BOAC for operation by East African Airways Corporation
13 August 1949	Restored as **G-AGNH** to Minister of Civil Aviation
19 April 1952	CofA lapsed
19 January 1954	To Ministry of Transport & Civil Aviation & based Baghdad West for British Air Attaché;
	likely since 1949
6 July 1956	Cancelled as sold to Aden and registered **VR-AAP** 3.56 for Aden Airways
February 1959	Stored at Salalah
November 1959	Broken up at Salalah

Arabian Airways Ltd

Short S.16 Scion 2

G-AEOY
Constructor's No: S.789

1935	Registered as **G-ADDS** but not taken up
23 August 1935	First flown
24 October 1935	Registered **VH-UUT** to Adelaide Airways Ltd, South Australia
22 January 1936	Overturned in forced landing at Meadows, South Australia.
26 February 1936	Registration cancelled. Shipped back to Shorts, Rochester and rebuilt
3 November 1936	Registered **G-AEOY** to Pobjoy Airmotors & Aircraft Ltd
8 May 1937	New CofA issued
5 August 1937	Leased or sold to Halal Shipping Co Ltd, Khormaksar
~30 September 1937	Damaged in forced landing near Mukalla, repaired
1 November 1937	Registered to Arabian Airways Ltd
17 December 1937	Crashed on take-off at Terim

G-AEIL
Constructor's No: PA1003

11 May 1936	Registered as **G-AEIL** to R J B Seaman, Ramsgate but not delivered
24 June 1936	Registered to Pobjoy Airmotors & Aircraft Ltd
4 March 1938	Registered to Arabian Airways Ltd, Khormaksar
16 December 1939	Impressed for Heliopolis Communications Squadron but rejected 23.12.39
10 April 1940	CofA renewed
~26 April 1940	Believed destroyed in crash, Mukeiras
4 January 1946	Registration cancelled at census

GAL Monospar ST-25 Universal

G-AEJB
Constructor's No: GAL/ST25/82

22 May 1936	Registered as **G-AEJB** to General Aircraft Ltd
~December 1936	Given as 'sold abroad' but in fact sold to Antonin Besse/Halal Shipping, October 1936
10 November 1937	Registered to Arabian Airways Ltd
9 January 1942	Sold to Forces Aériennes Françaises Libres (FAFL) in Ethiopia
28 January 1942	Crashed on take-off at Addis Ababa, Ethiopia (Also reported as crashed on 19 August 1943)
4 January 1946	Registration cancelled at census

ACCIDENT REPORTS

February 3rd 1951. DC-3 VR-AAB en route Nairobi to Aden via Mogadishu.

Crew: Captain   D Ward
       First Officer   W A Cory
       Radio Officer   F W Johnson
       Stewardess   P M Jones

Plus three passengers, two of whom were flying to Aden, and one to Mogadishu.

The flight was operating the AD 468 from Nairobi to Aden via Mogadishu and Hargeisa, when shortly after the aircraft had become airborne from Nairobi at 0730, local time, the Captain was advised by the tower that his starboard undercarriage had not fully retracted.

The aircraft returned to Nairobi, and after several unsuccessful attempts had been made to obtain the correct cockpit indications that the undercarriage was locked down, the aircraft landed on runway 06 at Nairobi. The touchdown was successful, but at the end of the landing roll the right-hand undercarriage collapsed. There were no injuries to either crew or passengers.

The Board of enquiry found that the most probable cause of the undercarriage malfunction was a distorted jack rod within the retraction mechanism which had then prevented the proper retraction process in the first place thus preventing the undercarriage from locking down when the cockpit selection was made prior to landing.

The aircraft was repaired and was back flying within a few weeks. It was subsequently leased to Arab Airways (Jerusalem) Ltd in Jordan.

July 2nd 1951. DC-3 VR-AAD en route from Kamaran Island to Asmara.

Crew: Captain   H C Walbran
       First Officer   M R Lovell
       Radio Officer   E J Hathway
       Stewardess   D K Dowle

Plus 10 passengers.

The flight was operating the AD 466 from Aden to Cairo via Kamaran Island, Asmara, Port Sudan and Jeddah. After getting airborne from Kamaran Island on the second sector of the flight, the Captain noticed that the rate of climb was very low, even though the cockpit indications were that the undercarriage was up. However, a visual check showed that the port undercarriage had not retracted after take-off.

Several selections were made to retract and extend the undercarriage, but without success, and the red cockpit warning light remained on indicating an unlocked system. The flight continued to Asmara where visual checks were made from the tower before a landing was attempted and though the touchdown was good, as the aircraft slowed at the end of the landing roll, the port undercarriage collapsed.

There were no injuries to either passengers or crew.

The Board of enquiry was inconclusive in its findings, and was of the opinion that the incident could have occurred as a result of a distorted jack rod, though whether this occurred before the flight, or during it, could not be discovered. Another possibility was that a "brush takeoff" might have occurred out of Kamaran, whereby after takeoff and with the undercarriage starting its retraction phase, the aircraft might have sunk momentarily onto the retracting wheel, damaging the jackrod in the process.

October 18th 1952. DC-3 VR-AAE en route from Benina to Assouan, Sudan.

Crew: Captain   J B Fussey
       First Officer   C Dinnie
       Radio Officer   A Burnett

Plus 4 passengers.

The aircraft was being ferried from the UK to Aden by a Scottish Airlines crew of three, plus four staff passengers returning to Aden from UK leave. The flight had departed Benina, on the north coast of Africa, for the five and a half hour flight to Wadi Halfa, where it was to night-stop prior to continuing to Aden the following day.

On approaching Wadi Halfa in darkness, the aircraft was neither able to receive the direction finding beacon nor find the airfield itself and, running low on fuel, the Captain elected to make a forced landing along a main road which was successful in that there were no injuries to either passengers or crew, though the aircraft was initially declared a write-off.

It was the practice in Aden Airways, that when an aircraft needed a major overhaul or renewal of the Certificate of Airworthiness, it was ferried to Prestwick, Scotland, where the work was carried out by Scottish Aviation, after which the aircraft would be ferried back to Aden. If staff, stores or equipment needed transporting either way they were placed on these flights, and it was for this reason that 4 staff passengers were on board on this occasion.

The aircraft had departed Aden for Prestwick on July 19th 1952 for a Certificate of Airworthiness renewal and for certain modifications to be done. It was declared ready on October 14th and on that day it flew to Bovingdon in order to collect the four passengers. During the flight south to the African coast, problems had been evident with the radios, and a diversion had been made to Paris in order to have these remedied, though these same problems had continued during the subsequent flight to Benina. An added complication on this last sector was that the frequency of the Wadi Halfa Non Directional Beacon had been changed the month before, a fact which had not been communicated to the crew at Benina.

The flight arrived over the Nile some five and a half hours after departure from Benina and, due to the lack of communication with

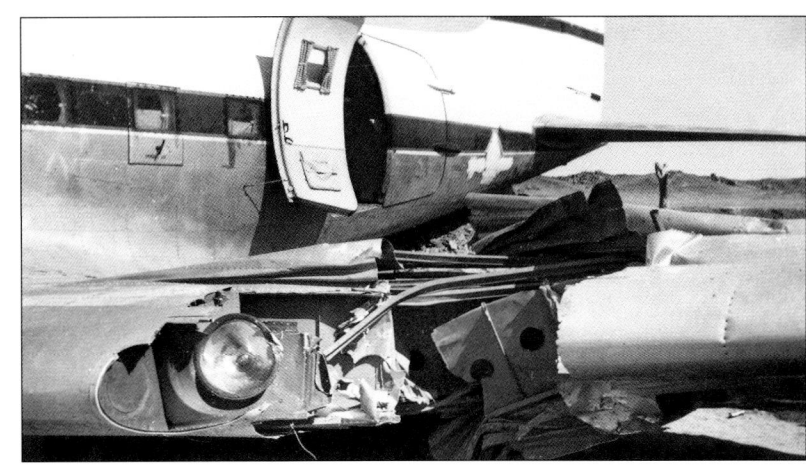

Individual Aircraft Histories, Accident Reports

The accident to VR-AAE (see also page 56):

Above, left: *The DC-3 touched down on this road, towards the camera, hit a tree with its left wing and slewed off the road.*

Above, right: *The damage to the left wing was considerable. (Both: British Airways Archives)*

Right: *The wings and tail surfaces were removed and the aircraft was towed out of the desert towards the river Nile. (Harry Pusey)*

Below: *VR-AAE nearing Heliopolis on its journey down the Nile for eventual repair. (Harry Pusey)*

anyone, the Captain decided to fly north, down the river, where after some 40 minutes the lights of a town which turned out to be Assouan became visible. By now the fuel situation was dire and the Captain elected to force-land along what appeared to be a main road. In this he was successful, though the aircraft hit a tree stump in the process which damaged it severely.

The subsequent Board of enquiry criticised Captain Fussey's decision to fly across a part of the desert with which he was unfamiliar, and at night as well, particularly when the route along the North coast of Africa to Cairo was the easier option. In addition, he further jeopardised the flight by insufficient briefing on the changes in radio aids on the chosen route, though questions were raised as to the adequacy of the way such changes were promulgated.

Though the aircraft had been declared a write-off, for which Aden Airways were paid £30,000, it was in fact sent to Cairo by river boat and repaired, though it never flew for Aden Airways again as shown in its individual history.

March 26th 1965. DC-3 VR-AAA at Hadibo Aerodrome, Socotra Island.

Crew: Captain   P E F Williamson
       First Officer   R Wigley
       Engineer   G Lazzarini
       Steward   S Ismail

Plus 14 passengers

The flight originated at Aden with first sector to Riyan flown by Captain Williamson and a landing effected on runway 06. Captain Williamson instructed Mr Wigley to fly the aircraft on the next sector to Hadibo operating from the left-hand seat. The aircraft took off from Riyan at 0657 hours for Hadibo on a special non-scheduled flight with fourteen passengers. The take-off and flight were normal and on arrival overhead at its destination at 0812 hours the aircraft was flown over the runway for inspection purposes. A fire was observed to one side of the runway but this consisted of flames without smoke and gave no indication of wind speed or direction. Hadibo is a single runway aerodrome, 2,900 feet long, 150 feet wide, bearing 01/19, height 10' AMSL.

Mr Wigley decided to approach from the north as a result of his surface wind observations and a long straight-in approach was made during which minor turbulence was experienced on crossing the coast. An approach from this direction was not disputed by Captain Williamson. Full flap was selected with power on approach at 80 knots IAS. Touch-down was executed in the almost stalled condition at a distance estimated to be 300 feet from the runway threshold and flaps retracted as the tail-wheel made contact with the ground. Normal brake application was applied and pressure steadily increased but this action had little effect in slowing down the aircraft. With maximum foot load applied to the brake pedals and with the aircraft approximately 500 feet from the southern threshold of the runway, Captain Williamson took over control of the aircraft.

It then became apparent that the aircraft would overshoot the runway and as the ground in this area formed a steep incline over boulder-strewn ground, a controlled swing of the aircraft to port was attempted. As the forward momentum was still excessive the swing developed into a partial ground-loop causing structural failure of the starboard main undercarriage assembly. The aircraft came to rest at 90° to its original path to the left of centre line of the runway, with the starboard mainplane resting on the ground outside the runway threshold.

The aircraft was quickly and safety evacuated and Captain Williamson observed that the surface wind speed and direction varied from calm conditions to 15 knot gusts from east backing to north. None of the occupants of the aircraft suffered any injury and fire did not occur.

Captain P E F Williamson held Airline Transport Pilot licence No. 26835 issued by the Ministry of Aviation, London and valid until 18th April 1965. His instrument rating was renewed on 18th December 1964 and his last check flight carried out on the 12th December 1964. His licence was validated for aircraft registered in the Federation of South Arabia. His total flying hours at the time of the accident were 16,836 of which 12,378 hours were in command of DC-3 aircraft. Captain Williamson had not previously made a landing at Hadibo aerodrome.

First Officer R Wigley held Airline Transport Pilot licence No. 44277 issued by the Ministry of Aviation, London and valid until 8th July 1965. His instrument rating was renewed on 15th January 1965 and his last check flight carried out on 8th February 1965. His licence was validated for aircraft registered in the Federation of South Arabia. His total flying hours at the time of the accident was 8,750 of which 4,300 hours were as First Officer on DC-3 aircraft.

Mr Wigley had been selected by Aden Airways as eligible for the next command vacancy on DC-3 aircraft. He had not previously landed at Hadibo aerodrome.

The weather during the flight from Riyan was fine with winds en route from the south-east. Low stratus cloud covered the high ground adjacent to the aerodrome, base 2,000 feet. The state of the off-shore sea was calm.

The physical characteristics of the runway at Hadibo were unknown to both pilots, neither having operated into this aerodrome before. Pre-flight briefing was carried out by Aden Airways operations branch and an aerodrome information sheet for Hadibo handed to the pilot. The information was incorrect in that mention was made of an up-slope from the threshold of the runway 19 for a distance of 400 feet but omitted the more important information of a pronounced down-slope for the final 1,500 feet of the runway. Under calm conditions all aircraft should approach to the 01 threshold and this information should have been included in the briefing sheet.

Although observations prior to landing indicated calm conditions it was probable that a strong down-wind component developed during the straight-in approach over the sea, which for lack of a wind indicator at the aerodrome, was unobserved by the pilots.

Whilst a landing distance of 2,900 feet was available, marks on the runway indicated that the touch down point was 450 feet in from the threshold, thus reducing the available run to 2,450 feet. A probable down-wind component of 10 knots, together with a down gradient and a poor braking surface, no doubt contributed to the build-up of a dangerous situation from which the Commander of the aircraft was unable to recover in time, by taking overshoot action.

This accident was judged to have resulted from a lack of knowledge of aerodrome runway characteristics on the part of the Captain combined with a down-wind component which was difficult to determine without adequate wind indication on the ground.

The aircraft had had its Certificate of Airworthiness renewed on the 6th June 1964 for a period of 12 months. Total airframe hours since manufacture were 28,850.

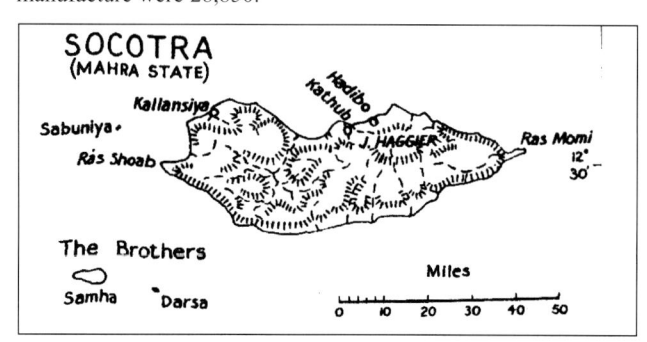

Socotra Island, showing Hadibo, the location of VR-AAA's accident.

VR-AAA ground looped at Hadibo, 26th March 1965. (Vic Spencer)

November 22nd 1966. DC-3 VR-AAN en route from Meifah to Aden.

Crew: In command   Captain P N D Skingley
        Co-pilot   Captain W L Wilson
        Flight Clerk   Mr Neguib
Plus 27 passengers including 2 infants

The aircraft was operating scheduled service AD447 from Meifah to Aden. It had departed Aden at 1100 hours under the command of Captain Skingley and arrived Meifah at 1235 hours where all commercial load is reported to have been removed. The aircraft was not refuelled as there was sufficient on board for the return flight to Aden, i.e. a total of 290 gallons of petrol and 23 gallons of oil in each engine.

27 passengers were embarked at Meifah together with their luggage – 400 kg, 2 pieces of freight – 60 kg and 2 packages of mail – 10 kg. At the time of departure the aircraft weight was 11,932 kg. (Regulated take off weight = 12,567 kg).

The aircraft departed Meifah at 1305 hours and at 1320 hours the Captain reported "airborne Meifah @ 1310Z for Aden estimating Lava 1339Z ADE 1400Z Aden @ 1416Z". The Air Traffic Controller reported that call strength was 2 and he cleared AD 447 F/L 80 AD10 to Aden. AD 447 replied he was VFR @ F/L 60. TNB not copied due to weak signal strength.

It was approximately five minutes after this that the explosion in the cabin occurred at 6,000 ft. No other communication was received from the aircraft. The fuselage disintegrated and the aircraft fell in pieces to the ground. All 27 passengers and 3 crew were killed. The explosion was not due to any defect in the aircraft but is attributed to an explosive charge in some hand baggage carried in the cabin on the port side just above the wing.

Eye witnesses have reported hearing an explosion and seeing the aircraft falling in pieces and on fire. They were the first people to arrive at the scene and reported that all passengers and crew were found to be dead. All victims were lying on the ground clear of the wreckage except for the Captain who was still in the control cabin.

All Arab victims, 25 passengers and the Fight Clerk, were taken by road to Meifah during the night of the accident. The two European passengers and the two pilots were taken to Aden by helicopter on 23rd November.

On examination the wreckage was found to be lying on a sand/gravel plain 130 nautical miles east of Aden and two miles from the coast. The wreckage trail was about 5,000 ft by 1,000 ft but most of the heavy pieces of wreckage were within 2,500 ft of the main wreckage. The location was confirmed as 13° 38' North 47° 04' East in the Federation of South Arabia two nautical miles NE of Hasn Valide.

Mr F W Bird, Deputy Superintendent of the CID Aden State Police who examined the wreckage on the morning immediately after the accident had taken away various pieces of debris for further examination. He has confirmed that there was an explosion in the cabin and that it was on the port side and was probably caused by 2 lb of TNT-type explosive.

An examination was made of the wreckage trail from which it soon became apparent that the aircraft had disintegrated in flight. Detailed examination of components of the aircraft and, in particular, the flooring, seats and fuselage skin on the port side had suffered severe burning and there was evidence of an explosive force having disrupted and brought about the fuselage disintegration.

A further detailed inspection of the structure which had been damaged by fire was carried out and certain portions of the aircraft salvaged and flown back to Aden for more detailed inspection and investigation.

The aircraft, Constructor's No. 4692, was purchased from Middle East Airlines in September 1956 at which time it had been in service 16,108 hours. At the time of the accident it had completed a total of 34,367 hours 35 minutes.

The Pilot-in-Command Captain Peter Norman Dunkin Skingley was born in Canterbury, Kent 13th October 1925. He held United Kingdom ALTP Licence No. 34469 valid in Part I for Dakota C-47 aircraft; the date of expiry was 16th August 1968. He was last medically examined on 8th August 1966. The licence was validated on 29th September 1966 for aircraft registered in the Federation of South Arabia. At the time of the accident Captain Skingley had completed a total flying time of 15,180 hours.

The Co-pilot Captain Warren Leonard Wilson was born in Sydney, Australia 29th June 1921. He held United Kingdom ALTP Licence No. 43270 valid in Part I for Dakota C-47 aircraft; the date of expiry was 11th September 1967. His medical certificate was valid to 14th March 1967 and the licence was validated on 7th November 1966 for aircraft registered in the Federation of South Arabia. At the time of the accident Captain Wilson had completed a total flying time of 15,854 hours.

BIBLIOGRAPHY

R Baram	Airlines and Airliners. Viscount 700. Aviation Hobby Shop.
W Bray	The history of BOAC. Wessex Press, 1975
G Cowell	Handley Page Herald. James Publishing Company, 1980
R E G Davies	A History of the World's Airlines. Oxford, 1964.
J M Davis	The Curtiss C-46 Commando. Air Britain, 1978.
J M Davis & H G Martin	The Curtiss C-46 Commando. Air Britain, 1981
P J Davis	East African: An Airline Story. Runnymede Malthouse Publishing, 1993.
P W Davis	The Vickers Viscount. Air Britain, 1981.
Jennifer Gradidge	The Douglas DC-3. Air Britain, 1984
Jennifer Gradidge	DC-1, DC-2, DC-3: The First Seventy Years. Air Britain, 2006
B R Guttery	Encyclopaedia of African Airlines. MacFarland Co Inc, 1998.
J F Hamlin	The De Havilland Dragon/Rapide Family. Air Britain, 2003.
P Hinchcliffe et al	Without Glory in Arabia. I B Tauris & Co Ltd, 2006.
Larry Milberry	The Canadair North Star. Canav Books, 1982
Harry Pusey	Civil Aviation in Jordan. Private publication, 1963.
P Richards	Return to Aden. G F Murray Creative Information Solutions, 1975.
Roadcap	World Airline Record. 1948, 1952, 1955, 1965.
John Stroud	Annals of British and Commonwealth Air Transport. Putnam, 1962.
A Szura	Folded Wings. History of Transocean Airlines. Pictorial Histories Publishing Co, 1989.
Richard Thruelsen	Transocean, the story of an unusual airline. Henry Holt & Co, 1953.
P StJohn Turner	Handbook of the Vickers Viscount. Ian Allan, 1968
Flight Magazine:	1947-1968.
Aeroplane Magazine:	1947-1968.
ABC Guide:	1946-1968.
Bradshaws Guide:	1946-1949
British Airways Archives:	BOAC Board Minutes 1946-1968.
	BOAC Associated Companies Board Minutes.
	BOAC Annual Reports 1946-1968.
Aden Airways	Annual Reports: 1950-1951
	1951-1952
	1963-1964

Evocative view of VR-AAA at Hargeisa, 1954. *(Vic Spencer)*

APPENDICES

1	Richard de Graaff Hunter,	Managing Director Aden Airways, 1948-1954	p194
2	Reflections on Aden:		
	Trevor Austin,	Staff and Administration Manager, 1963-1967.	p195
	Michael Hedges,	RAF Wireless operator Khormaksar, 1951-1954.	p201
	Mike Gardner,	Ground Engineer 1959-1963.	p202
	Pat Kennedy,	Traffic Officer, Junior Grade, 1957-1958.	p205
	David Willmott,	Temporary Captain Aden Airways, 1963.	p205
	Tony May,	First Officer Aden Airways, 1965-1967.	p206
3	Aden Airways Crews:		p209
	List of Chief Pilots of Aden Airways.		
	List of Pilots.		
	List of Air Hostesses.		
	List of Stewards and Flight Clerks.		
4	Flights which specifically allowed females.		p210

1. Richard de Graaff Hunter.

He was born on January 20, 1909 in Lahore, at that time in India, though today it is in Pakistan, where his Father was head of the India Survey. He followed a conventional, if privileged, upbringing within the system as it was then. Sent to boarding school in Cheltenham, England, followed by Cambridge where he read Aeronautical Engineering, a subject which was in itself unusual in those days. Unable to get a job with Imperial Airways Ltd, he went to work for a gentleman (whose name seems to have been forgotten by all) who had invented front wheel brakes for Rolls Royce cars; an unusual job since it involved visiting mainly stately homes in his suitably fitted Rolls Royce in order to persuade the owners of the virtues of this invention.

Once he had achieved some success in England, he was sent to Poland in order to convince the upper classes in the same way, but tiring of this he set off on his travels to the USA and Tahiti where he found employment on the MGM film set there shooting "Mutiny on the Bounty". Sadly, while the film was a great success, there was to be no career in Hollywood and after this disappointment he returned to the UK where he joined the Home Office.

When WW2 broke out in 1939, he was put in charge of a Civil Defence department near Sandringham, Norfolk, after which he was posted to Burma as Civil Defence Commissioner. Following the overrun of Burma he managed to get back to India where he was invited to join the Civil Intelligence department there. After some time he was sent to Bermuda as personal assistant to the Governor, Lord Knollys, who, when he became Chairman of BOAC in 1943 asked de Graaff Hunter to follow him in the same capacity.

In 1947 he was sent to the Middle East to work under Keith Granville, the General Manager there (and who was later to become Chairman of BOAC) with the intention that he should gain more airline experience, though there was a suggestion that his presence and role in London were resented by the established airline executives. Whatever the motives, he was selected to be the Managing Director of the new airline in Aden (though the base was to be in Asmara, Eritrea) where his considerable personal skills could come into play.

As with so many people of his intellect, he could appear to be somewhat mercurial. As his widow wrote: "His main strength was his brain; he was very clever and very well educated, and had a charm which few others were able to match." His approach to Aden Airways was of the "broad brush" variety and he had little time for the minute detail of everyday airline life, preferring instead to concentrate on issues within the Red Sea region and the role that the new airline could play. That he had vision and drive there was no doubt, demonstrated by the negotiations with Ethiopia in 1953 to manage Ethiopian Airlines and the setting up of Arab Airways (Jerusalem) Ltd during the same year. However, when he opened negotiations with other local Governments for traffic rights, he caused considerable anger back in London, both with BOAC and the Colonial Office.

Fortunately, he was supported by a capable team in Captain Steve Colvin, the Chief Pilot, A C Middleton, Chief Accountant and later Harry Pusey as Planning Officer. But his own personnel selection could be arbitrary; for instance, a representative was employed in Cairo simply because he was related to King Farouk, (though a relative close to the seat of power was considered essential in those days); a BOAC fireman became his Sales Promotion Superintendent on rather dubious grounds, and a BOAC navigator who helped him sail his yacht from Bermuda became Operations Superintendent, in the process replacing a very able man.

These factors, together with an ostentatiously opulent lifestyle, did cause resentment amongst employees. Nor did he always get on well with the British Government departments in Aden and elsewhere in the region.

But his formidable intellect helped him rise above all these "minor" problems. Because of his background and education he walked easily in the company of those in charge, engaging them in discussion and argument, often achieving on his own what Government agents had been unable to do for years.

He was also an innovative Manager; it was he who brought in male travelling traffic clerks, instead of female cabin crew, for the routes up into the Aden Protectorate thus avoiding any conflict with the male tribesmen from that region. Converting the DC-3s into a passenger cum freight layout made many of the routes highly flexible since the ratio of seats to freight could be varied relatively easily. When he lowered the fares between Aden and Mukalla and Mukeiras to realistic levels there was an increase in traffic not only in passengers, but goats and Qat as well, which made these hitherto unprofitable routes become valuable contributors to the bottom line financially. He was always full of new ideas for expanding the airline, whether it was trying to make BOAC lend four engined equipment in order to operate to India, or subleasing out the two Yorks from BOAC in 1952 which were meant for the Haj. (They did operate on the West African Haj, but had been subleased to West African Airways). Once again, though, his grasp of detail let him down at times, such as when he could not accept that the refusal of BOAC to lease him two further Yorks in 1952, in order to operate a freight company out of Asmara, was based on poor aircraft performance and not on spite.

With the benefit of hindsight, one must doubt his judgment when he involved Aden Airways in the creation of Arab Airways (Jerusalem) Ltd in 1953. True, BOAC had been invited to come to Jordan and set up an airline in that country and had walked away from it. They did, however, suggest to de Graaff Hunter that he might care to have a look at the situation in order to see whether the prospect was a viable one. In doing so, he was being handed a poisoned chalice which proved to be a serious drain upon the resources of Aden Airways until 1958, long after his departure from Aden. That is not to say that Arab Airways could not have become a sound airline, but one must question what Aden Airways was doing there; perhaps it fitted in with de Graaff Hunter's vision of expansion and influence within the region. To a large extent, it sowed the seeds of his demise in May 1954 when he was dismissed by BOAC.

He led a hard life in every respect and certainly appears to have lived it to the full. Eventually, though, BOAC became increasingly concerned at the way the management of the company was being conducted, and he was invited to resign.

If there was to be a final word on de Graaff Hunter, Robert Wigley's assessment is probably the most accurate: *"de Graaff Hunter was an extraordinary man, and may not have always fitted into the mould as an airline manager. But his vision and enthusiasm during those early years ensured the survival of the airline where, under a less imaginative manager, it would have foundered early"*.

2. Reflections on Aden

Trevor Austin:

a) Working for Aden Airways, 1963-67.

I think Aden Airways was actually quite an expensive operation in many ways. For example, there were a number of outstations – Hargeisa was an example - where the probity of local agents and employees was suspect and where local labour laws made it difficult to trim employment costs. This wasn't so surprising when it is remembered that Aden Airways was an expatriate firm operating in a country with extremely high unemployment. When we eventually closed Hargeisa I had to go there to try and get the release of the Aden Airways Land Rover which we wanted in Aden. This was quite a valuable vehicle but I had to go to the local court – where I was the only white face among at least 200 unfriendly locals objecting to our wishes - and it was made clear to me that unless some deal was arranged Aden Airways would not see its Land Rover, its money and probably its Staff and Admin Manager again! In the end we had to sell the vehicle at a knock-down price to the local agent who was probably related to the judge.

Aden Airways certainly had all kinds of difficulties getting revenue out of Somalia in particular and Abyssinia as well. The Marxist regime in Somalia was totally corrupt and perpetually short of cash and remittances of AA revenue were held up because the local Government put pressure on the bank to use deposits for other things. I know the Aden Airway's Accountant made several visits to Mogadishu and only managed to get any money out by bribing Government ministers with free tickets on BOAC and other carriers to Moscow and Havana; Amsterdam was also another popular destination and you will doubtless know why!

Back in Aden, the company followed a policy of Adenising as many jobs as possible which may have mildly pacified local opinion (though it threw up all kinds of problems with various ethnic groups in the colony) but which played havoc with productivity. Unemployment was very high in Aden and jobs with firms like Aden Airways were difficult to obtain. One of the first things I had to do when I arrived was to sack my Indian Employment Superintendent who I found was selling Aden Airways jobs at £50 a throw. His Adeni successor was a totally trustworthy chap and a good friend as well. On the other hand I am pretty sure there was a lot of feather-bedding and this was partly due to local tendencies anyway and partly due to the Company policy of running itself on BOAC lines instead of operating a budget service which the local circumstances really called for.

This was taking place amongst a belligerent attitude from local staff who were organised in the Aden Trade Union Congress which had openly Marxist and anti-British attitudes even though the bulk of employment in Aden depended on British firms. The breakdown of Aden Airways pay negotiations led to a very damaging go-slow and eventually a strike which had serious revenue implications for a while until one of the more sensible local supervisors and I conducted some back-street coffee shop negotiations and everyone went back to work. The great majority of the local staff were keen and diligent but there were a lot of them and the standard of expertise was not very good. This led to much effort and expense being devoted to training schemes to bring local staff up to an acceptable standard. I mentioned the recruitment of an Adeni second officer who was trained in the UK and the Company also opened a local Engineering Apprentice School which again was socially and politically desirable but financially expensive. It has to be remembered that as a British Colony Aden Airways operated under the rules of the local Directorate of Civil Aviation which was mostly run by expatriate civil servants.

Aden Airways had a most generous medical scheme for all staff and this was a heavy drain on company finances. It even included free hospital treatment and expensive medicines and I don't think the scheme really recovered from the heavy costs of sending a local labourer to a prestigious London hospital for several weeks' private treatment of a cancerous leg condition. There was quite high sickness absence rate that never seemed to be under control though I think this was largely endemic to the area. Even quite senior people absented themselves on quite trivial grounds which meant employing more people than necessary. I recall I had to employ two local staff doing nothing but staff travel because one of them, an Indian woman, had such enormous amounts of sick leave.

In those days all reservations were done manually and this meant a proliferation of offices in various parts of Aden with the objective of picking up bits of business and I suspect there was never any serious attempt to see if these were cost effective for fear of the difficulties that would arise if there was an attempt to close them down. In fairness, however, Aden Airways did try to reduce the number of ticket-selling outlets but didn't get very far. We had a large and expensive Head Office in Khormaksar, more offices and the Engineering, Operations and Catering facilities at the Airport and I think at least two offices in town (Crater and Maala).

I can't be sure but I think 1962 onwards was the time of the Wilson Labour government which was ideologically committed to shedding colonies and giving independence to local people. A kind of half-way house where the Government in London wanted to loosen but not sever the strings and to introduce independence gradually (on the grounds that locals didn't know how to run things themselves) was the concept of Federation. This was tried in several parts of the world such as Central Africa, Malaysia, the Caribbean and South Arabia. The last one at least leaned very heavily on local "aristocracy" like the Sultan of Lahej (Aden Airways had a couple of these individuals on the local Board) backed up by a British Colonial civil service that gradually brought in pro-British locals.

None of these Federations ever succeeded and the South Arabian Federation was an unsuccessful expensive experiment to try and replace British colonialism with a pro-British local set-up.

In the 1950s and 1960s Aden was still a big military, naval and air force base, partly because the services wanted to maintain their self perpetuating role of policing half the world and partly, I suspect, because the base was just there! The existence of any British military presence in the Middle East was anathema to the growing militancy of countries like Egypt, Iraq and Libya so there were continued attempts led by Egypt to undermine the British position. I don't think the military were facing up to the realities and instead were insisting they were needed in the region to protect British interests and pro-British locals i.e. the Sultans. In short, the base was a thorn in the flesh of the Arab nationalists who exploited every bit of anti-British publicity from it, often via the United Nations.

In the end the London Government were galvanised by United Nations as well as UK pressure to send out some sort of Commission and this led to an enquiry by a man called Sir Humphrey Trevelyan who was very far-seeing and sensible. He recommended giving full independence to Aden and was mercifully appointed the last Governor when he sensibly advanced the timetable so that the British could get out without too much trouble. This of course pleased the more militant Arabs who were glad to see the back of the British military. The repercussions on the very large Services' employment of local people were not always realised and I remember going to a meeting of the Aden Employers Association where the TUC asked in all seriousness for the NAAFI (which employed several hundreds of locals) to stay in Aden when the Services left!

As well as the external Arab pressures on London there were pressures from Aden militants as well on the Aden and Al Ittihad (Federal) Governments. On top of these were the inter-Arab conflicts between various pro-independence factions which eventually ended up in two major organisations called FLOSY (Front for the Liberation of South Yemen) and the NLF (National Liberation Front) fighting each other. Each tried to out-do the other in nastiness and anti-expatriate and anti-British actions and prominent Arabs supporting the Federal Government were often targets. This including the Aden Airways Manager, Abdul Raheem Kassem, a most delightful and wise individual, who was assassinated by militants.

Aden Airways was, despite its name, seen as a Government organisation and its staff and activities were clearly targets for those intent on pressurising the UK to grant independence as soon as possible. Thus we had to adopt all kinds of security measures to safeguard the staff as well as the aircraft. I was in charge of the Aden Airways security section and one of my early jobs was to remove for his own safety the section head who was silly enough to get involved with the local Special Branch police (all eventually bumped off by nationalists) who suspected Aden Airways was harbouring militants in its local staff (which was almost certainly true). BOAC replaced him with a splendid man called Bill McGarry who was sensible and effective and who stayed right to the very end of Aden Airways.

On the operational side we had to introduce an expensive search system of all passengers which was a disagreeable task with all kinds of sensitivities when dealing with women passengers for example. It worked well enough in Aden but someone managed to exploit the usual confusion at one of the up-country airstrips to secrete a bomb on a DC-3 which exploded killing all on board. The army eventually took over security at the Khormaksar Civil Airport but even that did not prevent the destruction of one of the Viscounts.

So there were operational constraints like the searching of passengers, the re-scheduling of a reduced fleet, the risks of serving some up-country places where aircraft had to be guarded by British military, and the effect on staff some of whom decided to leave while the going was still reasonably good. There were inevitably all kinds of restrictions on personal movement after a spate of attacks on expatriates and the Crater District was effectively out of bounds. The very lively social life among expatriates continued but there was an atmosphere of unease and caution. Nobody with any sense drove an open-topped car, anyone with any sense carried a hand-gun (including me), and great care was taken at restaurants or any gathering, even such innocent events as a badminton game, having one's hair cut or visiting the market and shops. Almost all expatriates employed local servants and tension sometimes arose because the militants pressurised some servants into giving information on expatriates' movements as well as, in at least one case, placing a bomb which exploded during a party.

Donald Classey, the Aden Airways General Manager, and I sent regular reports to AC in London about the security situation but I don't think they really appreciated what was going on. The AC Personnel Manager, Adrian Lee, was sent to make an assessment but he bounced gung-ho into the Aden Airways head office in full military combat gear (he was in the TA) and heavily armed so that we had to hide him in my office and smuggle him out as fast as possible lest any locals thought we were too closely connected with the military. Ray Cox, a Personnel Officer from AC, also came but I don't think his bosses fully accepted his report. Eventually, Gilbert Lee and John Linstead made a flying visit and were taken around by McGarry and me. They were visibly shaken and I think they eventually recommended BOAC to pull out.

Meanwhile, the UK government wanted Aden Airways to continue operating both its own services and handling BOAC VC-10 aircraft which served Aden via Nairobi or Khartoum carrying mainly service dependants but also many commercial and government passengers. At one time the BOAC aircraft were handled by Aden Airways staff (including me in emergencies) at the Civil Airport (and presumably there was a financial arrangement) but as the security situation became more dangerous the handling was done by RAF people at the military side of the airport. This meant a cumbersome and expensive business of non-military passengers checking in at the civil side and being bussed to the military side where there were further checks and security searches and so on.

Coming from an aviation background I loved being close to aircraft, even old-fashioned ones like the DC-3. Anyone from LHR would have been astonished at the way the expatriate staff and families became involved in operations - such as when the catering staff went on strike and the staff wives went down to the airport and made sandwiches for passengers. There was a BOAC Station Officer in Aden because they had twice-weekly services there but he did not mix with us and I found him difficult because he thought he should be able to give instructions to me and the Aden Airways staff who wouldn't have it! Aden Airways handled BOAC services and I invariably met incoming and departing aircraft to greet and say goodbye to our staff passengers. This allowed me access to the tarmac and I remember being roped in one morning by a hard-pressed engineer to check the tyre pressures on the VC-10.

While all this was going on the Aden Government was trying to mollify local nationalists by handing over Immigration Control to Adeni staff. This gave us many headaches in getting work permits for our staff and although permits were usually given fairly easily for pilots there were often difficulties put in the way of others. I remember being told to go to the Immigration Office in Crater about my own permit which I refused to do as it was clearly an attempt to lure me into an ambush. Eventually it was worked out and we solved most of the difficulties by a typically Arab arrangement whereby we employed as a stewardess the niece of the Controller of Immigration. This young lady was familiarly known as "Bechstein" because of the shape of her legs and she was so afraid of flying that she spent most flights curled up in a seat at the rear of the aircraft. An anecdote that still gives me pleasure concerned a stewardess, British through and through, who I successfully argued did not need a work permit because she had been born in Aden to a military family in transit some 20 years before. The Controller was very unhappy indeed but could not refute my argument!

The up-country airstrips I visited had a kind of shack where I thought the flight clerk sold tickets but Vic will know about that. There was chaos there when passengers were getting on and off, partly due to temperament and partly because they were trying to get things on board they shouldn't carry. That was probably how the bomb was planted on the DC-3, someone got on and left a bomb in a bag in the luggage rack or under a seat and then got off in the confusion and disappeared. I know there was some delay on take-off possibly because the two free-lance pilots were unused to the passenger habits. This meant that when the bomb exploded the wreckage fell on the seashore instead of out to sea as had been planned. Vic Spencer was, of course, much involved in the investigation and I had to return urgently from Australia where I was on holiday to deal with the staff casualties and related matters.

FLOSY (Front for the Liberation of South Yemen) was a secretive Arab Independence movement initially of a fairly non-violent type although they organised several strikes in Aden including some in Aden Airways. It was led by a shadowy character called Al-Asnag and I was taken furtively by one of my people to meet him in an office in an Aden back street. Bearing in mind what happened later to people like Terry Waite in Lebanon I must have been mad but I found Al-Asnag very intelligent and reasonable and we made an informal agreement about limiting strikes and damage to Aden

APPENDIX 2: REFLECTIONS ON ADEN

Airways. Unfortunately, FLOSY was upstaged by the much more militant NLF which promised independence more quickly and the two organisations competed in the violent incident business.

There was an amusing side of a report I made to London about an incident which FLOSY had perpetrated affecting Aden Airways. Communications between Aden Airways and BOAC were insecure (I suspected the Signals staff sent copies of all incoming and outgoing signals to FLOSY) and even the telephone was unreliable until we fitted a scrambler. Anything confidential was sent in Lloyds Commercial Code to which only Donald Classey and I had access. To encode FLOSY I used the symbols for "female dog" hoping someone in London had a dog called Flossie. When Gilbert Lee read this he reputedly said "the heat is sending Austin of his head – what is this female dog business?" Fortunately Adrian Lee realised what I meant and we all had a good laugh about it later.

I can't remember exactly when it happened but there was a serious belief in Government that Aden could be occupied by Arab forces via the land frontier with Yemen. This led to considerable tension and all expatriate companies including Aden Airways were required to have an evacuation officer (yes, I drew the short straw) to liaise with the military and plan for our expatriates and all their possessions including cars to be evacuated surreptitiously through the port to the aircraft carrier HMS *Bulwark* which was anchored off the harbour. In the end the plan was not needed and everyone left for London (or Rome in the case of the Italian engineers) by scheduled aircraft. Quite a lot of baggage went by cargo aircraft and several people sent their cars home by sea. At least it was a better idea than the one where the expatriates would have taken their cars by ship to Djibouti and then travelled by road and track to Nairobi or Cairo; the thought of doing that in a mini was very off-putting.

We also had to make plans to remove the aircraft and spares – Aden Airway's main assets - to Europe. This involved all kinds of mad flight plans across East and Central Africa – refuelling at Fort Lamy was one idea that sticks in my mind, but eventually saner counsel prevailed and I think the aircraft were sold locally.

Before the close-down decision was taken there was a serious diminution in passenger revenue and everyone with an ounce of perception could see Aden Airways was doomed. Government wanted us to maintain services as much as possible to keep up the communications with out-stations and up-country places. The number of attacks on expatriate civilians and military increased (my own cousin's Marine sergeant husband was killed by an Arab sniper at this time) and at some stage I know the Government wisely recommended the evacuation of all expatriate women and children. I think Aden Airways took some to places where they could pick up BOAC services but I am not sure how exactly. Most of the families were keen to go, but it made things a bit lonely.

b) Living in Aden.

Secondment conditions were excellent and included generous baggage and clothing allowances, a highly advantageous local currency adjustment, good pay levels with local income tax paid by AA which meant I could remit a high proportion to my UK savings account. I had 13 weeks annual leave, a throw-back to the times when staff travelled by sea and Aden attracted a high "hard-living" allowance. I never managed to take it all and the balance was paid to me in cash on de-secondment when my baggage allowance was enough to ship home a crate of furniture and carpets.

Mention of ties may surprise you and I should explain that staff who worked in air-conditioned offices wore long trousers, long sleeved shirts and ties and proper shoes. Where there was no air-conditioning the dress was shorts, short-sleeved shirts, no ties, knee-length socks and proper shoes. In our leisure time we wore shorts, short-sleeved shirts and flip-flops; few people wore hats or caps which is probably why I had a small skin cancer on my face. I don't suppose many people know nowadays what Red Sea Kit is or was? Well, this was what European civilian men wore in Aden for formal occasions and it consisted of long black tropical weight trousers, a short-sleeved open-necked white shirt and a black or dark coloured cummerbund. It was quite comfortable and I remember one party where the French Consul-General caused a sensation by turning up in black shorts and knee-length black socks.

The social life was great for a young bachelor such as myself. In the early days I was at other people's parties six nights a week and entertained at home on the seventh. Mostly it was dinner parties but often we made up a table of eight or ten people at the Rock Hotel which had an excellent restaurant (crepes georgette was a speciality) with live music and dancing. There were also informal curry lunches and formal dinners at the Classey's home, Ras Boradli, some of which were the company entertaining important contacts in the Colony. The major employers' top people sometimes invited me to their parties and I had some invitations to Government House as well. It was certainly very different to the social life in the southern suburbs of London.

There were opportunities to see unusual and remote places in Aden and the surrounding countries like the Queen of Sheba's water cisterns and the Sheikh Othman zoo, and I had flights to the up-country landing grounds where our military stood guard against the rebels in the surrounding hills. I had business trips to outstations like Cairo, Khartoum, Bahrein, Nairobi, Mogadishu and Hargeisa. When back in the UK on leave I dined out for weeks on stories about these places.

Although no great sportsman, I played a lot of tennis until the security people stopped it. Sporting life centred round the Goldmohur Club on a small beach protected by a shark net where most expatriate staff went after work. It was a little way out of Aden through several military camps and clubs and was a pleasant place for a morning or afternoon. You could get a light meal there on tick (once a month settlement) and the amount of Heineken consumed was prodigious! The swimming was fair, the waves were modest and there was a diving platform off shore. I enjoyed floating around on a lilo until one day after a good lunch I dropped off to sleep on this thing and was woken up abruptly fighting for air in 16 feet of water having been thrown off when it hit the shark net. Great merriment on shore of course when I got back coughing and spluttering. The other enjoyable sport was thanks to the Spencers who had a motor-boat and on Sundays they would invite a party to picnic with them on one of the several sea-access only beaches where the girls prepared lunch while the guys practiced with their handguns shooting beer cans off the rocks.

I enjoyed helping local staff prepare for independence and did my best as did Bill McGarry to train our local people. We got a long way forward on this probably because we knew we had a job waiting for us in London whereas the directly-engaged expatriates were going to be fishing for work when they had to leave.

We could use the RAF medical facilities if ill and I was lucky and only needed this twice in the time I was in Aden. It was also comforting to know that if the security worsened there were several thousand troops to protect us.

The deterioration in security was undoubtedly top anxiety as there were several nasty incidents. We were restricted in where we could go and there were several times when a curfew was imposed unless you had a special pass. I had one but worried about the military on road blocks getting jumpy though in fairness they always behaved impeccably to me. They took an Aden Airways pilot into custody one night because he was so sunburned they thought he was an Arab. It was dangerous, of course, and all expatriates were

Goldmohur Beach with its surrounding shark net in April 1956. (Vic Spencer)

potential targets. I remember one Sunday when Bill McGarry and I (we always travelled together so that one could drive and the other hold the gun ready) went into the Arab market to buy fruit before continuing to Goldmohur. We hadn't been there long before hearing that two young RAF men out of uniform had been assassinated in the market. I always thought we were the targets but luckily we had left before the gunmen and the unfortunate RAF lads arrived. Dinner parties were severely curtailed after one ended tragically when a bomb placed by the host's servant in the dining room sideboard exploded killing several people. The Rock Hotel closed because it was too easily infiltrated by terrorists and so we tended to socialise among ourselves in the Aden Airways Khormaksar compound. There was another Aden Airways compound in Maala where the stewardesses, Italian engineers and non-European expatriates lived and I was a regular visitor there for badminton evenings under floodlight until these were stopped because of the security risk.

The climate was terrible. Not only was it very hot – up to 110°F in the summer – but it was very humid so that you carried a small towel to keep mopping your brow. Cars needed loose Turkish towelling seat covers to absorb sweat and stop your posterior burning on the leather or plastic. The humidity corroded metal (we never washed a car properly but just sponged it down) and leather and cloth grew mildew if not brushed frequently. I recall sitting at my desk in the flat wearing just a pair of shorts and not moving though the sweat dripped steadily onto the letter I was writing. Add to that the pervasive Aden smell which was a mixture of rotting domestic rubbish, sewers and stagnant water. If people say "it never rained in Aden" it isn't quite true although it rained very infrequently – about every five or six years! I was there when it rained heavily one morning for an hour or so with the result that my flat was flooded with rain falling on the verandahs and the roads had no soakaways or rain gullies. The stagnant water stank for days.

The climate and facilities meant you had to take care of yourself to keep well. It was essential to keep the flat very clean and people who economised on disinfectant, and there were some, usually found they had cockroaches everywhere, even in the fridge. It was important to keep weight down and boil all water used in drinking and cooking. We had a case of typhoid in the compound through poor hygiene and several people had uncomfortable skin problems like prickly heat. Sunburn was common until you learned to respect the strength of the sun and the dermatologist who removed a skin cancer from my face a few years ago attributed it to my time in Aden. It was necessary to change clothes several times a day and put the soiled ones out to the dhobi rather than just drying them. Care in selecting your dhobi was important otherwise people could and did contract an unpleasant complaint called "Dhobi Itch". The worst trouble I had was a persistent cough which the RAF medical people could not cure so I had to go to see the BOAC medical unit in London. After coughing my way from Aden to Heathrow it stopped as soon as I took a breath of cold wet air and the eventual diagnosis was a grain of sand in the lung.

Although we could buy a fair range of food and drink (especially the latter which inevitably caused some alcohol problems with those who imbibed too generously) the quality was not very good and the pilots who went to Nairobi were good at bringing back fresh instead of frozen meat and so on. Adrian Lee was a real friend in that way and when he visited Aden always brought me cooking apples which you couldn't get locally.

When security got really bad – there was a mutiny by the South Arabian Army – as independence drew closer the Government evacuated the wives and families of all military and Government people and advised expatriate firms to do the same. Most of the AA families were only too glad to go because the European School had closed but it left a big gap in the social side and Goldmohur became very quiet with no children there. The only troublesome case I had was with a pilot who did not want his wife and small daughter to leave Aden because, being on a temporary posting, that would mean the end of his accompanied allowances and he needed these to pay the mortgage on his UK property. Eventually I had to ask BOAC AC to issue an instruction to him before he would pack up and leave Aden. After all the staff were paid off and I sold all the furniture and fittings at auction I too left and the only Aden Airways expatriate staff were Donald Classey, Bill Williams and Bill McGarry. After selling the flats to the Russian Navy they also left, so the only Aden Airways representative was the General Services Officer, Mohamed Obali, who later fell out with the independent government and was summarily executed.

I hope I have given a fair idea of expatriate life. Our office hours were 7am to 2pm six days a week but my work meant I was effectively on call any time of the day and night. One of the bugbears of the job was that staff (and their wives) who did not work office hours e.g. pilots thought nothing of nabbing me at the beach club or coming round to my flat later in the evening to discuss business things like redecorating or staff travel on behalf of their husbands. I went to the beach for a swim most days and usually put in an hour or two at the office in the evenings or took work back to my flat. Postal services were erratic for personal mail and I had a wide correspondence with family and friends all round the world so I kept a supply of UK stamps and persuaded friendly passengers to take my mail and post it in London. Confidential reports to London were sent in the same way. My spare time was fairly limited as I found business affairs taking more and more space. It was annoying when we could no longer play tennis or badminton and the occasional visit to the open air cinema in the RAF camp at Khormaksar was another casualty after someone threw a live grenade into the audience. There were always domestic odd jobs to do and I spent many evenings re-arranging and cataloguing a large collection of Commonwealth postage stamps. Ali, my houseboy, was a good plain cook but no more than that, so I enjoyed cooking reasonably elaborate meals when friends came round.

c) Attitudes in Aden

I think there were varying views among the locals towards the Company. Most of them felt it was a local company but they fully realised it was financed and mainly run by expatriates who were not going to be there for ever. Even the most radical, and there were some of those, wanted there to be a local airline of some kind but dreamed of it being run by local people. I have my doubts if they ever gave much thought as to how such a company would be financed.

The second factor was the sharpening attitude between those who wanted full independence with no reliance on the British and those who advocated some form of co-operation with the UK, at least until Aden could produce its own managers and technical staff. This last group were pushed aside pretty brutally (including Abdul Raheem Kassim the Aden Airways Traffic Manager and a Minister in the Federal Government, who was assassinated as mentioned earlier) and the militants also made it clear that non-Arabs, especially Indians, would be unwelcome in independent Aden even when they had lived there for generations.

The Traffic Department was entirely localised as was Catering but I reckon Engineering were very nervous of giving real authority to local engineers. However, there was no doubt in my mind that BOAC Associated Companies was determined to keep its hands firmly on the Chief Accountant job. Operations was a bit special as the pilots were all European until the Adeni second officer came along and I was able to persuade the Management Committee to recruit a few local stewardesses. This was far from easy because the Arab attitude to such things as handling alcohol, ham sandwiches and staying in the same hotels as male crew, was entirely negative.

When I arrived in Aden the attitude of expatriates to local staff was generally friendly in a kind of mildly patronising way. As long as they were good servants and helpful shop-keepers that was fine but the old habits of colonialism were still around especially in anything connected with the military. It was all rather cosy but the attitude changed as the incidents of anti-British behaviour increased. I expect you have read about the assassination of Sir Arthur Charles, the Speaker of the Assembly, the attempt to assassinate the Deputy Governor at the airport, the grenade thrown into a teenagers' dance near the RAF HQ, the bomb secreted in a sideboard at an expatriate party and several other incidents.

This led to distrust and great wariness and, sadly, indifference to the disadvantages and worries of the local staff most of whom only wanted to make a decent living. I remember having to stop visiting the Crater District, and the funny little zoo at Sheikh Othman was also out of bounds. I had to carry a handgun, watch the curfew, keep all the doors firmly locked and eventually move from my now vulnerable flat into the staff compound.

The centre of bad feeling was undoubtedly the Engineering Department where the militant Trade Union leaders worked (sometimes!). Some were very hard cases indeed but others were tough in public and surprisingly sensible and co-operative in private. The Union Chairman was an upholsterer by trade and from snarling at me during negotiations one day came the next day with a beautifully made set of loose seat covers for my car.

d) Dealing with security

The effect of the DC-3 incident was to heighten the uncertainty of the Company's future as well as its security of operations. A very visible military presence was put in place at the Airport and the Headquarters building. Passes for entry and exit were rigorously examined and local staff were liable to be stopped and searched without warning. There was also a night curfew and a special pass was needed by people like me who had occasionally to drive somewhere after curfew. Places like Crater, Sheikh Othman and Little Aden were virtually out of bounds.

Although this was mildly inconvenient almost everyone realised it was common sense and there were no objections that I recall. It did mean that staff had to be very vigilant about personal security as there were one or two assassinations of military and commercial personnel. We therefore started to bring the perimeter closer in the sense that anyone living outside Khormaksar and Maala compounds was required to move inside the protected area. I was one of those affected and had to move into the Compound, not that we felt it was any safer as it was wide open to infiltration from the beach and the guard at the entry barrier – just a pole actually – was no real protection.

It was unwise to travel around alone and most people had some arrangement where they drove the car and an armed passenger kept an eye out for attackers. This mean restricting freedom of shopping mainly to the few shops in Khormaksar but this seemed to be readily accepted. Within the compound there was still a fair amount of entertaining but the number of external visits, especially at night, certainly fell. I have a feeling there was some sort of arrangement whereby we could tell the military that we wanted a bit of extra protection at certain times and I remember travelling many times to Donald Classey's house at Ras Boradli during the curfew and being waved on by military checkpoints who had my car number.

I think it was about this time that it was decided not to have expatriate staff children out for the school holidays and this upset some people. There was one case of a young man who somehow got to see his parents in Aden and then proceeded to wander all over the place including Arab quarters which created quite a security scare until he was found and put under lock and key!

There were some food shortages from time to time but visitors from Nairobi and the UK were very good at bringing out goodies. More serious was the exhausting of the Aden Airways Club beer supply which was, I recall, topped up by courtesy of the Royal Air Force. It was still possible to eat at one of the restaurants in Steamer Point but everyone had an eye on the doors and windows.

It was realised that there would be no resolution of the uncertainty without a political decision about the future of the Colony and eventually the British Government announced a departure date which was then very sensibly brought forward by the last

Crater, Aden 1953.
(Michael Hedges)

Governor. Before then, of course, Aden Airways was expected to continue its up-country and international transport even though the pilots and passengers were understandably nervous.

I think at one time there was an idea that the Company could continue operating even when the British had departed. Maybe the local directors were pressing for something like this but eventually it was realised that no independent revolutionary Arab government would have any such arrangement and anyone who thought themselves to be indispensable, like pilots, could be supplied from elsewhere in the Arab world.

So, while Aden Airways staff carried on with such business as remained, almost everyone was thinking about the possibilities of employment after independence. Adenis felt generally that their knowledge and skill would be needed in a new local airline but those of other nationalities like Indians, Yemenis, Somalis and Europeans were looking for jobs elsewhere in other countries.

Although security was an ever-present and increasing concern, the majority of people tried to carry on their day to day lives as best as possible. I think there were still occasional dinner dances on the top floor of the Rock Hotel but if I remember correctly the details were passed from mouth to mouth of expatriates only rather than being advertised in the newspapers.

Increased security on Aden Airways flights was stepped up by our own security personnel who reported to me and I recall putting myself into uniform to help with the body and baggage searching as well as occasionally flying on the aircraft to see that all was handled properly at the other end. It was a rotten job and everyone hated it and, of course, we had to get some of our Arab female staff to body-search the female Arab passengers.

Aden Airways continued to handle non-military passengers on the BOAC VC10 services to London but as explained earlier the aircraft were restricted to the military side of the airfield. I almost always went over to the military side if any Aden Airways staff or dependents were flying to London and almost always took the opportunity of asking someone to take a letter and post it for me so that my family got mail much quicker than via the Aden Postal Service. This still operated but became unreliable and the main post office at Steamer Point was considered a risky place to go to.

The other case was when a United Nations delegation arrived to investigate accusations of cruelty by the security services to the Arabs they were holding in prison. On leaving Aden the representative from Mali refused to have his suitcase searched even when asked to do so by the captain of the aircraft who they said it would depart without the suitcase, if necessary. The passenger was most unpleasant and insisted the captain of the aircraft personally opened the suitcase because there on the top was apparently a forbidden bottle of whisky.

All the time the company operated flights the daily routine was much the same and it was the social side that was restricted although we were able to go to Goldmohur beach most afternoons. I can't remember exactly when and how the decision was made to stop operations but I do remember being recalled to London for a meeting with Gilbert Lee and John Linstead at which I gave the opinion that a British-owned airline was not viable post independence.

When the government ordered all expatriate families to leave Aden I was heavily involved with seeing that our people packed up their wives and families and baggage and got away in good order. It was fairly lonely, of course, for many of the men who were left and really put an end to social meetings although we tended to eat together where possible. I can't remember exact dates but a lot of the deprivations of a declining colony came gradually and spasmodically rather than in a lump. From time to time there were interruptions in the electricity supply or the telephone system became unreliable, but I don't remember any difficulties with water supply or sanitation. It was wise to keep car petrol tanks topped us as the supply was a bit spasmodic and it was a potentially dangerous business filling up as Arab snipers found that was a time when expatriates were vulnerable.

I can't remember exactly how the announcement of the company closure was made but I think it was done by a carefully organised cascade communication exercise which sensibly arranged for everyone bar a few essential people to have their jobs terminated very quickly. There was a kind of inevitability about the affair and most staff were well occupied in making sure they got their correct redundancy pay which was based on the Colony Labour Ordinance plus some rounding up which ensured there was no trouble.

The very first to leave were the temporary pilots and one of the few sour tastes was the way they left hurriedly owing debts to local Arab traders who had expected, vainly, Aden Airways to pay up. Associated Companies tried to recover these debts from the people on arrival but I don't think any succeeded. For security reasons we terminated the local staff as quickly as possible and they were not allowed back into the premises. Some thought they would be able to survive with the gratuity they had from the company and others asked for, and received, help with airline tickets to investigate employment opportunities in Bahrain, Kuwait and the UK.

The older expatriate pilots knew they would not be able to convert to modern aircraft and most of them either retired or found jobs with small airlines in various countries. Several were offered jobs by BOAC whose Flight Operations Department foolishly did not take up my offer to comment on those they were taking on. The result was that they employed a number of junior pilots whose technical expertise was suspect and whose mental stability was in doubt. It caused BOAC a lot of grief for many years and it served them right.

Repatriation of expatriate staff went smoothly on the whole as most of them anticipated the time was coming when they would have to pack up their possessions and use the very generous accompanied and unaccompanied baggage allowance to transport them to the UK or, in the case of the Italian engineers, to Rome. Most of this stuff went by air but some people had bought expensive luxury cars which had to be sent by sea. I don't remember anything going wrong with this apart from when one pilot, who hadn't been very generous with tips anyway, unwisely interfered with the labourers loading his Mercedes. Nobody was surprised or sorry when they managed to accidentally drop the car 20 ft off the quayside which caused a fair amount of damage.

My task was to see that all local and expatriate staff departed safely and after my Chinese secretary left for the UK I had some very competent ladies helping me from the military and when that ended, I did it myself with the help of my most loyal Personnel Superintendent, Yassin Fara. I was also tasked with disposing of all assets other than aircraft and engineering stores so knowing how easily anything not nailed down in a locked room could disappear in a place like Aden, I collected all office equipment in rooms to which I held the key.

We had to empty all the expatriates' flats of, firstly, any rubbish they had left behind and, secondly, the company-supplied furniture. What to do with all this stuff was a real headache until Yassin arranged for a local contractor, who was hoping to make a fast rupee or two, to buy all the office equipment including my own desk and chair! Household furniture was another problem until I had the bright idea of holding an auction for ex-Aden Airways staff to buy whatever they wanted. This excited the Arabs no end and almost everything was sold at very high prices. Anything left was torched.

With no families around - apart from a few who either had nowhere to go to or who (thinking of one BOAC seconded person) wanted to hold their accompanied families allowances until the end – Goldmohur was one of the few places of entertainment left and that was no more than a swimming club. I know I spent many evenings in my flat packing up the china and glass I had acquired and putting them in wooden crates which were sent to the airport for despatch as cargo to London.

We didn't feel threatened until the night when the Federal troops not far from the compound mutinied one evening and there was much firing of small arms. I turned the lights off and kept out of range of anything that might have come in one of the windows which meant sitting on the floor by the lavatory with the telephone handy, with which I rang all remaining staff to ensure they were safe even if shaken. After that we really were anxious to depart and I remember selling my almost new Mini to an Aden Government Customs Officer and thereafter used an old wreck of a Vauxhall Velox. This had been left behind by one of our captains because it needed a new radiator so cooling water was carried in a twenty-gallon drum on the back floor.

There was some uncertainty about arrangements for transferring funds from Aden to wherever and I had already arranged for salaries to be paid partly in London leaving just enough for everyday needs in Aden. In the end, however, there was no difficulty in transferring residual balances to London with the help of the Company's Indian accountant who did the paperwork to avoid the risk of going to the bank. It was still possible to take a chance and go on to one or other of the stores in Maala that were frantically trying to liquidate their remaining stocks and I went to a jeweller who sold me, at an incredibly low price, an Omega watch which I still wear every day plus some very pretty 18-carat gold jewellery for my family.

In the end it was very difficult to get fresh fruit and vegetables as these usually came from the Hadramaut which was cut off or from Nairobi; the Aden market was definitely an unsafe place to go. But I don't think we were anywhere near starvation level it was just that there was more canned food than before and, of course, anyone with any sense was extremely careful to boil any water used in cooking or drinking.

Fortunately, most people were pretty healthy in Aden if they avoided excessive alcohol and when Dr Keshani, the Aden Airways local doctor left, we were able to use the RAF medical facilities which had, in any case, always been available to expatriate staff.

I stayed in my flat right to the day of my departure leaving Donald Classey, Bill Williams and Bill McGarry as the only expatriates and Mustafa Obali (General Services Officer) as the only local employee. I paid off my houseboy with a new watch, two months pay and all my tropical clothing plus everything in the fridge and store cupboards; he was over the moon! My unaccompanied baggage in crates was awaiting shipment at the airport and I had 21 pieces of accompanied baggage which all reached London in one piece.

Michael Hedges:

Memories of a Wireless Operator, Aden 1951-54.

Morse code to me was something to be avoided at all costs. It was like learning Arabic or Chinese or Pitman's shorthand, quite unnatural. Nevertheless, in 1951 on entering the RAF for three years engagement, instead of the 18 months National Service, learn it I did!

On passing my WOP exam I was posted to RAF Khormaksar in Aden where after a few days adjusting to the heat I was introduced to the radio room situated in the Air Traffic Control Centre (ATCC). In those days, in simple terms, all military aircraft which embodied two or more engines normally had a basic crew of three or four, a pilot, flight engineer, navigator and wireless operator. The civil aviation authorities also for their aircraft were required to have the same crew plus an air-hostess or steward. I considered myself very fortunate as my job included both military and civil aircraft involvement. Very High Frequency (VHF) communication was used for nearby base landings and take off but after that, High Frequency (HF) communication in wireless telegraphy (W/T) was used as the aircraft moved out of VHF range. This was the norm in those days until HF was gradually handed over to satisfactory long-range radiotelephony (RT).

During those two years in Aden I remember Aden Airways, which was situated on the other side of the RAF base. It had its own apron, hanger and reception customs building with tall palm trees.

Every day you had the comings and goings of Aden airways Dakotas, BOAC Argonauts, Avro Yorks, Ethiopian Airlines Dakotas, Air France Junkers 52s and Air India Constellations. All these aircraft were communicated with by W/T throughout the day and night. The messages were all in Q code. I still remember them quite clearly since I hammered them out on the morse key for three years. A basic message would be sent by the Radio Officer of an Aden Airways Dakota call sign V-RAAA to me in morse. QTN KHORMAKSAR 1200Z, QAB ASMARA 1445Z QTK 200KNOTS QTI 350 DEG, QAH 2800 FT, QTH 1050N 4045E followed by a lot more dots and dashes keeping in touch until the plane landed safety the other end of its journey. Anybody who has been in the radio communication business would know what most of the Q-code meant and the thrill of communications.

I recall my mates and I visiting the Aden Airways bar where the beer tasted better than the NAFFI. Our visits there gave us opportunities to visit the civil aircraft hangers and roam through the cabins of the airliners which looked sheer luxury compared with military dull air force blue-grey interiors of the RAF planes. I got to know Frank Marlow employed by Adenair Radio who commanded the radio frequency of the civil airlines who operated in RT and I often used to tune into their channel to listen to the crews chatting about times of arrivals and departures etc.

But as an ex-WOP I still recall fondly the tones of morse code, tweeting away like birds, from the aeroplanes' radio transmitters relaying their positions in the Arabian sky.

Mike Gardner:

An engineering over-view of Aden Airways.

Joining Aden Airways from BOAC was something of a cultural shock. The engineering base was located at the eastern end of the strip of land which formed Khormaksar airfield with the RAF located to the western side of Khormaksar. With the sea at both ends of the main runway, the environment was not particularly well suited to aircraft maintenance especially as Aden Airways Engineering's base was confined to a single T2 Hanger with side workshops, stores, management offices etc.

A high priority therefore was a corrosion retention programme as part of the fleet maintenance schedule.

When I joined the airline in 1959, the fleet consisted of the six DC-3s (VR-AAA, -AAB, -AAC, -AAF, -AAM, -AAN) and two aircraft maintained for local businessmen; a Beech Twin Bonanza (VR-ABB) and an Aero Commander 680E (VR-ABC) maintained on behalf of the A Besse Group.

The engineering staff structure was made up of the following:-
  Chief Engineer (seconded from BOAC)
  Deputy Chief Engineer/Quality Manager x 1
  Senior Aircraft Engineer – Airframes x 1
  Senior Aircraft Engineer – Engines x 1
  Licensed Aircraft Engineers x 6 **
  Licensed Avionics Engineers, Instruments/Electrical/Radio x 3 **
  Aircraft Mechanics (Italian) x 8
  Adeni/Somali/Indian assistant mechanics x 10
  Engineering Cleaning staff x 12
  Planning clerks x 2
  Stores and Purchasing Manager x 1
  Stores staff (Indian) x 4
** A minimal increase in these staffing levels took place with the introduction of the Argonaut fleet in 1960.

The above resources were to meet the following tasks:-
  All scheduled Base maintenance (excluding Major airframe and engine overhauls)
  All Line Maintenance – Aden Airways fleet.
  All Line Maintenance – Visiting Operators.
  En route aircraft unserviceability and third party maintenance.

From the above you can see that the majority of scheduled and unscheduled maintenance was carried out at Khormaksar; much of the time under very difficult conditions. These were the days before air-conditioned hangars were heard of and apart from the telling heat and humidity, there was always the Shamals (dust storms) to contend with. In the hot season, Shamals were a regular occurrence in Aden, usually late in the afternoon when they would leave everything covered in dust and sand; not the best conditions for aircraft maintenance!

On the aircraft utilisation programme operated by Aden airways, minor maintenance checks requiring a scheduled hangar input usually occurred about once every four weeks per aircraft. Due to the climatic conditions, scheduled maintenance work on the aircraft would be planned from 0630 hours to 1300 hours as, particularly in the hot season, it was impossible to work in the hangar through the hottest part of the day. Of course, there would be exceptions to this when operational, or fleet unserviceability required it. (With the introduction of the Argonaut fleet in 1960, the exceptions unfortunately became the rule!)

The T2 hangar was not generous in its accommodation space and one DC-3 hangared at a time was the maximum although this usually left some room for the two customer light aircraft. This problem was compounded by the fact that the hangar only had access to the airport apron at one end with the non-access end being used for bulk storage etc.

Aden Airways intentionally scheduled aircraft departures and arrivals outside of the hottest parts of the day. The Line Maintenance shifts, which worked an early and late daily roster, would usually get an afternoon 'rest period' between operations if the serviceability of the fleet allowed. However that could not always be guaranteed as apart from the AA operations, they also handled all visiting aircraft with the exceptions of Air India (one service per week from Bombay to Nairobi via Aden) and Ethiopian Airlines (daily service from Asmara) which utilised their own station engineers.

The number of airlines which used Aden either as a termination point or en route stopover was considerable. Aden Airways Engineering provided line maintenance support to BOAC consisting initially of one, but then upgraded to two, London terminating services per week using Britannia 100 series aircraft. This was also supplemented by BOAC at peak travel times by additional DC-7C flights. All flights operated by BOAC required crew night stops as no slip crews were available. In the early 1960s these services were taken over by the Comet 4C. Other airlines supported by AA were BUA (on MoD troop flights to Aden, Indian Ocean and Australian flights using either DC-6 or Britannia aircraft), British Eagle (DC-6 or Britannia aircraft), Aviation Traders (DC-4 and ATL Carvair aircraft), East African Airways Nairobi/Aden services using DC-3 or DC-4M Argonauts, Lloyd International (DC-4 or Britannia aircraft) and Middle East Airlines using Viscount or Comet 4C aircraft.

The T2 hangar formed the base of Aden Airways Engineering. As already outlined, the prime use was for DC-3 'Base Checks' and casualty rectification, and hangarage for the customer aircraft. Extensive side workshops attached to the hangar on the airfield side accommodated the engineering offices, engine shop, hydraulic workshop, metal workshop and all avionics shops. On the opposite of the hangar was located the main stores, cabin interior workshop and wheel bay. It was a compact operation and effective in its support of the aircraft.

All DC-3 major checks were carried out in Beirut by MASCO (Middle East Aircraft Servicing Company). With the aircraft away on major inputs at MASCO, Aden Airways chartered in wet leased DC-3 capacity from an organisation in India (Indamer). Major check downtime was approximately six weeks and was planned for one aircraft a year, so the Indian aircraft became a regular part of the operation.

Overhaul of the DC-3s' Pratt & Whitney R1830-922 engines was carried out by East African Airways (EAAC) in Nairobi, as was the propellers maintenance. Bare engines and dismantled propellers, were shipped to EAAC with the Aden Airways Engine Shop carrying out the overhaul of the power plant in house and the strip and rebuild of propellers.

The Arrival of the Argonauts
The DC-3s were doing stirling work on the domestic routes within the Aden Protectorate, for which the rugged structure and reliability of the airplane was an important issue. However, the same aircraft that had operated internal flights with passengers carrying everything but the kitchen sink, were also required to operate international services to places like Djibouti, Hargeisa, Mogadishu and Asmara etc. With additional turnaround cleaning between flights, these services were operated to an improved cabin service level. However, in late 1959 it was decided that the prime Aden Airways routes to Nairobi, Khartoum, Cairo and Bahrain, required a larger aircraft and improved cabin service so the decision was made to acquire three ex-BOAC DC-4M Argonauts primarily for these services.

Another contributory factor at about the same time was that the RAF was in discussions with the airline about capacity to operate trooping leave charters to leave centres in Nairobi and Mombassa. The prime requirement being that these flights were to be operated by four engined, pressurised aircraft!

The ex-BOAC aircraft were readily available being in store at London Heathrow (LHR) and the transfer from the 'mother' airline was quick once the decision had been made. The Argonauts went through a maintenance alignment pre-delivery programme at LHR with the first aircraft arriving in early 1960. Additional resources were brought in by the airline to cover this operation including flight crew, cabin staff and engineers, but not in large numbers as some aircrew were transferred from the DC-3 fleet. In addition to the aircraft, Aden Airways acquired a large spares holding from BOAC which was an essential part of the deal considering our location in the Middle East.

The introduction of the Argonauts had a major impact on the engineering department as the aircraft was known to be labour intensive compared to the DC-3. Prior the arrival of the first aircraft, we employed four experienced Licensed Aircraft Engineers familiar with the DC-4M. We did have some in house engineers who had knowledge of the type including the Chief Engineer and myself, so were able, with the assistance of BOAC, to instigate in-house training for the other key engineering staff. Although the airframe was a Canadair-built unit, it was basically a Douglas airplane with similarities to others of the breed particularly the DC-6 with its pressurised fuselage. However, the DC-4M apart from its pressurised fuselage was powered by the Rolls-Royce Merlin and these engines were of a type unknown to many of the engineering staff.

Aviation in Aden was administered by the ARB (Colonial) in Nairobi and the introduction of the 'new' type was greatly helped by the attitude of the resident ARB surveyor, responsible for Aden.

One of our major problems was that our T2 hangar could not accommodate an aircraft the size of an Argonaut and as periodic checks would have to be carried out on base, agreement with the ARB was essential on the maintenance support we could provide. The agreed solution was that on base maintenance, the Argonaut would be towed up to the open hangar doors which at least allowed the four engines and forward fuselage some under-cover protection. At least Aden wasn't concerned about rainfall as, on average, it only rained for approximately one day a year but we still had to contend with the Shamals, high humidity and the heat!

In general, the maintenance arrangements for the aircraft worked well. The 'periodic' checks were broken down into smaller elements usually requiring an approximate two-day downtime per aircraft per month.

Aden Airways contracted East African Airways (EAA) in Nairobi, for all major checks on the aircraft and they were integrated into the EAA maintenance programme as the same aircraft type, ex-BOAC machines, were operated by them. EAA also provided a replacement aircraft (usually VP-KOI) on dry lease whilst our aircraft were on major inputs and they also overhauled the Rolls-Royce Merlins.

Initially, maintaining the Argonauts was something of a headache for the engineering department. Apart from the learning curve, spares provisions did cause problems, particularly on consumable items such as 'O' rings, filters, AGS items etc. With the very limited scheduled airline services from London in those days, spares replenishment could be a very time consuming problem. EAA were always very supportive to us and with more Aden - Nairobi services available to us than flights from London, they usually became our first supplier for 'nil stock' items.

As part of the spares package acquired with the aircraft, we did have two Merlin QEC power plant units and several serviceable Merlin bare engines. Soon after initial introduction of the aircraft, we ran into a severe bout of engine problems. In my opinion, the RR Merlin really didn't like the Middle East, with major over-temperature problems, block backs etc. Our spare QECs were quickly utilised and during the periods when none were available we had to resort to carrying out bare engine changes on the wing! This became a routine for us and we got it off to a fine art with the engineering team, including the Chief Engineer, stripped to the waist and being supplied with non-stop cold beverages from the airport café, achieving the task usually overnight!

There were other incidents where we would have to resort to carrying out block changes on the Merlin's also 'on the wing' when the task was achieved similarly to the bare engine changes. Engine problems manifested themselves usually when the aircraft returned to base off-service at the end of the day so resources to handle engine failures involved calling in available staff including, if necessary, people like the Chief Engineer. As our hangar staff only covered 0600 through 1330 hours, and the line maintenance shifts only covered the period 0500 through 2300 hours approximately, there was no other solution other than staff call out to handle emergencies.

My memories of such events are of huge 'job satisfaction' whenever these situations arose and there was always great team spirit in getting the job done. I don't think that modern attitudes to 'health and safety' would have allowed us to accomplish what we achieved in those days!

DC-3: The Mogadishu Engine Change
The reliability of the Douglas DC-3, especially in the harsh terrains Aden Airways had to operate in, is legendary. The reliability of the Pratt & Whitney R1830-92 engines was a key factor. However, virtually all destinations that the aircraft operated to saw an engine

failure from time to time. The Engineering response was always quick with the relief aircraft carrying the repair team and equipment, plus the replacement power plant. We got the away-from-base engine changes down to a fine art even when it required assembling and operation of the shear legs crane on soft sandy surfaces; this was extremely hard work in the prevailing conditions.

Under very trying conditions, the team always had to be self-contained and it was essential that you took everything you would need to achieve the task as there was usually no easy way, without flying an aircraft from Aden, to get anything you had not bought with you!

A classic example of this took place in Mogadishu in 1963 when the aircraft operating the scheduled service, had an engine failure on take-off and returned to the airfield. The casualty team was flown from Aden with the usual equipment and spares required to replace the engine. The relief aircraft then positioned back to Aden with the passengers.

It was about this time that the sensitive political issues were surfacing in Aden and we were beginning to experience some friction within the engineering section, especially with some of the Yemeni staff. The problem was that in order to achieve away-from-base aircraft repairs quickly, we would always utilise a team of our best engineers; this was usually made up of English Licensed Aircraft Engineers, Italian and sometimes, Indian mechanics.

There was a reluctance to use the Adeni (Yemeni) mechanics away from base as they were less experienced and not always good team players. The requirement to carry out the engine change at Mogadishu brought the matter of team selection to a head. Once the team was known, there was some verbal complaint from the Adeni mechanics but nothing more than that. However, the subject brought about what I think was the first example of sabotage within the airline.

Having installed the replacement engine into the aircraft in Mogadishu, as soon as we managed to start the engine, it misfired badly and it was impossible to accelerate it without severe vibration. We elected to replace the spark plugs but on removing the plugs, noted that in several cylinders, the removed plugs indicated impact damage from which could only have been foreign objects in the cylinders.

Mogadishu is a long way from Aden so we had to make a decision as to the quickest way to get the aircraft back to base. This was a classic example of the 'ARB Jungle' so we came up with the plan to replace the affected cylinders and pistons using items from the removed engine! Had we elected to call up spares from Aden, it would have taken several days to get the required spares package together plus the need to take another aircraft out of the operational programme to fly the spares to us.

On removal of the first cylinder, it was evident that small nuts and bolts had been put into the cylinders through the spark plug holes! It took us two days of hard work to get the aircraft serviceable by changing four cylinders with all parts coming off the u/s engine.

A full inquiry took place on our return to Aden and a specialist security man was positioned from London. Unfortunately, we never did establish who had been the culprit but departmental security was immediately upgraded and with it, the level of trust that had existed between the different nationalities, unfortunately ebbed away!

The Goldmohur Low Flying Incident
Aden Airways expatriate staff used the Goldmohur Beach Club for leisure activities, mainly the opportunity to have a safe swim in the sea.

On one public holiday, when the club was full of families enjoying the beach, an Aden Airways DC-3 made what became infamously known as the 'Goldmohur Beat-up'. It turned out that the aircraft and crew were engaged on crew training out of Khormaksar! The beach club nestled up against a rock outcrop which separated Goldmohur Bay from the Ras Tarshine Bay and at its extremity, housed the signal station for shipping using Aden harbour.

On the day of the incident, the aircraft approached the club from the direction of Steamer Point harbour and when I saw it, it could not have had an altitude of more than about 50 feet, maybe less.

It headed straight for the beach club leaving those on the beach mesmerised. I have to admit that the crew left it until the very last minute to climb the aircraft, just clearing the top of the rock face. The majority opinion was that this was a reckless act and too close for comfort. The incident made news for all the wrong reasons and was not appreciated by the senior management of the airline!

VR-AAA Ground Accident at Khormaksar
Late one evening, an Argonaut returning from service lost hydraulic system pressure as it approached the ramp area at the airport and just at it was required to take a right turn to avoid the parked DC-3s. Unfortunately, before the crew could stop the aircraft the port wing tip hit the fuselage of VR-AAA just forward of the flight deck, ripping out instrumentation, auto-pilot components, etc.

To repair the aircraft, we needed to locate a replacement cockpit section of fuselage for the DC-3 and eventually located the required section near an airport in the Egyptian Canal Zone. It had once belonged to an aircraft that had been cannibalised! After ensuring the required section would be acceptable from an airworthiness point of view, we sent a team to remove the section and we flew it to Aden on a chartered Bristol 170 freighter. Repairs to the aircraft took several weeks but it did eventually return to service.

Argonaut CofA Air Tests
As part of the airworthiness control programme for the Argonaut fleet, agreed with the ARB in Nairobi, it was necessary to carry out a CofA air test per year. It was agreed that a candidate aircraft would be selected to establish the fleet average performance criteria with all the fleet having undergone such a test over a three year period.

The CofA air test is very demanding on the aircraft and I am sure that when the type was operated by BOAC it was never envisaged that such a performance test would be carried out in the Middle East! I think I drew the short straw in crew selection as I was rostered as the Flight Engineer on all such tests carried out whilst I was with the airline!

To give the aircraft a chance of meeting its performance criteria take-off would be scheduled for first light, usually 0600 hours and if possible, scheduled during the 'cool season'. A minimum crew consisted of Captain, two Senior First Officers and Flight Engineer.

As I have already mentioned, the Rolls-Royce Merlin, being a liquid cooled engine, was not ideally suited to Middle East operations and with very high ambient temperatures various aspects of the CofA air test were extremely difficult to achieve. The following is a good example. Apart from prolonged ground tests prior to take off, the first airworthiness check required one outboard engine to be throttled back to idle as soon as the aircraft was airborne. It was then timed to climb to an altitude of 1,000 ft. This was virtually impossible to achieve as by sustaining power on the three operating engines to maintain the climb, radiator temperatures would reach the 130°C maximum and the header tanks would begin to vent overboard.

This check, along with several others requiring sustained high engine power, had to be modified to prevent engine operating parameters from being exceeded. The compromise solution relating to the above check was to time the aircraft to a point where the radiator temperatures reached maximum and then, on return to base, compare the figures to those achieved at the previous air test. This compromise, along with several similar requirements, was the only way of overcoming the effects of the high ambient temperatures on the requirements of the CofA air test for satisfactory submission to the ARB. In other words, it was a juggling act!

Conclusions
There was no doubt about it that the aircraft operated by Aden Airways, at that time, were the best available for the unique operational requirements of the airline. The DC-3 with its excellent record of operating into rough terrains and flexibility in operation was the backbone of the airline. The introduction of the Argonaut fleet filled the gap for the scheduled service airliner and although probably not the best performer in the Middle East, it did do sterling service on the airline routes and with the military charters that became a large element of its operations.

In 1961, Aden Airways did place an order for the Avro 748 and along with others, I went on the Rolls-Royce Dart Engine course at Derby. However, the order was cancelled in 1962 before we had taken delivery of any aircraft, due to the 748's failure to meet the operational requirements of Aden Airways! Viscount aircraft were eventually acquired to take over from the Argonauts.

Pat Kennedy:

Administration and Traffic 1957-1958.

Joining in 1957, following an interview with BOAC Associated Companies, I was offered the position of Traffic Officer, Junior Grade.

The structure consisted of a General Manager, Captain Alger, a pleasant and effective man who, I believe, had considerable flying experience during the early days of Imperial Airways and before the outbreak of World War II. His number two, the Commercial Manager, was Leslie Bennett, a former Wing Commander and a member of the RAF Regiment. General knowledge seems to suggest his attachment to an armoured car detachment in Mesopotamia. Again, some of his service was carried out before the outbreak of war.

Under this umbrella, the traffic and sales departments operated. My arrival coincided with the departure of the Traffic Superintendent, an Australian by the name of Queckett (??); self inflicted removal I understand through an over-indulgence in alcohol, not an uncommon problem in those parts. Mike Brady was the remaining European Traffic Supervisor – a Cambridge University man with a misplaced sense of his own superiority. The Sales Officer, Tony Pike, operated his own agenda, reporting directly to the Commercial Manager.

Normal practice was a morning prayer meeting attended by the above and chaired by Leslie Bennett. Discussion centred on the success, or otherwise, of the previous day's operation and any forward activities which merited attention. Worth a mention is the character of Bennett, a tall, quietly-spoken man, slightly portly with a dark semi-handlebar moustache and always impeccably turned out. At these morning gatherings he invariably placed his chair away from his desk, crossed his legs and stroking his moustache would mutter regularly the phrase 'brave little show' if the reports were favourable. He was never put out by events and always polite.

The only other European members of staff, apart from the flying personnel, were Eric Pickles, Personnel Manager, a Lancastrian and thoroughly sound chap. A man by the name of Gill was the Accountant who I believe, operated from the Crater office.

I almost overlooked the redoubtable Sheila McGann, the Catering Manager. Aged late 40s or early 50s and unmarried who, at some previous time, had been chef at Government House. Intelligence had it that she had been born into an Irish well-to-do family and demonstrated those attributes associated with a solid middle-class background. Marriage was possibility something she had never considered, being a 'four square' woman with personality to match - amusing, hearty and with an insatiable intake of alcohol which to me never appeared to have any effect! Invariably dressed in her white Aden Airways dress, the hem above the knees, when seated, with a glass in her hand and her legs akimbo, she was a sight to behold. She was a charming, witty and delightful character!

The duties of Mike Brady and myself were split to give 24-hour coverage though it was not necessary to have a physical presence at Khormaksar Airport whilst doing duty. The day-to-day operation traffic duties were carried out by the local Adeni staff. Those employed were of high calibre and efficient. Along with BP, Aden Airways had the pick of local staff because of perceived status and relatively high pay scales. Abdul Raheem was the Senior Officer – capable, respected and held in esteem by the others. My duties were purely to oversee the operation and to attend as and when European presence was thought necessary. In fact, the position was irrelevant and would not be countenanced today.

Captain David Willmott:

Flying as a short-term pilot in 1963.

I need to start with a brief background of how I became involved with Aden Airways (a BOAC Associated Company).

During the years 1952 – 54 I served my National Service in the Royal Air Force as a trainee pilot (Tiger Moth, Chipmunk and Airspeed Oxford). My first civilian employment was as a summer season pilot with East Anglian Flying Services (Channel Airways) on DH Rapides and Austers at Portsmouth Airport.

In the autumn of 1955, having passed my M.T.C.A. Instrument Rating, I joined Freddie Laker's Air Charter Ltd as a co-pilot on Bristol 170 Freighter/Wayfarer (car ferry Southend, British Army Accra and cargo operations Berlin). Progress was made on to Avro Tudor (Cargo Operations Berlin and MOD Contracts World Wide) Avro York (Berlin) and later Douglas DC-4 (scheduled services Berlin and MOD Trooping contracts).

In 1958 I was offered a more senior position with Overseas Aviation at Southend, on Vickers Vikings and ex-BOAC Canadair C-4 Argonauts. By 1960 this company were in financial difficulties and, on advice from BALPA, I joined Cunard Eagle Airways as a First Officer on the Douglas DC-6 A/B fleet. I was promoted, out of seniority, at the age of 28 years, in 1962 to become a long-haul Captain on this fleet operating to the Middle and Far East, Australia and the USA.

On the 1st April 1963 a new company BOAC– Cunard was formed and absorbed the Boeing 707 aircraft from Cunard Eagle taking the very minimum of crew members, thus leaving the resultant Eagle Airways (to be renamed British Eagle) with a surplus of pilots. Redundancies occurred from the seniority list, mostly co-pilots, which was to be rebalanced by demotion of some captains, myself included.

On the very day my demotion letter arrived an advertisement appeared in *"Flight International"* for six-monthly contracts for qualified Argonaut Captains, for unaccompanied positions with Aden Airways. By volunteering to be seconded to Aden Airways I saved a co-pilot's redundancy and retained my position on British Eagle's seniority list as well as negotiating the possibility of taking my family (wife, three year-old and one year-old daughters) with me, to be accommodated at my expense.

We arrived in Aden on 25th April 1962 via Nairobi, on Air India. My log book totalled 4,900 hours with some 450 hours in command of DC-6 and a Group I rating on the Argonaut. The first couple of nights in Aden were spent at the Crater Hotel with my one year-old daughter sleeping in the bath. Although against the contracted terms Aden Airways decided to provide my family with a two-bedroom flat next to a small hotel, named the Khormaksar Palace. This hotel was used by British Eagle crews, so I remained in touch with my parent company while serving my six months in Aden. Aden Airways subsequently provided like accommodation for the other temporary contract pilots plus transport to and from duty flights.

On 28th April I undertook a six-monthly base check and instrument rating on Argonaut VR-AAT with Captain George Dyer. Five days later I was to do my first route familiarisation flight with Captain Bill Burman, the Chief Pilot. I had been issued with a set of BOAC rules with regard to uniform and while having no difficulty in obtaining khaki shirts, trousers and cap, I found no source of supply for khaki socks and therefore expecting some adverse comment of my wearing black ones. However, I was pleasantly surprised when following Bill Burman up the aircraft steps to notice he was wearing bright yellow socks!

Further route training was with Captain Dicky Larcombe quickly followed by a final line check with Captain Jack Lawson. One of the redundant British Eagle First Officers, Eric Atkinson, who had joined Cunard Eagle on the same DC-6 course as myself, arrived in Aden to join the DC-3 fleet on a permanent basis. His family soon linked up with mine and social life revolved around use of the military officers' beach club at Tarshine and the civilian beach club at Goldmohur.

The Argonaut aircraft was operated with two pilots and two cabin crew. The cabin stewardesses were usually recruited from the many military families based in Aden. The temporary pilots were needed to help keep the Argonaut services flying while the permanent pilots were being trained on the up-dated replacement Viscount aircraft.

In the six months from April 1963, I flew more than 600 hours on the following routes:-
  Aden – Mombassa – Aden
  Aden – Jeddah – Cairo (night stop) – Jeddah – Aden
  Aden – Mogadishu – Nairobi (night stop) – Mogadishu – Aden
  Aden – Riyan – Bahrain (night stop) – Riyan – Aden

Early morning arrivals at Mogadishu airport would usually find that radio calls to Air Traffic control would awaken the Control Officer, in bed in town, who would cycle to the airport and give breathless taxi-in instructions, after our second approach. The first approach and go around had to be made to get the domestic cattle off the runway!

The Argonaut fleet was obviously ready for retirement with the liquid cooled Rolls-Royce Merlin suffering in the hot, dusty climate. I suffered the five following engine failures:-
6th July 1963 Argonaut VP-KOI No.4 engine feathered out of Aden.
11th July 1963 Argonaut VP-KOI No.3 engine coolant loss, feathered Aden.
20th July 1963 Argonaut VR-AAS No.3 engine low oil pressure, high oil temperature, feathered – return to Aden.
24th July 1963 Argonaut VR-AAS No.2 engine fire – feathered – extinguished, returned to Aden. This was the last flight of VR-AAS.
1st October 1963 Argonaut VP-KOJ No.4 engine fire – supercharger failed Cairo – returned to Cairo. 3 days for engine change!

I had taken delivery of VP-KOJ from East African Airways at Nairobi on 8th August and this delivery flight was operated into Dire Dawa, Ethiopia, to collect a DC-3 cargo load of the chewable drug Qat, which was a regular DC-3 schedule, for the local inhabitants of Aden (6d a bunch).

The First Officers I flew with were all experienced four-engine pilots, but other than Bob Wigley and Frank Hewitt their names escape me, after 45 years.

The end of the Argonaut fleet was complete on 27th October 1963 when, with my family, I operated VP-KOJ back to EAA at Nairobi, where we subsequently returned to my DC-6, later Bristol Britannia, and Captain's employment with British Eagle at London Heathrow.

Aden Airways was an excellent employer. My company flat did not have air-conditioning in my children's bedroom but, on buying a unit, Aden Airways fitted it through the wall. Midway through my contract, my family's travel costs to/from the UK were unexpectedly reimbursed by Aden Airways as they had covered the travel costs of the other temporary pilot families.

Tony May:

Flying as a First Officer 1965-1967.

The first time I actually saw a DC-3 was when I arrived in Aden! I departed from Heathrow and was given my ticket by a Mr Cox of BOAC.AC. My interview for the job consisted of him trying to put me off by saying it was hot, he was totally unable to give any information about the flying or conditions out in Aden. He had never been there. I asked if he had been to Egypt, but received the negative reply. When I said that our family had lived there for the best part of two years, his reply was that I obviously knew more than him so was able to make up my own mind. He didn't know even the colour of the uniforms, what shoes were worn etc. Ah well ….

Alan (Pappy) Jennings was the Fleet Captain and it was he who introduced me to the machine. I suppose I'm telling you what you already know, but the machines, although abbreviated to DC-3, were actually C-47s. They had two large rectangular cargo doors at the rear, whereas the DC-3, as far as I know, had a smaller oval passenger door. I arrived in Aden on the 8th August. On the 14th for my conversion and GP2 type (1179 or whatever it's called), I seem to remember that we went out over the sea and did the stalls, (with and without flaps and gear), steep turns and an ADF approach, (there being no ILS at Khormaksar), then I did 10 landings at Khormaksar. Ernest K Gann in his book *'Flying*

Appendix 2: Reflections on Aden

Circus' has described the DC-2 and its landings. I think that nothing had changed with the DC-3. My first couple must have been the same as everyone's, a series of bounces until the aircraft ran out of flying speed. The ground effect was so great that airspeed loss took forever and I was thankful the runway was a reasonable length. The total time was two hours. It took eleven days before I received my stamped licence and could fly up-route. Then followed a series of flights with Pappy taking me into most of the Protectorate fields. The one which stands out most of all was the first. It was into Mukeiras, which is a dirt strip to the NE at the edge of the escarpment at a height of 6,500 feet. As we touched down a series of spurts of dust ran down the side of the runway just in front of the aircraft. "Look Sir, I've never seen a series of dust devils before, is that because we are so high". "Don't be bloody stupid, some bastard is firing at us!" was the retort.

Being at that height, there were problems both landing and with take-off procedures. Landings were made with power on; closing the throttles meant one just fell out of the sky! In the event of EFTO, ('cos the thing wouldn't fly on one), we had set drills. So, up to a certain point the drill was a standard abandon. After that, if still on the ground, the routine was to raise the gear and let it slide on its belly, it was thought to stop quicker that fashion! After about 100 feet, if the engine failed, it was possible to dive into a small ravine. This led to the escarpment, and safety. Landing at Mukeiras was virtually always towards the East, and take-off definitely was towards the ravine. Being shown the way round the various fields and having certain rocks and other features pointed out was the 'training'. The other things strange to me were the hand-cranked ADP (days of the A/N range beacons) and the drift sight, which had to be set on the roll by the co-pilot.

The first lesson had been learnt. Sneak in and sneak out and do not stray to the North! This applied to Dhala, Beihan and Abu Wain as well. Dhala was up the Wadi Radfan and housed a detachment of soldiers from both the local (Federal Army) forces and the British ones. They were supplied daily by Aden Airways and occasionally by the RAF. The runway, which faced directly into the cliff face, sloped dramatically uphill. At the bottom, just to the right of the runway, was another small hill, around which one had to fly. One was out of sight of the runway right until the last moment. Firstly one had to fly at 1,500 feet (i.e. at 6,000 feet above sea level, the runway being at 4,500 feet at the top end and 4,200 feet at the bottom) overhead the guard tent which was at the top of the runway. The guards would then jump into their Jeep and roar off down one side of the runway checking for mines, and roar back up again on the other side doing the same thing. If all was clear, they would fire a green flare from their Very pistol. If not clear, a red flare would appear above the hill. Instead of coming round the hill with wheels down, we would continue in a circuit, and wait for confirmation. Either the danger was over and we landed or we returned to Aden.

Taking off, things were different. We taxied to the top of the hill and applied the brakes. With full power set, the brakes were released and slowly we trundled to take-off speed. The engines were not very powerful at height and in that heat. The briefing for the take-off always included the reminder of what to do in the event of a power failure "LIFT THE GEAR and we'll slide to a halt on its belly whilst shutting down the other engine. Try to move the feathered engine into a position so that the props do not foul the ground." If an engine stopped after we were airborne, there was a small gully down which we could slip and hopefully, before the valley bottom, gain flying speed proper. We would then chase down the valley as quickly as we could (there were rebel tribesmen in the valley ready to shoot at anything), back to our base.

Soon I had been cleared by Alan to fly with any Captain and now began the process of learning the country. There were no roads going up country, only tracks. Towns were few and made of bricks and mud from the local ground. Only the more prosperous places had any paint on their walls to distinguish them from the earth on which they were built. However, there were wadis (dried streams), the occasional group of trees and rock formations that stood out.

The DC-3 had a device called a drift sight. As one taxied straight down the taxiway, or as one was "tearing" down the runway, it was the job of the person in the co-pilot's seat to align with the ground, the marker lines and pointer of the sight (by looking down a small "telescope"). This established the fore-and-aft axis of the aircraft and the marker lines were locked into position as one got airborne. The pointer was free to move. After take-off, and with the aircraft headed on the track angle, one could look down the telescope again and realign the pointer with the ground. The difference between the plate locked to the aircraft side and the telescope pointer was the drift angle. Now, if one turned the aircraft by the amount of drift, one had a heading to fly. Once flying this heading, one checked again and made any small adjustment necessary to ensure the track made good was the same as the required track. In the desert it was an invaluable aid …. but only as long as one could see the ground, of course!

We flew at 122 knots indicated airspeed. This worked out at 145 knots true airspeed. Due to compressibility of the air, the ambient pressure and temperature, the indicated and true airspeeds differed. It is only with vastly more expensive modern instruments has this problem been solved, such that what one sees, is what one is experiencing. At this speed the ground passed by relatively slowly, and there was plenty of time to look around, observe and mark one's map with relatively distinguishable features. We were all issued with our own maps! A large patch of land coloured white (due to some reason or other, it might have been salt), that could be seen from a distance and from any angle, comes to mind.

Other than Beihan, (into which the RAF flew Beverleys and Hunters) and Khormaksar, all other strips into which we flew were dirt strips. Some had the beginning of the runway marked by oil drums and others by cairns of stones three of four feet high. Occasionally there were painted markers. I learnt how to recognise the strips from various angles, how the runway was aligned, which was the preferable direction for landing, and any problem areas. (Out in Aden, the wind was rarely a factor and one often landed with a slight tail wind for ease of operation). The idea was to land, slow and taxi the shortest distance to the area at which we dropped off and picked up our passengers. Take-off was made in a similar fashion, taxi the shortest distance to the runway and take-off directly back to Aden without a heading change.

The routes flown by the DC-3 were to all the main towns of the 17 States of the Federation and to some other RAF strips. Then the other places were Djibouti (to collect Qat, the narcotic leaf that grows on the mountains of Ethiopia), Berbera, Burao, Hargeisa and Erigavo (to provide a service for those Somali servants working in Aden, and to import piles of duty free goods from the port). The three islands we went to were Perim, Kamaran and Socotra. Normally all our flights were out and back, but for fuel purposes RAF Riyan, at Mukalla, was the eastern refuelling station and it was from here that we serviced the Wadi Hadramaut towns of Ghuraf, Shibam, Qatn and Al Hauta. I note from my logbook that I went from Riyan to Al Gheida and cannot remember where that place is, only that the times were 1.30 out and 1.25 back. It was from Al Gheida that we went out to Hadibo (Socotra) but diverted one time, due to rainstorm and landed in Ras Karma. From the depths of somewhere I seem to remember that Al Gheida was the capital of the far eastern State, but that the Sultan was so afraid of being assassinated that he remained on his island at Hadibo. This gained some sort of notoriety by being the place into which a pilot flew, (without checking the runway), and then on touchdown, failed to realise the length of the strip and tried to stop by the top of the hill. In so doing, he burst a tyre. Most of the runway was on the other side! The RAF rescued the crew, but the rescue Aden Airways DC-3 was too late with the spare wheel. The locals had used the stranded aircraft for target practice and left it unflyable. I assume it is still there to this day?

It was from Riyan that we supplied the Pan American Oil exploration teams. They set up strips in the desert (The Empty Quarter) and marked them with 45 gallon oil drums at each corner. The landing strips were flattened by their Land Rovers being driven up and down. They would then fix their position by sextant and send us this position. (Western1, Western2, Western L, and '88' etc). We would work out a track and distance and set off from Riyan by using the drift sight to maintain track. When they heard the sound of our engines they would set fire to oil and a black smoke would rise giving not only their location, but also a wind vector. The other things that helped us to navigate were the watershed lines on our maps. As you may know, dunes move and change shape quite a lot, but the watershed lines remain virtually constant.

Initially when operating these Pan Am trips no flight clerk was carried since they were all inclusive charter flights. Our crews were supplied with flasks of coffee and teas and hot meals in a large topped vacuum flask. However, all this changed just before I arrived. It seems that about an hour into the flight one of the Arabs came up to the front and asked if the two pilots would like some tea. "Ethnin chai effendhi?" Without thinking, they both replied, "Yes". Then it dawned on them that the circuit breaker to the electric urn at the front door, was pulled. (This circuit breaker panel was just behind the skipper's shoulder.) The skipper went back to find the passengers sitting round a fire made of wood on the cargo floor, heating up their water in a cooking pot! By luck, this floor section had been reinforced and covered with a steel sheet. Adroit use of the fire extinguisher ended the party and all were confined to their seats. After that scare a flight clerk was carried on all flights ..... except for the "gold runs".

The names of the strips of the Federation were Dhala (up in the Radfan), Mukeiras (on the top of the escarpment), Lodwar (below, on the plain), Raudha, Nisab, Beihan, Wadi Ain, Ataq, Mafidh, Ahwar, Maifah, Ahwar, Dathina and El Gheida. All of the federation strips were just dirt/sand compacted and sprayed with old sump oil, except for the one at Beihan. This was asphalt and used by the RAF for their Hunter operations and supplied by the Beverleys. I know I said that most operations were out and back, but from Beihan we flew into Wadi Ain and to Nisab. Before taking-off for Wadi Ain we had to have a telephone call to say that all was well on the strip. The take-off would be to the East. Then we would receive a negative signal from the Federation troops stationed at the gap in the hills though which we flew, i.e. no signal, and all was still well. We flew North through the gap and made a sharp 90 degree left turn, lowering the gear and flap for a 'blind' landing onto the strip. If a red Very flare was fired from the strip it meant the strip had just come under attack and we had to tighten our turn into a split-arsed one, through another 90 degrees and get out through the same gap we had just entered, raising the gear but keeping the flaps lowered. Landing was on an uphill slope. Take off was back down the slope, a sharp turn to the South through the gap and escape to the West down the valley back to Beihan. The one thing we did not do was climb the aircraft above the hills in that area. We would then be sitting ducks for the Yemeni malcontents.

After landing, as pilots, we used to get out and stand in a wide trench out of the way of any person who just might chance his arm with a shot. This meant the aircraft was loaded and unloaded by the Federal troops. To whom they owed allegiance, FLOSY or the NLF, only they as individuals knew. Generally Aden Airways was recognised as an essential tool for all in the Federation, but, just occasionally, someone would think we were the RAF and thus, legitimate targets!

The other spectacular landing was at Dhala. This airfield was at a height of 4,500 feet and was a strip that headed directly into the mountain that was sheer up to 9,000 feet. We used to fly over the top at 6,000 feet, scraping along the cliff face with our left wing. The Army troops stationed at the strip would then run their jeeps down and back up the strip to check that no mines had been laid in the night, or whilst there backs were turned (Dhala was normally an early morning flight). As we saw them leave, we would turn downwind and start our descent. Turning base and finals was done behind a hill without the field in sight. As we turned onto finals at about 300 feet with gear down and full flap, the strip would emerge and we landed between 300 and 400 feet below the guard tent at the top of the strip. Once again the flight was controlled by Very flare.

Take off was the same as Mukeiras with yet another ravine which led down the Radfan valley as a safety outlet for low level engine failure. Actually the only occasion I had an emergency going into this place was when we had a Green and then found a string of camels emerge from the 'bundu' on our right, crossing the runway, just as the wheels touched. Luckily Marion (Kozubski) was flying and doing one of his three pointers! He was the only pilot who could do this and pissed off everybody else with his handling skills! He managed to stop in about one third of the normal distance, much to the astonishment of the camel driver (Allah Kareem!), the guards (who hadn't spotted the train) and myself! The lead camel was a little surprised as well, since we did a bit of a ground loop to avoid him!

Ghuraf in the Wadi Hadramaut had the one and only airport building in the whole of the Federation, other than those at Khormaksar. Normally, all transactions took place outside the aircraft alongside the cargo-loading floor. (Just occasionally there would be a tent someone had erected because of the departure of someone special). A balance was suspended from the top of the cargo doorframe and people's luggage was weighed and entered onto a form. The flight clerk, whom we carried, took the money, accepted the cargo, issued the tickets and gave the passengers instructions. We did the load sheet when given the figures and left the copy with a "responsible person on the ground". There must be a paper trail of tech log pages showing our routes across the whole of the Federation! Somebody responsible must have found them! Someone else must have devoured all the sausages that were discarded along the routes. I know of no one who actually liked these bullet hard things. Mind you, I did like the scrambled egg made with egg powder, but maybe I was desperate.

Some of these strips were hard to spot. Nisab, in particular, tended to blend in with the surrounding land and could only be spotted by associating it with a bearing and distance from the buildings. In that village they had been having a feud with others since time immemorial and I think it still continued despite the best efforts of the British Political Officers. I think it was there that a tribe of extremely black people existed. These wore only a loincloth and carried crossed bandoliers of bullets, AK47s and the traditional knives worn at chest height. Their features reminded me of the people of Fiji but with big 'afro' hairstyles. There was no way these people were of Arab descent, indeed the local Arabs seemed to fear them. Maybe they were descendants of a band, which, in the past, had escaped their slavers. Mukalla had been a slave port and a point of entry to the Wadi Hadramaut and, from there, to the whole of Saudia.

Flying conditions were generally blue skies and since there were only two ADFs in the area, one at Aden and other at Riyan, that was very fortunate. When the rainy season did come, all we had were cumulus clouds, but these were free from the cell structures associated with viciousness found in other parts of the world. I assume that this was due to the dryness of the area. However, the Cbs one met around the escarpment in Somalia between Berbera and Hargeisa were some of the worst in the world.

3. Aden Airways Crews

Chief Pilots

J Banks	1949	-	1950
S Colvin	1950	-	1953
J Pascoe	1953	-	1955
H Mills	1955	-	1958
G Dyer	1958	-	1961
W Burman	1961	-	1964
V Spencer	1964	-	1967

List of Pilots in Aden Airways at starting date.

Captains	Starting Date	Copilots	Starting Date
Walbran	1949	Clayton	1949
Ward	1949	Croskell	1949
Beale	1949	Painter	1949
Mills	1949	Perry	1949
Pascoe	1949	Downing	1949
Banks	1949	Skinner	1949
Colvin	1949	Buckley	1949
Maxwell-Lipkin	1949	Castle	1949
Beatty	1949	Bodger	1949
Bodger (Former copilot)	1949	O'Neill	1954
Spencer	1951	Jennings	1954
MacDonald	1953	Barnes	1954
Creigh	1954	Robinson	1954
Gauss	1954	Rush	1954
Harris	1954	Borsberry	1954
Adams	1954	McMurchy	1954
Branson	1955	Wood	1954
Lawson	1955	Lorimer	1955
Parker	1956	Elgee	1955
Mister	1956	Grove	1955
Larcombe	1956	Goows	1955
Williamson	1956	Hamblin	1955
Dyer	1957	Kay	1955
Ball	1958	Wigley	1956
Dinnie (Former copilot)	1956	Benton	1956
Wigley (Former copilot)	1956	Cubitt	1956
Manlove	1958	Ball	1956
Fox	1958	Scott	1956
Williamson	1959	Hayes	1957
Wood	1955	Stewart	1957
Elgee (Former copilot)	1955	Warrington	1958
Whittaker (Former copilot)	1958	Whittaker	1958
Murray (Former copilot)	1959	Smith	1958
Nanit	1959	Rose	1958
Burman	1960	Woodhill	1959
Barnes	1960	Austin	1959
Pike (Former copilot)	1954	Thomas	1959
Van Elst	1962	Turvill	1959
Wilmot	1962	Shields	1959
Hamblin	1963	Pearman	1959
Emsley (Former copilot)	1955	Emmett	1960
		Knight	1960
		Keene	1961
		Johns	1961
		Gordon	1961
		Wallis	1961
		Duir	1961
		Brent	1961
		Watson	1961

Captains	Starting Date	Copilots	Starting Date
Johns (Former copilot)	1963	Musgrove	1962
		Emsley	1963
Atkinson (Former copilot)	1964	Hewitt	1963
		Slaughter	1963
Jennings	1964	Carson	1963
Duir (Former copilot)	1955	Marlow	1963
		Steven	1964
Van der Laan	1961	Cooper	1964
(Former copilot)		Slugget	1964
MacDonald	1965	Gilpin	1964
Gilpin (Former copilot)	1966	Browne	1964
		Chapman	1965
Kozubski (Former copilot)	1966	Bidwell	1965
		Hampson	1965
Broadhurst	1966	Spouse	1965
Colman	1966	Smith	1965
Webb	1966	Bailey	1965
Dunsmore	1966	May	1965
		Wahed	1966
		Dordi	1966
		Armstrong	1966

Air Hostesses in Aden Airways with dates of starting.

	Date		Date
Jones	1950	Seton	1962
Attie	1954	Fisk	1962
Walker	1954	Turini	1962
Bishop	1954	Trimits	1962
Dowle	1954	Davidson	1962
Marao	1954	Emmet	1962
Merlo	1954	Staret	1962
Griffith	1954	Baker	1962
Moja	1954	Lazarini	1962
Hammond	1954	Coard	1962
Rizzi	1954	Reid	1963
Atkinson	1955	Burnet	1963
Anastasia	1956	Munro	1963
Lombardini	1956	Wood	1963
Doyle	1956	Chambers	1963
Tanzi	1956	Cole	1963
Cammasio	1956	Bharucha	1963
Baxter	1956	Hooper	1964
Jenschenak	1956	Crouch	1964
Deverall	1956	Flory	1964
Bomenti	1957	Dennys	1964
Franzel	1957	Watson	1964
Molinari	1957	Illot	1964
Caminabio	1958	Turnbull	1964
Nanut	1959	Anastasia	1964
Buckham	1960	Cawthorne	1964
Harvey	1960	Knight	1964
Jones	1960	Turnbull	1965
Old	1960	Aola	1965
Mauchafee	1960	Elliot	1965
Dent	1960	Landez	1965
Cahill	1960	Hillman	1965
Wilson	1960	Pcat	1965
Venning	1961	Asia	1965
Locke	1961	Flory	1965
Kerr	1961	Nagat	1966
Peyronel	1961	Lees	1966
Summers	1961	Nabiha	1966
Mordini	1962	Madge	1966

Majeiny	1966
Adla	1966
Hope	1967
Lander	1967

Adeni Stewards and Flight Clerks with starting dates.

Stewards

Sham Shan	1956
Tarish	1956
Adan	1956
Mohammed	1956
Abdi	1956
Magid	1957
Hamid	1958
Ahmed	1958
Hahara	1964
Tewfik	1966
Dayal	1967

Flight Clerks

Zokari	1956
Jummia	1956
Gamai	1956
Tayegali	1956
Jumai	1957
Yafai	1957
Musaid	1958
Nagi	1958
Kassim	1958
Kusais	1958
Saif	1959
Chaleb	1959
Murshed	1959
Khaid	1959
Ranniklan	1959
Nasser	1959
Obali	1960
Nagi	1960
Khalil	1961
Fara	1961
Hageb	1962
Ramaklan	1962
Nageeb	1962
Gamil	1963
Feisal	1964
Misri	1965
Barakat	1965
Hajib	1965
Rahman	1965
Reshed	1966

4. Carriage of Females on Domestic Services

ADEN AIRWAYS LIMITED

Carriage of Females on Domestic Services

Reference CPO/SE15/110 dated 26th January 1967. Effective Monday 6th February 1967 and until further notice females will be accepted on the following services:

AD450/1
ADEN/ATAQ	ATAQ/ADEN
Thursdays	Thursdays

AD454/5
ADEN/RIYAN	RIYAN/ADEN
Mondays	Mondays
Fridays	Fridays
Saturdays	Saturdays

AD456/7
ADEN/RIYAN/ALGAIDA	ALGAIDA/RIYAN/ADEN
Tuesdays	Tuesdays

AD458/9
ADEN/GHURAF	GHURAF/ADEN
Thursdays	Thursdays
Sundays	Sundays

AD460/1
ADEN/DHALA	DHALA/ADEN
Thursdays	Thursdays

AD462/3
ADEN/MUKEIRAS	MUKEIRAS/ADEN
Mondays	Mondays
Thursdays	Thursdays
Sundays	Sundays

AD470/1
ADEN/BEIHAN	BEIHAN/ADEN
Fridays	Fridays
Sundays	Sundays

Being a Muslim country, the airline was obliged to observe male sensitivities as to the mixing of male and female passengers. Certain flights into the Protectorates were mixed as above, while the majority were occupied by males only. This did not apply to International routes to Somalia and East Africa generally.

INDEX

Page numbers in *italics* refer to illustrations.

ABAMEL (Associated British Airlines (Middle East) Ltd) 15, 84, 120, 121
Abdul Manaf Mohager 61
Abdul Rahim *109*
Abu Talib 140
Adams, Trevor *95*
Addis Ababa 65, 105
    airport *14, 19, 47*
Addis Ababa to Aden services 23, *23*, 116
Addis Ababa to Cairo services 16, 23, 33
Aden Airways *see also* routes; timetables; *individual aircraft types; chapters by year.*
    proposals for, in 1946 survey 18
    requirements defined 24
    final arrangements for formation (1948) 25-26
    first flights planned 25, 31
    incorporation (1949) 32, *33*
    beginning of 32-34
    begins operations 33
    Aden Airways Board 33, 123, 136
Aden Colony *see also* Khormaksar Airport
    accommodation, lack of 57-58, 66
    Aden Airways offices in 37, *55*, 90
    aerial view *17*
    Air Ministry employees strike 155
    air travel promoted within 95
    airstrips, setting up 95-97
    aviation, early, in 11-12
    to be called "Aden and the Protectorate of South Arabia" 153
    closure of military base 169, 171
    considerations for airline base (1946) 18
    Crater district *17*, *38*, 90, 171, 177
    Crescent Hotel 90, 91, 132
    Department of Civil Aviation 46
    Director of Civil Aviation 32
    general strikes in 136-137, 146, 149, 169, 175, 177, 179
    Handa's House accommodation 37
    history 11
    Immigration Authorities 155
    independence 173
    industrial unrest in (1963) 152
    land acquisition in 89-90, 100
    Legislative Council 101, 140
    living in 90-91
    local air services planned (1945) 16
    local services, 1948/49: 25, 27
    as natural centre for region 15
    operators licences issued 21
    port *38*
    and the Protectorates in 1950: *11, 36*
    Steamer Point *11*, 90, *107*
    strike after arrest of Mr Al Asnag 149
    violence in 47-48, 163, 165, 166, 169, 171, 175, 177
    Yemen claims Protectorates 140
Aden Government 123
    civil aviation policies 89, 95
    limited renewal of Aden Airways' operating licence 129
    subsidy from 171-172
    use of Aden Airways by 99
Aden Protectorate Levies (enlisted men) 100
Aden to Addis Ababa service (1948) 23, *23*
Aden to Berbera freighter flight 39, 40
Aden to Bombay route 32
Aden to Cairo services *16*, 33
Aden to India route, proposed 32, 37, 44, 45, 47
Aden to London service,
    joint BOAC/Aden Airways 57-60, *59*
    timetable 60

Aden to Nairobi service 20, 27-28, *28*, 29, *29*, 32, 108, 163
    Tripartite Pool agreement 159
Adeni employees, attempts to bring in 175
Adeni pilots 155
Adila, Air Hostess 177
administration 91-92
advertisements *114*, *128*, *150*, *176*
Afar 124
agents 44
Ahwar 123
Air Djibouti 47, 51-53, *51*, 82-83
    Bahrain to Kabul route 53
    route map, 1951 *52*
    timetables 52, 53
Air France 11, 15, 21, 60
Air India 31, 32, 37, 47, 58, 59, 101, 159, 179
    L749 Constellation *101*
    Super Constellation *128*
Air Jordan 53, 81, 82, 83, *83*, 84, 85, 87, 88
Air Jordan of the Holy Land 88
Air Ministry 158, 159
Air Somali 136, 148, 161
aircrew *see also* pilots; stewardesses
    issued with termination notices 179
    resignations 169, 172, 173
    uncertainties after VR-AAN disaster 174
Airspeed Ambassador 121
Airspeed Consul 82, *83*
Airwork 15, 19
Al Asnag, Mr 149
Al Chark 33
Al Khaff 61
al Mansoura detention camp 177
ALA Littoria 11
Alam 117
Alawi Al Kaff 140
Alger, Capt Jimmy 122, 125, 137, 138, 140
Ali Abu Nawar, Col 87
Alitalia 21, *24*, 31-32, 148
Amerada Petroleum Corporation 111, 124
American commercial interests 14-15
Amman 86
Amman Airport *81*
    Airport Commandant *82, 83*
Anaqein 128
Anastasi, Air Stewardess 145
Anderson, Andy 91
Anglo-Egyptian bilateral agreements 26, 27, 33, 34, 37
Anglo-Iranian Oil Company 56, 73
Arab Airways 81
Arab Airways Association 43, 53, 81-82, 83-84, 86, 88
    Dragon Rapide *82*, 88
Arab Airways (Jerusalem) Ltd 53, 56, 61, 65, 67, 69, 71-72, 73, 78, 136
    1953-58: 81-88
    aftermath 88
    Avro York 88
    connecting servcies with Aden Airways, May 1954 86
    Douglas DC-3 JY-ABS *87*
    Douglas DC-3 TJ-ABN *81*, *85*, 86
    losses 121
    operational patterns 85
    operational record 86-88
        1953-56: 86-87
        1956-58: 87-88
    organisation 84-85
    relationship with Aden Airways put on sounder footing 92
    route structure, May 1954: 85, *92*
    structure 84
    UN charters 116
Arab-Israeli six day war (1967) 179

Arab-Jewish conflict 82
Arab Legion Air Force 82, 83
Arabian Airways Ltd 12, *12*, 21
ARAMCO 37
Armstrong, Capt W 26
Armstrong-Whitworth Ensign 13
Asmara, Eritrea 11, 13, 14, 15, 21, 25, *25*, *39*, 45, 46, 51-52, 55, 57, 59, 60, 62, 66, 71, 72, 73, 82, 122
    Aden Airways office *26*
    airport *37*, *39*, *65*, *68*
    Bahobescia Apartments *90*
    Palazzo Falletta flats 25
    vegetable charters 104, 119
Assam (catering officer) *165*
Associated British Airlines (Middle East) Ltd (ABAMEL) 15, 84, 120, 121
Ataq 94, *101*, 102, *145*, *153*, 171
    fort and camp *102*, *103*
Attie, Jean 71, *72*
Austin, Capt Peter 131, 142, 153
Austin, Trevor *180*
Aviation Traders Accountant 121
Avro 748: 129, 130, 131-132, 139, 142, 151
    advertisement *142*
    mock-up *132*
    routes planned after arrival of 131
Avro Anson 28, 29, 41, 45, 48. 66
Avro Lancastrian 32
Avro York 24, 48-49, 51, 61-62, 63, *90*, 93
    G-AGSO *63*
    G-AHFF *94*
    G-ANGL *94*
    JY-AAC (Arab Airways (J) Ltd) 88

Baghdad Pact 86
Baharoon, Mr (Chief Minister of Aden) 161, 162
Bahrain 45, 52, *52*, 53, *53*, *151*
    cholera outbreak 167
    route 159
    service 123
    service timetable, November 1959 *131*
Baldwin (Indamer owner) 51
BALPA (British Airline Pilots Association) 93, 117, 155, 162, 163
Bamberg, Harold 77
Banks, Capt J L C 24
Barnes, Capt Rex *74*, *172*
BEA (British European Airways) 66, 67
Beale, Capt Tom 35, 37
Beech Bonanza 97
Beihan 94, 95, *95*, 108, *110*, 117, *133*, *137*, *152*, 166
    hotel *152*
Beirut *67*, *78*
Benton, Howard 115
Berbera to Aden freighter flight 39, 40
Berryman, Ann 90-91, *91*
Besse, A, & Co (Aden) 11, 101
Besse, Antonin 11, 12, *12*, 39
Besse, Antonin (son) 140
Bilbeisi, Ismail 53
bird strike incident 123
Bishop, Chloe *93*
Blackburn Beverley (RAF) 162
BOAC (British Overseas Airways Corporation)
    Aden local services, 1948 *23*
    and Aden to Nairobi service 56
    and aircraft charters 77, 78
    and Arab Airways Association 81, 88
    Argonaut fleet 131
    Avro York *63*
    Cairo, routes from 13, 20
    Cairo base (Almaza) 14, 18, 22
    Cairo to Addis Ababa services, 1946 *16*
    Cairo to Aden services *16*, 20

Cairo to Karachi services 13, 14, *14*
charter agreement proposed 139
communications with Aden Airways 73-74
and de Graaff Hunter's plans for Aden Airways 31-32
Douglas DC-3 *23, 31*
load limits, declines to help on 156
early days 12-14
early years 14-16
East African traffic, surge in 57
Flight BO460/461 23
Flight No 15/16R (1948) 22
Flight No 17/18R (1948) 22
Flight No 19/20R (1948) 22
Flight No 21R (1948 - later BO 453) 23
Flight No 23R (1948 - later BO 451) 23
Flight No 27R (1948 - later BO 459) 23, *23*
flights in area, last (1948) 24-25, 26
and Haj flights 61-62, 63
Handley Page Hermes 57, *58, 60*
operation to Aden, 1952 57-60, *59*
and Jordan 92
and Kenyan services 28, 29
Lockheed Lodestar 13, *14, 18*
and London to Aden route 89
London to Nairobi route, proposed 59-60
timetable 60
No 1 Line 14, 21, 22, *23*
No 5 Line 14, *15*, 18, *18*, 19, 20, *20*, 22
and payments for carrying mail 48
personnel seconded to Aden Airways 25
plans for Red Sea operations, further (1947/48): 19-22
and possible transfer of Aden Airways to EAL 125-126
and proposed Cyprus Airways/Aden Airways merger 66, 67, 72, 73
Red Sea routes survey for MCA 17, 18
Red Sea services, 1948 *24*
reluctant to supply chief pilots for Associated Companies 158
revenue sources 151
security in Aden, concern for 166
Security Officer seconded 152
Technical Manager, Eastern Division 24
UN charters 115-116
BOAC.Associated Companies (BOAC.AC)
colour scheme *123*
creation of 120-122
engineering costs reduced 125
BOAC.Associated Companies Board 123, 129, 130, 153, 155
and alternative work for Viscounts 166
and Avro 748: 139
concern over Aden Airways financial situation (1960) 137-138
and Somalia 136
BOAC Board 89, 94, 97, 120, 123, 125
and Aden security situation 161
gives serious thought to future of company 171, 173
might withdraw interest in company in absence of Government support 168
offers company to Aden government 175
possible transfer of Associated Companies' shareholding in Aden Airways 162
requested sanction for purchase of Avro 748s 131-132
Bodger, Capt Alan 71
Boeing 707: 159
Bombay, proposed route to 18, 32
Booth, J W 129
Borsberry, F/O Eric *99*, 105
BP 167
Brancker, J W S 52
Branson, Capt R L C 127
Bristol 170 Wayfarer 18, 19, 20
Bristol Britannia 133

British Aviation Services (Engineering) Ltd 123
British Colonial Office 11
British Eagle Airways *153*
British International Airlines Ltd (BIAL) 15, 66, 102, 103
British Levant Airways 66-67
British West Indian Airways (BWIA) 71
Broad, Stephen 92, 98, 100
and Air India services 101
appointed General Manager 89
proposed use of Viscount 109, 110
and staff morale 93
Brothers Air Services 162
Buckham, Mavis *149*
Bulmer, Elsa 57
Bulmer, Capt Ken 57
Buran 119
Burley, John 163-164
Burman, Capt Bill 137, 139-140, 145, 158, 161

C. L. Air Surveys Ltd 28
cabin crew roster, Feb/March 1966 *170*
Cairo 12, 13, *13*, 14
airport 112
Almaza BOAC engineering base 14, 18, 37
flight (AD 472) 146
Ibn Tulun mosque *18*
as main engineering base for Aden Airways 24
proposed BOAC routes from (1947) 20
route 133, 136, 159, 161
Cairo to Addis Ababa services *16*, 23, 33
Cairo to Aden services *16*, 20, 33
Cairo to Karachi services 13, 14, *14*, 15
Cairo to London service (1948) 24
Cairo to Nairobi route 23, 27, 42, 48
camel train *117*
Camp 2 (oil exploration site, later Museifa) 108, 117
Campden, Vic 163
Canadair Argonaut 18, 59, *59*, 60, 89, 131, 132, 151
in Aden Airways service 132, 133-138
arrival in Aden 132
cockpit *134*
load factor 138
losses from operations 137
pilot training 132, 133
replacements considered 147, 150
technical problems 136, 139, 147, 153
G-ALHS (Derby Airways) *121*, 144, 145-146
VP-KNY (EAAC) 145
VP-KOI (EAAC) 150
VP-KOJ (EAAC) 153, *153*
VR-AAR 132, *132*, 133, 140, 142-143, 145, *146*, 150
VR-AAS 133, *134*, *136*, 139, 146, *148*, *151*, 152, 153
VR-AAT 133, *136*, 139, 144, *145*, 147, 152, 155
Castle, F/O Alan 71, 117
Central African Airways 130-131, 152, *156, 159*, 161
Chambers, Chris *151*, 174
Chambers, Jack 90
charter, Governor's 142
charter, tourist 168
charters 37, 46, 77, 96, *96*, 124, 128, 147-148, 175 see also drug, Qat, charter flights; oil charters; Royal Air Force charters; Service Leave charters; vegetable charter flights
charters, United Nations 92, 94, 115-116, *116*
Chennault, Maj Gen Claire 51
Chiang Kai-shek 51
cholera 23, 47
Civil Aviation Employees Union 152, 156, 161, 169

Clairways of Kenya 18, 20, 21, 22, 23, 27-29, 32, 41, 52
Nairobi and Aden, flights between (1948/49): *28, 29*
Classey, Donald 138, 140
Colvin, Capt Steve 35, 39, *42*, 62, *64*, 73, *73*, 92
company seal 33
company trademark 33
Convair CV-240: 32, 46, 47, 58, 60, 65, 69, 125, 145
ET-T-20 (Ethiopian Airlines) *58*
ET-T-21 (later ET-AAW) 60, *60*
and JATO 60, *60*
Cork, John 133, 135
Cox, Dave *169*
crewbus *168*
Cribbett, Sir George 121
Cumberbatch Trophy 146
Cumming, Sir Duncan 110, 116-117, 121, 122, 125, 162
Curtiss C-46 Commando 51, *51*, 52, *145*
Cyprus Airways 47, 77
DC-3 *67*
proposed merger with 66-67, 72, 73
Cyprus Government 67

Dathina 163
Davicos, Count 62
de Graaff Hunter, Richard 24, 26-27, 31, *32*, 34, 37-38, *40*, *42*, *50*, *64*, *84*, 89, 92
and Air Djibouti 51, 52-53
and aircraft charters 78
and aircraft purchase 77
appointed General Manager/Managing Director 13, 20, 23-24
and Arab Airways (Jerusalem) 69, 71, 81
BOAC, relations with 39
Board of Directors meetings, first 33
and Capt Colvin 73
and Cyprus Airways 67, 72
and employment of pilots 71
and Ethiopia, venture into 64, 65
fares, reduces 126
and financial problems 48, 72, 73, 74
and flights, naming of 41
and Haj flights 34, 61, 62, 63, 64, 92, 94
and passenger accommodation in Aden 58, 59
plans for running the company 31-32
resignation 72, 73, 75
and VR-AAE 56, 69, 77
de Graaff Hunter, Mrs *32, 40*
de Graaff Hunter, Sarah *40*
de Havilland Comet 1: 60, 132, 139, 142, 151, 159
G-ALYP 74
de Havilland DH.123: 129, 130
de Havilland Dragon Rapide 82, *82*, 85, *88*
de Havilland Dragon Rapide Mark IV 94, 98-99
TJ-AAE *82*
VR-AAL 98, *99*, 102, 105, *106*, 108, 109, 110, *114*, 117
VR-AAP 98
delivery flight from UK (G-AOJI) 115
Dent, Christine 147, *147, 149*
Derby Airways 144, 145-146, 147, 155
Dhahir 124
Dhala 106, *106*, 111, 140, 152-153, 162, 163, 168, 171, 179
Dhala, Amir of 111
Dhofar Air Services 96
Dhofar City Services 122
Dinnie, Capt Colin 142, *168*
Diplomatic Wireless Service 158
Dire Dawa 31, 46, 50, 55, 56, *105*, 123, 125, 144
disease 23, 47
Djibouti 12, 21, 51, 106, 119, 125, 131, 133
Dolal, Ethiopia 35, 37
Douet (Russell), Sue 156, 159

Douglas Dakota (RAF) 89, *153*
Douglas DC-2: 13
Douglas DC-3: 14, 18, 19-20, 21, 22, 23, 24, 26, 28, 29, 31, 32, 33, 38, 39, 41, 47, 57, 61, 66, 71, 77, 89, 92, 109
    28-seat 83
    40-seater conversion 50, 55
    Aden Airways 35, 68, *101, 127, 129, 133, 168*
    Arab Airways (Jerusalem) Ltd 84
    ARAMCO 96
    BOAC 23, *31*
    cockpit *102*
    colour scheme, early (1950) *30*
    fleet reduced 123
    galley *72*
    interior, Aden Airways 24, *25, 34, 42, 84, 100, 111*
    replacements considered 121-122, 129, 130-131
    restrictions imposed on 121, 148, 151, 156
    shortage of 165
    tailwheel change *103*
    ET-ABI (Ethiopian Airlines) *19*
    ET-ABX (Ethiopian Airlines) *47*
    ET-T-3 (Ethiopian) *106*
    G-AGNB *see* Douglas DC-3 VR-AAF
    G-AIWC (BIAL) *102*
    G-AKGX (Cyprus Airways) *67*
    G-AMVK *see* Douglas DC-3 VR-AAM
    G-AMYB (Eagle Aviation) 77, *78*
    G-AMYJ (Transair) 77
    G-ANAE (LAC) 71, *71*
    G-AOJI (later VR-AAO) 115, *122*
    JY-ABS (Arab Airways (Jerusalem) Ltd) *87*
    OD-AAM *see* Douglas DC-3 VR-AAZ
    TJ-ABN (Arab Airways (Jerusalem) Ltd) *81*, 85, *86*
    UN 351: 92, 116, *116*
    UN 601: 94
    UN 640: 92
    VP-KLA (EAAC) 126
    VP-TBJ (BWIA) 77
    VR-AAA 89, *94*, 96, 102, 117, 121, 124, *153, 157, 158*;
        damaged beyond repair 163, 164, *164*
    VR-AAB 132, 139
    VR-AAC *42, 45, 49, 68, 69*, 172, 174
    VR-AAD 46
    VR-AAE *44*, 55-56, *56, 68, 69, 72*, 77, 78
    VR-AAF *31, 35, 74*, 97, 99, 102, *105*, 108, 121, *125*, 131, *148*, 152, *165*, 171, *171*
    VR-AAI 71, 96, 99, 108, 117, 145, 153, 162, *162*, 165, 174, 175
    VR-AAK 108, 112, 123
    VR-AAM 103, 108, 109, *109*, 117, 125, 159
    VR-AAN 123, *123*, 124, 125, *125, 137*, 142, *148*, 165, 168, *175*;
        disaster 173-174
    VR-AAO 115, *122*
    VR-AAZ 161, 165, 173, 175, 179
    VT-DGP (Indamer) *78*, 94
    VT-DGQ (Indamer) 94
    VT-DGT (Indamer) 94, 116
    YE-AAC (Yemen) *60*
Douglas DC-4 47
Douglas DC-6A *153*
Douglas DC-6B 136, 142, 153, 159
    ET-T-26 (later ET-AAY) (Ethiopian Airlines) *137*
drug, Qat 31, 50, 55, 56, 105, *105*, 123
    ban on imports 143
    ban lifted 144
    charter flights 122, 123, 125, 126, 127, 133, 137, 139, 159, 131, 144
    embargo on Ethiopian supplies 161, 164

production affected by drought 148
Duirs, Capt 173
Dulles, John Foster 87
Dunsmore, Capt 172
Duqa 97, *104*, 106
Duqam 117
Durban 12, 13
Dutton, Barney 75, 89, 101-102, 122
Dyer, Capt George 124-125, 127, *127*, 128, 129, 132, 133, 137, *137*, 142
Dykes, J C 142

Eagle Aviation Ltd 71, 77, 78
East African Airways 18, 28, 29, 32, 59, 66, 101, 110, 113, 125, 136, 142, 145, 166
    Canadair Argonaut *153*
    maintenance by 147, 150
    possible transfer of Aden Airways to 125-126
    timetable *130, 135*
    Tripartite Pool agreement 159
Eastern Airways 81, 84
Edinburgh, HRH The Duke of *80*
Egglesfield, Capt L A 13
Egypt 86
    authorities in 43, 45
    difficulties with 34
    Saudi Arabia breaks off diplomatic relations with 158
    Saudi Arabia resumes diplomatic relations with 159
    support from Soviet Union 136, 140
Egyptian Aircraft Engineering Company (EAEC) 37
Egyptian Airways proposed 18, 19
El Aghil, Mr 140
El Gheida 97
Elgee, F/O (later Capt) 105, 152
Elizabeth II, HRH Queen *80*
Emergency Checklist 127-128
Emmett, Capt Alex *168*, 177
employees 37
see also aircrew; stewardesses; pilots
    bonus scheme 44
    dismissed 169
    expatriate allowances 155
    issued with termination notices 179
    local staff relations poor 159
    morale 93
    Yemeni 152
Emsley, Capt 162
engines, Pratt & Whitney *100, 110*, 115
English Electric Canberra 148
Entebbe 23
equator, "Crossing the Line" certificate *180*
Erigavo 119
Eritrea 15, 17, 21, 43-44, 49, 52, 55, 57, 64, 66, 82
Ethiopia 15, 17, 55, 64-65, 148
Ethiopian Air Force 64
Ethiopian Airlines 15, 18, 19, 20, 21, 31, 32, 42, 46, 47, 50, 52, 55, 58, 59, 66, 69, 82, 113, 122, 136, 139, 142, 145, 153
    Convair CV-240: *58, 60, 60*
    Douglas DC-3 *19, 47, 106*
    Douglas DC-6B *137*
    and JATO use 60, *60*
    pooling arrangement with 151-152
    possible take-over of (1952-53) 64-65
    Qat flights 123, 125
    services to Aden and Mukalla (1947) 21
Ethiopian Government 78, 125
Everest, F/O 77
Expatriate Staff Association 155

Fara, Flight Clerk 142
fares, reduced 40, 41, 58-59
Farnborough, SBAC show, 1960 *132*
Farqe, Emile 88

Farrell, Mr *96*
female passengers 175
Field Aircraft Services Ltd 142, 144
Fifth Freedom rights 138
flight information log *159*
Flight Planning and Performance Tables 155
Flights *see also* routes; timetables
    AD 454/455 "Assab Air Coach" *43*, 45
    AD 456/470 "Cairo Express" 41, *43*
    AD 458/459 "Addis Freighter" 41
    AD 460/461 "Mukalla Air Coach" 39, 41
    AD 462/463 "Mukeiras Air Coach" 39, 41, 56
    AD 464/465 "Hargeisa Air Coach" 41
    AD 466/467 "Nairobi Special" 41, *43*, 46, 47-48
    AD 468/469 "Nairobi Special" 41, 48
    AD 471/457 "Addis Express" 41, *43*
    AD 472/473 "Cairo Freighter" 34, 41, *43*, 47-48
    AD 474/475 "Sudan Special" 41, *43*, 47-48
    AD 478/479 "Levant Special" 34, 41, *43*, 45
FLOSY (Front for the Liberation Of South Yemen) 172, 174, 177
Flying Tigers 51
Fokker Friendship 121
freighter service (BO 476/477) 34-35
French Air Force 21
French Bureau de Securite 51
French colonial interests 11, 12, 15

Gauws, Capt Frank *104, 114*
General Aircraft Monospar ST-25 11, 12, *12*
General Post Office 48
Ghaba 128
Gharb 124
Ghudu 109
Ghuraf *49*, 61, *89*, 94, 99, *105*, 168, 175
    terminal *42*
Glover, T J 168
Glubb Pasha, Gen 87
Goldsmith, Joan 90
Gordon, F/O 145
Granville, Keith 16, 28, 64
Griffiths, R 17
Gross, Capt Jimmy *88, 169*, 177
Grove, F/O Roger *108*
Grumman Goose *145*
Guild of Air Pilots and Air Navigators (GAPAN) 146
Gulf Aviation (later Gulf Air) 45, 47, 48, 66, 110, 139

Habbanniya, Iraq 13
Habilayne *171*
Hadibo, Socotra Island 163-164, *164*
Hadramaut *163 see also* Wadi Hadramaut
    services into 56, *111*
"Hadramaut Route" 13, 14, 15
Hadramis 61
Haile Selassie, Emperor 64, *64*, 105
Haj pilgrimage flights 15, 18, 33-34, 42-43, 51, 53, 66, *90*, 102, 109-110, 118-119, 129, 145, 135, 159
    1952: 47, 61-64, *62*
    1954-55: 89, 92, 93-94
Hamble, College of Air Training 155, 163
Hamblin, Capt 159
Hamq 112
Handley Page Dart Herald 121, 129, 130
Handley Page Herald 121
Handley Page Hermes 48, 49, 56, 73, 89, *91*
    BOAC 57, *58*, *60*
    operation, April-December 1952 57-60
    G-ALDW (BOAC) *57*
Harare (formerly Salisbury) 152, 155
Hargeisa *47*, 108, 117, 124, 133, 159, 161, 165

Harman, H M 57-58
Harvey, Mr (BOAC Station Engineer) *121*
Hasanali, A S 93
Hawker Hunter T.7 *149*
Hawker Siddeley Trident 173
headquarters, transfer of 49
Heap, Capt 152
Heima 124
Henderson, Mr (Mukeiras Political Officer) 93
Hijman, Air Hostess 179
Hilary, Richard M 17, 18, 19, 20-21, 29, 32, 51, 52, 58
Hone, E D 74
Hornsby, E M 33
Horseshoe Route 12, 13
Houchen, H O 33
Houston, Capt 62
Hudson, Berry 90
Hunting Clan 83
Hussein, King of Jordan 87

IATA (International Air Transport Association) 126, 145
Ibn Saud, King Abdul Aziz 61
Ibri 124
Ilott, Air Hostess 177, 179
Ilyushin Il-14 140
Imperial Airways 11-12, 15
Indamer 51, 64, 69, 71, 84, 92, 104, 109, 116, *116*
    charters, 1953 77-78
    DC-3 VT-DGP *78*
India to Aden route, proposed 32, 37, 44, 45, 47
Indian Government 78
Indian Overseas Airlines (formerly Mistri) 21, 31, 32
Instrument Rating competency checks 161
International Aeradio Ltd 21
    wireless operators *72*
IPC (International Petroleum Company) 110, 137
Iraq 13, 87, 140
Israel 82
    Arab hostility towards 42
    Arab-Israeli six day war (1967) 179
    Arab-Jewish conflict 82
"Ivory route" 18, 31

Jeddah 47, 61, 63, 104-105, 118, 129
    see also Haj pilgrimage flights
Jennings, F/O (later Capt) Alan 96, *110*, *151*, 174, *174*, 179
Jet Assisted Take-Off (JATO) use 60, *60*
Jiwani 13
Johnson, Capt J 174
Jones, Miss (stewardess) *37*
Jordan 53, 61, 81, 83, 87, 92, 136
    airline Manager *84*
Jordan Airways 88
Jordan Government 82, 83, 84, 85, 88
Joshi, V K 33, 39, 101, *108*
Junkers Ju 52: 21

Kabul 52, 53, *53*
Kalundia airfield 82
Kamal Sindi 61
Kamaran Island 14, 17, *44*, 108, *114*, 129, 153, 161, 163
Karachi, routes to 13, 14, *14*, 15
Kashmir 116
Kassem, Gen 87
Kathir 128
Khalifa (Aden Airways employee) 156, 159
Khama 128
Khareba 109
Khartoum 11-12, 15, 16, 37, 63
    Airport *90*, 119
Khartoum route, pooling arrangement with EAL 151-152

Khasfa 119
Khormaksar Airport 11, *17*, 18, 19, 21, *38*, *69*, *121*, *125*, *128*, *129*, *145*, *148*, *153*, *155*, *156*, *158*, *162*, 165
    Aden Airways hangar 126, *126*, *127*
    as Aden Airways maintenance base 90
    Aden Airways mess *58*, *104*
    Aden Airways staff accommodation (Cambria House) 113, *113*, 116, *116*
    Aden Airways Planning Office 95
    Air Traffic Control Centre 70
    civil apron and aircraft *149*
    engineering department, security measures in 174, 179
    engineers *110*, *115*
    grenade attack on High Commissioner 156
    ground staff *45*
    RAF side *149*
    runway improvements 132
    sabotage of VR-AAV at *177*, 179
    security office blown up 168
    strike by Shell staff 166-167
    terminal building, 1959 *132*
Kilimanjaro, Mount *163*
KLM 11, 15
Knollys, Lord 13, 20
Koszarek (Indamer owner) 51
Kozubski, Capt Marian 174, 179
Kuwait 140
Kuwait Airways 173
Kuwait Oil Company 15, 66, 96
Kuwait Unit 66

La Anod 117
Lal Sikka *169*
Lambert, A J 74, 75
Lamsoon 96
Lancashire Aircraft Corporation 71, *71*
Larcombe, Capt Dick 133, *137*, 175
Lawson, Capt Jack *104*, *109*, 133, *169*, 174
Lazelle, Capt H 17
Lebanon 87-88
Lee, Gilbert 74, 75, 89, 92, 94, *108*, 120, 169, 173
Lightfoot, F/O John 77
Linstead, John 92
Lipkin, Capt M 77
Little Aden 77, 83, 86
livestock as cargo 94, 97, 98, 102, 105, 129
Lloyd, Col Charles 28, 29
load weighing 49
Lockheed 14: 13
Lockheed L749 Constellation 31, 32, 47, 58
    VT-DEO (Air India) *101*
Lockheed Lodestar 13, 14, 15, 17, 18, *18*, 21, 22, 27, 32, *145*
    G-AGBX 13
    G-AGCM *13*
    G-AGIL *14*
Lockheed Super Constellation 128
locusts, flying through 117
Lombardini, Engineer Peter 96, *96*
London (Heathrow) Airport *57*
London to Aden service, joint BOAC/Aden Airways 57-60, *59*
    timetable 60
London to Cairo service (1948) 24
London to Nairobi route, proposed (BOAC) 59-60
Lorrimer, F/O 109
Lovell, F/O 46
Luxor, Egypt 23, 47

Macmillan, Harold 147
Mahfid 123
mail, carrying 48
Main Line Service No 1: 25, 27, 31
Main Line Service Nos 2, 3 and 4: 25, 27

maintenance, Check IV 136, 139, 142, 144, 147, 150
Mardini, Fiammetta *147*
Marlow, Frank 70
Marmul 109
Martin, Mr (engineer) 92
MASCO (Mideast Aircraft Service Company) 120, 121, 126, 136, 139
Masirah Island 13, 102, 133, 135, 163
Masraq 117
Massawa 104, 119
Maxwell, Robert 13
McGarry, R/O 71, 102, *116*, 142, 175, 177
Meifah 173, 174
Merlo, Stewardess Vera 96, *96*
Middle East Air Transport Board (MEATB) 19
Middle East Airlines 15, 133, 137-138
Middleton, A C 53, 64, 69, 72-73, 74, 92
Mideast Aircraft Service Company (MASCO) 120, 121, 126, 136, 139
Midway airstrip 89, 97, 99-100, 102, 106, 117
MiG fighter, Yemeni 166
Mills, Capt Harry *4*, 25, *25*, *37*, *42*, *45*, 56, 71, *86*, *104*, 115, 117
    and Haj pilgrimage flights 42-43
    returns to BOAC 124
Mills, Joan *37*
Ministry of Civil Aviation (MCA) 14, 17, 18, 19, 26, 29, 42, 63
Ministry of Transport and Civil Aviation (MTCA) 116-117, 121, 122, 127-128, 137, 140
    load limitations on DC-3s 148, 151, 156, 156
Misr (later Misrair) 37, 43, 45, 46, *46*, 47, 113, 116
Mistri Airlines (later Indian Overseas Airlines) 21, 31, 32
Mogadishu, Somalia 159, 163, 165
Mombasa 140
    charters 133
    service to 56-57, 119, 126-127
monsoon season 94-95, 103-104
Mordini, Air Stewardess 145
Moretti, Carlo *57*, *151*, 179
Morton (Bahrain Resident) 52
Mukalla 12, 23, 27, 35, 39, 40, 179
Mukeiras 35, 39, 40, 56, *72*, *93*, 94, *94*, 95, *95*, *100*, 130, 140, 141, 142, 156, 163, 165, 171
    take-off weights out of 93
    terminal building *144*
Munro, Sheila *151*, *165*, *168*, 174, 179
Murray, Capt Mike 133
Muscat, Azaiba airport 110, 117, 124, 128
Museifa (formerly Camp 2) 108, 117

Nairobi, Kenya *58*
    Director of Civil Aviation 28, 29
    maintenance unit 126, 147, 150
    Office of Civil Affairs 28-29
Nairobi to Aden service 20, 27-28, *28*, 29, *29*, 32, 108, 163
    Tripartite Pool agreement 159
Nairobi to Cairo service 23, 27, 42, 48
Nairobi to London route, proposed (BOAC) 59-60
Nanga Parbat 116
Napoleon Bonaparte 11
Nasser, Col Gamal Abdel 71, 86, 112, 136, 140, 179
National Liberation Front (NLF) 149, 174, 177
Neguib, Flight Clerk 173-174
Nelson, Orvis 51, 52, 53, 81, 82
network, areas of responsibility 44
Newton, Colonel 162
Nicosia 66, 67
Nigeria, Haj flights from 62-63
night flying 109

INDEX

Nisab 73, 74, 94, 108, *123*, 128
NLF (National Liberation Front) 149, 174, 177

Obbia 117
oil charters 96, *96*, 97, 99-100, 102, 106, 108, 111, 112, 117, 124, 135, 137, 142, 153
oil exploration 89
    site airstrips, establishing and finding 153
    sites, 1955-65: *124*
Oman 119, 124, 128
O'Neill, F/O David *117*, 102, 174, 179
Operating Manuals 127, 128, 129
operating plan, initial (Nov. 1948) 27
Operating Procedures, Standard 127

Page, Mr (administrator) 92
Pamlat Rkhot 119
Pan American Airways 15
Pan American Hadramaut Drilling Company 163
Parker, Capt Jack 162, *162*
Parker, Capt Ted 105
Pascoe, Capt John *54*, 71, 77, 93, 94, 96-97, *98*
Pelly, Capt C N 20
People's Socialist Party 149
Perim Island 129
    listening post 158, 168
pilots *see also* aircrew
    employment of 71
    local 155, 163, 175
    newly-arrived, training 131
    seconded from BOAC 35, 37, 71
    tensions among 173
    "volunteer", for Aden Airways 25, *25*
pilots' children *116*
pilots' operating schedule, October 1953 78-79
plague, bubonic 47
Porter, Cole *87*
public confidence disappears 174-175
Purvis, Capt 77
Pusey, Harry 53, 61, 63, *83*, *84*, *86*
    car in DC-3 *84*
Putt, P B 33

Qat Importing Company 161 *see also* drug, Qat
Qatar (formerly Qaiti states) 142
Qatn 94, 109, *168*
quarantine requirements 23, 47

Radfan valley 161, 162
Ram, J 78
Ras Duqam 108
Rawalpindi, Flashman's Hotel 115
Rayda 128
Red Sea area routes, plans for 14, 15-16, 17, 18, 19-22
refuellers 98
revenue rate per hour 40
revenue sources comparison 151
Riyan 13, 15, 16, 18, 19, 20, 21, 22, 23, 27, *35*, 44, 45, 46, 47, 56, 66, 71, 94, 96, 99, 100, 102, 109, 117, 118, 119, 133, 135, 142, 145, 163, 165, *165*, 172, 173, 179
Rizzi, Fernanda *110*
Robinson, F/O Robby 102, *102*, 131, 168
routes *see also* timetables
    1946-47: *15*
    1949: *34*
    1950 international *40*
    1951: *46*
    1953: *71*
    1954: *92*, *99*
    with Arab Airways connecting services *85*, *86*
    1955: *107*
    1956 local *113*
    1957: *118*
    1963-64: *154*, *156*

1965 foreign destinations *166*
Royal Air Force 11, 12, 15, 17-18, 21, 27, 29, 163
    charters 126, 133, 135
    Douglas Dakota *89*, *153*
Royal Jordanian Airlines 88
Rujeima 128
Rush, F/O John *90*, 96
Rush, Mrs *90*
Russell (Douet), Sue 156, 159

Saad, Theresa *88*
Sahna 117
Said 156-157
Salalah, Oman 13, 96-97, *98*, 99, 100, 102, 106, 109, 117, *122*, *125*, 128, 133, 135, 163, *169*
Salalah, Wali of 104, *104*
Salameh, W 84
Salasil 119
Salisbury (now Harare) 152, 155
Saudi Arabia 112, 158, 159
    Government 42, 45, 61
Saudi Arabian Airlines 61
Saudia 15
Sauqira 124
Sayer, Jack 179
Scott, Mike 125
Scottish Aviation 50, 77
Seiyun 12
Senior First Officer rank introduced 163
Service Leave charters 126-127, *128*, 131, 155, 158, 159, 161, 163, 165
Seton, Air Stewardess 145
Shansan (steward) 164
Shaum 106
Sheikh Ottman, atrocity in 179
Shell 111, 112
    workers, strikes by 166-167, 168, 169
Short Scion 12, *12*
Silver City 15
single-engine approach and landing checks 129
Skingley, Capt Peter 173
Skyways Ltd 15, 28, 29, *90*, 93, 94, 123
Smallpiece, Basil 73, 74-75
Socotra Island 163-164, *164*
Somali Government 136, 148
Somali services, May 1956 *111*
Somalia (formerly British Somaliland) 15, 17, 20, 21, 39, 40, 43-44, 117, 119, 124, 165
    British Military Administration 28
    increasing unrest in 158
    independence 135-136
    political confusion in 152
    proposed services in 148
Somaliland, French 15, 21, 39, 51
Somaliland, Italian 135-136
Sorsbie, Capt Malin 28, 29
Soviet Union, support for Middle Eastern countries 136, 140
Spencer, Mary 99, *103*, *111*
Spencer, Capt Vic *71*, *93*, *96*, *151*
    in 1954-55: 98-100
    in 1955-56: 102, 104, 105, 108
    in 1956-57: 111, 112
    in 1957-58: 117, 118, 121
    in 1961-62: 142, 144
    in 1962-63: 145
    in 1963-64: 152, 153
    in 1966-67: 172, 173
    bird strike incident 123
    carries pistol 177, 179
    Chief Pilot, proposed as 137
    as Chief Pilot 168-169
    as Chief Pilot of Argonaut fleet 132, 136, 139
    death threats received 172, 177
    as Deputy Chief Pilot 139-140

    and end of company 179
    flies into Said 156
    flights to Dhala and Djibouti 106
    joins company 71, 95, 96
    and loss of VR-AAN 174
    and MTCA audit 127-128
    and Nisab DC-3 incident 165
    Operations Manager position, accepts 158, 161
    and problems at Khormaksar 166-167
    problems in Radfan 162
    promoted to Assistant Chief Pilot 125
    Qat flights 125
    and single-engine approach and landing checks 129
    and Socotra incident 164
    and staff termination notices 179
    training for Viscount 155
    training on Argonaut 132, 133
    and union trouble 149
    and violence in colony 163
    visits airstrips 109
    VR-AAV brought back from maintenance 175
Spouce, S/O 165
Srinagar 116, *116*
staff *see* aircrew; employees; pilots; stewardess/es
stewardess operating schedule, 1953 79
stewardesses 35 *see also individual entries*
    sickness rate 171
    uniform *125*
Stewart, F/O (later Capt) Ian 115, 116, *116*, 117, 124, 144
    experiences flying DC-3s 129-130
Stewart, R D 28, 29
Straight, Whitney 19, 52-53, 62, 72
Sudan Airways 18, 151
Suez Canal 11
Suez Crisis (1956): 87, 112, 116
Superintendents 44

Tassan, Gen Ibrahim 61, 63
Tedder, Air Marshal Arthur 13
Thamud 99, *99*
Thomas, Sir Miles, DFC 48, 67
timetables
    1949: *33*
    1950 international: *35*, *41*
    1951 international: *43*
    1953 international: *75*, *76*
    1953 local and African: *76*
    1953 temporary: *70*
    1954: *97*
    1955: *107*
    1956: *111*
    1956 international: *112*
    1956 Western Protectorate: *111*
    1957 Caravan Class: *120*
    1957 main line: *119*
    1959 Eastern Protectorate and Bahrain: *131*
    1959 international: *130*
    1960 international: *135*
    1960 Protectorate: *135*
    1961 Caravan Class: *144*
    1961 international: *138*, *141*, *143*
    1961 Protectorate: *140*
    1962 international: *146*
    1962 regional: *150*
    1962 Eastern Protectorate: *147*
    1963 Western Protectorate: *152*
    1964 international and regional: *160*
    1965 international: *166*
    1965 regional: *167*
    1966 regional: *172*
    1967 international and regional: *173*, *178*
tortoises, landing on 117
tourist charter flight 168

Trans World Airlines (TWA) 19, 52, 64, 66, 136
Transcontinental and Western Air (TWA) 14, 15
Transocean Air Lines Inc 15, 51, *51*, 52, 53, 81, 88
    background 82-84
Trevaskis, Kennedy 156
Tripartite Pool agreement (1964) 159
troop reinforcement flight 140
Tufluk (Party II - exploration site) 119
Turboméca Palas jet unit 60
TWA (Trans World Airlines) 19, 52, 64, 66, 136
Type Rating competency checks 161

uniform, Air Stewardess, 1958 *125*
United Arab Airlines 133, 136, 138
United Arab Republic, formation of 87
United Nations 55
    charters 92, 94, 115-116, *116*
    Mission to Aden 177
    UN 351: 92, 116, *116*
    UN 601: 94
    UN 640: 92
United States Government 51

van der Laan, Capt *165*
Van Elste, Capt 145-146
vegetable charter flights 101, 104, 119
    see also drug, Qat, charter flights
vehicles 100, *168*
Vennings, Jennifer *139*
Vickers Valetta *101*

Vickers Viking 46, 47, 83
    SU-AGO (Misr) *46*
Vickers Viscount 67, 116, 133, 150, 151, 155, 159, 161
    simulator course 155
    slipper tanks *156*
    training for 152, 155
    OD-ACT (MEA) 168-169
    VP-YNA (Central African Airways) *156*, 161
    VP-YNB (Central African Airways) *159*, 161
    VP-YNC (Central African Airways) 161
    VR-AAV 155, *155*, 168, 172, 173, 174, 175, 177, 179
        blown up *177*, 179
        in-flight log *159*
    VR-AAW 155, *156*, 168, 173, 177
Vincent, C 74, 92
Volpe, Engineer *109*
    family 90
Von Rosen, Count Gustav 64

Wadi Hadramaut 96, 129-130
Wadi Halfa 115
Wadi Seidna 119
Wahed, S/O 163, 175, 179
Walbran, Capt Ian 46
Ward, Capt Les 71
Warrington, Mike 135
weapons carried by expatriate staff 171, 172, *172*, 177
weather 46 *see also* monsoon season

West African Airways Corporation (WAAC) 15, 18, 34, 47, 64
    Accra to Khartoum service 34, *34*
"Western" oil sites 153
Whittaker, Capt Frank 116, *116*, 165
Wigley, F/O Bob 123, 125, 164
Williamson, Capt Pete 133, 161, *161*, 164, 165, 168
Wilson, Margaret *139*, 142
Wilson, R *165*
Wilson, Capt Warren 173
Wimpey, George 77
Winster, Lord 14
Wolfson, Capt V 66, 67, 74, 77, 120
Wood, Capt Jimmy 104, *172*
World War Two 12-14, 15
Wymeswold 142, 144

Yafai, Flight Clerk 152
Yemen
    Aden Protectorates claimed as part of 140
    Egyptian-backed coup in 148
    employees from 152
    proposed airline in 140-141
    royal flight 148
    support from Soviet Union 140
Yemen, Imam of 140
Yemen Airlines 148, 152, 161, 164
    Aden Airways agreement with 141
    DC-3 YE-AAC *60*
Yemeni MiG fighter 166
Young, Albert *97*